ST/ESA/STAT/SER.X/65

Department of Economic and Social Affairs
Statistics Division

National Accounts Statistics: Analysis of Main Aggregates, 2019

United Nations
New York, 2021

The Department of Economic and Social Affairs of the United Nations is a vital interface between global policies in the economic, social and environmental spheres and national action. The Department works in three main interlinked areas: (i) it compiles, generates and analyses a wide range of economic, social and environmental data and information on which United Nations Member States draw to review common problems and to take stock of policy options; (ii) it facilitates the negotiations of Member States in many intergovernmental bodies on joint courses of action to address ongoing or emerging global challenges; and (iii) it advises interested Governments on the ways and means of translating policy frameworks developed in United Nations conferences and summits into programmes at the country level and, through technical assistance, helps build national capacities.

NOTE

The designations employed and the presentation of the material in the present publication do not imply the expression of any opinion whatsoever on the part of the United Nations concerning the legal status of any country or of its authorities, or the delimitations of its frontiers. The term "country" as used in this report also refers, as appropriate, to territories or areas.

The designations of country groups are intended solely for statistical or analytical convenience and do not necessarily express a judgement about the stage reached by a particular country, territory or area in the development process. Mention of the names of firms and commercial products does not imply endorsement by the United Nations.

The symbols of United Nations documents are composed of capital letters and numbers. The first 14 editions of this publication were issued without series symbols.

ST/ESA/STAT/SER.X/65

UNITED NATIONS PUBLICATION

Sales No. E.21.XVII.1 H

ISBN 978-92-1-259152-0
eISBN 978-92-1-005185-9
Print ISSN 0259-3017
Online ISSN 2412-1827

Enquiries should be directed to:
SALES SECTION
UNITED NATIONS
NEW YORK, NY 10017
E-mail: publications@un.org
Internet: http://www.un.org/Pubs

CONTENTS

B. PERCENTAGE DISTRIBUTION OF MAIN NATIONAL ACCOUNTS AGGREGATES AT CURRENT PRICES: INDIVIDUAL COUNTRIES OR AREAS

C. GROWTH RATES OF MAIN NATIONAL ACCOUNTS AGGREGATES AT CONSTANT 2015 PRICES

D. IMPLICIT PRICE DEFLATORS OF GROSS DOMESTIC PRODUCT: INDIVIDUAL COUNTRIES OR AREAS (2015=100)

I. INTRODUCTION

A. BACKGROUND

1. This is the fiftieth issue of *National Accounts Statistics: Analysis of Main Aggregates*[1,2] presenting a series of analytical national accounts tables for more than 200 countries and areas of the world. Like the previous issues, it has been prepared by the Statistics Division of the Department for Economic and Social Affairs of the United Nations Secretariat with the generous co-operation of national statistical offices. It is issued in accordance with the recommendation of the Statistical Commission at its first session[3] that the Statistics Division should publish regularly the most recent available data on national accounts for as many countries and areas as possible.

2. This publication presents, in the form of analytical tables, a summary of the principal national accounts aggregates. These aggregates, based on official national account data and thus reported directly by countries to the Statistics Division, are supplemented with estimates prepared by the Statistics Division. The sources and methods used for each country's national accounts aggregates should be taken into consideration when using the data in this publication. Information on metadata is available on the Statistics Division website at: https://unstats.un.org/unsd/snaama/Metadata/.

3. The *National Accounts Statistics: Analysis of Main Aggregates* publication is published as the complementary part of the series of publications on national account data by the Statistics Division. The first part of this series is the *National Accounts Statistics: Main Aggregates and Detailed Tables*[4,5], which shows detailed national accounts statistics provided to the United Nations as official data. Prior to 1982, detailed national accounts statistics and analytical national accounts tables were published as two volumes of a single publication, the *Yearbook of National Accounts Statistics*.

B. SYSTEM OF NATIONAL ACCOUNTS

4. This publication is the twentieth issue based on the United Nations National Accounts Questionnaire (NAQ) introduced in October 1999, which in turn is based on the *System of National Accounts 1993* (1993 SNA)[6].

5. The 1993 SNA was unanimously recommended to the United Nations Economic and Social Council by its Statistical Commission at its 24th session in March 1993. Similar to the recommendation made in 1968 for its predecessor, *A System of National Accounts* (1968 SNA)[7], the Council in its resolution 1993/5 of 12 July 1993 recommends that Member States use the 1993 SNA in the international reporting of comparable national accounts data. However, it should be highlighted that the Council went a few steps further in 1993 and also recommends that Member States consider using the 1993 SNA: (a) as the standard for the compilation of their national accounts statistics, (b) to promote the integration of economic and related statistics, and (c) as an analytical tool. In 2003 the Statistical Commission called for an update of the 1993 SNA. The first 17 Chapters of the updated SNA, comprising the accounting rules, the accounts and tables, and their integration was approved by the Statistical Commission in 2008; Chapters 18 to 29, comprising the interpretations and extensions of the accounts and tables of the System, was approved by the Statistical Commission in 2009. The updated SNA, called the *System of National Accounts 2008* (2008 SNA)[8] was finalized in September 2009 and is available on the Statistics Division's website at: http://unstats.un.org/unsd/nationalaccount/sna2008.asp.
Beginning in October 2014, Member States of the European Union adopted the European System of Accounts 2010 (ESA 2010), which is a counterpart of the 2008 SNA. In addition to the European Union Member States, an increasing number of other countries have also adopted the 2008 SNA recommendations. Overall, 207 countries/ territories representing 99 percent of the world's gross national income (GNI), and 98 percent of the world population had implemented 1993 SNA or 2008 SNA.

7. The form and concepts of the statistical tables in the present publication generally conform to the 1993 SNA recommendations.

C. SCOPE OF PUBLICATION

8. The tables of the publication include analysis of data on gross domestic product (GDP) by different structural components. The types of analysis presented are classified into four major categories listed below:

I: Analysis of the level of total and per capita GDP
Table 1.A Estimates of gross domestic product in United States dollars by major area, region and country
Table 1.B Estimates of per capita gross domestic product in United States dollars by major area, region and country

II: Analysis of the percentage shares of GDP by type of expenditure and gross value added by kind of economic activity
Table 2 Gross domestic product by type of expenditure
Table 3 Gross value added by kind of economic activity

III: Analysis of economic development expressed in terms of real growth of GDP and its components by type of

expenditure and gross value added by kind of economic activity
Table 4 Average rate of growth of gross domestic product by major area, region and country
Table 5.A – 5.E Average rate of growth of components of gross domestic product by type of expenditure
Table 6.A – 6.G Average rate of growth of value added by kind of economic activity

IV: Analysis of price development reflected by implicit price deflators of GDP
Table 7 Implicit price deflators of gross domestic product

9. The analytical tables presented in this publication are based on a homogeneous data series for each country. These data series are based on official data and estimations that have been applied to produce a consistent time series for each country. The design of these data tables facilitates cross-table analysis, as well as, analysis and comparisons of multiple countries or regions.

10. The data provided in this publication, as well as additional analytical data, are available on the Statistics Division website at http://unstats.un.org/unsd/snaama or http://data.un.org.

D. COLLECTION OF DATA

11. To collect national accounts data, the Statistics Division annually sends the United Nations National Accounts Questionnaire (UN-NAQ) to countries and areas. The countries are requested to provide the latest available national accounts estimates and to indicate where the scope and coverage of the country estimates differ for conceptual or statistical reasons from the definitions and classifications recommended by the 1993 SNA. This additional metadata information is requested to provide a brief overview of the sources and methods of the compilation of national accounts. For countries for which data are not directly reported to the Statistics Division, data are supplemented by information gathered from additional correspondence with national statistical offices, from national source publications and other sources (see Section II).

12. In order to reduce the reporting burden of countries, UNSD obtains data from the Organisation for Economic Cooperation and Development (OECD), the United Nations Economic Commission for Europe (ECE) and the Caribbean Community (CARICOM) on behalf of their constituents.

E. COMPARABILITY OF THE NATIONAL ESTIMATES

13. Every effort has been made to present the estimates of the various countries or areas in a form designed to facilitate international comparability. To this end, important differences in concept, scope, coverage and classification have been described in the footnotes for individual countries. Such differences should be taken into account to avoid misleading comparisons.

14. Data contained in the tables relate to the calendar year t for which they are shown, except in the following cases:

A: Year beginning 1 July, t; ending 30 June, t+1
Australia, Sudan and Former Yemen Arab Republic

B: Year beginning 1 April, t; ending 31 March, t+1
India and New Zealand

C: Year beginning 21 March, t; ending 20 March, t+1
the Islamic Republic of Iran

D: Year beginning 1 July, t-1; ending 30 June, t
Bangladesh, Egypt, Nauru, Pakistan, Puerto Rico and Tonga

E: Year beginning 8 July, t-1; ending 7 July, t
Ethiopia and Former Ethiopia

F: Year beginning 16 July, t-1; ending 15 July, t
Nepal

G: Year beginning 1 October, t-1; ending 30 September, t
Haiti, Marshall Islands, Micronesia (Federated States of) and Palau

H: Year beginning 1 October, t; ending 30 September, t+1
Myanmar

F. NOMENCLATURE

15. The information for the countries and areas shown in this publication reflect what is provided to the Statistics Division as of December 2020.

16. Designations, which have changed in recent years, are as follows:

China, Hong Kong SAR - Pursuant to a Joint Declaration signed on 19 December 1984, the United Kingdom restored Hong Kong to the People's Republic of China with effect from 1 July 1997; the People's Republic of China resumed the exercise of sovereignty over the territory on that date.

China, Macao SAR - Pursuant to a Joint Declaration signed on 13 April 1987, Portugal restored Macao to the People's Republic of China with effect from 20 December 1999; the People's Republic of China resumed the exercise of sovereignty over the territory on that date.

Czech Republic, Slovakia - Data for Czech Republic and Slovakia are shown separately under the appropriate country name. For period prior to 1 January 1993, data for the former Czechoslovakia are shown under the country name Czechoslovakia (Former).

Yugoslavia (Former) - Following the adoption and the promulgation of the Constitutional Charter of Serbia and Montenegro by the Assembly of the Federal Republic of Yugoslavia on 4 February 2003, the name of the State of the Federal Republic of Yugoslavia was changed to Serbia and Montenegro. All data for former Yugoslavia prior to 1 January 1992 refer to the Socialist Federal Republic of Yugoslavia that was then composed of six republics. After that date, when available, data for the republics, Bosnia and Herzegovina, Croatia, Slovenia and North Macedonia are shown separately. On 3 June 2006, Serbia and Montenegro formally dissolved into Montenegro and Serbia which are now shown separately from 1990 onwards. Kosovo, formerly part of Serbia, is compiling its own National Accounts Statistics and included as a separate territory in this issue, starting in 1990.

USSR (Former) - In 1991, the Union of Soviet Socialist Republics formally dissolved into fifteen independent republics (Armenia, Azerbaijan, Belarus, Estonia, Georgia, Kazakhstan, Kyrgyzstan, Latvia, Lithuania, Republic of Moldova, Russian Federation, Tajikistan, Turkmenistan, Ukraine and Uzbekistan). When available, data are shown for the individual republics. All data for the former USSR are shown under the country name USSR (Former).

Germany - On October 1990, the Federal Republic of Germany and the German Democratic Republic united to form one sovereign State under the designation Germany.

Yemen - In May 1990, Yemen and Democratic Yemen united to form a single State. Since that date they have been represented as one country with the name "Yemen".

Ethiopia, Eritrea – In 1993 Eritrea separated from Ethiopia to form a new state. Ethiopia refers to Ethiopia excluding Eritrea while Ethiopia (Former) refers to Ethiopia including Eritrea.

Sudan, South Sudan – In 2011 South Sudan separated from Sudan to form a new country. Sudan refers to Sudan excluding South Sudan while Sudan (Former) refers to Sudan including South Sudan.

Netherlands Antilles – In 2010 the Netherlands Antilles dissolved into three separate entities within the Netherlands. Curaçao and Sint Maarten each became constituent entities that provide data separately while Bonaire, Sint Eustatius and Saba have been integrated into the Netherlands as special municipalities.

G. COUNTRY COVERAGE

17. The 1993 SNA defines economic territory as the relevant geographical area to which the concept of residence is applied. The 1993 SNA also indicates that the economic territory and geographical territory can be different. Within the analytical tables, the economic territory is usually consistent with the geographic territory; the exceptions include:

France - Includes French Guiana, Guadeloupe, Martinique, Mayotte and Réunion.

Cyprus - Excludes Northern Cyprus.

Serbia - Excludes Kosovo from 1999 onward.

United Republic of Tanzania - Excludes Zanzibar.

Morocco - Includes Western Sahara.

Indonesia - Excludes Timor-Leste from 1999 onward.

China - China is published in this yearbook in three sections: China (mainland); China, Hong Kong SAR; and China, Macao SAR.

H. COUNTRY GROUPINGS

18. There are two types of country groupings (or aggregates) presented in the tables: economic groupings and regional groupings. The tables of GDP and growth rates of GDP (Tables 1, 4, 5 and 6) include aggregations of data by economic and regional groupings as well as individual country data. Countries are presented alphabetically by region. The tables of percentage share of components of GDP and gross value added and the implicit price deflators (Tables 2, 3 and 7) only include individual country data presented alphabetically by region.

19. Standard country and area designations, as well as a basic classification of economic and regional groupings are posted on the United Nations website, https://unstats.un.org/sdgs/indicators/regional-groups. The designations employed and the material in this publication do not imply the expression of any opinion whatsoever on the part of the Secretariat of the United Nations concerning the legal status of any country, territory or area or its authorities, or concerning the delimitation of its frontiers or boundaries. The designation "developed" and "developing" groupings are intended for statistical convenience and do not necessarily express a judgment about the stage reached by a particular country or area in the development process.

20. A description of the economic and regional classifications employed in this publication is listed below:

World
Total of developed, developing and transition economies

Developed economies
Northern America, Europe (excluding Transition Economies in Europe), Japan, Australia and New Zealand

Developing economies
Africa, Americas excluding Northern America, Caribbean, Central America, South America, Asia excluding Japan and Transition Economies in Asia, and Oceania excluding Australia and New Zealand

Transition economies
Commonwealth of Independent Countries
Armenia, Azerbaijan, Belarus, Kazakhstan, Kyrgyzstan, Republic of Moldova, Russian Federation, Tajikistan, Turkmenistan, Ukraine and Uzbekistan

Other Asia
Georgia

Other Europe
Albania, Bosnia and Herzegovina, Croatia, Kosovo, Montenegro, Serbia, North Macedonia

REGIONAL CLASSIFICATION

Africa – comprised of Northern Africa and Sub-Saharan Africa (Eastern Africa, Middle Africa, Southern Africa and Western Africa)

Eastern Africa – Burundi, Comoros, Djibouti, Eritrea*, Ethiopia*, Kenya, Madagascar, Malawi, Mauritius, Mozambique, Rwanda, Seychelles, Somalia, South Sudan[†], Uganda, United Republic of Tanzania (mainland), Zambia, Zanzibar, Zimbabwe
Middle Africa – Angola, Cameroon, Central African Republic, Chad, Congo, Democratic Republic of the Congo, Equatorial Guinea, Gabon, Sao Tome and Principe
Northern Africa – Algeria, Egypt, Libyan Arab Jamahiriya, Morocco, Sudan, Tunisia
Southern Africa – Botswana, Eswatini, Lesotho, Namibia, South Africa
Western Africa – Benin, Burkina Faso, Cabo Verde, Cote d'Ivoire, Gambia, Ghana, Guinea, Guinea-Bissau, Liberia, Mali, Mauritania, Niger, Nigeria, Senegal, Sierra Leone, Togo

Americas – comprised of Latin America and the Caribbean (Caribbean, Central America and South America) and Northern America
Caribbean – Anguilla, Antigua and Barbuda, Aruba, Bahamas, Barbados, British Virgin Islands, Cayman Islands, Cuba, Curaçao[††], Dominica, Dominican Republic, Grenada, Haiti, Jamaica, Montserrat, Puerto Rico, Saint Kitts and Nevis, Saint Lucia, Saint Vincent and the Grenadines, Sint Maarten (Dutch part)[††], Trinidad and Tobago, Turks and Caicos Islands
Central America – Belize, Costa Rica, El Salvador, Guatemala, Honduras, Mexico, Nicaragua, Panama
South America – Argentina, Bolivia, Brazil, Chile, Colombia, Ecuador, Guyana, Paraguay, Peru, Suriname, Uruguay, Venezuela (Bolivarian Republic of)
Northern America – Bermuda, Canada, Greenland and United States of America

Asia – comprised of Central Asia, Eastern Asia, South-Eastern Asia, Southern Asia and Western Asia

Central Asia – Kazakhstan*, Kyrgyzstan*, Tajikistan*, Turkmenistan*, Uzbekistan*
Eastern Asia – China, Hong Kong Special Administrative Region of China, Macao Special Administrative Region of China, Democratic People's Republic of Korea, Japan, Mongolia, Republic of Korea
South-Eastern Asia – Brunei Darussalam, Cambodia, Indonesia, Lao People's Democratic Republic, Malaysia, Myanmar, Philippines, Singapore, Thailand, Timor-Leste**, Vietnam
Southern Asia – Afghanistan, Bangladesh, Bhutan, India, Iran (Islamic Republic of), Maldives, Nepal, Pakistan, Sri Lanka
Western Asia – Armenia*, Azerbaijan*, Bahrain, Cyprus, Georgia*, Iraq, Israel, Jordan, Kuwait, Lebanon, State of Palestine, Oman, Qatar, Saudi Arabia, Syrian Arab Republic, Turkey, United Arab Emirates, Yemen*

Europe – comprised of Eastern Europe, Northern Europe, Southern Europe and Western Europe

Eastern Europe – Belarus*, Bulgaria, Czech Republic*, Hungary, Poland, Republic of Moldova*, Romania, Russian Federation*, Slovakia*, Ukraine*
Southern Europe – Albania, Andorra, Bosnia and Herzegovina*, Croatia*, Greece, Italy, Kosovo**, Malta, Montenegro*, Portugal, San Marino, Serbia*, Slovenia, Spain, North Macedonia*
Northern Europe – Denmark, Estonia*, Finland, Iceland, Ireland, Latvia*, Lithuania*, Norway, Sweden, United Kingdom of Great Britain and Northern Ireland
Western Europe – Austria, Belgium, France, Germany, Liechtenstein, Luxembourg, Monaco, Netherlands and Switzerland

---

* since 1990
** since 1999
[†] since 2008
[††] since 2010

Oceania – comprised of Australia and New Zealand, Melanesia, Micronesia, and Polynesia

Australia and New Zealand – Australia, New Zealand
Melanesia – Fiji, New Caledonia, Papua New Guinea, Solomon Islands, Vanuatu
Micronesia – Kiribati, Marshall Islands, Micronesia (Federated States of), Nauru, Palau
Polynesia – Cook Islands, French Polynesia, Samoa, Tonga, Tuvalu

I. REVISIONS

21. The figures shown are the most recent estimates and revisions available at the time of compilation. In general, figures for the most recent year are to be regarded as provisional.

J. SYMBOLS AND DATA DISPLAY

22. The following symbols have been employed:

Data not available	...
Category not available	..
Data in units	(u)
Data in thousands	(t)

23. The sum of the components in the tables may not necessarily add up to totals shown because of rounding.

K. GENERAL INFORMATION

24. For further information visit the Statistics Division website at http://unstats.un.org/unsd/snaama. Queries regarding the AMA database or this publication can be sent to sna@un.org.

II. ESTIMATION METHODS

A. BACKGROUND

1. This section outlines the methodology employed to obtain a complete data series for each country, as well as for computing growth rates, indices and the economic and regional aggregates.

2. A basic description of the methodology related to the compilation of official national accounts data is provided in *National Accounts Statistics: Main Aggregates and Detailed Tables*. For full details on the 1968, 1993 or 2008 SNA, see *A System of National Accounts* (1968 SNA), *System of National Accounts 1993* (1993 SNA) and *System of National Accounts* 2008 (2008 SNA).

3. The System of National Accounts (SNA) consists of a coherent, consistent and integrated set of macroeconomic accounts; balance sheets and tables based on a set of internationally agreed concepts, definitions, classifications and accounting rules. It provides a comprehensive accounting framework within which economic data can be compiled and presented in a format that is designed for purposes of economic analysis, decision-taking and policy-making. The accounts themselves present in a condensed way a great mass of detailed information, organized according to economic principles and perceptions, about the working of an economy. They provide a comprehensive and detailed record of the complex economic activities taking place within an economy and of the interaction between the different economic agents, and groups of agents that takes place on markets or elsewhere. In practice the accounts are compiled for a succession of time periods, thus providing a continuing flow of information that is indispensable for the monitoring, analysis and evaluation of the performance of an economy over time. The SNA provides information not only about economic activities, but also about the levels of an economy's productive assets and the wealth of its inhabitants at particular points of time. Finally, the SNA includes an external account that displays the links between an economy and the rest of the world.

B. DATA SOURCES FOR ESTIMATION IN NATIONAL CURRENCY

4. Official data, as reported by countries to the United Nations through the Statistics Division's annual UN-NAQ, are published in the *National Accounts Statistics: Main Aggregates and Detailed Tables* publication.

5. For many countries a full set of official data is not available, thus estimation procedures are employed to obtain estimates for the entire time series. When full data is not available, a hierarchy of other data sources is used to gather information on the national accounts of a country. The data gathered are then either used directly or estimation procedures are applied to obtain the basic statistics presented in this publication.

B.1 HIERARCHY OF DATA SOURCES

6. If official data are not available, the selection of data sources is based on following hierarchy:

1) Official publications and websites of national statistical offices, central banks or relevant government ministries;

2) Official statistics disseminated by Eurostat, European Central Bank and the Organization for Economic Cooperation and Development (OECD) for their members;

3) Information provided by Permanent Missions to the United Nations;

4) Economic surveys and estimates prepared by United Nations' Regional Economic Commissions (i.e. UNECE, ECLAC, ESCAP, UNECA and ESCWA);

5) Publications of international organizations with a strong focus on statistical data collection (including regional development banks). The most common sources used for their respective countries are listed below.

   Asia: Asian Development Bank, ASEAN, Arab Monetary Fund, Secretariat of the Pacific Community

   Africa: African Development Bank, Afristat, Banque des Etats de l'Afrique Centrale (BEAC), Union Economique Monetaire Ouest Africain (UEMOA)

   Americas: CARICOM, Caribbean Development Bank, Eastern Caribbean Central Bank (ECCB)

   Other: OECD for some non-member countries, Statistical Committee of the Commonwealth of Independent States

6) Estimates and indicators from other international organizations. The most common sources used are the International Monetary Fund (IMF) and the World Bank;

7) Publications or websites of specialized groups. The most common sources used are the Gulf Cooperation Council, the Asia-Pacific Economic Cooperation (APEC), the Committee of Central Bank Governors in SADC; the Islamic Development Bank, and the Statistical, Economic and Social Research and Training Centre for Islamic Countries;

8) Economic data from commercial providers and other sources. The most common sources used are the Economic Intelligence Unit and the United States Central Intelligence Agency;

9) Information from neighbouring countries where no alternative source is available (Switzerland for Liechtenstein; France for Monaco; Italy for San Marino; Spain for Andorra; and some Pacific Islands for other Pacific Islands).

C. BACKCASTING OF OFFICIAL DATA

7. From time to time countries provide revised data without revising a full historical time series. In these cases the data series are backcasted to derive a single, consistent time series.

8. Official data are often reported as multiple sets of time series versions. Each time series version represents a unique methodology used to compile the national accounts data (for example, a difference between two time series versions could reflect a change in currency, a switch from 1968 SNA to 1993 SNA, a change in the office responsible for compiling national accounts, etc.). These time series versions may not be comparable, especially when a country has shifted from the 1968 SNA to 1993 SNA or 2008 SNA.

9. When a single time series version does not exist for the entire period (1970 to t-1), then estimation procedures are used to backcast the most recently reported time series version. Backcasting is only performed when time series overlap for at least one year. The overlapping year is used to create a ratio; this ratio is then applied backwards to the previous time series version. Note that if there is a change of fiscal year between two official data time series, the older series are converted to the fiscal year type of the most recent time series prior to backcasting.

10. The same backcasting methods are applied when constant price time series versions include multiple base years or when constant price time series versions are reported as constant prices of the previous year (CPPY). CPPY data are backcasted by using the officially reported current price data and the officially reported constant price data. The data are backcasted into a single series with a fixed base year.

D. ESTIMATION BASED ON SOURCES OTHER THAN OFFICIAL DATA

11. The methods involved in preparing data estimates using sources other than official data include trend extrapolation, using appropriate indices for inflating or deflating relevant data series, and share distribution of GDP. A hierarchical assessment is followed to determine which method should be used. Effort is made to keep data estimation methods consistent from year to year.

D.1 TREND EXTRAPOLATION

12. Trend extrapolation is the most frequent method used for estimating data. The trend from an alternative data source is applied to official data or other estimates by applying the growth rate forward or backward (data sources are used according to the hierarchy described in section B).

13. Trend extrapolation can also be used to form a bridge between two official data series for the purpose of backcasting. This is done when an overlapping year does not exist between two official data time series versions. The alternative source is used to create a time series version that includes an overlapping year with a second official data time series version. The backcasting procedures are then followed using this overlapping year.

14. In some cases there is no source available for some of the years in the estimation period. In these cases the average trend of the several years preceding or following a data item is used to extrapolate a value for a specific year. If there is missing data for the components of GDP for a period of time in the middle of the time series, then half of the missing years are calculated using the preceding years and the other half are calculated using the following years (when the gap covers an odd number of years then the middle year is calculated as the average of the preceding and following years).

D.2 PRICE INDICES

15. In cases when either data at current prices or constant prices are missing, an appropriate price index may be used to deflate or inflate the relevant data to obtain the missing data. This method is applied only when

other reliable data sources are not available. Under this method, GDP is deflated or inflated based on a price index and the components of GDP are calculated using the share to GDP.

D.3 SHARE DISTRIBUTION OF GDP

16. Another method for filling in data gaps is to apply the share distribution of GDP. Candidates for this method are countries where official GDP data exist, but data for some or all components are missing. This method requires a secondary data source for GDP and a breakdown of components. If the information is comparable, the share distribution of GDP from the secondary source is applied to the official GDP data.

17. If a secondary source is not available, but some of the years of available data include a breakdown by component, then the average share of the preceding or following five-year period is used to estimate missing data. If there are missing data for the components of GDP for a period of time in the middle of the time series, then half of the missing years are calculated using the preceding five years and the other half are calculated using the following five years (when the gap covers an odd number of years then the middle year is calculated as the average of the preceding and following five years).

E. CONVERSION TO UNITED STATES DOLLARS

18. GDP and per capita GDP data are converted to US dollars using appropriate annual monthly-average or annual average end-of month quotations of exchange rates. As a rule, market exchange rates (MERs) obtained from the International Monetary Fund publication, *International Financial Statistics* are used. These MERs are averages of the market rates communicated to the International Monetary Fund by the Monetary Authority of each member country or end-of-month quotations in the market of the country. MERs generally consist of three types of rates: a) market rates, determined largely by market forces; b) official rates, determined by government authorities; and c) principal rates, for countries maintaining multiple exchange rates arrangements.

19. When MERs from the International Monetary Fund are not available United Nations operational rates of exchange are used (United Nations operational rates were established for accounting purposes and are used in official transactions of the United Nations). These rates are based on official, commercial and/or tourist rates of exchange.

20. National Accounts data expressed in US dollars need to be used with caution as the data may be distorted by fluctuations in exchange rates and domestic inflation movements. To minimize such distortions, the data are examined to identify countries for which changes in the per capita GDP converted in US dollars are not consistent with the economic developments in the country as reflected by the relative movements of domestic and international inflation. To identify these countries, the GDP per capita of each country is evaluated.

21. A MER valuation index (MVI) is calculated for each country in order to review changes in the MER using the following formula:

Assuming,

r = *growth rate of per capita GDP between periods 1 and 2*

P_{US} = *price changes in the US*

$E(Y_2)$ = *expected per capita GDP (in US$) in period 2*

Y_1 = *per capita GDP in period 1*

Then,

$$E(Y_2) = r \times P_{US} \times Y_1$$

and

$$MVI = Y_2 / E(Y_2)$$

The MER of countries with an MVI above 1.2 or below 0.8 are considered for adjustment. For each country, graphs of the per capita GDP and the growth of the MVI over time are also evaluated to support the outcome of the numerical analysis.

22. Once possible countries for MER adjustment have been identified, each case is carefully considered taking into account the economic situation in each country during the identified period.

23. The assumption is that changes in the exchange rate of a country between two periods reflect changes in domestic prices relative to changes in United States prices. Taking this assumption into consideration price adjusted rates of exchange (PARE) are calculated for year t by adjusting the exchange rate in year $t+n$ with the changes, between year t and $t+n$, in the GDP deflator in national currency units relative to the US GDP deflator, where year $t+n$ is a year with a realistic GDP per capita expressed in US dollars (for example, the year after an economic crisis ended). The PARE rate is calculated using the following formula:

Assume,

X_t = *exchange rate for year t*
C_t = *current price GDP for year t*
K_t = *constant price GDP for year t*
d_t = *deflator for year t*

Then,

$$d_t = {}^{c_t}\!/_{k_t}$$

and

$$PARE_t = \frac{x_{t+n}}{\left(\dfrac{{}^{d_{t+n}}\!/_{d_t}}{{}^{d^{US}_{t+n}}\!/_{d^{US}_t}} \right)}$$

Where d^{US}_t = deflator for the United States for year t

24. For example: a country's GDP per capita in 1987 was 11,300 US dollars, while it was 549 in 1979 and 663 in 1990. Between 1984 and 1989 the country suffered from hyperinflation while MERs were not allowed to adjust adequately to market prices. Using 1990 as a base year and applying the PARE rates backwards to 1980 results in a GDP per capita series with a more plausible value of 740 for 1987, the year in question.

25. Notwithstanding these adjustments, the inter-country comparisons of national accounts data expressed in US dollars should be done with caution as all distortions may not be eliminated.

F. CONVERSION TO 2015 PRICES

26. Once all data have been compiled in national currency, the constant price data are converted to 2015 prices. Constant price data in national currency are converted to US dollars using the 2015 exchange rates.

G. ECONOMIC AND REGIONAL AGGREGATES

27. The economic and regional aggregates are defined as the sum of the data in US dollars for the countries, areas and territories within the economic or regional grouping. The growth rates and implicit price deflators are calculated from the economic and regional aggregates, not as an average of the country-level growth rates or implicit price deflators.

H. DATA QUALITY

28. All official data received by the United Nations Statistics Division are checked for errors prior to incorporation in the United Nations official data database. The checking involves ensuring that aggregate indicators are equal to the sum of their components and that indicators which are provided in multiple tables are represented consistently. Footnotes are added to the data when necessary.

29. Similarly, the estimated data in this yearbook are checked for consistency by ensuring that aggregate indicators are equal to the sum of their components and that indicators which are represented in multiple tables are represented consistently. The estimates derived for each year are compared to previous years to ensure that estimates are prepared consistently from year to year. Additionally, the growth rate from year to year is analyzed to identify anomalies in the data.

1 United Nations, 1968-1981, Yearbook of National Accounts Statistics. 14 volumes. New York: United Nations Publications.

2 United Nations, 1982-2018, National Accounts Statistics: Analysis of Main Aggregates. 36 volumes. New York: United Nations Publications.

3 United Nations, 1947, Official Records of the Economic and Social Council Supplement No. 6 (E/264), chap. VIII, para. 42. New York: United Nations Publications.

4 United Nations, 1957-1981, Yearbook of National Accounts Statistics. 25 volumes. New York: United Nations Publications.

5 United Nations, 1982-2018, National Accounts Statistics: Main Aggregates and Detailed Tables. 36 volumes. New York: United Nations Publications.

6 Commission of the European Communities, International Monetary Fund, Organisation for Economic Cooperation and Development, United Nations, and World Bank 1993, System of National Accounts 1993. New York: United Nations Publications Sales No. E.94.XVII.4.

7 United Nations, 1968, A System of National Accounts, Studies in Methods, Series F No.2, Rev.3. New York: United Nations Publications.

8 European Commission, International Monetary Fund, Organisation for Economic Cooperation and Development, United Nations, and World Bank, 2009, System of National Accounts 2008. New York: United Nations Publications Sales No. E.08.XVII.29.

III. Analytical Tables

A. Estimates of Main National Accounts Aggregates at Current Prices

Description of Analysis in Table 1A and Table 1B

A. Level of total and per capita gross domestic product.

Table 1A and Table 1B present estimates of total and per capita gross domestic product (GDP) expressed in current US dollars. The tables are intended to facilitate international comparisons of levels of income generated in production. Aggregations of data by economic and regional groupings as well as individual country data presented alphabetically by region are shown in rows. The columns list total and per capita GDP in terms of US dollars for 1970, 1980, 1990, 2000, 2010 and 2015 through 2019.

Official data and estimates of total and per capita GDP have been converted to US dollars as described in the section II (Estimation methods) of this publication.

For inter-country comparisons over time, it would be more appropriate to use the growth rate information based on constant price data, presented in Table 4 of the present volume, which are more indicative of inter-country and intra-grouping comparisons of trends in total GDP.

The nominal gross domestic product for each geographic region since 1970 (in billions of US dollars) and the share in world GDP of each geographic region are shown in the following graphs.

Figure 1. Nominal gross domestic product by region

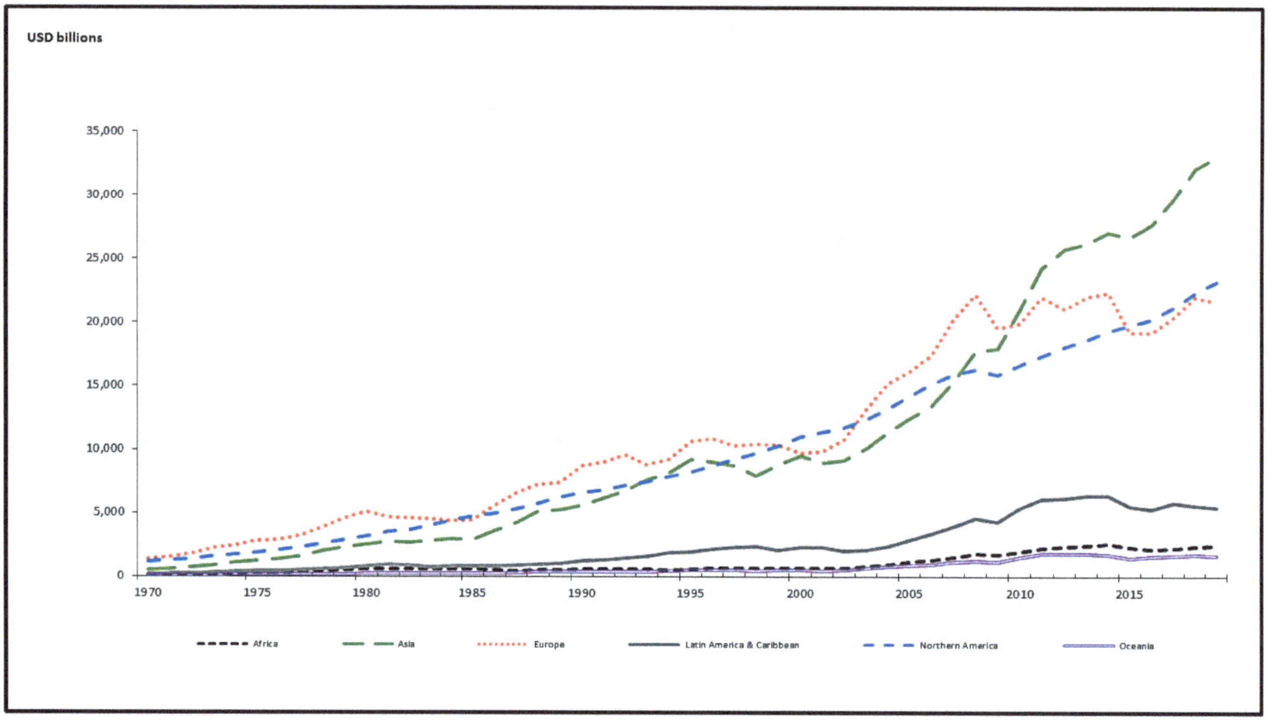

Figure 2. Share in nominal world GDP by region

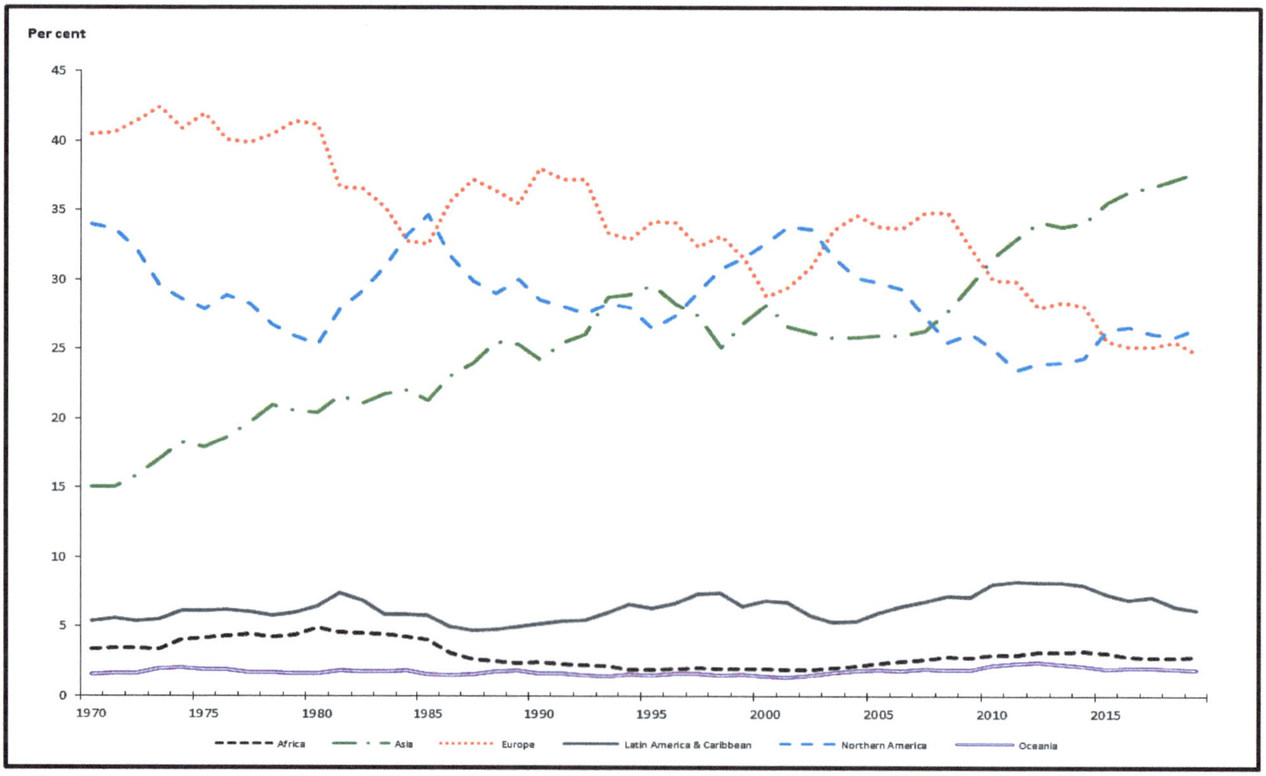

Table 1.A. Estimates of Gross Domestic Product in US Dollars at Current Prices by Major Area, Region and Country

Major area, region and country	(Millions of Dollars)									
	1970	1980	1990	2000	2010	2015	2016	2017	2018	2019
World	**3 418 983**	**12 372 905**	**23 008 701**	**33 636 794**	**66 272 559**	**74 985 744**	**76 173 813**	**81 056 929**	**86 115 347**	**87 445 234**
Developed economies	**2 368 119**	**8 549 115**	**18 106 170**	**25 842 527**	**42 023 752**	**43 466 835**	**44 649 958**	**46 554 758**	**49 309 295**	**49 824 107**
Developing economies	**600 633**	**2 811 651**	**4 065 074**	**7 388 329**	**22 055 636**	**29 464 522**	**29 619 804**	**32 246 240**	**34 398 476**	**35 141 741**
Transition economies	**450 232**	**1 012 139**	**837 458**	**405 938**	**2 193 172**	**2 054 388**	**1 904 051**	**2 255 930**	**2 407 576**	**2 479 386**
Africa	**116 433**	**610 574**	**554 677**	**655 205**	**1 969 815**	**2 314 902**	**2 163 422**	**2 244 978**	**2 368 474**	**2 460 599**
Northern Africa	*24 736*	*138 619*	*185 321*	*262 287*	*648 783*	*729 675*	*680 391*	*661 595*	*666 133*	*714 511*
Algeria	5 155	42 252	61 751	54 667	161 207	165 979	160 034	170 097	175 415	171 158
Egypt	8 143	20 119	35 995	95 684	214 630	317 745	270 254	195 135	249 751	317 359
Libya	3 979	38 186	31 088	38 471	80 942	17 666	15 320	24 805	34 737	32 600
Morocco	4 645	22 097	30 320	38 901	93 217	101 179	103 312	109 683	118 096	119 701
Sudan	...	...	...	...	54 735	83 933	89 671	122 073	48 363	34 895
Sudan (Former)	1 234	6 365	12 647	13 092	...	...	...	...	...	...
Tunisia	1 580	9 599	13 520	21 474	44 051	43 173	41 801	39 802	39 771	38 797
Sub-Saharan Africa	91 697	471 956	369 357	392 918	1 321 032	1 585 227	1 483 031	1 583 383	1 702 341	1 746 088
Eastern Africa	*19 506*	*58 344*	*71 962*	*79 691*	*217 614*	*313 147*	*324 673*	*356 325*	*384 242*	*407 967*
Burundi [1]	245	951	1 148	709	2 032	2 811	2 930	3 217	3 080	3 002
Comoros	37	259	511	422	907	966	1 012	1 077	1 179	1 166
Djibouti	71	301	457	546	1 244	2 445	2 619	2 767	2 923	3 166
Eritrea	...	...	332	706	1 590	2 013	2 174	1 904	2 006	1 982
Ethiopia	...	...	11 208	8 030	26 311	63 079	72 158	76 795	80 210	92 750
Ethiopia (Former)	2 559	5 889	11 540	...	...	...	...	...	...	...
Kenya	2 518	10 518	12 664	14 465	40 000	64 008	69 189	78 965	87 779	95 502
Madagascar	1 052	3 826	3 609	4 502	9 983	11 323	11 849	13 176	13 760	14 105
Malawi	579	2 236	3 166	3 150	6 960	6 431	5 310	6 348	7 180	8 099
Mauritius	206	1 211	2 735	4 869	10 004	11 692	12 232	13 259	14 182	14 180
Mozambique	4 027	6 379	3 924	5 656	11 105	15 951	11 937	13 219	14 845	15 297
Rwanda	228	1 326	2 435	2 068	6 124	8 533	8 697	9 253	9 637	10 355
Seychelles	22	178	445	747	970	1 377	1 427	1 525	1 586	1 699
Somalia	341	574	994	2 052	1 093	1 455	1 456	1 561	1 553	1 626
South Sudan	...	...	...	...	14 930	6 580	3 224	3 511	4 693	4 960
U.R. of Tanzania: Mainland	2 314	8 878	6 522	12 369	31 553	47 379	49 774	53 276	57 004	61 137
Uganda	1 424	3 246	4 318	6 779	19 683	25 098	25 423	27 115	29 688	32 609
Zambia	1 544	4 315	3 795	3 601	20 265	20 859	21 453	25 868	27 005	23 085
Zanzibar	...	...	137	298	820	1 184	1 262	1 448	1 621	1 806
Zimbabwe	2 337	8 257	13 560	8 721	12 042	19 963	20 549	22 041	24 312	21 441
Middle Africa	*11 277*	*42 234*	*54 050*	*43 748*	*189 153*	*238 018*	*222 087*	*245 763*	*244 834*	*225 405*
Angola	3 808	7 153	13 671	12 207	83 799	116 194	101 124	122 124	101 353	85 001
Cameroon	1 316	10 090	12 814	10 047	26 144	30 905	32 644	35 009	38 694	38 861
Central African Republic	276	1 163	1 507	957	2 141	1 695	1 825	2 072	2 221	2 220
Chad	355	789	1 834	1 576	10 971	11 690	10 392	10 394	11 372	11 272
Congo	284	1 846	3 073	3 359	13 678	11 751	10 152	11 012	13 360	12 397
D.R. of the Congo	4 772	15 638	14 829	8 342	21 566	37 918	40 338	37 642	47 146	47 320
Equatorial Guinea	21	56	170	1 511	16 299	13 176	11 241	12 201	13 278	11 025
Gabon	410	5 421	6 039	5 677	14 359	14 372	14 024	14 929	16 994	16 888
Sao Tome and Principe	35	78	113	72	197	318	348	379	415	422
Southern Africa	*19 563*	*88 407*	*125 049*	*150 618*	*406 125*	*349 554*	*328 659*	*385 996*	*407 504*	*389 192*
Botswana	67	852	3 721	5 788	12 787	14 421	15 646	17 406	18 663	18 341
Eswatini	155	806	1 254	1 738	4 439	4 073	3 841	4 446	4 718	4 594
Lesotho	79	414	588	822	2 269	2 372	2 165	2 403	2 575	2 460
Namibia	605	2 422	2 786	3 834	11 282	11 272	10 666	12 734	13 454	12 366
South Africa	18 656	83 913	116 699	138 436	375 348	317 416	296 341	349 007	368 094	351 431
Western Africa	*41 351*	*282 970*	*118 296*	*118 861*	*508 140*	*684 508*	*607 611*	*595 300*	*665 760*	*723 523*
Benin	322	1 484	1 993	2 569	6 970	11 380	11 821	12 702	14 262	14 403
Burkina Faso	506	2 174	3 524	2 961	10 100	11 823	12 833	14 107	16 060	15 991
Cabo Verde	73	162	350	613	1 664	1 596	1 663	1 770	1 967	1 982
Côte d'Ivoire [2]	1 501	10 176	11 893	10 682	26 264	45 780	47 964	51 588	58 011	58 540
Gambia	160	838	1 176	1 301	1 543	1 378	1 467	1 505	1 675	1 823
Ghana	4 698	6 924	13 214	10 570	42 587	49 182	55 010	58 995	65 535	66 999
Guinea	765	1 998	3 906	4 269	6 853	8 794	8 604	10 325	10 907	12 354
Guinea-Bissau	281	469	609	363	849	1 047	1 179	1 350	1 382	1 322
Liberia	316	935	595	645	1 292	2 669	2 757	2 763	2 745	2 582
Mali	320	1 651	2 732	2 954	10 679	13 095	14 043	15 366	17 071	17 433
Mauritania	457	1 857	2 289	1 780	5 629	6 167	6 399	6 758	7 049	7 594

Table 1.A. Estimates of Gross Domestic Product in US Dollars at Current Prices by Major Area, Region and Country

Major area, region and country	1970	1980	1990	2000	2010	2015	2016	2017	2018	2019
	(Millions of Dollars)									
Niger	569	3 594	3 515	2 301	7 620	9 659	10 288	11 170	12 821	12 928
Nigeria	29 388	243 851	61 536	69 449	363 360	494 583	404 649	375 770	421 821	474 517
Senegal	1 232	4 210	8 028	6 055	16 725	17 761	19 040	20 997	23 236	23 665
Sierra Leone	455	1 333	879	861	2 578	4 248	3 863	3 740	4 085	4 122
Togo	308	1 314	2 057	1 488	3 426	5 346	6 032	6 395	7 133	7 270
Americas	**1 348 342**	**3 931 364**	**7 755 212**	**13 308 052**	**21 964 966**	**25 299 796**	**25 553 758**	**26 983 229**	**27 923 866**	**28 619 048**
Latin America and the Caribbean	**185 469**	**796 597**	**1 192 831**	**2 306 284**	**5 346 509**	**5 496 213**	**5 270 832**	**5 780 761**	**5 579 784**	**5 433 941**
Caribbean	*17 287*	*59 706*	*95 823*	*161 788*	*290 604*	*346 466*	*353 745*	*365 378*	*376 124*	*388 983*
Anguilla	4	12	76	150	268	331	320	284	320	380
Antigua and Barbuda	34	134	459	826	1 149	1 337	1 437	1 468	1 605	1 662
Aruba	198	332	856	1 963	2 502	2 920	2 966	3 056	3 203	3 293
Bahamas	763	2 190	4 768	8 077	10 096	11 711	11 929	12 491	13 022	13 579
Barbados	218	1 034	2 055	3 152	4 530	4 715	4 830	4 978	5 087	5 209
British Virgin Islands	12	32	120	858	1 021	1 174	1 286	1 207	1 249	1 297
Cayman Islands	31	227	1 226	3 002	4 277	4 785	4 989	5 237	5 517	6 020
Cuba	5 693	19 913	28 645	30 566	64 328	87 206	91 370	96 851	100 023	105 355
Curaçao	...	...	...	...	2 951	3 152	3 122	3 117	3 128	3 102
Dominica	23	73	201	333	494	541	576	520	551	582
Dominican Republic	1 859	8 298	9 522	23 960	53 160	71 155	75 682	79 998	85 555	88 941
Former Netherlands Antilles	224	943	1 980	2 857	...	...	...	...	...	...
Grenada	19	88	236	520	771	997	1 062	1 126	1 169	1 212
Haiti	439	1 835	3 096	3 665	6 708	8 355	7 598	8 521	9 287	8 051
Jamaica	1 736	3 323	5 277	9 005	13 221	14 198	14 077	14 809	15 731	15 831
Montserrat	8	28	75	36	56	61	63	60	62	67
Puerto Rico	5 106	14 639	31 034	62 569	98 381	103 376	104 337	103 446	100 979	104 989
Saint Kitts and Nevis	25	68	217	421	760	923	971	997	1 011	1 051
Saint Lucia	41	181	557	936	1 487	1 808	1 865	1 999	2 066	2 122
Sint Maarten (Dutch part)	...	...	...	...	896	1 066	1 072	1 014	954	1 009
St. Vincent and the Grenadines	21	70	234	396	681	755	774	792	811	825
Trinidad and Tobago	824	6 253	5 082	8 176	22 182	24 960	22 386	22 385	23 680	23 209
Turks and Caicos Islands	10	32	106	319	687	942	1 032	1 022	1 113	1 197
Central America	*51 645*	*261 431*	*332 550*	*776 487*	*1 209 615*	*1 400 519*	*1 319 995*	*1 413 770*	*1 484 374*	*1 528 232*
Belize	28	216	449	832	1 377	1 724	1 775	1 837	1 871	1 880
Costa Rica	1 253	6 144	7 261	14 950	37 269	54 776	57 158	58 482	60 554	61 774
El Salvador	339	1 177	4 818	11 785	18 448	23 438	24 191	24 979	26 117	27 023
Guatemala	1 670	6 913	6 712	16 923	40 682	62 186	66 053	71 612	73 118	76 710
Honduras	824	3 061	3 637	7 187	15 839	20 980	21 718	23 136	24 024	25 095
Mexico	45 225	237 095	299 944	707 910	1 057 801	1 170 567	1 077 906	1 157 735	1 220 697	1 256 441
Nicaragua	1 140	2 706	3 555	5 093	8 759	12 757	13 286	13 786	13 064	12 521
Panama	1 165	4 119	6 174	11 808	29 440	54 092	57 908	62 203	64 928	66 788
South America	*116 537*	*475 460*	*764 458*	*1 368 009*	*3 846 290*	*3 749 227*	*3 597 091*	*4 001 614*	*3 719 286*	*3 516 726*
Argentina	33 985	81 764	153 186	308 148	426 487	644 903	557 532	642 696	519 872	449 664
Bolivia (Plurinational State of)	1 010	3 519	4 868	8 398	19 650	33 000	33 941	37 509	40 288	40 895
Brazil	35 214	191 125	406 897	652 360	2 208 838	1 802 212	1 795 693	2 062 838	1 885 469	1 847 796
Chile	9 680	30 721	34 918	78 363	218 538	243 919	250 440	277 045	298 258	282 318
Colombia	10 127	46 899	56 557	99 230	286 563	293 482	282 825	311 884	333 569	323 803
Ecuador	2 861	17 873	15 232	18 319	69 555	99 290	99 938	104 296	107 562	107 436
Guyana	427	943	632	1 137	3 433	4 280	4 483	4 748	4 788	5 174
Paraguay [3]	680	5 088	6 022	9 184	27 239	36 164	36 054	39 009	40 385	38 087
Peru	5 829	16 648	29 119	51 743	147 528	189 803	191 898	211 008	222 045	226 850
Suriname	356	1 089	752	1 157	4 368	4 787	3 129	3 216	3 465	3 697
Uruguay	2 538	10 642	9 239	22 823	40 285	53 274	52 688	59 530	59 597	56 046
Venezuela (Bolivarian Republic of)	13 830	69 147	47 036	117 146	393 806	344 112	288 469	247 836	203 990	134 960
Northern America	**1 162 873**	**3 134 767**	**6 562 381**	**11 001 768**	**16 618 456**	**19 803 583**	**20 282 927**	**21 202 468**	**22 344 082**	**23 185 108**
Bermuda	266	902	2 035	3 480	6 635	6 655	6 900	7 142	7 263	7 361
Canada	89 228	276 037	596 088	744 774	1 617 267	1 556 129	1 528 245	1 649 519	1 721 906	1 741 497
Greenland	76	520	1 113	1 167	2 503	2 499	2 707	2 827	3 052	3 024
United States	1 073 303	2 857 307	5 963 144	10 252 347	14 992 052	18 238 301	18 745 075	19 542 980	20 611 861	21 433 226
Asia	**515 800**	**2 527 344**	**5 575 446**	**9 493 268**	**20 965 666**	**26 712 943**	**27 735 626**	**29 762 753**	**32 112 976**	**33 081 821**
Central Asia	*...*	*...*	*55 852*	*41 975*	*227 976*	*316 820*	*268 993*	*279 120*	*286 518*	*304 653*
Kazakhstan	...	...	29 665	18 292	148 047	184 388	137 278	166 806	179 340	181 667

Table 1.A. Estimates of Gross Domestic Product in US Dollars at Current Prices by Major Area, Region and Country

(Millions of Dollars)

Major area, region and country	1970	1980	1990	2000	2010	2015	2016	2017	2018	2019
Kyrgyzstan	...	...	2 608	1 370	4 794	6 678	6 813	7 703	8 271	8 455
Tajikistan	...	...	2 839	861	5 642	7 855	6 953	7 536	7 765	8 333
Turkmenistan	...	...	3 071	4 932	22 583	36 052	36 169	37 915	40 749	48 276
Uzbekistan	...	...	17 670	16 520	46 909	81 847	81 779	59 160	50 393	57 921
Eastern Asia	*329 110*	*1 559 686*	*4 073 972*	*7 196 026*	*13 653 535*	*17 834 116*	*18 593 245*	*19 812 773*	*21 629 978*	*22 132 386*
China	92 603	306 167	394 566	1 211 331	6 087 192	11 061 573	11 233 315	12 310 490	13 894 907	14 342 934
China, Hong Kong SAR	3 812	28 862	76 929	171 669	228 639	309 386	320 840	341 242	361 697	365 711
China, Macao SAR	166	1 008	3 221	6 720	28 124	45 362	45 388	50 751	55 084	53 859
D.P.R. of Korea	4 927	9 879	14 702	10 608	13 945	16 283	16 786	17 365	17 487	16 331
Japan	212 609	1 105 386	3 132 818	4 887 520	5 700 098	4 389 476	4 922 538	4 866 864	4 954 807	5 082 466
Mongolia	202	691	1 749	1 318	7 189	11 750	11 187	11 426	13 109	13 853
Republic of Korea	9 005	65 398	283 366	576 179	1 144 067	1 465 773	1 500 112	1 623 901	1 724 755	1 646 539
South-Eastern Asia	*37 638*	*206 709*	*373 474*	*625 343*	*1 984 539*	*2 468 319*	*2 590 145*	*2 790 298*	*2 986 732*	*3 157 434*
Brunei Darussalam	225	6 190	3 901	6 650	13 707	12 930	11 400	12 128	13 567	13 469
Cambodia	768	715	1 698	3 667	11 242	18 050	20 017	22 177	24 572	27 098
Indonesia	10 440	84 791	133 858	175 702	755 094	860 854	931 877	1 015 619	1 042 240	1 119 191
Lao People's DR	119	333	902	1 806	7 313	14 390	15 806	17 071	18 142	18 823
Malaysia	3 864	24 488	44 025	93 790	255 018	301 355	301 255	319 109	358 712	364 684
Myanmar	2 726	6 232	6 173	8 694	44 847	63 835	66 971	68 062	73 617	76 785
Philippines	7 413	35 954	49 095	81 026	199 591	292 774	304 898	313 620	330 910	359 354
Singapore	1 921	12 082	38 892	96 077	239 808	307 999	318 642	341 857	373 206	372 074
Thailand	7 387	33 528	88 460	126 392	341 105	401 296	412 353	455 275	504 992	542 017
Timor-Leste	...	...	203	367	882	1 594	1 651	1 599	1 560	2 018
Viet Nam	2 775	2 396	6 472	31 173	115 932	193 241	205 276	223 780	245 214	261 921
Southern Asia	*98 425*	*341 222*	*522 589*	*739 628*	*2 541 613*	*3 127 927*	*3 341 790*	*3 773 763*	*3 931 515*	*4 194 216*
Afghanistan	1 731	3 647	3 560	3 342	14 699	18 713	18 038	18 623	17 987	17 877
Bangladesh	6 196	16 729	28 137	45 470	114 508	194 466	220 316	245 633	269 628	301 051
Bhutan	62	129	274	439	1 585	2 004	2 159	2 450	2 447	2 564
India	62 422	187 033	329 139	476 148	1 669 620	2 146 759	2 290 591	2 625 598	2 773 660	2 891 582
Iran (Islamic Republic of)	10 976	95 617	96 364	111 615	491 099	393 436	425 403	460 976	461 940	603 780
Maldives	42	93	281	886	2 588	4 109	4 379	4 754	5 301	5 642
Nepal	1 041	2 089	3 780	5 730	16 281	20 801	20 982	25 590	27 958	30 715
Pakistan	13 139	30 994	51 666	76 866	174 508	267 035	277 521	302 710	284 169	256 996
Sri Lanka	2 815	4 891	9 390	19 132	56 726	80 604	82 401	87 428	88 426	84 009
Western Asia	*50 627*	*419 727*	*549 558*	*890 296*	*2 558 002*	*2 965 760*	*2 941 453*	*3 106 799*	*3 278 232*	*3 293 133*
Armenia	...	...	2 302	2 039	9 875	10 553	10 546	11 527	12 458	13 673
Azerbaijan	...	...	6 518	5 273	52 906	53 076	37 867	40 867	47 112	48 048
Bahrain	422	3 764	4 909	9 063	25 713	31 126	32 268	35 474	37 653	38 574
Cyprus	616	2 416	6 258	9 963	25 707	19 771	20 876	22 638	24 963	24 565
Georgia	...	...	8 878	3 217	12 243	14 954	15 142	16 243	17 600	17 743
Iraq	3 289	17 541	23 877	23 657	138 517	166 774	166 602	190 644	215 489	225 232
Israel	6 020	23 964	58 801	132 342	233 996	299 813	318 951	353 253	370 588	395 099
Jordan	612	4 138	4 146	8 725	27 134	38 587	39 893	41 408	42 932	44 503
Kuwait	2 873	28 691	18 471	37 718	115 416	114 585	109 407	120 688	140 665	134 624
Lebanon	1 990	5 447	2 950	16 679	38 444	49 939	51 205	53 141	54 961	53 367
Oman	268	6 256	11 556	19 507	56 913	68 400	65 481	70 598	79 789	76 332
Qatar [4]	539	7 838	7 360	17 760	125 122	161 740	151 732	166 929	191 362	183 466
Saudi Arabia	5 377	164 540	117 473	189 515	528 207	654 270	644 936	688 586	786 522	792 967
State of Palestine	177	1 074	1 936	4 314	9 682	13 972	15 405	16 128	16 277	17 059
Syrian Arab Republic	1 756	13 146	11 159	19 000	60 465	19 090	12 377	13 341	16 361	20 379
Turkey	25 070	94 768	207 570	274 295	776 967	864 314	869 683	858 989	778 382	761 426
United Arab Emirates	1 067	44 169	51 364	105 701	289 787	358 135	357 045	385 606	422 215	421 142
Yemen	...	...	4 029	10 865	30 907	26 660	22 037	20 739	22 903	24 935
Yemen Arab Republic (Former)	398	1 620	3 595	...	...	...	...	...	...	...
Yemen Democratic (Former)	154	355	697	...	...	...	...	...	...	...
Europe	**1 384 584**	**5 098 123**	**8 740 836**	**9 701 151**	**19 889 619**	**19 188 074**	**19 177 842**	**20 395 507**	**21 991 871**	**21 644 995**
Eastern Europe	*506 091*	*1 119 751*	*913 920*	*658 925*	*2 867 785*	*2 629 553*	*2 557 988*	*3 008 402*	*3 281 110*	*3 354 841*
Belarus	...	...	19 480	10 770	57 232	56 455	47 724	54 725	60 031	63 081
Bulgaria	9 000	10 832	20 726	13 246	50 364	50 631	53 784	58 952	66 199	67 926
Czechia	...	...	40 728	61 823	209 070	188 033	196 272	218 629	248 909	250 681
Czechoslovakia (Former)	16 294	47 822	57 575	...	...	...	...	...	...	...
Hungary	6 389	25 483	37 193	47 218	131 917	125 074	128 471	142 962	160 419	163 469
Poland	28 277	59 108	66 050	172 220	479 834	477 812	472 632	526 504	587 409	595 862
Republic of Moldova	...	...	4 766	1 546	6 975	7 745	8 071	9 670	11 457	11 955
Romania	12 719	36 469	40 591	37 439	166 225	177 895	188 495	211 696	241 626	250 076
Russian Federation	...	...	574 068	261 567	1 539 845	1 366 410	1 279 528	1 577 580	1 668 456	1 692 930

Table 1.A. Estimates of Gross Domestic Product in US Dollars at Current Prices by Major Area, Region and Country

Major area, region and country	(Millions of Dollars)									
	1970	1980	1990	2000	2010	2015	2016	2017	2018	2019
Slovakia	...	...	16 847	20 719	90 311	88 468	89 655	95 494	105 702	105 080
Ukraine [b]	...	...	93 471	32 375	136 012	91 031	93 356	112 190	130 902	153 781
USSR (Former)	433 412	940 038	790 877	...	...	...	...	...	...	...
Northern Europe	*214 891*	*921 400*	*1 835 881*	*2 516 109*	*4 293 790*	*4 761 422*	*4 546 951*	*4 658 249*	*5 010 428*	*4 923 042*
Denmark	17 075	71 127	138 248	164 158	321 995	302 673	313 116	332 121	356 879	350 104
Estonia	...	...	5 653	5 698	19 694	23 049	24 260	26 952	30 631	31 471
Finland	11 302	53 649	141 446	125 707	249 181	234 440	240 608	255 232	275 947	269 296
Iceland	527	3 386	6 478	9 004	13 684	17 389	20 618	24 488	25 738	24 188
Ireland	4 397	21 751	49 315	99 871	222 071	291 522	299 556	339 341	386 156	398 590
Latvia	...	...	9 654	7 950	23 878	27 240	28 052	30 459	34 416	34 103
Lithuania	...	...	10 235	11 525	37 138	41 419	43 018	47 759	53 723	54 627
Norway	12 814	64 439	119 791	171 246	428 757	385 802	368 820	398 394	434 167	403 336
Sweden	38 092	142 093	261 847	262 834	495 813	505 104	515 655	541 019	555 455	530 884
United Kingdom	130 682	564 954	1 093 214	1 658 116	2 481 580	2 932 785	2 693 248	2 662 484	2 857 317	2 826 442
Southern Europe	*192 892*	*874 020*	*1 984 636*	*2 064 826*	*4 302 051*	*3 621 001*	*3 710 286*	*3 915 732*	*4 214 986*	*4 088 495*
Albania	2 266	2 142	2 146	3 488	11 927	11 387	11 861	13 020	15 147	15 278
Andorra	99	565	1 302	1 429	3 447	2 789	2 895	3 000	3 218	3 154
Bosnia and Herzegovina	...	...	7 755	5 693	17 176	16 212	16 913	18 081	20 184	20 164
Croatia	...	...	16 632	21 669	59 808	49 531	51 597	55 319	60 991	60 415
Greece	13 134	56 845	97 893	131 719	296 835	195 318	192 732	200 125	212 250	205 327
Italy	113 400	477 237	1 176 422	1 143 829	2 134 018	1 835 899	1 875 797	1 961 796	2 091 545	2 003 576
Kosovo	...	...	4 424	1 695	5 830	6 440	6 714	7 246	7 943	7 953
Malta	259	1 293	2 635	4 053	8 741	10 710	11 470	12 790	14 647	14 864
Montenegro	...	...	2 147	991	4 139	4 053	4 374	4 857	5 507	5 542
North Macedonia	...	...	2 912	3 773	9 407	10 065	10 672	11 307	12 629	12 695
Portugal	8 108	32 895	78 718	118 311	237 881	199 314	206 286	221 358	242 313	238 785
San Marino	80	338	832	1 141	2 139	1 419	1 467	1 529	1 655	1 602
Serbia [b]	...	...	40 531	9 866	41 819	39 656	40 693	44 179	50 641	51 475
Slovenia	...	...	18 184	20 291	48 161	43 090	44 736	48 587	54 162	54 174
Spain	40 992	232 747	536 528	596 877	1 420 722	1 195 119	1 232 076	1 312 539	1 422 154	1 393 491
Yugoslavia (Former)	14 554	69 959	88 161	...	...	...	...	...	...	...
Western Europe	*470 709*	*2 182 952*	*4 006 399*	*4 461 290*	*8 425 993*	*8 176 097*	*8 362 618*	*8 813 125*	*9 485 347*	*9 278 618*
Austria	15 373	82 055	166 468	196 800	391 893	381 818	395 569	417 238	455 095	445 075
Belgium	26 707	126 832	205 330	236 204	480 952	462 150	475 740	502 698	543 734	533 097
France	148 451	701 305	1 269 139	1 362 248	2 642 610	2 438 208	2 471 286	2 595 151	2 787 864	2 715 518
Germany	215 835	950 334	1 771 647	1 943 144	3 396 354	3 356 236	3 467 498	3 682 602	3 963 768	3 861 124
Liechtenstein	111	685	1 756	2 747	5 621	6 269	6 237	6 474	6 839	6 798
Luxembourg	1 509	6 232	13 229	21 263	53 212	57 744	60 691	64 182	70 920	71 105
Monaco	284	1 342	2 429	2 607	5 362	6 259	6 468	6 431	7 194	7 424
Netherlands	38 165	195 159	318 328	416 442	846 555	765 265	783 528	833 870	914 043	907 051
Switzerland	24 274	119 008	258 074	279 834	603 434	702 150	695 601	704 479	735 889	731 425
Oceania	**53 825**	**205 499**	**382 531**	**479 118**	**1 482 494**	**1 470 029**	**1 543 165**	**1 670 461**	**1 718 161**	**1 638 770**
Australia and New Zealand	*51 649*	*196 599*	*368 984*	*463 218*	*1 446 047*	*1 425 102*	*1 498 328*	*1 622 200*	*1 666 873*	*1 587 144*
Australia	45 152	173 234	323 544	408 775	1 299 463	1 247 634	1 310 105	1 416 784	1 458 953	1 380 208
New Zealand	6 497	23 365	45 440	54 443	146 584	177 468	188 224	205 416	207 921	206 936
Melanesia	*1 767*	*6 922*	*9 214*	*11 012*	*28 167*	*37 026*	*36 625*	*39 651*	*42 147*	*42 563*
Fiji	221	1 205	1 339	1 708	3 141	4 682	4 930	5 353	5 537	5 504
New Caledonia	378	1 182	2 529	3 412	9 355	8 790	9 002	9 459	10 174	9 880
Papua New Guinea	1 097	4 267	4 966	5 289	14 251	21 723	20 759	22 743	24 216	24 970
Solomon Islands	32	144	208	338	720	1 071	1 130	1 216	1 306	1 303
Vanuatu	38	124	171	265	701	760	804	880	915	907
Micronesia	*74*	*194*	*405*	*588*	*864*	*1 050*	*1 127*	*1 178*	*1 243*	*1 260*
Kiribati	20	33	40	75	156	169	182	187	197	195
Marshall Islands	8	27	79	111	168	181	198	208	221	237
Micronesia (FS of)	21	68	158	233	297	317	332	367	402	414
Nauru	15	42	49	22	59	104	118	129	138	133
Palau	9	24	79	148	183	279	297	288	285	280
Polynesia	*335*	*1 784*	*3 928*	*4 299*	*7 416*	*6 851*	*7 085*	*7 433*	*7 897*	*7 803*
Cook Islands	11	28	73	100	241	302	310	346	363	379
French Polynesia	263	1 558	3 568	3 757	6 081	5 324	5 493	5 757	6 175	6 023
Samoa	41	115	115	238	692	787	822	824	834	845
Tonga	17	79	162	191	371	403	421	461	480	508
Tuvalu	3	4	10	14	31	35	40	44	46	47

Notes for Table 1.A. Estimates of Gross Domestic Product in US Dollars at Current Prices by Major Area, Region and Country

1/ Burundi
1970, 1980, 1990
Refers to data compiled according to the 1968 SNA.

2/ Côte d'Ivoire
1970, 1980, 1990, 2000
Refers to data compiled according to the 1968 SNA.

3/ Paraguay
1970, 1980, 1990, 2000
Does not incorporate export of binational hydroelectric power at market prices.

4/ Qatar
1970, 1980, 1990
Refers to data compiled according to the 1968 SNA.

5/ Ukraine
2010-2019
The Government of Ukraine has advised the United Nations that it is not in a position to provide statistical data concerning the Autonomous Republic of Crimea and the city of Sevastopol.

6/ Serbia
1990
Includes data for Kosovo and Metohija

Table 1.B. Estimates of Per Capita Gross Domestic Product in US Dollars by Major Area, Region and Country

Major area, region and country	(Dollars)									
	1970	1980	1990	2000	2010	2015	2016	2017	2018	2019
World	**924**	**2 777**	**4 320**	**5 476**	**9 529**	**10 163**	**10 208**	**10 742**	**11 288**	**11 339**
Developed economies	**2 983**	**10 003**	**19 818**	**26 814**	**41 231**	**41 727**	**42 698**	**44 355**	**46 814**	**47 149**
Developing economies	**228**	**849**	**990**	**1 516**	**3 916**	**4 890**	**4 852**	**5 215**	**5 494**	**5 543**
Transition economies	**1 701**	**3 501**	**2 750**	**1 337**	**7 208**	**6 614**	**6 105**	**7 204**	**7 660**	**7 862**
Africa	**321**	**1 284**	**881**	**809**	**1 898**	**1 960**	**1 786**	**1 807**	**1 859**	**1 884**
Northern Africa	*288*	*1 247*	*1 278*	*1 480*	*3 205*	*3 267*	*2 987*	*2 849*	*2 814*	*2 962*
Algeria	356	2 198	2 397	1 761	4 481	4 178	3 946	4 110	4 154	3 976
Egypt	236	465	641	1 390	2 593	3 437	2 861	2 023	2 538	3 161
Libya	1 865	11 861	7 007	7 180	13 060	2 752	2 360	3 769	5 201	4 810
Morocco	290	1 105	1 222	1 351	2 882	2 919	2 941	3 083	3 278	3 282
Sudan	...	...	...	...	1 584	2 158	2 250	2 991	1 157	815
Sudan (Former)	90	335	493	391	...	...	...	...	...	...
Tunisia	312	1 506	1 640	2 212	4 142	3 862	3 698	3 481	3 439	3 318
Sub-Saharan Africa	331	1 295	763	621	1 581	1 656	1 508	1 567	1 041	1 039
Eastern Africa	*185*	*413*	*377*	*318*	*643*	*806*	*813*	*869*	*912*	*943*
Burundi [1]	71	229	211	111	234	277	279	297	276	260
Comoros	163	841	1 241	778	1 315	1 242	1 272	1 324	1 416	1 370
Djibouti	447	839	774	761	1 480	2 676	2 818	2 931	3 049	3 252
Eritrea	...	...	147	308	501	602	644	558	581	567
Ethiopia	...	...	234	121	300	626	696	722	734	828
Ethiopia (Former)	86	160	230	...	...	...	...	...	...	...
Kenya	223	641	534	453	952	1 337	1 411	1 572	1 708	1 817
Madagascar	160	439	311	286	472	467	476	515	524	523
Malawi	123	358	337	283	479	384	309	359	396	435
Mauritius	249	1 254	2 590	4 109	8 016	9 284	9 694	10 486	11 192	11 169
Mozambique	446	548	302	319	472	590	429	461	503	504
Rwanda	61	257	334	261	610	751	745	772	783	820
Seychelles	425	2 688	6 311	9 221	10 628	14 503	14 907	15 812	16 335	17 382
Somalia	99	91	138	231	91	105	103	107	104	105
South Sudan	...	...	...	...	1 570	614	298	322	428	448
U.R. of Tanzania: Mainland	171	479	266	380	732	947	965	1 003	1 041	1 084
Uganda	151	261	249	287	607	657	641	659	695	737
Zambia	370	737	472	346	1 489	1 314	1 311	1 535	1 556	1 292
Zanzibar	...	...	201	325	655	821	848	944	1 026	1 111
Zimbabwe	442	1 115	1 300	734	948	1 445	1 465	1 548	1 684	1 464
Middle Africa	*281*	*799*	*763*	*455*	*1 437*	*1 544*	*1 396*	*1 498*	*1 448*	*1 293*
Angola	646	858	1 154	745	3 588	4 167	3 506	4 096	3 290	2 671
Cameroon	202	1 170	1 088	648	1 285	1 326	1 364	1 425	1 534	1 502
Central African Republic	152	529	537	263	488	377	402	451	476	468
Chad	98	175	307	189	918	828	714	692	735	707
Congo	214	1 038	1 304	1 074	3 200	2 420	2 038	2 155	2 548	2 304
D.R. of the Congo	238	593	428	177	334	497	512	462	561	545
Equatorial Guinea	69	223	405	2 492	17 272	11 275	9 250	9 668	10 144	8 130
Gabon	696	7 464	6 361	4 621	8 841	7 379	6 984	7 230	8 019	7 773
Sao Tome and Principe	475	811	952	509	1 095	1 596	1 710	1 828	1 968	1 961
Southern Africa	*783*	*2 725*	*2 974*	*2 928*	*6 956*	*5 550*	*5 142*	*5 954*	*6 199*	*5 841*
Botswana	106	949	2 892	3 522	6 435	6 800	7 244	7 893	8 280	7 961
Eswatini	359	1 372	1 525	1 729	4 168	3 690	3 448	3 953	4 152	4 002
Lesotho	77	309	345	404	1 137	1 152	1 044	1 149	1 221	1 158
Namibia	740	2 290	1 944	2 136	5 325	4 869	4 523	5 300	5 495	4 957
South Africa	845	2 938	3 171	3 079	7 329	5 731	5 272	6 122	6 369	6 001
Western Africa	*390*	*2 054*	*655*	*506*	*1 655*	*1 946*	*1 682*	*1 604*	*1 747*	*1 848*
Benin	111	399	400	374	758	1 076	1 087	1 137	1 242	1 220
Burkina Faso	90	319	400	255	647	653	688	735	813	787
Cabo Verde	272	570	1 037	1 432	3 378	3 042	3 131	3 293	3 616	3 604
Côte d'Ivoire [2]	294	1 267	997	649	1 279	1 971	2 013	2 111	2 314	2 276
Gambia	345	1 314	1 231	987	861	661	683	680	735	776

Table 1.B. Estimates of Per Capita Gross Domestic Product in US Dollars by Major Area, Region and Country

Major area, region and country	(Dollars)									
	1970	1980	1990	2000	2010	2015	2016	2017	2018	2019
Ghana	538	626	894	548	1 719	1 766	1 931	2 026	2 202	2 203
Guinea	184	410	615	518	672	769	733	856	879	967
Guinea-Bissau	398	600	625	302	558	603	661	739	738	688
Liberia	226	505	287	226	332	597	601	588	570	523
Mali	54	233	323	270	710	751	782	830	895	887
Mauritania	398	1 206	1 125	677	1 611	1 524	1 537	1 578	1 601	1 678
Niger	126	600	438	203	463	483	495	517	571	555
Nigeria	525	3 321	646	568	2 292	2 730	2 176	1 969	2 154	2 361
Senegal	289	754	1 067	618	1 319	1 218	1 270	1 362	1 466	1 452
Sierra Leone	166	393	204	188	402	592	527	499	534	528
Togo	145	483	545	302	534	730	803	831	904	899
Americas	**2 609**	**6 399**	**10 747**	**15 974**	**23 532**	**25 823**	**25 853**	**27 066**	**27 778**	**28 239**
Latin America and the Caribbean	**649**	**2 210**	**2 700**	**4 429**	**9 060**	**8 826**	**8 381**	**9 104**	**8 705**	**8 400**
Caribbean	*706*	*2 069*	*2 890*	*4 357*	*7 221*	*8 315*	*8 448*	*8 689*	*8 911*	*9 178*
Anguilla	576	1 664	8 496	13 352	19 923	23 148	22 199	19 488	21 756	25 529
Antigua and Barbuda	528	2 173	7 348	10 871	13 049	14 286	15 198	15 383	16 673	17 113
Aruba	3 346	5 528	13 770	21 608	24 607	27 980	28 281	29 006	30 262	30 975
Bahamas	4 505	10 397	18 607	27 098	28 444	31 295	31 563	32 719	33 768	34 864
Barbados	912	4 095	7 874	11 609	16 056	16 525	16 900	17 392	17 746	18 149
British Virgin Islands	1 182	2 764	6 855	42 225	36 732	40 283	43 818	40 820	41 898	43 189
Cayman Islands	3 398	14 018	48 428	70 967	75 461	77 518	79 738	82 621	85 972	92 692
Cuba	653	2 022	2 703	2 747	5 730	7 700	8 061	8 541	8 822	9 296
Curaçao	...	...	...	...	19 782	19 718	19 387	19 239	19 219	18 980
Dominica	324	967	2 860	4 788	6 967	7 596	8 081	7 275	7 688	8 111
Dominican Republic	413	1 430	1 335	2 828	5 483	6 921	7 279	7 609	8 051	8 282
Former Netherlands Antilles	1 490	5 856	11 285	17 343	...	...	...	...	...	...
Grenada	202	990	2 451	5 057	7 258	9 097	9 628	10 153	10 486	10 818
Haiti	94	325	440	433	674	781	701	776	835	715
Jamaica	925	1 536	2 181	3 392	4 704	4 911	4 844	5 070	5 360	5 369
Montserrat	675	2 439	7 105	7 292	11 331	12 358	12 615	11 972	12 436	13 487
Puerto Rico	1 940	4 736	9 119	17 054	27 482	30 571	31 780	32 698	33 221	35 791
Saint Kitts and Nevis	554	1 585	5 397	9 553	15 509	18 029	18 812	19 155	19 275	19 896
Saint Lucia	396	1 538	4 032	5 973	8 540	10 094	10 362	11 047	11 358	11 611
Sint Maarten (Dutch part)	...	...	...	...	26 238	26 682	26 271	24 467	22 747	23 804
St. Vincent and the Grenadines	234	695	2 179	3 676	6 293	6 921	7 075	7 213	7 361	7 464
Trinidad and Tobago	872	5 764	4 161	6 453	16 702	18 214	16 251	16 174	17 038	16 637
Turks and Caicos Islands	1 674	4 079	8 745	15 842	21 028	26 182	28 241	27 546	29 555	31 353
Central America	*744*	*2 870*	*2 933*	*5 738*	*7 676*	*8 290*	*7 712*	*8 157*	*8 459*	*8 606*
Belize	228	1 496	2 394	3 364	4 271	4 776	4 818	4 888	4 885	4 815
Costa Rica	678	2 571	2 328	3 773	8 142	11 299	11 666	11 815	12 112	12 238
El Salvador	92	256	914	2 002	2 983	3 706	3 806	3 910	4 068	4 187
Guatemala	297	949	725	1 453	2 781	3 826	3 983	4 234	4 239	4 363
Honduras	303	832	734	1 093	1 904	2 302	2 343	2 454	2 506	2 575
Mexico	878	3 499	3 573	7 158	9 271	9 606	8 740	9 278	9 673	9 849
Nicaragua	474	829	852	1 005	1 504	2 050	2 108	2 159	2 021	1 913
Panama	767	2 082	2 499	3 897	8 082	13 630	14 344	15 146	15 545	15 728
South America	*607*	*1 977*	*2 589*	*3 928*	*9 804*	*9 098*	*8 649*	*9 536*	*8 787*	*8 238*
Argentina	1 423	2 931	4 696	8 358	10 429	14 971	12 814	14 628	11 719	10 041
Bolivia (Plurinational State of)	225	631	709	998	1 955	3 036	3 077	3 351	3 549	3 552
Brazil	370	1 584	2 731	3 732	11 286	8 814	8 710	9 925	9 001	8 755
Chile	989	2 690	2 630	5 108	12 808	13 574	13 754	14 999	15 925	14 896
Colombia	471	1 743	1 709	2 504	6 337	6 176	5 871	6 377	6 717	6 432
Ecuador	471	2 237	1 489	1 445	4 634	6 124	6 060	6 214	6 296	6 184
Guyana	606	1 209	850	1 522	4 581	5 577	5 811	6 125	6 146	6 610
Paraguay [3]	275	1 599	1 426	1 725	4 360	5 407	5 319	5 681	5 806	5 406
Peru	433	949	1 319	1 956	5 082	6 229	6 205	6 711	6 941	6 978
Suriname	969	3 029	1 856	2 456	8 256	8 562	5 539	5 638	6 015	6 360
Uruguay	903	3 650	2 971	6 875	11 992	15 614	15 387	17 322	17 278	16 190
Venezuela (Bolivarian Republic of)	1 214	4 554	2 396	4 842	13 847	11 439	9 664	8 429	7 062	4 733

Table 1.B. Estimates of Per Capita Gross Domestic Product in US Dollars by Major Area, Region and Country

Major area, region and country	(Dollars)									
	1970	1980	1990	2000	2010	2015	2016	2017	2018	2019
Northern America	**5 034**	**12 342**	**23 456**	**35 215**	**48 411**	**55 468**	**56 417**	**58 581**	**61 336**	**63 244**
Bermuda	5 052	15 675	33 017	53 532	101 462	104 480	108 897	113 282	115 742	117 768
Canada	4 175	11 305	21 643	24 348	47 361	43 194	42 004	44 907	46 444	46 550
Greenland	1 649	10 367	20 025	20 776	44 196	44 329	47 989	50 046	53 950	53 353
United States	5 123	12 451	23 652	36 393	48 516	56 839	58 031	60 117	63 015	65 134
Asia	**246**	**975**	**1 728**	**2 538**	**4 981**	**6 026**	**6 196**	**6 587**	**7 042**	**7 190**
Central Asia	...	...	*1 114*	*758*	*3 630*	*4 626*	*3 861*	*3 939*	*3 977*	*4 161*
Kazakhstan	...	...	1 811	1 226	9 109	10 493	7 699	9 226	9 790	9 793
Kyrgyzstan	...	...	596	278	884	1 121	1 122	1 244	1 312	1 318
Tajikistan	...	...	537	138	750	929	803	849	853	894
Turkmenistan	...	...	834	1 092	4 439	6 478	6 388	6 585	6 965	8 124
Uzbekistan	...	...	866	667	1 645	2 646	2 601	1 851	1 552	1 756
Eastern Asia	*330*	*1 304*	*2 925*	*4 735*	*8 508*	*10 841*	*11 252*	*11 938*	*12 981*	*13 233*
China	112	306	335	939	4 447	7 863	7 944	8 663	9 733	10 004
China, Hong Kong SAR	991	5 928	13 130	25 086	32 021	43 054	44 293	46 705	49 065	49 180
China, Macao SAR	676	4 234	9 368	15 710	52 253	75 341	74 061	81 517	87 208	84 097
D.P.R. of Korea	386	638	735	462	571	650	667	686	688	640
Japan	2 026	9 382	25 162	38 326	44 344	34 297	38 529	38 171	38 952	40 063
Mongolia	158	409	801	550	2 643	3 919	3 660	3 669	4 135	4 295
Republic of Korea	280	1 719	6 602	12 161	23 091	28 841	29 423	31 781	33 705	32 143
South-Eastern Asia	*134*	*578*	*840*	*1 191*	*3 324*	*3 891*	*4 038*	*4 303*	*4 558*	*4 769*
Brunei Darussalam	1 736	31 930	15 077	19 959	35 269	31 164	27 156	28 572	31 627	31 086
Cambodia	110	107	189	302	786	1 163	1 270	1 385	1 512	1 644
Indonesia	90	573	735	831	3 122	3 332	3 563	3 838	3 894	4 136
Lao People's DR	44	102	212	339	1 170	2 135	2 309	2 455	2 569	2 625
Malaysia	358	1 775	2 442	4 044	9 041	9 955	9 818	10 259	11 378	11 414
Myanmar	100	182	149	186	886	1 212	1 263	1 275	1 371	1 421
Philippines	207	759	793	1 039	2 124	2 867	2 941	2 982	3 103	3 324
Singapore	927	5 010	12 908	23 847	46 736	55 077	56 361	59 890	64 821	64 103
Thailand	200	708	1 564	2 008	5 076	5 840	5 979	6 578	7 274	7 785
Timor-Leste	...	...	275	415	806	1 333	1 354	1 286	1 230	1 561
Viet Nam	64	44	95	390	1 318	2 085	2 192	2 366	2 566	2 715
Southern Asia	*133*	*363*	*439*	*508*	*1 484*	*1 711*	*1 806*	*2 015*	*2 074*	*2 187*
Afghanistan	155	273	287	161	504	544	510	513	484	470
Bangladesh	96	210	273	356	776	1 245	1 395	1 538	1 671	1 846
Bhutan	208	316	515	743	2 313	2 753	2 931	3 287	3 243	3 361
India	112	268	377	451	1 353	1 639	1 729	1 961	2 051	2 116
Iran (Islamic Republic of)	385	2 474	1 710	1 701	6 658	5 012	5 347	5 714	5 647	7 282
Maldives	366	588	1 258	3 172	7 077	9 033	9 209	9 577	10 279	10 626
Nepal	86	139	200	239	603	770	770	926	995	1 074
Pakistan	226	397	480	540	973	1 339	1 363	1 456	1 339	1 187
Sri Lanka	225	325	542	1 019	2 800	3 855	3 920	4 138	4 165	3 940
Western Asia	*686*	*4 239*	*3 710*	*4 830*	*11 019*	*11 524*	*11 229*	*11 663*	*12 110*	*11 975*
Armenia	...	...	651	664	3 432	3 607	3 592	3 915	4 221	4 623
Azerbaijan	...	...	900	649	5 857	5 516	3 889	4 151	4 735	4 782
Bahrain	1 985	10 460	9 899	13 636	20 722	22 689	22 632	23 743	23 991	23 504
Cyprus	1 004	4 750	10 802	14 364	30 993	23 323	24 514	26 484	28 968	28 285
Georgia	...	...	1 641	737	2 987	3 716	3 771	4 052	4 397	4 439
Iraq	332	1 285	1 371	1 007	4 657	4 688	4 551	5 077	5 607	5 730
Israel	2 140	6 475	13 219	22 257	31 852	37 578	39 333	42 851	44 215	46 376
Jordan	355	1 740	1 163	1 703	3 737	4 164	4 175	4 231	4 308	4 405
Kuwait	3 859	20 962	8 815	18 443	38 576	29 874	27 650	29 755	33 999	31 999
Lebanon	866	2 104	1 052	4 340	7 762	7 645	7 626	7 793	8 013	7 784
Oman	371	5 419	6 377	8 601	18 713	16 029	14 619	15 131	16 521	15 343
Qatar [4]	4 921	35 048	15 454	29 976	67 403	63 039	57 163	61 264	68 794	64 782
Saudi Arabia	921	16 978	7 236	9 171	19 263	20 628	19 879	20 802	23 337	23 140
State of Palestine	157	711	921	1 338	2 387	3 085	3 323	3 397	3 347	3 424
Syrian Arab Republic	276	1 472	897	1 198	2 830	1 061	709	780	966	1 194

Table 1.B. Estimates of Per Capita Gross Domestic Product in US Dollars by Major Area, Region and Country

Major area, region and country	(Dollars)									
	1970	1980	1990	2000	2010	2015	2016	2017	2018	2019
Turkey	719	2 155	3 849	4 337	10 742	11 006	10 894	10 590	9 453	9 127
United Arab Emirates	4 551	43 324	28 092	33 727	33 893	38 663	38 142	40 645	43 839	43 103
Yemen	...	...	344	624	1 335	1 006	811	745	804	855
Yemen Arab Republic (Former)	84	264	392	...	...	...	...	...	...	...
Yemen Democratic (Former)	105	198	273	...	...	...	...	...	...	...
Europe	**1 968**	**6 798**	**12 104**	**13 342**	**26 945**	**25 760**	**25 704**	**27 294**	**29 390**	**28 896**
Eastern Europe	*1 540*	*3 132*	*2 950*	*2 168*	*9 725*	*8 932*	*8 693*	*10 231*	*11 168*	*11 433*
Belarus	...	...	1 919	1 091	6 075	5 981	5 052	5 791	6 351	6 674
Bulgaria	1 058	1 220	2 344	1 656	6 783	7 032	7 520	8 300	9 388	9 703
Czechia	...	...	3 939	6 008	19 842	17 737	18 483	20 546	23 337	23 452
Czechoslovakia (Former)	1 135	3 116	3 684	...	...	...	...	...	...	...
Hungary	616	2 370	3 584	4 620	13 288	12 791	13 172	14 693	16 525	16 879
Poland	866	1 663	1 740	4 467	12 519	12 563	12 441	13 872	15 490	15 727
Republic of Moldova	...	...	1 092	368	1 707	1 903	1 985	2 382	2 828	2 957
Romania	619	1 613	1 728	1 691	8 120	8 928	9 522	10 771	12 387	12 914
Russian Federation	...	...	3 891	1 787	10 732	9 424	8 808	10 840	11 449	11 606
Slovakia	...	...	3 186	3 837	16 711	16 276	16 475	17 529	19 384	19 256
Ukraine [5]	...	...	1 816	663	2 970	2 026	2 088	2 522	2 958	3 496
USSR (Former)	1 789	3 556	2 748	...	...	...	...	...	...	...
Northern Europe	*2 681*	*11 218*	*20 003*	*26 715*	*42 892*	*46 128*	*43 804*	*44 630*	*47 748*	*46 680*
Denmark	3 463	13 881	26 891	30 734	57 967	53 206	54 823	57 939	62 043	60 657
Estonia	...	...	3 612	4 073	14 784	17 523	18 427	20 427	23 154	23 740
Finland	2 450	11 204	28 310	24 230	46 439	42 772	43 765	46 310	49 967	48 678
Iceland	2 580	14 836	25 401	32 106	42 718	52 655	62 065	73 232	76 438	71 345
Ireland	1 512	6 426	14 046	26 399	48 761	62 660	63 793	71 391	80 137	81 637
Latvia	...	...	3 623	3 334	11 269	13 636	14 209	15 611	17 846	17 885
Lithuania	...	...	2 769	3 291	11 889	14 127	14 887	16 784	19 178	19 795
Norway	3 306	15 770	28 204	38 060	87 754	74 195	70 239	75 221	81 336	74 986
Sweden	4 729	17 086	30 563	29 593	52 801	51 726	52 425	54 621	55 704	52 896
United Kingdom	2 352	10 051	19 134	28 140	39 105	44 530	40 623	39 901	42 557	41 855
Southern Europe	*1 514*	*6 310*	*13 833*	*14 258*	*28 121*	*23 662*	*24 266*	*25 633*	*27 621*	*26 825*
Albania	1 053	798	653	1 115	4 046	3 939	4 109	4 514	5 254	5 303
Andorra	4 098	15 660	23 886	21 854	40 812	35 748	37 448	38 963	41 794	40 887
Bosnia and Herzegovina	...	...	1 737	1 518	4 635	4 727	4 995	5 395	6 072	6 109
Croatia	...	...	3 482	4 894	13 818	11 701	12 260	13 225	14 674	14 627
Greece	1 516	5 905	9 573	11 886	27 264	18 323	18 156	18 934	20 172	19 604
Italy	2 119	8 469	20 622	20 176	35 972	30 306	30 922	32 334	34 498	33 090
Kosovo	...	...	2 731	860	3 430	3 615	3 739	4 049	4 453	4 473
Malta	809	3 901	7 278	10 297	21 100	24 702	26 303	29 205	33 346	33 752
Montenegro	...	...	3 491	1 616	6 630	6 465	6 973	7 739	8 772	8 825
North Macedonia	...	...	1 459	1 854	4 543	4 840	5 129	5 431	6 063	6 093
Portugal	937	3 374	7 955	11 490	22 450	19 223	19 978	21 515	23 626	23 350
San Marino	4 173	15 730	34 491	41 540	68 505	42 643	43 796	45 399	48 997	47 313
Serbia [6]	...	...	4 259	1 313	5 735	5 589	5 765	6 275	7 215	7 359
Slovenia	...	...	9 063	10 208	23 570	20 804	21 568	23 400	26 066	26 062
Spain	1 210	6 174	13 686	14 620	30 273	25 607	26 420	28 137	30 458	29 816
Yugoslavia (Former)	720	3 176	3 772	...	...	...	...	...	...	...
Western Europe	*2 815*	*12 708*	*22 625*	*24 220*	*44 301*	*42 095*	*42 854*	*44 950*	*48 160*	*46 922*
Austria	2 045	10 783	21 552	24 389	46 599	43 995	45 222	47 306	51 184	49 701
Belgium	2 773	12 852	20 520	22 973	43 968	40 942	41 899	44 020	47 355	46 198
France	2 857	12 714	21 793	22 378	40 685	36 612	36 980	38 721	41 492	40 319
Germany	2 747	12 140	22 411	23 871	42 020	41 036	42 187	44 552	47 685	46 232
Liechtenstein	5 202	26 463	60 991	82 786	156 167	167 294	165 630	171 278	180 408	178 799
Luxembourg	4 443	17 120	34 650	48 758	104 772	101 889	104 773	108 432	117 370	115 481
Monaco	12 098	50 185	82 511	81 101	150 577	165 945	169 909	167 516	185 985	190 532
Netherlands	2 935	13 794	21 271	26 148	50 744	45 179	46 141	48 990	53 580	53 053
Switzerland	3 947	18 939	38 791	39 172	77 277	84 629	83 008	83 313	86 315	85 135

Table 1.B. Estimates of Per Capita Gross Domestic Product in US Dollars by Major Area, Region and Country

Major area, region and country	(Dollars)									
	1970	1980	1990	2000	2010	2015	2016	2017	2018	2019
Oceania	**2 721**	**8 918**	**14 138**	**15 388**	**40 518**	**37 150**	**38 439**	**41 028**	**41 624**	**39 173**
Australia and New Zealand	*3 308*	*11 085*	*18 124*	*20 272*	*54 517*	*49 921*	*51 806*	*55 390*	*56 235*	*52 929*
Australia	3 529	11 875	19 076	21 524	58 654	52 131	53 997	57 629	58 597	54 763
New Zealand	2 305	7 425	13 372	14 108	33 543	38 458	40 398	43 687	43 836	43 264
Melanesia	*483*	*1 473*	*1 543*	*1 473*	*3 066*	*3 658*	*3 550*	*3 771*	*3 933*	*3 898*
Fiji	424	1 896	1 838	2 106	3 653	5 391	5 651	6 101	6 267	6 185
New Caledonia	3 592	8 147	14 850	15 702	36 900	32 427	32 831	34 129	36 335	34 942
Papua New Guinea	394	1 195	1 076	905	1 949	2 679	2 510	2 695	2 814	2 845
Solomon Islands	200	623	667	820	1 363	1 776	1 823	1 911	2 001	1 945
Vanuatu	445	1 074	1 170	1 433	2 967	2 802	2 890	3 082	3 125	3 023
Micronesia	*492*	*1 064*	*1 684*	*2 163*	*2 978*	*3 440*	*3 650*	*3 775*	*3 941*	*3 950*
Kiribati	395	565	552	885	1 517	1 525	1 613	1 641	1 698	1 657
Marshall Islands	416	882	1 676	2 187	2 986	3 159	3 426	3 578	3 788	4 038
Micronesia (FS of)	343	933	1 640	2 171	2 885	2 906	3 015	3 290	3 568	3 640
Nauru	2 343	5 414	5 181	2 101	5 925	10 050	11 281	12 177	12 953	12 351
Palau	790	1 969	5 235	7 738	10 220	15 784	16 742	16 148	15 934	15 572
Polynesia	*918*	*4 180*	*8 100*	*7 955*	*12 671*	*11 493*	*11 829*	*12 340*	*13 031*	*12 790*
Cook Islands	524	1 590	3 990	5 576	13 093	17 183	17 682	19 741	20 705	21 603
French Polynesia	2 379	10 164	17 849	15 610	22 821	19 492	20 007	20 852	22 238	21 567
Samoa	289	741	708	1 362	3 722	4 066	4 224	4 220	4 250	4 285
Tonga	203	849	1 705	1 949	3 570	4 001	4 162	4 523	4 650	4 865
Tuvalu	451	563	1 070	1 473	2 982	3 157	3 523	3 862	4 001	4 036

Notes for Table 1.B. Estimates of Per Capita Gross Domestic Product in US Dollars by Major Area, Region and Country

1/ Burundi

1970, 1980, 1990

Refers to data compiled according to the 1968 SNA.

2/ Côte d'Ivoire

1970, 1980, 1990, 2000

Refers to data compiled according to the 1968 SNA.

3/ Paraguay

1970, 1980, 1990, 2000

Does not incorporate export of binational hydroelectric power at market prices.

4/ Qatar

1970, 1980, 1990

Refers to data compiled according to the 1968 SNA.

5/ Ukraine

2010-2019

The Government of Ukraine has advised the United Nations that it is not in a position to provide statistical data concerning the Autonomous Republic of Crimea and the city of Sevastopol.

6/ Serbia

1990

Includes data for Kosovo and Metohija

B. Percentage Distribution of Main National Accounts Aggregates at Current Prices: Individual Countries or Areas

Description of Analysis in Tables 2 and 3

B. Economic structure expressed in terms of percentage shares of gross domestic product and gross value added.

The tables included in this section of the publication disaggregate GDP and gross value added at current prices into component parts and express these as percentage shares that outline the economic structures in countries. The years of coverage are 1970, 1975, 1980, 1985, 1990, 1995, 2000, 2005, 2010 and 2015 through 2019.

GDP estimates by type of expenditure are shown in Table 2 and gross value added by kind of economic activity in Table 3. Differences in the concepts and coverage in classifications used are indicated in the footnotes. Both tables are designed to provide an overview of the structure of the economic system expressed in current prices.

GDP and gross value added estimates of the countries are expressed in millions of the national currency as indicated in the first column of Table 2 and Table 3, respectively. For tabulation purposes, the values of the GDP and gross value added estimates of some countries prior to a high inflation period might be qualified with unit (u) or thousand (t) to reflect the measurement in a single unit or thousands of units of national currency.

Table 2 features the distribution of GDP based on expenditure components. It shows what portion of income from production is spent by households or government on final consumption, what is spent on investment, and what part of GDP is exported after deducting the expenditures on imports.

It is noted that in some instances the shares for changes in inventories should be used with caution as countries may also include items such as statistical errors.

Table 3 presents the shares of the components of gross value added by kind of economic activity (in terms of ISIC Rev 3.1):

- Agriculture, hunting, forestry and fishing (ISIC A-B)
- Mining and quarrying, Manufacturing, Electricity, gas and water supply (ISIC C-E) Manufacturing (ISIC D) as a separate activity)
- Construction (ISIC F)
- Wholesale and retail trade; repair of motor vehicles, motorcycles and personal and household goods, Hotels and restaurants (ISIC G-H)
- Transport, storage and communications (ISIC I)
- Other activities which includes Financial intermediation, Real estate, renting and business activities, Public administration and defense; compulsory social security, Education, Health and social work, Other community, social and personal service activities, Private households with employed persons (ISIC J-P)

The distributive shares of gross value added are presented from each economic activity based on the classification by tabulation category of the International Standard Industrial Classification (ISIC 3) of all Economic Activities. This table reflects the economic structure of production in the country. For example, it identifies the value-added shares from different sources of production, e.g., oil, gas and other minerals. It also illustrates that many developing countries heavily depend on income mainly originating in agriculture, while relatively more developed countries generate a much larger portion of income in the industrial and services activities.

Note that the breakdown in shares of GDP in current prices by type of expenditure in Table 2 might not add up to 100 per cent due to statistical discrepancies.

The breakdown of nominal world GDP by type of expenditure and nominal world value added in current prices by type of economic activity since 1970 are shown in the following graphs.

Figure 3. Share in nominal world GDP by type of expenditure

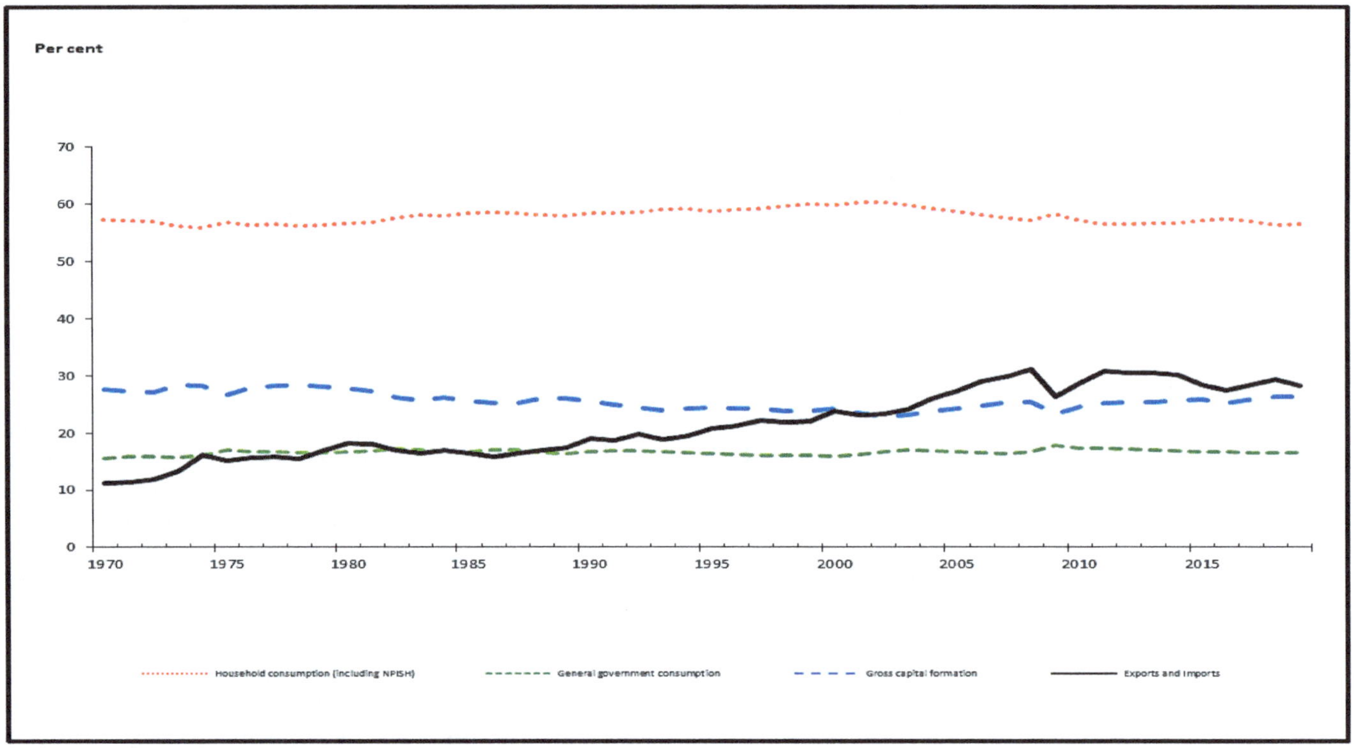

Figure 4. Share in nominal gross value added by kind of economic activity

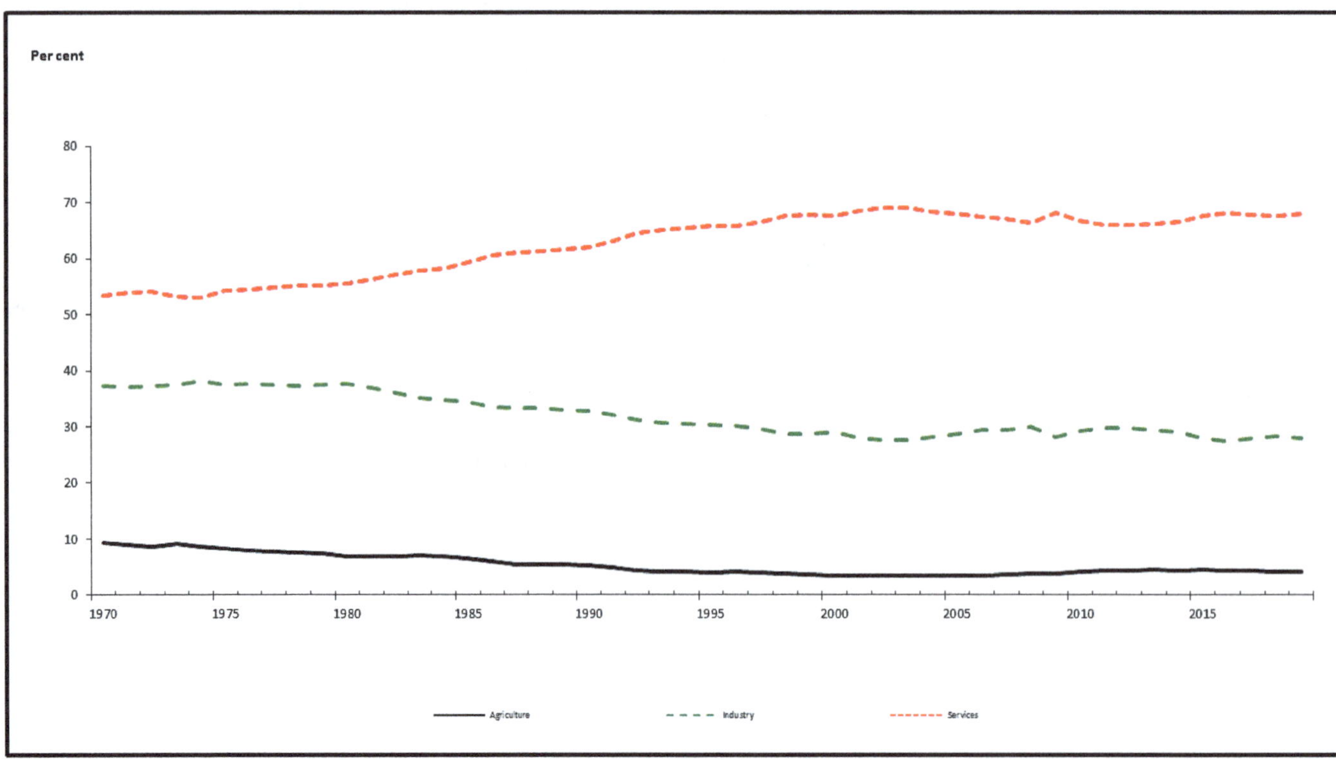

Table 2. Gross Domestic Product by Type of Expenditure: Individual Countries or Areas

Major area, region and country	Year	Gross Domestic Product (at current prices) Million	Percentage Distributtion: Household final consumption expenditure 1	General government final consumption expenditure 2	Gross fixed capital formation 3	Changes in inventories 4	Exports of goods and services 5	Imports of goods and services 6
Africa								
Algeria (Algerian Dinar)	1970	25 451	59.7	13.3	30.7	2.4	22.1	27.6
	1975	61 435	51.2	13.0	39.0	6.1	33.6	43.1
	1980	162 141	43.3	13.8	33.8	5.2	34.3	30.5
	1985	290 940	48.1	15.8	31.9	1.3	23.5	20.5
	1990	553 138	56.7	16.3	25.6	3.2	23.4	25.2
	1995	2 000 476	55.8	17.0	27.1	4.5	26.6	30.9
	2000	4 114 219	41.7	13.6	20.7	2.8	42.1	20.8
	2005	7 561 984	33.8	11.5	22.4	9.3	47.2	24.1
	2010	11 991 564	34.3	17.2	36.3	5.1	38.4	31.4
	2015	16 712 675	41.0	21.6	42.3	8.5	23.2	36.5
	2016	17 514 635	42.5	20.9	43.1	7.7	20.9	35.1
	2017	18 876 200	42.6	19.0	40.8	7.8	22.6	32.7
	2018	20 452 300	41.9	17.2	40.1	7.1	25.8	32.1
	2019	20 428 300	43.5	16.9	38.7	7.3	22.8	29.2
Angola (Kwanza)	1970	109 (u)	46.8	28.4	23.9	0.9	35.8	33.0
	1975	106 (u)	46.2	28.3	23.6	0.9	34.9	32.1
	1980	214 (u)	48.1	24.8	22.0	0.9	33.6	28.5
	1985	273 (u)	46.9	30.8	17.2	0.7	33.0	28.6
	1990	409 (u)	44.7	28.6	11.0	0.5	38.9	23.7
	1995	18	52.3	21.9	27.9	...	76.2	78.2
	2000	122 568	39.5	34.1	11.7	...	67.5	52.9
	2005	3 222 350	32.0	16.0	27.8	-0.2	65.5	41.1
	2010	7 701 651	35.8	17.0	28.2	0.0	61.5	42.6
	2015	13 950 291	52.7	16.4	28.2	6.0	29.8	33.1
	2016	16 549 565	56.0	13.9	26.2	1.0	28.1	25.2
	2017	20 262 296	57.2	12.9	23.2	0.9	29.0	23.3
	2018	25 627 742	56.4	10.5	17.2	0.7	40.8	25.5
	2019	31 010 417	57.4	12.6	16.6	0.7	42.4	29.6
Benin (CFA Franc BCEAO)	1970	89 017	54.7	23.4	15.4	0.4	40.3	32.8
	1975	144 438	59.9	21.5	21.2	2.5	39.5	46.0
	1980	313 634	63.2	16.0	20.6	1.4	35.3	43.1
	1985	507 478	75.0	16.7	12.6	3.0	31.4	38.9
	1990	542 610	75.7	17.6	12.6	1.4	19.2	26.5
	1995	1 170 413	76.6	13.5	25.8	5.6	22.3	42.5
	2000	1 829 207	78.1	12.1	24.6	-1.0	21.1	34.9
	2005	2 533 784	76.7	13.4	19.7	-1.9	18.9	26.9
	2010	3 452 207	73.4	16.9	23.3	-0.2	23.8	37.2
	2015	6 732 814	75.2	11.4	20.5	0.2	24.7	32.0
	2016	7 005 230	73.2	10.3	19.7	0.5	27.6	31.4
	2017	7 375 302	72.6	10.5	23.4	0.5	27.2	34.3
	2018	7 922 004	70.4	10.4	25.9	0.5	27.3	34.5
	2019	8 439 005	70.9	10.2	25.2	0.5	24.0	30.5
Botswana [1] (Pula)	1970	48	85.9	19.7	49.9	8.7	25.1	72.1
	1975	203	63.5	17.9	34.6	14.1	40.0	67.9
	1980	663	60.5	19.4	31.8	4.7	52.0	67.2
	1985	1 594	47.6	25.1	26.4	2.3	58.6	59.9
	1990	6 923	36.5	24.4	32.9	4.0	53.4	51.8
	1995	13 114	39.4	30.1	27.0	0.2	50.8	43.8
	2000	29 531	33.3	24.9	25.1	4.4	51.8	40.1
	2005	50 752	38.1	19.4	25.3	1.8	52.9	35.6
	2010	86 867	49.1	19.8	33.6	7.8	43.6	51.3
	2015	146 066	52.0	20.6	34.0	-1.4	49.8	56.1
	2016	170 564	47.3	18.2	31.1	-4.0	52.6	44.2
	2017	180 103	49.3	18.4	29.1	-1.5	39.7	35.9
	2018	190 365	49.4	18.2	30.2	-0.8	40.3	39.2
	2019	197 269	51.2	18.4	31.5	1.6	33.6	40.5
Burkina Faso (CFA Franc BCEAO)	1970	139 921	85.7	9.5	7.2	2.7	6.1	15.5
	1975	214 417	82.6	20.5	11.0	4.7	8.5	26.9

Table 2. Gross Domestic Product by Type of Expenditure: Individual Countries or Areas

Major area, region and country	Year	Gross Domestic Product (at current prices) Million	Percentage Distributtion: Household final consumption expenditure 1	General government final consumption expenditure 2	Gross fixed capital formation 3	Changes in inventories 4	Exports of goods and services 5	Imports of goods and services 6
	1980	459 373	78.3	19.5	19.2	3.0	9.4	29.4
	1985	792 557	80.8	17.3	19.1	3.8	9.9	31.0
	1990	959 477	73.5	21.1	17.7	1.2	11.0	24.5
	1995	1 349 563	72.2	16.9	20.1	2.3	12.3	29.3
	2000	2 108 160	88.8	14.1	16.5	-1.9	8.8	26.3
	2005	3 240 716	83.1	13.8	15.4	2.1	9.8	24.3
	2010	5 002 182	71.6	14.5	20.1	1.9	20.5	28.6
	2015	6 995 311	71.5	15.9	19.2	0.2	26.1	33.0
	2016	7 605 123	68.8	16.5	20.3	0.5	25.9	32.0
	2017	8 191 299	66.6	17.7	20.9	1.2	26.5	32.8
	2018	8 920 421	64.3	17.0	19.8	2.9	28.1	32.2
	2019	9 369 188	64.0	19.0	20.5	2.5	25.4	31.4
Burundi [2]	1970	21 476	86.8	9.7	4.0	0.5	10.6	11.5
(Burundi Franc)	1975	32 671	91.5	11.7	9.4	-1.7	8.4	19.3
	1980	85 607	81.9	16.1	12.8	1.1	8.6	20.4
	1985	141 347	77.5	16.1	14.2	0.1	9.9	17.7
	1990	196 656	83.0	19.5	16.4	-0.6	8.0	26.2
	1995	249 865	91.6	13.4	9.4	-0.1	12.9	27.3
	2000	511 039	91.1	14.8	7.5	...	7.8	21.3
	2005	1 208 240	91.4	13.0	18.4	-0.1	6.2	28.9
	2010	2 501 050	85.6	17.8	15.9	0.7	9.7	29.8
	2015	4 417 870	90.5	18.4	12.3	1.3	6.3	28.9
	2016	4 848 204	85.8	18.2	13.4	1.1	6.7	25.3
	2017	5 562 399	86.0	17.9	14.0	1.4	7.3	26.6
	2018	5 490 821	87.8	18.7	17.3	2.1	7.7	30.1
	2019	5 541 207	87.7	19.4	17.8	2.2	8.9	36.7
Cabo Verde	1970	2 097	71.2	14.8	43.3	5.5	36.1	72.5
(Cabo Verde Escudo)	1975	3 422	71.6	14.7	42.5	5.8	35.4	72.0
	1980	6 499	74.9	12.8	36.9	7.5	29.6	66.9
	1985	14 358	70.4	20.6	44.9	2.9	39.3	79.1
	1990	24 534	71.4	16.4	38.7	7.5	29.6	68.5
	1995	42 881	69.3	19.8	36.9	6.3	28.9	66.4
	2000	73 397	66.5	16.4	29.0	3.5	43.1	57.2
	2005	98 016	65.3	18.7	34.1	4.1	32.6	57.6
	2010	138 569	63.0	18.4	45.2	2.5	32.7	61.8
	2015	158 699	65.2	18.9	28.8	1.4	44.9	59.2
	2016	165 782	63.2	17.3	33.1	2.1	44.2	60.0
	2017	173 097	65.3	18.0	33.8	4.4	45.9	67.4
	2018	183 698	61.6	17.8	39.4	...	49.2	68.0
	2019	195 202	61.6	17.6	35.3	...	50.9	65.4
Cameroon	1970	363 702	73.7	13.0	22.8	2.9	29.4	43.8
(CFA Franc BEAC)	1975	777 135	71.1	10.9	27.1	1.8	31.2	42.4
	1980	2 131 725	69.7	8.9	33.2	2.5	26.6	39.1
	1985	4 311 624	64.9	11.8	34.3	0.4	24.2	32.1
	1990	3 488 859	68.9	11.0	22.3	-0.2	26.9	28.4
	1995	4 812 443	68.4	9.9	17.1	-0.4	28.2	21.8
	2000	7 153 015	67.4	10.4	19.6	-0.4	28.0	24.1
	2005	9 464 932	68.9	11.0	21.7	0.3	24.6	26.4
	2010	12 948 432	70.2	11.4	23.5	-0.3	22.2	27.0
	2015	18 285 382	70.7	12.3	23.0	-0.7	22.3	27.6
	2016	19 344 838	70.0	12.1	22.6	0.0	19.2	24.0
	2017	20 328 363	70.0	11.1	23.0	0.0	18.6	22.6
	2018	21 492 534	70.5	11.1	22.8	0.0	19.3	23.7
	2019	22 769 300	71.8	11.0	23.1	-0.1	20.1	25.9
Central African Republic	1970	76 277	71.6	20.1	18.0	...	31.9	41.6
(CFA Franc BEAC)	1975	118 425	87.9	17.1	13.8	...	21.1	39.9
	1980	245 747	93.7	15.1	6.9	0.1	25.2	41.1
	1985	406 531	72.8	22.8	14.0	0.4	23.9	33.0
	1990	410 412	74.3	23.2	13.3	0.3	18.6	27.0
	1995	582 516	70.8	22.5	14.7	0.4	24.2	29.5

Table 2. Gross Domestic Product by Type of Expenditure: Individual Countries or Areas

Major area, region and country	Year	Gross Domestic Product (at current prices) Million	Percentage Distributtion: Household final consumption expenditure 1	General government final consumption expenditure 2	Gross fixed capital formation 3	Changes in inventories 4	Exports of goods and services 5	Imports of goods and services 6
	2000	681 242	71.3	24.6	12.5	0.3	22.1	26.4
	2005	745 210	81.0	15.7	11.0	0.3	14.4	22.5
	2010	1 060 142	82.3	12.0	16.1	0.7	11.6	22.8
	2015	1 002 592	82.4	14.8	20.6	1.2	17.1	36.1
	2016	1 081 516	84.0	14.4	20.9	1.6	14.8	35.7
	2017	1 203 324	83.0	14.1	24.2	1.4	17.3	39.9
	2018	1 233 635	88.0	14.2	25.0	0.9	18.9	47.0
	2019	1 300 902	89.5	15.0	22.4	0.8	18.7	47.5
Chad	1970	98 207	71.4	20.5	11.2	-0.4	16.1	26.1
(CFA Franc BEAC)	1975	161 221	75.2	15.8	19.2	-0.2	11.8	29.3
	1980	166 715	82.1	5.4	9.6	2.0	15.3	14.5
	1985	443 374	105.4	9.0	8.2	1.9	13.7	38.5
	1990	499 245	97.5	8.6	13.4	1.2	13.7	36.2
	1995	820 239	99.4	8.1	11.8	-1.2	17.8	36.6
	2000	1 121 908	103.9	7.8	15.9	2.4	15.3	41.7
	2005	3 523 810	66.5	7.7	19.2	0.1	47.7	41.2
	2010	5 433 500	63.9	10.2	20.2	4.0	38.2	36.4
	2015	6 916 770	71.9	7.3	16.9	2.8	26.8	25.6
	2016	6 158 629	74.4	9.5	15.0	5.1	24.1	28.1
	2017	6 035 358	76.9	9.7	14.0	6.4	21.7	28.7
	2018	6 316 526	73.6	8.7	12.8	5.8	27.2	28.9
	2019	6 604 192	70.4	8.8	15.8	7.2	28.3	30.5
Comoros	1970	10 359	77.9	30.6	33.2	-8.0	13.9	51.6
(Comoro Franc)	1975	24 506	77.9	30.6	33.1	-7.9	13.8	51.5
	1980	54 673	78.2	30.7	34.4	-7.2	11.1	52.2
	1985	107 771	71.8	27.4	34.2	-7.3	21.6	50.3
	1990	139 061	78.6	25.6	14.7	1.7	15.0	37.5
	1995	180 894	83.1	22.3	19.5	...	19.8	44.6
	2000	225 310	94.0	11.7	10.1	...	16.7	32.5
	2005	311 472	87.1	8.9	14.0	0.3	7.3	17.6
	2010	336 947	92.8	9.3	17.9	0.3	9.6	29.9
	2015	428 346	93.3	10.6	13.5	0.1	10.1	27.7
	2016	450 159	92.6	10.6	12.5	0.1	10.7	26.5
	2017	469 217	92.1	10.8	13.3	0.1	11.9	28.3
	2018	490 958	91.3	10.3	14.9	0.1	13.2	29.8
	2019	512 344	90.3	10.3	15.9	...	12.8	29.3
Congo	1970	78 410	88.8	21.8	51.3	-0.4	29.3	96.0
(CFA Franc BEAC)	1975	158 499	83.2	24.9	49.0	-1.0	37.8	109.5
	1980	390 026	58.9	18.3	65.0	-3.4	55.9	116.0
	1985	1 050 666	59.7	17.1	56.3	-4.1	56.4	103.3
	1990	836 658	62.2	26.6	16.1	-1.2	46.6	43.5
	1995	1 101 811	62.3	25.0	39.7	1.2	54.4	76.6
	2000	2 391 498	34.2	15.5	17.7	1.7	79.9	47.2
	2005	3 349 307	33.8	14.1	23.8	0.4	77.3	48.1
	2010	6 774 405	28.1	10.1	49.4	0.1	65.8	53.3
	2015	6 952 360	38.1	20.4	80.5	-1.3	43.2	80.9
	2016	6 016 200	44.3	22.9	80.9	-7.1	45.3	86.3
	2017	6 393 990	40.8	19.4	36.5	0.3	58.5	55.6
	2018	7 420 823	39.1	14.9	25.2	-1.8	72.7	50.1
	2019	7 263 756	30.0	16.4	26.8	-0.9	70.5	48.1
Côte d'Ivoire [3]	1970	414 862	59.3	15.7	20.2	1.8	37.1	34.0
(CFA Franc BCEAO)	1975	834 545	62.0	16.9	22.0	0.4	37.8	39.1
	1980	2 149 886	64.6	16.6	24.4	2.2	36.0	43.7
	1985	3 134 800	58.6	14.1	11.8	1.2	46.8	32.4
	1990	3 238 000	69.1	20.7	7.7	-1.6	28.8	24.6
	1995	5 543 000	64.1	16.9	12.2	1.9	37.0	32.1
	2000	7 605 000	67.2	15.5	12.3	-1.0	39.8	33.8
	2005	9 011 755	68.4	14.4	9.2	2.2	49.9	44.0
	2010	13 007 967	66.9	12.0	12.7	1.1	48.0	41.2
	2015	27 086 150	65.2	9.3	23.7	-0.2	27.4	25.4

Table 2. Gross Domestic Product by Type of Expenditure: Individual Countries or Areas

Major area, region and country	Year	Gross Domestic Product (at current prices) Million	Percentage Distribution: Household final consumption expenditure 1	General government final consumption expenditure 2	Gross fixed capital formation 3	Changes in inventories 4	Exports of goods and services 5	Imports of goods and services 6
	2016	28 423 874	66.6	9.9	21.5	0.2	24.6	22.9
	2017	29 955 010	68.0	10.5	20.1	...	24.9	23.6
	2018	32 222 000	69.0	10.6	19.8	1.5	22.6	23.4
	2019	34 299 000	68.3	10.5	21.1	-1.0	23.8	22.6
D.R. of the Congo (Franc Congolais)	1970	0 (u)	44.0	28.4	21.6	4.5	44.2	42.7
	1975	0 (u)	63.6	23.6	28.5	3.4	27.1	46.1
	1980	0 (u)	60.7	16.0	20.0	4.9	35.5	37.1
	1985	1 (u)	47.8	11.6	21.7	7.7	72.2	61.1
	1990	36 (u)	79.1	11.5	12.8	-3.8	29.5	29.2
	1995	628	81.0	4.9	9.7	-0.3	28.5	23.7
	2000	470 942	87.6	2.1	14.4	0.0	11.4	15.6
	2005	5 670 100	87.7	6.9	11.7	0.1	22.9	29.4
	2010	19 536 700	70.1	9.7	28.7	0.1	41.1	49.6
	2015	35 111 200	69.9	14.4	19.4	0.2	27.7	31.6
	2016	40 753 100	79.4	10.4	17.4	0.2	22.1	29.4
	2017	55 124 300	77.5	5.5	20.6	0.2	35.6	39.4
	2018	76 495 499	76.5	6.3	20.6	0.2	34.1	37.7
	2019	77 971 389	70.8	7.0	25.1	0.3	32.1	35.2
Djibouti (Djibouti Franc)	1970	15 300	72.4	25.3	9.8	...	39.1	46.6
	1975	30 100	76.3	26.7	9.1	...	35.7	47.8
	1980	53 527	65.1	35.9	15.2	...	39.7	55.9
	1985	63 164	73.4	45.6	32.5	...	45.6	97.1
	1990	81 203	67.2	33.6	27.2	-0.1	81.4	109.3
	1995	90 572	62.6	35.4	18.9	-0.2	39.2	55.8
	2000	97 101	69.3	30.1	12.3	7.6	36.3	55.7
	2005	125 939	65.4	24.4	20.4	6.3	40.6	57.0
	2010	221 023	57.3	22.9	26.4	39.4	66.1	112.1
	2015	434 612	61.0	19.7	29.7	-11.5	140.6	139.5
	2016	465 375	61.1	22.1	27.3	13.9	100.0	124.4
	2017	491 728	62.3	21.7	25.9	21.5	147.0	178.4
	2018	519 540	60.7	20.5	27.2	2.1	153.7	164.2
	2019	562 720	61.1	20.6	27.6	19.0	150.2	178.5
Egypt (Egyptian Pound)	1970	3 540	65.5	24.7	11.5	2.4	14.2	18.8
	1975	4 961	63.9	25.2	15.3	6.5	20.4	31.3
	1980	14 083	66.1	16.2	29.4	4.7	26.6	43.0
	1985	40 896	68.2	17.2	25.2	1.5	19.9	32.0
	1990	97 991	71.7	11.0	25.6	5.5	22.0	35.8
	1995	223 065	74.5	10.5	19.2	1.0	22.5	27.7
	2000	332 218	76.8	11.1	17.0	0.7	19.1	24.7
	2005	545 847	72.9	11.1	16.9	0.7	31.3	32.9
	2010	1 206 640	74.6	11.2	19.2	0.3	21.3	26.6
	2015	2 443 856	82.4	11.8	13.7	0.6	13.2	21.7
	2016	2 709 400	83.1	11.4	15.0	...	10.3	19.9
	2017	3 470 000	86.8	10.1	15.3	...	16.3	28.5
	2018	4 437 400	85.4	8.4	16.7	...	18.9	29.4
	2019	5 322 300	82.6	7.7	18.0	...	17.5	25.8
Equatorial Guinea (CFA Franc BEAC)	1970	5 797	67.3	22.2	19.9	...	35.7	45.1
	1975	7 475	65.6	27.3	15.0	...	43.0	50.8
	1980	11 759	63.0	53.7	29.3	...	37.4	83.4
	1985	39 666	80.3	15.5	12.0	-4.5	27.3	30.5
	1990	46 212	55.4	10.3	47.7	-3.4	28.8	48.4
	1995	107 481	55.6	11.6	64.2	0.0	50.6	84.4
	2000	1 075 667	11.3	4.2	49.8	4.2	92.4	62.4
	2005	4 493 858	21.5	7.9	21.8	-0.5	83.6	33.2
	2010	8 072 290	23.4	11.7	42.3	-4.3	85.8	58.9
	2015	7 795 420	38.9	21.9	24.5	0.2	56.7	42.2
	2016	6 661 366	47.7	25.3	16.6	0.1	51.4	41.2
	2017	7 084 543	47.0	23.7	14.0	0.1	58.9	43.6
	2018	7 375 490	47.8	23.0	16.1	0.0	58.8	45.7
	2019	6 459 504	57.9	26.0	13.3	0.0	55.1	52.3

Table 2. Gross Domestic Product by Type of Expenditure: Individual Countries or Areas

Major area, region and country	Year	Gross Domestic Product (at current prices) Million	Percentage Distributtion: Household final consumption expenditure 1	General government final consumption expenditure 2	Gross fixed capital formation 3	Changes in inventories 4	Exports of goods and services 5	Imports of goods and services 6
Eritrea	1990	1 522	90.1	25.8	19.6	...	21.2	59.4
(Nakfa)	1995	3 943	96.1	38.4	22.3	...	21.0	77.8
	2000	6 799	71.7	54.8	22.0	...	9.7	58.2
	2005	16 880	93.2	35.2	20.3	...	6.2	54.9
	2010	24 439	81.3	26.5	18.2	...	6.4	32.4
	2015	30 953	65.0	19.9	10.3	...	31.5	26.6
	2016	33 366	73.8	18.8	6.9	...	21.0	20.6
	2017	28 702	62.0	22.9	8.7	...	31.7	25.3
	2018	30 235	70.0	22.8	2.9	...	32.8	28.5
	2019	29 876	71.2	22.5	4.0	...	31.5	29.3
Eswatini	1970	111	53.5	13.8	23.9	0.2	75.7	65.2
(Lilangeni)	1975	293	41.9	16.8	21.6	-1.0	80.4	57.9
	1980	628	76.0	20.1	33.3	...	70.2	99.6
	1985	1 198	78.7	18.9	21.7	...	64.3	83.5
	1990	3 246	79.9	14.7	15.5	...	60.6	70.8
	1995	6 897	81.2	15.5	17.0	...	60.2	73.9
	2000	12 062	70.0	14.5	23.5	...	68.8	82.5
	2005	20 211	75.8	17.1	17.4	...	60.4	72.3
	2010	32 497	81.3	20.9	14.5	...	46.5	59.6
	2015	51 972	66.9	21.9	12.5	...	43.0	40.8
	2016	56 496	63.0	24.3	12.8	...	43.8	42.3
	2017	59 285	65.5	24.9	12.7	...	43.1	43.8
	2018	62 474	66.4	22.8	13.0	...	40.4	43.8
	2019	66 396	62.4	23.1	11.3	...	45.2	42.0
Ethiopia	1990	23 200	71.4	15.0	10.5	...	5.6	9.7
(Ethiopian Birr)	1995	46 722	80.9	8.5	13.9	...	10.4	19.2
	2000	65 986	69.1	19.1	22.2	...	12.1	24.2
	2005	105 415	77.3	13.3	26.0	...	15.3	35.8
	2010	379 135	81.5	9.2	27.0	...	13.8	33.3
	2015	1 297 960	69.0	9.0	39.2	0.2	9.4	30.3
	2016	1 568 097	66.5	11.1	35.9	1.4	7.8	27.1
	2017	1 832 786	66.5	11.1	37.9	0.5	7.6	23.5
	2018	2 200 121	65.7	10.3	34.3	0.4	8.4	22.8
	2019	2 696 223	68.5	9.2	34.6	0.6	7.9	20.8
Gabon	1970	113 289	29.5	24.3	32.5	...	41.0	31.6
(CFA Franc BEAC)	1975	585 617	18.9	15.1	47.7	16.2	40.8	39.8
	1980	1 145 422	21.0	16.3	22.8	5.3	53.3	26.3
	1985	2 084 175	24.5	22.9	31.0	7.0	46.9	35.9
	1990	1 644 341	41.3	20.4	19.4	2.0	45.4	28.5
	1995	2 754 889	32.7	16.3	18.8	2.2	52.9	31.4
	2000	4 041 735	32.3	14.1	17.5	2.2	61.7	27.4
	2005	5 052 603	30.0	12.5	21.0	0.4	60.0	23.9
	2010	7 111 500	30.6	13.5	31.4	-1.7	57.7	31.5
	2015	8 503 500	37.8	14.8	29.2	...	46.0	27.9
	2016	8 310 600	40.4	14.6	27.0	...	44.0	26.1
	2017	8 668 900	40.0	13.2	21.4	...	50.2	24.8
	2018	9 439 300	37.9	12.1	21.0	...	50.9	21.9
	2019	9 894 800	37.6	12.0	20.6	...	51.5	21.7
Gambia	1970	334	86.3	12.4	12.5	...	33.3	44.5
(Dalasi)	1975	1 057	99.2	14.1	6.9	...	29.5	49.6
	1980	1 441	104.4	22.2	14.4	...	23.6	64.5
	1985	4 234	83.6	13.7	7.1	...	48.7	53.2
	1990	9 266	82.9	13.7	18.0	...	44.3	59.0
	1995	12 467	80.4	16.4	19.8	...	45.3	62.0
	2000	16 639	81.2	11.2	17.3	...	47.7	57.4
	2005	29 367	80.3	9.1	15.8	...	18.2	26.2
	2010	43 231	89.7	8.5	11.8	...	13.2	20.4
	2015	58 581	81.7	8.3	20.3	...	19.6	33.3
	2016	64 390	79.0	8.4	24.9	...	15.9	30.1

Table 2. Gross Domestic Product by Type of Expenditure: Individual Countries or Areas

Major area, region and country	Year	Gross Domestic Product (at current prices) Million	Household final consumption expenditure 1	General government final consumption expenditure 2	Gross fixed capital formation 3	Changes in inventories 4	Exports of goods and services 5	Imports of goods and services 6
			Percentage Distributtion					
	2017	70 142	86.0	7.9	23.0	...	16.8	36.5
	2018	80 649	84.8	8.1	18.8	...	16.3	33.0
	2019	91 649	82.8	8.1	21.2	...	17.5	34.4
Ghana..	1970	479 (t)	67.5	6.0	16.5	2.6	12.0	12.3
(Cedi)	1975	1 121 (t)	67.2	6.1	15.9	1.2	10.0	9.5
	1980	9 090 (t)	76.9	5.2	8.4	-0.8	4.4	4.7
	1985	73	76.0	4.4	13.1	-0.2	5.0	6.0
	1990	431	78.3	5.1	16.7	-0.2	8.0	12.4
	1995	1 644	68.8	5.6	30.5	-2.1	11.8	16.1
	2000	5 760	73.3	6.0	35.5	0.6	23.1	31.8
	2005	20 631	70.5	9.1	44.6	-1.0	17.3	29.2
	2010	60 944	74.9	8.3	24.0	2.1	22.3	32.7
	2015	180 399	74.9	9.7	29.2	0.8	32.0	43.6
	2016	215 077	73.3	10.0	27.0	0.9	31.9	37.5
	2017	256 671	70.2	8.8	20.6	1.7	35.3	38.4
	2018	300 596	72.0	9.0	23.2	1.4	35.3	36.4
	2019	349 480	69.0	8.9	19.6	6.9	36.0	35.4
Guinea..	1970	79 849	91.7	10.5	8.4	1.4	15.8	22.7
(Guinea Franc)	1975	126 732	91.5	10.4	8.4	1.4	16.0	22.7
	1980	185 712	89.7	10.2	8.5	1.4	16.8	22.7
	1985	556 988	93.6	10.7	7.9	1.3	15.4	22.7
	1990	2 578 486	83.5	9.6	14.4	3.5	16.7	27.0
	1995	5 214 978	96.5	8.4	10.4	2.3	10.7	21.0
	2000	7 458 153	86.6	7.0	14.9	3.9	11.2	20.2
	2005	14 807 353	83.4	6.3	21.1	7.4	19.4	36.1
	2010	39 243 444	80.0	12.6	19.1	1.2	30.3	43.2
	2015	65 829 149	85.8	19.5	24.0	0.2	21.5	50.9
	2016	77 087 903	83.5	16.9	52.4	0.3	29.7	82.4
	2017	93 833 884	74.4	15.3	25.8	-3.5	44.7	56.6
	2018	98 286 378	80.2	16.3	21.6	-2.6	37.6	53.0
	2019	113 461 288	79.5	16.2	16.8	-2.1	35.0	44.6
Guinea-Bissau.......................................	1970	124	76.3	20.6	26.4	...	3.6	27.2
(CFA Franc BCEAO)	1975	200	82.0	23.6	13.7	...	4.7	23.4
	1980	244	72.9	28.5	23.7	1.5	11.4	37.7
	1985	1 018	104.0	18.5	29.5	1.8	8.8	52.0
	1990	23 572	100.9	11.4	13.8	0.9	12.0	39.0
	1995	222 375	94.8	6.4	22.3	...	11.7	35.1
	2000	258 220	80.6	17.2	7.2	0.1	18.6	23.7
	2005	309 516	87.7	14.9	6.1	0.4	16.1	25.2
	2010	420 515	93.5	15.2	6.5	0.1	19.9	35.2
	2015	619 726	85.3	15.5	5.5	-1.4	27.5	32.5
	2016	698 685	86.8	13.3	4.8	0.1	26.5	31.6
	2017	783 989	84.1	14.3	6.1	0.1	26.5	31.0
	2018	767 879	86.9	14.6	6.8	-1.8	27.4	31.2
	2019	774 732	97.4	15.9	5.6	-0.2	21.9	37.4
Kenya...	1970	17 989	67.9	12.8	15.9	2.6	18.5	19.5
(Kenyan Shilling)	1975	35 444	76.3	14.7	16.8	-2.8	19.6	23.2
	1980	78 043	68.3	16.2	19.7	3.5	18.8	26.8
	1985	149 703	64.8	13.9	14.6	5.2	16.6	17.6
	1990	290 204	69.6	15.0	17.2	1.5	17.2	21.0
	1995	690 600	77.5	11.9	17.7	-0.9	21.5	26.0
	2000	1 101 863	79.0	12.5	17.1	1.1	18.9	26.0
	2005	1 624 831	76.3	14.2	19.0	-1.5	23.7	31.5
	2010	3 169 301	77.2	14.2	20.3	0.4	20.7	33.6
	2015	6 284 185	78.8	14.1	21.6	-0.1	16.6	27.6
	2016	7 022 963	78.8	12.9	17.6	0.6	14.3	23.4
	2017	8 165 842	81.6	12.9	18.3	0.8	13.2	24.2
	2018	8 892 111	82.4	13.1	17.3	0.7	13.2	23.0
	2019	9 740 360	82.5	13.1	16.8	0.6	12.0	21.4

Table 2. Gross Domestic Product by Type of Expenditure: Individual Countries or Areas

Major area, region and country	Year	Gross Domestic Product (at current prices) Million	Percentage Distributtion: Household final consumption expenditure 1	General government final consumption expenditure 2	Gross fixed capital formation 3	Changes in inventories 4	Exports of goods and services 5	Imports of goods and services 6
Lesotho	1970	57	99.7	13.4	10.6	-0.6	8.9	47.0
(Loti)	1975	120	137.1	23.5	22.9	-1.4	12.0	108.3
	1980	323	122.0	40.6	38.5	0.5	18.9	127.9
	1985	619	141.3	38.9	47.3	-2.0	11.9	145.5
	1990	1 521	135.0	27.3	57.3	-2.2	16.0	145.1
	1995	3 241	113.4	34.7	66.3	-3.2	20.2	142.1
	2000	5 705	118.0	35.3	44.5	-1.4	35.2	126.1
	2005	9 275	105.2	36.5	21.7	0.0	49.3	113.1
	2010	16 612	97.2	39.4	28.0	1.9	41.5	106.3
	2015	30 268	80.0	34.4	27.7	0.1	42.7	86.4
	2016	31 852	82.8	35.1	25.6	2.9	44.7	88.4
	2017	32 048	87.3	36.4	25.9	2.9	45.3	90.1
	2018	34 089	83.4	35.5	25.2	6.8	49.5	93.2
	2019	35 552	84.6	35.1	30.3	4.4	43.4	90.9
Liberia	1970	316	50.6	11.1	19.6	2.1	58.9	42.2
(US Dollar)	1975	622	42.3	12.0	26.4	9.1	66.2	61.0
	1980	936	40.9	19.9	21.4	5.4	66.9	67.0
	1985	1 076	67.0	13.0	12.0	0.7	44.6	30.6
	1990	595	69.8	13.0	10.5	0.3	34.2	27.8
	1995	209	69.6	13.0	10.4	0.3	35.7	29.0
	2000	645	92.5	7.5	7.5	...	31.4	38.9
	2005	706	221.5	11.2	19.5	...	59.1	211.3
	2010	1 292	95.1	21.7	18.7	...	16.6	52.2
	2015	2 669	62.5	24.5	40.8	...	28.8	56.6
	2016	2 757	61.7	23.8	40.2	...	29.2	54.9
	2017	2 763	65.7	23.9	34.6	...	29.2	53.5
	2018	2 745	63.4	24.5	30.9	-9.0	31.3	51.1
	2019	2 582	60.8	29.1	38.5	...	34.6	53.5
Libya	1970	1 421	31.0	14.2	17.6	0.2	78.2	34.3
(Libyan Dinar)	1975	4 041	32.9	23.6	26.9	2.5	64.9	49.9
	1980	11 305	28.3	19.0	22.5	0.8	73.8	40.2
	1985	8 848	39.2	27.1	18.9	0.4	44.7	30.2
	1990	8 804	48.4	24.4	13.9	4.7	39.7	31.1
	1995	11 830	58.8	22.3	11.7	0.5	29.2	22.4
	2000	19 704	46.4	20.6	12.6	0.4	35.2	15.3
	2005	59 468	21.9	10.5	27.8	...	69.7	29.9
	2010	102 537	16.0	20.6	37.9	...	71.1	45.6
	2015	24 400	37.4	59.1	37.6	...	37.1	71.2
	2016	21 300	56.8	58.7	33.7	...	18.9	68.1
	2017	34 573	28.0	41.8	32.0	...	55.1	57.0
	2018	47 414	28.4	40.4	32.2	...	54.7	55.7
	2019	45 584	27.5	37.5	31.7	...	56.0	52.7
Madagascar	1970	58 455	73.5	26.0	10.6	...	23.0	17.8
(Malagasy Ariary)	1975	92 629	83.6	21.5	8.7	...	19.1	17.2
	1980	161 678	83.7	24.0	16.0	...	14.2	23.0
	1985	364 092	87.1	18.6	9.0	...	14.4	16.8
	1990	1 078 541	69.8	12.5	14.7	...	15.3	19.6
	1995	3 129 559	73.8	10.4	9.7	0.1	22.1	23.7
	2000	6 003 055	68.0	12.2	14.4	0.1	28.5	28.9
	2005	11 716 571	70.8	13.9	19.7	0.1	25.9	34.0
	2010	20 863 368	74.0	13.1	25.9	1.1	21.9	36.0
	2015	33 216 176	73.3	15.1	19.0	-3.0	28.4	32.8
	2016	37 637 586	71.5	14.8	19.0	-2.6	29.1	31.7
	2017	41 058 843	71.6	16.1	18.1	-2.3	30.9	34.4
	2018	45 886 302	72.0	13.6	21.0	-0.3	31.5	36.3
	2019	51 035 217	70.9	15.1	21.2	1.4	28.4	34.2
Malawi	1970	483	70.7	10.6	23.5	11.9	12.9	21.9
(Kwacha)	1975	957	67.7	9.7	25.6	20.2	17.4	28.5
	1980	1 816	71.2	13.3	22.8	7.3	14.9	24.1

Table 2. Gross Domestic Product by Type of Expenditure: Individual Countries or Areas

Major area, region and country	Year	Gross Domestic Product (at current prices) Million	Percentage Distributtion					
			Household final consumption expenditure 1	General government final consumption expenditure 2	Gross fixed capital formation 3	Changes in inventories 4	Exports of goods and services 5	Imports of goods and services 6
	1985	3 486	72.8	12.4	13.8	4.4	14.6	18.6
	1990	8 641	76.1	11.2	17.6	5.7	15.2	22.5
	1995	37 807	70.9	15.1	12.2	3.9	19.3	23.7
	2000	187 585	79.6	10.1	12.7	7.0	15.0	21.9
	2005	432 930	90.4	12.7	14.3	5.1	16.9	39.3
	2010	1 047 336	97.5	9.1	15.3	1.0	17.5	37.8
	2015	3 213 173	83.9	9.2	12.6	9.9	23.8	39.5
	2016	3 812 567	88.3	9.7	13.3	10.4	22.7	44.5
	2017	4 635 556	86.1	9.5	12.9	10.2	20.2	38.8
	2018	5 258 469	86.0	9.5	12.9	10.2	18.7	37.3
	2019	5 976 584	85.1	9.4	12.8	10.1	16.7	34.0
Mali..........	1970	88 549	70.8	16.1	12.6	2.0	18.0	19.5
(CFA Franc BCEAO)	1975	150 290	100.4	3.9	17.8	3.3	18.1	43.5
	1980	348 858	90.3	4.6	17.4	1.1	19.5	33.0
	1985	566 224	78.5	26.0	20.1	-4.0	13.4	31.9
	1990	743 754	74.0	19.6	20.9	0.3	12.5	27.3
	1995	1 416 037	85.6	5.0	28.3	-2.0	19.8	36.7
	2000	2 103 270	76.9	16.4	17.7	-0.5	22.5	32.9
	2005	3 294 055	73.4	13.8	20.2	0.6	23.0	31.1
	2010	5 288 939	72.6	15.7	20.8	3.3	22.8	35.1
	2015	7 747 688	80.5	16.2	16.7	2.1	24.0	39.6
	2016	8 321 834	81.1	16.3	17.2	2.3	23.4	40.3
	2017	8 922 205	75.9	16.2	18.2	3.3	22.2	35.9
	2018	9 481 953	74.8	15.9	18.7	1.8	24.5	35.6
	2019	10 213 969	72.9	15.7	20.8	1.8	23.1	34.3
Mauritania..........	1970	2 538	56.2	17.0	38.1	-26.9	22.9	17.4
(Ouguiya)	1975	4 614	60.0	25.5	62.9	-40.8	21.1	33.0
	1980	8 528	79.4	25.1	37.8	-24.5	16.5	28.8
	1985	11 798	71.4	23.2	52.6	-36.5	32.0	41.4
	1990	18 448	83.1	17.2	24.2	-14.5	25.4	29.7
	1995	30 766	61.8	22.8	31.8	-21.7	25.9	24.7
	2000	42 517	76.0	20.6	31.9	-20.6	25.5	33.4
	2005	77 981	68.7	17.1	40.7	8.2	26.8	61.5
	2010	155 297	56.2	13.5	33.3	-1.0	45.7	47.7
	2015	200 221	63.9	14.6	34.3	4.2	30.2	47.2
	2016	225 473	60.6	13.4	29.0	2.3	33.9	39.2
	2017	241 913	58.9	12.8	22.7	7.7	38.3	40.6
	2018	251 497	59.9	13.3	29.9	-1.5	39.6	41.1
	2019	278 621	56.7	12.9	37.1	3.8	41.8	52.4
Mauritius..........	1970	1 142	64.8	16.7	12.7	0.2	47.4	45.7
(Mauritius Rupee)	1975	3 655	51.8	13.9	31.2	0.4	63.3	61.8
	1980	9 307	71.1	15.1	21.9	-2.2	48.8	58.2
	1985	17 783	63.1	12.4	17.5	4.8	51.0	52.5
	1990	40 653	61.6	12.6	29.3	-0.3	64.4	71.3
	1995	74 286	60.8	13.0	22.6	1.9	56.6	58.6
	2000	127 816	57.4	14.3	21.6	3.3	59.1	59.2
	2005	199 845	65.1	14.5	20.6	1.1	57.1	62.1
	2010	307 957	73.2	13.8	24.2	2.9	51.2	62.2
	2015	409 893	74.7	14.9	17.4	0.7	48.8	58.8
	2016	434 765	73.6	15.4	17.2	0.7	44.3	53.7
	2017	457 201	74.8	15.2	17.4	0.9	42.5	54.9
	2018	481 251	75.7	15.3	18.8	0.7	40.8	54.3
	2019	503 030	75.2	15.3	19.8	0.2	39.2	53.6
Morocco..........	1970	23 505	67.7	10.7	16.3	6.3	18.5	21.0
(Moroccan Dirham)	1975	42 749	63.6	14.4	27.1	4.0	24.2	33.2
	1980	86 988	62.3	16.4	24.3	5.3	18.4	27.3
	1985	152 057	60.9	14.1	25.3	7.9	26.0	33.5
	1990	249 905	60.2	13.8	26.2	4.7	25.7	30.2
	1995	330 744	63.9	15.9	23.4	1.9	23.9	30.0
	2000	413 346	60.6	17.7	26.7	-0.1	27.1	32.6

Table 2. Gross Domestic Product by Type of Expenditure: Individual Countries or Areas

Major area, region and country	Year	Gross Domestic Product (at current prices) Million	Percentage Distributtion					
			Household final consumption expenditure 1	General government final consumption expenditure 2	Gross fixed capital formation 3	Changes in inventories 4	Exports of goods and services 5	Imports of goods and services 6
	2005	554 460	56.6	18.6	28.3	1.7	31.2	37.1
	2010	784 624	58.8	17.9	30.7	3.4	32.2	43.0
	2015	987 950	57.5	19.3	28.4	2.4	34.8	42.4
	2016	1 013 229	58.5	19.3	30.0	2.4	35.4	45.5
	2017	1 063 045	57.9	19.0	28.6	4.0	37.2	46.8
	2018	1 108 463	58.0	19.0	28.4	5.0	38.8	49.2
	2019	1 151 170	57.4	19.4	27.7	4.5	39.1	48.0
Mozambique..	1970	116	82.2	17.4	12.4	...	3.0	18.2
(Metical)	1975	164	82.1	17.4	12.4	...	3.0	18.2
	1980	207	82.8	19.9	12.3	...	2.9	17.9
	1985	390	87.9	11.3	4.3	...	3.7	22.8
	1990	3 646	92.6	14.2	23.7	...	5.5	34.5
	1995	26 170	91.6	13.1	18.1	15.9	11.4	50.2
	2000	86 132	71.1	14.9	20.0	17.7	11.2	34.9
	2005	196 989	74.8	17.1	12.2	10.3	27.1	41.5
	2010	377 115	74.0	17.8	17.0	4.9	28.4	42.2
	2015	637 760	64.6	25.9	31.3	9.9	31.1	62.8
	2016	752 702	66.6	26.4	25.9	20.7	33.5	72.1
	2017	840 526	64.7	24.6	22.8	10.3	38.6	61.1
	2018	895 567	65.6	21.8	50.0	...	44.9	82.3
	2019	956 786	66.7	21.7	46.1	...	41.0	75.5
Namibia...	1970	434	62.2	17.6	24.1	-1.4	62.7	61.0
(Namibian Dollar)	1975	827	62.2	17.6	24.2	-1.4	62.8	61.1
	1980	1 886	49.6	14.2	25.1	-1.2	70.4	56.3
	1985	3 579	56.2	22.0	12.3	-2.3	51.7	40.2
	1990	7 208	53.4	23.5	18.5	8.6	43.6	50.3
	1995	14 300	58.4	25.1	19.9	-0.3	45.1	49.3
	2000	26 607	61.9	24.0	16.9	0.5	41.7	45.4
	2005	45 287	59.0	19.7	19.0	1.1	41.2	41.1
	2010	82 599	62.0	25.6	25.3	-1.2	49.0	60.7
	2015	145 207	68.5	27.4	31.0	-0.5	35.6	62.0
	2016	156 879	75.5	27.1	21.7	0.2	35.2	59.7
	2017	169 529	70.7	25.9	17.7	-0.2	34.0	48.2
	2018	178 052	69.6	25.8	16.7	-2.1	36.3	46.4
	2019	178 677	73.2	25.9	16.2	-3.4	35.8	47.7
Niger..	1970	157 210	81.9	16.0	5.4	2.1	11.1	15.7
(CFA Franc BCEAO)	1975	255 360	73.6	17.2	16.4	2.5	14.2	23.3
	1980	759 433	68.2	13.2	20.5	4.5	17.7	26.0
	1985	916 490	75.5	19.8	11.5	0.6	15.5	21.3
	1990	957 027	73.0	20.9	10.4	1.8	15.8	20.5
	1995	1 188 183	75.2	18.6	9.8	2.4	14.7	19.6
	2000	1 638 538	74.3	19.8	12.3	0.3	14.6	19.8
	2005	2 368 004	74.0	17.0	17.5	1.0	14.7	23.4
	2010	3 774 167	73.8	14.7	31.5	0.6	17.4	36.8
	2015	5 715 039	67.4	16.7	32.4	-0.3	14.3	30.5
	2016	6 096 438	68.9	15.1	27.2	0.5	12.8	24.6
	2017	6 485 968	70.1	15.1	28.1	0.2	12.8	26.3
	2018	7 121 376	69.2	15.1	29.0	0.4	12.1	25.8
	2019	7 574 455	70.6	15.2	30.2	0.3	11.7	28.0
Nigeria..	1970	20 991	9.5	1.4	79.3	-0.6	5.8	4.4
(Naira)	1975	60 368	9.1	1.5	73.0	3.0	9.0	6.6
	1980	133 333	8.6	1.7	77.0	0.2	10.2	7.2
	1985	187 831	47.9	1.9	46.4	0.0	7.1	3.3
	1990	494 644	34.6	1.2	53.1	0.1	21.0	9.9
	1995	3 100 235	52.8	1.2	37.2	0.0	24.2	15.4
	2000	7 062 751	40.7	2.1	34.0	0.1	36.0	13.0
	2005	23 121 879	60.3	4.5	25.0	1.2	21.0	12.0
	2010	54 612 264	68.7	8.8	16.8	0.7	25.7	17.7
	2015	95 177 736	79.0	6.7	14.8	0.7	10.7	10.8
	2016	102 575 418	81.6	5.4	14.7	0.6	9.2	11.5

Table 2. Gross Domestic Product by Type of Expenditure: Individual Countries or Areas

Major area, region and country	Year	Gross Domestic Product (at current prices) Million	Percentage Distributtion: Household final consumption expenditure 1	General government final consumption expenditure 2	Gross fixed capital formation 3	Changes in inventories 4	Exports of goods and services 5	Imports of goods and services 6
	2017	114 906 664	80.1	4.4	14.7	0.8	13.2	13.2
	2018	129 112 625	76.6	5.6	19.0	0.8	15.5	17.5
	2019	145 639 139	73.5	5.9	25.4	0.8	14.2	19.8
Rwanda	1970	22 781	79.6	16.0	6.4	0.4	9.5	11.8
(Rwanda Franc)	1975	55 758	76.2	19.3	11.1	1.4	7.0	13.7
	1980	114 104	81.2	14.5	10.3	4.4	11.1	20.4
	1985	183 535	78.5	13.1	13.1	2.7	8.3	15.3
	1990	203 822	80.8	19.9	10.4	...	5.9	14.8
	1995	322 516	96.3	18.0	10.2	...	6.1	30.6
	2000	806 000	88.3	16.1	12.3	...	5.5	22.1
	2005	1 636 000	81.3	16.4	15.2	...	10.7	23.5
	2010	3 571 000	82.2	13.1	19.9	0.6	10.7	26.5
	2015	6 152 000	80.8	13.8	24.0	0.3	13.1	32.0
	2016	6 847 000	77.9	15.1	27.1	-1.5	15.5	34.1
	2017	7 694 000	73.8	15.0	22.7	1.1	20.5	33.1
	2018	8 298 000	76.2	14.7	23.0	-0.3	21.1	34.7
	2019	9 313 000	71.5	15.8	26.9	0.2	21.8	36.1
Sao Tome and Principe	1970	1 017 (t)	74.8	18.2	8.8	...	18.5	20.4
(Dobra)	1975	1 460 (t)	85.7	12.7	8.9	...	12.9	20.2
	1980	2 700 (t)	77.1	34.5	11.4	...	22.4	50.8
	1985	3 509 (t)	77.1	41.2	11.4	...	17.1	50.8
	1990	16	100.8	27.6	31.3	...	14.5	72.5
	1995	140	83.8	27.6	68.1	...	20.6	100.1
	2000	578	92.4	31.6	35.8	...	35.1	95.0
	2005	1 332	94.9	13.0	26.8	-5.0	13.0	42.8
	2010	3 653	81.8	29.0	37.5	0.8	13.3	62.5
	2015	7 031	80.4	25.2	35.4	2.5	11.8	55.4
	2016	7 698	79.6	13.0	26.8	5.1	27.8	52.3
	2017	8 231	78.1	11.7	26.2	5.0	27.5	48.6
	2018	8 619	85.7	17.5	21.7	...	23.6	48.5
	2019	9 230	88.9	15.3	18.1	...	22.8	45.2
Senegal [4]	1970	340 475	75.0	13.8	11.8	-5.8	16.7	16.4
(CFA Franc BCEAO)	1975	576 298	73.6	14.1	13.2	-6.3	22.3	21.7
	1980	889 552	79.9	20.8	15.1	-7.6	19.1	26.9
	1985	1 631 737	81.4	17.2	13.3	-6.7	20.3	26.0
	1990	2 185 840	73.5	15.1	14.9	-5.6	17.4	19.2
	1995	3 147 384	75.9	12.7	17.5	-6.2	22.0	25.5
	2000	4 310 994	72.0	11.4	20.8	0.9	21.6	28.8
	2005	5 943 033	73.7	11.8	21.6	4.4	20.9	32.9
	2010	8 283 317	74.5	13.1	20.6	2.9	19.3	31.2
	2015	10 508 650	72.6	14.3	23.2	2.6	22.7	35.4
	2016	11 283 396	71.6	14.0	24.1	1.2	21.6	32.5
	2017	12 191 796	70.4	13.6	26.0	3.8	21.9	35.8
	2018	12 906 359	69.1	13.7	26.2	5.4	23.0	37.5
	2019	13 865 300	66.7	14.3	27.4	4.6	25.2	38.1
Seychelles	1970	124	31.9	35.4	38.3	1.0	76.9	86.7
(Seychelles Rupee)	1975	348	29.2	36.2	39.3	0.7	78.3	85.4
	1980	1 138	37.8	43.7	36.5	1.1	49.7	71.8
	1985	1 456	39.8	52.8	22.7	-0.4	48.2	63.7
	1990	2 377	35.6	42.2	23.0	1.2	62.5	66.7
	1995	2 924	34.9	42.1	30.1	-0.5	66.7	75.4
	2000	4 267	33.5	42.2	27.6	...	78.3	81.6
	2005	5 055	51.4	34.6	35.7	...	78.3	100.0
	2010	11 705	59.0	27.2	35.4	...	86.7	108.3
	2015	18 340	53.9	20.3	36.9	...	79.3	86.1
	2016	19 002	55.9	21.7	36.3	...	80.6	93.0
	2017	20 806	58.3	20.6	38.6	...	88.6	100.7
	2018	22 064	59.4	22.9	34.6	...	84.1	98.3
	2019	23 841	59.4	21.4	31.2	...	99.8	105.8

Table 2. Gross Domestic Product by Type of Expenditure: Individual Countries or Areas

Major area, region and country	Year	Gross Domestic Product (at current prices) Million	Percentage Distributtion					
			Household final consumption expenditure 1	General government final consumption expenditure 2	Gross fixed capital formation 3	Changes in inventories 4	Exports of goods and services 5	Imports of goods and services 6
Sierra Leone (Leone)	1970	380	76.9	9.0	13.8	1.6	31.8	32.8
	1975	678	84.8	10.4	12.9	1.0	25.0	34.0
	1980	1 399	90.7	7.6	16.7	1.1	22.9	39.1
	1985	7 010	83.5	6.9	9.4	1.3	10.7	11.8
	1990	133 166	84.0	7.8	9.6	0.5	22.4	23.8
	1995	890 069	95.1	14.0	5.6	...	18.6	26.5
	2000	1 800 588	98.9	14.3	6.9	...	18.1	39.3
	2005	4 769 248	90.4	9.9	10.9	0.5	17.6	29.3
	2010	10 255 614	76.0	10.5	30.7	0.5	16.8	34.5
	2015	21 583 562	102.3	10.2	15.4	0.0	19.2	47.1
	2016	24 296 286	97.2	11.8	18.0	1.1	23.7	51.9
	2017	27 614 660	93.1	10.4	18.0	0.5	26.1	48.0
	2018	32 401 626	97.7	9.2	13.1	1.8	17.5	39.2
	2019	37 137 732	100.2	8.4	12.0	1.1	16.0	37.5
Somalia [5] (Somali Shilling)	1970	2 436	80.7	10.4	9.1	5.0	11.6	16.8
	1975	4 765	71.1	20.7	15.6	7.4	16.0	30.7
	1980	17 341	89.2	13.8	9.8	-0.7	4.9	17.0
	1985	87 290	90.5	10.6	8.9	2.9	4.2	17.0
	1990	1 738 800	71.0	10.3	23.0	0.6	0.9	5.7
	1995	6 424 840	72.2	8.5	20.6	0.1	0.3	1.7
	2000	19 641 182	72.3	8.6	20.4	0.1	0.3	1.7
	2005	35 315 000	72.4	8.7	20.3	0.1	0.3	1.7
	2010	34 171 000	72.7	8.7	19.9	0.1	0.3	1.7
	2015	32 375 000	72.6	8.7	20.0	0.1	0.3	1.7
	2016	33 571 409	72.6	8.7	19.9	0.1	0.3	1.7
	2017	36 053 071	72.6	8.7	20.0	0.1	0.3	1.7
	2018	37 747 295	72.6	8.7	20.0	0.1	0.3	1.7
	2019	39 519 160	72.6	8.7	20.0	0.1	0.3	1.7
South Africa (Rand)	1970	13 326	59.0	12.7	25.1	3.2	21.0	24.3
	1975	28 466	54.9	14.7	29.9	1.7	26.7	28.9
	1980	65 354	49.4	14.2	26.7	3.9	34.1	26.3
	1985	132 935	53.5	18.1	23.5	-2.4	30.3	21.7
	1990	301 939	59.5	19.5	19.8	-1.5	23.4	18.0
	1995	571 026	61.0	18.2	16.4	2.3	22.0	21.2
	2000	960 720	61.8	18.0	15.4	0.7	26.9	23.9
	2005	1 639 254	62.0	19.5	17.2	1.1	26.4	26.7
	2010	2 748 008	59.0	20.2	19.3	0.2	28.6	27.4
	2015	4 049 884	59.8	20.5	20.3	0.6	30.2	31.5
	2016	4 359 061	59.3	20.8	19.4	-0.3	30.6	30.1
	2017	4 653 579	59.2	20.8	18.8	0.0	29.6	28.3
	2018	4 873 899	59.9	21.3	18.2	-0.2	29.9	29.6
	2019	5 077 625	60.2	21.3	17.9	-0.3	29.9	29.4
South Sudan (South Sudanese Pound)	2010	34 428	47.8	17.0	11.1	0.0	62.3	38.3
	2015	26 909	188.9	64.6	21.4	0.1	38.5	213.5
	2016	150 649	151.9	20.6	13.9	0.1	63.0	149.5
	2017	399 064	151.7	16.8	18.1	0.0	70.7	157.3
	2018	663 517	88.7	16.7	8.4	...	62.8	76.7
	2019	783 637	85.4	12.3	17.2	...	63.6	78.5
Sudan (Sudanese Pound)	2010	126 219	76.3	4.9	22.1	2.4	4.8	10.5
	2015	505 761	87.1	6.3	11.3	1.0	6.5	12.1
	2016	605 409	90.8	5.9	8.6	0.3	5.3	10.9
	2017	815 856	88.4	6.8	10.4	0.3	6.5	12.5
	2018	1 176 630	85.9	7.7	15.8	...	6.0	15.5
	2019	1 607 295	88.8	7.9	12.5	...	8.5	17.7
Togo (CFA Franc BCEAO)	1970	85 014	76.7	14.0	9.7	4.3	36.1	35.0
	1975	149 068	74.7	20.9	17.5	10.1	33.9	52.1
	1980	277 535	65.9	20.2	22.5	12.5	46.3	62.0
	1985	386 317	66.1	19.8	17.6	9.6	59.0	64.5

Table 2. Gross Domestic Product by Type of Expenditure: Individual Countries or Areas

Major area, region and country	Year	Gross Domestic Product (at current prices) Million	Household final consumption expenditure 1	General government final consumption expenditure 2	Gross fixed capital formation 3	Changes in inventories 4	Exports of goods and services 5	Imports of goods and services 6
			Percentage Distributtion					
	1990	560 070	71.2	14.8	14.5	8.9	31.9	41.1
	1995	830 035	77.9	12.8	11.8	8.8	27.7	40.3
	2000	1 059 553	76.6	12.5	14.7	8.5	28.2	40.4
	2005	1 202 931	81.1	13.0	16.1	5.5	35.6	51.2
	2010	1 696 830	80.6	13.4	21.2	0.4	37.8	53.4
	2015	3 162 836	79.2	15.0	23.2	-0.2	28.7	45.4
	2016	3 574 379	77.8	13.8	22.5	-1.1	26.9	40.0
	2017	3 713 574	76.4	12.9	16.9	1.5	25.3	32.9
	2018	3 961 763	78.9	14.1	16.4	0.5	24.3	32.8
	2019	4 259 581	78.8	13.8	16.3	1.1	23.8	32.7
Tunisia..	1970	830	67.8	17.5	19.7	-0.1	19.7	23.7
(Tunisian Dinar)	1975	1 912	63.4	15.1	24.7	1.2	27.7	32.1
	1980	3 887	62.8	15.0	27.2	0.0	36.5	41.4
	1985	7 705	60.5	17.7	27.0	0.9	28.3	34.2
	1990	11 875	64.9	16.9	23.4	1.7	38.9	45.3
	1995	18 721	64.2	16.9	23.2	-0.3	40.1	43.7
	2000	29 433	60.6	16.7	25.2	0.7	39.7	42.9
	2005	41 871	61.8	16.9	21.4	0.2	44.9	45.3
	2010	63 055	62.9	16.6	24.6	1.0	49.5	54.7
	2015	84 689	71.3	19.5	19.8	0.1	40.1	50.9
	2016	89 789	71.8	20.5	19.3	-0.9	40.0	50.8
	2017	96 298	72.2	20.9	18.8	0.5	43.8	56.2
	2018	105 268	72.3	20.0	18.6	2.3	48.4	61.5
	2019	113 848	72.1	20.4	18.9	0.6	44.1	56.2
U.R. of Tanzania: Mainland....................	1970	16 530	58.1	29.8	27.8	-1.6	14.0	13.9
(Tanzanian Shilling)	1975	34 258	62.1	38.7	25.3	-0.8	10.6	15.1
	1980	72 767	66.3	30.7	25.1	-1.4	8.0	13.4
	1985	193 502	65.5	35.7	20.7	-1.5	4.1	8.6
	1990	1 272 166	62.4	23.1	47.0	-3.6	8.7	19.8
	1995	4 137 288	76.8	16.3	27.0	-1.6	18.7	26.3
	2000	9 900 611	78.4	8.0	18.7	-1.1	11.4	14.5
	2005	19 387 990	66.4	12.0	28.2	-1.9	17.8	21.4
	2010	44 467 109	66.8	10.4	32.1	1.2	19.7	28.1
	2015	94 349 316	63.9	9.9	32.8	-0.1	17.1	23.7
	2016	108 362 324	59.9	9.1	33.8	-1.6	16.3	19.1
	2017	118 744 498	60.2	8.5	36.3	-2.3	15.2	17.1
	2018	129 043 901	59.9	8.1	40.0	-1.6	14.8	17.9
	2019	139 893 804	58.6	7.8	43.5	-3.8	16.0	17.0
Uganda..	1970	102	62.8	12.2	49.8	-8.8	31.5	48.6
(Uganda Shilling)	1975	243	70.6	13.7	26.0	-3.6	11.3	26.0
	1980	1 931	78.6	14.7	9.2	...	5.7	17.9
	1985	31 876	68.1	14.4	9.0	1.2	9.2	9.6
	1990	1 851 754	74.1	10.0	16.7	2.2	5.8	15.3
	1995	6 926 228	70.3	12.0	21.5	0.1	9.2	16.8
	2000	11 147 493	73.2	14.1	23.9	0.4	9.1	20.4
	2005	19 868 905	70.6	13.2	27.3	0.3	12.7	23.3
	2010	42 861 170	76.7	11.6	25.2	0.3	17.6	31.4
	2015	81 333 382	78.0	8.4	24.4	0.5	19.3	30.5
	2016	86 950 826	74.5	8.8	23.7	0.5	17.7	25.2
	2017	97 918 886	75.0	9.8	22.6	0.5	18.3	26.2
	2018	110 649 303	73.1	11.7	24.8	0.4	18.8	28.9
	2019	120 785 779	74.7	10.2	25.7	0.4	16.8	27.9
Zambia..	1970	1 103 (t)	47.2	18.6	15.2	-6.0	77.9	64.8
(Kwacha)	1975	1 710 (t)	70.5	36.3	14.7	-5.8	42.2	78.6
	1980	3 403 (t)	66.8	30.8	11.4	-4.5	46.7	62.2
	1985	8 704 (t)	69.7	26.8	9.6	-3.8	39.5	47.2
	1990	115	60.8	18.3	19.0	-7.5	46.2	55.2
	1995	3 290	75.3	8.6	15.2	6.1	33.8	40.9
	2000	11 201	84.3	5.2	20.8	3.9	19.5	31.9
	2005	37 189	64.0	9.7	25.8	4.1	30.6	35.6

Table 2. Gross Domestic Product by Type of Expenditure: Individual Countries or Areas

Major area, region and country	Year	Gross Domestic Product (at current prices) Million	Percentage Distribution: Household final consumption expenditure 1	General government final consumption expenditure 2	Gross fixed capital formation 3	Changes in inventories 4	Exports of goods and services 5	Imports of goods and services 6
	2010	97 216	54.6	9.4	25.9	4.0	37.0	30.9
	2015	180 062	51.6	15.1	39.1	4.4	37.8	48.0
	2016	221 242	50.2	15.7	35.6	1.7	34.5	37.7
	2017	246 252	47.0	13.7	38.8	2.2	35.0	36.6
	2018	282 423	43.2	12.4	34.7	3.7	37.0	36.0
	2019	297 553	46.8	13.9	35.9	1.4	36.4	33.8
Zanzibar	1990	26 660	62.4	23.1	47.0	-21.5	8.7	19.8
(Tanzanian Shilling)	1995	106 849	76.8	16.3	27.0	-12.5	18.7	26.3
	2000	238 352	78.4	8.0	18.7	-2.0	11.4	14.5
	2005	493 994	66.2	12.0	28.2	-2.7	17.8	21.4
	2010	1 155 920	66.8	10.4	32.1	-0.9	19.7	28.1
	2015	2 356 960	63.9	9.9	31.9	0.9	17.1	23.7
	2016	2 747 160	59.9	9.1	32.8	1.0	16.3	19.1
	2017	3 227 050	60.2	8.5	35.5	-2.2	15.2	17.1
	2018	3 668 630	59.9	8.1	39.0	-4.0	14.8	17.9
	2019	4 131 986	58.6	7.8	42.6	-7.9	16.0	17.0
Zimbabwe	1970	2 337	63.0	15.3	2.5	15.0	23.3	20.8
(US Dollar)	1975	5 421	56.3	16.8	3.7	21.7	23.8	23.0
	1980	8 257	59.3	25.8	2.4	15.3	24.5	24.9
	1985	8 720	56.8	26.5	2.2	14.5	17.9	16.5
	1990	13 560	58.0	25.5	2.9	13.5	18.5	17.1
	1995	11 063	54.5	23.5	3.9	20.0	30.7	30.5
	2000	8 721	59.9	24.3	11.8	1.8	38.2	35.9
	2005	7 189	92.2	15.2	2.0	-0.5	33.5	42.5
	2010	12 042	89.8	15.3	17.0	1.8	29.6	53.5
	2015	19 963	89.5	18.9	10.0	0.0	19.2	37.6
	2016	20 549	83.3	18.1	9.8	0.1	19.9	31.3
	2017	22 041	79.4	21.7	9.7	0.0	19.7	30.4
	2018	24 312	77.0	25.6	9.3	0.0	19.0	31.0
	2019	21 441	79.9	21.8	9.6	0.0	19.5	30.9
Latin America and the Caribbean								
Anguilla	1970	7 818 (t)	39.6	12.8	45.8	...	45.4	50.8
(East Caribbean Dollar)	1975	16	39.7	12.8	45.7	...	45.3	50.7
	1980	33	40.1	12.9	44.8	...	45.3	50.5
	1985	73	41.1	12.6	40.8	...	49.0	51.5
	1990	204	46.4	11.3	38.5	...	54.5	57.4
	1995	280	69.6	14.9	27.4	...	54.8	72.1
	2000	406	81.1	14.5	40.9	...	46.2	82.6
	2005	618	77.7	12.1	35.0	...	49.6	74.5
	2010	723	80.1	17.9	24.1	...	47.6	69.7
	2015	892	78.7	16.8	25.2	...	62.9	83.5
	2016	865	83.4	16.3	20.8	...	65.0	85.5
	2017	767	64.0	19.0	21.6	...	98.3	102.9
	2018	865	80.5	15.8	46.0	...	73.9	116.2
	2019	1 025	102.4	14.1	19.1	...	72.4	93.7
Antigua and Barbuda	1970	68	79.8	15.1	15.3	...	57.7	66.2
(East Caribbean Dollar)	1975	185	79.2	15.2	16.0	...	59.8	69.1
	1980	363	92.2	15.8	18.3	...	63.5	87.6
	1985	661	96.0	14.9	16.3	...	71.4	94.5
	1990	1 241	57.1	15.3	26.6	...	75.2	74.1
	1995	1 559	63.9	18.3	24.3	...	69.6	76.0
	2000	2 231	57.4	17.3	29.0	...	56.5	60.3
	2005	2 762	69.3	16.5	26.9	...	53.3	66.7
	2010	3 101	67.5	17.9	28.1	...	45.6	59.1
	2015	3 609	68.1	16.2	24.5	...	43.7	51.2
	2016	3 879	74.1	15.6	24.8	...	41.8	51.6
	2017	3 964	83.6	15.9	24.9	...	38.8	53.1
	2018	4 334	74.6	15.9	39.6	...	36.8	55.7
	2019	4 487	71.5	14.6	35.9	...	38.9	53.2

Table 2. Gross Domestic Product by Type of Expenditure: Individual Countries or Areas

Major area, region and country	Year	Gross Domestic Product (at current prices) Million	Percentage Distributtion: Household final consumption expenditure 1	General government final consumption expenditure 2	Gross fixed capital formation 3	Changes in inventories 4	Exports of goods and services 5	Imports of goods and services 6
Argentina	1970	1 (u)	68.1	8.6	20.0	1.5	6.3	5.9
(Argentine Peso)	1975	21 (u)	60.6	10.9	24.5	2.4	5.4	5.3
	1980	4 161 (u)	66.2	11.0	21.0	2.2	4.7	5.9
	1985	5 749 (t)	66.3	11.6	14.6	1.5	10.8	5.7
	1990	74 692	70.1	11.2	11.6	1.2	9.5	4.2
	1995	279 632	70.2	13.3	14.9	1.6	9.0	9.3
	2000	307 994	71.0	13.8	13.4	1.4	10.2	10.6
	2005	582 538	63.0	12.1	17.4	1.5	23.2	17.3
	2010	1 661 721	64.2	15.2	16.6	1.1	18.9	16.0
	2015	5 954 511	65.9	18.1	15.6	1.5	10.7	11.8
	2016	8 228 160	65.7	17.7	14.3	3.4	12.5	13.6
	2017	10 644 779	66.3	17.7	15.0	1.2	11.2	14.0
	2018	14 605 790	65.1	16.1	14.4	1.5	14.3	16.4
	2019	21 650 351	64.4	15.3	13.1	1.0	17.3	15.1
Aruba	1970	354	53.7	13.1	29.3	0.3	93.0	85.9
(Aruban Guilder)	1975	459	53.7	13.1	29.3	0.3	93.0	85.9
	1980	595	53.7	13.1	29.3	0.3	93.0	85.9
	1985	771	53.7	13.1	29.3	0.3	93.0	85.9
	1990	1 532	53.9	13.2	29.2	0.4	93.3	86.5
	1995	2 477	54.2	14.2	29.2	1.6	95.2	91.3
	2000	3 514	53.0	15.3	24.8	0.4	83.4	74.6
	2005	4 372	56.6	16.5	33.1	0.1	76.9	82.3
	2010	4 478	65.0	19.4	28.6	...	68.1	81.7
	2015	5 226	62.0	17.0	20.1	1.4	73.5	74.1
	2016	5 309	61.4	16.8	20.0	1.4	71.3	70.8
	2017	5 471	60.8	16.7	19.4	1.4	73.3	71.6
	2018	5 734	61.4	16.8	19.8	1.4	72.7	72.2
	2019	5 895	61.2	16.8	19.7	1.4	72.4	71.6
Bahamas	1970	764	55.5	12.0	20.7	0.0	77.1	68.5
(Bahamian Dollar)	1975	1 101	56.5	10.9	20.7	0.0	77.3	62.2
	1980	2 190	38.7	11.6	21.2	...	77.6	52.9
	1985	3 306	43.1	14.1	21.2	...	72.6	59.5
	1990	4 768	59.1	9.4	20.7	3.3	46.9	43.6
	1995	5 165	64.0	10.1	20.6	2.0	42.9	42.7
	2000	8 077	57.3	9.3	28.0	2.1	38.0	41.6
	2005	9 836	59.4	9.8	26.2	1.2	38.8	42.6
	2010	10 096	61.7	12.5	26.7	1.3	35.0	43.7
	2015	11 711	62.5	12.3	23.9	1.1	37.9	38.3
	2016	11 929	61.7	11.6	24.9	1.0	36.6	37.3
	2017	12 491	64.4	12.6	26.2	1.1	36.3	40.0
	2018	13 022	64.1	12.1	24.2	1.1	39.4	38.4
	2019	13 579	59.6	14.2	25.0	1.0	39.2	36.7
Barbados	1970	436	84.8	14.2	19.7	1.8	42.6	62.7
(Barbados Dollar)	1975	970	76.3	11.5	14.6	0.4	43.6	49.9
	1980	2 067	64.3	10.3	17.8	1.3	60.7	59.5
	1985	2 879	59.6	13.1	11.8	0.2	58.6	49.6
	1990	4 109	65.4	14.0	14.8	-0.1	42.5	42.7
	1995	4 594	70.2	12.0	11.3	0.4	45.5	43.7
	2000	6 304	68.9	13.1	17.5	0.1	42.0	46.0
	2005	7 871	68.1	16.2	18.2	0.1	43.5	51.2
	2010	9 060	74.6	15.4	15.7	0.2	38.9	48.0
	2015	9 430	77.0	13.6	16.7	0.2	40.1	47.4
	2016	9 660	78.0	13.4	16.2	0.2	36.6	42.1
	2017	9 956	76.5	12.2	15.4	0.2	35.8	40.7
	2018	10 173	74.4	11.8	14.1	0.2	35.1	39.7
	2019	10 418	74.2	11.3	15.5	0.2	35.7	41.7
Belize	1970	47	63.7	11.8	22.7	4.0	37.0	44.2
(Belize Dollar)	1975	209	60.4	9.9	25.4	3.8	45.6	51.5
	1980	431	70.3	14.1	20.5	1.3	31.8	41.2

Table 2. Gross Domestic Product by Type of Expenditure: Individual Countries or Areas

Major area, region and country	Year	Gross Domestic Product (at current prices) Million	Percentage Distributtion: Household final consumption expenditure 1	General government final consumption expenditure 2	Gross fixed capital formation 3	Changes in inventories 4	Exports of goods and services 5	Imports of goods and services 6
	1985	463	50.2	18.7	15.7	3.8	53.7	53.8
	1990	898	54.5	13.0	23.5	0.1	54.5	55.3
	1995	1 240	61.6	15.1	21.8	-1.0	48.5	51.4
	2000	1 664	74.1	12.9	28.7	3.0	53.0	73.7
	2005	2 204	72.8	14.6	18.7	2.4	55.3	63.4
	2010	2 754	71.2	16.2	15.5	-2.1	59.1	58.6
	2015	3 448	71.2	15.6	20.6	1.1	58.8	66.3
	2016	3 550	74.4	16.8	21.4	0.1	52.6	61.6
	2017	3 673	70.4	16.7	18.7	-0.6	55.0	58.4
	2018	3 742	69.3	17.5	19.0	-0.6	57.7	58.0
	2019	3 759	69.3	17.5	19.0	-0.6	57.7	58.0
Bolivia (Plurinational State of) [6] (Boliviano)	1970	12 (t)	75.0	8.3	16.7	...	25.0	25.0
	1975	48 (t)	72.9	10.4	18.8	4.2	25.0	33.3
	1980	123 (t)	66.7	13.0	14.6	0.8	26.0	20.3
	1985	2 867	62.5	8.3	11.7	5.2	29.0	16.7
	1990	15 443	76.9	11.8	12.6	0.0	22.8	23.9
	1995	32 235	75.8	13.6	15.5	-0.3	22.6	27.2
	2000	51 928	76.4	14.5	17.0	0.3	18.3	27.3
	2005	77 024	66.3	16.0	13.0	1.3	35.5	32.1
	2010	137 876	62.3	13.8	16.6	0.4	41.2	34.3
	2015	228 031	68.4	17.5	21.4	-1.1	30.9	37.1
	2016	234 533	68.9	17.5	20.7	0.4	24.5	31.9
	2017	259 185	67.7	17.0	21.3	1.0	24.9	31.8
	2018	278 388	67.0	17.5	20.2	0.4	26.0	31.1
	2019	282 587	68.4	18.1	19.0	0.9	25.0	31.4
Brazil (Brazilian Real)	1970	0 (u)	68.6	11.3	18.8	1.7	7.0	7.4
	1975	0 (u)	67.9	10.2	23.3	2.4	7.2	11.0
	1980	4 (u)	75.0	8.3	25.0	...	8.3	8.3
	1985	503 (u)	65.8	9.9	16.9	2.2	12.1	7.2
	1990	12	60.8	17.6	22.3	-2.3	7.5	6.0
	1995	713 993	62.4	20.5	20.0	-0.5	7.3	9.4
	2000	1 193 443	64.2	18.7	18.3	1.4	10.1	12.6
	2005	2 170 585	60.5	18.9	17.1	0.1	15.2	11.8
	2010	3 885 847	60.2	19.0	20.5	1.3	10.7	11.8
	2015	5 995 787	64.0	19.8	17.8	-0.4	12.9	14.1
	2016	6 269 328	64.3	20.4	15.5	-0.6	12.5	12.1
	2017	6 583 319	64.5	20.2	14.6	0.1	12.5	11.8
	2018	6 889 176	64.7	20.1	15.2	-0.4	14.9	14.5
	2019	7 256 926	64.9	20.3	15.4	-0.2	14.3	14.7
British Virgin Islands (US Dollar)	1970	12	86.1	9.9	49.9	6.1	27.5	63.5
	1975	16	80.9	8.7	26.7	3.0	47.3	61.4
	1980	32	51.3	8.9	28.5	2.6	65.9	66.7
	1985	53	51.8	12.7	29.0	1.2	94.0	90.5
	1990	120	45.4	14.0	24.4	1.4	101.0	86.2
	1995	453	49.9	13.9	24.7	0.8	92.2	81.4
	2000	858	40.5	10.5	24.1	-0.9	104.4	78.6
	2005	994	37.1	9.2	24.0	-1.6	108.9	77.7
	2010	1 021	35.3	8.6	23.9	-1.9	111.3	77.2
	2015	1 174	34.8	8.4	23.9	-2.0	111.9	77.0
	2016	1 286	34.8	8.4	23.9	-2.0	111.9	77.0
	2017	1 207	34.8	8.4	23.9	-2.0	111.9	77.0
	2018	1 249	34.8	8.4	23.9	-2.0	111.9	77.0
	2019	1 297	34.8	8.4	23.9	-2.0	111.9	77.0
Cayman Islands (Cayman Islands Dollar)	1970	26	54.1	10.1	14.6	...	78.1	57.1
	1975	78	54.1	10.1	14.6	...	78.1	57.1
	1980	189	54.1	10.1	14.5	...	77.9	56.9
	1985	457	54.2	10.2	12.8	...	76.6	55.4
	1990	1 022	53.9	8.9	13.6	...	70.5	46.2
	1995	1 424	53.8	9.5	13.9	...	64.8	41.7
	2000	2 502	53.8	9.5	13.9	...	64.8	41.7

Table 2. Gross Domestic Product by Type of Expenditure: Individual Countries or Areas

Major area, region and country	Year	Gross Domestic Product (at current prices) Million	Percentage Distributtion					
			Household final consumption expenditure 1	General government final consumption expenditure 2	Gross fixed capital formation 3	Changes in inventories 4	Exports of goods and services 5	Imports of goods and services 6
	2005	3 341	53.8	9.5	13.9	...	64.8	41.7
	2010	3 464	53.9	9.5	13.9	...	64.7	41.7
	2015	3 923	54.0	9.3	13.7	0.1	64.3	41.4
	2016	4 091	54.0	9.6	13.7	0.1	64.1	41.3
	2017	4 294	53.0	9.6	14.1	0.3	67.8	43.5
	2018	4 598	51.6	9.5	15.8	0.0	66.6	44.3
	2019	5 017	52.9	9.6	14.5	0.1	66.1	43.0
Chile	1970	109	68.3	14.6	17.9	-1.2	14.4	13.4
(Chilean Peso)	1975	39 486	69.4	17.3	20.7	-7.3	24.0	25.7
	1980	1 198 109	68.6	13.7	19.5	2.0	21.5	25.3
	1985	3 053 850	65.6	13.5	17.9	-0.2	25.7	22.8
	1990	10 646 702	60.6	9.8	24.6	1.2	31.6	27.9
	1995	29 797 310	61.3	9.9	25.4	1.1	27.9	25.5
	2000	42 283 777	64.2	11.8	20.8	1.2	30.2	28.2
	2005	68 831 700	58.9	10.6	22.2	-0.3	40.2	31.5
	2010	111 509 000	58.3	12.1	21.6	1.6	37.7	31.3
	2015	159 553 348	63.4	13.0	23.8	0.0	29.4	29.6
	2016	169 537 388	63.4	13.8	22.7	-0.5	28.1	27.5
	2017	179 756 126	63.4	14.1	21.0	0.2	28.4	27.2
	2018	191 265 952	63.4	14.5	21.3	0.9	28.6	28.8
	2019	198 440 707	63.0	14.6	22.4	0.3	28.2	28.6
Colombia	1970	186 773	79.5	6.9	26.6	1.7	9.1	14.8
(Colombian Peso)	1975	568 744	79.7	6.8	22.6	1.2	10.9	14.3
	1980	2 217 399	77.1	7.7	24.7	1.8	11.1	15.5
	1985	6 973 782	76.4	8.2	25.8	0.7	9.2	12.7
	1990	28 406 296	72.2	7.9	24.5	1.3	13.8	15.1
	1995	100 027 254	74.4	10.3	26.9	3.2	10.8	19.7
	2000	207 183 527	71.4	14.7	15.1	0.9	16.0	18.2
	2005	337 958 000	67.9	14.0	21.0	0.7	17.0	20.5
	2010	544 060 000	65.9	13.8	22.0	-0.2	16.3	17.9
	2015	804 692 000	68.5	14.8	23.4	0.4	15.7	22.7
	2016	863 782 000	69.1	14.5	22.1	1.0	14.7	21.5
	2017	920 471 000	68.5	14.9	21.7	-0.1	15.1	20.1
	2018	985 931 000	68.0	15.4	21.4	0.0	15.9	20.7
	2019	1 062 342 495	68.5	15.5	21.6	0.7	15.9	22.2
Costa Rica	1970	8 298	90.2	10.1	16.9	-1.6	24.4	33.6
(Costa Rican Colon)	1975	21 371	87.7	12.3	19.0	-3.0	26.3	37.5
	1980	52 657	80.3	14.7	20.7	-1.0	23.2	35.8
	1985	251 700	73.6	12.7	16.7	2.5	26.9	31.6
	1990	664 920	75.2	14.6	19.4	1.0	29.9	40.1
	1995	2 068 165	70.9	12.9	19.9	-0.2	38.3	41.9
	2000	4 607 291	66.1	13.8	19.8	1.0	43.1	43.8
	2005	9 532 875	69.7	13.6	20.0	-1.0	43.7	46.0
	2010	19 596 937	65.4	16.8	19.7	0.1	33.2	35.0
	2015	29 281 373	65.0	17.5	18.6	-0.2	30.8	31.7
	2016	31 136 211	64.2	17.2	18.2	0.1	32.1	31.8
	2017	33 189 221	63.8	17.2	17.3	2.1	32.8	33.1
	2018	34 937 936	63.2	16.9	17.5	2.1	33.5	33.2
	2019	36 279 504	63.3	17.4	16.1	1.8	33.8	32.4
Cuba [7]	1970	5 693	54.6	31.7	25.4	0.5	32.6	44.2
(Cuban Peso)	1975	10 682	54.6	31.7	25.4	0.5	32.6	44.2
	1980	14 337	54.2	31.6	25.4	0.9	32.8	44.3
	1985	20 993	51.6	31.1	25.3	3.5	33.7	45.0
	1990	21 541	53.9	31.0	24.5	0.3	30.2	40.9
	1995	23 835	70.5	24.4	7.8	-0.7	13.4	15.9
	2000	30 566	60.9	29.6	11.9	0.6	14.1	16.9
	2005	42 644	53.3	33.6	9.0	1.8	21.0	18.3
	2010	64 328	50.3	34.8	8.6	1.4	22.6	17.7
	2015	87 133	55.7	32.2	8.6	0.7	17.1	14.5
	2016	91 370	55.8	31.9	8.8	0.7	15.0	12.3

Table 2. Gross Domestic Product by Type of Expenditure: Individual Countries or Areas

Major area, region and country	Year	Gross Domestic Product (at current prices) Million	Percentage Distributtion: Household final consumption expenditure 1	General government final consumption expenditure 2	Gross fixed capital formation 3	Changes in inventories 4	Exports of goods and services 5	Imports of goods and services 6
	2017	96 851	56.0	30.8	9.9	0.4	14.5	11.7
	2018	100 023	56.0	30.1	11.5	0.6	14.5	12.6
	2019	105 355	55.9	30.9	10.0	0.6	14.7	12.2
Curaçao	2005	4 197	64.0	16.1	24.9	11.0	59.5	75.4
(Netherlands Antillian Guilder)	2010	5 283	69.6	16.2	29.1	17.9	55.9	88.7
	2015	5 642	66.0	15.6	21.9	11.5	62.5	77.5
	2016	5 589	66.4	15.8	23.2	11.4	57.4	74.1
	2017	5 579	71.1	16.8	24.9	10.4	55.1	78.4
	2018	5 599	72.9	17.3	25.1	11.9	61.5	88.6
	2019	5 552	66.2	15.7	23.1	10.6	58.9	74.5
Dominica	1970	46	68.7	26.9	25.5	3.6	35.4	59.7
(East Caribbean Dollar)	1975	92	80.4	18.2	17.0	...	33.8	49.7
	1980	197	105.4	22.8	33.0	3.1	17.9	75.1
	1985	323	84.0	19.1	20.6	...	30.1	49.5
	1990	544	74.8	17.4	28.8	0.8	41.6	62.5
	1995	741	71.6	17.1	22.0	...	40.7	53.5
	2000	900	72.8	10.0	20.0	...	43.3	54.9
	2005	983	82.5	15.7	20.1	...	35.5	53.8
	2010	1 333	82.9	16.7	18.4	...	35.6	53.6
	2015	1 460	78.5	21.3	13.3	...	47.3	60.5
	2016	1 556	78.2	19.1	15.2	...	44.6	57.2
	2017	1 404	79.9	24.2	16.9	...	41.0	62.0
	2018	1 487	88.4	27.6	33.0	...	29.4	78.4
	2019	1 572	82.2	23.6	21.7	...	38.4	65.8
Dominican Republic	1970	1 859	74.5	9.7	15.7	5.6	27.7	37.0
(Dominican Peso)	1975	4 504	67.4	5.2	21.1	6.2	45.1	42.3
	1980	8 298	74.9	6.4	22.6	5.3	30.9	43.6
	1985	17 487	75.4	6.7	18.6	3.7	47.1	52.4
	1990	81 181	77.3	3.0	19.4	3.6	41.9	44.9
	1995	214 123	78.6	4.8	17.9	2.2	35.2	38.7
	2000	393 303	71.7	8.7	25.0	2.8	35.5	43.8
	2005	1 083 445	72.1	8.1	22.6	2.2	28.3	33.3
	2010	1 983 202	74.3	9.9	25.2	1.2	22.7	33.3
	2015	3 205 655	70.9	10.3	23.3	0.2	23.8	28.4
	2016	3 487 293	70.5	10.3	22.9	0.0	23.9	27.7
	2017	3 802 656	69.5	10.9	23.7	-1.3	23.7	26.5
	2018	4 235 847	68.3	10.9	25.8	0.0	23.6	28.5
	2019	4 562 235	67.8	11.1	26.8	-0.8	23.1	27.9
Ecuador	1970	2 861	74.3	9.7	15.7	3.8	9.4	13.0
(US Dollar)	1975	7 728	61.7	20.9	18.5	2.1	16.1	19.3
	1980	17 873	57.1	18.3	18.9	6.5	17.1	17.9
	1985	17 141	62.6	14.8	16.8	2.2	19.7	16.0
	1990	15 232	62.7	12.3	18.3	5.8	22.8	21.8
	1995	24 421	72.3	11.2	17.3	2.5	21.3	24.6
	2000	18 319	64.6	9.4	19.0	2.3	32.1	27.3
	2005	41 507	68.5	10.7	20.4	1.2	27.6	28.5
	2010	69 555	63.3	13.2	24.6	3.4	27.9	32.4
	2015	99 290	61.4	14.4	26.6	0.3	21.3	24.0
	2016	00 038	59.9	14.6	25.1	-0.1	19.5	19.0
	2017	104 296	59.9	14.6	25.4	0.9	20.8	21.6
	2018	107 562	59.7	14.7	25.6	1.2	22.6	23.8
	2019	107 436	60.5	14.5	25.0	0.0	23.4	23.3
El Salvador	1970	339	75.3	10.7	11.9	1.3	24.8	24.5
(US Dollar)	1975	591	73.3	11.1	22.9	-0.9	32.9	38.1
	1980	1 177	71.9	13.9	13.5	-0.3	34.0	33.1
	1985	1 892	81.3	15.4	12.0	-1.2	22.2	29.8
	1990	4 818	88.9	9.9	13.7	0.1	18.5	31.1
	1995	8 922	85.5	9.8	19.1	1.9	21.6	37.8
	2000	11 785	84.3	13.1	17.7	0.0	26.8	41.9

Table 2. Gross Domestic Product by Type of Expenditure: Individual Countries or Areas

Major area, region and country	Year	Gross Domestic Product (at current prices) Million	Percentage Distributtion: Household final consumption expenditure 1	General government final consumption expenditure 2	Gross fixed capital formation 3	Changes in inventories 4	Exports of goods and services 5	Imports of goods and services 6
	2005	14 698	86.6	14.0	16.3	2.3	25.3	44.4
	2010	18 448	87.3	15.7	14.8	1.9	26.9	46.6
	2015	23 438	85.1	16.5	15.7	0.3	29.5	47.1
	2016	24 191	83.6	16.3	15.5	0.5	28.5	44.4
	2017	24 979	83.4	16.1	16.0	0.6	29.0	45.3
	2018	26 117	83.4	15.9	17.1	3.2	28.8	48.4
	2019	27 023	83.0	16.0	17.8	1.3	29.5	47.6
Grenada	1970	38	63.8	24.7	18.9	...	51.9	59.3
(East Caribbean Dollar)	1975	110	72.2	21.8	6.5	...	60.5	61.1
	1980	238	84.9	20.6	26.1	4.2	52.9	88.7
	1985	367	77.2	21.9	31.2	-1.7	47.9	76.4
	1990	637	64.9	20.5	38.9	3.1	44.4	71.8
	1995	751	69.5	13.4	30.3	...	36.2	49.5
	2000	1 404	64.7	11.7	37.9	...	45.3	59.6
	2005	1 878	76.2	13.0	46.3	...	21.4	57.0
	2010	2 082	87.2	16.2	22.0	...	23.8	49.2
	2015	2 692	67.3	12.6	17.7	1.5	50.8	50.0
	2016	2 866	68.3	12.4	19.1	...	49.5	49.2
	2017	3 039	67.2	11.7	22.7	...	51.9	53.4
	2018	3 155	66.0	11.9	26.0	...	53.7	57.1
	2019	3 271	69.8	12.5	22.1	...	52.7	56.5
Guatemala	1970	1 670	76.2	11.3	15.7	0.3	25.8	25.3
(Quetzal)	1975	3 199	76.6	9.8	19.6	0.5	30.2	33.4
	1980	6 913	76.7	11.3	20.6	-0.7	30.9	35.4
	1985	9 809	80.8	9.9	13.7	0.6	25.7	28.6
	1990	30 107	81.2	9.7	16.3	0.7	27.5	33.7
	1995	74 711	83.2	7.9	18.2	0.6	26.8	36.1
	2000	131 374	81.5	10.0	20.2	2.1	28.1	41.1
	2005	204 432	86.7	9.1	19.4	2.9	23.2	40.8
	2010	327 807	85.1	11.2	15.7	0.1	23.9	36.2
	2015	476 023	84.3	11.1	14.5	0.3	19.8	30.1
	2016	502 002	84.6	10.4	13.9	0.0	18.8	27.6
	2017	526 200	84.9	10.6	13.6	0.0	18.5	27.6
	2018	549 790	85.8	11.0	13.8	0.1	18.2	28.9
	2019	590 417	84.9	11.1	14.2	0.3	17.7	28.2
Guyana	1970	854	74.8	10.6	14.3	...	28.9	27.6
(Guyana Dollar)	1975	1 894	58.9	12.3	20.7	...	38.4	35.9
	1980	2 405	65.7	18.1	18.7	...	35.4	39.0
	1985	3 132	66.9	22.4	13.1	...	27.1	30.6
	1990	24 981	75.8	8.5	26.5	...	33.5	49.2
	1995	140 766	57.7	10.0	28.5	...	48.4	53.2
	2000	207 332	62.0	17.3	24.1	...	40.0	51.5
	2005	395 403	91.4	16.9	20.3	...	53.7	75.8
	2010	699 064	87.4	15.1	25.4	...	50.1	78.0
	2015	883 787	76.1	17.0	23.5	...	43.1	61.0
	2016	925 677	63.2	17.5	30.2	...	47.7	55.2
	2017	980 498	67.4	17.2	31.1	...	46.9	62.9
	2018	994 472	66.4	18.9	29.6	...	45.8	60.9
	2019	1 078 729	69.2	18.8	33.2	...	44.4	65.2
Haiti	1970	2 196	86.2	9.9	11.7	...	10.0	17.6
(Gourde)	1975	4 518	85.1	9.1	18.4	...	14.5	27.0
	1980	9 176	89.1	11.0	20.8	...	19.6	40.6
	1985	13 324	84.1	11.4	19.3	...	17.1	32.3
	1990	15 481	94.2	8.4	19.9	...	11.9	34.5
	1995	40 729	85.3	8.1	26.1	...	9.1	28.7
	2000	77 580	87.3	6.1	27.3	...	12.7	33.4
	2005	163 681	102.0	2.1	28.1	...	14.4	44.1
	2010	266 952	121.8	2.2	25.4	...	15.3	64.7
	2015	423 644	96.1	2.0	32.4	...	20.0	50.5
	2016	481 212	99.3	2.1	30.5	...	20.7	52.6

Table 2. Gross Domestic Product by Type of Expenditure: Individual Countries or Areas

Major area, region and country	Year	Gross Domestic Product (at current prices) Million	Percentage Distributtion					
			Household final consumption expenditure 1	General government final consumption expenditure 2	Gross fixed capital formation 3	Changes in inventories 4	Exports of goods and services 5	Imports of goods and services 6
	2017	551 911	106.4	2.3	29.0	...	18.8	56.5
	2018	631 829	110.1	2.3	29.0	...	17.1	58.5
	2019	715 066	111.6	2.2	27.6	...	16.9	57.5
Honduras (Lempira)	1970	1 649	73.2	12.8	19.1	1.0	37.3	42.7
	1975	2 682	78.2	13.2	20.9	-3.4	39.5	47.6
	1980	6 122	69.5	13.5	24.2	-1.4	48.6	53.0
	1985	8 684	74.5	14.0	16.7	-0.8	32.8	35.9
	1990	14 956	67.0	13.8	19.9	1.2	48.6	48.1
	1995	44 745	63.6	10.0	23.6	5.4	57.0	57.8
	2000	106 654	70.8	13.4	25.8	2.5	54.0	66.4
	2005	183 747	75.3	15.5	24.9	2.7	59.0	77.5
	2010	299 286	78.1	17.9	21.6	0.3	45.8	63.7
	2015	460 405	77.5	14.3	23.7	1.4	45.2	62.1
	2016	495 922	76.9	14.1	22.0	1.3	42.7	57.1
	2017	543 403	76.8	13.5	23.3	1.6	43.6	58.7
	2018	574 243	79.5	13.6	24.2	1.6	41.8	60.8
	2019	615 051	80.3	13.5	22.5	-0.2	40.2	56.4
Jamaica (Jamaican Dollar)	1970	1 446	54.9	10.0	25.1	0.3	27.8	23.5
	1975	3 225	59.8	15.6	18.7	2.0	29.4	28.5
	1980	5 920	59.5	17.2	11.5	1.2	42.4	33.1
	1985	14 479	62.6	13.2	18.4	2.0	48.6	42.8
	1990	37 910	56.2	11.9	21.8	0.5	43.3	35.0
	1995	231 148	69.8	10.0	24.9	0.3	51.3	56.4
	2000	387 089	74.5	14.0	23.2	0.3	38.8	50.7
	2005	700 276	78.8	14.2	26.7	0.2	35.3	55.2
	2010	1 152 781	81.9	16.1	19.9	0.3	31.3	49.6
	2015	1 659 677	81.1	13.8	21.2	0.1	29.9	46.2
	2016	1 760 976	77.7	13.8	21.2	0.1	31.8	44.6
	2017	1 895 025	78.3	13.4	22.1	0.4	34.7	48.9
	2018	2 027 251	76.1	13.4	23.3	0.0	38.6	51.4
	2019	2 110 433	76.2	13.6	24.1	0.2	38.0	52.1
Mexico (Mexican Peso)	1970	565	74.2	5.8	20.6	4.4	6.9	9.9
	1975	1 400	70.9	8.3	22.1	4.0	6.1	9.9
	1980	5 442	64.0	8.7	24.9	6.0	11.1	13.8
	1985	57 691	63.4	8.0	19.2	4.9	16.0	11.0
	1990	843 623	70.2	7.5	18.7	5.1	16.3	17.3
	1995	2 311 458	67.2	8.6	16.4	4.6	24.1	22.2
	2000	6 693 683	69.4	9.5	21.5	1.5	25.4	27.0
	2005	9 562 648	68.6	10.5	20.7	0.9	26.2	27.7
	2010	13 366 377	65.3	11.8	21.6	1.2	29.7	31.1
	2015	18 551 459	65.6	12.3	22.5	0.8	34.6	36.6
	2016	20 118 101	65.6	12.0	22.9	0.8	37.1	39.0
	2017	21 911 894	65.3	11.6	22.1	0.8	37.7	39.5
	2018	23 491 507	64.8	11.7	22.1	0.7	39.3	41.2
	2019	24 203 617	65.4	11.6	20.9	0.5	39.2	39.2
Montserrat (East Caribbean Dollar)	1970	16	104.6	20.1	32.1	0.4	21.6	85.6
	1975	31	103.9	20.2	30.6	-0.8	19.9	80.7
	1980	76	117.2	16.0	25.4	...	20.9	79.6
	1985	118	94.5	16.9	22.4	...	28.2	62.1
	1990	204	30.9	15.8	100.5	...	25.4	72.5
	1995	186	79.4	19.8	18.1	...	53.4	70.7
	2000	97	73.0	49.7	45.0	...	48.2	115.9
	2005	132	91.7	48.2	32.2	...	34.1	106.3
	2010	150	82.1	48.7	24.1	...	22.1	76.8
	2015	166	86.9	47.7	16.4	...	27.2	81.6
	2016	170	89.9	50.3	23.4	...	29.3	94.1
	2017	161	86.4	49.5	22.5	...	28.3	88.4
	2018	168	87.7	49.2	20.8	...	28.3	88.0
	2019	182	88.0	49.7	22.3	...	28.6	90.1

Table 2. Gross Domestic Product by Type of Expenditure: Individual Countries or Areas

Major area, region and country	Year	Gross Domestic Product (at current prices) Million	Percentage Distributtion: Household final consumption expenditure 1	General government final consumption expenditure 2	Gross fixed capital formation 3	Changes in inventories 4	Exports of goods and services 5	Imports of goods and services 6
Nicaragua (Cordoba Oro)	1970	2 (u)	67.7	7.1	12.3	2.9	16.1	16.0
	1975	5 (u)	71.5	6.7	17.0	0.6	16.8	20.2
	1980	9 (u)	76.6	13.9	9.9	2.7	13.8	22.5
	1985	50 (u)	43.9	26.6	15.6	3.4	8.9	11.9
	1990	501	60.5	24.9	16.2	0.7	15.5	25.2
	1995	31 073	78.7	12.3	16.9	3.3	18.6	31.5
	2000	64 596	79.7	14.2	24.1	4.4	23.3	46.4
	2005	105 424	81.8	15.4	23.8	3.8	28.2	53.3
	2010	187 053	80.5	14.1	21.2	3.7	40.5	59.9
	2015	347 707	70.5	14.1	29.3	4.2	40.1	58.1
	2016	380 261	70.4	14.5	27.6	3.6	38.9	54.9
	2017	414 279	69.4	14.4	26.8	3.2	41.3	55.0
	2018	412 207	70.2	15.2	22.9	0.9	42.2	51.5
	2019	414 714	72.1	15.6	17.5	-0.4	45.1	50.0
Panama (Balboa)	1970	1 165	69.2	12.7	20.7	5.8	72.1	81.5
	1975	2 115	64.5	16.3	23.3	5.8	90.8	106.2
	1980	4 119	62.9	16.1	19.4	6.7	85.8	91.5
	1985	5 817	72.0	18.0	13.1	1.1	60.4	63.3
	1990	6 174	62.3	15.4	6.7	7.8	76.6	69.4
	1995	9 188	56.5	12.9	20.4	5.7	89.1	86.4
	2000	11 808	59.0	13.0	20.8	2.9	71.4	68.7
	2005	15 714	61.1	12.9	16.6	1.5	74.3	68.0
	2010	29 440	57.4	12.6	29.6	8.6	70.0	78.2
	2015	54 092	51.5	10.3	39.4	3.3	47.7	52.3
	2016	57 908	52.0	11.0	38.4	2.1	42.0	45.4
	2017	62 203	50.7	11.4	39.3	2.4	41.8	45.6
	2018	64 928	51.2	11.7	38.6	2.8	42.7	47.0
	2019	66 788	51.4	12.0	37.4	1.9	40.7	43.4
Paraguay [8] (Guarani)	1970	85 705	64.3	11.2	18.8	4.8	18.0	15.6
	1975	217 850	62.3	7.8	26.9	11.8	15.9	18.1
	1980	641 128	59.1	7.7	35.2	10.9	16.7	19.5
	1985	1 594 517	62.9	8.0	26.7	8.5	26.7	25.5
	1990	7 406 322	64.0	7.7	28.5	8.2	40.1	38.3
	1995	20 494 394	73.6	8.3	27.8	7.3	45.5	54.2
	2000	32 019 820	76.9	10.5	20.6	4.9	29.2	37.1
	2005	69 849 376	59.7	7.7	19.5	3.5	44.5	35.0
	2010	128 989 495	64.5	8.8	21.3	2.5	40.4	37.5
	2015	188 230 723	64.8	11.6	19.4	2.7	33.0	31.5
	2016	204 447 278	63.3	11.1	19.1	1.1	35.4	30.0
	2017	219 188 417	63.9	10.8	19.2	2.0	36.4	32.3
	2018	231 489 278	64.8	11.2	19.9	2.9	35.9	34.8
	2019	237 688 558	66.2	12.1	21.3	0.8	34.4	34.8
Peru (Nuevo Sol)	1970	226 (u)	71.4	17.4	13.4	-0.1	22.6	20.2
	1975	536 (u)	75.2	17.5	20.2	0.9	13.7	27.7
	1980	4 809 (u)	62.2	15.9	21.5	2.0	28.3	28.1
	1985	159 (t)	63.2	16.1	19.6	-1.1	25.3	19.3
	1990	5 471	71.2	11.6	19.2	-1.1	15.2	14.6
	1995	120 263	71.1	9.9	24.0	0.8	12.6	18.3
	2000	180 584	70.9	11.5	19.7	0.0	16.8	18.8
	2005	250 749	64.9	11.4	17.1	0.2	26.8	20.5
	2010	416 784	61.7	10.5	23.5	0.2	27.8	23.8
	2015	604 416	65.3	13.0	23.1	1.2	21.3	23.9
	2016	647 668	65.0	13.2	21.4	0.6	22.6	22.8
	2017	687 989	64.1	13.2	20.6	0.1	24.7	22.8
	2018	729 773	63.7	13.1	21.0	0.3	25.4	23.5
	2019	757 060	64.6	13.3	21.2	-0.3	24.2	22.9
Puerto Rico (US Dollar)	1970	5 106	74.4	15.2	27.8	1.0	44.3	62.8
	1975	8 313	79.4	19.4	25.0	1.7	48.8	75.1
	1980	14 639	74.9	15.6	14.1	2.8	66.1	73.9

Table 2. Gross Domestic Product by Type of Expenditure: Individual Countries or Areas

Major area, region and country	Year	Gross Domestic Product (at current prices) Million	Percentage Distributtion					
			Household final consumption expenditure 1	General government final consumption expenditure 2	Gross fixed capital formation 3	Changes in inventories 4	Exports of goods and services 5	Imports of goods and services 6
	1985	20 574	74.6	14.9	11.4	0.8	68.5	70.4
	1990	31 034	65.2	14.3	15.4	1.3	76.8	73.2
	1995	43 246	61.1	13.7	15.2	1.5	69.7	61.3
	2000	62 569	58.9	11.6	18.9	0.5	73.2	63.2
	2005	83 915	56.1	12.0	14.2	0.4	81.7	64.4
	2010	98 381	57.7	11.0	9.1	0.1	75.5	53.4
	2015	103 376	59.6	8.8	8.5	0.1	75.3	52.4
	2016	104 337	58.4	8.2	8.0	0.1	77.5	52.2
	2017	103 446	60.4	8.8	8.0	-0.2	77.7	54.6
	2018	100 979	64.2	8.0	15.7	0.0	72.0	59.9
	2019	104 989	65.4	8.7	14.6	0.0	70.9	59.6
Saint Kitts and Nevis...............................	1970	50	89.2	18.2	19.1	...	42.4	69.0
(East Caribbean Dollar)	1975	110	77.0	16.4	12.7	...	63.2	69.3
	1980	185	84.5	9.4	27.5	...	47.4	68.9
	1985	300	79.9	11.6	25.0	...	40.7	57.3
	1990	587	62.9	9.3	57.2	...	41.2	69.0
	1995	846	61.3	10.5	48.0	...	41.0	62.1
	2000	1 137	64.3	10.9	51.2	...	36.2	62.7
	2005	1 477	54.5	17.8	42.2	...	41.7	56.2
	2010	2 052	75.8	17.6	33.6	...	29.5	56.5
	2015	2 493	66.4	19.3	30.7	...	37.7	54.2
	2016	2 622	69.7	19.1	31.6	...	36.1	56.5
	2017	2 692	67.3	19.1	30.6	...	37.0	53.9
	2018	2 729	67.8	19.1	31.0	...	36.9	54.9
	2019	2 838	68.2	19.1	31.1	...	36.6	55.1
Saint Lucia...	1970	82	77.6	17.4	40.8	...	47.3	82.4
(East Caribbean Dollar)	1975	208	78.3	18.8	46.1	...	41.8	85.1
	1980	489	85.7	11.8	28.3	...	55.1	77.6
	1985	805	77.1	13.3	17.1	...	43.6	50.4
	1990	1 503	79.0	10.4	20.6	...	57.3	65.3
	1995	1 995	66.4	11.9	20.6	...	58.2	58.8
	2000	2 528	69.4	12.8	24.9	...	45.0	53.3
	2005	3 023	67.1	11.6	26.9	...	52.4	59.4
	2010	4 014	75.2	12.5	25.2	...	44.1	57.0
	2015	4 882	68.9	12.3	20.4	...	40.1	41.7
	2016	5 037	73.1	12.4	22.1	...	36.8	44.3
	2017	5 398	67.7	11.9	23.2	...	38.7	42.8
	2018	5 578	65.2	11.4	22.9	...	40.6	42.2
	2019	5 731	62.3	10.8	23.0	...	40.4	39.2
Sint Maarten (Dutch part).......................	2005	1 267	82.5	15.5	9.1	...	127.0	133.6
(Netherlands Antillian Guilder)	2010	1 605	75.3	15.5	8.9	...	104.0	103.9
	2015	1 909	61.2	16.8	14.0	...	114.4	106.4
	2016	1 919	64.9	17.3	14.3	...	109.0	105.6
	2017	1 815	72.4	19.4	17.7	...	92.0	101.5
	2018	1 708	66.2	17.8	15.3	...	105.2	104.5
	2019	1 806	67.8	18.2	15.7	...	102.1	103.8
St. Vincent and the Grenadines.............	1970	42	93.6	21.0	22.7	...	24.5	55.3
(East Caribbean Dollar)	1975	83	103.3	22.3	23.1	...	19.9	60.2
	1980	189	90.7	20.1	33.7	...	47.3	83.7
	1985	360	59.6	17.0	21.5	2.8	61.7	61.6
	1990	632	70.6	18.0	25.5	1.1	55.6	60.1
	1995	843	66.0	17.4	25.9	...	43.6	51.6
	2000	1 070	61.3	16.7	23.4	...	45.3	46.7
	2005	1 487	75.7	15.6	25.1	...	36.4	52.9
	2010	1 839	80.6	19.3	29.0	0.9	27.4	57.1
	2015	2 040	80.3	22.0	25.3	0.5	37.8	54.3
	2016	2 091	81.4	20.0	26.0	0.6	37.6	57.7
	2017	2 139	79.4	21.0	25.7	0.5	34.9	54.7
	2018	2 191	80.7	21.1	25.1	0.5	36.0	56.6
	2019	2 229	83.1	21.4	18.9	0.4	37.7	54.8

Table 2. Gross Domestic Product by Type of Expenditure: Individual Countries or Areas

Major area, region and country	Year	Gross Domestic Product (at current prices) Million	Percentage Distributtion: Household final consumption expenditure 1	General government final consumption expenditure 2	Gross fixed capital formation 3	Changes in inventories 4	Exports of goods and services 5	Imports of goods and services 6
Suriname..	1970	672 (t)	53.4	23.4	18.4	...	56.7	52.9
(Surinam Dollar)	1975	1 138 (t)	52.8	20.9	27.1	5.3	62.1	68.1
	1980	1 944 (t)	57.6	21.3	21.5	4.9	68.8	74.2
	1985	2 136 (t)	55.0	33.7	17.9	-3.4	36.7	39.9
	1990	4 750 (t)	56.7	25.8	15.0	2.0	22.4	21.7
	1995	374	20.3	24.8	32.9	5.8	75.1	65.8
	2000	1 530	57.6	14.3	43.1	...	49.2	60.0
	2005	5 991	53.7	12.3	45.6	...	51.3	59.3
	2010	11 993	35.9	13.3	37.5	-1.3	52.5	38.4
	2015	16 357	36.8	12.9	42.1	0.2	50.3	42.4
	2016	19 489	36.9	12.9	41.9	0.1	50.6	42.4
	2017	24 082	36.9	12.9	42.1	0.2	50.5	42.6
	2018	25 855	36.9	12.9	42.0	0.2	50.4	42.5
	2019	27 575	36.9	12.9	42.0	0.2	50.5	42.5
Trinidad and Tobago..............................	1970	1 648	61.9	13.1	20.9	4.9	46.3	49.0
(Trinidad and Tobago Dollar)	1975	5 314	43.9	12.3	20.5	6.9	57.4	41.4
	1980	15 006	47.3	12.1	28.1	2.5	54.6	45.8
	1985	18 120	56.1	22.7	20.2	-1.5	35.3	33.4
	1990	21 597	54.8	16.2	13.8	0.0	49.1	33.4
	1995	31 782	48.8	15.9	18.9	1.8	53.8	39.1
	2000	51 509	57.4	12.0	15.6	1.2	59.2	45.2
	2005	100 953	31.4	11.6	28.6	1.5	65.8	38.9
	2010	141 424	47.2	11.2	18.4	...	53.7	30.5
	2015	159 179	57.0	14.0	20.6	...	50.0	41.7
	2016	149 294	66.4	16.1	20.0	...	41.5	44.1
	2017	151 762	64.1	15.6	16.4	...	46.4	42.5
	2018	160 332	66.1	16.1	8.6	...	47.6	38.5
	2019	156 756	69.6	17.0	7.6	...	38.7	32.9
Turks and Caicos Islands.......................	1970	9 775 (t)	49.2	28.1	30.1	...	61.3	69.3
(US Dollar)	1975	18	49.2	28.1	30.1	...	61.3	69.3
	1980	32	49.2	28.1	30.2	...	61.4	69.4
	1985	58	49.5	28.1	30.3	...	61.5	69.8
	1990	106	51.0	27.6	30.8	...	62.2	71.9
	1995	191	57.0	25.7	32.9	...	64.1	79.7
	2000	319	30.8	15.2	26.3	...	78.5	50.8
	2005	579	43.0	17.2	38.7	...	63.9	62.7
	2010	687	24.0	24.7	20.4	...	81.5	50.7
	2015	942	41.2	21.3	16.4	...	77.5	56.6
	2016	1 032	39.5	21.7	16.4	...	77.8	55.7
	2017	1 022	40.5	21.6	16.3	...	77.6	56.1
	2018	1 113	40.4	21.5	16.4	...	77.6	56.1
	2019	1 197	40.1	21.6	16.4	...	77.7	56.0
Uruguay..	1970	629 (t)	71.5	14.3	15.9	2.3	11.0	13.9
(Peso Uruguayo)	1975	8 551 (t)	73.4	12.8	18.5	2.9	14.6	20.4
	1980	97	72.8	11.7	23.2	4.3	13.6	21.3
	1985	529	70.9	12.9	10.7	1.9	22.7	20.8
	1990	10 805	71.5	12.4	12.0	0.2	22.2	19.8
	1995	135 311	75.4	10.6	15.0	2.0	16.1	18.8
	2000	276 152	76.5	12.4	14.3	0.1	16.7	20.0
	2005	425 018	69.4	10.9	16.5	1.2	30.4	28.5
	2010	808 079	67.0	12.6	19.1	0.3	26.3	25.4
	2015	1 455 848	66.8	13.8	19.8	-0.1	22.5	22.9
	2016	1 589 195	66.1	14.5	19.0	-1.2	21.4	19.9
	2017	1 707 109	67.2	14.5	16.5	-1.3	21.4	18.3
	2018	1 831 132	66.8	14.6	16.5	0.1	21.0	19.0
	2019	1 975 921	66.4	15.0	17.2	-1.0	21.7	19.3
Venezuela (Bolivarian Republic of)........	1970	61	37.6	19.8	33.8	13.3	22.1	17.5
(Bolivar Fuerte)	1975	138	33.4	20.5	39.5	8.5	31.2	23.4
	1980	297	37.8	21.3	38.5	0.0	31.6	23.5

Table 2. Gross Domestic Product by Type of Expenditure: Individual Countries or Areas

Major area, region and country	Year	Gross Domestic Product (at current prices) Million	Percentage Distributtion: Household final consumption expenditure 1	General government final consumption expenditure 2	Gross fixed capital formation 3	Changes in inventories 4	Exports of goods and services 5	Imports of goods and services 6
	1985	450	44.8	20.2	23.6	0.8	25.7	15.9
	1990	2 206	46.6	16.8	19.2	-5.8	40.6	20.4
	1995	13 243	54.1	14.8	22.4	1.4	27.9	22.1
	2000	79 656	51.7	12.4	21.0	3.2	29.7	18.1
	2005	304 087	46.8	11.1	20.3	2.7	39.7	20.5
	2010	1 016 830	55.9	11.2	18.7	3.3	28.5	17.6
	2015	6 025 330	121.3	12.9	39.5	2.6	7.7	84.0
	2016	21 059 374	115.1	18.7	22.8	-22.6	6.7	36.4
	2017	150 606 855	133.6	20.4	27.8	-32.9	6.4	48.6
	2018	79 260 044 396	105.1	14.7	26.7	-6.3	0.0	0.2
	2019	10 306 909 440 075	104.3	15.8	27.0	-6.9	0.0	0.2
Northern America								
Bermuda (Bermudian Dollar)	1970	266	68.2	9.8	14.1	-0.2	51.3	42.6
	1975	492	68.2	9.8	14.7	-0.2	51.2	43.0
	1980	902	67.5	9.6	17.6	-0.2	51.5	44.5
	1985	1 428	65.7	11.7	20.9	-0.3	47.2	43.0
	1990	2 035	68.6	12.3	17.1	-0.2	47.6	43.4
	1995	2 557	65.1	11.9	14.1	-0.2	46.0	37.1
	2000	3 480	53.9	10.9	19.5	0.6	46.8	40.9
	2005	4 868	51.2	15.5	17.2	0.0	46.5	31.4
	2010	6 635	46.8	13.8	13.0	...	50.8	23.8
	2015	6 655	48.3	12.5	11.9	...	50.0	23.3
	2016	6 900	48.5	12.1	12.8	...	49.3	23.4
	2017	7 142	48.9	11.6	13.8	...	48.5	24.0
	2018	7 263	47.9	11.7	13.3	...	51.0	25.1
	2019	7 361	48.2	11.9	14.9	...	51.1	26.0
Canada (Canadian Dollar)	1970	93 236	55.6	20.9	21.6	0.3	21.6	19.4
	1975	178 045	54.6	22.4	24.3	0.5	21.9	23.8
	1980	322 747	53.4	21.4	23.9	-0.2	27.4	25.7
	1985	500 027	54.1	22.1	20.7	0.8	27.5	25.3
	1990	695 501	55.8	22.6	21.7	-0.4	25.1	24.9
	1995	831 621	55.8	21.7	18.3	1.0	36.1	33.0
	2000	1 106 071	54.5	19.1	19.6	1.0	44.2	38.6
	2005	1 421 590	54.3	19.1	21.8	0.8	36.9	32.9
	2010	1 666 048	57.0	21.5	23.5	0.0	29.2	31.0
	2015	1 990 441	57.8	20.9	23.9	0.0	31.8	34.3
	2016	2 025 535	58.5	21.0	22.8	0.0	31.5	33.9
	2017	2 140 641	58.0	20.7	22.7	0.9	31.5	33.6
	2018	2 231 168	57.9	20.9	22.6	0.6	32.3	34.2
	2019	2 310 712	57.8	21.1	22.3	0.7	31.9	33.5
Greenland (Danish Krone)	1970	570	113.2	25.6	46.4	...	31.3	116.6
	1975	1 326	67.1	20.3	41.3	...	65.2	93.8
	1980	2 932	79.3	38.7	27.1	...	60.6	105.7
	1985	4 781	80.0	44.0	20.8	...	65.4	110.1
	1990	6 891	33.6	45.6	19.0	...	68.9	67.1
	1995	7 401	44.9	46.1	16.3	...	47.8	55.1
	2000	9 434	42.9	44.8	25.0	...	39.7	52.4
	2005	11 093	47.3	45.8	24.0	...	41.1	58.6
	2010	14 078	43.1	46.8	52.2	...	34.1	70.4
	2015	16 814	39.5	44.2	24.0	...	37.6	45.5
	2016	18 224	37.3	42.3	25.3	...	40.8	45.1
	2017	18 664	36.7	43.1	23.0	...	40.9	44.0
	2018	19 270	36.0	44.1	23.8	...	40.8	45.0
	2019	20 166	36.7	43.2	24.0	...	40.8	44.7
United States (US Dollar)	1970	1 073 303	60.3	18.0	21.2	0.2	5.6	5.2
	1975	1 684 904	61.2	17.6	20.6	-0.4	8.2	7.3
	1980	2 857 307	61.3	15.9	23.5	-0.2	9.8	10.3
	1985	4 338 979	62.5	15.9	23.7	0.5	7.0	9.6
	1990	5 963 144	63.9	15.9	21.3	0.2	9.3	10.6

Table 2. Gross Domestic Product by Type of Expenditure: Individual Countries or Areas

Major area, region and country	Year	Gross Domestic Product (at current prices) Million	Percentage Distribution: Household final consumption expenditure 1	General government final consumption expenditure 2	Gross fixed capital formation 3	Changes in inventories 4	Exports of goods and services 5	Imports of goods and services 6
	1995	7 639 749	65.0	14.9	20.9	0.4	10.6	11.8
	2000	10 252 347	66.0	14.0	23.1	0.5	10.7	14.4
	2005	13 036 637	67.1	15.1	22.9	0.4	10.0	15.5
	2010	14 992 052	67.9	16.7	18.4	0.4	12.3	15.7
	2015	18 238 301	67.4	14.3	20.4	0.7	12.4	15.3
	2016	18 745 075	68.1	14.2	20.3	0.2	11.9	14.6
	2017	19 542 980	68.3	14.0	20.5	0.1	12.2	15.0
	2018	20 611 861	67.9	14.0	20.8	0.3	12.3	15.2
	2019	21 433 226	67.9	14.0	20.8	0.2	11.7	14.6
Asia								
Afghanistan (Afghani)	1970	78	89.6	6.5	5.5	...	9.6	11.3
	1975	104	85.7	6.2	9.6	...	13.0	14.4
	1980	161	83.6	6.0	13.2	...	11.6	14.4
	1985	169	83.5	6.0	13.3	...	11.5	14.4
	1990	180	83.5	6.0	13.4	...	11.5	14.4
	1995	2 297	100.9	7.3	12.8	...	22.9	43.9
	2000	158 271	118.4	8.5	12.2	...	34.3	73.4
	2005	307 885	115.9	11.5	19.6	...	33.0	68.7
	2010	682 800	96.0	19.6	14.4	...	18.3	34.7
	2015	1 144 181	80.0	22.2	13.7	...	16.2	33.2
	2016	1 224 144	79.6	23.0	12.6	...	17.3	32.4
	2017	1 266 867	72.1	21.5	14.9	...	23.6	32.0
	2018	1 296 559	89.0	19.5	15.5	...	17.0	41.0
	2019	1 389 686	96.8	24.1	12.3	...	12.7	46.0
Armenia (Armenian Dram)	1990	50	50.1	16.8	44.3	2.8	35.0	46.3
	1995	556 946	104.8	9.6	16.2	2.2	26.8	61.0
	2000	1 099 842	95.7	10.1	18.5	0.1	26.2	49.6
	2005	2 391 859	74.4	9.0	29.8	0.5	32.3	42.4
	2010	3 690 038	80.8	11.2	33.5	-0.7	23.4	44.4
	2015	5 043 633	78.1	13.1	20.6	0.1	29.7	41.9
	2016	5 067 294	77.3	13.5	17.4	0.7	33.1	42.8
	2017	5 564 493	80.0	12.3	17.6	1.6	37.3	49.5
	2018	6 017 035	81.8	11.5	16.7	5.7	37.7	53.4
	2019	6 569 031	84.5	12.5	15.8	1.7	38.5	52.9
Azerbaijan (Azerbaijanian Manat)	1990	293 (t)	52.6	17.6	20.3	6.3	43.9	39.2
	1995	2 134	84.3	12.8	15.6	8.1	32.5	53.4
	2000	4 718	64.4	15.2	23.1	-2.5	40.2	38.4
	2005	12 523	42.1	10.4	41.3	0.2	62.9	52.9
	2010	42 465	39.4	10.9	18.2	-0.1	54.3	20.7
	2015	54 380	56.7	12.4	27.8	0.1	37.8	34.8
	2016	60 425	58.7	12.8	25.0	0.6	46.4	43.6
	2017	70 338	57.6	11.3	23.8	0.6	48.5	41.9
	2018	80 092	54.1	10.5	20.7	-0.6	54.1	37.6
	2019	81 681	56.7	10.8	19.4	0.8	49.2	36.9
Bahrain (Bahraini Dinar)	1970	201	67.7	11.0	33.9	-4.8	85.1	88.9
	1975	468	65.6	12.4	22.8	-0.3	89.9	89.6
	1980	1 419	52.6	11.1	28.5	16.9	80.8	89.3
	1985	1 683	43.6	25.1	27.9	4.5	67.1	71.2
	1990	1 846	53.3	21.6	23.2	-3.0	80.4	79.0
	1995	2 552	49.5	19.1	20.2	1.3	70.7	60.7
	2000	3 408	44.7	16.0	16.4	0.4	79.2	56.6
	2005	6 004	39.7	13.7	25.7	1.4	83.9	64.4
	2010	9 668	41.2	12.9	26.0	1.2	69.5	50.9
	2015	11 703	45.5	17.6	24.0	1.5	82.9	71.7
	2016	12 133	45.1	17.1	25.7	3.4	74.1	65.4
	2017	13 338	42.1	16.6	28.3	4.6	75.8	67.3
	2018	14 157	39.7	16.3	29.6	6.8	79.6	71.8
	2019	14 504	40.1	15.8	29.6	3.2	76.6	65.3

Table 2. Gross Domestic Product by Type of Expenditure: Individual Countries or Areas

Major area, region and country	Year	Gross Domestic Product (at current prices) Million	Percentage Distributtion					
			Household final consumption expenditure 1	General government final consumption expenditure 2	Gross fixed capital formation 3	Changes in inventories 4	Exports of goods and services 5	Imports of goods and services 6
Bangladesh	1970	45 099	98.4	1.3	5.6	...	5.8	8.8
(Taka)	1975	164 008	95.8	1.5	8.7	0.2	2.2	6.3
	1980	258 535	85.7	4.3	21.3	0.6	5.4	15.3
	1985	536 630	86.8	3.9	18.0	0.5	5.8	13.9
	1990	972 648	84.6	4.5	20.2	-2.0	6.3	14.0
	1995	1 525 180	82.0	4.6	19.1	...	10.9	17.3
	2000	2 370 860	77.5	4.6	23.0	...	14.0	19.2
	2005	3 707 070	74.4	5.5	24.5	...	16.6	23.0
	2010	7 975 387	74.1	5.1	26.2	...	16.0	21.8
	2015	15 158 022	72.4	5.4	28.9	...	17.2	25.7
	2016	17 328 637	69.1	5.9	29.7	...	16.6	21.3
	2017	19 758 154	68.7	6.0	30.5	...	15.0	20.3
	2018	22 504 793	70.8	6.4	31.2	...	14.8	23.4
	2019	25 424 826	68.7	6.3	31.6	...	15.3	21.4
Bhutan	1970	463	73.2	21.4	33.2	-0.9	14.4	43.1
(Ngultrum)	1975	727	73.1	21.4	33.2	-0.9	14.4	43.1
	1980	1 011	70.0	23.7	32.5	-1.3	14.1	39.0
	1985	2 130	66.0	23.3	43.1	0.4	14.7	50.2
	1990	4 789	54.2	17.5	31.8	4.5	28.9	33.0
	1995	9 376	41.6	18.6	46.3	2.4	38.9	43.9
	2000	19 736	47.7	21.9	50.0	-1.8	29.4	48.3
	2005	36 112	40.4	21.9	52.1	0.0	38.2	64.4
	2010	72 497	43.8	20.0	61.2	0.5	42.5	70.7
	2015	128 535	49.8	18.3	55.7	-0.3	34.4	67.8
	2016	145 073	48.2	17.3	56.4	0.6	29.6	55.8
	2017	159 572	48.4	16.8	52.1	-0.1	30.1	52.7
	2018	167 327	51.5	17.1	47.2	0.3	30.8	55.9
	2019	180 589	52.9	18.3	44.3	0.3	29.0	50.4
Brunei Darussalam	1970	689	15.7	9.1	3.9	0.1	90.8	19.6
(Brunei Dollar)	1975	3 480	17.3	11.0	4.9	0.1	90.1	23.4
	1980	13 255	8.3	7.0	3.0	0.1	93.4	11.7
	1985	9 737	9.2	15.7	11.9	0.1	61.3	16.6
	1990	7 070	16.8	21.8	27.7	0.2	51.2	31.7
	1995	7 435	23.3	26.4	54.3	0.4	49.4	47.5
	2000	11 464	15.8	25.5	19.2	0.3	55.7	30.5
	2005	17 578	14.3	18.2	16.8	0.1	58.1	23.2
	2010	18 690	14.7	22.2	23.5	0.2	67.4	28.0
	2015	17 778	19.8	25.1	35.0	0.2	52.2	37.7
	2016	15 748	21.2	26.2	34.4	0.3	49.6	37.7
	2017	16 748	20.5	26.5	34.6	0.2	49.6	35.6
	2018	18 301	19.5	24.1	40.9	0.2	51.9	42.0
	2019	18 375	20.5	25.0	38.5	0.2	57.9	50.6
Cambodia	1970	12 944	95.0	4.0	9.3	...	2.3	14.4
(Riel)	1975	10 674	95.0	4.0	9.3	...	2.3	14.4
	1980	10 149	95.0	4.0	9.3	...	2.2	14.3
	1985	20 508	95.9	3.6	9.3	...	1.6	13.9
	1990	723 653	90.4	7.2	8.3	...	2.4	8.4
	1995	8 110 680	90.9	5.1	13.2	0.2	32.7	43.9
	2000	14 002 000	88.8	5.2	18.3	-0.8	49.8	61.8
	2005	25 754 300	84.3	5.8	18.9	-0.4	64.1	72.7
	2010	47 048 000	81.3	6.3	16.2	1.2	54.1	59.5
	2015	73 422 700	76.8	5.4	21.4	1.0	61.7	66.1
	2016	81 241 900	76.1	5.2	21.7	1.0	61.3	65.7
	2017	89 830 525	73.4	5.1	21.9	1.0	60.7	64.1
	2018	99 544 275	70.6	4.9	22.6	0.9	61.6	63.3
	2019	110 014 048	69.4	4.8	23.4	0.9	61.1	62.5
China	1970	227 970	52.9	10.9	24.8	8.7	2.9	2.8
(Yuan Renminbi)	1975	303 950	50.3	11.7	29.8	6.0	5.5	5.5
	1980	458 760	50.9	13.7	29.3	6.0	6.9	7.3

Table 2. Gross Domestic Product by Type of Expenditure: Individual Countries or Areas

Major area, region and country	Year	Gross Domestic Product (at current prices) Million	Percentage Distributtion					
			Household final consumption expenditure 1	General government final consumption expenditure 2	Gross fixed capital formation 3	Changes in inventories 4	Exports of goods and services 5	Imports of goods and services 6
	1985	909 890	50.9	14.2	31.3	8.6	9.4	13.4
	1990	1 887 290	50.0	13.6	24.6	10.2	14.0	11.3
	1995	6 133 990	45.8	13.2	33.2	6.5	19.2	17.5
	2000	10 028 010	46.9	16.6	33.4	1.0	23.1	20.7
	2005	18 731 890	40.2	14.0	40.5	0.9	33.8	28.4
	2010	41 211 930	35.4	12.8	45.1	2.6	26.3	22.7
	2015	68 885 820	37.8	16.2	42.1	1.1	21.4	18.1
	2016	74 639 510	38.7	16.4	41.6	1.1	19.6	17.3
	2017	83 203 590	38.5	16.3	41.9	1.2	19.7	17.9
	2018	91 928 110	38.5	16.5	42.8	1.0	19.1	18.3
	2019	99 086 510	38.9	16.7	42.6	0.7	18.8	17.3
China, Hong Kong SAR	1970	23 106	66.2	5.7	19.7	0.7	93.2	85.5
(Hong Kong Dollar)	1975	49 589	65.5	6.0	21.5	1.5	83.4	77.8
	1980	143 619	60.0	5.6	32.2	2.6	88.7	89.3
	1985	278 128	61.5	7.0	21.0	0.5	103.9	93.9
	1990	599 256	57.5	6.8	26.2	1.0	117.3	108.7
	1995	1 119 006	62.2	8.0	30.2	4.1	126.2	130.7
	2000	1 337 501	58.6	9.4	26.5	1.1	126.0	121.6
	2005	1 412 125	57.5	9.2	21.4	-0.3	177.5	165.2
	2010	1 776 332	61.4	8.9	21.8	2.1	205.3	199.4
	2015	2 398 280	66.4	9.6	22.4	-0.9	195.9	193.5
	2016	2 490 438	66.3	10.0	21.5	0.0	187.0	184.7
	2017	2 659 384	67.1	9.8	21.7	0.4	188.9	187.9
	2018	2 835 161	68.3	9.9	21.6	0.4	188.4	188.6
	2019	2 865 679	68.7	10.8	19.1	-0.2	177.5	175.8
China, Macao SAR	1970	1 007	59.0	5.9	20.1	3.0	113.0	100.9
(Pataca)	1975	2 278	58.9	5.9	20.1	3.0	113.0	100.9
	1980	5 135	59.1	5.8	20.0	3.3	113.0	101.3
	1985	10 789	56.0	7.3	20.0	2.9	106.9	93.2
	1990	25 835	45.7	10.3	22.5	0.5	99.0	78.0
	1995	55 743	41.1	9.6	26.1	0.5	74.5	51.7
	2000	53 938	46.0	12.6	10.3	0.1	90.0	59.0
	2005	96 872	31.9	9.8	25.0	0.7	84.9	52.3
	2010	225 051	23.4	8.2	12.5	0.8	87.8	32.7
	2015	362 213	26.1	9.6	24.6	0.5	77.9	38.7
	2016	362 876	26.4	10.4	21.6	0.0	76.1	34.5
	2017	407 328	24.3	9.7	19.7	-0.2	79.9	33.3
	2018	444 666	23.8	9.5	16.7	0.5	82.8	33.2
	2019	434 670	25.4	10.4	13.7	0.5	83.5	33.4
Cyprus	1970	439	76.4	7.4	31.4	1.3	53.7	63.7
(Euro)	1975	497	82.0	13.5	26.2	4.0	50.3	76.1
	1980	1 457	63.8	10.5	45.0	0.8	64.7	85.4
	1985	2 838	61.0	10.9	35.8	1.0	69.8	79.8
	1990	4 898	57.3	13.4	32.4	0.4	73.7	77.2
	1995	7 678	61.9	12.4	25.3	1.3	66.8	67.6
	2000	10 595	61.9	15.1	20.3	0.2	70.0	67.5
	2005	14 822	61.6	16.5	21.6	0.8	55.7	56.2
	2010	19 410	65.8	18.5	22.6	1.5	50.4	58.7
	2015	17 827	67.9	16.4	13.1	-0.1	70.3	67.7
	2016	18 873	66.0	15.3	17.8	-0.8	70.8	69.0
	2017	20 040	65.5	15.0	21.0	-1.1	73.0	73.4
	2018	21 138	65.2	14.9	19.2	-0.1	73.1	72.3
	2019	21 944	64.9	16.4	19.2	-0.1	71.1	71.5
D.P.R. of Korea	1970	12 663	...	...	...	...	5.4	8.3
(North Korean Won)	1975	20 768	...	...	...	...	5.4	8.3
	1980	25 389	...	...	...	...	5.4	8.3
	1985	30 447	...	...	...	...	5.4	8.3
	1990	31 904	...	...	...	...	7.5	11.8
	1995	10 329	...	...	...	...	3.8	5.7
	2000	22 807	...	...	...	...	4.2	10.0

Table 2. Gross Domestic Product by Type of Expenditure: Individual Countries or Areas

Major area, region and country	Year	Gross Domestic Product (at current prices) Million	Percentage Distributtion					
			Household final consumption expenditure 1	General government final consumption expenditure 2	Gross fixed capital formation 3	Changes in inventories 4	Exports of goods and services 5	Imports of goods and services 6
	2005	1 801 509	...	...	...	...	6.0	11.1
	2010	1 405 640	...	...	...	...	5.9	11.1
	2015	1 751 302	...	...	...	...	5.9	11.1
	2016	1 808 781	...	...	...	...	5.9	11.1
	2017	1 870 904	...	...	...	...	5.9	11.1
	2018	1 834 778	...	...	...	...	5.9	11.1
	2019	1 756 121	...	...	...	...	5.9	11.1
Georgia	1990	15 (t)	63.2	16.8	23.7	...	40.0	45.7
(Lari)	1995	3 885	87.8	5.8	18.9	3.9	13.2	27.0
	2000	6 357	89.2	6.2	24.9	0.4	21.7	37.5
	2005	12 225	72.5	12.6	27.5	4.4	31.8	48.8
	2010	21 822	81.2	15.3	18.9	1.6	33.0	49.9
	2015	33 935	76.5	14.3	24.4	1.9	40.9	57.9
	2016	35 836	69.8	15.3	26.5	3.6	40.8	56.0
	2017	40 762	69.8	13.9	25.5	1.8	46.5	57.5
	2018	44 599	69.3	13.2	25.1	3.0	50.6	61.2
	2019	50 002	69.3	12.8	23.7	3.1	54.0	62.9
India	1970	468 169	79.7	8.9	15.5	0.8	3.8	3.9
(Indian Rupee)	1975	852 124	77.7	9.5	17.7	0.9	5.6	6.6
	1980	1 470 629	77.8	9.7	19.7	1.1	6.1	9.2
	1985	2 845 341	73.0	10.9	21.8	0.5	5.3	7.6
	1990	5 761 092	67.1	11.3	26.1	2.1	7.1	8.5
	1995	12 055 827	63.7	10.5	25.1	2.2	10.8	12.0
	2000	21 398 857	63.7	11.9	26.7	-0.5	13.0	13.9
	2005	36 321 250	57.4	10.4	33.9	2.5	19.6	22.4
	2010	76 344 720	54.7	11.0	35.4	4.4	22.4	26.9
	2015	137 718 739	59.0	10.4	30.2	1.9	19.8	22.1
	2016	153 916 690	59.3	10.3	29.3	2.7	19.2	20.9
	2017	170 983 040	59.0	10.8	29.4	4.9	18.8	21.9
	2018	189 712 370	59.3	11.1	30.0	2.2	19.9	23.6
	2019	203 625 140	60.5	11.0	27.9	2.6	17.9	20.4
Indonesia	1970	3 787 867	73.9	8.1	12.4	0.6	12.6	14.4
(Rupiah)	1975	14 789 993	64.1	8.9	17.9	0.9	21.6	19.8
	1980	53 163 493	56.1	9.3	18.4	0.9	28.8	19.7
	1985	113 468 718	54.7	10.1	20.3	5.7	20.9	18.2
	1990	246 674 584	52.7	8.0	25.0	3.4	23.9	21.1
	1995	531 696 932	56.5	7.0	25.0	4.5	24.8	24.6
	2000	1 479 724 635	61.3	6.5	19.2	3.4	40.5	29.8
	2005	2 953 850 193	64.0	8.0	22.9	2.6	33.7	29.3
	2010	6 864 133 100	56.2	9.0	31.0	1.9	24.3	22.4
	2015	11 526 332 800	57.5	9.7	32.8	1.3	21.2	20.8
	2016	12 401 728 500	57.8	9.5	32.6	1.3	19.1	18.3
	2017	13 589 825 700	57.3	9.1	32.2	1.5	20.2	19.2
	2018	14 838 311 500	57.0	9.0	32.3	2.3	21.0	22.0
	2019	15 833 943 400	57.9	8.8	32.3	1.4	18.4	18.9
Iran (Islamic Republic of)	1970	831 451	57.7	17.4	36.8	3.8	18.5	21.2
(Iranian Rial)	1975	3 529 378	45.5	23.8	42.2	-0.8	40.7	35.4
	1980	6 753 980	57.7	21.0	36.9	10.9	13.7	28.7
	1985	15 808 050	67.0	15.9	32.9	-8.6	8.9	14.3
	1990	37 986 542	67.9	10.8	27.0	6.0	13.3	23.8
	1995	197 370 155	50.0	14.3	24.7	5.5	21.7	13.5
	2000	639 664 897	48.8	13.5	30.7	5.0	21.1	19.4
	2005	2 029 907 700	41.2	12.1	28.6	10.2	30.3	24.1
	2010	5 035 812 300	42.9	10.8	27.4	12.9	24.4	19.4
	2015	11 414 167 000	50.3	12.7	22.7	11.3	19.7	19.3
	2016	13 151 259 100	49.4	13.3	20.3	12.9	22.4	20.8
	2017	15 316 529 600	47.6	13.4	19.7	15.0	24.9	23.8
	2018	18 876 880 802	43.5	11.7	18.5	19.4	23.3	19.5
	2019	25 358 741 372	45.6	12.5	18.0	20.7	9.8	9.8

Table 2. Gross Domestic Product by Type of Expenditure: Individual Countries or Areas

Major area, region and country	Year	Gross Domestic Product (at current prices) Million	Percentage Distribution: Household final consumption expenditure 1	General government final consumption expenditure 2	Gross fixed capital formation 3	Changes in inventories 4	Exports of goods and services 5	Imports of goods and services 6
Iraq	1970	5 273	22.7	15.1	10.9	-4.0	71.9	16.6
(Iraqi Dinar)	1975	17 156	14.9	12.2	20.1	-7.1	91.7	31.8
	1980	66 891	7.9	7.5	18.3	-8.8	95.1	20.1
	1985	64 984	22.6	13.4	16.4	1.9	160.3	114.8
	1990	97 711	21.3	12.1	16.4	0.7	118.6	69.1
	1995	8 140 901	66.3	21.6	3.5	1.4	24.1	16.8
	2000	56 609 817	16.8	14.7	3.6	32.5	93.9	61.6
	2005	73 533 599	51.7	27.5	19.1	11.4	74.9	84.6
	2010	162 064 566	52.6	22.4	19.2	-0.4	46.6	40.3
	2015	194 680 972	59.1	19.8	27.6	-6.0	36.7	37.3
	2016	196 924 142	60.0	19.4	15.4	3.5	29.7	28.0
	2017	225 722 376	54.9	17.4	15.6	3.5	36.2	27.6
	2018	254 870 185	49.9	18.1	13.6	0.3	46.6	28.5
	2019	266 224 666	51.4	17.2	15.5	...	42.4	29.2
Israel	1970	2 107 (t)	53.4	36.4	29.1	0.7	21.8	40.1
(New Israeli Sheqel)	1975	9 183 (t)	50.2	42.0	31.0	0.8	24.2	46.6
	1980	123	49.6	37.0	24.3	-0.2	37.3	47.8
	1985	32 310	53.3	32.4	20.4	-0.4	37.3	43.3
	1990	118 553	57.2	27.3	21.0	-0.5	29.9	35.0
	1995	302 289	55.5	26.4	24.9	0.9	27.5	35.2
	2000	539 602	53.0	24.3	21.2	1.6	35.6	35.7
	2005	639 627	55.4	24.2	19.0	1.5	40.8	40.9
	2010	874 904	56.6	22.7	18.8	0.0	34.7	32.8
	2015	1 165 324	54.5	22.5	19.2	0.8	31.2	28.2
	2016	1 224 951	54.8	22.4	20.7	0.5	29.7	28.1
	2017	1 271 555	54.7	22.7	20.8	0.7	28.7	27.5
	2018	1 330 618	54.7	23.0	21.4	0.4	29.4	29.0
	2019	1 408 340	54.2	22.9	20.6	0.5	28.9	27.1
Japan	1970	76 539 308	46.5	11.1	37.7	3.3	10.4	9.2
(Yen)	1975	154 787 118	50.8	15.0	34.5	0.0	12.3	12.3
	1980	250 636 100	52.4	14.7	33.6	0.4	13.1	14.1
	1985	333 686 000	52.5	14.3	29.5	0.5	13.9	10.7
	1990	453 608 500	51.2	13.5	34.1	0.4	10.2	9.4
	1995	512 541 700	53.5	15.4	29.5	0.3	9.0	7.7
	2000	526 706 000	54.4	16.9	27.4	-0.1	10.6	9.2
	2005	524 132 800	55.6	18.1	24.6	0.1	14.0	12.5
	2010	500 353 900	57.8	19.5	21.3	0.0	15.0	13.6
	2015	531 319 800	56.6	19.8	23.8	0.2	17.6	18.0
	2016	535 537 200	55.7	19.9	23.3	0.1	16.3	15.3
	2017	545 897 400	55.4	19.6	23.8	0.2	17.8	16.8
	2018	547 125 500	55.6	19.8	24.1	0.2	18.5	18.3
	2019	554 037 900	55.2	20.0	24.3	0.2	17.5	17.2
Jordan [9]	1970	218	74.2	31.3	14.7	0.0	8.2	35.2
(Jordanian Dinar)	1975	402	80.3	31.8	27.8	4.2	30.2	74.8
	1980	1 233	71.3	23.0	41.1	6.5	38.8	78.0
	1985	2 083	84.9	22.4	21.6	2.9	38.4	72.1
	1990	2 752	70.8	21.2	29.4	8.6	61.4	89.9
	1995	4 862	61.5	20.1	33.5	5.8	51.3	70.7
	2000	6 186	76.8	20.2	23.9	2.8	41.5	66.4
	2005	9 204	83.7	16.6	34.7	6.1	52.3	91.4
	2010	19 265	67.6	19.2	30.9	3.9	47.0	67.2
	2015	27 397	80.4	17.8	21.8	3.0	36.5	58.8
	2016	28 324	80.0	17.3	20.0	3.4	34.4	54.3
	2017	29 400	79.6	17.5	20.4	3.4	34.5	55.4
	2018	30 482	77.1	17.1	20.4	3.4	35.1	53.0
	2019	31 597	73.7	16.2	19.3	3.2	36.5	49.2
Kazakhstan	1990	96	67.1	12.4	39.0	7.7	7.8	30.5
(Tenge)	1995	1 014 190	71.1	13.6	23.1	0.3	39.0	43.5
	2000	2 599 902	61.9	12.1	17.3	0.8	56.6	49.1

Table 2. Gross Domestic Product by Type of Expenditure: Individual Countries or Areas

Major area, region and country	Year	Gross Domestic Product (at current prices) Million	Percentage Distributtion: Household final consumption expenditure 1	General government final consumption expenditure 2	Gross fixed capital formation 3	Changes in inventories 4	Exports of goods and services 5	Imports of goods and services 6
	2005	7 590 594	49.9	11.2	28.0	3.0	53.2	44.6
	2010	21 815 517	45.4	10.8	24.3	1.0	44.2	29.9
	2015	40 884 134	53.7	11.6	22.9	5.0	28.5	24.5
	2016	46 971 150	54.5	11.6	22.7	5.1	31.8	28.5
	2017	54 378 858	52.6	10.5	21.7	4.7	32.4	24.4
	2018	61 819 536	52.1	8.3	21.2	4.1	37.6	25.9
	2019	69 532 627	52.0	9.1	23.0	3.7	36.2	27.7
Kuwait [10]	1970	1 026	38.6	13.5	12.3	-0.2	59.8	24.2
(Kuwaiti Dinar)	1975	3 485	21.7	11.1	12.0	0.7	80.5	26.0
	1980	7 755	30.0	11.2	12.5	1.4	78.2	33.2
	1985	6 450	47.8	22.4	19.8	-0.9	53.7	42.7
	1990	5 328	58.6	38.6	15.6	0.2	44.8	57.8
	1995	7 925	41.3	33.0	13.9	1.2	53.6	43.0
	2000	11 570	41.5	21.5	10.5	0.2	56.5	30.1
	2005	23 593	32.2	15.7	14.6	1.8	64.0	28.3
	2010	33 079	28.9	17.1	16.0	1.6	66.7	30.4
	2015	34 473	41.5	24.2	25.5	-0.1	53.8	44.9
	2016	33 056	45.2	25.7	29.3	0.7	47.0	48.5
	2017	36 611	43.3	24.4	27.0	0.7	51.2	46.6
	2018	42 475	39.2	22.7	24.4	0.7	56.7	43.8
	2019	40 873	46.1	26.3	21.4	0.6	53.5	48.0
Kyrgyzstan	1990	43	71.3	25.0	23.1	0.9	29.2	49.5
(Som)	1995	16 145	75.0	19.5	20.7	-2.3	29.5	42.4
	2000	65 358	65.7	20.0	18.3	1.7	41.8	47.6
	2005	100 899	84.5	17.5	16.2	0.2	38.3	56.8
	2010	220 369	84.6	18.1	28.1	-0.7	51.6	81.7
	2015	430 489	90.5	17.8	33.0	1.7	35.2	75.8
	2016	476 331	82.8	17.4	32.2	1.7	35.8	70.0
	2017	530 476	82.1	17.1	31.9	1.0	34.3	66.4
	2018	569 386	82.5	17.2	32.1	4.0	31.6	67.3
	2019	590 042	82.0	16.8	31.9	1.0	37.4	65.7
Lao People's DR	1970	175	90.2	8.1	7.6	...	4.4	10.3
(Kip)	1975	738	90.2	8.0	7.6	...	4.4	10.2
	1980	5 540	90.2	8.0	7.4	...	4.3	10.0
	1985	87 928	90.0	8.7	7.0	...	4.0	9.8
	1990	638 246	89.1	7.3	16.8	...	11.3	24.5
	1995	1 490 613	90.1	7.3	16.7	...	23.2	37.3
	2000	14 245 301	93.5	6.7	13.9	...	30.1	44.2
	2005	31 393 853	69.9	8.2	34.3	2.1	25.8	39.0
	2010	60 400 108	72.7	11.6	26.8	...	34.5	48.1
	2015	117 252 000	71.2	15.1	31.6	...	34.0	51.8
	2016	129 279 000	65.7	14.0	29.0	...	33.2	41.9
	2017	140 749 142	65.2	12.9	29.0	...	34.3	41.5
	2018	152 414 196	67.4	14.0	29.9	...	33.8	45.1
	2019	163 369 000	66.1	13.6	29.3	...	33.8	42.8
Lebanon	1970	6 504	86.3	10.5	14.4	4.2	23.6	39.0
(Lebanese Pound)	1975	10 024	93.1	11.6	19.1	...	15.2	38.9
	1980	18 717	92.2	25.1	15.7	...	39.0	72.0
	1985	37 356	100.4	32.0	26.3	...	23.0	69.0
	1990	2 050 649	100.5	35.8	29.7	...	31.3	82.1
	1995	18 655 913	87.8	14.2	37.5	...	15.4	53.7
	2000	25 142 897	85.6	17.6	21.0	-0.6	13.6	37.1
	2005	32 407 235	82.0	14.5	22.0	1.0	36.6	56.1
	2010	57 954 190	87.9	12.2	25.0	-0.1	35.0	60.1
	2015	75 283 608	90.8	12.5	21.7	0.5	23.1	48.7
	2016	77 191 722	88.6	13.0	22.2	0.5	21.7	45.9
	2017	80 109 512	90.0	13.2	21.0	0.4	21.9	46.4
	2018	82 854 123	90.6	15.3	20.1	0.7	20.7	47.4
	2019	80 450 816	86.7	15.2	18.4	...	21.7	41.9

Table 2. Gross Domestic Product by Type of Expenditure: Individual Countries or Areas

Major area, region and country	Year	Gross Domestic Product (at current prices) Million	Percentage Distributtion: Household final consumption expenditure 1	General government final consumption expenditure 2	Gross fixed capital formation 3	Changes in inventories 4	Exports of goods and services 5	Imports of goods and services 6
Malaysia [11]	1970	11 829	60.0	18.3	17.5	...	45.6	41.3
(Malaysian Ringgit)	1975	22 332	58.6	17.6	25.1	-1.7	45.5	45.1
	1980	53 308	50.5	16.5	31.1	-0.7	57.5	55.0
	1985	77 470	52.0	15.3	29.8	-2.3	54.9	49.8
	1990	119 081	51.8	13.8	33.0	-0.7	74.5	72.4
	1995	222 473	47.9	12.4	43.6	0.1	94.1	98.0
	2000	356 401	43.8	10.2	25.3	1.6	119.8	100.6
	2005	543 578	44.2	11.5	22.3	0.1	112.9	91.0
	2010	821 434	48.1	12.6	22.4	1.0	86.9	71.0
	2015	1 176 941	54.0	13.1	25.9	-0.4	69.4	61.9
	2016	1 249 698	54.8	12.6	25.5	0.5	66.8	60.1
	2017	1 372 310	55.4	12.2	25.1	0.5	70.0	63.1
	2018	1 447 451	57.4	11.9	24.2	-0.3	68.6	61.9
	2019	1 510 693	59.8	11.7	23.0	-1.9	65.2	57.8
Maldives	1970	201	50.4	12.0	16.0	-0.2	71.3	55.6
(Rufiyaa)	1975	310	49.9	12.1	16.2	-0.2	71.3	55.6
	1980	703	46.8	12.7	17.1	...	71.3	55.6
	1985	1 178	47.7	14.0	22.0	-0.8	71.3	55.6
	1990	2 681	47.8	14.1	22.0	-0.8	71.3	55.7
	1995	6 666	48.6	13.7	21.9	-0.9	71.8	56.2
	2000	10 431	43.8	18.8	18.3	-0.6	69.4	52.1
	2005	14 891	43.0	21.8	34.1	-0.7	66.4	73.8
	2010	33 129	35.9	20.9	28.6	0.4	67.5	65.8
	2015	63 147	41.1	18.2	33.0	0.5	78.4	71.2
	2016	67 300	44.0	17.8	39.2	4.0	72.0	77.1
	2017	73 153	47.0	14.7	40.2	5.0	72.3	79.3
	2018	81 586	47.0	14.8	46.5	5.3	70.1	83.7
	2019	86 788	46.0	15.4	40.6	6.9	69.0	78.0
Mongolia	1970	7 132	55.5	18.3	51.6	...	12.4	34.1
(Tugrik)	1975	9 354	55.6	18.4	51.6	...	12.3	34.2
	1980	12 495	58.7	18.6	46.5	...	12.1	32.5
	1985	17 572	54.2	18.8	53.4	...	14.4	37.3
	1990	18 825	66.3	21.1	38.8	-5.0	13.4	30.2
	1995	772 062	67.5	10.7	25.6	0.4	33.8	37.0
	2000	1 419 295	76.9	14.3	28.0	2.0	46.1	61.7
	2005	3 526 502	56.9	11.0	30.8	7.9	50.2	57.8
	2010	9 756 590	55.2	12.7	35.9	6.2	46.7	56.7
	2015	23 150 400	59.1	13.5	21.2	5.2	45.6	44.6
	2016	23 942 866	54.8	14.6	20.5	5.2	50.2	45.4
	2017	27 876 297	53.5	12.7	24.6	6.7	59.8	57.4
	2018	32 411 224	54.3	11.7	29.4	10.2	58.5	64.0
	2019	36 897 640	55.3	12.2	31.5	4.4	61.3	64.4
Myanmar [12]	1970	12 980	80.7	13.4	11.3	1.7	4.0	12.7
(Kyat)	1975	25 452	77.9	12.9	7.9	2.3	5.1	6.0
	1980	40 744	70.7	11.5	19.5	2.8	8.1	12.6
	1985	57 509	77.1	12.2	15.0	-1.0	4.3	7.6
	1990	169 372	73.7	13.4	14.7	-0.3	1.7	3.2
	1995	698 355	79.4	8.3	14.4	-1.3	12.7	32.6
	2000	3 050 601	72.6	15.6	11.7	0.2	29.6	34.0
	2005	14 569 762	78.1	7.6	13.2	0.3	33.0	19.0
	2010	43 042 326	59.2	5.8	26.3	0.2	17.3	15.5
	2015	74 215 746	53.3	21.7	32.5	0.8	23.0	30.9
	2016	82 700 024	54.5	20.3	32.0	2.4	25.9	35.1
	2017	92 588 955	55.4	19.0	31.2	1.1	28.2	34.2
	2018	105 258 501	55.3	15.1	29.9	0.7	30.4	30.3
	2019	116 578 512	55.1	18.1	31.0	1.4	28.2	33.2
Nepal	1970	10 538	90.9	6.5	6.0	...	4.9	8.3
(Nepalese Rupee)	1975	17 790	87.9	6.3	13.6	-0.2	9.0	14.2
	1980	25 068	87.8	5.6	15.9	1.0	11.6	19.8

Table 2. Gross Domestic Product by Type of Expenditure: Individual Countries or Areas

Major area, region and country	Year	Gross Domestic Product (at current prices) Million	Percentage Distributtion					
			Household final consumption expenditure 1	General government final consumption expenditure 2	Gross fixed capital formation 3	Changes in inventories 4	Exports of goods and services 5	Imports of goods and services 6
	1985	50 013	82.4	7.8	20.4	-0.2	11.7	21.2
	1990	111 021	89.1	7.2	16.6	0.4	10.6	22.3
	1995	235 293	81.1	7.7	22.3	1.0	24.5	36.6
	2000	407 394	81.0	7.4	19.5	3.0	23.5	34.3
	2005	589 412	79.5	8.9	19.9	6.5	14.6	29.5
	2010	1 192 770	78.6	10.0	22.2	16.1	9.6	36.4
	2015	2 130 150	79.9	10.9	28.0	11.1	11.6	41.5
	2016	2 253 163	84.4	11.5	28.7	5.2	9.5	39.3
	2017	2 674 493	75.4	11.2	31.4	15.4	9.0	42.4
	2018	3 044 927	71.7	11.6	34.5	19.4	8.9	46.2
	2019	3 458 793	69.5	11.6	33.7	22.9	8.7	46.3
Oman	1970	112	19.4	12.8	13.8	...	73.7	19.7
(Rial Omani)	1975	758	15.9	31.6	35.6	...	67.6	50.7
	1980	2 161	34.4	14.7	26.2	2.7	46.9	29.8
	1985	3 551	33.0	22.8	32.5	3.2	38.0	29.5
	1990	4 443	33.7	27.4	15.9	1.7	37.4	22.8
	1995	5 248	39.9	28.3	19.4	1.9	34.9	29.4
	2000	7 501	35.4	21.5	16.6	-0.1	53.7	25.9
	2005	11 951	30.6	20.8	22.0	-0.6	58.3	31.1
	2010	21 883	33.5	18.7	24.7	-1.9	67.5	42.6
	2015	26 300	38.6	28.4	28.1	1.5	47.4	44.0
	2016	25 177	41.4	30.0	33.0	-4.1	39.2	39.5
	2017	27 145	41.6	28.0	27.4	0.1	44.6	41.8
	2018	30 679	37.2	24.7	23.2	1.2	52.1	38.4
	2019	29 349	40.7	24.6	23.3	-2.7	54.3	40.0
Pakistan	1970	62 568	80.5	7.6	13.7	1.2	5.8	7.9
(Pakistan Rupee)	1975	145 682	85.8	8.0	13.9	1.5	8.9	15.7
	1980	306 843	87.0	7.5	16.0	0.6	9.6	17.7
	1985	618 665	85.5	9.0	15.7	1.5	8.1	17.2
	1990	1 121 537	74.8	11.3	16.5	1.3	11.3	15.4
	1995	2 444 906	75.9	8.8	16.2	1.2	12.8	14.7
	2000	4 123 718	78.0	8.3	13.7	1.3	12.5	13.6
	2005	7 005 354	79.6	7.6	15.1	1.6	14.6	18.2
	2010	14 866 996	79.7	10.3	14.2	1.6	13.5	19.4
	2015	27 443 022	79.8	11.0	14.1	1.6	10.6	17.1
	2016	29 075 633	80.0	11.3	14.1	1.6	9.1	16.2
	2017	31 922 303	81.9	11.3	14.6	1.6	8.3	17.6
	2018	34 618 576	82.5	11.7	15.1	1.6	8.8	19.7
	2019	38 558 769	82.1	12.6	13.8	1.6	9.7	19.9
Philippines [13]	1970	43 770	63.8	9.1	20.0	4.2	18.2	19.0
(Philippine Peso)	1975	119 607	60.2	10.6	27.3	7.7	17.7	24.5
	1980	270 063	61.1	8.9	30.2	2.8	19.9	25.8
	1985	633 620	70.8	7.5	18.2	-2.0	20.3	19.8
	1990	1 193 528	68.5	10.0	25.6	1.8	23.2	30.1
	1995	2 111 705	71.3	11.2	24.6	0.9	30.7	40.0
	2000	3 580 714	72.2	11.4	22.1	-3.7	51.4	53.4
	2005	5 677 750	75.0	9.0	19.9	1.6	46.1	51.7
	2010	9 003 480	71.6	9.7	20.5	0.0	34.8	36.6
	2015	13 322 041	73.8	10.9	22.0	-0.8	28.4	34.3
	2016	14 480 349	73.7	11.2	24.0	-0.2	28.1	37.4
	2017	15 807 596	73.5	11.2	25.0	0.1	31.0	40.9
	2018	17 426 202	73.8	11.9	26.8	0.2	31.7	44.4
	2019	18 613 044	74.6	12.7	26.3	-0.7	30.1	42.1
Qatar [14]	1970	2 566	21.4	20.5	22.7	0.5	64.4	29.5
(Qatari Rial)	1975	9 707	22.9	20.7	23.3	0.5	63.0	30.3
	1980	28 663	15.7	19.6	16.6	0.4	73.7	26.1
	1985	22 398	25.1	35.2	17.7	0.1	51.4	29.5
	1990	26 792	27.8	32.9	17.0	1.0	53.5	32.1
	1995	29 622	32.1	31.9	30.0	5.0	44.3	43.3
	2000	64 646	15.2	19.7	19.5	0.7	67.3	22.3

Table 2. Gross Domestic Product by Type of Expenditure: Individual Countries or Areas

Major area, region and country	Year	Gross Domestic Product (at current prices) Million	Percentage Distributtion					
			Household final consumption expenditure 1	General government final consumption expenditure 2	Gross fixed capital formation 3	Changes in inventories 4	Exports of goods and services 5	Imports of goods and services 6
	2005	162 091	16.0	14.3	32.0	2.3	65.1	29.7
	2010	455 445	16.2	14.0	31.3	...	62.3	23.8
	2015	588 733	22.3	20.2	37.1	...	57.1	36.6
	2016	552 305	25.7	19.5	48.9	...	47.7	41.8
	2017	607 620	24.6	17.0	44.6	...	51.0	37.3
	2018	696 558	22.1	15.9	42.9	...	53.6	34.4
	2019	667 817	23.5	18.4	44.4	...	50.2	36.4
Republic of Korea [15] (Won)	1970	2 796 600	73.7	9.9	25.8	0.5	11.4	21.1
	1975	10 543 600	69.1	11.1	27.2	1.3	22.7	31.3
	1980	39 725 100	62.7	11.9	32.9	1.2	28.4	37.1
	1985	88 129 700	55.9	10.6	29.5	2.8	26.9	25.8
	1990	200 556 200	50.2	11.0	37.3	2.2	25.0	25.8
	1995	436 988 800	52.0	10.0	37.1	1.8	25.7	26.7
	2000	651 634 400	54.5	10.9	31.8	1.1	33.9	32.2
	2005	957 447 800	52.3	12.9	30.5	2.0	35.3	33.0
	2010	1 322 611 200	50.4	14.2	30.2	2.3	47.1	44.3
	2015	1 658 020 400	48.5	15.1	29.0	0.5	43.0	36.1
	2016	1 740 779 600	48.0	15.2	29.7	0.4	40.1	33.5
	2017	1 835 698 200	47.5	15.4	31.5	0.8	40.9	36.2
	2018	1 898 192 600	48.0	16.1	30.4	1.1	41.7	37.3
	2019	1 919 039 900	48.5	17.2	30.0	1.4	39.9	37.0
Saudi Arabia (Saudi Riyal)	1970	24 198	32.5	15.9	12.7	9.7	50.8	21.6
	1975	164 530	16.5	14.5	17.4	0.0	73.3	21.7
	1980	547 381	25.0	15.9	20.7	2.2	63.5	27.3
	1985	376 318	53.2	31.9	22.3	-0.8	30.1	36.6
	1990	440 525	46.3	29.0	18.9	-3.2	40.3	31.4
	1995	536 820	46.6	23.5	19.2	1.0	37.3	27.7
	2000	710 681	36.2	25.9	17.4	2.0	43.4	24.8
	2005	1 230 771	26.3	21.3	19.3	0.9	57.1	24.9
	2010	1 980 777	32.3	20.2	24.4	6.5	49.6	33.0
	2015	2 453 512	40.3	30.0	29.9	5.3	33.3	38.8
	2016	2 418 508	42.8	25.8	26.1	4.8	31.1	30.7
	2017	2 582 198	41.2	24.4	24.5	4.4	34.9	29.3
	2018	2 949 457	37.9	24.6	21.0	3.3	39.9	26.7
	2019	2 973 626	38.9	23.8	22.1	5.7	35.5	26.1
Singapore (Singapore Dollar)	1970	5 879	67.1	11.8	32.1	6.1	126.0	145.0
	1975	13 729	60.1	10.5	34.9	3.9	137.1	146.4
	1980	25 870	50.5	9.6	39.5	5.5	202.0	208.9
	1985	40 863	44.8	13.4	40.8	0.3	152.2	151.9
	1990	70 492	44.6	9.5	31.7	3.9	177.2	167.1
	1995	124 463	40.9	8.3	33.2	0.7	181.1	164.3
	2000	165 632	41.9	10.5	32.3	2.8	188.4	176.0
	2005	212 723	39.8	9.9	23.2	-1.7	225.2	195.3
	2010	326 980	36.3	9.7	25.6	2.1	198.0	171.7
	2015	423 444	37.2	10.2	27.2	-1.9	178.4	151.1
	2016	440 218	36.5	10.3	26.3	0.4	165.1	138.9
	2017	472 079	35.3	10.2	25.4	1.9	170.7	145.3
	2018	503 395	34.8	10.1	23.1	2.4	177.7	149.3
	2019	507 568	36.0	10.3	23.1	1.7	173.5	145.6
Sri Lanka (Sri Lanka Rupee)	1970	16 757	75.9	6.2	15.1	6.4	20.8	23.3
	1975	31 601	85.8	5.3	11.9	6.0	23.1	29.4
	1980	80 863	82.7	5.1	29.2	7.1	26.5	45.1
	1985	186 679	79.2	6.4	21.4	5.2	22.7	33.4
	1990	376 173	79.1	6.9	18.3	4.7	25.8	32.6
	1995	783 793	74.8	7.7	22.8	5.5	30.3	38.5
	2000	1 473 246	74.5	7.5	22.7	5.8	33.4	42.3
	2005	2 807 109	72.5	7.1	21.4	7.7	28.3	36.1
	2010	6 413 668	68.5	8.5	24.5	5.9	19.6	26.8
	2015	10 950 621	67.4	9.0	26.0	5.1	21.0	28.5
	2016	11 996 083	71.0	8.5	27.5	0.4	21.2	28.5

Table 2. Gross Domestic Product by Type of Expenditure: Individual Countries or Areas

Major area, region and country	Year	Gross Domestic Product (at current prices) Million	Percentage Distributtion: Household final consumption expenditure 1	General government final consumption expenditure 2	Gross fixed capital formation 3	Changes in inventories 4	Exports of goods and services 5	Imports of goods and services 6
	2017	13 328 103	67.1	8.5	27.4	4.2	21.8	29.1
	2018	14 366 103	67.8	9.1	26.3	4.1	22.9	30.3
	2019	15 016 142	69.3	9.4	27.4	-0.1	23.1	29.2
State of Palestine....................................	1970	177	103.9	37.0	15.2	0.8	10.4	58.2
(US Dollar)	1975	579	107.7	26.5	31.8	1.7	16.5	82.3
	1980	1 074	88.9	19.4	43.9	2.3	15.5	67.6
	1985	1 005	97.5	20.5	38.1	2.0	14.5	70.5
	1990	1 936	98.4	21.3	38.5	2.0	14.5	71.7
	1995	3 283	100.1	18.4	36.0	2.0	17.1	74.4
	2000	4 314	89.6	25.5	30.6	0.9	20.5	67.1
	2005	5 126	102.9	27.0	23.9	0.4	14.1	69.7
	2010	9 682	93.2	25.8	18.8	1.0	14.1	54.4
	2015	13 972	88.4	25.0	23.7	1.4	16.1	54.7
	2016	15 405	87.9	23.5	24.0	1.3	14.3	51.1
	2017	16 128	88.7	20.8	26.0	1.6	15.7	52.7
	2018	16 277	88.9	22.0	26.8	1.5	16.0	55.4
	2019	17 059	90.5	20.2	25.5	1.5	15.5	53.7
Syrian Arab Republic..............................	1970	6 848	72.5	17.3	13.1	0.6	17.4	20.9
(Syrian Pound)	1975	20 711	63.0	20.9	24.9	3.7	21.3	33.8
	1980	51 270	66.0	23.2	28.0	...	18.2	35.4
	1985	83 225	65.7	23.8	24.1	...	12.0	25.4
	1990	268 328	68.7	14.3	16.5	...	28.3	28.0
	1995	570 975	66.2	13.4	27.2	...	31.0	37.9
	2000	904 623	63.4	12.4	17.3	...	36.1	29.2
	2005	1 506 437	65.9	13.7	23.0	-4.6	41.0	39.1
	2010	2 791 775	60.6	12.4	20.8	5.9	32.7	32.3
	2015	4 524 911	59.8	12.1	19.2	9.4	32.1	32.5
	2016	5 696 999	59.7	12.1	19.2	9.3	32.3	32.6
	2017	6 572 147	59.7	12.1	19.1	9.5	32.3	32.6
	2018	7 100 793	59.7	12.1	19.1	9.4	32.3	32.6
	2019	9 121 460	59.7	12.1	19.1	9.4	32.3	32.6
Tajikistan..	1990	72 (t)	75.8	9.3	5.4	4.6	62.3	64.1
(Somoni)	1995	69	72.0	14.8	16.9	6.4	121.6	162.1
	2000	1 787	87.7	11.6	7.4	2.0	92.4	100.2
	2005	7 207	81.1	14.6	11.1	0.5	54.3	72.8
	2010	24 707	84.7	11.3	24.5	-0.6	26.8	59.0
	2015	48 409	82.5	15.0	28.2	0.6	10.3	42.3
	2016	54 479	78.8	14.1	30.7	0.4	13.3	42.8
	2017	64 434	77.9	14.3	26.6	0.6	15.7	40.9
	2018	71 059	90.4	16.4	21.2	...	14.8	42.8
	2019	79 418	76.0	10.9	28.3	...	14.9	40.9
Thailand..	1970	153 658	64.6	11.9	26.2	2.1	14.5	18.7
(Baht)	1975	316 229	64.3	10.9	25.3	4.3	17.7	22.2
	1980	686 536	61.5	13.1	27.8	1.5	23.3	29.5
	1985	1 094 856	58.4	14.4	27.2	1.2	22.5	25.2
	1990	2 263 299	53.1	10.0	40.4	1.1	33.0	40.5
	1995	4 217 614	51.3	11.3	41.3	1.5	41.5	48.2
	2000	5 069 820	54.1	13.6	21.6	0.7	64.8	56.5
	2005	7 614 413	55.8	13.7	27.7	2.7	68.4	69.5
	2010	10 808 142	52.2	15.8	24.0	1.4	66.5	60.8
	2015	13 743 463	51.0	17.1	24.5	-2.2	68.7	57.2
	2016	14 554 569	49.8	16.9	23.8	-2.8	68.4	53.6
	2017	15 451 959	48.7	16.4	23.2	-0.3	68.2	54.3
	2018	16 316 417	48.7	16.2	22.8	2.2	66.8	56.5
	2019	16 828 330	49.4	16.6	22.7	1.1	61.5	51.0
Timor-Leste...	1990	203	73.1	111.3	31.7	-3.7	27.2	139.5
(US Dollar)	1995	416	77.0	117.2	33.4	-3.9	20.8	146.9
	2000	367	87.5	133.3	38.0	-4.5	10.6	164.9
	2005	462	92.0	52.6	15.7	0.1	7.1	67.5

Table 2. Gross Domestic Product by Type of Expenditure: Individual Countries or Areas

Major area, region and country	Year	Gross Domestic Product (at current prices) Million	Percentage Distributtion: Household final consumption expenditure 1	General government final consumption expenditure 2	Gross fixed capital formation 3	Changes in inventories 4	Exports of goods and services 5	Imports of goods and services 6
	2010	882	71.4	103.2	42.7	0.0	8.6	125.8
	2015	1 594	58.2	58.8	35.5	1.3	3.0	56.9
	2016	1 651	58.8	55.3	38.0	1.6	3.1	56.8
	2017	1 599	63.2	54.6	32.7	1.6	2.4	54.5
	2018	1 560	66.8	56.4	32.8	1.5	2.9	60.5
	2019	2 018	54.3	47.4	23.1	2.5	28.2	55.5
Turkey...	1970	284 (t)	68.0	7.7	17.6	-0.4	3.9	4.2
(New Turkish Lira)	1975	928 (t)	67.7	9.6	18.9	-1.2	4.3	8.0
	1980	7 206 (t)	75.5	7.0	15.2	-0.5	4.6	8.3
	1985	48	66.4	7.5	20.8	0.0	13.9	13.1
	1990	541	64.1	9.2	21.8	-0.6	11.3	12.4
	1995	10 694	65.7	9.0	22.7	-0.6	16.9	17.2
	2000	171 494	66.9	11.9	22.2	1.5	19.9	22.5
	2005	680 276	63.4	12.2	26.4	0.4	21.9	24.3
	2010	1 167 664	62.7	14.9	24.6	2.1	21.2	25.5
	2015	2 350 941	60.0	13.8	29.6	-1.4	24.5	26.6
	2016	2 626 560	59.4	14.7	29.1	-1.1	23.1	25.2
	2017	3 133 704	58.6	14.4	29.9	0.8	26.0	29.7
	2018	3 758 316	56.2	14.7	29.7	-0.4	31.2	31.3
	2019	4 320 191	56.9	15.5	25.9	-1.1	32.7	29.9
Turkmenistan...	1990	3 040 (u)	49.1	8.8	30.2	9.4	111.2	107.5
(Turkmenistan Manat)	1995	130	60.6	8.4	23.3	10.3	142.5	145.0
	2000	5 130	37.1	14.5	35.4	...	97.2	82.4
	2005	17 861	46.6	13.2	22.9	...	65.0	47.8
	2010	64 362	5.0	9.3	51.9	...	76.3	44.5
	2015	125 299	11.7	9.0	49.1	...	74.1	44.2
	2016	126 593	10.6	9.0	49.8	...	74.4	44.1
	2017	132 703	11.0	9.0	49.6	...	74.2	44.1
	2018	142 622	11.1	9.0	49.5	...	74.2	44.1
	2019	168 968	10.9	9.0	49.6	...	74.3	44.1
United Arab Emirates.............................	1970	5 082	14.1	6.1	25.9	2.9	55.9	20.2
(UAE Dirham)	1975	59 075	17.7	4.9	35.0	0.4	49.9	18.8
	1980	163 750	19.5	6.5	31.5	1.4	52.2	22.1
	1985	151 004	31.6	11.6	27.7	0.9	38.1	19.7
	1990	188 557	42.7	9.6	21.9	1.4	43.0	25.7
	1995	244 499	52.3	9.4	24.8	1.7	45.9	37.0
	2000	388 187	49.3	9.2	20.1	1.4	51.0	34.1
	2005	671 986	49.0	7.8	18.2	1.8	66.7	45.7
	2010	1 064 244	42.2	10.0	24.8	2.4	82.2	61.6
	2015	1 315 251	35.4	12.4	23.4	2.3	100.9	74.4
	2016	1 311 248	36.2	12.5	24.5	1.6	101.0	75.7
	2017	1 416 136	37.3	13.2	19.0	6.3	99.6	75.4
	2018	1 550 585	38.3	11.8	17.3	6.2	93.0	66.7
	2019	1 546 645	38.9	13.3	17.6	6.2	92.5	68.5
Uzbekistan...	1990	39	71.4	21.4	29.3	4.3	24.0	38.1
(Uzbekistan Sum)	1995	363 544	58.8	18.7	31.6	-6.3	26.3	22.8
	2000	3 908 859	72.0	15.7	23.0	-2.5	22.1	21.3
	2005	18 897 787	54.3	14.8	19.4	7.1	31.9	23.1
	2010	74 042 027	57.0	13.3	24.1	2.4	27.9	19.7
	2015	210 183 102	61.4	14.3	23.3	2.8	15.3	15.1
	2016	242 495 523	63.0	14.9	22.8	3.5	14.9	14.9
	2017	302 536 816	59.9	13.2	25.6	3.9	21.8	23.9
	2018	406 648 543	55.9	14.1	32.9	4.7	28.0	38.6
	2019	511 838 093	54.4	16.4	40.0	-0.2	31.2	41.8
Viet Nam..	1970	2 775	90.0	6.7	12.5	2.0	25.9	36.5
(Dong)	1975	3 896	90.0	6.7	12.5	2.0	25.9	36.5
	1980	7 899	90.0	6.7	12.5	2.0	25.9	36.5
	1985	138 909	90.2	6.5	12.4	2.0	26.1	36.8
	1990	41 955 000	89.6	7.5	13.1	1.3	26.4	35.7

Table 2. Gross Domestic Product by Type of Expenditure: Individual Countries or Areas

Major area, region and country	Year	Gross Domestic Product (at current prices) Million	Percentage Distributtion					
			Household final consumption expenditure 1	General government final consumption expenditure 2	Gross fixed capital formation 3	Changes in inventories 4	Exports of goods and services 5	Imports of goods and services 6
	1995	228 892 000	73.6	8.2	25.4	1.7	32.8	41.9
	2000	441 646 000	66.5	6.4	27.6	2.0	55.0	57.5
	2005	914 001 000	65.5	5.5	31.3	2.5	63.7	67.0
	2010	2 157 828 000	66.6	6.0	32.6	3.0	72.0	80.2
	2015	4 192 862 309	68.0	6.3	24.7	3.0	89.8	89.0
	2016	4 502 732 989	68.5	6.5	23.7	2.9	93.6	91.1
	2017	5 005 975 000	68.0	6.5	23.8	2.8	101.6	98.8
	2018	5 542 331 870	67.6	6.5	23.9	2.7	105.8	102.5
	2019	6 037 347 631	68.2	6.5	26.8	...	106.8	103.6
Yemen	1990	148 155	79.1	16.1	11.1	-0.5	12.2	17.1
(Yemeni Rial)	1995	588 100	91.2	13.6	18.4	-3.2	19.0	36.7
	2000	1 756 999	60.3	13.0	15.7	4.6	36.7	30.3
	2005	3 646 557	57.4	11.4	18.3	8.5	36.0	31.5
	2010	6 786 814	72.2	13.1	19.8	-0.7	30.0	34.4
	2015	5 729 031	90.8	18.2	16.7	-4.2	7.0	28.6
	2016	5 316 938	101.3	14.1	15.4	2.2	4.2	37.2
	2017	5 190 032	100.9	12.2	15.5	-0.2	9.0	37.4
	2018	5 731 456	99.6	11.9	15.0	1.1	9.3	36.9
	2019	6 240 082	105.0	13.3	16.7	1.3	11.5	46.3
Europe								
Albania	1970	11 328	57.9	9.1	33.9	2.6	22.4	22.3
(Lek)	1975	13 051	58.0	9.1	33.8	2.5	22.5	22.3
	1980	14 993	58.4	9.3	34.2	0.7	23.1	22.1
	1985	16 271	60.7	9.6	34.4	0.5	16.2	17.9
	1990	16 228	75.3	10.6	35.8	-10.5	14.9	22.5
	1995	221 803	90.4	13.6	21.0	...	12.5	34.5
	2000	501 199	82.7	9.7	31.9	...	20.1	43.3
	2005	804 163	76.9	11.0	37.9	...	23.0	47.9
	2010	1 239 645	78.1	11.2	28.4	1.9	28.0	48.6
	2015	1 434 307	80.7	11.1	24.4	1.4	27.3	44.5
	2016	1 472 479	81.0	11.3	24.4	0.9	29.0	45.8
	2017	1 550 645	79.6	11.5	24.6	0.5	31.6	46.6
	2018	1 635 715	78.9	11.3	23.9	0.2	31.6	45.3
	2019	1 678 309	80.3	11.5	22.3	...	31.5	45.2
Andorra	1970	42	63.8	9.9	26.9	1.5	12.1	13.7
(Euro)	1975	96	64.1	10.9	27.3	2.8	12.4	16.7
	1980	243	65.4	13.6	22.8	1.6	14.3	17.3
	1985	448	63.1	15.2	20.5	0.3	20.9	20.0
	1990	798	61.3	16.2	25.8	1.1	15.7	19.9
	1995	1 118	61.0	17.6	21.9	0.6	21.8	22.9
	2000	1 551	59.6	16.7	25.9	0.7	28.6	31.5
	2005	2 541	58.1	17.3	29.0	0.4	25.0	29.8
	2010	2 602	58.1	20.6	21.8	0.5	26.0	27.0
	2015	2 515	58.5	19.5	18.0	1.0	33.6	30.6
	2016	2 617	58.2	19.1	18.0	0.8	33.9	29.9
	2017	2 656	58.4	18.6	18.7	0.7	35.1	31.5
	2018	2 725	58.2	18.7	19.5	1.0	35.1	32.4
	2019	2 818	57.3	18.9	19.9	0.9	34.9	31.9
Austria	1970	29 047	55.1	14.3	27.2	3.8	27.4	27.5
(Euro)	1975	50 703	56.7	16.8	28.1	-0.9	28.1	28.5
	1980	77 152	56.5	17.5	27.4	1.4	31.7	35.1
	1985	104 330	57.7	18.6	23.9	0.6	34.9	35.2
	1990	137 549	55.9	18.0	25.6	1.1	35.7	35.8
	1995	176 609	54.9	19.6	25.6	1.1	33.5	34.7
	2000	213 606	53.9	19.2	25.7	0.2	43.3	42.0
	2005	254 075	53.8	19.3	23.1	0.7	48.6	45.4
	2010	295 897	53.5	20.5	22.1	0.5	51.3	47.8
	2015	344 269	52.7	19.8	23.3	0.5	53.1	49.3
	2016	357 608	52.3	19.7	23.5	0.7	52.4	48.6

Table 2. Gross Domestic Product by Type of Expenditure: Individual Countries or Areas

Major area, region and country	Year	Gross Domestic Product (at current prices) Million	Percentage Distributtion: Household final consumption expenditure 1	General government final consumption expenditure 2	Gross fixed capital formation 3	Changes in inventories 4	Exports of goods and services 5	Imports of goods and services 6
	2017	369 341	52.5	19.5	24.1	0.7	54.1	50.9
	2018	385 362	51.9	19.3	24.4	1.1	55.7	52.4
	2019	397 575	51.7	19.4	25.0	0.5	55.6	52.2
Belarus	1990	448 (u)	48.0	22.8	21.7	4.5	44.4	42.2
(Belarussian Ruble)	1995	13	60.0	19.8	24.4	0.0	48.0	52.3
	2000	944	57.8	18.7	24.9	0.2	62.6	66.0
	2005	6 727	52.9	20.0	26.2	1.9	57.8	57.2
	2010	17 047	55.6	16.0	38.8	1.8	51.4	64.5
	2015	89 910	52.9	14.9	28.7	0.4	58.0	57.9
	2016	94 949	54.5	15.7	25.4	1.0	62.5	62.7
	2017	105 748	54.5	15.7	26.2	1.9	66.8	66.6
	2018	122 320	53.6	15.7	26.2	1.9	70.5	68.9
	2019	131 952	55.1	15.9	27.0	2.0	66.4	66.9
Belgium	1970	33 102	51.2	16.8	26.9	2.7	45.0	42.8
(Euro)	1975	59 879	52.6	21.1	26.6	0.0	45.9	45.6
	1980	91 939	54.7	22.9	24.8	1.7	50.1	52.9
	1985	126 978	57.3	22.8	18.8	0.1	62.5	61.4
	1990	170 097	54.2	20.2	24.0	0.4	61.6	59.9
	1995	210 489	53.1	21.3	21.2	0.5	60.1	56.3
	2000	256 376	52.3	21.0	22.5	1.3	72.5	69.7
	2005	310 038	50.2	22.1	22.2	1.5	74.3	70.2
	2010	363 140	51.4	23.7	22.2	1.0	75.9	74.1
	2015	416 701	51.3	23.6	23.0	0.7	77.8	76.4
	2016	430 085	51.3	23.3	23.2	1.0	79.4	78.2
	2017	444 991	51.5	23.0	23.2	1.3	83.2	82.2
	2018	460 419	51.7	23.0	23.8	1.7	83.0	83.3
	2019	476 203	51.4	23.0	24.2	0.8	81.8	81.2
Bosnia and Herzegovina	1990	892 (t)	101.2	21.4	23.2	7.5	22.7	76.0
(Convertible Marks)	1995	2 932	108.3	22.8	12.3	7.7	20.4	71.5
	2000	12 086	98.2	20.8	27.5	...	28.5	75.1
	2005	17 650	94.5	21.6	27.1	0.1	31.6	71.6
	2010	25 365	84.7	23.1	17.4	-1.1	29.7	51.3
	2015	28 589	81.6	22.0	18.2	0.8	35.5	53.8
	2016	29 904	79.6	21.0	17.8	2.3	36.3	52.9
	2017	31 376	77.9	20.3	18.9	3.0	40.8	57.0
	2018	33 444	76.1	19.8	19.6	2.0	42.1	57.1
	2019	35 229	75.5	19.5	19.5	2.1	40.1	55.2
Bulgaria	1970	11	61.6	5.9	27.0	6.3	37.2	38.0
(Bulgarian Lev)	1975	14	61.6	5.9	27.1	6.3	37.2	38.2
	1980	26	62.2	5.6	28.3	5.7	37.4	39.3
	1985	33	61.5	8.5	26.4	5.8	44.9	47.0
	1990	45	66.8	7.2	21.3	9.1	34.7	39.1
	1995	1 276	57.5	15.3	16.7	1.1	32.3	22.9
	2000	28 125	66.5	19.8	16.7	2.3	36.2	41.5
	2005	47 017	68.8	18.2	25.7	2.1	42.5	57.2
	2010	74 407	63.6	16.6	22.3	0.3	50.4	53.3
	2015	89 333	61.9	16.1	20.9	0.1	64.0	63.0
	2016	95 092	60.4	15.6	18.5	0.5	64.1	59.1
	2017	102 308	60.1	15.6	18.4	1.5	67.3	63.0
	2018	109 695	59.7	16.5	18.8	2.5	65.9	63.3
	2019	118 669	59.5	17.5	18.3	1.2	63.6	60.1
Croatia	1990	334	63.7	20.8	12.4	0.5	45.2	45.4
(Croatian Kuna)	1995	117 261	66.4	24.9	14.4	2.5	27.6	35.8
	2000	179 371	62.7	21.4	20.0	0.4	35.2	39.8
	2005	270 015	63.3	18.5	25.4	1.6	36.7	45.5
	2010	328 824	60.1	20.5	21.2	-0.1	36.2	37.9
	2015	339 696	59.1	20.1	19.5	1.1	46.4	46.2
	2016	351 169	58.3	19.6	20.1	1.0	47.6	46.5
	2017	366 426	58.1	19.5	20.0	1.8	50.0	49.4

Table 2. Gross Domestic Product by Type of Expenditure: Individual Countries or Areas

Major area, region and country	Year	Gross Domestic Product (at current prices) Million	Percentage Distributtion: Household final consumption expenditure 1	General government final consumption expenditure 2	Gross fixed capital formation 3	Changes in inventories 4	Exports of goods and services 5	Imports of goods and services 6
	2018	382 965	58.2	19.4	20.0	3.2	50.5	51.3
	2019	400 102	58.1	19.6	20.7	2.1	51.1	51.7
Czechia	1990	731 207	49.3	21.9	25.0	-0.4	32.9	30.6
(Czech Koruna)	1995	1 596 306	48.7	20.2	33.9	0.2	40.2	43.3
	2000	2 386 289	50.4	19.5	31.3	0.6	48.1	50.0
	2005	3 285 601	47.8	20.3	28.9	0.7	61.8	59.5
	2010	3 992 870	49.0	20.5	27.2	0.1	65.5	62.5
	2015	4 625 378	47.2	18.9	26.7	1.3	80.6	74.6
	2016	4 796 873	47.4	19.0	25.1	0.9	79.1	71.5
	2017	5 110 743	47.3	18.8	25.0	1.3	79.0	71.5
	2018	5 408 766	47.5	19.4	26.5	0.7	77.0	71.0
	2019	5 748 668	47.3	19.7	26.4	0.6	74.4	68.4
Denmark	1970	128 066	55.1	21.0	25.4	1.3	27.2	30.0
(Danish Krone)	1975	232 574	53.9	24.6	22.5	0.0	29.4	30.3
	1980	400 868	54.1	26.3	20.6	-0.5	32.5	33.0
	1985	663 955	52.5	24.6	20.8	1.3	36.4	35.7
	1990	855 557	40.7	20.9	20.6	0.2	36.4	30.9
	1995	1 036 483	50.6	24.1	19.6	1.1	36.7	32.0
	2000	1 326 912	47.1	23.9	21.6	0.7	44.8	38.1
	2005	1 585 984	47.8	24.5	21.3	0.9	47.5	41.9
	2010	1 810 926	47.6	27.4	18.3	-0.2	50.5	43.6
	2015	2 036 356	47.1	25.5	20.0	0.6	55.4	48.6
	2016	2 107 808	46.7	24.9	21.2	0.6	53.4	46.7
	2017	2 192 960	46.4	24.4	21.4	0.7	55.1	47.9
	2018	2 253 558	46.7	24.3	22.2	1.0	56.3	50.4
	2019	2 335 002	46.1	23.8	22.1	0.6	58.3	51.0
Estonia	1990	51	64.4	13.2	23.8	6.5	42.0	49.9
(Euro)	1995	2 858	55.9	24.6	26.5	-0.1	66.0	73.3
	2000	6 180	54.2	19.8	26.7	1.7	61.5	64.8
	2005	11 336	54.2	17.0	32.9	0.5	65.5	70.5
	2010	14 861	52.1	20.1	21.1	0.4	74.4	68.1
	2015	20 782	51.3	20.0	24.3	0.5	76.9	73.0
	2016	21 931	51.4	20.2	24.2	0.7	76.4	72.8
	2017	23 858	50.3	19.8	24.9	1.8	75.6	71.7
	2018	25 938	50.2	19.7	24.6	2.2	74.1	71.5
	2019	28 112	49.0	19.9	26.2	1.5	72.9	68.9
Finland	1970	7 983	54.6	14.3	27.5	3.9	24.0	25.7
(Euro)	1975	18 145	53.1	16.9	33.0	2.7	22.2	28.3
	1980	33 657	51.9	17.7	27.3	3.9	30.8	32.1
	1985	58 245	52.1	19.7	26.7	0.3	28.0	27.3
	1990	90 959	50.1	20.9	29.7	0.5	22.1	23.7
	1995	98 549	51.0	21.9	19.3	1.0	35.8	28.3
	2000	136 442	47.8	19.7	23.1	0.8	42.0	32.9
	2005	164 687	49.6	21.4	23.0	1.6	40.3	36.3
	2010	188 143	52.6	23.7	22.3	-0.2	38.4	37.1
	2015	211 385	54.5	24.4	21.3	0.5	35.4	36.0
	2016	217 518	54.3	23.7	22.8	0.5	34.8	36.1
	2017	225 933	53.2	22.8	23.4	0.6	37.6	37.6
	2018	233 664	50.0	22.9	24.2	1.2	38.5	39.6
	2019	240 556	52.4	23.0	23.9	0.3	40.2	39.9
France [16]	1970	125 698	54.3	17.0	25.7	2.5	16.0	15.4
(Euro)	1975	235 876	54.6	19.6	25.4	-0.5	18.8	17.9
	1980	451 770	54.7	21.0	24.4	1.3	21.0	22.5
	1985	757 689	56.6	22.6	21.2	0.0	23.3	23.7
	1990	1 053 546	55.2	21.2	23.4	1.0	21.0	21.8
	1995	1 218 273	54.7	23.2	20.1	0.4	22.6	21.0
	2000	1 478 585	53.9	22.3	21.5	1.0	28.6	27.3
	2005	1 765 905	54.4	23.1	21.8	0.7	27.0	26.9
	2010	1 995 289	55.4	24.0	22.1	-0.2	26.8	28.1

Table 2. Gross Domestic Product by Type of Expenditure: Individual Countries or Areas

Major area, region and country	Year	Gross Domestic Product (at current prices) Million	Percentage Distributtion: Household final consumption expenditure 1	General government final consumption expenditure 2	Gross fixed capital formation 3	Changes in inventories 4	Exports of goods and services 5	Imports of goods and services 6
	2015	2 198 432	54.0	23.8	21.5	1.2	30.6	31.2
	2016	2 234 129	54.3	23.7	21.8	0.8	30.2	30.9
	2017	2 297 242	54.0	23.6	22.5	0.9	30.9	32.0
	2018	2 360 687	53.9	23.3	22.9	1.0	31.7	32.8
	2019	2 425 708	53.7	23.1	23.6	0.5	31.8	32.8
Germany (Euro)	1970	403 898	55.6	16.3	29.7	3.0	15.1	16.6
	1975	617 172	58.2	20.9	24.2	0.3	17.1	18.8
	1980	883 200	58.9	20.9	26.6	0.6	18.6	23.2
	1985	1 102 612	58.6	20.6	23.1	0.0	22.9	25.0
	1990	1 463 578	56.3	19.1	24.9	-0.1	22.8	23.0
	1995	1 894 610	55.8	19.4	23.7	0.6	22.0	21.6
	2000	2 109 090	56.3	19.0	23.2	1.3	30.8	30.7
	2005	2 288 310	56.5	18.8	19.2	0.3	38.1	32.9
	2010	2 564 400	55.1	19.6	19.7	0.4	42.6	37.3
	2015	3 026 180	53.0	19.7	20.2	-0.5	46.9	39.3
	2016	3 134 740	52.8	19.9	20.4	-0.4	46.1	38.7
	2017	3 259 860	52.3	19.9	20.6	0.2	47.2	40.2
	2018	3 356 410	52.3	20.0	21.3	0.3	47.4	41.2
	2019	3 449 050	52.4	20.4	21.8	-0.4	46.9	41.1
Greece (Euro)	1970	1 156	61.0	12.6	27.6	8.8	7.9	15.2
	1975	2 684	58.2	14.9	25.6	10.8	14.1	21.2
	1980	7 109	60.5	15.6	30.7	0.0	19.3	25.3
	1985	19 382	59.6	19.3	23.6	7.8	16.1	24.3
	1990	45 539	66.7	17.5	24.8	2.8	14.8	25.3
	1995	93 064	68.0	17.8	20.0	2.4	14.4	22.7
	2000	141 247	66.9	18.3	24.7	1.1	23.7	34.7
	2005	199 242	66.2	20.0	20.9	1.2	21.3	29.6
	2010	224 124	67.3	22.4	16.7	1.3	21.8	29.4
	2015	176 110	68.5	20.4	10.8	1.3	32.2	33.2
	2016	174 237	68.2	20.4	11.0	1.8	31.3	32.8
	2017	177 152	68.7	20.4	11.7	0.7	35.0	36.5
	2018	179 727	69.2	19.6	10.8	2.5	39.0	41.1
	2019	183 413	69.3	19.7	10.1	2.6	40.1	41.7
Hungary (Forint)	1970	383 334	48.3	18.6	36.9	-3.3	23.6	24.2
	1975	555 008	48.9	18.8	40.9	-3.1	32.3	36.3
	1980	829 025	49.8	19.7	35.3	-4.6	30.4	30.6
	1985	1 188 476	50.5	20.5	27.5	-2.5	32.8	29.7
	1990	2 350 797	48.7	21.3	22.8	2.7	24.8	21.6
	1995	5 836 483	54.0	22.9	21.9	1.3	39.2	39.2
	2000	13 324 052	54.4	21.2	25.6	2.5	66.9	70.5
	2005	22 549 020	54.8	22.2	24.0	1.3	62.6	65.0
	2010	27 431 270	52.8	21.4	20.2	0.3	81.3	76.0
	2015	34 937 313	49.1	19.7	22.3	0.9	87.6	79.6
	2016	36 167 453	50.2	20.0	19.7	1.5	86.5	77.8
	2017	39 233 430	50.2	20.2	22.4	0.5	86.0	79.2
	2018	43 347 041	49.3	19.6	24.9	1.7	83.9	79.5
	2019	47 513 912	49.1	19.6	27.4	0.8	82.2	79.1
Iceland (Iceland Krona)	1970	464	60.1	13.2	28.6	-0.9	44.2	42.7
	1975	2 166	56.8	16.7	37.6	1.8	32.7	41.1
	1980	16 247	56.4	17.0	29.7	0.4	34.9	35.0
	1985	124 047	61.9	17.7	24.1	-1.0	39.6	39.5
	1990	377 589	59.0	19.2	21.7	-0.6	33.1	31.9
	1995	461 533	57.2	21.2	17.5	0.7	34.9	31.5
	2000	707 830	59.4	22.5	24.6	0.4	32.2	39.1
	2005	1 058 882	58.5	23.8	29.7	-0.2	30.4	42.2
	2010	1 672 719	51.5	24.7	14.1	-0.2	52.0	42.1
	2015	2 293 948	50.0	23.3	19.4	0.2	51.8	44.7
	2016	2 490 936	49.6	22.9	21.1	0.1	47.6	41.4
	2017	2 616 306	50.4	23.5	22.0	0.0	46.1	42.0
	2018	2 787 386	51.0	24.0	21.6	0.4	47.5	44.5

Table 2. Gross Domestic Product by Type of Expenditure: Individual Countries or Areas

Major area, region and country	Year	Gross Domestic Product (at current prices) Million	Percentage Distributtion					
			Household final consumption expenditure 1	General government final consumption expenditure 2	Gross fixed capital formation 3	Changes in inventories 4	Exports of goods and services 5	Imports of goods and services 6
	2019	2 965 617	50.8	24.3	20.2	-0.1	45.3	40.6
Ireland (Euro)	1970	2 326	70.1	16.3	22.5	1.5	33.1	41.3
	1975	5 445	65.3	20.7	22.5	0.4	38.2	44.8
	1980	13 440	67.0	22.2	28.3	-1.0	44.4	57.9
	1985	25 543	60.7	20.7	18.8	0.8	54.0	53.7
	1990	37 858	57.5	17.2	19.2	2.3	54.7	50.3
	1995	54 767	52.4	17.3	18.1	0.8	73.5	62.6
	2000	108 400	46.9	14.7	23.8	0.8	94.5	80.6
	2005	170 231	43.6	16.0	29.8	0.5	79.6	68.7
	2010	167 674	47.3	18.8	17.6	-0.3	103.1	86.4
	2015	262 853	32.9	12.5	24.1	1.7	122.0	93.2
	2016	270 809	33.6	12.7	35.8	1.8	121.2	105.6
	2017	300 387	31.3	12.2	33.1	1.4	119.7	97.9
	2018	326 986	30.2	12.0	28.4	0.4	122.3	93.9
	2019	356 051	29.3	11.9	45.6	0.4	126.1	113.8
Italy (Euro)	1970	36 604	59.0	15.0	25.3	0.7	15.2	14.9
	1975	76 779	60.4	16.0	20.1	-2.3	18.7	18.7
	1980	211 091	59.6	16.5	25.7	1.0	20.2	22.8
	1985	445 932	59.2	18.3	22.4	0.7	21.1	21.5
	1990	727 932	57.9	19.7	22.2	0.2	18.4	18.3
	1995	988 243	58.9	17.4	19.4	0.6	24.7	21.0
	2000	1 241 513	60.5	17.7	20.8	0.0	25.6	24.8
	2005	1 493 635	59.3	19.6	21.4	-0.2	24.6	24.7
	2010	1 611 279	60.7	20.6	20.1	0.5	25.1	26.9
	2015	1 655 355	60.8	19.1	17.0	0.1	29.7	26.7
	2016	1 695 787	60.1	19.0	17.3	0.3	29.3	26.0
	2017	1 736 593	60.3	18.8	17.6	0.5	30.7	27.9
	2018	1 771 063	60.2	18.9	18.0	0.6	31.4	29.0
	2019	1 789 747	60.1	18.7	18.2	-0.1	31.5	28.5
Kosovo (Euro)	1990	3 655	92.2	31.6	26.6	...	14.7	65.1
	1995	3 886	92.2	31.7	26.7	...	14.7	65.2
	2000	1 840	102.8	34.5	29.3	...	17.9	85.3
	2005	2 959	86.1	23.3	22.5	4.5	11.2	48.0
	2010	4 402	86.2	16.4	29.6	3.4	19.9	55.5
	2015	5 807	85.5	15.4	25.8	1.8	21.9	50.4
	2016	6 070	86.0	14.1	25.5	1.6	23.7	50.9
	2017	6 414	84.1	13.4	26.9	1.4	26.7	52.5
	2018	6 726	85.7	14.0	28.1	1.4	26.4	55.6
	2019	7 104	82.5	14.4	28.7	1.4	29.1	56.1
Latvia (Euro)	1990	97	54.8	8.2	24.1	18.2	39.4	43.5
	1995	4 057	65.3	23.6	14.2	1.7	34.6	39.3
	2000	6 860	62.4	20.9	25.0	-0.3	36.8	44.8
	2005	13 627	61.2	17.7	31.1	4.3	43.1	57.4
	2010	18 023	63.1	18.3	19.1	1.6	53.5	55.5
	2015	24 561	59.7	18.2	21.9	1.9	60.3	62.0
	2016	25 360	60.5	18.0	19.3	1.9	59.6	59.3
	2017	26 962	60.4	18.1	20.6	1.5	61.6	62.3
	2018	29 143	59.0	18.0	22.1	1.6	61.4	62.2
	2019	30 463	59.4	19.1	22.2	0.2	60.1	61.0
Liechtenstein (Swiss Franc)	1970	484	57.2	8.3	33.4	4.6	42.1	42.2
	1975	737	59.7	10.0	29.2	-2.1	40.4	35.0
	1980	1 148	61.7	10.0	28.9	3.2	47.2	49.3
	1985	1 674	60.2	10.7	28.5	-0.8	48.6	45.7
	1990	2 439	55.6	11.6	31.1	1.6	42.1	41.6
	1995	3 187	56.3	11.7	26.6	1.4	40.0	36.0
	2000	4 640	56.5	11.1	27.1	-0.2	51.3	45.8
	2005	5 038	55.8	11.2	26.4	-0.1	53.6	46.9
	2010	5 862	52.9	11.1	24.4	0.7	64.4	53.5
	2015	6 033	52.2	11.4	25.2	-0.6	62.4	50.7

Table 2. Gross Domestic Product by Type of Expenditure: Individual Countries or Areas

Major area, region and country	Year	Gross Domestic Product (at current prices) Million	Percentage Distributtion					
			Household final consumption expenditure 1	General government final consumption expenditure 2	Gross fixed capital formation 3	Changes in inventories 4	Exports of goods and services 5	Imports of goods and services 6
	2016	6 146	52.3	11.4	25.4	-0.6	65.7	54.1
	2017	6 375	52.7	11.3	26.0	-0.9	65.1	54.2
	2018	6 688	51.8	11.1	25.4	-0.8	66.2	53.7
	2019	6 756	52.0	11.2	25.5	-1.0	66.0	53.7
Lithuania	1990	41	54.3	21.0	26.3	6.7	38.7	47.4
(Euro)	1995	7 761	63.8	24.0	20.4	2.4	37.2	47.8
	2000	13 351	64.9	22.4	19.2	-0.3	38.6	44.8
	2005	20 980	64.4	18.5	23.5	0.8	55.1	62.4
	2010	28 034	64.0	19.8	16.9	1.2	63.9	65.9
	2015	37 346	62.5	17.2	19.7	1.6	68.8	69.8
	2016	38 890	63.1	17.0	19.9	-0.7	67.6	66.9
	2017	42 276	62.2	16.3	20.2	-1.0	73.6	71.3
	2018	45 491	61.5	16.4	21.0	-0.7	75.2	73.4
	2019	48 797	60.5	16.8	21.4	-4.0	77.5	72.2
Luxembourg	1970	1 871	45.6	10.8	21.1	1.4	88.1	68.6
(Euro)	1975	2 948	52.2	15.3	25.4	-5.4	91.6	79.8
	1980	4 518	53.0	17.1	24.8	-2.8	87.7	80.8
	1985	6 975	53.2	16.1	16.2	1.5	107.5	93.7
	1990	10 959	46.5	15.8	23.6	1.8	97.8	85.1
	1995	15 777	42.8	15.9	21.2	-0.2	102.5	82.1
	2000	23 079	37.9	14.8	21.3	1.0	148.5	123.5
	2005	30 031	36.3	17.1	20.7	0.3	161.7	136.1
	2010	40 178	32.2	17.0	17.1	0.8	174.5	141.6
	2015	52 066	30.1	16.5	18.5	0.8	221.2	187.2
	2016	54 867	29.7	15.9	18.2	0.8	213.0	177.6
	2017	56 814	29.8	16.4	18.2	0.4	217.6	182.5
	2018	60 053	29.8	16.7	16.8	0.8	211.6	175.5
	2019	63 516	29.5	17.1	16.8	0.6	208.8	172.8
Malta	1970	252	76.9	17.0	22.2	9.6	64.7	97.6
(Euro)	1975	440	70.7	16.1	17.1	5.7	108.0	118.1
	1980	1 040	63.9	14.2	16.8	7.1	118.6	118.2
	1985	1 263	69.2	15.5	20.0	7.3	94.5	108.3
	1990	1 950	62.0	15.4	24.0	8.5	111.1	121.3
	1995	3 041	60.4	18.0	24.1	6.9	122.3	131.7
	2000	4 137	62.9	17.7	22.6	4.0	119.3	126.5
	2005	5 149	63.0	18.1	22.1	-0.8	104.4	106.8
	2010	6 600	57.8	19.5	21.1	2.5	153.3	154.2
	2015	9 657	48.3	17.5	24.9	-0.4	153.8	144.2
	2016	10 370	46.5	16.1	23.6	0.1	151.6	137.8
	2017	11 322	44.4	15.3	20.6	-1.5	149.2	128.0
	2018	12 403	44.0	16.0	19.0	-0.4	144.4	123.0
	2019	13 277	42.9	17.3	19.5	-0.2	140.8	120.3
Monaco	1970	241	54.3	17.0	25.7	2.5	16.0	15.4
(Euro)	1975	451	54.6	19.6	25.4	-0.5	18.8	17.9
	1980	865	54.7	21.0	24.4	1.3	21.0	22.5
	1985	1 450	56.6	22.6	21.2	0.0	23.3	23.7
	1990	2 016	55.2	21.2	23.4	1.0	21.0	21.8
	1995	2 332	54.7	23.2	20.1	0.4	22.6	21.0
	2000	2 830	53.9	22.3	21.5	1.0	28.6	27.3
	2005	3 380	54.4	23.1	21.8	0.7	27.0	26.9
	2010	4 049	55.4	24.0	22.1	-0.2	26.8	28.1
	2015	5 644	54.0	23.8	21.5	1.2	30.6	31.2
	2016	5 848	54.3	23.7	21.8	0.8	30.2	30.9
	2017	5 693	54.0	23.6	22.5	0.9	30.9	32.0
	2018	6 092	53.9	23.3	22.9	1.0	31.7	32.8
	2019	6 632	53.7	23.1	23.6	0.5	31.8	32.8
Montenegro	1990	1 774	89.2	16.6	17.4	3.4	30.5	55.0
(Euro)	1995	890	89.1	16.6	17.5	3.4	30.5	55.1
	2000	1 076	85.0	15.5	17.6	3.4	30.2	50.0

Table 2. Gross Domestic Product by Type of Expenditure: Individual Countries or Areas

Major area, region and country	Year	Gross Domestic Product (at current prices) Million	Percentage Distribution: Household final consumption expenditure 1	General government final consumption expenditure 2	Gross fixed capital formation 3	Changes in inventories 4	Exports of goods and services 5	Imports of goods and services 6
	2005	1 832	84.8	21.2	18.8	-2.1	35.8	59.8
	2010	3 125	81.8	22.1	21.6	0.1	37.0	62.7
	2015	3 655	79.2	19.2	20.1	-0.1	42.1	60.6
	2016	3 954	76.8	19.6	23.2	2.9	40.5	62.9
	2017	4 299	74.8	18.4	26.9	3.3	41.1	64.5
	2018	4 663	73.4	18.5	29.2	2.7	42.9	66.7
	2019	4 951	69.2	17.8	27.3	4.6	43.7	64.8
Netherlands	1970	62 693	53.3	18.3	28.8	0.9	43.1	43.3
(Euro)	1975	115 500	51.6	21.5	23.0	-0.2	47.3	42.8
	1980	176 066	52.5	23.1	23.3	0.3	50.4	49.4
	1985	216 804	51.0	22.4	22.0	-0.5	59.9	54.6
	1990	263 037	49.4	21.7	23.5	0.7	54.4	49.6
	1995	329 547	49.2	22.4	21.1	0.6	57.2	50.6
	2000	452 007	50.3	20.6	22.5	0.1	66.0	59.5
	2005	550 883	48.8	22.3	20.2	0.2	65.6	57.2
	2010	639 187	45.4	26.2	19.6	0.6	69.8	61.7
	2015	690 008	45.0	25.0	22.1	0.3	82.7	75.2
	2016	708 337	44.0	24.7	20.0	0.4	79.5	69.3
	2017	738 146	44.3	24.3	20.2	0.4	83.4	72.6
	2018	773 987	44.1	24.4	20.4	0.5	84.7	74.1
	2019	810 247	43.8	24.5	21.0	0.3	83.3	72.9
North Macedonia	1990	508	71.7	18.5	24.2	-4.5	18.4	28.0
(Denar)	1995	178 311	71.3	17.3	20.7	-0.3	22.4	31.8
	2000	248 646	75.5	16.9	20.4	1.5	32.9	47.2
	2005	308 447	80.2	16.2	19.2	0.7	34.8	51.0
	2010	437 296	75.5	18.3	23.1	1.3	39.8	58.1
	2015	558 954	68.8	17.0	23.9	6.5	48.7	65.0
	2016	594 795	66.9	15.4	24.4	8.1	50.7	65.5
	2017	618 106	66.7	14.9	22.6	9.7	55.1	69.0
	2018	658 053	65.9	14.8	19.9	12.1	60.6	73.2
	2019	697 545	64.8	15.0	34.1	...	61.7	75.6
Norway	1970	91 530	52.0	15.7	28.0	4.9	36.5	37.1
(Norwegian Krone)	1975	171 849	50.2	18.1	34.8	2.7	36.1	41.9
	1980	318 279	47.0	18.7	27.9	0.4	42.8	36.7
	1985	562 402	47.4	17.9	26.0	1.5	42.0	34.8
	1990	749 860	48.9	20.3	22.8	1.7	39.4	33.2
	1995	963 138	48.9	21.0	21.4	2.7	37.2	31.1
	2000	1 507 283	42.5	18.9	19.8	2.0	45.7	28.9
	2005	1 989 987	41.9	19.4	20.4	2.2	43.4	27.4
	2010	2 591 479	42.0	21.3	20.8	4.7	39.8	28.5
	2015	3 111 168	43.5	23.2	23.8	3.6	37.8	32.1
	2016	3 098 148	45.6	24.4	25.2	2.9	35.5	33.5
	2017	3 295 382	44.7	24.0	24.6	3.3	36.3	32.8
	2018	3 530 860	43.4	23.4	24.1	3.2	38.4	32.6
	2019	3 549 360	44.8	24.4	26.1	2.9	36.9	35.2
Poland	1970	113	62.9	19.7	21.8	-1.4	22.9	26.0
(Zloty)	1975	163	62.8	19.7	22.3	-1.6	23.4	26.8
	1980	261	62.7	19.6	25.3	-3.2	28.1	34.1
	1985	1 079	56.4	21.2	21.8	1.5	18.3	18.6
	1990	62 747	47.0	21.1	19.6	5.9	25.9	19.4
	1995	345 060	59.3	18.9	17.4	2.2	22.9	20.8
	2000	748 483	63.8	18.1	23.7	0.9	27.2	33.7
	2005	990 530	63.1	18.3	18.9	1.0	34.6	35.9
	2010	1 446 844	61.5	19.2	20.3	1.2	39.9	42.1
	2015	1 801 112	58.6	18.1	20.1	0.5	49.1	46.3
	2016	1 863 487	58.6	17.9	18.0	1.7	51.9	48.2
	2017	1 989 835	58.6	17.7	17.5	2.4	54.2	50.4
	2018	2 121 555	58.4	17.7	18.2	2.6	55.2	52.2
	2019	2 287 738	57.5	18.0	18.5	1.2	55.5	50.8

Table 2. Gross Domestic Product by Type of Expenditure: Individual Countries or Areas

Major area, region and country	Year	Gross Domestic Product (at current prices) Million	Percentage Distributtion: Household final consumption expenditure 1	General government final consumption expenditure 2	Gross fixed capital formation 3	Changes in inventories 4	Exports of goods and services 5	Imports of goods and services 6
Portugal	1970	1 163	65.8	12.0	24.9	3.2	19.1	24.1
(Euro)	1975	2 467	76.9	13.0	27.7	-8.3	16.0	25.6
	1980	8 214	67.4	12.7	30.6	3.4	21.5	32.8
	1985	23 046	67.9	13.5	23.3	-1.9	29.2	32.3
	1990	55 973	63.9	15.2	26.8	0.9	29.2	35.9
	1995	89 029	64.7	17.5	23.4	0.8	26.8	33.1
	2000	128 414	63.4	18.9	28.1	0.7	28.2	39.2
	2005	158 553	64.4	21.0	23.2	0.1	27.1	35.9
	2010	179 611	65.9	20.6	20.6	0.5	30.1	37.7
	2015	179 713	65.6	17.9	15.6	0.3	40.6	39.9
	2016	186 490	65.4	17.6	15.6	0.3	40.2	39.1
	2017	195 947	64.6	17.2	16.9	0.4	42.7	41.7
	2018	205 184	64.3	17.0	17.6	0.7	43.4	43.0
	2019	213 301	63.9	16.9	18.3	0.7	43.5	43.3
Republic of Moldova	1990	16	57.2	8.2	21.9	6.7	33.0	37.2
(Moldovan Leu)	1995	7 777	54.9	21.3	15.9	9.3	42.7	52.0
	2000	19 226	85.2	12.0	15.4	8.9	35.2	58.6
	2005	45 189	90.1	13.5	24.5	6.8	36.3	70.3
	2010	86 275	90.2	18.2	22.5	1.3	27.8	60.1
	2015	145 754	87.4	14.5	24.3	-0.7	31.9	57.4
	2016	160 815	86.2	14.9	22.2	-0.2	32.3	55.3
	2017	178 881	85.6	15.0	22.3	0.5	31.1	54.5
	2018	192 509	84.8	15.2	24.3	1.3	30.1	55.7
	2019	210 099	84.7	13.7	25.6	0.7	30.5	55.2
Romania	1970	28	56.0	16.9	25.5	2.9	2.6	2.7
(New Leu)	1975	46	51.1	17.0	30.0	3.4	15.9	18.5
	1980	66	53.2	12.3	34.9	3.9	20.7	20.3
	1985	87	51.9	10.7	30.5	1.7	26.5	18.3
	1990	91	67.0	12.3	19.8	9.5	15.4	24.0
	1995	7 657	68.7	12.7	21.4	2.1	25.5	30.5
	2000	81 275	68.3	17.2	19.3	0.5	32.7	38.0
	2005	286 862	71.1	16.2	23.4	-0.4	24.5	34.8
	2010	528 247	63.8	15.5	26.1	1.1	32.4	38.8
	2015	712 588	61.8	13.7	24.8	0.4	41.0	41.6
	2016	765 135	62.5	15.1	22.9	0.5	41.2	42.1
	2017	857 896	63.0	15.7	22.4	1.0	41.5	43.6
	2018	952 397	63.5	16.8	21.0	1.8	41.6	44.6
	2019	1 059 803	63.6	17.3	23.7	-0.7	40.4	44.2
Russian Federation	1990	602	48.6	19.9	30.9	1.1	19.1	19.0
(Russian Ruble)	1995	1 438 694	51.7	18.6	22.9	4.1	29.1	25.7
	2000	7 357 666	45.8	14.7	18.3	1.5	43.7	23.9
	2005	21 821 317	49.5	16.2	19.4	1.8	34.9	21.3
	2010	46 761 885	50.9	18.0	23.2	0.7	28.9	20.9
	2015	83 265 815	51.9	18.1	20.4	1.6	28.6	20.6
	2016	85 799 945	52.8	18.5	21.7	1.2	25.8	20.6
	2017	92 040 416	52.3	18.3	21.8	1.6	26.0	20.7
	2018	104 559 040	49.5	17.3	20.2	1.6	30.5	20.6
	2019	109 596 334	50.9	17.8	21.0	1.9	28.4	20.8
San Marino	1970	26	59.0	15.0	25.3	0.7	284.5	286.9
(Euro)	1975	54	60.4	16.0	26.0	-2.3	284.5	286.9
	1980	149	59.6	16.5	25.7	1.1	284.5	286.9
	1985	315	59.2	18.3	22.4	0.8	284.3	286.7
	1990	515	57.9	19.7	22.1	0.2	283.1	285.5
	1995	858	68.5	9.5	28.3	-10.3	236.7	232.7
	2000	1 238	36.1	14.8	26.8	4.9	202.8	186.2
	2005	1 630	32.3	12.0	33.1	1.8	192.7	175.3
	2010	1 615	34.0	17.2	23.8	-1.3	197.5	171.2
	2015	1 279	40.4	20.0	17.3	-5.2	174.5	146.9
	2016	1 327	38.5	19.7	19.0	-3.3	173.1	147.1

Table 2. Gross Domestic Product by Type of Expenditure: Individual Countries or Areas

Major area, region and country	Year	Gross Domestic Product (at current prices) Million	Percentage Distributtion: Household final consumption expenditure 1	General government final consumption expenditure 2	Gross fixed capital formation 3	Changes in inventories 4	Exports of goods and services 5	Imports of goods and services 6
	2017	1 353	37.3	19.9	20.4	-1.2	168.8	145.1
	2018	1 402	36.3	19.4	20.3	0.3	166.6	142.9
	2019	1 431	35.3	18.6	21.6	-0.2	168.4	144.1
Serbia [17]	1990	0 (u)	71.9	18.8	11.1	3.2	8.6	13.6
(Serbian Dinar)	1995	59 587	71.0	18.4	11.1	2.5	5.2	8.2
	2000	434 319	76.4	19.3	12.2	-3.0	8.8	13.7
	2005	1 846 853	74.9	19.5	19.4	3.3	28.0	45.1
	2010	3 250 581	75.5	19.1	17.7	-0.1	32.3	44.5
	2015	4 315 020	71.9	16.4	17.0	1.7	45.2	52.2
	2016	4 528 192	70.8	16.0	17.1	1.0	48.5	53.3
	2017	4 760 686	70.9	16.1	17.7	1.8	50.5	57.1
	2018	5 072 932	69.4	16.5	20.0	2.6	50.4	59.1
	2019	5 417 725	68.2	16.6	22.5	2.6	51.0	61.0
Slovakia	1990	10 040	55.3	26.3	30.9	-1.6	23.8	33.4
(Euro)	1995	19 768	53.3	23.8	26.1	-2.4	53.9	54.6
	2000	31 661	54.6	20.7	26.2	0.9	53.2	55.6
	2005	50 486	55.0	18.5	26.2	3.4	72.3	75.4
	2010	68 189	57.1	19.4	21.1	2.7	77.2	77.5
	2015	79 768	54.0	18.6	23.8	0.5	92.0	88.9
	2016	81 051	55.1	18.9	21.0	2.0	93.7	90.8
	2017	84 532	55.9	18.9	21.2	1.7	95.2	92.9
	2018	89 506	56.2	18.7	21.1	2.1	96.2	94.3
	2019	93 865	56.4	19.7	21.4	2.1	92.4	92.0
Slovenia [18]	1990	859	52.3	16.3	20.8	-1.6	81.0	71.1
(Euro)	1995	10 561	59.0	17.8	23.1	2.3	45.4	47.7
	2000	18 853	56.3	18.5	27.4	1.5	50.1	53.8
	2005	29 114	53.3	18.9	26.6	1.9	59.8	60.5
	2010	36 364	56.2	20.4	21.1	1.3	64.3	63.2
	2015	38 853	54.0	18.8	18.7	0.5	77.1	69.1
	2016	40 443	54.0	19.0	17.4	1.0	77.6	69.1
	2017	43 009	52.6	18.4	18.3	1.7	83.1	74.2
	2018	45 863	52.1	18.2	19.2	1.9	84.8	76.3
	2019	48 393	52.4	18.4	19.6	1.1	83.7	75.3
Spain	1970	17 246	63.8	9.9	26.9	1.5	12.1	13.7
(Euro)	1975	39 598	64.1	10.9	27.3	2.8	12.4	16.7
	1980	100 299	65.4	13.6	22.8	1.6	14.3	17.3
	1985	184 771	63.1	15.2	20.5	0.3	20.9	20.0
	1990	328 696	61.3	16.2	25.8	1.1	15.7	19.9
	1995	460 588	61.0	17.6	21.9	0.6	21.8	22.9
	2000	647 851	59.6	16.7	25.9	0.7	28.6	31.5
	2005	927 357	58.1	17.3	29.0	0.4	25.0	29.8
	2010	1 072 709	58.1	20.6	21.8	0.5	26.0	27.0
	2015	1 077 590	58.5	19.5	18.0	1.0	33.6	30.6
	2016	1 113 840	58.2	19.1	18.0	0.8	33.9	29.9
	2017	1 161 867	58.4	18.6	18.7	0.7	35.1	31.5
	2018	1 204 241	58.2	18.7	19.5	1.0	35.1	32.4
	2019	1 244 772	57.3	18.9	19.9	0.9	34.9	31.9
Sweden	1970	197 060	49.2	20.2	28.5	5.1	22.0	22.3
(Swedish Krona)	1975	344 157	47.9	22.5	26.5	5.2	25.6	25.7
	1980	600 993	48.7	27.2	25.6	2.1	27.2	28.7
	1985	981 908	48.1	25.5	25.9	0.9	32.7	31.3
	1990	1 549 815	47.6	25.2	29.0	0.6	27.9	27.9
	1995	1 906 773	48.0	25.5	19.7	1.1	37.1	31.5
	2000	2 408 151	47.5	24.5	22.3	0.6	43.3	38.2
	2005	2 931 085	46.5	24.9	22.4	-0.2	45.0	38.7
	2010	3 573 581	46.9	25.0	22.5	0.4	44.7	39.6
	2015	4 260 470	46.0	25.7	23.8	0.7	43.8	40.0
	2016	4 415 031	45.9	26.4	24.2	0.5	42.7	39.6
	2017	4 625 094	45.7	26.0	25.2	0.6	43.7	41.2

Table 2. Gross Domestic Product by Type of Expenditure: Individual Countries or Areas

Major area, region and country	Year	Gross Domestic Product (at current prices) Million	Percentage Distributtion: Household final consumption expenditure 1	General government final consumption expenditure 2	Gross fixed capital formation 3	Changes in inventories 4	Exports of goods and services 5	Imports of goods and services 6
	2018	4 828 306	45.7	26.1	25.2	0.8	45.7	43.4
	2019	5 021 285	45.4	25.9	24.5	0.7	47.0	43.5
Switzerland [19]	1970	106 151	57.2	8.3	33.4	4.6	42.1	42.2
(Swiss Franc)	1975	164 093	59.7	10.0	29.2	-2.1	40.4	35.0
	1980	199 422	61.7	10.0	29.3	2.8	47.2	49.3
	1985	264 792	60.2	10.7	27.1	0.5	48.6	45.7
	1990	358 506	55.6	11.6	31.2	1.4	42.1	41.6
	1995	417 579	56.3	11.7	26.2	1.8	40.0	36.0
	2000	472 596	56.5	11.1	26.2	0.7	51.3	45.8
	2005	523 663	55.8	11.2	26.7	-0.3	53.6	46.9
	2010	629 325	52.9	11.1	25.4	-0.3	64.4	53.5
	2015	675 736	52.2	11.4	25.0	-0.3	62.4	50.7
	2016	685 441	52.3	11.4	25.7	-0.9	65.7	54.1
	2017	693 694	52.7	11.3	26.2	-1.1	65.1	54.2
	2018	719 614	51.8	11.1	25.0	-0.4	66.2	53.7
	2019	726 921	52.0	11.2	25.2	-0.6	66.0	53.7
Ukraine [20]	1990	1 731 (t)	57.9	15.9	24.1	3.5	26.7	27.7
(Hryvnia)	1995	56 458	55.8	20.4	23.5	3.3	45.5	48.4
	2000	176 128	57.4	17.9	19.8	0.0	60.3	55.4
	2005	457 325	59.2	17.5	21.9	0.6	47.7	46.9
	2010	1 079 346	63.8	19.4	17.1	3.8	47.1	51.1
	2015	1 988 544	67.8	18.9	13.6	2.4	52.6	55.2
	2016	2 385 367	66.6	18.6	15.5	6.2	49.3	56.2
	2017	2 983 882	67.1	20.7	15.8	4.2	48.0	55.7
	2018	3 560 596	69.4	20.8	17.7	0.9	45.2	53.9
	2019	3 974 564	75.3	19.9	18.1	-5.5	41.2	49.0
United Kingdom	1970	54 451	67.3	17.8	23.5	0.7	21.8	21.0
(Pound Sterling)	1975	109 274	69.2	22.5	25.5	-1.7	25.4	27.1
	1980	243 097	65.6	21.4	22.8	-1.5	26.6	24.4
	1985	381 251	65.9	20.4	21.7	0.1	27.9	26.8
	1990	615 673	66.7	18.6	23.5	-0.5	23.1	24.9
	1995	850 181	64.0	17.1	18.0	0.5	25.6	25.3
	2000	1 095 900	66.5	16.8	18.0	0.5	25.2	27.0
	2005	1 393 038	65.0	19.8	17.4	0.3	25.1	27.5
	2010	1 606 027	64.0	21.6	16.1	0.2	28.3	30.2
	2015	1 919 641	64.3	19.5	17.2	0.5	27.3	28.7
	2016	1 994 712	64.8	19.1	17.7	0.1	28.2	30.0
	2017	2 068 757	64.5	18.7	18.1	0.2	30.1	31.6
	2018	2 141 792	64.7	18.6	17.9	0.0	30.9	32.1
	2019	2 214 362	64.0	19.1	18.0	0.3	31.2	32.6
Oceania								
Australia	1970	40 314	54.5	13.9	30.7	1.5	12.7	12.9
(Australian Dollar)	1975	83 234	55.8	17.9	26.2	0.2	13.5	13.4
	1980	152 142	56.1	17.8	28.4	0.3	14.9	16.7
	1985	260 240	56.4	19.0	28.2	0.3	15.0	18.1
	1990	414 478	57.2	18.2	24.6	-0.3	16.1	16.2
	1995	527 599	57.6	18.0	24.2	0.6	18.9	19.4
	2000	705 066	58.7	17.8	23.3	0.2	22.2	22.1
	2005	996 430	56.7	17.5	27.9	-0.3	19.9	21.7
	2010	1 416 622	54.7	17.8	26.1	0.5	21.4	20.5
	2015	1 660 714	58.2	18.7	25.3	0.1	19.3	21.5
	2016	1 762 371	56.7	18.6	24.0	0.1	21.2	20.6
	2017	1 848 560	56.4	18.7	24.3	0.2	21.8	21.4
	2018	1 952 680	55.3	19.0	23.2	0.0	24.1	21.6
	2019	1 985 438	53.7	20.3	22.5	-0.3	23.9	20.1
Cook Islands	1970	9 958 (t)	80.3	32.0	15.9	10.3	67.8	106.3
(New Zealand Dollar)	1975	14	88.4	39.5	28.8	...	55.5	112.1
	1980	29	76.3	44.4	24.9	...	68.1	113.8

Table 2. Gross Domestic Product by Type of Expenditure: Individual Countries or Areas

Major area, region and country	Year	Gross Domestic Product (at current prices) Million	Percentage Distributtion: Household final consumption expenditure 1	General government final consumption expenditure 2	Gross fixed capital formation 3	Changes in inventories 4	Exports of goods and services 5	Imports of goods and services 6
	1985	62	69.8	45.5	22.7	...	64.9	102.8
	1990	122	57.9	44.8	18.9	...	64.3	85.9
	1995	176	46.1	38.5	15.0	...	49.3	48.9
	2000	220	45.2	31.4	14.7	...	76.8	68.0
	2005	283	43.1	32.3	14.0	...	66.8	56.2
	2010	334	32.2	32.1	10.5	...	81.4	56.1
	2015	433	33.7	32.3	11.0	...	84.5	55.6
	2016	445	33.9	32.3	11.1	...	91.1	56.4
	2017	486	34.0	32.3	11.1	...	78.2	69.7
	2018	524	33.9	32.3	11.0	...	84.6	60.6
	2019	575	33.9	32.3	11.0	...	84.6	62.2
Fiji	1970	192	56.3	14.2	23.5	6.1	49.6	49.7
(Fiji Dollar)	1975	563	58.6	12.1	23.6	3.7	44.1	42.0
	1980	986	42.2	16.2	32.8	9.3	49.6	50.1
	1985	1 318	53.1	19.4	23.4	1.8	45.4	43.1
	1990	1 983	59.0	17.7	21.4	2.9	63.8	64.7
	1995	2 803	66.1	16.1	16.1	1.8	56.0	56.2
	2000	3 636	63.8	17.2	19.6	3.0	58.6	62.2
	2005	5 040	77.0	15.9	19.6	1.4	54.1	63.7
	2010	6 025	72.3	15.0	15.9	2.9	57.4	63.8
	2015	9 822	58.7	20.1	17.3	2.4	48.8	52.4
	2016	10 327	63.5	18.9	17.5	1.7	46.6	50.5
	2017	11 065	61.0	18.3	17.8	2.1	46.0	50.9
	2018	11 557	59.3	19.9	17.8	...	48.3	56.0
	2019	11 892	61.3	19.1	17.4	0.0	47.9	52.4
French Polynesia	1970	26 541	62.6	32.2	31.9	0.6	29.2	52.3
(CFP Franc)	1975	55 658	53.3	27.4	40.5	1.7	25.7	41.0
	1980	119 713	54.9	28.2	34.7	-0.3	15.8	35.4
	1985	280 357	46.7	24.0	48.8	1.6	19.6	32.4
	1990	353 256	53.1	27.3	24.5	0.6	17.6	26.6
	1995	401 188	50.6	26.0	20.4	0.6	22.3	23.3
	2000	486 621	53.3	27.4	20.8	0.6	28.8	30.7
	2005	547 222	61.3	31.8	24.0	0.8	20.5	38.4
	2010	547 877	66.7	33.4	21.4	-0.2	16.4	37.7
	2015	572 812	65.3	31.1	19.9	0.0	19.6	36.0
	2016	592 618	64.8	31.2	18.6	-0.2	19.6	34.0
	2017	608 162	64.7	31.0	19.8	...	20.2	35.8
	2018	623 974	64.5	30.9	20.2	...	21.0	36.4
	2019	642 024	64.7	31.0	19.5	...	20.3	35.4
Kiribati	1970	18	52.0	26.5	8.3	1.5	51.1	39.1
(Australian Dollar)	1975	59	39.2	17.7	6.6	1.3	64.3	29.5
	1980	29	92.8	36.4	44.0	...	22.5	95.7
	1985	43	112.7	43.3	48.6	0.3	21.1	125.9
	1990	51	129.6	49.8	55.9	0.3	11.6	147.2
	1995	76	88.2	33.9	38.0	0.2	11.6	71.9
	2000	129	98.8	38.0	42.6	0.2	12.9	92.5
	2005	147	108.2	41.6	46.7	0.3	14.4	111.2
	2010	170	91.4	35.1	39.4	0.2	12.2	78.4
	2015	225	105.1	40.4	45.3	0.3	15.6	106.7
	2016	211	104.0	40.3	45.2	0.3	19.2	109.7
	2017	244	103.6	39.9	44.7	0.3	15.7	104.2
	2018	263	97.2	37.4	41.9	0.2	9.7	86.6
	2019	280	96.3	37.0	41.5	0.2	9.4	84.5
Marshall Islands	1970	8 487 (t)	75.5	62.9	14.9	...	58.6	87.8
(US Dollar)	1975	17	75.4	62.9	14.8	...	59.4	87.7
	1980	27	78.2	63.9	11.2	...	59.2	82.8
	1985	44	80.0	57.2	18.8	...	51.8	94.6
	1990	79	80.9	54.2	29.9	...	27.9	110.8
	1995	121	73.0	58.6	19.0	...	31.7	85.7
	2000	111	72.9	58.6	19.4	...	31.9	86.2

Table 2. Gross Domestic Product by Type of Expenditure: Individual Countries or Areas

Major area, region and country	Year	Gross Domestic Product (at current prices) Million	Percentage Distributtion					
			Household final consumption expenditure 1	General government final consumption expenditure 2	Gross fixed capital formation 3	Changes in inventories 4	Exports of goods and services 5	Imports of goods and services 6
	2005	140	73.1	58.0	19.1	...	36.7	92.7
	2010	168	74.2	54.8	42.9	...	44.0	107.1
	2015	181	73.0	56.7	18.7	...	49.1	93.6
	2016	198	70.4	57.2	20.0	...	41.3	82.2
	2017	208	73.2	57.1	22.1	...	47.4	90.7
	2018	221	73.5	56.3	20.9	...	40.6	87.1
	2019	237	72.4	56.9	21.0	...	45.3	89.0
Micronesia (FS of) (US Dollar)	1970	21	75.2	52.3	31.8	2.0	18.2	79.5
	1975	49	75.2	52.3	31.8	2.0	18.2	79.5
	1980	68	75.2	52.3	31.8	2.0	18.2	79.5
	1985	108	75.2	52.2	31.8	2.0	18.2	79.4
	1990	158	74.8	52.0	31.6	2.0	18.1	78.5
	1995	222	71.9	49.9	30.4	1.9	18.2	72.3
	2000	233	71.5	49.7	30.2	1.9	18.0	71.3
	2005	251	73.7	51.2	31.2	2.0	16.7	74.8
	2010	297	73.4	51.0	31.0	2.0	23.5	80.9
	2015	317	70.4	48.9	29.8	1.9	26.2	77.2
	2016	332	67.8	47.1	28.7	1.8	26.4	71.9
	2017	367	69.0	47.9	29.2	1.9	26.2	74.1
	2018	402	69.1	48.0	29.2	1.9	26.3	74.4
	2019	414	68.6	47.7	29.0	1.8	26.3	73.4
Nauru (Australian Dollar)	1970	14	52.0	26.5	8.3	1.5	51.1	39.1
	1975	26	39.2	17.7	6.6	1.3	64.3	29.5
	1980	37	92.8	36.4	44.0	...	22.5	95.7
	1985	47	112.7	43.3	48.6	0.3	21.1	125.9
	1990	63	129.6	49.8	55.9	0.3	11.6	147.2
	1995	47	88.2	33.9	38.0	0.2	11.6	71.9
	2000	37	98.8	38.0	42.6	0.2	12.9	92.5
	2005	34	108.2	41.6	46.7	0.3	14.4	111.2
	2010	65	91.4	35.1	39.4	0.2	12.2	78.4
	2015	139	105.1	40.4	45.3	0.3	15.6	106.7
	2016	159	104.8	40.3	45.2	0.3	19.2	109.7
	2017	168	103.6	39.9	44.7	0.3	15.7	104.2
	2018	185	97.2	37.4	41.9	0.2	9.7	86.6
	2019	191	96.3	37.0	41.5	0.2	9.4	84.5
New Caledonia (CFP Franc)	1970	38 204	51.5	7.5	47.6	1.2	51.4	64.0
	1975	63 643	52.3	19.7	29.2	...	41.9	43.9
	1980	90 847	54.6	27.9	22.4	-0.7	35.1	40.8
	1985	139 650	54.8	37.8	15.4	-1.4	33.4	39.7
	1990	250 427	57.3	32.6	24.4	-1.1	22.0	35.4
	1995	329 296	69.2	28.3	21.1	0.7	17.5	36.8
	2000	441 872	65.1	26.8	21.8	1.1	22.8	37.6
	2005	598 402	63.6	25.6	28.4	1.4	21.5	40.4
	2010	842 913	61.5	23.8	43.1	-0.6	20.2	48.0
	2015	945 740	65.0	24.0	34.9	-0.4	18.0	41.7
	2016	971 123	63.9	23.9	35.9	0.6	17.4	41.7
	2017	999 157	63.9	23.8	35.3	0.3	18.0	41.3
	2018	1 028 000	64.3	23.9	35.4	0.2	17.8	41.6
	2019	1 053 068	64.0	23.8	35.5	0.3	17.7	41.5
New Zealand (New Zealand Dollar)	1970	5 801	63.9	15.2	23.4	0.9	22.1	25.1
	1975	11 506	62.2	17.3	29.9	-2.5	22.9	29.7
	1980	23 988	59.8	19.6	21.8	-0.1	28.9	30.0
	1985	48 779	57.7	17.7	27.1	-0.3	29.0	31.1
	1990	76 167	60.2	18.4	20.7	-0.2	26.7	25.8
	1995	96 235	57.7	16.8	22.4	1.2	29.4	27.5
	2000	119 838	58.0	17.0	20.9	1.2	35.7	32.8
	2005	162 935	58.2	17.9	24.7	0.7	28.3	29.7
	2010	203 434	58.1	19.5	19.7	0.4	30.3	28.0
	2015	254 484	57.2	18.6	22.9	0.3	27.9	26.9
	2016	270 388	57.7	18.2	22.7	0.5	26.5	25.7

Table 2. Gross Domestic Product by Type of Expenditure: Individual Countries or Areas

Major area, region and country	Year	Gross Domestic Product (at current prices) Million		Percentage Distributtion				
			Household final consumption expenditure 1	General government final consumption expenditure 2	Gross fixed capital formation 3	Changes in inventories 4	Exports of goods and services 5	Imports of goods and services 6
	2017	289 104	57.1	18.0	23.1	0.7	27.5	26.4
	2018	300 499	57.5	18.5	23.6	0.4	28.0	28.0
	2019	314 104	115.0	18.4	23.8	-0.3	27.8	27.8
Palau (US Dollar)	1970	9 329 (t)	95.4	37.5	13.0	...	12.3	56.0
	1975	15	95.4	37.5	13.0	...	12.3	56.0
	1980	24	95.4	37.5	13.0	...	12.3	56.0
	1985	41	95.4	37.5	12.9	...	12.4	56.0
	1990	79	96.1	37.4	12.7	...	12.3	56.0
	1995	110	105.2	36.0	13.5	...	9.1	57.6
	2000	148	58.5	43.4	67.2	1.5	37.1	110.3
	2005	184	65.7	31.3	42.5	0.4	47.0	78.6
	2010	183	70.1	37.5	23.8	0.7	49.8	77.1
	2015	279	66.4	28.7	27.3	-1.9	58.6	76.0
	2016	297	66.3	29.0	27.1	-0.7	52.3	73.0
	2017	288	68.7	30.4	29.9	0.3	49.6	77.5
	2018	285	69.3	32.6	27.4	0.1	46.8	76.8
	2019	280	67.5	33.4	30.4	...	41.9	78.8
Papua New Guinea (Kina)	1970	980	62.0	30.0	47.7	6.7	15.8	56.7
	1975	1 773	49.2	33.5	14.3	4.1	39.8	41.6
	1980	2 863	55.3	24.8	19.5	3.4	42.6	46.1
	1985	3 704	58.4	25.2	16.9	2.7	45.0	49.1
	1990	4 743	51.8	26.3	22.9	1.1	43.0	45.4
	1995	9 364	42.7	17.1	19.5	2.4	59.3	41.1
	2000	14 715	44.6	16.6	20.4	1.5	66.2	49.2
	2005	22 815	48.0	16.1	16.5	1.0	74.5	56.1
	2010	38 752	61.8	15.1	23.0	1.4	63.6	64.9
	2015	60 139	54.6	20.9	7.5	0.6	57.9	41.5
	2016	65 038	58.6	19.1	7.5	0.6	58.6	44.4
	2017	72 522	53.2	21.5	7.5	0.5	58.5	41.3
	2018	79 405	55.2	22.1	7.5	0.5	55.3	40.6
	2019	84 586	56.7	22.4	7.5	0.5	52.1	39.2
Samoa (Tala)	1970	30	86.3	26.2	19.7	...	25.8	58.4
	1975	54	86.3	26.1	19.7	...	25.9	58.5
	1980	106	86.3	25.6	19.7	...	26.4	58.6
	1985	197	87.6	28.1	21.0	...	36.5	72.7
	1990	266	82.6	27.7	22.9	...	28.0	61.2
	1995	498	80.5	23.8	19.6	...	31.8	55.7
	2000	781	85.2	24.0	14.2	...	30.6	53.9
	2005	1 211	91.6	22.4	10.4	...	29.9	54.3
	2010	1 720	92.9	20.3	9.0	...	30.8	53.0
	2015	2 015	93.8	18.9	9.0	...	33.0	54.7
	2016	2 107	93.6	19.0	9.0	...	32.3	53.8
	2017	2 106	93.6	18.9	9.0	...	32.4	54.0
	2018	2 157	93.7	18.9	9.0	...	32.6	54.2
	2019	2 237	93.6	18.9	9.0	...	32.4	54.0
Solomon Islands (Solomon Islands Dollar)	1970	29	81.5	19.2	14.7	...	24.8	35.0
	1975	50	64.5	29.0	26.7	...	23.8	44.0
	1980	119	53.2	24.0	22.0	...	51.0	51.6
	1985	207	64.2	28.1	21.1	5.1	51.1	69.6
	1990	526	57.4	31.1	17.4	2.7	46.5	56.8
	1995	1 242	48.9	32.9	17.6	1.5	57.7	58.8
	2000	1 721	48.5	31.8	18.3	1.3	59.1	59.1
	2005	3 234	64.5	38.4	16.0	1.2	32.9	52.0
	2010	5 803	59.9	44.8	20.3	1.1	45.9	76.1
	2015	8 476	58.8	29.9	15.2	4.9	50.3	60.2
	2016	8 978	56.6	29.7	15.7	5.0	50.4	57.7
	2017	9 589	56.5	29.0	17.0	5.2	51.4	59.3
	2018	10 386	59.8	30.8	10.8	3.8	53.8	60.0
	2019	10 647	63.3	32.8	11.2	3.9	46.4	59.9

Table 2. Gross Domestic Product by Type of Expenditure: Individual Countries or Areas

Major area, region and country	Year	Gross Domestic Product (at current prices) Million	Percentage Distributtion: Household final consumption expenditure 1	General government final consumption expenditure 2	Gross fixed capital formation 3	Changes in inventories 4	Exports of goods and services 5	Imports of goods and services 6
Tonga (Pa'anga)	1970	15	89.5	15.4	21.3	2.4	35.2	63.8
	1975	32	89.1	12.9	23.0	4.4	41.5	71.0
	1980	69	94.1	13.0	23.8	2.3	26.7	59.9
	1985	105	99.8	16.0	23.3	3.1	30.1	72.2
	1990	207	93.7	18.7	17.7	0.5	33.2	63.8
	1995	265	93.6	16.4	25.7	0.6	17.0	54.2
	2000	336	92.1	18.1	20.0	0.5	15.2	46.3
	2005	507	103.3	15.9	22.1	0.3	17.8	58.4
	2010	708	96.3	18.7	29.1	0.5	12.5	58.3
	2015	849	101.0	21.3	23.3	2.0	17.0	64.5
	2016	933	96.6	20.4	24.2	0.5	21.7	63.3
	2017	1 018	96.3	20.1	26.7	1.2	22.2	65.8
	2018	1 073	101.1	19.2	22.6	2.1	21.4	66.1
	2019	1 164	95.5	20.3	24.4	1.0	22.0	65.2
Tuvalu (Australian Dollar)	1970	2 308 (t)	30.8	64.6	74.8	...	7.7	77.9
	1975	2 939 (t)	30.8	64.6	74.8	...	7.8	78.0
	1980	3 773 (t)	30.8	64.5	74.9	...	8.2	78.4
	1985	5 034 (t)	31.1	64.5	75.5	...	11.9	83.0
	1990	12	28.5	55.2	68.6	...	2.8	55.1
	1995	16	34.9	49.9	82.3	...	2.3	69.4
	2000	24	16.5	130.4	10.6	...	1.8	59.4
	2005	28	97.2	75.0	3.6	...	16.1	91.9
	2010	34	112.1	88.3	17.2	...	14.1	131.7
	2015	47	139.0	95.5	27.0	...	10.5	172.0
	2016	53	71.0	94.6	34.8	...	10.4	110.8
	2017	57	94.7	90.4	22.2	...	10.0	117.3
	2018	62	101.6	93.5	28.0	...	10.3	133.4
	2019	68	89.1	92.8	28.3	...	10.2	120.5
Vanuatu (Vatu)	1970	3 838	67.7	37.5	23.7	-2.1	50.6	70.9
	1975	5 563	67.7	37.5	23.7	-2.1	50.6	70.9
	1980	8 476	67.7	37.5	23.7	-2.1	50.6	70.9
	1985	14 056	67.5	38.3	18.1	2.5	52.9	74.0
	1990	20 074	75.2	30.1	32.3	-0.8	48.1	78.3
	1995	30 565	56.0	27.1	23.8	-0.6	45.8	54.8
	2000	36 472	65.5	15.9	28.5	0.5	36.3	48.2
	2005	43 148	67.2	13.2	23.4	0.7	45.4	54.8
	2010	67 912	62.0	17.5	33.9	0.8	46.6	52.7
	2015	82 798	65.9	15.8	32.9	0.8	44.3	64.5
	2016	87 250	65.1	14.5	24.7	0.9	47.4	58.9
	2017	94 887	61.9	17.4	27.2	0.7	47.7	57.9
	2018	100 771	59.0	16.9	26.4	0.4	56.6	60.0
	2019	103 590	62.0	16.3	26.1	0.7	50.6	58.9

Notes for Table 2. Gross Domestic Product by Type of Expenditure: Individual Countries or Areas

1/ Botswana

General government final consumption expenditure
2005, 2010, 2015-2019
Excludes individual consumption of general government.

2/ Burundi

(a) Gross Domestic Product
1970, 1975, 1980, 1985, 1990
Refers to data compiled according to the 1968 SNA.

(b) Household final consumption expenditure
1970, 1975, 1980, 1985, 1990
Refers to data compiled according to the 1968 SNA.

(c) General government final consumption expenditure
1970, 1975, 1980, 1985, 1990
Refers to data compiled according to the 1968 SNA.

(d) Gross fixed capital formation
1970, 1975, 1980, 1985, 1990
Refers to data compiled according to the 1968 SNA.

(e) Changes in inventories
1970, 1975, 1980, 1985, 1990
Refers to data compiled according to the 1968 SNA.

(f) Exports of goods and services
1970, 1975, 1980, 1985, 1990
Refers to data compiled according to the 1968 SNA.

(g) Imports of goods and services
1970, 1975, 1980, 1985, 1990
Refers to data compiled according to the 1968 SNA.

3/ Côte d'Ivoire

(a) Gross Domestic Product
1970, 1975, 1980, 1985, 1990, 1995, 2000
Refers to data compiled according to the 1968 SNA.

(b) Household final consumption expenditure
1970, 1975, 1980, 1985, 1990, 1995, 2000
Refers to data compiled according to the 1968 SNA.

(c) General government final consumption expenditure
1970, 1975, 1980, 1985, 1990, 1995, 2000
Refers to data compiled according to the 1968 SNA.
2010, 2015-2019
Includes NPISH final consumption expenditure.

(d) Gross fixed capital formation
1970, 1975, 1980, 1985, 1990, 1995, 2000
Refers to data compiled according to the 1968 SNA.

(e) Changes in inventories
1970, 1975, 1980, 1985, 1990, 1995, 2000
Refers to data compiled according to the 1968 SNA.

(f) Exports of goods and services
1970, 1975, 1980, 1985, 1990, 1995, 2000
Refers to data compiled according to the 1968 SNA.

(g) Imports of goods and services
1970, 1975, 1980, 1985, 1990, 1995, 2000
Refers to data compiled according to the 1968 SNA.

4/ Senegal
Changes in inventories
2019
Includes Acquisitions less disposals of valuables.

5/ Somalia
(a) Exports of goods and services
1970, 1975, 1980, 1985, 1990, 1995
Exports of goods only.

(b) Imports of goods and services
1970, 1975, 1980, 1985, 1990, 1995
Refers to imports of goods and non-factor services.

6/ Bolivia (Plurinational State of)
General government final consumption expenditure
2000, 2005, 2010, 2015-2019
Excludes individual consumption of general government.

7/ Cuba
General government final consumption expenditure
2000, 2005, 2010, 2015-2019
Includes NPISH final consumption expenditure.

8/ Paraguay
(a) Gross Domestic Product
1970, 1975, 1980, 1985, 1990, 1995, 2000
Does not incorporate export of binational hydroelectric power at market prices.

(b) Exports of goods and services
1970, 1975, 1980, 1985, 1990, 1995, 2000
Does not incorporate export of binational hydroelectric power at market prices.

9/ Jordan
General government final consumption expenditure
1990
capital development expenditure of the central government is included in fixed capital formation.

10/ Kuwait
Changes in inventories
2000, 2005, 2010, 2015-2019
Includes Acquisitions less disposal of valuables.

11/ Malaysia
Changes in inventories
1975, 1980, 1985, 1990, 1995, 2000, 2005, 2010, 2015-2019
Includes Acquisitions less disposals of valuables.

12/ Myanmar
(a) Exports of goods and services
1970, 1975, 1980, 1985, 1990, 1995
Country used official exchange rates rather than market exchange rates in compiling imports and exports data.

(b) Imports of goods and services
1970, 1975, 1980, 1985, 1990, 1995
Country used official exchange rates rather than market exchange rates in compiling imports and exports data.

13/ Philippines

Gross fixed capital formation

1970, 1975, 1980, 1985, 1990, 1995, 2000, 2005, 2010, 2015-2019

Includes intellectual property products.

14/ Qatar

(a) Gross Domestic Product

1970, 1975, 1980, 1985, 1990

Refers to data compiled according to the 1968 SNA.

(b) General government final consumption expenditure

1970, 1975, 1980, 1985, 1990

Refers to data compiled according to the 1968 SNA.

(c) Changes in inventories

1970, 1975, 1980, 1985, 1990

Refers to data compiled according to the 1968 SNA.

(d) Exports of goods and services

1970, 1975, 1980, 1985, 1990

Refers to data compiled according to the 1968 SNA.

(e) Imports of goods and services

1970, 1975, 1980, 1985, 1990

Refers to data compiled according to the 1968 SNA.

15/ Republic of Korea

Changes in inventories

1970, 1975, 1980, 1985, 1990, 1995, 2000, 2005, 2010, 2015-2019

Includes Acquisitions less disposals of valuables.

16/ France

Changes in inventories

1970, 1975, 1980, 1985, 1990, 1995, 2000, 2005, 2010, 2015-2019

Includes Acquisitions less disposals of valuables.

17/ Serbia

(a) Gross Domestic Product

1990, 1995

Includes data for Kosovo and Metohija

(b) Exports of goods and services

1990, 1995, 2000, 2005, 2010, 2015-2019

Includes exports of goods and services to Montenegro.

(c) Imports of goods and services

1990, 1995, 2000, 2005, 2010, 2015-2019

Includes imports of goods and services from Montenegro.

18/ Slovenia

Changes in inventories

1990, 1995, 2000, 2005, 2010, 2015-2019

Includes Acquisitions less disposal of valuables.

19/ Switzerland

Changes in inventories

1970, 1975

Includes Acquisitions less disposals of valuables.

20/ Ukraine

(a) Gross Domestic Product

2010-2019

The Government of Ukraine has advised the United Nations that it is not in a position to provide statistical data concerning the Autonomous Republic of Crimea and the city of Sevastopol.

(b) Household final consumption expenditure

2010-2019

The Government of Ukraine has advised the United Nations that it is not in a position to provide statistical data concerning the Autonomous Republic of Crimea and the city of Sevastopol.

(c) General government final consumption expenditure

2010-2019

The Government of Ukraine has advised the United Nations that it is not in a position to provide statistical data concerning the Autonomous Republic of Crimea and the city of Sevastopol.

(d) Gross fixed capital formation

2010-2019

The Government of Ukraine has advised the United Nations that it is not in a position to provide statistical data concerning the Autonomous Republic of Crimea and the city of Sevastopol.

(e) Changes in inventories

2010-2019

The Government of Ukraine has advised the United Nations that it is not in a position to provide statistical data concerning the Autonomous Republic of Crimea and the city of Sevastopol.

(f) Exports of goods and services

2010-2019

The Government of Ukraine has advised the United Nations that it is not in a position to provide statistical data concerning the Autonomous Republic of Crimea and the city of Sevastopol.

(g) Imports of goods and services

2010-2019

The Government of Ukraine has advised the United Nations that it is not in a position to provide statistical data concerning the Autonomous Republic of Crimea and the city of Sevastopol.

Table 3. Gross Value Added by Kind of Economic Activity: Individual Countries or Areas

Major area, region and country	Year	Gross Value Added (at current prices) Million	Percentage Distributtion						
			Agriculture, hunting, forestry, fishing A-B	Mining, Manufacturing, Utilities C-E	Of which: Manufacturing D	Construction F	Wholesale, retail trade, restaurants and hotels G-H	Transport, storage and communication I	Other Activities J-P
Africa									
Algeria (Algerian Dinar)	1970	26 283	12.8	26.4	11.4	6.8	17.4	4.8	31.7
	1975	61 835	11.2	37.8	8.3	8.6	9.5	4.6	28.4
	1980	162 141	8.1	43.6	9.1	10.2	11.7	4.5	22.0
	1985	290 940	8.4	37.0	11.6	12.7	13.8	4.7	23.3
	1990	529 810	12.0	37.5	11.9	10.8	13.5	4.9	21.4
	1995	1 913 449	10.4	37.9	9.2	10.0	16.2	4.9	20.6
	2000	3 957 614	8.8	49.4	6.2	7.4	12.2	6.6	15.7
	2005	7 258 407	8.0	52.8	4.6	7.0	10.2	8.9	13.2
	2010	11 776 661	8.6	41.3	4.3	10.1	11.9	7.9	20.1
	2015	16 014 700	12.1	25.7	4.6	11.6	15.4	10.4	24.8
	2016	16 851 500	12.7	24.2	4.6	11.8	15.3	10.7	25.2
	2017	18 155 000	12.2	26.6	4.5	11.7	14.8	10.9	23.9
	2018	19 722 400	12.3	29.2	4.4	11.4	14.1	10.9	22.1
	2019	19 622 100	12.9	26.7	4.6	12.2	14.0	11.4	22.7
Angola [1] (Kwanza)	1970	107 (u)	14.0	35.5	9.3	4.7	13.1	4.7	28.0
	1975	104 (u)	14.4	35.6	9.6	4.8	12.5	4.8	28.8
	1980	211 (u)	14.2	35.5	9.0	4.7	12.8	4.3	28.0
	1985	269 (u)	13.8	38.7	9.7	4.8	13.0	4.8	24.9
	1990	406 (u)	18.0	38.2	4.0	3.0	10.8	3.2	27.1
	1995	18	7.4	63.9	4.0	3.5	9.3	2.4	13.5
	2000	120 960	5.7	70.3	2.9	2.8	7.6	1.9	11.6
	2005	3 261 048	5.0	54.1	3.9	5.6	11.1	2.9	21.3
	2010	7 735 211	6.2	43.1	5.0	9.0	16.8	4.4	20.5
	2015	13 910 605	9.1	29.1	6.0	12.9	21.2	5.3	22.3
	2016	16 459 491	9.9	29.0	6.9	13.8	20.6	4.7	22.0
	2017	20 049 050	10.1	28.8	6.8	13.8	22.3	4.1	20.8
	2018	25 562 697	8.6	37.3	6.1	10.7	20.7	3.4	19.3
	2019	30 819 134	9.5	31.7	6.6	12.8	21.2	4.1	20.7
Benin [2,28] (CFA Franc BCEAO)	1970	78 922	34.4	10.8	8.8	3.7	16.0	7.4	27.8
	1975	135 109	27.4	12.1	9.8	4.2	17.6	8.1	30.6
	1980	280 805	32.9	9.2	7.5	3.2	17.1	7.9	29.8
	1985	467 358	32.4	11.5	9.4	4.0	16.3	7.5	28.3
	1990	531 491	35.4	9.5	7.5	3.2	16.0	7.3	28.6
	1995	1 057 268	23.7	24.3	22.9	8.2	16.2	5.1	22.5
	2000	1 641 828	25.5	24.1	23.4	7.3	15.7	5.8	21.5
	2005	2 309 034	27.1	22.2	21.3	8.1	14.2	6.4	21.9
	2010	3 091 278	25.4	16.9	15.4	7.9	12.4	9.5	28.0
	2015	6 195 406	28.7	12.8	10.9	5.0	17.9	11.5	24.1
	2016	6 420 917	30.3	12.1	10.8	5.1	17.7	11.8	23.1
	2017	6 785 100	31.0	11.7	10.5	4.7	17.5	11.7	23.4
	2018	7 249 173	30.7	11.2	10.0	4.8	17.3	11.7	24.3
	2019	7 698 146	29.4	12.2	10.8	5.6	17.4	11.7	23.5
Botswana (Pula)	1970	52	36.3	15.6	5.9	8.2	9.2	4.4	26.2
	1975	180	33.3	18.2	7.4	11.2	8.9	3.9	24.5
	1980	566	15.4	36.4	6.6	8.9	9.0	2.8	27.4
	1985	1 354	7.4	47.2	6.5	7.1	7.3	3.2	27.8
	1990	6 245	4.6	48.3	5.8	8.2	7.7	3.1	28.1
	1995	12 387	4.9	39.9	5.6	6.6	10.3	4.0	34.4
	2000	27 061	3.0	45.1	6.1	5.4	11.0	3.6	31.9
	2005	45 660	2.0	42.3	5.5	5.3	12.0	4.0	34.3
	2010	77 623	2.8	29.1	7.1	6.5	16.9	5.8	38.9
	2015	131 938	2.4	25.9	6.4	7.3	18.0	6.5	39.9
	2016	155 414	2.2	28.4	5.7	6.8	19.9	6.2	36.4
	2017	163 785	2.2	25.8	5.6	7.0	21.4	6.5	37.1
	2018	172 970	2.2	25.2	5.7	7.3	21.2	6.7	37.5
	2019	178 808	2.2	23.7	5.8	7.5	21.4	6.8	38.4
Burkina Faso [29] (CFA Franc BCEAO)	1970	165 160	21.0	22.7	16.2	8.0	19.0	2.7	26.7
	1975	235 622	24.8	25.9	18.7	6.7	13.1	2.2	27.2
	1980	538 361	20.7	28.1	14.3	5.3	18.1	3.2	24.6
	1985	783 041	28.3	24.1	16.8	2.5	15.4	3.0	26.8
	1990	952 121	23.2	22.3	18.0	2.8	14.8	2.8	34.2
	1995	1 305 002	28.3	20.8	17.0	3.1	15.5	2.6	29.7
	2000	1 992 800	26.4	19.1	16.2	4.0	12.9	3.5	34.2
	2005	2 964 809	29.3	18.3	14.6	3.7	13.5	4.0	31.1
	2010	4 617 997	26.2	22.9	13.1	5.4	12.9	4.0	28.7

Table 3. Gross Value Added by Kind of Economic Activity: Individual Countries or Areas

Major area, region and country	Year	Gross Value Added (at current prices) Million	Agriculture, hunting, forestry, fishing A-B	Mining, Manufacturing, Utilities C-E	Of which: Manufacturing D	Construction F	Wholesale, retail trade, restaurants and hotels G-H	Transport, storage and communication I	Other Activities J-P
			Percentage Distributtion						
	2015	6 358 100	24.9	23.1	12.8	3.7	13.8	4.4	30.2
	2016	6 875 188	24.0	23.5	12.3	4.0	12.7	4.6	31.2
	2017	7 347 088	23.0	24.1	11.4	3.9	12.5	4.9	31.6
	2018	8 030 677	25.6	23.8	10.8	3.4	12.1	4.3	30.7
	2019	8 458 670	22.3	24.7	11.2	3.7	11.8	4.5	33.0
Burundi [3,47]	1970	19 882	68.2	7.1	6.8	2.3	8.0	1.2	13.3
(Burundi Franc)	1975	30 467	64.8	7.7	7.3	3.2	9.6	1.4	13.1
	1980	77 430	61.8	9.3	9.0	4.9	8.7	2.2	13.2
	1985	138 789	55.8	12.8	12.4	4.1	11.6	2.3	13.4
	1990	192 050	52.4	17.6	16.8	3.4	4.9	3.1	18.5
	1995	217 969	48.2	12.7	12.1	6.6	6.0	4.8	21.9
	2000	454 646	40.5	14.3	13.2	4.5	8.1	8.5	24.1
	2005	1 147 062	43.0	14.3	12.5	3.5	10.3	3.1	25.8
	2010	2 361 257	40.7	11.9	10.8	4.4	7.0	3.7	32.3
	2015	4 157 046	37.5	12.7	11.6	3.7	7.2	4.9	34.1
	2016	4 494 924	38.3	14.2	13.2	4.0	5.9	4.3	33.2
	2017	5 217 993	39.7	13.8	12.6	3.9	5.8	4.2	32.6
	2018	5 136 071	38.5	13.6	12.5	3.9	6.3	4.5	33.3
	2019	5 172 914	38.9	13.8	12.8	3.9	6.0	4.3	33.0
Cabo Verde [29]	1970	1 809	21.0	5.8	7.9	16.4	24.9	10.2	21.6
(Cabo Verde Escudo)	1975	2 956	21.4	5.9	7.9	16.4	24.8	10.0	21.5
	1980	5 668	25.2	6.0	7.9	16.1	23.7	8.2	20.7
	1985	12 737	17.3	11.0	10.0	14.5	22.2	13.1	21.8
	1990	23 745	17.6	18.6	11.7	14.3	15.3	12.5	21.7
	1995	44 265	15.6	19.3	10.0	10.6	11.8	13.1	29.5
	2000	70 804	15.8	16.4	7.9	9.2	14.5	16.3	27.8
	2005	89 322	11.7	11.6	6.1	11.1	15.6	18.5	31.4
	2010	120 970	9.2	8.4	6.2	12.4	18.5	17.4	34.2
	2015	138 667	10.0	11.7	7.5	9.1	16.9	15.2	37.2
	2016	144 090	9.2	10.3	6.8	9.4	17.8	15.0	38.3
	2017	149 154	7.8	10.4	7.1	10.8	20.2	15.0	35.8
	2018	157 010	6.2	11.4	7.9	11.2	20.6	14.6	36.0
	2019	167 142	5.4	11.2	7.8	11.7	20.8	14.8	36.1
Cameroon [29]	1970	342 516	20.8	14.7	12.7	6.0	21.8	8.1	28.5
(CFA Franc BEAC)	1975	741 113	22.1	13.0	11.3	7.6	16.0	8.9	32.4
	1980	2 016 950	18.2	20.0	12.3	9.0	12.1	6.5	34.3
	1985	4 212 885	14.8	20.9	13.9	10.3	15.0	6.7	32.4
	1990	3 424 343	15.6	22.6	15.5	6.3	14.5	7.9	33.1
	1995	4 523 352	17.5	22.5	16.0	6.2	16.6	8.7	28.6
	2000	6 560 480	16.5	28.4	17.0	5.0	14.7	8.7	26.6
	2005	8 786 608	15.2	24.5	15.0	5.8	18.0	8.6	28.0
	2010	12 090 545	15.1	24.5	15.5	4.6	21.3	8.5	26.1
	2015	16 828 100	16.1	22.2	15.9	5.2	21.2	8.5	26.9
	2016	17 794 087	15.8	21.3	16.2	5.3	21.0	8.8	27.8
	2017	18 662 559	15.7	21.9	16.5	5.6	21.2	8.5	27.1
	2018	19 737 316	15.7	22.1	15.5	5.9	20.9	8.3	27.1
	2019	20 941 900	15.9	21.9	15.5	6.2	21.2	8.2	26.6
Central African Republic	1970	72 531	29.7	26.2	18.0	1.0	15.1	1.3	26.8
(CFA Franc BEAC)	1975	120 448	30.7	25.7	19.4	0.8	15.0	1.3	26.6
	1980	253 922	32.4	23.6	18.4	0.6	15.8	1.4	26.2
	1985	413 743	35.7	21.3	16.4	0.9	15.9	1.4	24.8
	1990	428 949	36.0	24.7	18.9	1.7	13.9	1.6	22.2
	1995	590 782	36.1	24.2	17.9	2.6	14.3	1.4	21.4
	2000	676 390	41.4	17.2	10.9	1.6	12.7	2.3	24.7
	2005	717 185	44.6	16.5	11.5	1.9	14.3	2.6	20.0
	2010	994 796	39.8	21.9	19.6	4.2	14.2	1.8	18.1
	2015	971 353	32.5	21.4	20.4	1.5	17.7	3.3	23.6
	2016	1 041 698	33.1	21.1	20.2	1.4	18.5	2.8	23.1
	2017	1 160 862	34.0	19.9	19.1	1.6	19.2	2.5	22.9
	2018	1 169 556	33.0	19.9	19.1	1.8	19.7	1.8	23.9
	2019	1 247 111	33.4	20.3	19.5	1.6	19.1	2.4	23.3
Chad [3]	1970	113 005	32.3	10.0	10.0	4.7	32.3	8.2	12.5
(CFA Franc BEAC)	1975	185 532	32.3	10.0	10.0	4.7	32.3	8.2	12.5
	1980	192 499	32.5	9.7	9.7	4.8	32.5	8.2	12.4
	1985	497 359	31.7	9.8	9.8	5.1	32.9	6.4	14.0
	1990	568 947	27.1	9.0	9.0	7.8	31.7	9.0	15.2

Table 3. Gross Value Added by Kind of Economic Activity: Individual Countries or Areas

Major area, region and country	Year	Gross Value Added (at current prices) Million	Percentage Distributtion: Agriculture, hunting, forestry, fishing A-B	Mining, Manufacturing, Utilities C-E	Of which: Manufacturing D	Construction F	Wholesale, retail trade, restaurants and hotels G-H	Transport, storage and communication I	Other Activities J-P
	1995	943 191	27.7	9.2	9.1	5.9	36.0	6.1	15.1
	2000	1 247 499	33.3	7.5	7.5	5.7	34.1	5.2	14.2
	2005	3 488 889	26.0	30.9	5.5	4.2	20.3	3.6	14.9
	2010	4 729 882	35.9	31.3	7.3	5.4	5.6	6.5	15.3
	2015	6 819 393	29.5	28.3	9.5	3.4	15.7	6.9	16.2
	2016	6 672 849	33.5	22.9	9.5	1.1	18.4	6.7	17.5
	2017	6 036 719	34.0	18.8	11.9	1.3	20.4	6.5	19.0
	2018	6 663 637	30.8	18.3	11.4	1.0	21.3	7.9	20.7
	2019	7 223 696	28.5	17.8	11.1	0.9	22.9	8.1	21.8
Comoros [4]	1970	10 049	24.6	8.9	6.9	7.6	21.7	4.8	32.3
(Comoro Franc)	1975	23 774	24.6	8.9	6.9	7.6	21.7	4.8	32.3
	1980	53 058	24.6	9.0	7.0	7.6	21.7	4.8	32.2
	1985	103 474	26.5	9.1	6.6	8.5	20.6	4.6	30.7
	1990	133 486	30.3	8.0	6.3	3.1	20.7	5.7	32.2
	1995	171 916	31.9	7.6	5.9	4.1	19.8	7.6	29.0
	2000	218 795	37.0	8.1	6.2	3.4	15.5	5.8	30.1
	2005	302 740	37.3	7.5	5.7	3.4	15.6	5.6	30.7
	2010	324 133	31.6	10.0	7.4	2.3	20.7	6.4	29.1
	2015	413 111	31.7	8.9	7.5	1.9	21.0	8.3	28.2
	2016	431 552	32.7	8.9	7.5	1.4	20.7	7.9	28.3
	2017	449 563	33.3	8.5	7.2	1.0	21.2	7.4	28.5
	2018	469 238	34.2	8.5	7.1	0.8	21.2	7.0	28.4
	2019	490 624	34.5	8.5	7.1	0.8	21.1	7.0	28.2
Congo [5]	1970	100 081	19.9	17.5	16.3	3.4	12.1	15.0	32.1
(CFA Franc BEAC)	1975	195 673	14.3	24.2	13.5	2.0	12.2	13.0	34.3
	1980	454 332	11.5	32.4	10.3	2.8	10.6	13.9	28.8
	1985	1 154 622	7.8	36.8	8.2	3.8	13.2	11.8	26.6
	1990	1 008 710	12.3	30.1	11.4	1.1	14.4	12.7	29.4
	1995	1 368 916	10.2	32.9	11.3	1.4	13.7	12.7	29.1
	2000	2 386 883	6.5	56.8	6.0	3.1	8.5	7.3	17.7
	2005	3 388 904	5.5	55.9	6.9	3.8	8.7	8.7	17.4
	2010	6 329 807	4.2	59.3	5.5	8.7	8.7	7.4	11.7
	2015	6 589 575	6.3	30.5	8.4	19.4	12.6	7.8	23.3
	2016	5 652 293	7.5	27.5	11.3	10.9	18.0	7.6	28.5
	2017	6 190 151	7.7	37.7	11.5	6.4	13.6	7.0	27.7
	2018	7 242 384	7.2	51.3	7.8	1.2	14.0	5.8	20.5
	2019	6 981 890	7.5	39.0	10.2	6.1	15.2	6.8	25.5
Côte d'Ivoire [6,48]	1970	392 201	28.7	15.5	14.1	7.1	21.7	8.1	19.0
(CFA Franc BCEAO)	1975	792 078	30.4	15.7	13.8	6.9	18.8	9.1	19.1
	1980	2 059 958	29.9	13.6	11.7	7.2	19.0	7.8	22.4
	1985	2 998 413	28.1	16.0	12.1	4.5	18.7	7.6	25.1
	1990	3 208 000	29.8	22.3	19.9	1.8	16.1	7.4	22.7
	1995	5 110 000	26.6	20.2	18.1	2.2	20.8	5.4	24.9
	2000	7 323 000	24.8	24.3	22.4	2.9	19.0	5.5	23.5
	2005	8 395 784	24.3	22.1	17.0	2.4	13.1	7.5	30.6
	2010	12 234 998	25.2	20.8	13.7	1.8	14.1	8.5	29.7
	2015	25 086 000	19.8	16.2	11.7	4.9	14.1	13.8	31.1
	2016	26 480 000	21.2	16.3	9.7	4.2	13.7	14.4	30.2
	2017	27 728 000	20.2	18.1	10.9	4.0	14.5	11.4	31.8
	2018	30 072 000	22.0	18.6	12.8	3.9	14.0	10.5	30.9
	2019	32 064 000	22.1	18.7	12.6	4.0	14.1	10.1	31.1
D.R. of the Congo [7,46]	1970	0 (u)	17.5	32.7	8.6	4.9	11.7	8.3	24.4
(Franc Congolais)	1975	0 (u)	20.5	22.1	10.5	6.1	17.9	4.5	29.0
	1980	0 (u)	26.8	30.0	15.2	5.0	15.1	14.6	8.4
	1985	1 (u)	31.8	25.8	10.5	5.2	14.7	14.2	8.2
	1990	35 (u)	31.0	24.5	11.3	4.5	15.9	15.3	8.9
	1995	623	57.0	13.9	4.9	3.1	10.3	9.9	5.7
	2000	466 329	32.3	19.7	10.0	2.9	17.6	18.4	9.1
	2005	5 487 300	22.3	28.9	17.0	3.9	14.1	14.3	16.5
	2010	18 656 500	22.4	39.4	17.0	1.1	11.1	11.2	14.7
	2015	32 716 700	19.7	43.9	18.4	0.9	11.3	10.9	13.3
	2016	38 063 500	20.6	42.2	20.3	0.9	12.3	10.0	13.9
	2017	52 699 527	20.8	42.5	20.6	1.0	12.7	9.0	13.9
	2018	73 377 361	20.0	44.5	18.6	1.5	12.1	8.5	13.4
	2019	74 906 380	20.8	40.9	20.8	1.5	12.9	8.9	14.9

Table 3. Gross Value Added by Kind of Economic Activity: Individual Countries or Areas

Major area, region and country	Year	Gross Value Added (at current prices) Million	Percentage Distributtion: Agriculture, hunting, forestry, fishing A-B	Mining, Manufacturing, Utilities C-E	Of which: Manufacturing D	Construction F	Wholesale, retail trade, restaurants and hotels G-H	Transport, storage and communication I	Other Activities J-P
Djibouti [9,31]	1970	13 566	5.0	10.5	7.0	4.1	50.7	8.5	21.2
(Djibouti Franc)	1975	26 733	4.1	10.5	6.9	8.3	42.3	10.3	24.5
	1980	44 523	4.2	12.7	9.7	6.2	21.8	10.9	44.2
	1985	52 776	4.4	11.6	7.2	9.3	17.9	13.1	43.7
	1990	70 151	3.1	10.8	3.7	11.2	18.1	17.1	39.8
	1995	77 847	3.2	9.8	2.9	5.5	15.2	22.1	44.2
	2000	84 803	3.6	8.4	2.9	6.8	16.4	26.3	38.5
	2005	112 023	3.6	8.6	2.6	7.6	20.7	26.7	32.7
	2010	202 081	2.8	6.2	2.5	9.9	24.8	25.8	30.5
	2015	403 334	1.3	7.8	2.9	4.3	32.4	24.8	29.4
	2016	433 055	1.4	7.5	3.0	4.3	31.4	24.9	30.5
	2017	456 923	1.5	8.2	3.3	4.2	32.4	23.5	30.1
	2018	483 307	1.4	7.6	2.9	4.2	31.9	25.3	29.7
	2019	523 336	1.4	7.7	3.0	4.1	32.1	24.9	29.9
Egypt [10]	1970	3 041	29.4	25.5	21.7	2.7	11.0	4.1	27.3
(Egyptian Pound)	1975	4 690	30.5	21.6	17.8	3.1	14.0	4.3	26.6
	1980	13 477	21.0	30.3	13.7	6.0	14.3	7.4	21.0
	1985	38 814	18.4	26.4	15.2	5.4	20.2	8.9	20.8
	1990	90 843	19.5	24.1	18.0	5.5	21.9	9.2	19.8
	1995	213 428	16.8	27.7	17.4	5.0	18.6	10.3	22.0
	2000	311 835	13.8	28.6	18.0	4.7	17.2	8.5	27.1
	2005	518 918	14.4	32.7	17.3	4.1	14.2	11.4	23.2
	2010	1 150 590	14.0	33.0	16.9	4.6	15.1	9.6	23.8
	2015	2 473 100	11.3	31.4	16.5	4.8	15.3	8.2	29.0
	2016	2 674 410	11.9	27.4	17.1	5.4	15.8	8.6	30.8
	2017	3 417 149	11.7	28.6	16.7	5.7	15.7	9.3	29.1
	2018	4 334 900	11.5	29.9	16.6	5.9	16.2	9.2	27.4
	2019	5 170 107	11.4	30.5	16.4	6.2	16.4	8.9	26.7
Equatorial Guinea [5]	1970	5 448	15.1	18.5	3.9	0.8	28.1	17.0	20.5
(CFA Franc BEAC)	1975	7 031	15.1	18.5	3.9	0.8	28.1	17.1	20.5
	1980	11 116	15.0	18.6	3.9	0.8	27.9	17.4	20.3
	1985	38 609	14.5	19.9	4.2	0.7	26.4	20.8	17.7
	1990	41 545	14.2	14.9	3.2	0.9	24.9	16.3	28.8
	1995	96 670	12.5	34.5	6.4	1.3	17.7	10.4	23.6
	2000	1 046 041	5.8	69.2	11.2	1.9	7.7	4.3	11.2
	2005	4 486 467	1.5	77.4	6.9	3.9	5.4	2.9	8.8
	2010	8 115 758	1.1	66.0	20.9	8.4	8.3	3.6	12.7
	2015	7 804 088	1.9	49.7	17.8	9.3	8.7	6.2	24.2
	2016	6 650 922	2.3	45.4	18.5	7.0	9.1	7.6	28.5
	2017	7 090 044	2.3	51.7	25.7	5.1	7.6	6.7	26.6
	2018	7 383 744	2.2	52.9	25.3	4.6	8.1	6.1	26.1
	2019	6 442 533	2.5	46.6	19.6	4.0	9.0	7.6	30.3
Eritrea	1990	1 344	26.3	9.1	8.5	4.8	23.0	12.4	24.4
(Nakfa)	1995	3 543	20.9	9.8	9.0	7.0	23.8	12.9	25.6
	2000	6 330	15.1	12.4	11.2	10.5	19.7	12.6	29.6
	2005	15 758	24.2	8.8	7.3	13.1	17.5	11.2	25.2
	2010	23 569	19.1	15.5	6.0	15.4	11.0	12.0	27.1
	2015	31 449	17.2	15.5	6.0	15.7	11.5	12.3	27.8
	2016	34 503	17.3	15.6	6.0	15.7	11.4	12.3	27.7
	2017	29 073	17.2	15.6	6.0	15.7	11.4	12.3	27.7
	2018	30 870	17.3	15.6	6.0	15.7	11.4	12.3	27.7
	2019	30 554	17.3	15.6	6.0	15.7	11.4	12.3	27.7
Eswatini [29]	1970	129	20.9	19.4	11.0	3.6	24.1	5.9	26.1
(Lilangeni)	1975	277	21.1	20.7	15.1	5.1	20.7	5.2	27.1
	1980	624	20.3	23.5	19.9	6.7	16.9	4.4	28.2
	1985	1 199	14.5	19.4	13.8	5.4	20.5	4.7	35.5
	1990	3 223	8.3	35.4	31.3	4.2	16.5	4.2	31.4
	1995	6 777	7.9	36.2	33.2	5.0	18.3	4.0	28.6
	2000	11 732	12.7	36.7	34.8	3.8	14.7	4.7	27.4
	2005	19 669	11.3	36.9	35.2	4.0	16.4	4.5	26.9
	2010	31 657	10.4	35.2	33.4	3.5	15.5	5.1	30.3
	2015	49 468	9.8	34.3	33.2	3.1	15.3	4.6	32.9
	2016	54 055	9.3	33.4	32.4	3.3	15.7	4.7	33.6
	2017	56 571	8.7	32.2	30.9	3.0	15.6	4.8	35.7
	2018	59 446	9.0	31.7	30.3	3.0	15.4	4.8	36.1
	2019	62 097	9.1	32.0	30.6	3.4	15.6	4.8	35.1

Table 3. Gross Value Added by Kind of Economic Activity: Individual Countries or Areas

Major area, region and country	Year	Gross Value Added (at current prices) Million	Percentage Distributtion: Agriculture, hunting, forestry, fishing A-B	Mining, Manufacturing, Utilities C-E	Of which: Manufacturing D	Construction F	Wholesale, retail trade, restaurants and hotels G-H	Transport, storage and communication I	Other Activities J-P
Ethiopia [4]	1990	22 064	52.0	6.8	4.9	3.0	14.7	3.8	19.7
(Ethiopian Birr)	1995	44 079	55.0	7.0	5.2	2.8	13.5	3.5	18.1
	2000	63 013	47.8	8.4	5.8	4.0	14.5	3.8	21.5
	2005	97 795	45.2	7.7	5.1	5.4	14.6	5.6	21.5
	2010	353 058	45.3	6.1	4.2	4.3	19.4	3.6	21.3
	2015	1 207 369	38.8	5.9	4.7	11.6	20.0	4.4	19.3
	2016	1 463 883	37.2	7.3	6.1	16.2	16.7	4.8	17.9
	2017	1 722 668	35.9	7.7	6.6	17.4	15.7	4.5	18.8
	2018	2 088 668	32.9	7.1	6.1	21.7	15.6	4.0	18.8
	2019	2 575 507	35.5	6.7	5.8	19.2	16.6	3.9	18.1
Gabon [11]	1970	91 242	16.0	45.8	9.2	8.0	9.6	4.2	16.4
(CFA Franc BEAC)	1975	514 033	7.3	48.8	5.9	12.5	6.5	4.7	20.2
	1980	1 102 478	5.6	48.7	5.3	4.3	6.3	4.4	30.7
	1985	1 890 349	5.0	54.1	6.2	4.4	5.9	5.5	25.1
	1990	1 671 999	6.6	39.7	5.4	4.0	10.5	8.9	30.3
	1995	2 557 588	7.3	51.2	4.4	3.3	7.7	6.3	24.1
	2000	3 699 913	5.7	58.2	3.6	2.0	5.7	5.6	22.8
	2005	4 836 222	5.2	60.0	4.7	2.7	5.7	5.1	21.4
	2010	6 589 700	4.2	55.5	4.8	4.1	5.0	4.8	26.5
	2015	7 881 600	4.7	45.0	6.7	6.3	5.6	6.0	31.8
	2016	7 731 318	5.3	41.9	7.8	6.5	5.8	6.7	33.7
	2017	8 202 517	5.6	43.3	7.3	4.8	5.4	9.2	31.8
	2018	8 978 377	5.7	44.7	7.8	6.0	5.4	7.0	31.2
	2019	9 326 397	5.5	43.3	7.7	5.8	5.5	7.6	32.2
Gambia [29]	1970	327	53.3	3.7	3.3	2.4	30.1	0.8	9.7
(Dalasi)	1975	1 190	36.2	7.2	6.9	4.9	35.7	1.1	14.9
	1980	1 594	29.8	8.7	8.5	6.6	34.8	1.6	18.5
	1985	5 006	25.6	5.0	4.5	4.2	50.1	1.6	13.6
	1990	11 247	19.3	7.6	7.1	4.2	55.5	1.9	11.6
	1995	13 561	23.0	7.8	7.0	4.9	45.7	2.8	15.8
	2000	17 823	26.9	7.1	5.9	5.7	42.3	3.3	14.7
	2005	27 701	34.0	8.2	6.7	3.9	33.6	5.6	14.6
	2010	40 733	37.4	6.8	4.8	3.6	32.6	5.5	14.1
	2015	53 451	24.3	9.4	7.0	9.4	35.0	6.9	15.0
	2016	58 978	23.9	8.4	6.1	14.5	32.6	6.6	14.0
	2017	64 755	22.7	7.0	4.8	12.4	37.2	7.1	13.6
	2018	74 314	23.7	7.4	4.7	9.1	38.1	7.4	14.3
	2019	83 218	20.1	6.9	4.7	10.6	39.3	7.7	15.3
Ghana [29]	1970	499 (t)	34.6	27.5	25.5	2.0	6.9	8.2	20.9
(Cedi)	1975	1 240 (t)	33.1	32.5	30.5	2.0	6.3	7.1	19.1
	1980	8 491 (t)	47.6	21.6	20.3	1.3	10.5	5.7	13.3
	1985	74	34.1	29.3	27.7	1.4	14.1	10.6	10.5
	1990	437	32.1	26.7	24.0	1.4	14.5	10.2	15.1
	1995	1 598	30.6	31.6	25.3	3.4	11.9	7.6	14.9
	2000	5 602	27.8	30.9	24.4	3.9	13.6	8.4	15.4
	2005	20 391	29.1	29.2	23.0	4.0	14.2	8.6	14.9
	2010	55 931	28.9	21.7	15.9	6.5	16.0	7.3	19.7
	2015	165 015	22.1	25.3	12.4	9.3	15.9	8.2	19.1
	2016	198 505	22.7	22.9	12.1	7.6	17.7	8.8	20.2
	2017	238 267	21.2	24.6	11.3	8.2	17.9	9.3	18.8
	2018	278 973	19.7	26.9	11.3	7.1	18.9	9.9	17.5
	2019	326 562	18.5	27.8	11.2	6.4	18.6	10.1	18.5
Guinea [1]	1970	86 223	18.1	23.3	3.0	8.4	33.8	4.5	11.9
(Guinea Franc)	1975	136 851	18.1	23.3	3.0	8.4	33.9	4.6	11.9
	1980	200 585	18.1	23.3	3.0	8.4	33.9	4.5	11.8
	1985	602 595	18.3	23.4	3.0	8.4	33.8	4.5	11.6
	1990	2 821 955	19.7	24.8	3.0	8.8	32.8	3.9	10.0
	1995	5 602 178	25.7	18.8	2.9	8.4	30.5	4.9	11.7
	2000	7 171 698	22.7	21.5	3.0	11.2	27.8	5.1	11.7
	2005	14 400 105	14.9	26.3	10.5	8.6	24.2	7.0	19.0
	2010	36 963 700	18.6	27.3	11.3	7.1	21.2	5.2	20.8
	2015	60 520 608	20.1	22.7	13.2	5.9	23.2	5.4	22.6
	2016	70 680 972	19.2	27.4	11.9	5.4	21.9	4.7	21.4
	2017	86 206 362	22.3	30.1	10.9	4.3	19.3	4.3	19.6
	2018	90 873 418	26.2	22.7	11.4	4.2	21.0	4.7	21.2
	2019	104 391 262	22.6	26.7	11.4	4.6	20.7	4.6	20.7

Table 3. Gross Value Added by Kind of Economic Activity: Individual Countries or Areas

Major area, region and country	Year	Gross Value Added (at current prices) Million	Percentage Distributtion						
			Agriculture, hunting, forestry, fishing A-B	Mining, Manufacturing, Utilities C-E	Of which: Manufacturing D	Construction F	Wholesale, retail trade, restaurants and hotels G-H	Transport, storage and communication I	Other Activities J-P
Guinea-Bissau (CFA Franc BCEAO)	1970	124	47.5	13.1	11.4	8.2	20.7	3.0	7.6
	1975	200	47.8	15.6	13.5	9.8	17.8	2.6	6.5
	1980	244	42.2	11.3	9.7	7.4	26.0	3.7	9.4
	1985	1 018	46.5	8.8	6.9	6.8	25.5	3.6	8.8
	1990	23 572	44.6	8.2	3.9	10.0	25.7	3.7	7.8
	1995	209 217	55.1	10.2	7.9	2.0	18.1	3.2	11.4
	2000	251 999	43.4	14.4	13.9	0.3	23.7	3.6	14.6
	2005	302 448	45.4	13.7	13.1	1.0	19.9	3.8	16.2
	2010	410 401	46.2	12.2	11.6	1.2	18.9	4.5	17.0
	2015	591 654	49.0	11.9	11.2	1.0	18.5	5.0	14.6
	2016	665 261	48.7	12.5	11.9	0.7	20.1	4.6	13.4
	2017	740 206	52.1	11.9	11.2	1.5	16.7	4.4	13.4
	2018	770 326	49.9	11.9	11.0	1.4	18.3	4.6	13.8
	2019	808 770	51.0	11.7	11.0	1.2	18.2	4.5	13.5
Kenya [1,29] (Kenyan Shilling)	1970	17 870	32.1	22.0	15.3	3.6	5.6	5.7	31.0
	1975	34 415	30.2	23.2	17.5	3.4	5.7	5.3	32.2
	1980	73 930	28.2	25.2	18.9	3.6	5.7	5.3	32.0
	1985	144 530	28.7	22.2	17.0	3.0	6.2	6.3	33.7
	1990	275 078	25.5	21.7	17.0	3.1	5.9	6.7	37.2
	1995	639 100	27.6	18.3	14.4	2.6	8.7	7.3	35.5
	2000	988 893	28.2	17.4	14.1	3.2	9.4	7.6	34.2
	2005	1 464 002	23.2	17.8	14.4	4.5	9.6	9.4	35.5
	2010	2 899 327	27.1	15.4	12.3	4.9	10.1	9.8	32.6
	2015	5 888 886	32.2	13.2	10.0	5.2	8.9	10.2	30.2
	2016	6 615 436	33.0	13.5	9.9	5.5	8.4	10.1	29.4
	2017	7 671 760	37.1	12.0	8.6	5.9	8.6	9.3	27.2
	2018	8 326 277	36.4	11.7	8.3	5.8	8.8	10.1	27.2
	2019	9 108 881	36.5	11.3	8.1	5.9	8.9	10.4	26.9
Lesotho [29] (Loti)	1970	50	24.4	7.0	5.2	1.2	21.2	3.4	42.9
	1975	99	22.8	8.9	7.1	2.5	20.5	6.9	38.5
	1980	260	19.2	15.4	6.7	4.5	12.0	3.7	45.2
	1985	511	16.9	11.4	9.6	5.5	13.6	5.1	47.5
	1990	1 279	13.6	15.9	12.9	9.8	12.1	5.3	43.3
	1995	3 034	9.3	16.9	12.2	17.3	12.3	4.8	39.5
	2000	5 304	8.3	24.2	17.4	15.0	11.5	4.5	36.5
	2005	8 618	6.1	34.2	24.2	5.9	12.4	6.3	35.1
	2010	15 004	5.3	26.4	14.3	7.9	14.0	6.2	40.2
	2015	26 971	4.2	31.9	16.9	5.7	12.7	5.9	39.6
	2016	28 386	6.3	28.8	18.3	4.7	13.4	6.0	40.8
	2017	28 451	6.1	27.5	17.0	4.6	13.7	5.7	42.3
	2018	30 158	5.0	31.3	18.4	4.3	12.1	5.4	42.0
	2019	31 168	5.0	30.0	18.2	4.8	13.0	5.7	41.5
Liberia [12] (US Dollar)	1970	297	24.7	35.6	4.0	4.8	11.1	8.3	15.4
	1975	575	11.1	49.1	6.4	5.1	8.7	7.2	18.7
	1980	829	19.6	30.7	9.5	4.0	9.7	7.5	28.5
	1985	999	35.9	21.4	6.6	3.3	6.1	7.3	26.0
	1990	562	53.4	13.2	11.2	3.3	6.4	9.8	13.8
	1995	197	80.5	3.6	2.7	1.5	3.1	4.7	6.6
	2000	603	71.7	0.5	0.3	0.1	16.5	4.7	6.4
	2005	587	68.8	6.5	5.6	3.2	4.9	6.6	9.9
	2010	991	64.5	9.9	5.8	2.6	5.0	5.4	7.4
	2015	2 287	69.5	8.4	5.6	2.1	5.6	6.1	8.3
	2016	2 411	73.7	6.6	5.0	1.2	5.2	5.7	7.7
	2017	2 410	73.6	7.0	4.7	1.6	5.0	5.5	7.4
	2018	2 442	72.5	7.2	4.4	2.1	5.1	5.6	7.5
	2019	2 360	74.0	6.8	4.1	1.9	4.8	5.3	7.1
Libya (Libyan Dinar)	1970	1 384	2.6	64.4	1.8	5.8	2.8	3.4	20.9
	1975	3 956	2.3	55.4	1.8	10.1	4.7	4.8	22.6
	1980	10 994	1.8	66.0	1.9	7.8	3.7	3.5	17.1
	1985	8 792	3.5	49.2	4.5	9.6	5.3	4.9	27.4
	1990	9 871	6.8	33.9	6.6	5.8	7.5	7.0	39.1
	1995	13 276	6.7	35.1	7.2	5.2	7.4	7.1	38.5
	2000	21 020	6.5	40.6	5.4	7.0	6.2	6.0	33.6
	2005	66 921	2.2	71.7	4.7	4.0	4.0	3.6	14.6
	2010	103 071	2.5	66.2	5.6	7.8	4.3	4.3	15.0
	2015	19 708	0.9	65.6	3.7	1.5	4.7	3.4	23.8

Table 3. Gross Value Added by Kind of Economic Activity: Individual Countries or Areas

Major area, region and country	Year	Gross Value Added (at current prices) Million	Percentage Distributtion: Agriculture, hunting, forestry, fishing A-B	Mining, Manufacturing, Utilities C-E	Of which: Manufacturing D	Construction F	Wholesale, retail trade, restaurants and hotels G-H	Transport, storage and communication I	Other Activities J-P
	2016	19 936	0.9	65.6	3.7	1.5	4.7	3.4	23.8
	2017	31 621	0.9	65.6	3.7	1.5	4.7	3.4	23.8
	2018	42 013	0.9	65.6	3.7	1.5	4.7	3.4	23.8
	2019	41 582	0.9	65.6	3.7	1.5	4.7	3.4	23.8
Madagascar [1]	1970	66 721	27.3	12.1	8.8	3.4	18.8	9.9	28.5
(Malagasy Ariary)	1975	104 262	38.5	11.9	8.7	3.3	15.2	8.0	23.0
	1980	181 736	33.9	12.0	8.8	3.4	16.5	8.7	25.6
	1985	406 958	39.4	10.6	7.8	3.0	16.6	8.8	21.6
	1990	993 107	36.9	11.6	8.5	3.3	18.0	9.5	20.7
	1995	2 924 446	38.0	11.4	8.2	3.0	17.3	10.4	19.9
	2000	5 596 922	33.5	11.2	8.3	4.0	18.8	10.0	22.5
	2005	10 826 200	32.3	11.6	9.7	6.6	17.4	9.8	22.2
	2010	19 995 396	30.3	11.8	9.3	7.0	16.1	9.7	25.0
	2015	31 708 923	27.0	13.2	8.9	6.7	16.6	8.5	28.1
	2016	35 964 268	26.3	14.0	10.7	6.3	17.7	7.7	28.0
	2017	39 298 162	25.7	14.1	9.6	6.9	16.3	9.3	27.8
	2018	43 222 482	25.5	15.7	9.9	7.1	14.0	8.2	29.6
	2019	48 588 154	24.1	15.8	10.6	7.8	14.2	8.0	30.1
Malawi [29,32]	1970	566	69.2	11.8	10.7	6.4	3.0	1.6	8.1
(Kwacha)	1975	1 037	52.7	17.0	16.0	9.7	5.0	3.3	11.7
	1980	1 905	49.4	21.6	19.9	12.4	3.4	2.0	11.1
	1985	2 996	50.0	23.3	21.6	4.8	4.6	2.3	14.9
	1990	8 356	46.0	25.4	21.8	5.2	6.3	2.4	14.7
	1995	34 926	31.9	19.7	18.2	2.2	12.5	4.8	28.9
	2000	177 944	41.4	16.8	14.9	2.7	10.7	4.3	24.0
	2005	384 015	37.1	13.6	11.6	3.2	12.8	5.0	28.3
	2010	971 608	31.9	13.2	10.7	3.2	18.7	6.7	26.3
	2015	2 844 563	32.4	13.2	10.8	3.2	20.3	7.9	23.0
	2016	3 365 184	31.6	13.1	10.7	3.2	20.3	8.1	23.6
	2017	4 086 291	32.0	12.7	10.4	3.2	20.3	8.2	23.6
	2018	4 616 277	31.1	12.7	10.4	3.2	20.4	8.4	24.1
	2019	5 225 399	30.8	12.7	10.4	3.2	20.3	8.6	24.3
Mali [1]	1970	98 557	76.3	7.4	6.7	2.0	4.7	1.7	7.9
(CFA Franc BCEAO)	1975	180 224	74.3	6.9	6.1	2.2	5.5	2.0	9.2
	1980	367 955	54.9	8.4	6.8	4.6	10.6	3.7	17.7
	1985	572 250	36.1	10.6	9.1	4.1	12.5	5.7	31.1
	1990	735 418	44.2	11.6	10.3	3.6	13.1	5.3	22.1
	1995	1 362 982	38.8	11.7	10.1	6.3	11.9	7.0	24.3
	2000	1 951 527	34.9	16.2	14.5	7.6	12.3	6.9	22.2
	2005	3 000 492	34.4	16.4	14.2	9.5	13.1	6.2	20.3
	2010	4 892 761	34.9	17.4	16.1	8.0	12.9	5.6	21.2
	2015	7 253 263	39.8	14.7	13.8	4.6	13.3	5.8	21.8
	2016	7 645 349	40.1	15.3	14.3	4.7	12.5	5.6	21.7
	2017	8 227 587	40.0	16.1	15.2	4.9	12.0	5.4	21.5
	2018	8 800 949	40.0	17.7	16.8	4.6	11.5	5.2	21.0
	2019	9 488 005	39.8	18.6	17.7	4.6	11.1	5.1	20.8
Mauritania [29]	1970	2 531	36.2	31.0	4.4	2.1	3.1	2.7	24.9
(Ouguiya)	1975	4 376	34.5	27.1	4.5	1.9	6.2	2.5	27.7
	1980	8 493	42.4	19.9	5.0	2.0	4.9	3.5	27.3
	1985	10 723	27.0	32.1	12.1	2.5	7.7	3.5	27.2
	1990	17 512	35.8	28.4	9.3	1.9	7.3	2.8	23.8
	1995	28 162	33.6	29.8	10.3	2.3	8.6	3.4	22.3
	2000	40 454	26.1	30.0	10.4	1.5	13.9	3.7	24.9
	2005	73 258	21.4	31.8	10.3	3.6	15.7	5.6	22.0
	2010	147 339	17.6	37.0	7.1	3.3	12.5	5.2	24.4
	2015	179 937	23.0	18.7	8.3	6.6	15.9	6.7	29.1
	2016	204 828	23.9	22.5	6.7	5.3	14.0	7.3	27.1
	2017	218 735	23.1	23.6	8.5	4.6	15.1	7.1	26.6
	2018	225 971	22.3	22.8	8.7	4.4	15.6	7.1	27.8
	2019	250 342	20.8	23.4	8.1	4.9	15.4	7.4	28.1
Mauritius [53]	1970	912	24.3	19.3	16.0	5.3	10.0	11.8	29.3
(Mauritius Rupee)	1975	3 090	33.5	20.6	18.3	7.0	9.0	9.1	20.8
	1980	7 946	12.0	23.3	20.6	6.7	14.0	10.6	33.3
	1985	14 939	14.8	27.3	24.6	4.9	12.9	10.1	30.1
	1990	33 811	11.8	27.7	26.1	6.2	16.4	10.3	27.5
	1995	62 314	9.8	25.0	22.5	6.3	16.7	11.3	30.9

Table 3. Gross Value Added by Kind of Economic Activity: Individual Countries or Areas

Major area, region and country	Year	Gross Value Added (at current prices) Million	Agriculture, hunting, forestry, fishing A-B	Mining, Manufacturing, Utilities C-E	Of which: Manufacturing D	Construction F	Wholesale, retail trade, restaurants and hotels G-H	Transport, storage and communication I	Other Activities J-P
			Percentage Distributtion						
	2000	107 325	6.5	24.3	22.5	5.3	17.4	12.7	33.8
	2005	168 216	5.7	21.2	19.2	5.4	19.1	11.9	36.8
	2010	273 999	4.1	18.5	15.9	6.8	18.0	11.0	41.7
	2015	363 549	3.6	17.3	14.7	4.4	18.5	10.6	45.7
	2016	385 903	3.6	16.8	14.0	4.2	18.8	10.6	46.1
	2017	402 998	3.5	15.7	13.4	4.3	19.3	10.6	46.5
	2018	422 315	3.2	15.2	12.9	4.7	19.6	10.6	46.7
	2019	440 031	3.3	14.9	12.6	4.9	19.4	10.7	46.7
Morocco	1970	20 204	21.6	24.3	19.8	3.9	20.8	5.8	23.7
(Moroccan Dirham)	1975	38 427	18.5	29.7	20.0	5.7	17.4	5.6	23.0
	1980	75 538	19.7	26.1	20.3	5.6	15.0	7.1	26.3
	1985	135 116	17.4	27.8	21.9	5.0	14.5	8.5	26.8
	1990	220 968	18.6	26.3	21.8	4.7	13.5	8.3	28.5
	1995	298 080	15.1	25.8	21.4	3.8	13.6	8.1	33.5
	2000	368 636	13.3	25.3	20.5	4.7	14.5	7.6	34.6
	2005	498 589	13.1	22.8	18.6	6.1	12.9	8.0	37.1
	2010	703 312	14.4	22.7	17.4	5.9	11.8	7.9	37.1
	2015	873 979	14.3	23.3	18.2	6.2	11.2	6.6	38.4
	2016	894 601	13.6	22.9	17.8	6.5	11.7	6.6	38.8
	2017	940 888	14.0	23.2	17.7	6.3	11.8	6.6	38.1
	2018	978 016	13.8	23.2	17.8	6.1	11.9	6.6	38.3
	2019	1 018 022	13.8	22.6	16.9	6.1	11.9	6.9	38.8
Mozambique [54]	1970	107	35.9	30.7	29.1	3.2	9.2	9.2	11.8
(Metical)	1975	150	35.9	30.7	29.2	3.2	9.2	9.2	11.8
	1980	189	37.1	31.2	29.6	3.3	8.7	8.7	11.1
	1985	391	47.5	12.0	11.4	1.2	12.0	12.0	15.3
	1990	3 350	37.1	16.5	15.6	1.9	12.9	13.8	17.7
	1995	25 676	32.3	11.2	10.7	3.0	18.6	14.8	20.2
	2000	71 433	23.0	17.3	15.4	4.3	19.1	16.4	19.9
	2005	174 848	25.7	18.9	15.2	1.5	12.4	13.6	27.8
	2010	340 299	29.8	16.1	11.1	2.1	13.4	13.2	25.4
	2015	564 123	25.9	18.3	9.3	2.1	14.3	11.6	27.7
	2016	666 945	25.8	21.2	9.6	1.9	13.9	9.8	27.4
	2017	756 527	27.8	25.0	9.1	1.7	13.1	9.5	22.9
	2018	805 241	27.3	26.6	9.7	1.6	12.4	9.9	22.2
	2019	849 446	29.3	24.3	10.2	1.4	12.4	9.9	22.7
Namibia [29]	1970	414	8.7	41.2	9.6	4.8	9.0	5.9	30.3
(Namibian Dollar)	1975	789	8.7	41.2	9.6	4.8	9.0	5.9	30.2
	1980	1 791	8.4	46.3	8.9	4.9	8.4	6.2	25.8
	1985	3 379	7.8	37.2	9.8	2.4	7.8	6.3	38.4
	1990	6 640	9.8	29.5	11.3	2.2	8.6	6.8	43.1
	1995	12 975	10.5	21.4	11.3	2.8	10.0	6.7	48.6
	2000	24 799	11.8	23.6	10.7	2.2	12.6	5.7	44.2
	2005	42 360	11.3	24.1	11.4	3.0	14.2	7.3	40.1
	2010	77 518	9.1	26.3	13.3	3.4	13.8	5.7	41.7
	2015	133 754	6.7	24.0	12.4	6.0	14.3	5.0	44.0
	2016	144 232	6.8	26.6	12.7	3.4	13.7	5.3	44.3
	2017	156 441	7.6	25.6	12.9	2.6	13.8	5.2	45.2
	2018	164 499	7.5	26.8	13.0	2.3	12.7	5.0	45.7
	2019	165 315	7.1	26.4	12.7	2.3	13.4	4.8	45.9
Niger [29]	1970	150 549	46.5	16.7	7.8	3.2	12.5	2.7	18.5
(CFA Franc BCEAO)	1975	245 275	45.5	16.6	8.9	3.0	12.0	3.0	19.8
	1980	769 090	37.4	18.9	4.1	6.1	13.5	2.9	21.1
	1985	910 318	32.9	20.1	8.0	3.7	18.8	2.9	21.6
	1990	953 299	30.3	17.8	7.5	2.8	21.2	3.5	24.4
	1995	1 177 935	32.0	14.6	7.6	2.3	23.3	4.5	23.2
	2000	1 562 779	37.0	12.5	7.6	2.6	19.8	4.8	23.2
	2005	2 213 520	41.2	11.2	7.0	2.8	18.3	5.1	21.4
	2010	3 568 586	39.2	16.9	6.0	3.0	17.6	4.7	18.6
	2015	5 342 090	34.9	19.6	7.2	3.5	16.4	4.9	20.6
	2016	5 774 792	37.9	17.5	7.0	3.5	16.3	5.1	19.7
	2017	6 149 734	38.0	17.7	7.0	3.7	16.3	5.2	19.3
	2018	6 718 536	40.7	15.2	6.6	4.0	15.6	5.2	19.4
	2019	7 172 882	40.3	15.9	6.5	3.6	15.9	5.1	19.2

Table 3. Gross Value Added by Kind of Economic Activity: Individual Countries or Areas

Major area, region and country	Year	Gross Value Added (at current prices) Million	Percentage Distributtion: Agriculture, hunting, forestry, fishing A-B	Mining, Manufacturing, Utilities C-E	Of which: Manufacturing D	Construction F	Wholesale, retail trade, restaurants and hotels G-H	Transport, storage and communication I	Other Activities J-P
Nigeria [29]	1970	20 283	19.6	21.9	15.5	9.5	9.7	13.0	26.3
(Naira)	1975	58 854	15.1	29.1	19.4	7.5	8.9	11.6	27.8
	1980	123 039	13.7	33.8	20.3	7.5	9.9	14.8	20.2
	1985	185 976	18.4	30.8	21.3	3.0	10.1	13.5	24.2
	1990	489 766	21.8	32.5	18.0	3.3	14.4	7.4	20.7
	1995	3 069 432	25.7	35.2	20.2	1.7	17.5	4.1	15.8
	2000	6 990 619	21.6	32.6	14.1	1.6	14.8	4.5	24.9
	2005	22 884 896	26.4	25.0	10.2	3.5	16.2	5.4	23.5
	2010	54 612 264	23.9	22.4	6.6	2.9	16.9	12.2	21.7
	2015	94 144 960	20.9	16.7	9.5	3.7	20.1	12.9	25.8
	2016	101 489 492	21.2	14.8	8.8	3.6	21.3	12.9	26.3
	2017	113 719 048	21.1	18.8	8.8	3.8	19.8	11.9	24.7
	2018	127 762 546	21.4	21.3	9.7	4.7	18.1	12.0	22.5
	2019	144 210 492	22.1	21.4	11.6	6.2	16.6	12.8	20.8
Rwanda [29]	1970	18 731	72.9	12.5	7.3	2.0	6.4	0.5	5.8
(Rwanda Franc)	1975	50 626	62.4	11.4	6.5	2.9	7.9	0.4	14.9
	1980	97 209	62.0	11.1	8.6	3.2	8.7	0.9	14.1
	1985	174 328	50.7	13.6	6.9	5.6	6.5	1.8	21.8
	1990	199 512	41.3	18.4	12.3	4.2	6.8	2.3	27.0
	1995	307 210	42.9	10.3	8.2	3.6	0.7	2.3	31.4
	2000	745 000	33.7	13.8	10.5	4.4	7.7	4.4	36.0
	2005	1 493 000	37.0	11.5	9.6	4.9	10.1	5.3	31.2
	2010	3 231 000	26.9	11.6	9.2	6.5	12.6	7.1	35.4
	2015	5 608 000	26.3	10.9	7.6	8.3	12.4	7.1	35.0
	2016	6 250 000	27.6	10.9	7.4	7.6	12.0	7.0	34.9
	2017	7 042 000	28.8	12.4	8.4	6.5	11.0	6.9	34.4
	2018	7 606 000	26.9	12.3	8.3	6.6	12.0	8.0	34.2
	2019	8 525 000	25.7	12.5	9.2	8.2	11.9	8.9	32.9
Sao Tome and Principe [3,8]	1970	1 017 (t)	27.6	9.8	7.7	8.1	25.4	11.8	17.3
(Dobra)	1975	1 460 (t)	27.6	9.8	7.7	8.1	25.4	11.8	17.3
	1980	2 700 (t)	27.6	9.8	7.7	8.1	25.4	11.8	17.3
	1985	3 509 (t)	27.6	9.8	7.7	8.1	25.4	11.8	17.3
	1990	16	27.6	9.8	7.7	8.1	25.4	11.8	17.3
	1995	140	26.4	10.7	8.4	8.9	25.2	11.7	17.1
	2000	578	20.0	9.7	7.6	7.6	28.9	13.7	20.1
	2005	1 340	18.3	7.5	5.3	7.4	24.8	18.3	23.7
	2010	3 498	11.8	12.4	8.9	5.7	33.5	13.1	23.5
	2015	6 868	12.2	8.8	6.5	6.9	31.4	11.6	29.0
	2016	7 550	11.6	9.5	7.2	6.5	31.5	11.4	29.5
	2017	8 077	11.1	10.2	7.6	6.3	31.6	10.9	29.9
	2018	8 425	11.4	9.3	6.7	5.3	31.2	11.8	31.1
	2019	9 071	12.4	8.6	6.2	4.2	30.2	12.3	32.3
Senegal [29]	1970	310 745	22.3	20.4	18.7	0.8	17.7	6.2	32.6
(CFA Franc BCEAO)	1975	520 551	28.3	22.9	21.0	0.9	13.7	6.1	28.1
	1980	810 968	17.8	22.1	20.2	1.3	15.0	6.0	37.8
	1985	1 516 706	17.3	25.7	24.0	1.4	16.3	5.7	33.6
	1990	2 095 552	17.8	26.0	23.9	1.5	15.1	5.5	34.1
	1995	2 989 149	18.3	27.3	24.7	1.7	16.3	5.5	31.0
	2000	3 966 042	18.2	23.4	20.6	2.4	16.9	6.1	33.0
	2005	5 399 807	16.0	23.8	21.2	2.5	15.8	9.5	32.4
	2010	7 555 644	16.6	23.3	19.5	2.3	15.2	9.9	32.6
	2015	9 384 878	16.0	23.9	19.1	2.5	16.0	9.6	32.0
	2016	10 124 160	16.1	23.0	18.3	3.0	15.2	9.7	33.0
	2017	11 025 109	16.6	22.7	17.5	3.0	15.8	9.5	32.4
	2018	11 770 786	16.5	23.3	17.2	3.3	15.8	8.6	32.6
	2019	12 570 700	16.5	22.8	16.7	3.4	15.4	8.8	33.0
Seychelles [1,29]	1970	104	9.7	3.0	2.4	3.4	32.7	3.8	47.3
(Seychelles Rupee)	1975	293	9.6	3.1	2.5	3.2	33.6	4.1	46.4
	1980	953	7.5	3.5	3.3	3.3	35.3	4.4	45.9
	1985	1 212	6.7	6.6	4.6	2.7	36.2	4.6	43.3
	1990	1 840	5.8	6.1	5.0	2.2	41.1	4.1	40.7
	1995	2 474	5.9	9.3	7.3	4.2	16.6	11.9	52.1
	2000	3 600	4.5	14.0	12.6	5.1	18.6	14.3	43.4
	2005	4 277	3.8	12.1	10.3	7.3	18.1	16.7	41.9
	2010	9 922	2.7	11.2	9.5	5.4	28.1	12.8	39.9
	2015	15 483	2.4	10.3	7.1	3.7	23.0	19.2	41.4

Table 3. Gross Value Added by Kind of Economic Activity: Individual Countries or Areas

Major area, region and country	Year	Gross Value Added (at current prices) Million	Agriculture, hunting, forestry, fishing A-B	Mining, Manufacturing, Utilities C-E	Of which: Manufacturing D	Construction F	Wholesale, retail trade, restaurants and hotels G-H	Transport, storage and communication I	Other Activities J-P
			Percentage Distributtion						
	2016	16 017	2.4	10.0	6.8	3.4	23.2	19.1	41.8
	2017	17 292	2.3	10.0	7.1	3.4	23.2	18.8	42.4
	2018	18 343	2.4	10.7	8.1	3.7	22.9	18.5	41.9
	2019	20 389	2.7	9.9	7.2	3.1	22.5	19.6	42.2
Sierra Leone [1]	1970	347	29.0	26.9	9.1	4.0	12.8	10.2	16.8
(Leone)	1975	627	36.0	20.7	7.9	3.0	12.8	10.7	16.9
	1980	1 298	32.4	18.5	7.5	4.3	13.3	15.1	16.5
	1985	6 680	41.0	17.9	4.5	2.5	14.8	9.4	14.4
	1990	126 287	48.2	6.7	3.5	2.4	9.8	7.1	25.9
	1995	838 283	48.1	6.7	3.5	2.4	9.8	7.1	25.9
	2000	1 716 063	48.3	7.1	3.3	2.4	9.8	7.0	25.4
	2005	4 620 614	51.0	9.5	2.6	2.1	9.6	6.5	21.4
	2010	9 843 866	55.2	6.7	2.3	1.4	9.6	6.0	21.2
	2015	20 960 687	60.5	3.5	1.8	1.1	9.7	4.2	21.0
	2016	23 631 324	59.4	5.9	2.0	1.0	9.7	3.9	20.0
	2017	26 860 304	62.0	4.3	2.0	1.0	9.7	3.6	19.4
	2018	31 284 231	61.0	4.6	2.2	0.8	9.4	3.3	20.7
	2019	33 683 835	59.9	5.0	2.0	0.8	9.6	3.5	21.3
Somalia [16]	1970	2 232	57.6	7.6	6.1	5.7	9.3	7.1	12.7
(Somali Shilling)	1975	4 478	56.4	5.0	3.7	5.5	11.0	8.5	13.5
	1980	16 550	67.4	5.1	4.7	2.8	9.5	4.3	10.9
	1985	84 049	66.1	5.4	4.9	2.2	10.1	6.7	9.5
	1990	1 767 373	69.3	2.4	2.0	3.6	9.1	6.5	9.1
	1995	6 658 677	60.1	3.1	2.5	4.2	10.6	9.7	12.3
	2000	17 866 358	60.2	3.1	2.5	4.2	10.6	9.3	12.6
	2005	31 019 046	60.1	3.1	2.5	4.2	10.6	9.7	12.3
	2010	30 036 000	60.2	3.2	2.5	4.2	10.6	9.4	12.5
	2015	28 447 000	60.2	3.2	2.5	4.2	10.6	9.4	12.5
	2016	29 498 794	60.2	3.2	2.5	4.2	10.6	9.4	12.5
	2017	31 678 553	60.2	3.2	2.5	4.2	10.6	9.4	12.5
	2018	33 167 595	60.2	3.2	2.5	4.2	10.6	9.4	12.5
	2019	34 724 527	60.2	3.2	2.5	4.2	10.6	9.4	12.5
South Africa	1970	12 452	7.1	33.2	22.6	4.4	15.0	10.2	30.1
(Rand)	1975	26 853	7.5	35.2	22.4	5.5	14.0	9.9	27.9
	1980	60 973	6.1	44.1	21.4	3.4	12.1	9.3	25.0
	1985	121 203	5.1	39.0	21.6	3.8	11.5	9.2	31.4
	1990	272 743	4.6	35.6	23.4	3.5	14.8	8.9	32.5
	1995	521 285	3.8	30.5	20.9	3.4	14.8	9.7	37.9
	2000	876 089	3.2	28.2	18.6	2.7	15.1	10.4	40.5
	2005	1 469 239	2.7	27.4	18.1	2.9	14.2	10.9	42.0
	2010	2 494 860	2.6	26.3	14.4	3.8	14.9	9.2	43.2
	2015	3 624 907	2.3	25.0	13.4	4.1	15.0	10.2	43.3
	2016	3 891 558	2.5	25.4	13.5	4.0	14.9	9.9	43.3
	2017	4 173 328	2.6	25.4	13.4	3.9	15.0	9.8	43.2
	2018	4 341 290	2.4	25.1	13.2	3.9	15.0	9.8	43.7
	2019	4 523 580	2.1	25.4	13.2	3.8	15.1	9.8	43.8
South Sudan [5]	2010	33 782	5.1	49.1	2.3	6.3	7.6	5.8	26.0
(South Sudanese Pound)	2015	26 526	4.2	38.6	2.2	6.4	10.9	10.6	29.4
	2016	148 557	3.9	39.6	2.2	6.2	9.4	11.4	29.6
	2017	393 595	2.9	44.4	2.6	5.7	8.0	10.5	28.6
	2018	654 270	2.5	50.4	1.9	4.3	7.4	9.8	25.6
	2019	772 788	3.3	47.8	2.0	4.0	7.7	9.8	27.4
Sudan [13]	2010	123 850	42.6	9.9	9.9	4.2	16.8	11.0	15.5
(Sudanese Pound)	2015	505 761	32.0	12.6	6.5	3.6	17.5	10.7	23.5
	2016	605 409	24.3	14.5	7.4	3.8	21.7	10.0	25.6
	2017	815 855	22.6	14.7	6.9	3.0	20.6	8.3	30.9
	2018	1 176 630	21.5	20.6	11.0	3.3	16.3	9.0	29.4
	2019	1 607 295	20.2	18.3	8.3	3.6	16.5	8.8	32.6
Togo [14]	1970	83 283	30.9	24.8	13.8	1.4	14.6	7.1	21.1
(CFA Franc BCEAO)	1975	133 487	22.5	28.9	11.6	3.1	11.3	7.6	26.5
	1980	235 455	25.7	26.1	12.2	3.5	13.4	7.1	24.2
	1985	333 531	30.9	23.3	10.5	2.4	12.9	6.7	23.8
	1990	439 313	30.5	25.8	15.2	2.0	12.4	6.5	22.9
	1995	646 020	34.2	25.6	15.2	2.0	11.4	5.9	21.1
	2000	951 966	30.4	19.6	12.6	1.8	15.1	7.7	25.3

Table 3. Gross Value Added by Kind of Economic Activity: Individual Countries or Areas

Major area, region and country	Year	Gross Value Added (at current prices) Million	Percentage Distributtion						
			Agriculture, hunting, forestry, fishing A-B	Mining, Manufacturing, Utilities C-E	Of which: Manufacturing D	Construction F	Wholesale, retail trade, restaurants and hotels G-H	Transport, storage and communication I	Other Activities J-P
	2005	1 084 585	34.0	14.5	10.1	2.0	14.9	10.1	24.5
	2010	1 543 809	33.8	12.5	8.4	3.5	11.6	12.8	25.8
	2015	2 805 003	24.2	17.9	13.6	2.3	8.2	14.5	33.0
	2016	3 216 930	23.1	19.4	15.6	2.9	8.3	13.3	33.0
	2017	3 328 400	23.0	19.0	15.6	3.1	8.6	13.8	32.6
	2018	3 608 823	22.4	19.1	15.4	2.7	8.5	14.1	33.3
	2019	3 844 161	22.0	19.2	15.5	2.9	8.6	13.9	33.4
Tunisia [1,10]	1970	790	15.2	14.3	8.7	5.2	11.7	8.4	45.2
(Tunisian Dinar)	1975	1 637	18.4	19.7	10.5	6.7	14.3	7.2	33.8
	1980	3 338	14.0	24.7	13.6	6.7	12.8	7.3	34.5
	1985	7 152	14.4	28.3	17.7	6.5	10.7	8.9	31.3
	1990	10 744	14.8	25.7	18.5	4.4	14.9	9.9	30.3
	1995	17 239	10.5	24.4	19.6	5.2	15.4	10.6	33.9
	2000	26 500	11.1	25.0	18.1	4.8	15.0	11.7	32.4
	2005	38 493	10.0	23.9	17.0	4.9	14.9	13.0	33.4
	2010	58 762	8.1	26.5	17.7	4.6	13.9	14.1	32.8
	2015	79 604	10.9	22.0	16.2	4.6	14.5	11.6	36.5
	2016	83 666	10.1	21.2	16.0	4.5	14.6	11.7	37.9
	2017	90 786	10.3	20.9	16.2	4.2	14.7	11.7	38.2
	2018	99 496	11.2	20.5	16.1	4.2	15.0	11.7	37.5
	2019	107 955	10.9	19.9	15.6	4.1	16.4	11.2	38.5
U.R. of Tanzania: Mainland [55]	1970	15 454	17.6	14.5	12.0	4.5	15.0	9.1	39.2
(Tanzanian Shilling)	1975	32 006	17.7	14.0	12.4	3.9	15.1	9.0	40.4
	1980	67 948	21.5	13.4	11.8	3.2	13.4	8.8	39.7
	1985	179 479	27.6	10.5	9.3	2.4	16.7	8.5	34.2
	1990	1 299 608	25.6	15.0	12.9	5.1	18.0	12.7	23.6
	1995	4 077 079	29.2	15.6	11.0	4.5	18.5	13.4	18.9
	2000	9 468 982	27.6	15.1	10.6	5.8	15.5	11.9	24.2
	2005	17 996 115	26.3	15.8	9.9	9.0	13.8	11.3	23.8
	2010	41 141 829	27.6	15.4	9.4	10.2	13.2	10.8	22.8
	2015	86 484 736	29.2	14.6	8.6	12.1	11.8	10.0	22.4
	2016	99 423 658	29.9	14.8	8.5	12.3	11.5	9.3	22.2
	2017	108 956 774	31.3	14.0	8.4	13.3	11.4	8.9	21.0
	2018	118 874 163	30.3	15.1	8.8	14.3	11.3	8.7	20.4
	2019	128 608 262	28.9	15.6	9.2	15.5	10.9	9.1	20.0
Uganda [29]	1970	97	45.6	10.3	7.8	2.3	14.7	3.3	23.8
(Uganda Shilling)	1975	231	45.6	10.3	7.8	2.3	14.7	3.3	23.8
	1980	1 810	46.3	10.1	7.7	2.2	15.0	3.3	23.0
	1985	28 850	50.2	7.7	5.8	1.8	16.1	2.8	21.3
	1990	1 727 779	46.4	10.2	7.0	2.9	14.9	4.0	21.6
	1995	6 430 903	40.2	13.3	8.6	3.7	14.5	3.9	24.3
	2000	10 402 095	31.8	16.1	10.1	4.8	14.6	5.3	27.4
	2005	18 522 451	28.7	16.6	9.9	5.6	14.3	6.7	28.1
	2010	39 727 367	26.3	14.2	10.2	6.3	16.8	8.7	27.7
	2015	74 828 825	25.8	14.2	9.8	8.0	17.4	6.9	27.6
	2016	80 062 160	25.4	14.6	9.8	8.1	16.9	5.8	29.2
	2017	90 373 980	27.0	14.2	9.5	7.5	16.2	5.6	29.4
	2018	103 143 281	23.6	14.3	9.9	8.6	17.7	6.2	29.6
	2019	110 302 120	22.7	14.9	9.7	8.9	17.3	6.0	30.1
Zambia [6,53]	1970	901 (t)	11.0	42.2	15.0	4.1	13.3	7.5	21.8
(Kwacha)	1975	1 493 (t)	13.3	37.9	19.7	3.7	14.5	7.3	23.3
	1980	3 058 (t)	11.5	35.7	18.7	2.5	19.3	6.3	24.7
	1985	7 563 (t)	13.3	48.9	27.5	1.9	12.2	4.6	19.1
	1990	102	17.0	45.7	29.4	2.4	14.0	4.3	16.7
	1995	3 067	15.1	33.0	9.8	3.8	17.0	6.9	24.2
	2000	10 414	17.4	20.6	10.2	4.4	22.7	8.3	26.7
	2005	34 945	15.5	20.9	10.5	7.7	24.2	6.8	24.9
	2010	91 836	10.0	23.5	8.0	10.6	20.9	7.9	27.1
	2015	173 953	5.3	24.8	7.9	10.6	25.4	7.3	26.8
	2016	205 916	6.5	25.8	8.1	10.8	23.6	7.0	26.2
	2017	230 054	4.3	29.8	8.7	10.2	22.0	8.1	25.6
	2018	260 605	3.0	28.6	8.4	9.9	24.3	9.6	24.7
	2019	278 686	3.4	27.4	8.1	9.4	25.7	9.5	24.7
Zanzibar [4,17,55]	1990	24 155	26.5	12.9	11.2	6.5	22.0	4.8	27.3
(Tanzanian Shilling)	1995	94 879	21.3	14.4	12.2	8.1	23.2	5.7	27.3
	2000	210 666	24.1	13.3	11.7	2.8	23.8	5.9	30.1

Table 3. Gross Value Added by Kind of Economic Activity: Individual Countries or Areas

Major area, region and country	Year	Gross Value Added (at current prices) Million	Agriculture, hunting, forestry, fishing A-B	Mining, Manufacturing, Utilities C-E	Of which: Manufacturing D	Construction F	Wholesale, retail trade, restaurants and hotels G-H	Transport, storage and communication I	Other Activities J-P
			Percentage Distributtion						
	2005	452 460	23.0	12.0	10.0	5.5	22.3	8.0	29.2
	2010	1 050 454	25.2	10.5	9.4	8.3	25.4	7.1	23.5
	2015	2 151 002	24.2	10.9	8.4	9.2	22.9	7.2	25.6
	2016	2 499 780	24.1	10.9	7.8	10.2	22.5	6.4	25.8
	2017	2 933 697	23.7	10.2	7.2	11.4	22.9	5.0	26.9
	2018	3 370 842	23.1	9.3	6.5	10.1	27.3	4.5	25.7
	2019	3 768 508	23.2	10.6	7.5	9.5	27.6	5.0	24.2
Zimbabwe [1]	1970	2 236	12.1	26.9	17.8	4.7	24.6	7.5	24.2
(US Dollar)	1975	5 237	13.7	28.9	20.4	4.3	22.4	6.6	24.1
	1980	7 903	11.2	31.1	21.5	2.4	22.9	5.7	26.7
	1985	8 353	17.7	21.6	16.7	2.1	28.1	4.5	26.0
	1990	12 746	12.9	25.5	19.2	2.7	27.1	5.2	26.7
	1995	10 557	11.5	21.9	17.7	1.9	33.1	5.4	26.2
	2000	8 508	19.8	14.8	11.7	1.9	26.0	7.8	29.6
	2005	6 403	10.7	36.4	5.6	0.4	18.9	3.0	30.7
	2010	10 613	10.9	21.8	10.4	1.7	24.6	15.5	25.4
	2015	17 826	9.3	22.6	13.3	2.4	21.1	11.7	32.9
	2016	18 576	8.7	22.1	12.8	2.4	22.2	11.3	33.3
	2017	19 911	9.2	21.2	12.2	2.5	22.7	11.3	33.0
	2018	21 936	9.2	20.3	11.7	2.6	22.5	11.5	33.9
	2019	19 366	9.0	21.2	12.3	2.5	22.5	11.4	33.4
Latin America and the Caribbean									
Anguilla [1]	1970	6 794 (t)	5.3	5.3	2.7	13.1	33.9	11.6	30.8
(East Caribbean Dollar)	1975	14	5.3	5.3	2.7	13.1	33.8	11.6	30.8
	1980	29	5.4	5.3	2.7	12.8	34.0	11.6	30.9
	1985	64	5.6	5.0	2.9	11.5	36.2	11.8	29.9
	1990	181	4.7	3.9	1.9	14.1	36.6	9.2	31.5
	1995	245	3.3	4.7	2.0	9.8	39.7	10.8	31.7
	2000	347	2.4	7.0	3.4	11.0	29.3	11.7	38.7
	2005	527	2.7	8.7	3.1	11.1	29.9	11.7	35.9
	2010	641	2.1	8.2	2.8	7.9	23.9	9.0	49.0
	2015	764	2.3	7.1	2.3	8.7	26.0	10.3	45.7
	2016	739	3.1	7.1	2.1	6.7	27.6	11.2	44.3
	2017	638	2.4	4.1	2.2	7.6	27.0	11.0	47.9
	2018	748	1.5	4.5	2.0	17.1	23.2	9.7	44.0
	2019	861	2.9	5.1	1.8	6.7	34.8	10.4	40.1
Antigua and Barbuda [1]	1970	61	4.5	9.1	7.2	6.0	25.6	14.7	40.1
(East Caribbean Dollar)	1975	169	5.1	8.7	6.8	5.2	28.1	14.3	38.7
	1980	335	3.2	6.3	4.2	6.7	35.5	15.4	32.8
	1985	623	2.2	5.8	3.4	5.6	34.9	16.2	35.3
	1990	1 094	2.0	6.5	2.9	9.2	33.8	15.3	33.0
	1995	1 372	1.9	6.0	1.9	8.5	34.2	15.7	33.7
	2000	2 057	1.7	5.4	1.8	9.6	29.6	15.7	37.9
	2005	2 455	2.0	6.0	2.0	10.4	29.7	14.2	37.8
	2010	2 746	1.8	7.5	2.4	10.8	26.4	12.2	41.2
	2015	3 174	1.8	8.7	3.1	10.0	26.2	11.9	41.3
	2016	3 415	1.8	9.1	3.1	11.2	25.8	12.0	40.1
	2017	3 504	2.0	8.4	2.8	13.3	24.8	11.0	40.4
	2018	3 843	2.0	7.7	2.8	16.1	23.3	10.7	40.2
	2019	4 020	2.0	7.6	2.6	16.5	23.5	10.8	39.6
Argentina	1970	1 (u)	8.7	36.8	33.5	6.3	18.0	4.6	25.7
(Argentine Peso)	1975	19 (u)	6.2	37.8	35.1	8.3	16.4	3.6	27.7
	1980	3 844 (u)	6.0	30.7	27.1	7.4	18.9	3.6	33.5
	1985	5 159 (t)	7.4	32.6	28.0	5.1	19.4	0.4	35.1
	1990	70 021	7.5	29.5	24.3	3.8	17.6	4.1	37.5
	1995	245 624	5.3	21.3	16.7	4.7	19.2	6.2	43.3
	2000	271 274	4.6	21.6	15.9	4.2	18.6	7.1	43.9
	2005	495 456	9.3	29.5	21.6	4.1	16.4	7.3	33.2
	2010	1 393 953	8.5	24.9	18.9	5.2	17.1	7.1	37.2
	2015	5 009 211	6.1	22.1	16.9	5.4	18.6	6.4	41.3
	2016	6 947 933	7.4	21.6	16.0	4.5	18.3	6.3	41.8
	2017	8 975 171	6.5	20.8	15.2	5.1	18.3	6.7	42.6
	2018	12 349 017	7.2	22.4	15.0	4.8	17.7	6.9	41.0
	2019	18 177 409	8.6	23.0	15.3	4.5	17.5	7.1	39.3

Table 3. Gross Value Added by Kind of Economic Activity: Individual Countries or Areas

Major area, region and country	Year	Gross Value Added (at current prices) Million	Percentage Distributtion						
			Agriculture, hunting, forestry, fishing A-B	Mining, Manufacturing, Utilities C-E	Of which: Manufacturing D	Construction F	Wholesale, retail trade, restaurants and hotels G-H	Transport, storage and communication I	Other Activities J-P
Aruba [29,30]	1970	338	0.0	6.5	1.7	5.4	35.7	7.7	44.6
(Aruban Guilder)	1975	439	0.0	6.5	1.7	5.4	35.7	7.7	44.6
	1980	569	0.0	6.5	1.7	5.4	35.7	7.7	44.6
	1985	737	0.0	6.5	1.7	5.4	35.8	7.7	44.6
	1990	1 466	0.0	6.5	1.7	5.4	35.6	7.7	44.8
	1995	2 396	0.0	6.6	2.2	5.3	33.8	8.0	46.3
	2000	3 390	0.0	7.5	3.3	5.0	33.3	7.3	46.9
	2005	4 106	0.0	9.6	3.2	5.5	29.3	7.2	48.5
	2010	4 320	0.0	7.9	3.6	4.1	26.0	8.0	54.0
	2015	4 947	0.0	8.7	3.9	5.0	27.0	8.7	50.6
	2016	5 043	0.0	8.7	3.9	5.2	26.7	8.5	50.8
	2017	5 174	0.0	8.6	4.2	5.0	27.0	8.2	51.2
	2018	5 432	0.0	8.7	4.0	5.1	26.9	8.5	50.8
	2019	5 586	0.0	8.7	4.1	5.1	26.9	8.4	50.9
Bahamas [29]	1970	682	2.2	7.3	3.1	6.6	30.1	6.5	47.3
(Bahamian Dollar)	1975	982	2.2	7.3	3.1	6.6	30.1	6.5	47.3
	1980	1 949	2.2	7.3	3.1	6.6	30.1	6.5	47.3
	1985	2 875	2.2	7.4	3.1	6.5	29.9	6.5	47.6
	1990	4 556	1.5	5.7	2.4	5.7	33.9	7.0	46.2
	1995	6 078	1.9	7.6	2.2	3.7	26.7	6.0	54.1
	2000	7 363	1.5	7.1	3.2	6.2	26.8	6.6	51.8
	2005	9 250	1.1	5.8	2.5	5.7	27.1	8.1	52.1
	2010	9 457	1.2	5.4	2.3	6.9	25.3	7.1	54.1
	2015	10 481	0.9	6.2	2.8	6.6	23.6	10.4	52.2
	2016	10 830	1.0	7.0	3.6	7.5	22.1	9.8	52.6
	2017	11 109	0.9	6.5	3.4	8.5	21.3	8.7	54.1
	2018	11 261	0.8	6.9	2.7	7.7	22.9	8.5	53.2
	2019	11 495	0.7	6.6	2.7	8.6	23.1	7.5	53.4
Barbados [1,29]	1970	415	7.4	12.3	10.9	9.1	26.0	5.8	39.4
(Barbados Dollar)	1975	907	9.0	15.2	14.1	6.4	25.0	5.9	38.5
	1980	1 964	6.8	18.4	16.6	7.5	30.2	4.7	32.5
	1985	2 813	4.3	17.5	14.6	5.2	28.4	7.0	37.7
	1990	3 762	3.7	13.7	11.2	6.4	29.1	6.9	40.1
	1995	4 053	3.5	11.7	8.8	4.8	29.1	8.3	42.6
	2000	5 474	2.2	11.4	8.7	5.7	28.4	7.8	44.4
	2005	6 837	1.8	10.5	7.8	6.1	26.2	10.8	44.6
	2010	8 032	1.5	9.5	6.6	6.3	24.2	12.3	46.2
	2015	8 350	1.5	9.1	6.2	6.4	23.5	12.3	47.3
	2016	8 442	1.5	8.9	6.1	5.8	24.2	13.2	46.5
	2017	8 610	1.5	8.9	6.0	5.7	24.8	12.7	46.4
	2018	8 790	1.7	9.0	6.1	6.0	25.7	11.7	45.9
	2019	9 107	1.5	9.0	6.1	6.1	24.4	12.4	46.6
Belize [1]	1970	42	23.8	10.0	8.7	4.5	21.7	6.3	33.7
(Belize Dollar)	1975	183	28.6	11.3	10.1	5.4	20.8	5.9	28.0
	1980	341	27.3	12.2	10.8	5.0	23.6	5.1	26.8
	1985	417	17.8	17.3	14.3	4.1	18.9	8.5	33.4
	1990	784	18.8	16.3	13.2	6.0	22.7	9.5	26.8
	1995	1 098	17.4	15.5	11.0	4.8	20.5	9.9	32.0
	2000	1 491	16.4	15.1	10.6	5.6	22.1	9.5	31.4
	2005	1 996	14.9	12.6	8.6	4.1	21.6	11.2	35.6
	2010	2 508	12.8	18.1	13.6	2.9	20.7	10.7	34.8
	2015	3 002	14.7	12.5	8.1	3.8	23.9	9.5	35.7
	2016	3 079	12.0	12.1	7.6	4.1	24.4	10.0	37.3
	2017	3 195	12.9	11.7	7.7	3.9	23.1	10.4	38.1
	2018	3 257	11.0	10.1	6.4	3.6	24.2	10.7	40.4
	2019	3 272	11.0	10.2	6.4	3.6	24.7	10.7	39.9
Bolivia (Plurinational State of) [1]	1970	11 (t)	17.7	27.6	17.7	8.8	8.8	8.8	28.2
(Boliviano)	1975	46 (t)	21.7	27.3	13.0	4.3	13.0	6.5	27.0
	1980	122 (t)	18.9	31.1	14.8	4.1	10.7	5.7	29.5
	1985	2 904	28.7	24.3	11.8	4.2	10.7	10.5	21.6
	1990	14 416	16.4	30.9	18.2	3.3	13.0	10.0	26.4
	1995	29 248	16.4	28.9	18.4	3.3	12.5	11.1	27.9
	2000	47 186	14.3	25.0	14.6	3.3	11.4	12.5	33.6
	2005	65 379	13.9	28.4	13.7	2.6	11.0	13.3	30.9
	2010	115 934	12.4	32.7	13.4	3.2	11.7	10.7	29.4
	2015	185 659	12.6	27.3	12.5	3.6	10.6	10.8	35.1

Table 3. Gross Value Added by Kind of Economic Activity: Individual Countries or Areas

Major area, region and country	Year	Gross Value Added (at current prices) Million	Percentage Distributtion: Agriculture, hunting, forestry, fishing A-B	Mining, Manufacturing, Utilities C-E	Of which: Manufacturing D	Construction F	Wholesale, retail trade, restaurants and hotels G-H	Transport, storage and communication I	Other Activities J-P
	2016	202 403	12.9	25.6	12.7	3.7	11.0	11.2	35.6
	2017	224 706	13.4	27.0	12.1	3.4	11.0	10.7	34.5
	2018	241 703	13.2	26.9	11.9	3.3	10.8	10.6	35.1
	2019	249 106	13.9	25.3	11.9	3.3	10.8	10.6	36.2
Brazil [15,54] (Brazilian Real)	1970	0 (u)	11.5	30.4	27.4	5.4	16.4	4.3	31.9
	1975	0 (u)	10.7	34.2	31.3	6.2	14.6	4.0	30.3
	1980	4 (u)	10.1	34.1	31.3	6.8	10.9	4.7	33.4
	1985	516 (u)	11.0	36.8	31.6	5.4	8.5	5.0	33.1
	1990	12	10.1	29.9	25.5	7.1	7.1	4.9	40.9
	1995	626 959	5.5	20.7	17.2	5.3	10.6	3.7	54.3
	2000	1 022 807	5.5	21.4	16.2	5.4	11.3	6.2	50.2
	2005	1 842 818	5.5	23.9	17.4	4.6	12.4	8.0	45.6
	2010	3 302 840	4.8	21.1	15.0	6.3	14.7	8.1	44.9
	2015	5 155 601	5.0	16.8	12.2	5.7	15.7	7.8	49.0
	2016	5 419 822	5.7	16.2	12.5	5.1	15.3	7.7	50.2
	2017	5 669 766	5.3	16.8	12.4	4.3	15.6	7.8	50.2
	2018	5 894 500	5.2	15.9	11.4	5.3	15.6	7.8	50.2
	2019	6 212 777	5.2	15.6	11.0	5.4	15.6	7.8	50.5
British Virgin Islands [1,29,33] (US Dollar)	1970	9 068 (t)	1.1	3.2	2.3	5.3	27.4	7.1	55.9
	1975	15	1.2	2.8	1.8	2.3	33.5	5.7	54.6
	1980	33	0.8	2.0	1.4	1.2	40.0	5.2	50.8
	1985	55	0.7	2.8	1.4	1.6	34.0	4.8	56.1
	1990	115	0.5	3.4	1.9	1.8	33.1	7.8	53.5
	1995	444	0.3	3.9	2.9	2.6	28.4	8.8	56.1
	2000	870	0.2	3.5	2.7	2.2	27.1	8.9	58.1
	2005	1 000	0.2	3.3	2.3	2.2	27.0	8.9	58.4
	2010	1 057	0.1	3.3	2.1	1.5	25.0	8.3	61.8
	2015	1 214	0.1	4.3	2.3	2.4	18.7	8.4	66.1
	2016	1 336	0.1	4.2	2.2	3.0	19.1	8.8	64.8
	2017	1 261	0.1	3.6	2.1	3.0	18.8	8.2	66.2
	2018	1 297	0.1	4.0	2.2	2.8	18.9	8.4	65.7
	2019	1 350	0.1	3.9	2.2	2.9	18.9	8.5	65.6
Cayman Islands [29] (Cayman Islands Dollar)	1970	23	0.3	3.7	1.5	8.5	10.5	7.9	69.0
	1975	69	0.3	3.7	1.5	8.5	10.5	7.9	69.0
	1980	167	0.3	3.7	1.5	8.5	10.5	8.0	69.1
	1985	404	0.3	3.7	1.4	7.4	10.4	8.3	69.8
	1990	948	0.3	3.7	0.9	7.1	11.6	6.8	70.6
	1995	1 339	0.3	3.6	0.9	6.6	10.7	6.6	72.2
	2000	2 351	0.3	3.6	0.9	6.6	10.7	6.6	72.2
	2005	3 145	0.3	3.6	0.9	6.5	10.7	6.5	72.4
	2010	3 290	0.3	3.8	0.8	3.7	10.5	6.3	75.4
	2015	3 720	0.4	3.6	0.9	3.8	11.9	6.6	73.7
	2016	3 868	0.4	3.7	0.9	4.0	11.9	6.6	73.3
	2017	4 067	0.4	3.6	0.9	4.0	12.0	6.6	73.4
	2018	4 317	0.4	3.6	0.9	4.1	12.3	6.4	73.2
	2019	4 735	0.4	3.6	0.9	4.0	12.1	6.5	73.3
Chile [29] (Chilean Peso)	1970	98	5.9	32.8	18.9	7.7	14.9	6.6	32.2
	1975	36 669	5.2	29.4	14.5	7.9	13.9	7.1	36.5
	1980	1 148 381	5.6	27.1	14.8	7.3	13.2	6.2	40.7
	1985	2 831 868	5.9	31.3	15.7	6.0	11.9	6.8	38.0
	1990	9 508 800	6.9	34.8	19.2	7.1	12.8	7.8	30.6
	1995	26 360 202	5.9	32.7	20.3	8.7	12.0	7.7	33.0
	2000	37 775 943	5.7	30.8	19.9	6.8	10.9	8.9	36.9
	2005	62 990 215	4.5	34.6	15.6	5.7	10.1	10.4	34.8
	2010	102 687 580	3.9	32.3	11.7	6.5	10.6	9.0	37.7
	2015	145 684 359	4.0	25.4	12.8	7.2	12.4	9.1	42.0
	2016	155 091 605	4.4	24.1	12.0	7.4	12.7	8.8	42.5
	2017	164 234 628	4.4	25.2	11.4	7.0	12.8	8.1	42.5
	2018	174 540 429	3.9	25.3	11.5	7.2	12.8	7.6	43.2
	2019	181 744 208	3.9	24.5	11.0	7.5	12.3	7.7	44.0
Colombia [29] (Colombian Peso)	1970	179 572	17.5	22.1	19.7	3.3	12.8	7.2	37.1
	1975	557 164	16.6	24.3	22.2	3.0	13.3	6.6	36.3
	1980	2 159 186	13.5	25.1	22.3	4.1	13.1	7.0	37.1
	1985	6 659 680	12.1	26.0	20.9	6.1	14.1	6.6	35.2
	1990	26 778 466	11.7	29.2	19.8	4.4	14.4	7.4	32.8
	1995	95 625 540	9.2	23.3	16.6	6.9	15.1	8.0	37.6

Table 3. Gross Value Added by Kind of Economic Activity: Individual Countries or Areas

Major area, region and country	Year	Gross Value Added (at current prices) Million	Percentage Distribution: Agriculture, hunting, forestry, fishing A-B	Mining, Manufacturing, Utilities C-E	Of which: Manufacturing D	Construction F	Wholesale, retail trade, restaurants and hotels G-H	Transport, storage and communication I	Other Activities J-P
	2000	191 306 406	8.8	26.9	17.1	3.5	13.7	8.2	39.0
	2005	307 697 000	8.3	28.6	17.6	4.7	12.7	9.1	36.6
	2010	495 613 000	6.9	28.4	15.3	6.0	12.2	8.7	37.7
	2015	730 543 000	6.6	23.5	13.7	7.9	13.0	8.9	40.1
	2016	787 719 000	7.2	22.2	13.5	8.2	13.8	8.8	39.8
	2017	835 906 000	7.0	21.8	12.6	7.7	14.1	8.6	40.7
	2018	894 790 000	6.9	22.4	12.3	7.3	14.0	8.6	40.9
	2019	961 807 673	7.4	22.0	12.1	7.0	14.1	8.5	40.9
Costa Rica [29]	1970	7 614	17.0	22.4	20.7	5.8	20.4	6.5	27.8
(Costa Rican Colon)	1975	19 569	15.4	25.1	23.0	7.1	18.6	7.3	26.5
	1980	47 422	13.7	23.7	21.4	8.7	19.9	6.6	27.3
	1985	228 539	14.4	28.6	25.2	5.0	20.1	7.7	24.3
	1990	608 871	11.9	25.1	21.9	4.4	19.6	7.8	31.1
	1995	1 893 120	14.0	24.4	20.9	4.8	17.6	7.1	32.1
	2000	4 171 293	10.3	24.1	20.3	4.1	16.5	6.3	38.8
	2005	8 640 624	9.6	22.5	18.7	4.4	15.3	7.7	40.5
	2010	17 956 520	7.2	19.2	15.8	6.2	13.4	7.7	46.4
	2015	26 871 746	5.4	15.8	12.4	5.3	13.6	9.3	50.5
	2016	28 577 693	5.6	15.9	12.4	5.0	13.4	9.4	50.7
	2017	30 571 954	5.4	15.9	12.7	4.6	13.4	9.8	50.8
	2018	32 301 480	4.9	15.9	12.7	4.9	13.4	10.0	50.9
	2019	33 489 590	4.6	15.7	12.4	4.3	13.0	10.3	52.1
Cuba	1970	6 240	10.2	13.6	11.4	6.8	28.2	9.9	31.3
(Cuban Peso)	1975	11 708	10.2	13.6	11.4	6.8	28.2	9.9	31.3
	1980	15 710	10.1	13.6	11.5	6.8	28.5	9.9	31.1
	1985	22 927	9.5	13.6	11.8	7.1	30.8	9.5	29.6
	1990	23 967	10.8	12.5	10.2	7.6	27.4	8.7	32.9
	1995	23 472	6.4	21.0	18.5	4.9	28.7	6.1	32.8
	2000	30 170	6.7	20.0	16.6	5.8	25.2	9.3	32.9
	2005	42 150	4.4	16.1	14.1	5.7	23.9	8.9	41.0
	2010	63 670	3.7	18.1	15.8	5.0	23.8	8.3	41.1
	2015	86 216	3.9	17.1	15.1	5.4	24.0	8.7	40.9
	2016	90 393	4.0	16.1	14.0	7.1	24.8	9.3	38.7
	2017	95 857	3.8	15.7	13.6	8.9	25.3	9.2	37.0
	2018	98 898	3.8	15.0	13.0	10.2	25.0	9.1	36.9
	2019	104 224	3.9	15.6	13.5	8.7	25.1	9.2	37.5
Curaçao [34]	2005	3 945	0.6	10.8	6.4	5.6	14.7	7.9	60.4
(Netherlands Antillian Guilder)	2010	4 886	0.5	10.3	6.6	6.0	15.0	10.9	57.4
	2015	5 149	0.5	13.8	11.8	6.4	16.0	11.9	51.4
	2016	5 061	0.4	13.5	11.4	6.6	15.6	11.4	52.5
	2017	5 038	0.4	13.4	11.2	6.8	15.4	11.3	52.7
	2018	5 073	0.4	12.1	9.8	6.5	16.0	11.4	53.7
	2019	5 024	0.4	13.0	10.8	6.6	15.7	11.3	53.0
Dominica [1]	1970	39	41.0	2.9	1.7	4.1	9.6	1.1	41.3
(East Caribbean Dollar)	1975	83	22.0	7.7	4.1	4.3	13.1	5.7	47.3
	1980	182	23.2	7.7	4.3	7.1	10.1	6.4	45.5
	1985	282	21.0	9.2	5.8	3.7	10.7	11.3	44.1
	1990	471	18.9	10.2	6.4	4.2	13.0	13.6	40.1
	1995	656	13.7	11.3	6.4	5.0	14.0	14.6	41.4
	2000	809	13.2	13.1	7.6	4.5	13.8	13.9	41.4
	2005	840	13.5	11.0	4.7	4.3	13.8	14.3	43.3
	2010	1 113	13.7	9.0	2.8	5.1	16.6	13.6	42.0
	2015	1 245	16.5	10.8	4.7	3.9	13.4	15.6	39.8
	2016	1 325	19.1	9.3	3.1	4.8	12.4	15.9	38.5
	2017	1 195	15.8	7.9	2.3	5.1	12.0	15.8	43.3
	2018	1 195	13.8	7.2	2.7	12.5	15.3	17.9	33.3
	2019	1 284	16.0	7.7	2.7	11.0	15.2	17.7	32.4
Dominican Republic [29]	1970	1 863	17.3	37.6	33.5	3.7	16.6	8.7	16.2
(Dominican Peso)	1975	4 668	15.5	40.2	36.6	5.0	16.3	6.6	16.4
	1980	7 859	15.9	33.3	29.3	5.7	17.3	6.5	21.2
	1985	16 955	13.4	37.0	32.6	4.9	17.4	9.7	17.6
	1990	74 906	13.9	29.8	26.5	6.5	15.4	8.0	26.4
	1995	196 541	10.7	27.1	23.7	7.9	17.4	6.6	30.2
	2000	356 038	7.4	26.4	23.2	8.6	15.5	8.2	33.8
	2005	1 010 305	7.7	23.0	19.7	9.5	18.7	9.7	31.4
	2010	1 849 807	6.5	19.1	16.4	10.8	18.6	11.2	33.8

Table 3. Gross Value Added by Kind of Economic Activity: Individual Countries or Areas

Major area, region and country	Year	Gross Value Added (at current prices) Million	Percentage Distributtion						
			Agriculture, hunting, forestry, fishing A-B	Mining, Manufacturing, Utilities C-E	Of which: Manufacturing D	Construction F	Wholesale, retail trade, restaurants and hotels G-H	Transport, storage and communication I	Other Activities J-P
	2015	2 982 624	5.9	19.6	15.8	11.0	19.5	10.0	33.9
	2016	3 240 875	5.9	19.5	15.5	10.2	20.0	9.9	34.5
	2017	3 530 288	5.8	18.9	15.2	11.3	19.6	10.0	34.4
	2018	3 921 807	5.6	18.8	15.3	12.3	19.4	9.9	34.0
	2019	4 224 604	5.6	18.5	14.9	12.9	18.8	9.9	34.3
Ecuador [29]	1970	2 722	27.4	25.8	24.4	3.1	15.5	5.2	23.1
(US Dollar)	1975	7 462	23.2	22.6	19.5	3.9	13.2	5.2	31.9
	1980	17 205	16.7	22.3	19.1	5.6	11.2	7.8	36.5
	1985	16 479	19.6	27.2	22.5	3.5	12.7	9.3	27.7
	1990	14 588	21.4	28.3	23.3	3.1	15.9	9.1	22.2
	1995	23 654	22.6	25.4	22.9	2.6	12.1	8.0	29.3
	2000	17 273	16.3	30.4	23.7	5.2	17.1	9.5	21.4
	2005	39 205	10.0	25.9	15.0	7.5	13.8	10.7	32.1
	2010	66 499	10.2	26.5	14.0	9.8	12.9	8.1	32.5
	2015	92 043	10.2	22.3	15.6	12.1	13.4	7.3	34.7
	2016	93 038	10.2	21.5	15.6	12.9	12.6	7.9	34.9
	2017	97 083	10.0	22.5	15.4	12.5	12.6	7.5	34.9
	2018	98 989	9.7	22.7	15.2	12.2	12.6	7.6	35.1
	2019	100 041	9.7	23.0	15.0	11.7	12.6	7.6	35.5
El Salvador [18,29]	1970	861	28.8	19.3	17.6	2.7	23.7	5.2	20.4
(US Dollar)	1975	1 497	23.3	18.8	17.3	4.7	27.6	4.4	21.3
	1980	2 977	28.2	16.3	14.0	3.3	24.0	3.7	24.5
	1985	4 795	18.4	17.8	15.3	3.0	28.5	4.5	27.9
	1990	4 528	17.0	21.5	19.9	3.3	18.7	7.5	31.9
	1995	8 147	12.6	23.1	21.0	4.8	19.6	7.8	32.0
	2000	10 916	7.7	24.1	21.1	4.9	16.7	8.8	37.7
	2005	13 402	6.8	21.7	18.2	5.1	15.9	10.1	40.4
	2010	16 928	7.6	22.2	17.6	5.3	15.1	8.8	40.9
	2015	21 289	6.1	22.3	18.0	5.6	16.1	8.7	41.3
	2016	21 990	6.3	21.8	17.9	5.6	15.9	9.1	41.4
	2017	22 651	5.9	22.0	17.7	5.8	15.8	8.8	41.6
	2018	23 627	5.6	22.2	17.7	6.0	15.8	8.7	41.6
	2019	24 495	5.6	21.9	17.4	6.4	15.7	8.7	41.7
Grenada [1]	1970	32	20.0	5.6	4.5	14.2	18.2	9.3	32.7
(East Caribbean Dollar)	1975	93	28.7	6.3	4.5	7.1	18.1	9.7	30.1
	1980	203	23.6	5.6	3.5	6.8	17.6	12.5	33.9
	1985	302	16.1	8.7	5.7	7.5	17.2	13.6	36.9
	1990	517	12.5	10.0	6.1	6.7	16.9	18.6	35.3
	1995	677	9.5	11.1	6.1	7.5	19.7	21.7	30.4
	2000	1 233	5.9	9.6	5.2	10.8	16.0	17.1	40.6
	2005	1 641	3.4	7.1	3.3	19.0	10.9	15.9	43.6
	2010	1 823	5.2	8.7	3.9	8.1	11.8	12.9	53.4
	2015	2 329	8.6	8.1	4.0	6.2	13.9	11.7	51.5
	2016	2 417	7.4	7.7	4.0	6.7	15.1	11.5	52.8
	2017	2 552	6.4	7.1	3.7	8.0	15.2	11.7	52.9
	2018	2 635	6.3	7.3	3.8	8.9	15.7	11.9	51.4
	2019	2 782	5.8	7.4	4.0	8.5	15.3	12.4	50.7
Guatemala [29]	1970	1 517	18.1	21.6	19.9	2.1	16.3	5.2	36.7
(Quetzal)	1975	2 896	18.7	21.1	19.1	2.4	16.2	5.2	36.4
	1980	6 387	16.2	23.7	20.6	3.7	15.8	5.0	35.5
	1985	8 982	17.0	22.0	19.8	2.7	16.3	5.2	36.7
	1990	27 586	17.0	21.6	18.8	3.3	16.3	5.2	36.6
	1995	68 957	15.8	20.8	17.5	3.9	16.7	5.3	37.6
	2000	122 016	14.8	20.1	16.2	4.7	17.0	5.4	38.1
	2005	190 179	13.0	19.6	15.2	5.3	18.9	6.3	37.0
	2010	308 491	11.4	19.7	15.0	4.5	20.1	8.1	36.2
	2015	448 192	10.6	19.0	15.2	5.2	22.5	7.9	34.9
	2016	472 698	10.3	18.7	15.1	5.4	23.2	7.8	34.7
	2017	495 007	10.3	18.2	15.0	5.1	23.7	7.5	35.2
	2018	516 272	10.1	17.8	14.9	5.1	23.8	7.4	35.8
	2019	554 651	10.0	17.7	14.7	5.6	23.7	7.3	35.7
Guyana [1,53]	1970	825	10.8	37.0	17.8	8.7	18.9	4.8	19.9
(Guyana Dollar)	1975	1 926	18.7	38.0	23.1	8.0	15.2	3.9	16.1
	1980	2 344	14.4	37.1	19.5	8.6	15.6	5.0	19.3
	1985	2 860	20.0	22.2	16.5	9.3	15.5	7.3	25.7
	1990	24 241	31.0	21.4	9.6	6.3	14.0	7.9	19.5

Table 3. Gross Value Added by Kind of Economic Activity: Individual Countries or Areas

Major area, region and country	Year	Gross Value Added (at current prices) Million	Percentage Distributtion: Agriculture, hunting, forestry, fishing A-B	Mining, Manufacturing, Utilities C-E	Of which: Manufacturing D	Construction F	Wholesale, retail trade, restaurants and hotels G-H	Transport, storage and communication I	Other Activities J-P
	1995	129 718	37.1	27.0	7.6	6.3	9.7	5.5	14.4
	2000	189 658	27.7	25.1	6.6	7.5	10.0	8.6	21.1
	2005	368 056	37.2	15.0	7.2	8.7	7.8	7.0	24.4
	2010	664 080	30.0	16.2	6.0	10.0	9.4	6.2	28.1
	2015	833 118	27.0	18.2	6.3	8.0	8.2	6.2	32.4
	2016	870 804	21.7	23.2	5.3	8.1	8.0	6.3	32.8
	2017	914 690	24.4	19.9	5.1	8.2	8.3	6.2	33.0
	2018	912 424	21.3	20.0	5.1	8.7	8.7	6.7	34.7
	2019	981 621	19.3	22.9	5.5	8.6	8.7	5.9	34.5
Haiti (Gourde)	1970	2 064	46.9	16.5	13.9	2.8	17.4	1.9	14.6
	1975	4 353	42.5	16.3	14.2	5.2	17.4	2.0	16.5
	1980	8 775	33.7	21.1	19.1	5.6	19.5	1.9	18.1
	1985	12 791	33.3	18.0	16.9	6.7	18.7	1.7	21.6
	1990	14 918	30.9	16.9	14.2	7.1	23.1	4.7	17.4
	1995	39 422	24.3	21.4	19.8	10.0	17.7	7.5	19.1
	2000	74 876	23.5	10.9	10.0	21.1	19.0	10.1	15.6
	2005	159 798	18.9	17.2	16.1	19.6	19.8	12.9	11.5
	2010	264 209	25.7	8.5	7.5	18.9	20.9	17.1	8.9
	2015	414 869	17.3	9.3	8.0	25.4	26.4	13.4	8.3
	2016	470 742	17.7	9.7	8.5	23.8	27.4	13.0	8.3
	2017	541 613	18.6	9.8	8.7	22.3	28.4	12.9	7.9
	2018	616 965	18.6	9.4	8.4	22.3	28.9	12.9	7.9
	2019	673 365	19.9	10.5	9.3	24.7	25.7	11.8	7.3
Honduras [1] (Lempira)	1970	1 642	28.5	16.8	15.7	5.8	17.2	9.0	22.7
	1975	2 691	25.2	18.4	17.1	6.0	18.5	9.4	22.5
	1980	6 129	21.7	17.4	16.1	6.6	19.4	9.8	25.1
	1985	8 443	20.4	17.5	15.9	6.3	16.5	9.3	30.1
	1990	14 563	21.0	20.2	18.0	5.9	14.4	9.3	29.1
	1995	42 056	20.4	23.5	19.9	6.4	15.2	7.1	27.4
	2000	100 781	15.2	24.9	21.7	6.2	15.6	8.1	30.1
	2005	174 758	13.1	22.2	20.1	5.4	17.3	7.5	34.5
	2010	292 743	11.9	20.0	16.9	6.1	16.8	6.9	38.4
	2015	445 207	12.6	21.2	18.1	5.3	17.5	7.4	35.9
	2016	477 365	12.5	21.1	17.8	5.7	17.4	7.6	35.7
	2017	521 983	13.2	21.5	17.8	6.1	17.4	7.2	34.6
	2018	548 951	12.1	21.5	17.6	6.6	17.9	7.1	34.8
	2019	588 460	11.2	22.0	17.1	6.6	17.7	7.4	35.1
Jamaica [1] (Jamaican Dollar)	1970	1 400	6.0	24.3	13.1	8.8	24.6	6.4	29.8
	1975	3 189	6.7	22.0	13.8	6.3	24.8	6.9	33.3
	1980	5 861	7.5	26.2	13.5	3.8	23.9	5.8	32.9
	1985	14 062	5.4	22.7	15.8	5.7	26.8	9.1	30.3
	1990	38 762	5.7	24.7	15.2	7.4	23.2	9.4	29.6
	1995	215 689	9.2	21.6	13.1	7.8	25.0	8.3	28.0
	2000	358 729	6.7	17.1	10.1	7.2	23.7	10.3	34.9
	2005	641 127	5.7	15.8	8.5	8.2	23.4	10.9	36.1
	2010	1 035 161	5.9	13.0	8.6	7.0	22.3	9.7	42.1
	2015	1 450 858	7.2	14.5	9.1	7.6	23.3	7.9	39.5
	2016	1 531 281	7.6	14.3	8.8	7.7	23.0	7.9	39.6
	2017	1 626 796	7.7	15.0	9.0	7.7	22.7	7.7	39.2
	2018	1 747 288	7.6	15.8	8.9	7.8	22.4	7.6	38.7
	2019	1 816 746	8.2	14.4	9.0	7.9	22.8	7.5	39.1
Mexico [29] (Mexican Peso)	1970	605	9.9	25.3	19.6	7.6	25.5	4.6	27.2
	1975	1 465	9.3	26.0	19.7	8.8	25.3	5.5	25.2
	1980	5 835	6.8	32.5	19.0	9.2	22.9	6.2	22.4
	1985	63 676	7.3	38.2	19.5	6.1	22.4	6.3	10.8
	1990	891 054	6.5	32.0	20.4	5.7	21.8	7.1	26.9
	1995	2 215 491	4.6	28.2	20.1	6.0	19.7	7.4	34.0
	2000	6 381 264	3.5	28.5	20.1	7.6	20.5	8.5	31.6
	2005	9 166 843	3.2	26.3	16.5	8.0	19.5	8.6	34.4
	2010	12 824 132	3.4	25.7	16.3	8.0	18.9	9.0	35.0
	2015	17 478 364	3.4	24.2	18.3	7.7	21.6	8.7	34.5
	2016	18 859 734	3.6	23.7	18.2	7.8	22.5	8.5	34.0
	2017	20 699 790	3.6	24.8	18.4	7.8	22.6	8.4	32.8
	2018	22 191 164	3.6	24.9	18.4	7.9	22.6	8.5	32.5
	2019	23 073 202	3.6	24.7	18.3	8.1	22.4	8.4	32.8

Table 3. Gross Value Added by Kind of Economic Activity: Individual Countries or Areas

Major area, region and country	Year	Gross Value Added (at current prices) Million	Percentage Distributtion						
			Agriculture, hunting, forestry, fishing A-B	Mining, Manufacturing, Utilities C-E	Of which: Manufacturing D	Construction F	Wholesale, retail trade, restaurants and hotels G-H	Transport, storage and communication I	Other Activities J-P
Montserrat [1]	1970	14	4.4	11.0	9.2	10.0	32.8	5.6	36.1
(East Caribbean Dollar)	1975	26	4.7	11.8	9.8	10.8	32.3	5.8	34.7
	1980	69	3.5	10.9	9.3	7.6	30.9	5.6	41.6
	1985	107	4.0	11.1	8.8	6.6	31.2	9.6	37.6
	1990	181	2.2	5.2	3.9	30.4	19.9	9.4	32.8
	1995	164	4.9	6.8	4.9	5.5	25.8	13.2	43.8
	2000	86	1.3	3.7	1.3	13.7	11.0	12.5	57.8
	2005	118	0.9	5.4	1.7	11.3	9.3	10.8	62.3
	2010	138	1.1	5.1	1.7	8.2	7.5	6.7	71.4
	2015	148	1.4	6.5	1.8	5.8	10.0	7.6	68.7
	2016	150	1.5	7.1	2.6	6.9	9.6	7.2	67.7
	2017	143	1.4	7.6	2.6	4.8	9.2	7.9	69.1
	2018	148	1.2	8.2	2.7	4.9	9.5	8.2	67.9
	2019	163	1.1	8.3	2.8	7.0	9.2	8.3	66.2
Nicaragua	1970	2 (u)	14.7	18.5	16.6	4.4	15.5	10.6	36.3
(Cordoba Oro)	1975	5 (u)	13.1	19.5	17.8	7.5	15.7	10.6	33.6
	1980	9 (u)	14.3	24.3	21.6	4.2	14.5	11.7	30.9
	1985	47 (u)	14.9	26.3	23.9	7.4	13.5	9.3	28.6
	1990	451	19.6	16.8	15.2	4.5	18.9	8.6	31.5
	1995	28 012	22.4	16.7	15.1	5.2	18.8	7.1	29.7
	2000	58 525	19.7	16.0	13.6	6.1	16.9	5.8	35.4
	2005	95 969	17.8	17.3	14.7	5.6	16.0	6.5	36.8
	2010	169 629	18.7	20.4	15.7	3.9	16.7	6.2	34.2
	2015	314 393	17.8	21.9	15.7	6.5	16.2	5.8	31.8
	2016	342 901	16.5	22.4	15.7	6.2	16.6	5.8	32.5
	2017	373 231	16.6	21.3	15.1	6.3	17.1	5.7	33.0
	2018	376 532	16.7	22.4	15.4	5.8	15.1	5.7	34.2
	2019	373 945	17.1	23.8	15.7	4.0	15.1	5.6	34.4
Panama	1970	1 175	11.6	20.8	19.0	4.3	16.8	6.9	39.6
(Balboa)	1975	2 253	8.8	20.2	18.4	4.9	17.3	7.6	41.2
	1980	4 341	7.7	16.9	14.4	4.4	17.4	12.4	41.2
	1985	6 256	7.0	19.3	15.9	2.6	12.5	13.1	45.4
	1990	5 861	8.7	16.7	13.1	0.9	14.3	14.3	45.2
	1995	8 559	7.1	15.9	12.4	3.7	18.1	12.9	42.3
	2000	11 259	6.8	13.3	9.6	4.9	16.4	13.6	45.0
	2005	14 753	6.6	11.6	7.2	4.5	17.2	16.2	44.0
	2010	28 180	3.8	11.0	7.4	9.1	23.6	15.5	37.1
	2015	52 022	2.9	10.4	6.6	18.3	24.4	12.3	31.7
	2016	55 605	2.7	10.3	6.4	19.3	24.0	11.7	31.9
	2017	59 923	2.5	10.1	6.3	20.4	23.3	11.8	32.0
	2018	62 717	2.3	9.8	6.1	20.7	23.2	11.7	32.2
	2019	64 637	2.2	10.3	5.9	20.3	22.7	12.2	32.3
Paraguay [19,29]	1970	91 634	16.5	29.7	29.1	2.2	12.6	5.8	33.3
(Guarani)	1975	221 308	20.0	29.6	28.7	3.1	12.5	6.2	28.8
	1980	666 531	15.6	31.0	29.5	4.9	13.8	6.4	28.3
	1985	1 674 536	15.1	30.2	28.8	4.7	13.6	6.2	30.1
	1990	7 346 845	15.4	34.1	32.5	4.6	16.2	6.1	23.7
	1995	20 369 340	13.2	32.4	30.0	4.8	16.0	6.1	27.5
	2000	32 885 791	10.5	30.8	28.0	4.2	13.6	8.1	32.9
	2005	68 999 198	11.6	40.8	22.0	3.8	13.7	7.9	22.2
	2010	119 910 931	14.0	31.2	20.0	6.0	15.6	7.7	25.4
	2015	174 405 865	10.2	30.8	21.0	6.5	13.9	7.9	30.6
	2016	189 759 707	11.6	30.4	20.6	6.8	13.6	7.6	30.0
	2017	202 840 324	11.1	30.4	21.0	6.8	14.4	7.5	29.8
	2018	214 113 015	11.0	30.5	20.9	6.7	14.0	7.7	30.2
	2019	219 812 973	11.2	29.4	20.1	6.5	14.2	7.2	31.5
Peru [29]	1970	212 (u)	20.0	30.3	14.4	2.9	15.7	9.3	21.8
(Nuevo Sol)	1975	500 (u)	17.7	26.1	14.7	3.7	20.5	11.7	20.4
	1980	5 672 (u)	8.7	48.5	11.7	2.2	16.8	9.1	14.7
	1985	173 (t)	8.7	42.5	15.3	2.9	18.5	9.1	18.3
	1990	5 045	7.9	28.5	20.0	3.9	22.6	9.1	27.9
	1995	108 299	8.9	25.2	17.0	7.1	21.2	8.9	28.6
	2000	164 568	8.9	26.4	16.7	5.5	18.5	9.2	31.6
	2005	228 300	7.5	32.6	18.2	5.2	15.3	8.0	31.5
	2010	381 539	7.5	32.3	17.0	6.8	15.2	8.7	29.5
	2015	552 594	7.7	25.6	15.1	7.6	16.5	9.6	33.0

Table 3. Gross Value Added by Kind of Economic Activity: Individual Countries or Areas

Major area, region and country	Year	Gross Value Added (at current prices) Million	Percentage Distributtion						
			Agriculture, hunting, forestry, fishing A-B	Mining, Manufacturing, Utilities C-E	Of which: Manufacturing D	Construction F	Wholesale, retail trade, restaurants and hotels G-H	Transport, storage and communication I	Other Activities J-P
	2016	594 546	7.6	26.1	14.5	7.2	16.4	9.6	33.1
	2017	632 991	7.4	26.9	14.1	7.1	16.3	9.3	33.0
	2018	671 598	7.5	26.8	14.1	7.4	16.2	8.9	33.3
	2019	696 760	7.6	25.4	13.3	7.4	16.5	9.1	34.0
Puerto Rico [20]	1970	4 920	4.1	30.1	26.0	9.2	16.6	3.8	36.1
(US Dollar)	1975	8 369	4.5	33.1	28.6	6.5	15.0	3.9	37.0
	1980	14 154	3.7	41.7	37.8	3.0	14.6	4.3	32.7
	1985	20 032	2.5	43.4	39.8	1.9	14.2	4.1	34.0
	1990	30 471	2.0	43.5	40.1	2.7	14.1	3.9	33.8
	1995	42 987	1.0	44.9	41.9	2.7	12.8	3.8	34.8
	2000	61 179	1.2	42.6	39.7	3.6	12.6	3.3	36.7
	2005	83 774	0.6	44.8	42.5	2.5	10.8	3.5	37.8
	2010	98 676	0.8	49.2	47.2	1.5	9.4	3.6	35.4
	2015	103 005	0.8	50.1	48.1	1.0	9.5	3.6	35.0
	2016	104 655	0.8	50.2	48.3	0.8	9.5	3.9	34.8
	2017	102 917	0.8	49.7	47.6	0.8	10.0	3.1	35.7
	2018	100 802	0.7	49.1	47.1	1.0	10.1	3.1	35.9
	2019	104 372	0.7	49.7	47.3	1.0	10.0	3.2	35.4
Saint Kitts and Nevis [1]	1970	44	11.7	11.4	10.8	7.8	7.3	6.7	55.0
(East Caribbean Dollar)	1975	98	11.2	11.5	10.9	8.2	8.1	7.0	53.9
	1980	161	9.7	10.4	9.8	11.4	11.7	8.1	48.7
	1985	274	5.4	8.7	8.0	9.5	17.4	9.3	49.8
	1990	527	3.9	9.7	8.8	16.9	17.7	11.4	40.3
	1995	771	3.2	8.5	7.3	14.3	19.4	11.7	42.8
	2000	1 084	1.6	8.6	7.3	19.5	13.0	10.0	47.2
	2005	1 370	1.8	8.7	6.9	15.3	17.0	8.7	48.5
	2010	1 884	1.4	10.8	9.2	14.4	17.4	10.8	45.2
	2015	2 255	1.1	9.0	7.5	17.1	16.4	11.6	44.8
	2016	2 393	1.0	7.9	6.5	20.1	16.0	10.7	44.4
	2017	2 543	1.2	7.2	6.0	22.3	15.4	11.0	42.9
	2018	2 581	1.2	7.4	6.1	20.3	16.2	11.3	43.6
	2019	2 703	1.4	7.3	6.0	20.1	16.7	11.4	43.1
Saint Lucia [29]	1970	75	11.5	8.7	6.6	5.7	23.2	5.7	45.3
(East Caribbean Dollar)	1975	187	11.6	8.2	6.0	5.7	21.2	5.3	47.9
	1980	442	9.5	10.6	8.5	6.9	26.3	9.6	37.0
	1985	714	11.5	9.7	7.1	4.3	23.7	13.2	37.6
	1990	1 351	11.1	9.0	6.7	4.4	27.3	13.0	35.3
	1995	1 854	7.1	8.4	5.6	5.4	26.4	13.9	38.7
	2000	2 288	5.5	8.0	4.0	6.2	22.7	11.5	46.0
	2005	2 665	3.3	8.6	5.0	7.2	23.8	12.5	44.6
	2010	3 553	3.0	7.2	3.8	6.3	27.5	11.6	44.4
	2015	4 248	2.5	7.4	3.4	5.2	34.0	9.3	41.7
	2016	4 381	2.4	7.7	3.6	4.9	34.1	9.6	41.3
	2017	4 724	2.0	7.5	3.5	5.1	35.5	9.9	40.0
	2018	4 861	2.1	7.3	3.7	4.3	35.5	9.4	41.4
	2019	4 995	2.3	7.3	3.9	4.1	34.9	10.7	40.7
Sint Maarten (Dutch part) [3]	2005	1 199	0.3	7.5	1.5	9.0	22.9	13.1	47.3
(Netherlands Antillian Guilder)	2010	1 511	0.1	6.5	1.4	6.9	23.7	13.3	49.4
	2015	1 754	0.1	4.4	1.0	5.4	25.6	12.5	52.0
	2016	1 773	0.1	4.0	0.9	5.2	25.7	12.5	52.5
	2017	1 693	0.1	4.6	0.8	6.3	24.4	11.4	53.2
	2018	1 580	0.1	4.3	0.9	5.6	25.2	12.2	52.6
	2019	1 675	0.1	4.3	0.9	5.7	25.1	12.0	52.8
St. Vincent and the Grenadines [1]	1970	38	14.1	10.6	8.2	8.4	12.6	11.8	42.5
(East Caribbean Dollar)	1975	75	14.3	10.7	8.3	8.2	12.6	11.8	42.4
	1980	180	10.7	11.6	9.5	9.3	12.1	11.5	44.8
	1985	318	15.1	14.1	10.8	5.5	11.4	12.7	41.3
	1990	557	16.7	12.3	8.2	6.9	11.9	14.5	37.7
	1995	735	11.2	12.5	8.1	8.4	15.5	14.6	37.8
	2000	938	8.5	11.2	5.7	8.3	17.8	14.3	39.9
	2005	1 308	6.2	10.4	5.9	8.3	17.8	15.0	42.4
	2010	1 577	7.1	10.4	5.6	8.8	16.1	13.8	43.8
	2015	1 740	7.3	10.1	5.7	7.9	15.3	13.4	46.0
	2016	1 753	8.2	9.9	5.9	7.7	15.2	14.1	45.7
	2017	1 780	8.3	10.0	6.1	8.0	15.4	13.9	45.5
	2018	1 827	8.7	10.2	6.0	7.8	15.9	13.4	44.8

Table 3. Gross Value Added by Kind of Economic Activity: Individual Countries or Areas

Major area, region and country	Year	Gross Value Added (at current prices) Million	Percentage Distributtion: Agriculture, hunting, forestry, fishing A-B	Mining, Manufacturing, Utilities C-E	Of which: Manufacturing D	Construction F	Wholesale, retail trade, restaurants and hotels G-H	Transport, storage and communication I	Other Activities J-P
	2019	1 857	8.6	9.1	4.8	7.6	15.6	14.3	45.4
Suriname [21]	1970	568 (t)	8.0	33.5	19.9	6.2	18.3	6.1	28.0
(Surinam Dollar)	1975	932 (t)	7.7	34.8	20.0	4.4	18.7	6.3	28.0
	1980	1 728 (t)	8.7	30.6	17.6	6.3	19.3	5.1	30.0
	1985	2 021 (t)	8.6	22.6	12.5	5.9	16.2	6.9	39.8
	1990	4 802 (t)	17.3	16.6	12.5	6.8	27.4	5.0	26.9
	1995	380	29.9	23.7	15.9	3.8	25.0	6.6	11.0
	2000	1 536	20.6	23.2	18.7	3.8	21.1	7.8	23.6
	2005	5 629	11.3	32.8	23.5	4.6	21.3	8.3	21.7
	2010	11 138	10.2	32.7	22.6	5.2	23.8	6.4	21.8
	2015	14 772	10.0	17.9	11.0	10.1	25.0	12.0	25.0
	2016	18 179	10.6	22.7	14.4	8.6	19.8	12.6	25.7
	2017	22 539	12.3	27.8	16.9	8.1	16.6	10.9	24.2
	2018	23 902	12.0	26.8	15.9	8.6	16.2	9.7	26.8
	2019	25 401	10.2	23.6	12.8	8.6	18.6	8.3	30.7
Trinidad and Tobago [1,29]	1970	1 787	7.8	36.0	22.8	6.4	15.7	14.4	19.7
(Trinidad and Tobago Dollar)	1975	5 383	5.6	47.5	15.1	8.3	12.0	7.4	19.2
	1980	15 187	3.9	43.4	9.0	12.6	8.5	10.4	21.3
	1985	18 986	5.0	30.2	8.5	11.7	12.1	9.1	31.9
	1990	21 414	4.4	37.0	13.9	9.4	13.9	8.8	26.5
	1995	32 050	3.3	35.2	16.5	7.7	17.4	9.9	26.6
	2000	52 848	2.1	39.0	16.9	7.2	17.0	8.9	25.8
	2005	99 453	0.9	49.1	22.1	7.6	13.9	6.2	22.3
	2010	140 192	0.7	45.6	20.2	6.7	18.8	6.2	22.0
	2015	155 299	1.1	33.8	15.8	6.3	25.7	6.0	27.1
	2016	145 719	1.2	32.0	19.3	6.4	25.6	6.4	28.5
	2017	150 709	1.2	34.2	18.7	5.9	23.8	6.2	28.7
	2018	157 193	1.1	36.8	19.6	5.8	22.6	6.0	27.7
	2019	154 619	1.0	35.2	18.8	5.7	23.1	6.1	28.9
Turks and Caicos Islands [1]	1970	10	1.3	9.0	4.4	7.3	38.2	10.4	33.8
(US Dollar)	1975	19	1.3	9.0	4.4	7.3	38.2	10.4	33.8
	1980	34	1.3	9.0	4.4	7.3	38.2	10.4	33.8
	1985	61	1.3	9.0	4.4	7.3	38.2	10.4	33.8
	1990	111	1.3	9.0	4.4	7.4	38.0	10.4	33.9
	1995	196	1.3	8.9	4.3	7.5	37.5	10.5	34.3
	2000	307	1.5	8.1	3.5	7.6	36.4	11.0	35.5
	2005	535	1.2	7.6	2.2	12.1	33.4	10.2	35.5
	2010	659	0.6	6.4	1.3	6.0	37.6	7.4	41.9
	2015	818	0.6	5.9	0.8	5.2	43.6	10.6	34.1
	2016	905	0.5	5.6	0.7	5.2	45.8	10.7	32.2
	2017	902	0.5	5.3	0.7	6.9	42.4	10.7	34.1
	2018	981	0.4	5.1	0.6	7.4	41.8	11.4	34.0
	2019	1 049	0.4	5.1	0.6	8.5	41.2	11.4	33.4
Uruguay [1]	1970	543 (t)	16.7	23.1	21.2	5.6	12.9	7.7	33.9
(Peso Uruguayo)	1975	7 505 (t)	15.3	25.9	23.6	6.8	14.7	6.7	30.5
	1980	86	14.0	26.2	24.3	7.5	14.2	5.5	32.5
	1985	499	12.5	27.5	24.6	3.3	12.9	5.8	38.0
	1990	10 077	10.6	24.2	22.2	3.7	13.2	6.4	41.9
	1995	125 607	8.1	20.0	16.7	5.9	16.0	7.2	42.9
	2000	257 820	6.4	16.8	13.4	6.8	14.3	9.1	46.5
	2005	379 260	9.8	20.4	16.6	6.2	14.3	9.3	40.0
	2010	727 071	8.0	19.1	15.0	8.2	15.2	7.9	41.7
	2015	1 323 347	6.7	17.5	14.6	10.5	14.3	6.2	44.8
	2016	1 448 134	6.5	17.5	14.1	10.6	14.3	5.9	45.3
	2017	1 550 770	5.6	16.4	12.9	10.9	15.3	6.1	45.8
	2018	1 664 782	6.2	16.0	12.8	10.9	15.1	5.9	45.9
	2019	1 797 774	6.5	15.9	12.9	10.7	14.9	5.9	46.1
Venezuela (Bolivarian Republic of) [1]	1970	58	6.1	40.7	24.5	11.2	9.5	3.6	29.0
(Bolivar Fuerte)	1975	138	4.8	44.3	23.4	14.0	7.9	3.1	25.8
	1980	300	4.6	42.8	23.4	15.0	6.8	3.2	27.7
	1985	447	6.4	44.1	29.2	7.8	9.8	3.7	28.2
	1990	2 213	5.9	51.5	27.1	5.8	10.7	3.2	23.0
	1995	12 808	5.9	40.9	23.4	6.2	11.4	5.6	30.0
	2000	76 305	4.1	40.4	19.3	8.1	9.5	6.9	31.0
	2005	283 770	4.0	50.0	16.2	6.9	11.1	5.8	22.2
	2010	965 490	5.7	42.4	13.6	8.5	15.5	5.7	22.1

Table 3. Gross Value Added by Kind of Economic Activity: Individual Countries or Areas

Major area, region and country	Year	Gross Value Added (at current prices) Million	Percentage Distributtion						
			Agriculture, hunting, forestry, fishing A-B	Mining, Manufacturing, Utilities C-E	Of which: Manufacturing D	Construction F	Wholesale, retail trade, restaurants and hotels G-H	Transport, storage and communication I	Other Activities J-P
	2015	5 510 384	6.3	22.7	17.7	7.8	27.5	6.6	29.1
	2016	19 696 616	5.6	30.6	14.6	8.5	22.1	5.7	27.5
	2017	140 024 986	5.7	28.0	15.2	8.5	23.5	5.9	28.4
	2018	73 436 139 498	5.9	27.2	15.8	8.3	24.3	6.1	28.3
	2019	9 590 750 262 237	5.7	28.6	15.2	8.4	23.3	5.9	28.1
Northern America									
Bermuda [6,36,43,53]	1970	264	0.8	4.8	2.4	5.6	17.6	7.2	64.0
(Bermudian Dollar)	1975	489	0.8	4.8	2.4	5.6	17.6	7.2	64.0
	1980	898	0.8	4.8	2.4	5.6	17.6	7.2	64.0
	1985	1 421	0.8	4.8	2.4	5.6	17.6	7.2	64.0
	1990	2 025	0.8	4.8	2.4	5.6	17.6	7.2	64.1
	1995	2 551	0.8	4.7	2.4	5.7	17.3	7.1	64.4
	2000	3 511	0.7	4.6	2.4	6.3	15.9	7.0	65.4
	2005	4 992	0.8	3.2	1.6	6.5	13.0	6.0	70.5
	2010	6 356	0.3	2.5	0.9	4.4	10.0	5.4	77.4
	2015	6 373	0.2	2.1	0.5	3.3	10.1	4.8	79.5
	2016	6 609	0.3	2.1	0.4	3.5	10.2	4.7	79.1
	2017	6 820	0.3	2.2	0.5	3.5	11.0	5.0	78.0
	2018	6 942	0.3	2.2	0.6	4.0	10.8	5.3	77.5
	2010	7 039	0.3	2.1	0.5	3.7	10.7	5.0	78.2
Canada [56]	1970	86 021	4.5	28.8	21.7	7.3	14.4	8.8	36.3
(Canadian Dollar)	1975	167 485	4.9	28.0	19.8	8.4	14.4	7.9	36.3
	1980	307 598	4.0	30.3	18.8	7.4	13.3	8.1	36.9
	1985	471 399	3.5	29.1	17.9	6.0	13.6	8.0	39.9
	1990	645 629	2.9	24.5	16.9	6.8	14.5	7.2	44.1
	1995	771 246	2.9	25.8	18.4	4.9	13.4	7.3	45.6
	2000	1 027 444	2.3	26.6	18.3	5.0	12.3	7.6	46.2
	2005	1 323 863	2.0	25.3	14.4	5.8	12.6	7.8	46.5
	2010	1 559 053	1.6	20.5	10.7	7.4	12.6	7.4	50.5
	2015	1 856 809	2.0	17.8	10.7	8.0	12.5	7.6	52.0
	2016	1 886 102	2.0	17.0	10.7	7.6	12.8	7.8	52.7
	2017	1 998 139	1.9	18.5	10.5	7.9	12.5	7.6	51.6
	2018	2 080 531	2.0	17.8	10.6	7.9	12.6	7.6	52.1
	2019	2 154 414	2.0	17.8	10.6	7.8	12.7	7.7	52.1
Greenland [29]	1970	562	17.5	10.4	7.4	5.0	11.5	12.6	43.0
(Danish Krone)	1975	1 309	17.5	10.4	7.4	5.0	11.5	12.6	43.0
	1980	2 894	17.5	10.4	7.4	5.0	11.5	12.6	43.0
	1985	4 720	17.5	10.4	7.4	5.0	11.5	12.6	43.0
	1990	6 802	17.5	10.4	7.4	5.0	11.5	12.6	43.0
	1995	7 303	17.5	10.4	7.4	5.0	11.5	12.6	42.9
	2000	9 080	18.0	10.5	7.4	5.2	11.7	13.0	41.5
	2005	10 751	17.5	11.7	8.6	5.0	10.5	12.9	42.3
	2010	13 670	13.8	8.1	4.5	10.6	9.4	13.4	44.8
	2015	16 313	17.6	8.1	4.2	9.5	11.9	11.9	41.1
	2016	17 592	19.1	8.5	4.7	9.9	11.4	12.3	39.0
	2017	18 038	19.9	6.7	3.0	10.9	11.4	11.9	39.1
	2018	18 509	18.6	7.6	4.6	10.8	11.4	12.2	39.5
	2019	19 442	19.2	7.6	4.1	10.5	11.4	12.1	39.2
United States [24,29,49]	1970	1 061 322	2.4	27.2	23.5	4.9	16.5	9.8	39.3
(US Dollar)	1975	1 658 615	2.8	26.0	21.4	4.6	16.6	9.8	40.2
	1980	2 845 960	2.0	26.2	20.6	4.6	15.9	9.8	41.5
	1985	4 319 985	1.6	24.0	18.6	4.4	16.0	9.5	44.6
	1990	5 957 893	1.5	21.6	17.5	4.2	15.1	8.9	48.7
	1995	7 636 976	1.2	20.5	16.0	3.8	15.3	9.3	49.9
	2000	10 252 200	1.0	18.2	15.1	4.5	15.6	9.3	51.4
	2005	13 036 400	1.0	16.5	13.0	5.0	15.0	9.3	53.2
	2010	14 991 900	1.0	16.2	12.0	3.5	14.3	9.6	55.4
	2015	18 238 400	1.0	15.0	11.7	3.8	14.9	10.0	55.3
	2016	18 745 100	0.9	14.2	11.2	4.0	14.8	10.2	55.9
	2017	19 543 100	0.9	14.4	11.2	4.1	14.6	10.2	55.7
	2018	20 611 800	0.9	14.7	11.2	4.1	14.4	10.3	55.6
	2019	21 433 600	0.8	14.2	10.9	4.2	14.4	10.6	55.8

Table 3. Gross Value Added by Kind of Economic Activity: Individual Countries or Areas

Major area, region and country	Year	Gross Value Added (at current prices) Million	Percentage Distributtion: Agriculture, hunting, forestry, fishing A-B	Mining, Manufacturing, Utilities C-E	Of which: Manufacturing D	Construction F	Wholesale, retail trade, restaurants and hotels G-H	Transport, storage and communication I	Other Activities J-P
Asia									
Afghanistan [57]	1970	78	50.2	21.8	21.4	2.7	13.1	4.8	7.4
(Afghani)	1975	104	50.2	21.8	21.4	2.7	13.1	4.8	7.4
	1980	161	50.3	21.8	21.4	2.7	13.1	4.8	7.4
	1985	169	50.9	22.0	21.6	2.8	11.9	5.0	7.5
	1990	180	42.4	19.5	19.2	3.0	23.0	5.8	6.4
	1995	2 297	66.3	5.7	5.6	5.0	9.4	6.2	7.4
	2000	157 803	57.5	16.6	16.3	6.0	4.3	8.3	7.3
	2005	290 317	37.3	13.8	13.2	7.6	9.9	10.4	21.1
	2010	636 152	33.2	8.4	7.0	4.6	9.9	12.1	31.9
	2015	1 071 361	27.3	6.9	4.2	3.9	11.3	10.8	39.8
	2016	1 165 815	27.7	7.1	3.8	3.4	10.7	9.9	41.2
	2017	1 200 037	27.0	7.6	3.3	3.5	11.4	9.5	41.0
	2018	1 228 947	23.7	9.5	5.5	3.6	11.9	9.2	42.1
	2019	1 320 687	26.9	9.4	5.0	3.4	11.4	8.7	40.2
Armenia [4,55]	1990	46	17.3	34.5	33.5	19.1	5.7	7.9	15.5
(Armenian Dram)	1995	527 227	40.3	22.0	19.3	6.5	10.3	4.6	16.4
	2000	996 374	24.0	26.7	17.5	10.6	10.5	8.1	20.0
	2005	2 150 293	19.9	23.2	14.2	20.6	12.3	6.7	17.3
	2010	3 299 956	17.8	16.5	10.3	18.3	14.4	7.6	25.5
	2015	4 596 994	18.9	17.9	10.1	10.3	13.3	6.5	33.1
	2016	4 655 734	17.8	19.4	11.2	8.4	12.1	6.9	35.3
	2017	5 095 354	16.4	20.2	11.6	7.9	13.6	7.0	34.9
	2018	5 494 466	15.3	19.9	12.3	7.2	14.4	7.0	36.2
	2019	5 945 603	13.2	20.0	13.0	6.8	14.8	7.3	37.8
Azerbaijan [55]	1990	268 (t)	29.7	24.0	19.3	8.9	3.6	8.9	24.9
(Azerbaijanian Manat)	1995	2 012	26.9	28.9	12.2	3.9	6.3	18.4	15.5
	2000	4 454	17.0	38.1	5.6	6.9	7.1	12.7	18.1
	2005	11 649	9.8	53.1	7.0	10.1	7.1	8.0	11.8
	2010	39 813	5.9	55.2	5.1	8.8	8.1	8.0	14.0
	2015	49 877	6.7	35.9	5.4	13.0	13.4	8.7	22.2
	2016	55 885	6.1	40.1	5.3	11.3	13.7	9.2	19.6
	2017	65 718	6.0	42.9	5.0	10.3	13.6	8.9	18.3
	2018	74 283	5.6	48.0	5.0	8.3	12.8	8.3	16.9
	2019	74 953	6.2	45.2	5.5	7.9	13.5	8.5	18.7
Bahrain [20]	1970	183	0.9	39.5	11.0	10.8	12.5	5.1	31.1
(Bahraini Dinar)	1975	410	1.0	44.0	12.6	7.6	11.9	5.0	30.5
	1980	1 361	0.8	43.0	11.2	7.2	10.0	5.7	33.3
	1985	1 825	0.8	30.0	6.1	8.9	6.6	7.0	46.7
	1990	1 806	0.7	31.5	11.3	6.3	8.2	6.0	47.3
	1995	2 504	0.7	31.1	15.9	5.0	9.7	7.0	46.5
	2000	3 352	0.6	37.6	10.9	3.5	6.5	6.4	45.2
	2005	5 945	0.3	35.7	12.9	7.1	8.2	5.5	43.1
	2010	9 567	0.3	37.9	14.6	7.5	7.4	6.8	40.0
	2015	11 594	0.3	33.2	17.5	7.5	7.1	7.6	44.3
	2016	12 035	0.3	31.7	18.2	7.9	7.1	7.5	45.4
	2017	13 205	0.3	33.4	18.7	8.2	7.0	7.5	43.6
	2018	14 051	0.3	35.1	17.8	8.3	6.6	7.5	42.2
	2019	14 380	0.3	33.4	18.2	8.1	6.9	7.5	43.7
Bangladesh	1970	42 441	41.8	8.8	8.4	3.8	16.2	9.8	19.7
(Taka)	1975	153 358	52.2	11.6	11.3	3.4	14.0	6.1	12.8
	1980	251 758	34.9	17.6	17.0	4.9	14.8	9.3	18.6
	1985	516 985	35.7	15.7	15.1	5.7	14.7	9.1	19.0
	1990	938 539	31.5	15.3	13.4	6.0	13.2	8.3	25.7
	1995	1 464 380	26.4	17.9	15.3	6.6	13.5	9.2	26.3
	2000	2 287 606	25.5	17.6	15.2	7.7	13.4	8.6	27.2
	2005	3 555 936	20.1	19.1	16.5	8.2	14.8	10.8	27.0
	2010	7 612 980	17.8	19.6	16.9	6.5	14.9	10.6	30.6
	2015	14 652 541	15.3	20.4	17.4	7.4	14.2	11.6	31.2
	2016	16 473 107	14.8	21.1	17.9	7.7	14.0	10.3	32.1
	2017	18 699 230	14.2	21.5	18.3	7.8	14.1	10.0	32.4
	2018	21 283 290	13.8	22.2	19.0	8.0	14.2	9.6	32.2
	2019	24 198 911	13.3	23.0	19.9	8.1	14.4	9.3	31.8

Table 3. Gross Value Added by Kind of Economic Activity: Individual Countries or Areas

Major area, region and country	Year	Gross Value Added (at current prices) Million	Percentage Distributtion						
			Agriculture, hunting, forestry, fishing A-B	Mining, Manufacturing, Utilities C-E	Of which: Manufacturing D	Construction F	Wholesale, retail trade, restaurants and hotels G-H	Transport, storage and communication I	Other Activities J-P
Bhutan	1970	459	43.2	5.2	4.2	13.2	8.2	4.7	25.4
(Ngultrum)	1975	720	43.2	5.2	4.2	13.2	8.2	4.7	25.4
	1980	1 009	45.0	3.8	2.9	10.7	8.1	4.7	27.6
	1985	2 133	42.3	7.0	5.7	14.4	6.4	5.0	25.0
	1990	4 796	37.1	17.8	8.2	8.4	4.5	6.9	25.3
	1995	9 048	33.2	23.6	10.9	9.9	5.2	7.5	20.5
	2000	19 312	27.4	21.7	8.4	14.3	5.0	9.3	22.3
	2005	33 827	21.0	20.0	7.6	18.4	6.8	11.5	22.4
	2010	67 888	15.4	30.5	9.3	15.2	6.4	10.2	22.3
	2015	122 805	15.1	27.7	8.6	16.8	10.4	9.7	20.4
	2016	138 210	15.1	27.1	8.0	17.6	10.6	9.5	20.1
	2017	151 485	15.8	26.9	7.9	17.2	11.2	10.0	18.9
	2018	157 487	16.9	25.6	8.0	15.1	12.1	10.6	19.7
	2019	171 151	15.9	26.5	8.0	16.6	11.3	10.0	19.6
Brunei Darussalam [29]	1970	689	0.4	91.8	17.2	0.6	0.9	0.5	5.8
(Brunei Dollar)	1975	3 704	0.4	91.1	18.6	0.7	1.0	0.6	6.2
	1980	13 689	0.2	89.9	19.4	0.6	3.7	0.4	5.2
	1985	9 737	0.4	77.8	17.1	0.8	4.4	1.3	15.3
	1990	7 070	0.9	61.4	13.8	1.8	5.7	3.8	26.3
	1995	7 136	1.1	47.6	16.1	5.8	7.5	4.6	33.4
	2000	11 790	1.0	62.8	18.5	1.7	4.8	3.3	26.4
	2005	18 012	0.9	70.5	14.8	1.5	3.7	2.5	20.9
	2010	19 043	0.7	65.6	14.6	1.8	4.7	3.1	24.1
	2015	18 115	1.1	57.8	14.3	2.4	6.0	3.8	28.9
	2016	15 979	1.2	54.0	11.3	2.5	6.5	4.0	31.9
	2017	17 025	1.1	56.3	12.5	2.5	6.2	3.9	30.1
	2018	18 593	1.0	59.8	13.8	2.5	5.8	3.5	27.5
	2019	18 683	1.0	59.0	13.4	2.4	6.2	3.6	27.8
Cambodia [1]	1970	13 227	46.6	10.7	8.3	2.9	16.6	5.7	17.6
(Riel)	1975	10 907	46.6	10.7	8.3	2.9	16.6	5.7	17.6
	1980	10 374	46.6	10.7	8.3	2.9	16.6	5.7	17.6
	1985	20 983	47.0	10.8	8.3	2.8	16.2	5.7	17.5
	1990	735 520	50.1	9.4	7.3	2.4	13.4	6.7	18.0
	1995	7 788 350	51.4	8.1	7.4	4.8	15.8	5.8	14.1
	2000	13 367 185	37.8	17.6	16.9	5.5	15.2	7.0	17.0
	2005	24 409 691	32.4	19.7	18.8	6.7	14.3	7.8	19.2
	2010	44 248 971	36.0	16.8	15.6	6.4	14.6	8.1	18.0
	2015	69 085 282	28.2	19.0	17.0	10.4	15.2	8.6	18.6
	2016	76 432 855	26.3	19.2	17.0	12.1	15.0	8.7	18.6
	2017	84 379 855	24.9	19.6	17.2	13.2	15.0	8.6	18.7
	2018	93 366 970	23.5	20.0	17.4	14.5	14.8	8.5	18.8
	2019	103 448 380	22.0	20.1	17.3	16.3	14.7	8.3	18.6
China [24,45,49]	1970	227 960	35.1	36.7	...	3.7	8.3	4.4	11.8
(Yuan Renminbi)	1975	303 950	32.2	41.3	...	4.1	6.3	4.9	11.1
	1980	458 770	29.9	43.9	...	4.3	5.3	4.7	12.0
	1985	909 890	28.2	38.2	...	4.6	10.3	4.6	14.0
	1990	1 887 280	26.8	36.6	...	4.6	8.3	6.2	17.5
	1995	6 133 980	19.8	40.8	...	6.1	9.7	5.3	18.3
	2000	10 028 020	14.9	40.1	...	5.5	10.3	6.1	23.0
	2005	18 731 880	12.0	41.6	32.1	5.6	9.7	5.7	25.5
	2010	41 211 930	9.6	40.1	31.6	6.6	10.6	4.6	28.6
	2015	68 885 810	8.7	34.1	29.4	6.9	11.6	4.4	34.2
	2016	74 639 500	8.4	32.9	28.7	6.9	11.7	4.4	35.7
	2017	83 203 600	7.8	33.1	28.9	7.0	11.6	4.5	36.2
	2018	91 928 100	7.3	32.8	28.5	7.1	11.5	4.4	36.9
	2019	99 086 510	7.4	32.0	27.9	7.2	11.5	4.3	37.6
China, Hong Kong SAR [35]	1970	22 248	0.9	21.3	19.7	6.9	19.1	8.1	43.7
(Hong Kong Dollar)	1975	47 755	0.9	21.4	19.8	6.9	19.1	8.1	43.7
	1980	137 417	1.0	22.0	20.5	6.5	19.7	8.1	42.8
	1985	261 578	0.6	21.9	19.1	4.8	21.8	9.0	41.8
	1990	584 961	0.3	17.3	14.9	5.1	23.7	10.4	43.1
	1995	1 091 375	0.2	9.2	6.8	5.0	24.6	10.8	50.4
	2000	1 283 036	0.1	7.7	4.8	4.9	24.5	10.9	51.8
	2005	1 378 003	0.1	5.8	2.9	2.8	28.8	11.7	50.7
	2010	1 737 297	0.1	3.7	1.8	3.3	27.0	11.1	54.8
	2015	2 325 443	0.1	2.6	1.1	4.6	26.1	9.9	56.7

Table 3. Gross Value Added by Kind of Economic Activity: Individual Countries or Areas

Major area, region and country	Year	Gross Value Added (at current prices) Million	Percentage Distributtion						
			Agriculture, hunting, forestry, fishing A-B	Mining, Manufacturing, Utilities C-E	Of which: Manufacturing D	Construction F	Wholesale, retail trade, restaurants and hotels G-H	Transport, storage and communication I	Other Activities J-P
	2016	2 418 028	0.1	2.5	1.1	5.2	25.0	9.7	57.5
	2017	2 552 791	0.1	2.4	1.1	5.1	24.8	9.4	58.2
	2018	2 700 426	0.1	2.3	1.0	4.5	24.7	9.3	59.2
	2019	2 747 982	0.1	2.4	1.0	4.2	23.2	9.4	60.8
China, Macao SAR [38]	1970	897	...	17.2	14.9	4.5	10.6	3.5	64.2
(Pataca)	1975	2 029	...	17.2	14.9	4.5	10.6	3.5	64.2
	1980	4 574	...	17.2	14.9	4.5	10.6	3.5	64.2
	1985	9 611	...	17.2	14.9	4.5	10.7	3.5	64.2
	1990	22 782	...	18.9	16.5	4.4	11.2	3.5	62.1
	1995	48 148	...	9.7	7.6	5.1	8.9	3.4	72.8
	2000	43 487	...	11.9	9.2	2.2	9.1	7.0	69.8
	2005	71 516	...	6.1	4.2	8.8	10.1	4.7	70.3
	2010	147 530	...	1.9	0.8	5.5	14.3	3.6	74.7
	2015	263 059	...	1.7	0.8	8.8	14.5	3.7	71.3
	2016	265 059	...	1.8	0.8	7.2	14.6	3.8	72.6
	2017	289 009	...	1.8	0.8	5.2	15.7	3.6	73.8
	2018	313 969	...	1.6	0.8	4.2	16.3	3.6	74.3
	2019	310 940	...	1.7	0.8	5.5	15.5	3.7	73.6
Cyprus [29]	1970	414	15.8	17.2	10.3	7.8	12.5	13.0	33.6
(Euro)	1975	464	15.8	16.8	13.3	8.2	12.5	9.9	36.8
	1980	1 374	9.8	17.5	15.2	14.7	14.4	12.3	31.3
	1985	2 670	7.6	16.0	13.6	11.0	17.7	14.5	33.2
	1990	4 625	7.0	14.2	12.2	10.4	20.2	14.0	34.3
	1995	7 008	5.2	12.6	10.4	9.4	20.9	12.7	39.2
	2000	9 654	4.0	11.2	8.9	8.2	20.8	13.0	42.8
	2005	12 950	3.1	10.1	7.8	10.4	18.0	10.7	47.6
	2010	17 109	2.3	8.1	5.7	8.3	16.5	11.1	53.5
	2015	15 609	2.1	7.6	4.8	4.0	16.9	12.7	56.7
	2016	16 517	2.4	7.9	5.2	4.5	17.6	13.1	54.4
	2017	17 373	2.3	7.9	5.6	5.2	18.3	13.6	52.7
	2018	18 261	2.3	7.9	5.6	6.2	18.3	13.4	51.9
	2019	19 072	2.3	8.0	5.7	7.0	18.1	13.4	51.2
D.P.R. of Korea	1970	12 663	28.3	40.3	26.7	8.1	...	...	23.2
(North Korean Won)	1975	20 768	28.3	40.3	26.7	8.1	...	...	23.2
	1980	25 389	28.3	40.3	26.7	8.1	...	...	23.2
	1985	30 446	28.3	40.3	26.7	8.1	...	...	23.2
	1990	31 904	27.4	45.9	31.8	8.6	...	...	18.0
	1995	10 329	27.6	35.3	22.5	6.7	...	...	30.3
	2000	22 807	30.4	30.2	17.7	6.9	...	...	32.5
	2005	1 801 516	25.0	33.2	19.0	9.6	...	...	32.2
	2010	1 405 645	20.8	40.2	21.9	8.0	...	...	31.0
	2015	1 751 307	21.6	37.2	20.4	9.0	...	...	32.2
	2016	1 808 776	21.7	38.4	20.6	8.8	...	...	31.1
	2017	1 870 904	22.8	36.9	20.1	8.6	...	...	31.7
	2018	1 834 778	23.3	34.8	18.8	8.9	...	...	33.0
	2019	1 756 116	21.2	35.0	18.7	9.7	...	...	34.1
Georgia [39,55]	1990	14 (t)	31.5	27.0	24.6	9.2	7.0	7.4	17.8
(Lari)	1995	3 895	48.5	10.5	8.3	1.5	27.1	8.7	3.6
	2000	6 380	23.8	16.7	10.6	2.6	15.5	14.5	26.9
	2005	11 132	18.8	16.1	11.5	6.2	16.9	14.0	28.0
	2010	19 286	9.6	14.9	10.3	4.2	19.5	11.6	40.2
	2015	30 197	8.8	13.9	10.0	7.6	17.0	9.3	43.4
	2016	31 556	8.3	13.0	8.8	8.8	17.2	8.6	44.1
	2017	35 348	7.2	14.2	9.9	9.1	18.1	9.2	42.2
	2018	38 779	7.8	14.6	10.2	8.3	18.6	9.1	41.6
	2019	43 320	7.2	14.4	10.1	8.6	19.2	9.5	41.1
India [29]	1970	431 778	43.7	17.6	15.1	4.9	5.4	3.6	24.9
(Indian Rupee)	1975	766 476	39.6	20.0	17.0	4.6	6.9	3.8	25.1
	1980	1 310 822	37.4	22.2	18.1	5.0	7.4	3.9	24.0
	1985	2 494 187	32.6	24.4	18.4	5.6	8.2	5.0	24.2
	1990	5 084 423	30.6	25.1	19.3	6.1	8.1	5.9	24.2
	1995	10 752 994	27.4	26.2	20.1	5.5	8.9	6.4	25.6
	2000	18 827 021	24.0	23.5	17.8	6.6	9.4	7.1	29.3
	2005	33 269 140	19.2	23.3	17.4	9.0	10.6	7.7	30.2
	2010	70 836 700	18.4	24.2	18.4	8.9	10.5	6.3	31.7
	2015	125 744 996	17.7	22.1	17.1	7.9	11.4	6.8	34.1

Table 3. Gross Value Added by Kind of Economic Activity: Individual Countries or Areas

Major area, region and country	Year	Gross Value Added (at current prices) Million	Agriculture, hunting, forestry, fishing A-B	Mining, Manufacturing, Utilities C-E	Of which: Manufacturing D	Construction F	Wholesale, retail trade, restaurants and hotels G-H	Transport, storage and communication I	Other Activities J-P
			Percentage Distributtion						
	2016	139 651 990	18.0	21.6	16.7	7.7	11.5	6.7	34.4
	2017	155 131 240	18.0	21.5	16.4	7.7	11.8	6.3	34.7
	2018	171 399 610	17.1	21.1	16.1	7.8	12.1	6.2	35.7
	2019	184 490 016	17.7	21.4	16.4	7.8	11.8	6.4	34.9
Indonesia [29]	1970	3 561 594	42.7	14.6	9.6	2.7	21.6	3.4	15.1
(Rupiah)	1975	13 832 546	27.9	27.1	9.4	4.0	21.9	4.7	14.3
	1980	49 432 297	22.1	35.4	12.4	4.8	18.6	5.0	14.1
	1985	109 836 131	19.8	28.5	16.4	4.6	20.2	7.0	19.9
	1990	243 842 872	16.2	31.3	20.8	4.6	21.1	6.9	19.9
	1995	531 003 450	14.2	32.1	24.0	6.2	20.5	7.3	19.8
	2000	1 453 608 197	14.5	37.6	25.2	5.0	19.7	5.4	17.8
	2005	2 918 963 148	12.1	36.8	24.7	6.3	18.9	7.4	18.5
	2010	6 683 679 800	14.3	34.6	22.6	9.4	16.8	7.5	17.4
	2015	11 163 205 700	13.9	30.8	21.7	10.5	16.8	8.8	19.1
	2016	11 958 855 500	14.0	30.0	21.3	10.8	16.7	9.1	19.4
	2017	13 066 595 800	13.7	30.2	21.0	10.8	16.5	9.6	19.3
	2018	14 237 381 500	13.4	30.4	20.7	11.0	16.5	9.5	19.2
	2019	15 183 730 400	13.3	29.4	20.5	11.2	16.5	9.9	19.7
Iran (Islamic Republic of) [1]	1970	799 634	13.5	35.3	12.9	6.9	10.2	4.7	29.4
(Iranian Rial)	1975	3 587 602	6.6	18.6	9.0	7.2	7.8	4.8	25.0
	1980	6 844 727	10.9	23.8	9.7	10.9	8.4	8.0	38.0
	1985	15 363 213	13.1	20.9	9.1	10.6	15.3	7.5	32.7
	1990	37 412 496	12.7	26.7	14.7	6.6	19.4	7.0	27.6
	1995	201 228 279	12.4	32.6	15.1	6.1	16.7	5.7	26.5
	2000	629 849 497	8.8	34.4	16.4	5.1	16.5	7.4	28.0
	2005	2 113 536 700	6.2	42.3	14.4	5.3	11.8	8.1	26.2
	2010	5 128 777 600	6.4	36.3	12.6	7.1	11.4	10.0	28.8
	2015	11 341 177 500	10.6	27.0	12.5	6.1	13.2	10.8	32.3
	2016	12 985 166 000	9.8	29.2	12.0	5.1	13.0	10.3	32.6
	2017	15 127 029 600	9.6	30.3	12.1	5.0	12.8	10.0	32.1
	2018	18 679 325 813	10.0	28.8	12.2	5.4	13.0	10.4	32.3
	2019	25 058 940 646	9.8	29.5	12.1	5.2	13.0	10.2	32.4
Iraq [1,37]	1970	5 534	16.2	41.6	9.7	3.4	8.2	5.9	24.6
(Iraqi Dinar)	1975	18 946	7.6	57.2	6.6	8.7	5.1	4.5	16.9
	1980	73 466	4.7	65.4	4.5	7.9	5.1	4.2	12.8
	1985	71 918	13.9	33.1	9.5	9.1	12.4	5.0	26.6
	1990	112 606	18.9	23.1	8.4	6.9	14.2	8.6	28.3
	1995	10 394 631	12.3	65.5	1.0	0.5	5.8	9.1	6.8
	2000	50 359 239	4.6	84.1	0.9	0.5	3.6	4.7	2.4
	2005	73 911 130	6.9	59.7	1.3	3.6	5.7	8.0	16.2
	2010	163 104 664	5.1	49.1	2.3	6.3	7.6	5.8	26.0
	2015	196 203 013	4.2	38.6	2.2	6.4	10.9	10.6	29.4
	2016	198 774 369	3.9	39.6	2.2	6.2	9.4	11.4	29.6
	2017	228 692 989	2.9	44.4	2.6	5.7	8.0	10.5	28.6
	2018	258 035 200	2.5	50.4	1.9	4.3	7.4	9.8	25.6
	2019	266 190 571	3.3	47.8	2.0	4.0	7.7	9.8	27.4
Israel [29,38]	1970	2 176 (t)	5.8	27.1	23.5	9.4	10.3	11.5	35.9
(New Israeli Sheqel)	1975	8 886 (t)	5.5	23.9	20.1	9.6	11.0	9.9	40.1
	1980	117	5.2	21.6	17.0	7.4	11.7	9.2	44.9
	1985	30 038	4.3	24.8	21.6	3.8	12.5	10.2	44.4
	1990	107 984	2.9	23.3	20.9	5.7	10.0	10.7	47.4
	1995	266 084	2.0	20.4	18.1	7.6	10.1	9.2	50.6
	2000	482 841	1.4	20.6	18.8	5.4	11.1	13.9	47.5
	2005	570 765	1.8	19.4	17.1	4.7	10.9	12.6	50.5
	2010	780 373	1.7	18.3	16.1	5.4	10.8	11.3	52.0
	2015	1 043 771	1.3	16.6	14.6	6.0	11.9	12.1	52.2
	2016	1 097 938	1.3	15.4	13.5	6.1	12.3	12.5	52.4
	2017	1 147 418	1.3	15.2	13.4	6.3	11.9	12.3	53.0
	2018	1 201 893	1.3	15.0	13.2	6.5	11.5	12.7	53.1
	2019	1 278 171	1.2	14.5	12.6	6.4	11.7	13.3	52.9
Japan [20,29]	1970	75 350 665	5.6	38.6	35.5	6.8	16.2	8.8	24.0
(Yen)	1975	150 705 687	5.1	32.9	30.1	8.6	16.8	8.4	28.2
	1980	250 263 903	3.3	31.9	28.4	8.2	17.0	7.8	31.8
	1985	331 419 711	2.9	32.6	28.8	6.9	14.9	8.2	34.4
	1990	447 326 192	2.3	30.5	27.4	8.9	15.1	8.2	35.0
	1995	508 932 100	1.7	26.8	23.6	7.8	17.0	8.8	37.9

Table 3. Gross Value Added by Kind of Economic Activity: Individual Countries or Areas

Major area, region and country	Year	Gross Value Added (at current prices) Million	Percentage Distribution: Agriculture, hunting, forestry, fishing A-B	Mining, Manufacturing, Utilities C-E	Of which: Manufacturing D	Construction F	Wholesale, retail trade, restaurants and hotels G-H	Transport, storage and communication I	Other Activities J-P
	2000	527 526 800	1.5	25.8	22.5	6.9	16.2	9.5	40.1
	2005	525 650 900	1.1	24.6	21.6	5.6	17.1	10.0	41.7
	2010	499 136 100	1.1	23.7	20.9	4.8	16.4	10.2	43.8
	2015	528 288 500	1.1	23.6	20.9	5.6	16.4	10.2	43.1
	2016	533 449 600	1.2	23.5	20.8	5.6	16.4	10.1	43.1
	2017	542 379 200	1.2	23.6	20.9	5.7	16.6	10.0	42.8
	2018	545 073 600	1.2	23.5	20.8	5.7	16.3	10.1	43.2
	2019	550 992 614	1.2	23.3	20.7	5.6	16.5	10.2	43.2
Jordan [1,29]	1970	201	8.1	14.7	12.6	4.1	17.9	7.2	48.1
(Jordanian Dinar)	1975	370	7.3	16.4	12.2	5.5	16.6	6.7	47.5
	1980	1 077	6.7	17.4	13.4	9.6	16.4	8.0	41.8
	1985	1 893	6.1	19.7	15.5	5.6	15.9	10.5	42.1
	1990	2 586	8.9	27.1	19.9	3.0	8.8	10.4	41.8
	1995	3 974	5.4	22.0	17.1	5.4	11.3	10.7	45.2
	2000	5 185	2.9	22.4	17.9	2.8	12.1	11.5	48.4
	2005	8 280	3.7	24.1	19.8	3.3	10.9	11.0	47.0
	2010	17 186	4.0	25.7	21.2	3.7	10.7	9.7	46.2
	2015	24 593	4.9	24.7	20.5	3.4	10.7	9.3	47.0
	2016	25 454	5.0	24.1	20.0	3.4	10.6	9.4	47.5
	2017	26 451	5.3	24.1	20.1	3.2	10.5	9.6	47.3
	2018	27 459	5.4	24.1	19.9	3.1	10.5	9.7	47.2
	2019	28 533	5.4	24.0	19.6	3.0	10.4	9.8	47.3
Kazakhstan [2,55]	1990	103	31.8	13.7	7.0	10.6	8.0	8.8	27.2
(Tenge)	1995	972 178	12.9	23.9	12.3	6.3	18.8	11.1	27.0
	2000	2 450 879	8.6	34.6	17.5	5.5	13.8	12.2	25.3
	2005	7 288 444	6.6	31.0	12.5	8.2	13.3	12.3	28.6
	2010	21 115 891	4.7	34.0	11.7	8.0	14.3	11.5	27.6
	2015	38 783 900	5.0	26.2	10.8	6.3	19.1	11.8	31.6
	2016	44 337 586	4.8	27.7	12.0	6.2	19.0	10.9	31.3
	2017	51 195 859	4.8	28.5	12.0	5.8	19.1	10.8	30.9
	2018	57 706 553	4.7	30.2	12.2	5.7	19.2	10.8	29.4
	2019	64 681 605	4.8	29.6	12.3	5.9	19.5	10.7	29.5
Kuwait [22]	1970	1 019	0.2	65.7	4.2	2.7	8.3	2.8	20.2
(Kuwaiti Dinar)	1975	3 461	0.2	77.1	5.6	2.1	6.4	1.7	12.5
	1980	7 694	0.2	70.7	5.5	3.6	7.7	2.4	15.4
	1985	6 517	0.6	52.4	5.9	4.0	8.7	4.2	30.1
	1990	5 372	0.9	49.9	11.5	1.8	7.5	3.6	36.2
	1995	8 022	0.4	49.8	11.1	3.0	7.7	4.5	34.5
	2000	11 969	0.3	55.1	6.7	2.1	5.8	4.6	32.0
	2005	24 472	0.3	58.4	7.0	1.8	4.8	5.0	29.6
	2010	37 564	0.4	56.2	5.3	1.9	4.3	6.3	30.8
	2015	39 612	0.5	46.2	6.1	2.5	4.9	6.4	39.6
	2016	37 473	0.5	43.4	6.4	2.6	5.3	6.4	41.8
	2017	41 346	0.5	46.4	6.6	2.9	4.9	5.5	39.9
	2018	47 131	0.4	51.1	6.2	2.6	4.3	5.3	36.3
	2019	45 818	0.4	48.8	6.2	2.5	4.5	5.4	38.4
Kyrgyzstan [4,55]	1990	42	33.6	30.2	27.6	7.9	4.8	6.1	17.4
(Som)	1995	15 219	43.1	15.3	12.5	6.5	12.0	5.1	17.9
	2000	61 066	36.6	27.0	19.3	4.5	13.7	4.2	14.1
	2005	91 775	31.3	19.1	14.1	3.0	21.0	7.6	18.0
	2010	205 058	18.8	22.3	18.1	5.9	18.5	9.8	24.8
	2015	392 988	15.4	18.3	15.4	9.2	22.6	8.9	25.6
	2016	426 456	14.3	20.3	17.2	9.3	22.0	8.2	25.9
	2017	476 129	13.9	20.9	16.7	9.6	21.7	7.8	26.1
	2018	506 306	13.1	20.8	16.0	10.1	22.0	7.2	26.8
	2019	530 671	13.4	19.9	15.9	10.8	22.2	7.1	26.6
Lao People's DR [29]	1970	174	41.6	9.4	3.9	5.1	14.5	6.1	23.3
(Kip)	1975	734	41.6	9.4	3.9	5.1	14.5	6.1	23.3
	1980	5 517	41.3	9.7	3.9	4.9	14.5	6.2	23.3
	1985	88 954	39.1	12.9	4.0	3.4	15.0	6.5	23.1
	1990	609 669	46.7	6.6	4.2	6.3	13.1	3.9	23.5
	1995	1 398 552	42.8	8.4	6.1	7.3	15.0	4.1	22.4
	2000	13 640 398	33.6	19.9	8.7	4.2	15.3	3.9	23.0
	2005	28 319 851	29.1	22.2	9.9	4.0	17.6	4.5	22.6
	2010	56 400 820	23.6	26.6	11.6	4.4	16.8	4.0	24.7
	2015	104 882 418	19.7	24.7	9.2	6.3	17.0	3.4	29.0

Table 3. Gross Value Added by Kind of Economic Activity: Individual Countries or Areas

Major area, region and country	Year	Gross Value Added (at current prices) Million	Percentage Distributtion: Agriculture, hunting, forestry, fishing A-B	Mining, Manufacturing, Utilities C-E	Of which: Manufacturing D	Construction F	Wholesale, retail trade, restaurants and hotels G-H	Transport, storage and communication I	Other Activities J-P
	2016	114 368 969	19.5	26.2	8.8	6.3	16.1	3.4	28.5
	2017	124 759 761	18.3	28.0	8.4	6.8	15.9	3.3	27.7
	2018	135 420 896	17.7	27.6	8.4	7.8	16.7	3.3	26.8
	2019	145 154 601	17.2	27.6	8.4	7.1	16.5	3.4	28.1
Lebanon [29]	1970	6 285	3.9	19.1	9.9	3.4	11.2	12.3	50.1
(Lebanese Pound)	1975	9 667	3.9	19.9	9.9	3.1	11.4	11.3	50.3
	1980	18 706	4.0	19.3	8.1	2.7	10.8	5.6	57.7
	1985	37 499	3.7	20.6	8.7	2.9	10.6	5.5	56.7
	1990	2 058 873	3.7	20.6	8.7	2.9	10.6	5.5	56.7
	1995	17 227 038	5.7	23.6	8.8	8.8	12.4	4.5	45.1
	2000	24 397 974	4.7	21.7	7.4	4.1	11.4	5.2	52.8
	2005	28 998 582	4.0	12.6	8.4	3.9	16.0	6.5	57.0
	2010	51 888 190	4.3	11.5	8.6	3.9	20.6	6.5	53.2
	2015	69 861 561	3.6	11.7	8.7	5.3	18.7	6.4	54.3
	2016	71 704 642	3.1	12.0	9.0	5.2	17.5	6.1	56.1
	2017	74 624 540	3.1	11.7	8.9	4.5	17.9	5.8	57.0
	2018	78 001 312	3.4	11.1	8.1	4.0	16.9	5.3	59.2
	2019	75 648 626	5.6	9.8	7.3	3.8	17.5	5.8	57.5
Malaysia [23,55]	1970	11 422	29.8	24.4	15.2	3.9	12.4	5.4	24.1
(Malaysian Ringgit)	1975	22 332	30.7	31.0	18.7	4.3	9.5	4.5	19.2
	1980	53 308	23.0	37.2	21.9	4.6	9.9	4.9	20.4
	1985	77 470	20.3	35.5	19.7	3.7	10.8	6.1	23.7
	1990	120 995	15.0	37.7	23.8	3.8	13.4	5.8	24.3
	1995	227 442	12.7	34.5	25.8	6.0	15.0	6.6	25.2
	2000	367 881	8.3	43.0	29.9	3.8	13.0	6.8	25.1
	2005	537 206	8.4	43.9	27.9	3.0	13.9	6.8	24.0
	2010	813 764	10.2	37.4	23.7	3.5	16.5	8.4	24.0
	2015	1 162 242	8.4	34.2	22.6	4.8	18.9	9.0	24.7
	2016	1 233 169	8.6	33.2	22.1	5.0	19.3	9.2	24.8
	2017	1 353 029	8.7	33.7	22.2	4.9	19.4	9.1	24.1
	2018	1 429 964	7.6	33.9	21.8	4.9	20.1	9.3	24.2
	2019	1 493 632	7.3	33.1	21.7	4.7	20.8	9.6	24.5
Maldives [29]	1970	163	22.8	4.7	3.7	3.3	26.2	15.3	27.6
(Rufiyaa)	1975	253	21.3	5.0	3.9	3.9	25.9	15.6	28.4
	1980	576	17.8	5.8	4.5	5.7	22.9	16.7	31.1
	1985	1 159	10.7	5.0	3.9	3.2	33.6	2.7	44.8
	1990	2 570	9.0	5.1	4.0	3.5	34.5	6.9	41.1
	1995	5 900	7.5	5.7	4.7	4.1	38.4	8.6	35.8
	2000	9 447	6.0	6.9	4.9	4.5	36.6	11.7	34.3
	2005	13 258	8.7	7.6	5.3	5.6	27.3	13.2	37.6
	2010	30 730	6.1	4.5	2.5	5.7	35.3	12.4	36.1
	2015	55 934	6.3	4.0	2.2	8.1	35.4	11.2	35.1
	2016	58 386	6.5	4.3	2.4	8.6	33.1	11.4	36.1
	2017	62 917	6.2	4.4	2.5	8.7	33.4	10.8	36.5
	2018	70 444	6.1	4.5	2.5	10.3	33.3	10.2	35.7
	2019	75 471	6.0	4.3	2.3	9.1	34.0	9.8	36.8
Mongolia [29]	1970	6 859	9.5	26.5	16.0	11.5	22.9	10.5	19.1
(Tugrik)	1975	8 995	9.5	26.5	16.0	11.5	22.9	10.5	19.1
	1980	12 014	9.7	26.8	16.2	11.6	22.7	10.4	18.9
	1985	16 889	8.8	27.9	16.9	12.1	22.2	10.2	18.7
	1990	18 445	9.5	33.0	20.0	10.7	22.6	9.3	14.9
	1995	737 720	28.0	32.4	19.2	4.2	14.8	6.0	14.6
	2000	1 283 120	24.9	21.5	7.9	5.0	16.6	10.4	21.6
	2005	3 216 393	17.8	31.5	6.7	5.9	12.9	11.5	20.4
	2010	8 758 230	13.1	34.1	7.6	2.9	14.3	10.7	25.0
	2015	21 264 700	14.5	29.2	8.3	4.6	13.6	8.0	30.1
	2016	21 952 100	12.7	32.6	8.0	4.3	13.2	7.9	29.3
	2017	25 336 269	11.3	38.1	9.9	4.1	12.4	7.3	26.7
	2018	28 892 751	12.1	39.7	10.6	4.1	11.6	7.2	25.3
	2019	32 884 996	12.4	39.8	10.8	4.0	11.5	7.1	25.2
Myanmar [24,46,50]	1970	10 636	38.6	11.6	9.7	1.7	23.8	7.5	16.8
(Kyat)	1975	25 630	47.8	9.7	8.9	0.8	28.4	3.8	9.4
	1980	41 073	48.0	10.2	8.9	1.5	24.7	4.6	11.0
	1985	58 089	50.1	10.3	9.0	1.5	22.6	4.9	10.6
	1990	171 294	59.1	7.7	6.9	1.8	21.7	3.3	6.4
	1995	707 873	60.9	7.4	6.6	2.1	22.0	4.1	3.5

Table 3. Gross Value Added by Kind of Economic Activity: Individual Countries or Areas

Major area, region and country	Year	Gross Value Added (at current prices) Million	Percentage Distributtion						
			Agriculture, hunting, forestry, fishing A-B	Mining, Manufacturing, Utilities C-E	Of which: Manufacturing D	Construction F	Wholesale, retail trade, restaurants and hotels G-H	Transport, storage and communication I	Other Activities J-P
	2000	2 999 027	58.0	7.9	7.3	1.9	23.6	5.7	2.9
	2005	14 274 315	45.9	14.3	13.1	3.5	21.0	12.0	3.3
	2010	42 016 866	35.3	23.9	19.2	4.3	19.4	12.8	4.3
	2015	74 215 746	26.7	28.0	21.3	5.9	19.1	13.6	6.6
	2016	82 700 024	24.9	29.3	23.0	6.2	19.7	13.3	6.6
	2017	92 788 955	23.0	30.5	24.2	6.3	20.2	13.2	6.8
	2018	105 258 501	21.4	31.6	24.8	6.4	20.6	13.2	6.9
	2019	116 578 512	23.1	30.4	24.0	6.3	20.1	13.3	6.8
Nepal [1]	1970	9 990	70.2	4.3	3.9	4.2	4.7	2.8	13.8
(Nepalese Rupee)	1975	16 650	70.8	4.7	4.3	2.3	5.7	3.9	12.7
	1980	22 654	61.5	4.9	4.5	4.5	6.9	6.4	15.8
	1985	47 864	49.0	6.5	5.7	5.1	16.8	5.3	17.4
	1990	107 470	48.4	6.9	6.0	5.4	17.2	5.0	17.1
	1995	226 567	38.9	11.1	9.3	6.6	18.9	5.8	18.7
	2000	396 310	37.7	11.2	9.2	6.1	19.0	7.0	19.0
	2005	566 578	35.2	10.7	7.9	6.5	15.7	9.1	23.0
	2010	1 118 570	35.4	8.2	6.3	6.9	16.0	8.5	25.0
	2015	1 971 705	31.7	7.8	6.0	7.1	16.7	8.4	28.3
	2016	2 077 655	31.6	7.4	5.8	6.8	16.1	8.1	30.0
	2017	2 442 930	29.6	7.3	5.5	7.2	15.5	7.6	32.8
	2018	2 745 778	28.6	7.4	5.5	7.5	15.8	7.1	33.6
	2019	3 049 460	27.5	7.5	5.7	7.6	16.2	7.2	34.0
Oman [1]	1970	115	15.6	55.1	0.4	12.9	1.7	0.5	14.2
(Rial Omani)	1975	803	2.7	54.4	0.6	12.4	5.8	2.2	22.5
	1980	2 249	2.7	61.6	0.6	8.4	5.5	2.2	19.7
	1985	3 657	2.3	53.2	2.2	10.1	7.5	3.0	23.9
	1990	4 497	2.7	53.1	2.9	3.8	7.4	3.4	29.6
	1995	5 260	2.9	45.4	4.7	4.3	9.4	4.7	33.3
	2000	7 605	2.2	56.3	5.6	2.1	8.2	4.8	26.5
	2005	12 221	1.6	58.4	8.4	3.7	7.9	5.3	23.0
	2010	22 998	1.4	56.9	10.1	5.7	8.1	5.2	22.7
	2015	27 796	1.9	43.2	9.4	7.4	9.1	5.7	32.7
	2016	26 107	2.2	37.0	8.8	8.8	9.4	5.8	36.8
	2017	28 261	2.2	40.4	9.6	7.4	9.1	5.9	35.1
	2018	31 822	2.0	47.1	10.1	6.1	7.9	5.4	31.4
	2019	30 586	2.3	45.5	10.0	6.1	7.8	5.6	32.8
Pakistan [29]	1970	58 023	39.7	14.0	10.9	2.9	18.9	7.3	17.2
(Pakistan Rupee)	1975	138 911	34.8	14.3	10.4	3.3	20.3	7.7	19.6
	1980	280 890	31.9	16.6	10.8	3.9	20.3	7.9	19.4
	1985	574 047	30.5	14.0	10.7	2.8	19.9	9.6	23.3
	1990	1 013 085	28.1	16.6	11.9	2.9	21.5	8.6	22.2
	1995	2 243 614	28.1	15.4	11.0	2.5	20.7	11.0	22.3
	2000	3 853 394	29.2	15.6	10.5	2.3	19.5	11.6	21.8
	2005	6 538 373	24.5	18.8	13.5	2.4	20.2	13.0	21.1
	2010	14 248 548	24.3	18.5	13.6	2.1	19.8	13.5	21.9
	2015	26 089 690	25.1	18.0	13.5	2.1	19.3	12.4	23.1
	2016	27 402 295	24.6	17.2	12.8	2.2	18.6	13.4	24.0
	2017	29 977 560	24.4	16.7	12.8	2.3	19.3	12.9	24.4
	2018	32 385 295	24.4	16.8	13.0	2.4	19.2	11.4	25.7
	2019	35 952 419	23.0	18.0	13.3	2.2	19.1	11.0	26.7
Philippines [24,29,49]	1970	43 255	26.0	30.5	27.0	4.4	12.0	3.6	23.6
(Philippine Peso)	1975	118 689	26.6	31.0	27.7	7.3	12.0	3.9	19.2
	1980	271 463	21.8	31.9	27.4	9.9	13.9	4.8	17.7
	1985	639 281	21.2	32.6	26.7	5.4	16.5	5.7	18.6
	1990	1 195 747	19.0	31.0	26.6	6.5	16.7	5.1	21.8
	1995	2 111 809	18.8	29.0	24.7	6.0	16.3	4.8	25.0
	2000	3 578 929	14.0	28.8	24.5	5.7	17.5	6.1	27.9
	2005	5 675 240	12.7	29.1	24.1	4.7	18.0	7.8	27.7
	2010	9 003 480	12.3	26.5	21.4	6.1	19.0	6.5	29.6
	2015	13 322 041	10.3	24.1	20.0	6.8	19.9	6.4	32.5
	2016	14 480 349	9.7	23.6	19.7	7.1	20.1	6.3	33.2
	2017	15 807 596	9.7	23.4	19.5	7.0	20.3	6.1	33.5
	2018	17 426 202	9.3	23.1	19.1	7.7	20.4	5.9	33.6
	2019	18 613 044	8.3	22.3	18.3	8.1	20.8	5.9	34.6

Table 3. Gross Value Added by Kind of Economic Activity: Individual Countries or Areas

Major area, region and country	Year	Gross Value Added (at current prices) Million	Percentage Distributtion						
			Agriculture, hunting, forestry, fishing A-B	Mining, Manufacturing, Utilities C-E	Of which: Manufacturing D	Construction F	Wholesale, retail trade, restaurants and hotels G-H	Transport, storage and communication I	Other Activities J-P
Qatar [1,20,29]	1970	2 582	0.7	68.8	3.1	8.7	5.1	1.7	15.0
(Qatari Rial)	1975	9 778	0.7	71.6	2.6	7.9	3.9	1.6	14.3
	1980	28 662	0.5	70.6	3.3	5.5	4.6	1.4	17.5
	1985	22 141	1.0	51.8	8.0	6.0	5.4	2.0	33.8
	1990	26 477	0.8	52.4	13.0	4.3	5.7	2.6	34.3
	1995	29 430	1.0	46.3	8.5	6.7	8.0	3.7	34.3
	2000	64 590	0.4	66.6	5.4	3.6	5.9	3.1	20.4
	2005	161 098	0.1	69.1	9.9	5.5	4.6	3.4	17.3
	2010	458 492	0.1	61.5	8.9	6.0	7.0	4.0	21.4
	2015	610 342	0.2	45.5	8.6	9.9	9.5	5.2	29.8
	2016	575 321	0.2	37.7	8.1	13.4	9.1	6.0	33.6
	2017	633 305	0.2	40.3	8.3	14.4	8.4	5.6	31.2
	2018	723 728	0.2	45.2	8.9	13.6	7.5	5.2	28.3
	2019	696 757	0.2	41.9	8.2	13.4	7.9	5.6	31.0
Republic of Korea [29]	1970	2 550 900	29.0	22.1	19.0	5.1	15.9	7.1	20.8
(Won)	1975	9 568 500	27.0	24.9	22.2	4.5	18.7	6.5	18.4
	1980	35 431 100	16.0	28.3	24.7	7.7	14.7	8.4	24.9
	1985	79 238 700	13.1	31.2	26.9	6.5	14.9	7.8	26.4
	1990	181 332 600	8.4	30.6	27.7	9.6	14.3	7.4	29.8
	1995	[illegible] 011 500	5.9	31.1	28.3	9.0	12.5	7.5	34.1
	2000	587 979 800	4.3	32.4	29.3	6.1	12.5	9.1	35.6
	2005	867 918 900	2.9	31.1	28.4	6.5	10.8	9.6	39.0
	2010	1 203 035 900	2.4	32.5	30.2	5.0	11.0	8.4	40.7
	2015	1 520 907 900	2.2	31.9	29.0	5.3	10.5	8.4	41.6
	2016	1 593 082 600	2.0	31.7	28.8	5.7	10.6	8.4	41.5
	2017	1 679 018 700	2.0	32.0	29.5	6.0	10.4	8.0	41.5
	2018	1 736 540 600	1.9	31.3	29.1	5.9	10.4	7.9	42.6
	2019	1 756 621 100	1.8	29.9	27.7	6.0	10.3	8.1	44.0
Saudi Arabia [1,29]	1970	23 978	4.3	55.4	8.3	3.5	4.6	4.5	27.8
(Saudi Riyal)	1975	164 618	0.9	65.5	5.0	6.3	3.2	1.6	22.5
	1980	549 725	1.0	63.7	4.1	7.5	4.0	2.5	21.4
	1985	378 651	3.6	32.4	7.9	8.8	8.2	5.0	42.0
	1990	442 100	5.7	42.5	8.5	6.5	6.4	4.5	34.4
	1995	539 849	5.9	42.1	9.5	6.8	6.6	4.6	34.1
	2000	714 363	4.9	48.0	9.6	5.8	6.7	4.1	30.4
	2005	1 237 396	3.2	57.1	9.5	4.7	6.2	3.5	25.3
	2010	1 985 704	2.6	53.7	11.0	4.6	8.8	5.1	25.2
	2015	2 449 589	2.6	38.7	12.7	6.7	11.4	6.3	34.3
	2016	2 415 126	2.7	36.6	12.9	6.6	11.4	6.6	36.0
	2017	2 581 646	2.5	39.9	12.9	6.0	10.7	6.4	34.6
	2018	2 953 321	2.2	44.3	12.8	5.1	9.5	5.8	33.0
	2019	2 976 768	2.2	41.9	12.5	5.5	10.0	6.1	34.3
Singapore [29,30,36]	1970	5 557	2.7	21.5	18.5	7.0	27.8	11.4	29.6
(Singapore Dollar)	1975	13 241	2.2	24.4	22.2	7.9	24.8	11.6	29.0
	1980	24 910	1.6	30.0	27.5	6.2	21.0	14.4	26.8
	1985	39 324	1.0	23.2	20.9	10.3	15.4	14.3	35.9
	1990	67 225	0.3	27.6	25.6	4.8	16.4	14.0	36.9
	1995	116 069	0.2	27.5	25.7	6.3	16.0	13.5	36.5
	2000	154 395	0.1	29.5	27.7	5.3	15.9	13.7	35.5
	2005	203 227	0.1	29.9	28.3	3.0	19.0	14.1	33.9
	2010	309 047	0.0	23.5	22.0	4.7	21.1	11.8	38.8
	2015	399 187	0.0	20.6	19.2	5.1	18.6	11.5	44.1
	2016	413 701	0.0	20.0	18.7	4.8	20.2	10.8	44.2
	2017	443 249	0.0	20.9	19.6	4.0	20.5	11.3	43.2
	2018	476 891	0.0	23.1	21.0	3.6	20.2	10.6	42.5
	2019	481 666	0.0	22.1	20.9	3.7	19.4	11.0	43.8
Sri Lanka [29]	1970	12 425	31.2	19.8	18.3	5.2	11.0	10.6	22.3
(Sri Lanka Rupee)	1975	24 033	24.0	33.2	30.7	4.0	11.7	9.9	17.1
	1980	58 571	23.3	26.7	23.5	8.5	11.2	11.9	18.4
	1985	132 118	22.2	24.8	22.0	6.9	12.7	13.2	20.1
	1990	267 453	20.7	26.9	22.8	6.2	13.1	11.6	21.6
	1995	569 804	16.6	26.3	22.5	6.4	14.5	11.0	25.1
	2000	1 080 956	14.2	27.4	23.8	6.0	16.1	12.3	24.0
	2005	2 493 591	8.8	25.7	22.0	5.4	16.4	11.3	32.4
	2010	5 758 102	9.5	23.8	20.1	5.8	13.8	12.1	35.0
	2015	10 154 807	8.8	21.1	17.5	8.2	13.4	13.6	34.8

Table 3. Gross Value Added by Kind of Economic Activity: Individual Countries or Areas

Major area, region and country	Year	Gross Value Added (at current prices) Million	Percentage Distribution: Agriculture, hunting, forestry, fishing A-B	Mining, Manufacturing, Utilities C-E	Of which: Manufacturing D	Construction F	Wholesale, retail trade, restaurants and hotels G-H	Transport, storage and communication I	Other Activities J-P
	2016	10 999 589	8.1	21.8	17.9	8.5	13.2	13.8	34.5
	2017	12 089 481	8.6	20.9	16.9	8.6	13.3	13.3	35.2
	2018	13 165 327	8.6	21.0	17.3	8.0	13.4	13.2	35.7
	2019	13 972 593	8.0	21.4	17.6	8.0	13.4	13.2	35.9
State of Palestine [29] (US Dollar)	1970	167	13.2	20.5	17.2	10.1	14.5	3.7	37.9
	1975	546	13.2	20.5	17.2	10.1	14.5	3.7	37.9
	1980	1 013	13.2	20.5	17.2	10.1	14.5	3.7	37.9
	1985	949	13.2	20.6	17.3	10.1	14.5	3.7	37.9
	1990	1 834	13.1	20.8	17.5	10.1	14.6	3.7	37.7
	1995	3 072	12.6	21.9	18.7	9.6	14.3	3.4	38.1
	2000	3 860	10.8	15.9	11.7	8.1	13.8	5.3	46.1
	2005	4 474	10.3	17.9	13.0	6.1	12.5	5.9	47.3
	2010	8 261	10.6	17.5	14.3	4.4	21.2	8.3	38.1
	2015	11 949	8.7	13.6	10.9	5.6	24.6	6.8	40.8
	2016	13 221	8.9	14.2	11.7	5.9	24.4	6.0	40.6
	2017	13 752	8.3	16.3	13.7	6.3	25.8	5.9	37.4
	2018	14 099	8.5	15.3	13.3	7.0	27.7	5.9	35.6
	2019	14 654	8.5	15.2	12.9	6.4	26.0	6.0	37.9
Syrian Arab Republic [24,49] (Syrian Pound)	1970	6 848	20.2	22.8	19.2	2.9	20.4	10.7	23.0
	1975	20 711	17.9	20.1	7.4	4.6	22.2	11.6	23.5
	1980	51 270	20.2	16.3	3.6	7.0	24.8	6.9	24.8
	1985	83 224	21.0	15.0	7.7	6.8	22.2	9.8	25.0
	1990	268 328	28.3	20.4	5.5	3.8	22.7	9.5	15.4
	1995	570 975	28.2	13.8	6.2	4.3	26.0	11.6	16.0
	2000	904 623	24.7	30.1	1.5	3.2	14.9	12.6	14.5
	2005	1 506 437	20.3	27.3	2.5	3.8	20.2	10.7	17.6
	2010	2 791 775	19.7	27.0	4.8	3.7	22.4	9.6	17.6
	2015	4 524 910	20.7	26.6	4.7	3.4	22.5	9.5	17.3
	2016	5 696 998	20.5	26.8	4.7	3.4	22.5	9.5	17.3
	2017	6 572 146	20.6	26.8	4.7	3.4	22.5	9.5	17.3
	2018	7 100 792	20.6	26.7	4.7	3.4	22.5	9.5	17.3
	2019	9 121 458	20.6	26.8	4.7	3.4	22.5	9.5	17.3
Tajikistan [40] (Somoni)	1990	75 (t)	26.9	34.6	34.6	6.6	4.6	6.4	20.9
	1995	75	31.6	46.6	46.6	1.8	4.3	4.0	11.7
	2000	1 642	27.3	36.1	36.1	2.3	11.8	5.2	17.3
	2005	6 428	23.8	25.6	25.6	5.1	18.5	8.3	18.7
	2010	22 151	21.8	16.4	16.4	11.4	22.6	12.5	15.3
	2015	42 980	24.7	15.0	15.0	12.5	16.7	14.0	17.1
	2016	48 955	22.7	16.9	16.9	13.4	17.1	14.1	15.8
	2017	58 097	22.5	22.1	22.1	13.2	13.9	13.6	14.7
	2018	64 040	21.9	23.5	23.5	14.7	14.1	12.1	13.7
	2019	72 205	22.8	24.1	24.1	12.5	15.0	8.3	17.3
Thailand [20,55] (Baht)	1970	153 658	25.9	20.0	15.9	5.3	23.3	6.2	19.2
	1975	316 229	26.9	22.0	18.7	3.8	23.8	5.5	18.0
	1980	686 536	23.2	24.2	21.5	4.4	22.8	5.3	20.0
	1985	1 094 856	15.8	26.7	21.9	5.1	23.9	7.4	21.0
	1990	2 262 473	10.0	30.9	27.1	6.0	23.0	7.2	22.9
	1995	4 217 614	9.1	30.0	26.2	7.3	21.2	7.3	25.1
	2000	5 069 820	8.5	33.7	28.4	3.0	20.6	8.7	25.5
	2005	7 614 413	9.2	35.5	29.6	3.0	17.5	8.3	26.5
	2010	10 808 142	10.5	37.1	30.9	2.8	16.9	7.7	25.0
	2015	13 743 463	8.9	33.4	27.4	2.8	18.7	8.1	28.2
	2016	14 554 569	8.4	32.9	27.2	2.8	19.8	8.0	28.0
	2017	15 451 959	8.3	32.7	27.2	2.6	20.8	8.0	27.6
	2018	16 023 688	8.3	33.0	27.4	2.6	22.5	7.6	26.0
	2019	16 727 692	8.3	32.9	27.3	2.6	21.0	7.9	27.2
Timor-Leste [56] (US Dollar)	1990	208	20.7	33.1	2.1	14.6	6.9	6.1	18.6
	1995	369	25.1	18.8	2.7	17.7	8.2	8.1	22.1
	2000	351	29.8	4.5	2.7	12.4	20.0	1.0	32.5
	2005	450	29.7	3.4	2.5	2.0	21.6	5.8	37.4
	2010	913	24.7	1.1	1.0	7.6	21.5	4.9	40.1
	2015	1 589	17.8	1.1	1.0	17.2	18.3	2.3	43.2
	2016	1 682	16.6	1.2	1.1	17.5	19.1	2.5	43.1
	2017	1 622	16.7	1.7	1.5	13.7	18.2	2.4	47.2
	2018	1 593	17.4	1.8	1.7	14.3	16.5	2.6	47.5
	2019	2 026	14.1	18.4	1.5	10.8	14.9	2.7	39.0

Table 3. Gross Value Added by Kind of Economic Activity: Individual Countries or Areas

Major area, region and country	Year	Gross Value Added (at current prices) Million	Percentage Distribution: Agriculture, hunting, forestry, fishing A-B	Mining, Manufacturing, Utilities C-E	Of which: Manufacturing D	Construction F	Wholesale, retail trade, restaurants and hotels G-H	Transport, storage and communication I	Other Activities J-P
Turkey [29]	1970	243 (t)	31.1	22.3	20.6	6.9	11.0	6.7	22.0
(New Turkish Lira)	1975	792 (t)	28.3	23.1	21.3	6.3	13.5	7.7	21.2
	1980	6 385 (t)	21.1	24.2	22.1	6.4	14.3	9.3	24.6
	1985	42	16.2	27.2	24.1	6.8	17.4	10.9	21.5
	1990	482	14.0	31.5	28.3	7.1	17.0	9.9	20.4
	1995	9 633	12.4	32.0	28.8	6.1	18.0	10.5	20.9
	2000	153 640	11.2	24.0	20.9	5.9	16.1	12.6	30.1
	2005	594 883	10.5	22.5	19.3	6.3	16.5	14.3	29.9
	2010	1 027 561	10.2	21.0	17.1	6.9	15.3	12.0	34.7
	2015	2 073 021	7.8	22.4	18.9	9.2	16.2	12.0	32.4
	2016	2 316 930	7.0	22.2	18.8	9.6	15.9	11.7	33.6
	2017	2 779 809	6.8	23.3	19.8	9.6	16.4	12.0	32.0
	2018	3 369 141	6.4	24.9	21.2	7.9	17.1	12.2	31.5
	2019	3 891 944	7.1	24.2	20.3	6.0	17.5	12.4	32.7
Turkmenistan [25]	1990	3 100 (u)	32.3	25.4	25.0	3.6	8.7	11.9	18.1
(Turkmenistan Manat)	1995	125	16.9	59.2	58.1	6.1	4.3	5.0	8.6
	2000	5 130	22.9	35.0	33.0	6.8	3.5	6.6	25.1
	2005	17 600	18.8	31.1	29.4	6.5	5.1	7.9	30.6
	2010	63 471	11.5	49.9	47.0	10.0	3.4	5.1	20.1
	2015	123 466	0.4	40.1	45.4	9.7	3.8	5.9	23.0
	2016	124 736	8.8	51.0	48.1	10.3	3.5	5.4	21.0
	2017	130 750	8.9	50.1	47.2	10.1	3.6	5.5	21.7
	2018	140 526	9.1	49.8	46.9	10.0	3.7	5.6	21.9
	2019	166 485	8.9	50.3	47.4	10.1	3.6	5.5	21.6
United Arab Emirates	1970	4 972	0.5	54.1	1.7	16.2	15.0	3.9	10.3
(UAE Dirham)	1975	57 967	0.5	58.4	0.8	14.8	14.5	3.3	8.5
	1980	160 199	0.4	59.7	3.4	12.2	14.7	3.6	9.4
	1985	145 942	0.9	48.7	8.2	12.1	15.5	4.4	18.5
	1990	183 766	1.0	48.0	6.8	10.5	17.7	5.2	17.7
	1995	237 992	1.6	36.1	8.9	11.4	20.5	6.8	23.6
	2000	376 084	2.1	42.6	11.9	8.9	18.9	7.0	20.6
	2005	661 946	1.3	45.7	9.5	8.4	14.8	8.2	21.7
	2010	1 064 244	0.8	41.5	7.9	11.0	13.7	8.7	24.3
	2015	1 315 251	0.7	34.2	8.8	9.7	14.7	9.7	30.9
	2016	1 311 248	0.8	32.0	9.0	9.4	15.4	9.2	33.2
	2017	1 416 136	0.8	33.5	9.2	9.0	15.5	9.0	32.1
	2018	1 550 585	0.7	38.5	8.7	8.5	14.4	8.4	29.5
	2019	1 546 645	0.7	37.7	8.7	8.4	14.5	8.8	29.8
Uzbekistan [5,54]	1990	33	33.0	25.9	16.6	10.5	5.8	5.9	18.7
(Uzbekistan Sum)	1995	343 127	47.2	16.7	10.7	5.9	8.6	6.4	15.3
	2000	3 653 437	50.7	11.1	7.1	5.0	10.0	7.0	16.3
	2005	17 517 619	45.3	16.8	10.8	4.1	8.3	9.8	15.7
	2010	65 161 690	32.6	19.9	12.3	5.8	9.2	11.3	21.2
	2015	192 359 446	33.6	20.0	14.7	5.9	8.4	10.0	22.1
	2016	222 610 509	33.6	20.4	15.7	5.9	8.4	9.5	22.2
	2017	271 748 059	33.5	21.9	16.1	5.6	7.9	9.3	21.8
	2018	369 047 514	30.8	26.0	18.7	6.0	7.2	8.3	21.7
	2019	478 177 244	27.3	29.2	20.9	6.3	6.7	7.5	23.0
Viet Nam [29,51]	1970	3 056	38.8	18.3	14.5	3.0	11.5	2.3	26.0
(Dong)	1975	4 291	38.8	18.3	14.5	3.0	11.6	2.3	26.0
	1980	8 700	38.8	18.3	14.5	3.0	11.5	2.3	26.0
	1985	153 086	39.0	18.5	14.8	2.9	11.1	2.3	26.2
	1990	46 440 041	35.1	17.2	11.0	3.5	15.4	3.2	25.7
	1995	254 394 052	24.5	19.9	13.4	6.2	17.0	0.7	27.8
	2000	483 310 727	22.5	29.1	16.9	4.9	15.7	3.7	24.1
	2005	914 003 000	19.3	32.3	18.8	5.8	15.4	4.2	23.0
	2010	1 887 082 497	21.0	29.7	14.8	7.0	13.3	4.3	24.6
	2015	3 772 552 309	18.9	30.9	15.2	6.0	15.4	3.8	24.9
	2016	4 050 629 544	18.1	30.1	15.9	6.2	15.9	3.8	25.8
	2017	4 505 601 442	17.0	30.7	17.0	6.4	16.2	3.7	26.0
	2018	4 989 887 500	16.3	31.5	17.8	6.5	16.3	3.8	25.6
	2019	5 438 720 893	15.5	31.7	18.3	6.6	16.6	3.8	25.8
Yemen	1990	138 991	22.6	20.7	7.4	2.5	11.7	14.0	28.5
(Yemeni Rial)	1995	582 759	17.3	23.7	11.2	3.6	15.7	11.4	28.3
	2000	1 726 601	12.2	38.1	5.3	4.0	15.6	11.0	19.2

Table 3. Gross Value Added by Kind of Economic Activity: Individual Countries or Areas

Major area, region and country	Year	Gross Value Added (at current prices) Million	Percentage Distributtion: Agriculture, hunting, forestry, fishing A-B	Mining, Manufacturing, Utilities C-E	Of which: Manufacturing D	Construction F	Wholesale, retail trade, restaurants and hotels G-H	Transport, storage and communication I	Other Activities J-P
	2005	3 593 369	9.6	39.3	5.8	4.5	17.6	11.0	17.9
	2010	6 717 393	12.1	33.2	8.5	5.4	19.6	11.1	18.5
	2015	5 659 795	18.2	15.8	10.4	4.3	19.0	13.8	28.9
	2016	5 227 362	18.7	16.1	11.0	4.6	20.1	14.9	25.6
	2017	5 113 328	19.1	15.6	11.3	4.6	20.3	15.4	24.9
	2018	5 647 945	19.3	15.8	10.9	4.7	20.6	15.3	24.3
	2019	6 143 991	19.0	15.9	11.1	4.6	20.3	15.2	24.9
Europe									
Albania [29]	1970	11 729	36.9	33.9	16.8	10.2	9.1	1.9	8.1
(Lek)	1975	13 513	36.9	33.9	16.8	10.2	9.1	1.9	8.1
	1980	15 579	37.5	34.4	17.1	10.4	8.4	1.8	7.5
	1985	16 908	38.7	33.2	16.5	9.9	8.7	1.9	7.7
	1990	17 062	39.6	38.3	19.0	9.1	6.2	1.3	5.5
	1995	230 955	54.3	12.2	6.3	14.3	9.0	2.1	8.2
	2000	442 127	27.8	9.1	4.9	12.8	21.3	6.4	22.6
	2005	703 494	21.5	11.1	5.1	17.5	15.8	8.8	25.3
	2010	1 077 485	20.7	13.8	6.3	14.9	14.6	8.5	27.5
	2015	1 259 726	22.5	14.6	6.5	10.1	14.3	6.9	31.5
	2016	1 291 203	22.6	14.0	6.5	10.2	14.7	7.0	31.6
	2017	1 354 490	21.8	12.8	7.0	10.5	14.8	7.2	32.9
	2018	1 430 677	21.1	14.1	7.0	10.3	15.0	7.0	32.6
	2019	1 464 603	21.3	13.2	7.2	9.7	15.4	7.4	32.9
Andorra [29]	1970	35	0.5	6.6	4.4	11.7	40.6	3.7	36.9
(Euro)	1975	80	0.5	6.6	4.4	11.7	40.6	3.7	36.9
	1980	203	0.5	6.6	4.4	11.7	40.5	3.7	36.9
	1985	374	0.5	6.6	4.4	11.7	40.5	3.7	37.0
	1990	666	0.5	6.6	4.4	11.8	40.5	3.7	37.0
	1995	939	0.5	6.7	4.5	12.1	40.3	3.5	36.9
	2000	1 426	0.6	5.4	4.2	10.7	27.5	4.4	51.4
	2005	2 308	0.4	5.0	3.8	12.7	27.5	4.9	49.5
	2010	2 357	0.5	5.0	4.1	9.5	26.0	5.3	53.8
	2015	2 242	0.6	5.4	4.2	5.8	24.4	5.7	58.1
	2016	2 323	0.6	5.5	4.2	5.9	24.5	6.1	57.4
	2017	2 359	0.6	5.5	4.2	6.2	25.4	6.0	56.3
	2018	2 433	0.6	5.5	4.0	6.9	25.4	5.9	55.7
	2019	2 506	0.6	5.5	4.2	6.3	25.1	6.0	56.4
Austria [29]	1970	27 331	7.4	34.6	30.4	8.8	15.7	8.7	24.8
(Euro)	1975	44 867	5.8	32.0	27.4	10.1	15.4	8.3	28.3
	1980	68 616	4.9	28.7	23.8	8.3	17.6	9.2	31.3
	1985	92 031	3.6	27.5	22.7	7.0	17.1	9.0	35.9
	1990	122 159	3.5	26.2	22.0	7.1	17.5	9.2	36.5
	1995	158 820	2.4	24.1	19.9	8.0	16.9	8.9	39.8
	2000	190 625	1.8	24.2	20.4	7.5	17.0	9.0	40.4
	2005	225 888	1.4	23.4	19.6	7.0	17.1	9.3	41.8
	2010	263 633	1.4	22.2	18.5	6.5	17.9	8.8	43.3
	2015	307 038	1.3	22.0	18.7	6.2	17.3	9.2	44.0
	2016	318 953	1.2	22.3	19.1	6.3	17.1	9.2	43.9
	2017	329 396	1.4	22.1	18.9	6.4	16.7	9.2	44.2
	2018	344 338	1.3	22.0	18.9	6.5	17.1	9.2	43.9
	2019	355 359	1.2	21.7	18.6	6.8	16.8	9.3	44.1
Belarus [55]	1990	422 (u)	23.5	40.8	37.9	8.3	5.0	6.6	15.9
(Belarussian Ruble)	1995	11	16.8	31.7	29.0	5.8	11.1	13.0	21.5
	2000	805	14.0	34.9	26.8	7.2	12.6	10.2	21.0
	2005	5 711	9.7	36.0	28.1	7.7	11.7	9.2	25.6
	2010	14 960	10.1	29.6	25.7	10.7	13.9	9.0	26.7
	2015	77 967	7.2	28.7	23.8	9.0	15.0	11.1	29.0
	2016	82 014	8.0	29.3	23.3	6.6	13.7	12.2	30.3
	2017	91 741	8.7	30.3	24.9	6.1	12.9	12.5	29.5
	2018	104 787	7.7	30.3	24.8	6.2	12.7	13.1	30.0
	2019	114 668	7.8	29.6	24.5	6.4	11.8	14.0	30.4
Belgium [29]	1970	28 610	4.3	36.6	34.7	7.6	12.7	8.5	30.3
(Euro)	1975	51 091	3.5	32.4	29.9	7.9	13.5	9.2	33.4
	1980	80 813	2.6	27.3	23.6	7.9	12.5	9.5	40.2
	1985	116 989	2.6	26.0	22.4	5.3	12.0	9.0	45.1
	1990	152 598	2.2	25.7	22.6	5.6	14.0	9.5	42.9

Table 3. Gross Value Added by Kind of Economic Activity: Individual Countries or Areas

Major area, region and country	Year	Gross Value Added (at current prices) Million	Percentage Distributtion: Agriculture, hunting, forestry, fishing A-B	Mining, Manufacturing, Utilities C-E	Of which: Manufacturing D	Construction F	Wholesale, retail trade, restaurants and hotels G-H	Transport, storage and communication I	Other Activities J-P
	1995	189 743	1.4	23.6	20.3	5.3	13.6	9.6	46.5
	2000	228 625	1.3	22.8	19.7	5.2	12.9	9.9	47.9
	2005	276 829	0.9	20.4	17.8	4.9	15.1	10.2	48.5
	2010	324 347	0.9	17.9	14.9	5.5	14.5	10.3	51.0
	2015	373 302	0.8	16.8	14.2	5.2	13.8	9.8	53.7
	2016	384 033	0.7	16.5	13.8	5.1	14.2	9.7	53.8
	2017	396 979	0.7	16.5	13.9	5.1	13.6	9.8	54.3
	2018	410 567	0.6	15.9	13.6	5.3	13.6	9.9	54.7
	2019	425 002	0.7	16.0	13.6	5.4	13.5	9.9	54.5
Bosnia and Herzegovina [7,56] (Convertible Marks)	1990	732 (t)	23.0	24.2	14.0	7.2	10.1	8.2	27.2
	1995	2 407	22.0	24.4	14.1	7.4	10.3	8.2	27.7
	2000	10 288	10.7	20.0	11.7	7.0	13.1	9.7	39.5
	2005	14 891	9.8	20.2	11.8	5.2	17.0	10.2	37.6
	2010	21 499	8.0	21.3	12.8	5.2	17.9	9.3	38.2
	2015	24 312	7.3	21.9	13.7	4.7	18.1	9.7	38.3
	2016	25 428	7.5	22.6	14.5	4.7	18.2	9.4	37.6
	2017	26 761	6.6	23.3	15.4	4.8	18.8	9.4	37.1
	2018	28 542	6.9	23.9	15.5	4.8	18.8	9.0	36.5
	2019	29 640	6.7	23.4	15.4	5.1	19.4	9.7	35.9
Bulgaria [29] (Bulgarian Lev)	1970	10	16.7	37.0	25.0	7.5	10.4	11.3	16.1
	1975	14	16.7	37.9	25.2	7.5	10.5	11.3	16.2
	1980	25	15.5	38.0	25.3	7.4	11.9	11.2	16.1
	1985	31	13.0	46.0	30.7	7.9	6.1	10.5	16.4
	1990	45	19.4	35.9	23.9	6.5	8.1	11.8	18.3
	1995	1 178	10.0	15.9	10.7	3.4	8.4	6.7	55.7
	2000	24 709	12.5	20.9	13.8	5.1	12.8	11.5	37.2
	2005	40 028	8.6	22.4	16.0	6.1	14.4	11.1	37.3
	2010	64 658	4.6	19.6	12.8	7.2	14.3	11.4	42.9
	2015	77 125	4.7	23.1	15.4	4.4	16.4	11.4	40.1
	2016	81 887	4.7	24.2	16.4	3.9	16.2	12.3	38.8
	2017	88 369	4.7	24.0	16.5	4.1	16.8	11.6	38.8
	2018	95 119	3.9	21.6	15.5	4.2	17.7	12.3	40.4
	2019	103 588	3.7	21.1	14.7	4.5	17.4	12.5	40.9
Croatia [55] (Croatian Kuna)	1990	301	7.2	38.2	31.3	6.3	15.6	9.2	23.5
	1995	97 165	6.9	26.4	22.4	5.9	16.0	10.4	34.5
	2000	147 823	6.1	24.7	20.4	4.9	14.7	10.0	39.6
	2005	227 099	4.6	21.3	17.1	7.7	17.1	10.4	38.8
	2010	279 151	4.4	19.9	15.5	6.2	16.3	9.6	43.6
	2015	281 466	3.6	20.8	15.6	5.0	18.3	8.9	43.4
	2016	291 037	3.8	20.7	15.8	5.0	18.1	9.1	43.4
	2017	302 659	3.6	20.2	15.6	5.0	18.5	9.4	43.3
	2018	314 886	3.5	19.7	15.2	5.2	19.0	9.5	43.2
	2019	328 236	3.4	19.2	14.6	5.4	19.1	9.7	43.2
Czechia [55] (Czech Koruna)	1990	614 018	8.5	39.2	32.5	7.7	13.4	6.4	24.8
	1995	1 450 345	4.4	31.3	23.7	7.7	13.9	9.9	32.8
	2000	2 173 796	3.6	30.6	25.7	6.2	15.0	11.6	33.1
	2005	2 971 553	2.5	30.5	25.0	6.7	13.8	11.7	34.8
	2010	3 613 528	1.7	29.6	23.2	7.1	12.6	11.2	37.8
	2015	4 165 174	2.5	31.9	26.6	5.7	12.9	10.9	36.3
	2016	4 314 719	2.3	31.7	26.7	5.5	12.8	11.1	36.7
	2017	4 592 620	2.3	30.9	26.2	5.5	13.3	11.3	36.7
	2018	4 874 217	2.1	29.7	25.2	5.6	13.1	11.5	38.0
	2019	5 188 440	2.1	29.2	24.8	5.6	13.0	11.5	38.5
Denmark [29] (Danish Krone)	1970	112 400	5.2	21.4	19.2	8.6	18.3	8.8	37.7
	1975	208 104	4.9	20.8	18.6	7.0	17.5	7.9	41.9
	1980	346 701	4.7	20.6	18.5	6.3	15.0	7.9	45.5
	1985	571 841	4.9	21.7	18.5	4.8	15.9	8.4	44.4
	1990	742 722	3.8	21.1	17.1	5.0	14.3	9.6	46.3
	1995	897 366	3.3	20.9	17.0	4.6	14.6	9.5	47.2
	2000	1 143 122	2.5	22.0	16.4	5.5	13.6	10.6	45.8
	2005	1 347 651	1.3	20.8	14.2	5.4	13.3	11.2	48.0
	2010	1 562 744	1.4	18.4	12.7	4.4	13.6	10.6	51.5
	2015	1 767 126	1.1	18.1	14.3	5.0	14.6	10.5	50.7
	2016	1 829 138	1.1	18.4	14.9	5.4	14.4	9.9	50.8
	2017	1 906 875	1.5	18.3	15.0	5.6	14.6	10.0	50.1
	2018	1 955 864	1.2	18.2	14.8	6.0	14.6	9.6	50.3

Table 3. Gross Value Added by Kind of Economic Activity: Individual Countries or Areas

Major area, region and country	Year	Gross Value Added (at current prices) Million	Percentage Distributtion						
			Agriculture, hunting, forestry, fishing A-B	Mining, Manufacturing, Utilities C-E	Of which: Manufacturing D	Construction F	Wholesale, retail trade, restaurants and hotels G-H	Transport, storage and communication I	Other Activities J-P
	2019	2 037 658	1.5	18.2	15.2	6.0	14.8	9.5	49.9
Estonia [55] (Euro)	1990	51	15.7	39.6	32.8	7.2	8.0	6.4	23.1
	1995	2 530	4.7	24.5	19.2	6.4	13.0	12.6	38.7
	2000	5 519	4.3	21.9	17.3	5.9	14.2	15.9	37.7
	2005	10 042	3.7	21.2	16.6	8.5	16.0	13.3	37.3
	2010	13 013	3.6	21.9	15.6	5.8	12.9	14.4	41.4
	2015	18 030	3.3	21.2	15.9	6.1	13.8	14.1	41.6
	2016	18 917	2.4	21.1	16.0	6.5	14.6	13.4	41.9
	2017	20 687	2.7	20.7	15.4	6.5	14.9	13.2	41.9
	2018	22 552	2.2	20.5	15.3	6.8	15.5	13.5	41.6
	2019	24 446	2.9	19.0	14.7	6.4	15.5	14.3	42.0
Finland [29] (Euro)	1970	7 111	12.4	29.2	25.4	9.1	11.8	9.6	27.9
	1975	16 490	10.7	28.9	25.4	10.1	12.6	8.5	29.1
	1980	30 084	9.6	30.7	27.1	7.4	12.5	9.8	30.0
	1985	51 312	7.8	28.1	24.6	7.0	13.0	9.9	34.2
	1990	79 033	6.2	25.3	22.5	8.4	12.5	9.8	37.9
	1995	86 345	4.3	28.8	25.4	4.8	10.7	10.1	41.2
	2000	119 381	3.4	30.0	27.6	6.2	10.5	11.0	39.0
	2005	143 921	2.6	27.0	24.3	6.4	11.4	10.7	41.8
	2010	164 663	2.8	23.4	19.4	6.5	11.0	10.1	46.2
	2015	182 599	2.6	20.5	17.0	6.5	11.0	10.5	48.9
	2016	187 394	2.7	20.3	16.9	7.0	10.8	10.5	48.7
	2017	195 339	2.7	21.0	17.5	7.2	10.9	10.5	47.7
	2018	201 626	2.8	20.4	17.0	7.4	10.8	10.6	48.0
	2019	208 050	2.7	20.5	17.0	7.5	10.7	10.6	48.0
France [29] (Euro)	1970	111 374	7.5	24.6	22.3	7.9	14.2	8.0	37.8
	1975	211 381	5.4	23.9	21.6	7.8	13.8	7.9	41.1
	1980	403 017	4.0	23.7	20.7	7.4	13.5	8.3	43.0
	1985	674 602	3.7	22.9	19.4	5.9	13.5	8.6	45.4
	1990	943 857	3.5	21.1	18.1	6.2	14.0	9.0	46.2
	1995	1 090 701	2.7	19.7	16.6	5.3	13.9	9.0	49.4
	2000	1 326 342	2.3	18.9	16.1	4.9	13.6	9.6	50.8
	2005	1 586 086	1.9	16.4	13.6	5.4	13.6	9.9	52.8
	2010	1 797 789	1.8	13.8	11.5	6.0	13.2	9.8	55.5
	2015	1 967 467	1.8	14.3	11.7	5.5	13.1	9.6	55.8
	2016	1 996 791	1.6	14.1	11.5	5.4	13.1	9.7	56.0
	2017	2 046 131	1.7	13.8	11.4	5.5	13.1	9.9	55.9
	2018	2 099 319	1.9	13.6	11.1	5.6	13.2	9.8	56.0
	2019	2 157 110	1.8	13.5	11.0	5.8	13.1	10.0	55.9
Germany [29] (Euro)	1970	369 397	3.2	39.2	34.2	8.8	13.9	6.8	28.1
	1975	568 125	2.7	35.1	30.6	7.0	13.6	6.6	35.0
	1980	808 985	2.1	33.5	29.3	7.6	13.4	6.5	36.9
	1985	1 010 411	1.7	33.3	28.8	6.0	12.9	6.3	39.9
	1990	1 335 181	1.3	31.5	27.8	6.1	12.8	6.2	42.1
	1995	1 720 878	1.1	25.9	22.6	6.9	11.8	7.8	46.6
	2000	1 907 274	1.1	25.5	22.7	5.1	11.7	8.7	47.8
	2005	2 075 552	0.8	25.2	22.1	3.9	11.9	9.1	49.2
	2010	2 311 665	0.9	25.5	21.8	4.3	11.2	8.8	49.3
	2015	2 728 847	0.8	25.5	22.6	4.6	11.2	9.1	48.8
	2016	2 829 452	0.8	25.9	22.9	4.7	11.4	9.0	48.3
	2017	2 943 907	0.9	25.8	22.6	4.7	11.5	9.0	48.1
	2018	3 031 817	0.7	25.4	22.2	4.9	11.5	9.2	48.2
	2019	3 113 755	0.8	24.2	21.2	5.4	11.7	9.3	48.6
Greece [29] (Euro)	1970	1 211	10.5	20.1	16.7	8.1	19.1	9.2	32.9
	1975	2 780	10.8	20.3	17.5	6.6	22.1	9.7	30.5
	1980	7 040	10.4	20.3	17.4	7.9	20.8	9.5	31.1
	1985	18 857	10.2	21.1	16.4	6.0	21.4	9.3	32.1
	1990	42 841	8.4	19.1	14.5	6.7	20.1	9.3	36.3
	1995	84 679	8.1	16.0	12.1	5.6	21.7	8.7	39.9
	2000	126 181	6.1	14.0	10.6	7.0	20.9	10.6	41.5
	2005	178 821	4.8	13.5	9.6	6.4	18.1	11.6	45.7
	2010	197 729	3.4	12.3	8.9	4.6	17.8	10.3	51.6
	2015	155 577	4.4	14.2	9.4	2.2	18.5	9.2	51.5
	2016	151 939	4.0	14.4	9.3	2.3	18.0	9.5	51.7
	2017	154 593	4.4	14.3	9.3	1.5	18.7	10.2	51.0
	2018	155 780	4.2	13.8	9.1	1.5	19.7	10.4	50.4

Table 3. Gross Value Added by Kind of Economic Activity: Individual Countries or Areas

Major area, region and country	Year	Gross Value Added (at current prices) Million	Percentage Distributtion						
			Agriculture, hunting, forestry, fishing A-B	Mining, Manufacturing, Utilities C-E	Of which: Manufacturing D	Construction F	Wholesale, retail trade, restaurants and hotels G-H	Transport, storage and communication I	Other Activities J-P
	2019	159 037	4.4	13.5	8.9	1.4	20.1	10.8	49.9
Hungary [29]	1970	352 928	17.0	36.1	25.5	8.3	8.2	9.2	21.3
(Forint)	1975	551 735	15.4	37.7	26.7	8.6	8.1	9.0	21.1
	1980	715 047	17.1	35.0	25.0	8.3	8.6	9.3	21.7
	1985	1 052 046	16.0	34.6	24.3	7.8	8.8	8.4	24.5
	1990	2 037 836	12.9	28.4	20.1	6.4	12.3	8.0	31.9
	1995	4 942 722	8.5	25.5	21.5	5.0	10.7	9.7	40.6
	2000	11 348 447	5.8	26.6	22.4	5.1	11.9	10.8	39.9
	2005	19 403 624	4.3	25.8	22.1	5.8	12.0	10.4	41.7
	2010	23 278 960	3.6	25.6	21.3	4.2	11.4	11.3	43.9
	2015	29 431 865	4.5	27.1	24.0	4.2	12.0	11.3	40.8
	2016	30 675 148	4.6	26.5	23.1	3.6	11.7	11.5	42.2
	2017	33 285 449	4.4	25.5	22.6	4.2	12.0	11.1	42.8
	2018	36 620 653	4.1	24.8	22.0	5.1	12.3	11.0	42.8
	2019	39 981 253	4.0	24.0	21.0	5.6	12.2	11.4	42.7
Iceland [29]	1970	421	11.0	21.9	18.7	15.5	10.7	12.9	28.0
(Iceland Krona)	1975	1 923	10.1	20.9	16.8	14.2	10.4	14.8	29.6
	1980	13 774	11.8	24.9	20.1	11.7	11.4	10.7	29.6
	1985	109 218	10.8	24.5	18.1	10.3	11.8	10.7	31.9
	1990	334 015	10.0	20.8	16.4	10.3	14.1	10.3	33.7
	1995	409 869	10.5	20.5	16.0	8.5	13.8	11.5	35.3
	2000	612 256	8.1	17.3	13.4	9.2	13.0	11.5	41.0
	2005	902 363	5.6	13.9	10.2	10.4	12.3	10.0	47.8
	2010	1 505 443	7.0	19.9	14.3	4.5	10.0	9.7	49.0
	2015	2 056 184	5.9	17.0	11.8	5.4	12.2	11.2	48.2
	2016	2 226 572	5.1	15.1	10.4	6.8	13.4	11.6	47.9
	2017	2 315 023	4.2	14.8	10.0	7.4	13.5	11.1	49.1
	2018	2 472 627	4.3	14.5	9.5	7.8	13.1	11.3	49.0
	2019	2 642 837	4.7	14.5	9.7	7.3	13.1	11.1	49.3
Ireland [29]	1970	2 048	15.5	19.6	16.5	9.9	16.0	12.0	27.1
(Euro)	1975	4 874	16.4	19.5	16.4	10.3	14.5	12.1	27.1
	1980	12 496	10.9	20.7	18.2	11.5	14.1	9.2	33.6
	1985	23 236	9.1	23.7	20.8	6.9	14.8	9.2	36.2
	1990	34 427	7.8	23.4	21.3	5.9	16.0	10.3	36.6
	1995	49 472	6.2	26.1	22.9	5.9	12.8	10.1	38.9
	2000	96 639	2.8	28.2	26.0	7.2	13.6	11.8	36.4
	2005	149 460	1.2	24.4	22.3	9.8	12.3	10.4	41.9
	2010	152 538	1.0	24.1	21.4	1.5	12.6	12.9	47.8
	2015	244 344	1.0	39.3	37.5	2.0	9.7	12.0	36.1
	2016	251 921	1.0	37.4	35.6	2.3	10.4	12.4	36.5
	2017	279 887	1.2	36.5	34.8	2.6	10.1	13.6	35.9
	2018	307 778	0.9	36.5	34.9	2.6	9.6	14.8	35.5
	2019	334 828	1.0	35.0	33.5	2.6	9.3	16.9	35.2
Italy [29]	1970	33 476	8.8	28.8	26.2	9.2	15.0	7.2	31.0
(Euro)	1975	72 969	7.5	28.6	26.1	8.7	15.1	7.4	32.8
	1980	198 699	6.0	29.6	27.5	7.1	16.6	8.0	32.6
	1985	418 587	4.7	26.6	23.9	6.4	17.3	8.2	36.8
	1990	668 096	3.5	24.9	22.0	6.1	16.8	8.1	40.7
	1995	893 037	3.3	23.9	21.0	5.2	17.1	8.4	42.0
	2000	1 112 456	2.9	22.3	19.6	4.9	16.5	9.2	44.2
	2005	1 346 105	2.3	19.9	17.3	5.9	15.4	9.6	46.8
	2010	1 449 430	2.0	18.7	15.8	5.6	14.9	9.6	49.2
	2015	1 488 049	2.3	18.9	16.0	4.3	15.2	9.1	50.2
	2016	1 522 754	2.1	19.3	16.5	4.3	15.5	9.3	49.4
	2017	1 557 796	2.2	19.5	16.6	4.2	15.8	9.4	48.8
	2018	1 589 263	2.2	19.7	16.7	4.2	15.8	9.3	48.9
	2019	1 603 736	2.1	19.6	16.6	4.3	15.8	9.4	48.8
Kosovo [55]	1990	2 978	7.7	21.0	12.7	16.2	13.0	4.8	37.3
(Euro)	1995	3 396	7.2	19.5	12.1	13.0	12.7	4.2	43.3
	2000	1 539	8.8	15.9	10.7	10.3	12.5	4.2	48.4
	2005	2 492	17.2	17.9	11.9	8.7	12.7	3.9	39.7
	2010	3 687	16.2	20.7	13.3	7.7	15.4	5.6	34.4
	2015	4 740	12.6	20.8	13.2	8.4	16.3	6.7	35.2
	2016	4 880	13.0	21.5	13.6	8.1	16.8	6.8	33.8
	2017	5 163	11.4	21.8	13.6	9.9	17.1	6.9	33.0
	2018	5 434	8.9	21.8	14.0	10.8	17.7	7.2	33.6

Table 3. Gross Value Added by Kind of Economic Activity: Individual Countries or Areas

Major area, region and country	Year	Gross Value Added (at current prices) Million	Percentage Distributtion						
			Agriculture, hunting, forestry, fishing A-B	Mining, Manufacturing, Utilities C-E	Of which: Manufacturing D	Construction F	Wholesale, retail trade, restaurants and hotels G-H	Transport, storage and communication I	Other Activities J-P
	2019	5 746	9.5	22.1	14.4	10.6	17.7	7.0	33.2
Latvia [55] (Euro)	1990	93	21.7	35.7	33.5	10.3	6.3	12.4	13.7
	1995	3 598	8.8	25.4	19.9	4.8	9.9	16.5	34.6
	2000	6 137	5.0	19.4	15.2	7.0	15.6	17.5	35.4
	2005	12 102	4.2	16.0	12.9	6.8	18.4	16.9	37.8
	2010	16 002	4.6	18.2	13.4	4.9	17.8	15.1	39.4
	2015	21 565	4.0	15.7	11.9	6.1	16.6	14.0	43.7
	2016	22 117	3.7	15.9	11.7	5.4	16.6	14.0	44.4
	2017	23 510	4.1	16.0	12.0	5.9	16.6	14.1	43.4
	2018	25 248	4.1	15.2	12.2	6.4	16.4	14.4	43.5
	2019	26 507	4.3	14.9	11.9	6.5	16.5	13.9	44.0
Liechtenstein [29] (Swiss Franc)	1970	452	2.4	26.7	23.2	7.8	18.2	9.1	35.9
	1975	689	2.4	26.7	23.2	7.8	18.2	9.1	35.9
	1980	1 072	2.4	27.2	23.7	7.8	18.1	9.1	35.4
	1985	1 564	2.3	24.6	21.3	7.9	18.1	9.1	38.0
	1990	2 279	2.0	23.1	20.3	8.4	17.8	8.5	40.2
	1995	3 004	1.4	23.2	19.6	6.8	16.2	8.7	43.7
	2000	4 115	0.2	40.1	37.9	3.9	5.3	3.4	47.2
	2005	4 579	0.1	41.8	40.2	3.9	5.6	3.5	45.1
	2010	5 422	0.1	40.8	39.2	3.7	6.3	3.4	45.7
	2015	5 844	0.1	39.1	37.6	4.0	5.7	3.5	47.6
	2016	5 945	0.1	39.5	38.1	3.9	5.6	3.5	47.4
	2017	6 107	0.1	41.7	40.4	4.3	7.4	3.1	43.4
	2018	6 421	0.1	38.5	37.2	4.0	9.2	3.6	44.5
	2019	6 498	0.1	39.9	38.6	4.1	7.4	3.4	45.1
Lithuania [55] (Euro)	1990	40	25.5	18.9	16.2	9.4	8.6	7.6	29.9
	1995	6 936	11.1	24.4	18.7	7.1	17.5	8.7	31.2
	2000	11 881	6.3	23.6	18.9	6.0	18.1	13.2	32.8
	2005	19 010	4.8	24.9	20.2	7.8	18.7	13.6	30.3
	2010	25 137	3.4	23.3	18.8	5.8	18.8	15.7	33.0
	2015	33 604	3.8	22.2	19.1	7.4	19.6	15.1	31.9
	2016	35 001	3.5	22.1	18.8	6.7	19.8	15.3	32.7
	2017	37 975	3.9	22.1	18.9	6.7	19.6	15.7	32.0
	2018	40 678	3.2	21.4	18.4	7.0	19.7	15.9	32.7
	2019	43 850	3.6	20.8	17.9	7.3	19.6	15.6	33.1
Luxembourg [29] (Euro)	1970	1 356	3.7	48.0	40.7	6.3	14.2	8.6	19.2
	1975	2 342	2.9	30.8	25.2	7.9	16.5	7.8	34.1
	1980	3 365	2.3	30.3	26.1	7.3	18.4	9.1	32.5
	1985	6 574	2.0	23.7	20.9	4.4	14.8	7.2	48.0
	1990	9 287	1.5	21.6	19.3	6.9	15.8	9.3	44.9
	1995	14 270	1.0	14.9	12.9	6.2	13.1	9.7	54.9
	2000	20 619	0.7	12.6	10.8	6.0	11.9	11.7	57.1
	2005	26 668	0.4	10.8	8.9	5.7	10.3	11.4	61.4
	2010	36 137	0.3	7.4	5.8	5.3	12.3	11.1	63.6
	2015	47 057	0.2	6.7	5.1	5.5	11.8	11.0	64.7
	2016	49 771	0.2	7.3	5.9	5.5	12.4	10.9	63.6
	2017	51 599	0.3	6.9	5.5	5.5	11.9	11.0	64.4
	2018	54 378	0.3	7.0	5.7	6.0	11.3	11.9	63.6
	2019	57 611	0.2	6.5	5.0	6.0	10.9	11.3	65.0
Malta [29] (Euro)	1970	215	7.3	20.6	19.4	11.7	28.4	6.3	25.7
	1975	413	6.0	27.1	26.3	11.0	23.6	7.8	24.5
	1980	986	3.6	28.2	27.2	8.0	23.2	10.8	26.2
	1985	1 190	4.4	25.9	24.8	7.3	25.1	9.6	27.6
	1990	1 759	3.5	25.0	23.3	7.0	23.9	10.1	30.6
	1995	2 679	2.8	22.3	21.0	6.2	22.1	11.8	34.8
	2000	3 654	2.3	23.4	21.6	5.9	20.2	12.4	35.9
	2005	4 443	2.2	15.7	14.7	7.3	17.9	11.5	45.4
	2010	5 710	1.7	14.2	13.1	4.7	15.6	11.7	52.1
	2015	8 479	1.2	9.4	8.5	3.9	16.3	12.9	56.3
	2016	9 078	1.4	9.0	8.2	3.6	15.4	13.4	57.3
	2017	9 913	0.9	9.1	8.3	3.7	15.1	13.3	57.9
	2018	10 829	1.0	9.2	8.4	3.6	15.0	13.1	58.0
	2019	11 672	0.9	8.9	8.1	3.9	14.8	13.0	58.6

Table 3. Gross Value Added by Kind of Economic Activity: Individual Countries or Areas

Major area, region and country	Year	Gross Value Added (at current prices) Million	Percentage Distributtion: Agriculture, hunting, forestry, fishing A-B	Mining, Manufacturing, Utilities C-E	Of which: Manufacturing D	Construction F	Wholesale, retail trade, restaurants and hotels G-H	Transport, storage and communication I	Other Activities J-P
Monaco [20]	1970	245	...	6.1	6.1	6.7	39.9	9.4	37.8
(Euro)	1975	459	...	6.1	6.1	6.7	39.9	9.4	37.8
	1980	880	...	6.1	6.1	6.7	39.9	9.4	37.8
	1985	1 476	...	6.1	6.1	6.7	39.9	9.4	37.8
	1990	2 052	...	6.1	6.1	6.7	39.9	9.4	37.8
	1995	2 372	...	6.1	6.1	6.7	39.9	9.4	37.8
	2000	2 879	...	6.1	6.1	6.7	39.9	9.5	37.8
	2005	3 438	...	5.8	5.8	6.4	39.8	9.3	38.6
	2010	4 049	...	5.8	5.8	7.1	25.9	9.6	51.6
	2015	5 644	...	4.9	4.9	12.7	22.2	8.0	52.3
	2016	5 848	...	3.9	3.9	14.3	20.8	7.9	53.1
	2017	5 693	...	4.1	4.1	8.7	22.7	9.2	55.3
	2018	6 091	...	3.7	3.7	9.5	23.2	8.5	55.1
	2019	6 631	...	3.1	3.1	9.9	22.8	8.5	55.7
Montenegro [55]	1990	1 613	12.1	21.3	11.4	4.1	15.7	12.4	34.5
(Euro)	1995	810	12.1	21.3	11.4	4.1	15.6	12.5	34.5
	2000	980	12.3	20.6	10.3	4.2	16.5	11.1	35.3
	2005	1 536	10.3	18.6	9.9	3.5	15.7	12.1	39.7
	2010	2 608	9.2	14.6	5.4	5.9	19.6	12.4	38.3
	2015	3 021	9.0	12.8	4.9	4.5	23.9	9.5	39.4
	2016	3 271	9.0	12.3	4.5	6.7	23.2	9.6	39.3
	2017	3 519	8.4	11.3	4.7	6.9	25.0	9.7	38.8
	2018	3 816	8.2	12.5	4.9	7.0	24.4	9.6	38.3
	2019	4 022	7.9	11.9	4.6	7.9	25.0	9.5	37.8
Netherlands [29]	1970	57 415	5.6	28.2	24.8	8.9	14.3	8.4	34.5
(Euro)	1975	105 181	4.7	26.6	21.0	7.4	13.0	7.7	40.7
	1980	160 661	3.8	25.4	17.9	6.8	12.7	7.5	43.8
	1985	199 310	4.1	27.3	17.5	4.9	12.8	7.5	43.4
	1990	242 010	4.4	23.0	18.2	5.5	14.3	8.5	44.3
	1995	299 274	3.4	21.3	16.9	5.2	14.3	8.4	47.4
	2000	405 832	2.6	18.9	14.9	5.3	15.6	9.4	48.2
	2005	491 394	2.1	18.1	13.8	5.4	14.9	9.9	49.6
	2010	574 280	2.0	16.7	11.7	5.3	14.2	9.4	52.6
	2015	620 835	1.9	16.0	12.0	4.3	15.4	9.7	52.8
	2016	634 824	2.0	15.2	12.1	4.4	15.7	9.8	52.9
	2017	661 566	2.1	15.2	12.3	4.5	15.8	9.8	52.6
	2018	692 632	1.8	15.2	12.4	4.7	15.9	9.8	52.6
	2019	722 150	1.8	14.9	12.3	5.0	15.9	9.7	52.6
North Macedonia [27,55]	1990	434	9.1	27.7	19.0	8.4	8.4	7.2	39.2
(Denar)	1995	156 999	12.5	18.9	11.2	5.8	12.3	6.3	44.2
	2000	209 602	12.0	18.7	10.6	6.7	11.9	9.7	41.1
	2005	264 847	11.3	17.6	11.3	6.2	15.0	7.9	42.0
	2010	377 199	11.7	17.9	11.4	6.5	14.1	8.3	41.5
	2015	488 408	11.1	19.3	13.5	8.1	16.6	7.9	37.1
	2016	515 600	10.6	19.7	14.2	8.0	17.4	8.1	36.3
	2017	535 726	9.1	20.5	14.5	7.5	18.4	8.5	36.1
	2018	571 210	9.8	21.4	15.3	6.2	18.2	8.5	36.0
	2019	608 908	10.0	21.2	14.8	6.2	18.3	8.5	35.7
Norway [29]	1970	79 884	5.8	24.3	20.3	6.4	16.6	16.5	30.3
(Norwegian Krone)	1975	151 295	4.7	26.5	20.2	6.2	16.5	12.6	33.4
	1980	284 568	4.1	33.2	15.0	5.0	13.5	11.1	33.1
	1985	494 928	3.2	36.0	12.9	4.6	12.8	9.9	33.5
	1990	666 420	3.4	28.9	11.6	4.4	12.3	12.2	38.9
	1995	835 217	3.0	29.1	12.5	4.1	12.0	11.0	40.0
	2000	1 329 434	2.1	37.5	10.0	3.9	10.1	10.6	35.8
	2005	1 775 602	1.6	37.8	9.1	4.7	9.0	10.0	36.9
	2010	2 308 033	1.8	33.7	8.1	5.3	9.1	9.7	40.4
	2015	2 768 846	1.7	28.5	7.7	6.4	9.2	9.7	44.5
	2016	2 739 686	2.4	24.9	7.4	6.7	9.7	9.6	46.7
	2017	2 919 814	2.2	27.0	7.2	6.6	9.4	9.1	45.6
	2018	2 899 686	2.3	31.9	7.2	7.1	9.4	9.4	39.8
	2019	3 150 407	2.2	26.1	7.0	6.7	9.4	9.2	46.4
Poland [29]	1970	112	13.7	40.9	30.9	11.1	9.4	5.4	19.5
(Zloty)	1975	161	13.7	40.9	30.9	11.1	9.4	5.4	19.5
	1980	259	13.8	40.9	30.9	11.1	9.4	5.3	19.5

Table 3. Gross Value Added by Kind of Economic Activity: Individual Countries or Areas

Major area, region and country	Year	Gross Value Added (at current prices) Million	Percentage Distributtion: Agriculture, hunting, forestry, fishing A-B	Mining, Manufacturing, Utilities C-E	Of which: Manufacturing D	Construction F	Wholesale, retail trade, restaurants and hotels G-H	Transport, storage and communication I	Other Activities J-P
	1985	1 071	14.6	40.4	30.5	11.0	9.4	5.3	19.3
	1990	65 544	6.8	41.5	31.4	10.2	11.8	6.3	23.4
	1995	304 362	6.3	29.6	22.0	8.3	19.8	7.1	28.9
	2000	664 322	3.5	24.2	18.1	8.2	21.1	8.7	34.2
	2005	870 463	3.3	25.0	18.2	7.6	19.8	10.2	34.1
	2010	1 273 022	3.2	24.4	17.4	8.4	20.4	9.3	34.2
	2015	1 598 028	2.7	26.0	19.7	8.0	18.8	10.5	34.1
	2016	1 646 287	2.9	26.4	20.3	7.0	18.7	10.6	34.4
	2017	1 747 525	3.3	25.2	19.1	7.1	19.0	11.0	34.5
	2018	1 857 482	2.7	24.9	19.1	7.6	19.1	11.3	34.4
	2019	2 010 603	2.7	24.7	18.9	7.2	19.0	11.4	35.1
Portugal [29]	1970	1 001	29.4	22.7	20.2	4.4	13.8	7.8	21.9
(Euro)	1975	2 092	26.5	22.9	20.9	5.9	13.7	8.5	22.5
	1980	7 768	17.5	20.7	18.7	6.2	21.2	6.7	27.7
	1985	22 134	13.3	21.9	18.8	4.9	21.5	9.2	29.1
	1990	50 250	8.6	22.5	18.9	5.9	19.5	7.2	36.3
	1995	78 453	5.4	21.6	18.1	6.5	18.8	7.2	40.4
	2000	112 522	3.5	20.3	17.2	7.6	18.5	7.7	42.3
	2005	137 486	2.7	17.7	14.5	6.9	18.3	7.9	46.5
	2010	157 971	2.2	16.8	13.2	5.8	18.1	8.3	48.7
	2015	156 517	2.4	18.3	13.9	4.1	19.8	8.3	47.1
	2016	161 993	2.4	18.2	14.0	4.0	19.9	8.3	47.2
	2017	169 642	2.4	18.0	14.3	4.0	19.7	8.5	47.3
	2018	177 466	2.4	18.1	14.2	4.2	19.4	8.5	47.5
	2019	184 531	2.4	17.5	13.8	4.3	19.6	8.6	47.6
Republic of Moldova [55]	1990	15	33.0	29.8	25.8	13.2	5.0	5.4	13.6
(Moldovan Leu)	1995	6 978	30.2	27.4	24.3	7.8	9.5	4.5	20.6
	2000	17 168	26.4	18.2	15.3	6.0	14.3	8.4	26.7
	2005	38 841	17.7	18.3	14.9	7.7	12.9	11.3	32.2
	2010	74 311	13.0	15.9	11.6	7.8	15.8	11.0	36.4
	2015	127 064	13.2	17.8	13.7	8.3	17.0	10.8	32.9
	2016	140 887	13.0	17.6	13.6	7.8	17.5	11.0	33.1
	2017	154 815	13.3	17.3	13.3	8.0	18.5	10.8	32.1
	2018	166 472	11.9	17.0	13.0	9.1	18.8	11.1	32.0
	2019	182 595	11.3	16.3	12.5	9.9	19.5	11.0	32.0
Romania [58]	1970	27	16.0	49.1	43.0	8.8	3.1	5.1	17.9
(New Leu)	1975	44	14.1	50.7	44.4	6.4	5.9	4.9	17.9
	1980	62	13.3	48.4	42.4	7.3	6.0	7.1	17.9
	1985	78	15.5	46.9	41.0	7.1	5.5	6.3	18.6
	1990	82	22.0	40.5	36.4	5.6	6.1	5.8	20.0
	1995	7 217	19.2	31.7	25.2	6.7	9.9	7.5	25.1
	2000	73 027	12.0	27.7	21.9	5.8	13.9	11.8	28.8
	2005	254 391	9.6	28.5	24.0	7.9	12.9	12.7	28.4
	2010	471 396	5.6	33.5	25.7	8.9	6.1	11.5	34.3
	2015	626 482	4.8	27.4	22.3	6.7	12.0	13.1	36.1
	2016	686 373	4.5	26.8	22.4	6.7	12.7	12.7	36.5
	2017	776 642	4.8	26.2	22.0	5.7	13.3	13.0	36.9
	2018	860 767	4.8	25.2	20.7	6.1	13.1	12.8	38.0
	2019	958 377	4.5	24.1	20.1	7.1	13.2	13.0	38.1
Russian Federation	1990	553	16.5	40.4	27.1	10.2	6.6	10.2	16.2
(Russian Ruble)	1995	1 322 972	7.1	30.4	20.1	9.1	21.2	12.0	20.2
	2000	6 471 893	6.3	33.3	22.7	6.5	23.7	8.9	21.3
	2005	18 701 468	4.9	32.9	18.5	5.3	20.2	10.0	26.7
	2010	40 462 643	3.8	28.3	15.0	6.4	20.8	8.9	31.7
	2015	74 627 452	4.3	26.1	13.9	7.2	17.3	7.7	37.4
	2016	77 475 287	4.3	25.6	13.3	7.1	17.3	7.8	37.9
	2017	83 155 588	3.9	26.3	13.5	7.5	17.3	7.7	37.3
	2018	92 799 527	3.5	27.7	13.8	8.2	16.7	7.5	36.3
	2019	98 416 647	3.9	26.5	13.5	7.6	17.1	7.7	37.2
San Marino [29]	1970	27	0.1	35.9	35.9	5.0	18.6	2.8	37.7
(Euro)	1975	56	0.1	35.9	35.9	5.0	18.6	2.8	37.7
	1980	153	0.1	35.9	35.9	5.0	18.6	2.8	37.7
	1985	324	0.1	35.9	35.9	5.0	18.6	2.8	37.7
	1990	529	0.1	35.9	35.9	5.0	18.6	2.8	37.7
	1995	880	0.1	35.8	35.8	5.0	18.6	2.8	37.7
	2000	1 284	0.1	35.7	35.7	5.0	18.6	2.8	37.9

Table 3. Gross Value Added by Kind of Economic Activity: Individual Countries or Areas

Major area, region and country	Year	Gross Value Added (at current prices) Million	Percentage Distributtion						
			Agriculture, hunting, forestry, fishing A-B	Mining, Manufacturing, Utilities C-E	Of which: Manufacturing D	Construction F	Wholesale, retail trade, restaurants and hotels G-H	Transport, storage and communication I	Other Activities J-P
	2005	1 526	0.1	32.0	32.0	6.2	17.6	2.9	41.2
	2010	1 489	0.1	29.5	29.5	6.1	16.3	3.2	44.8
	2015	1 191	0.0	30.7	30.7	3.7	13.6	5.6	46.3
	2016	1 241	0.0	30.7	30.7	3.9	14.2	6.3	44.8
	2017	1 272	0.0	30.6	30.6	3.9	14.7	6.3	44.4
	2018	1 318	0.0	34.4	34.4	4.1	14.2	6.8	40.4
	2019	1 326	0.0	34.2	34.2	4.2	14.2	7.0	40.4
Serbia [55] (Serbian Dinar)	1990	0 (u)	18.2	29.8	24.0	6.1	9.1	5.7	31.2
	1995	55 843	17.5	30.6	25.0	6.9	9.5	5.8	29.7
	2000	402 362	18.4	35.1	29.3	3.0	9.4	4.2	29.8
	2005	1 533 639	8.1	30.6	23.5	4.5	10.7	6.7	39.4
	2010	2 716 990	7.9	26.2	18.3	4.1	15.0	8.7	38.1
	2015	3 597 767	8.1	26.4	17.7	4.5	14.8	10.2	35.9
	2016	3 755 978	8.2	26.4	17.9	4.7	15.0	10.4	35.3
	2017	3 952 670	7.2	26.5	18.2	5.0	15.5	10.7	35.2
	2018	4 202 926	7.7	25.4	17.5	5.4	15.5	10.5	35.5
	2019	4 480 900	7.2	24.0	16.5	6.9	15.4	10.4	36.0
Slovakia [55] (Euro)	1990	8 486	3.5	46.7	30.9	8.2	9.4	4.5	27.6
	1995	17 117	2.6	27.5	22.0	4.5	11.7	8.1	45.5
	2000	27 967	1.9	27.6	22.0	5.7	15.2	10.8	38.8
	2005	44 621	1.8	29.7	23.3	6.5	16.2	10.4	35.5
	2010	61 755	1.8	25.2	20.0	8.6	15.5	9.6	39.3
	2015	71 786	2.9	26.1	21.7	7.8	12.4	11.8	38.9
	2016	73 022	3.0	24.8	20.6	7.7	11.9	11.6	41.0
	2017	75 781	2.7	24.0	20.0	8.3	12.2	11.5	41.3
	2018	80 217	2.7	24.7	21.2	7.9	12.0	11.0	41.8
	2019	83 986	2.8	24.5	20.3	7.6	11.7	11.4	42.1
Slovenia [55] (Euro)	1990	777	6.2	35.0	31.1	5.1	12.7	9.7	31.3
	1995	9 069	4.7	28.7	25.1	5.8	13.8	7.8	39.3
	2000	16 464	3.5	28.4	24.8	6.5	13.1	9.0	39.5
	2005	25 569	2.8	27.4	23.5	6.5	14.0	9.2	40.1
	2010	31 693	2.2	24.1	20.1	6.3	14.4	9.6	43.4
	2015	33 592	2.4	27.0	23.1	5.4	14.1	10.3	40.7
	2016	35 030	2.3	27.1	23.3	5.2	14.3	10.4	40.8
	2017	37 372	2.1	27.3	23.7	5.4	14.4	10.5	40.4
	2018	39 946	2.6	26.7	23.3	5.7	14.6	10.3	40.0
	2019	42 343	2.3	27.0	23.6	6.0	14.5	10.4	39.8
Spain [29] (Euro)	1970	15 794	10.4	30.7	25.4	11.0	15.5	7.3	25.1
	1975	37 508	9.1	30.1	24.9	11.3	15.7	7.3	26.5
	1980	95 199	6.8	28.3	23.4	9.9	17.3	8.1	29.6
	1985	173 574	5.7	27.0	22.3	7.8	18.3	8.6	32.6
	1990	309 366	5.1	23.8	19.7	10.6	18.2	8.5	33.9
	1995	426 438	4.2	21.3	17.6	9.3	19.6	9.0	36.6
	2000	588 988	4.1	20.7	17.9	10.1	19.0	9.2	36.9
	2005	832 410	3.1	18.4	15.3	11.9	18.3	8.6	39.7
	2010	985 479	2.6	16.3	12.4	8.9	17.9	8.4	45.8
	2015	978 469	3.0	16.4	12.4	5.8	18.6	8.5	47.7
	2016	1 010 688	3.1	16.2	12.4	5.9	19.1	8.3	47.5
	2017	1 053 180	3.1	16.2	12.5	5.9	19.3	8.3	47.2
	2018	1 089 802	3.1	16.1	12.3	6.1	19.0	8.4	47.4
	2019	1 129 010	2.9	16.1	12.3	6.4	18.8	8.5	47.2
Sweden [29] (Swedish Krona)	1970	169 806	7.8	29.0	25.9	7.0	11.3	11.1	33.7
	1975	301 262	8.1	30.1	26.9	6.3	11.9	10.6	33.0
	1980	550 014	5.3	26.3	22.8	6.1	11.1	10.4	40.7
	1985	884 379	5.4	27.3	23.6	5.6	11.7	9.2	40.6
	1990	1 368 656	4.3	24.5	20.8	6.2	11.4	10.4	43.2
	1995	1 661 913	3.3	26.1	22.4	4.4	11.2	10.2	44.8
	2000	2 126 870	2.2	25.4	22.7	4.1	11.0	11.6	45.5
	2005	2 576 227	1.4	23.2	19.4	4.9	11.8	12.5	46.2
	2010	3 149 564	1.9	21.4	16.8	5.6	12.3	12.8	46.0
	2015	3 776 075	1.6	18.7	15.3	6.2	12.5	13.3	47.7
	2016	3 911 759	1.6	18.4	15.1	6.3	12.7	12.6	48.5
	2017	4 096 431	1.6	18.3	14.8	6.7	12.7	12.4	48.4
	2018	4 284 080	1.6	18.7	15.0	6.8	12.6	12.5	47.9
	2019	4 460 184	1.6	18.2	14.7	6.8	12.6	12.5	48.3

Table 3. Gross Value Added by Kind of Economic Activity: Individual Countries or Areas

Major area, region and country	Year	Gross Value Added (at current prices) Million	Percentage Distributtion						
			Agriculture, hunting, forestry, fishing A-B	Mining, Manufacturing, Utilities C-E	Of which: Manufacturing D	Construction F	Wholesale, retail trade, restaurants and hotels G-H	Transport, storage and communication I	Other Activities J-P
Switzerland [29]	1970	106 039	2.4	26.7	23.2	7.8	18.2	9.1	35.9
(Swiss Franc)	1975	163 916	2.4	26.7	23.2	7.8	18.2	9.1	35.9
	1980	199 310	2.4	27.2	23.7	7.8	18.1	9.1	35.4
	1985	264 396	2.3	24.6	21.3	7.9	18.1	9.1	38.0
	1990	356 807	2.0	23.1	20.3	8.4	17.8	8.5	40.2
	1995	405 161	1.4	23.2	19.6	6.8	16.2	8.7	43.7
	2000	451 845	1.1	21.6	18.5	5.2	16.5	8.4	47.3
	2005	504 281	0.8	21.8	19.6	5.1	17.5	8.5	46.1
	2010	606 824	0.7	21.0	18.8	4.9	19.3	8.1	46.0
	2015	654 755	0.6	20.1	18.0	5.1	17.7	8.4	48.0
	2016	665 145	0.7	20.1	18.3	5.1	17.4	8.4	48.4
	2017	672 741	0.6	20.2	18.4	5.0	17.6	8.4	48.1
	2018	699 245	0.6	20.5	18.6	4.9	17.3	8.3	48.3
	2019	706 744	0.7	20.7	18.7	4.9	16.6	8.4	48.7
Ukraine [52,55]	1990	1 643 (t)	24.8	36.7	35.3	8.9	5.4	7.8	16.4
(Hryvnia)	1995	51 831	14.5	34.1	32.6	7.8	7.4	13.3	23.0
	2000	150 320	16.3	33.0	20.4	4.1	10.4	13.8	22.3
	2005	404 474	10.0	29.7	20.9	4.4	14.4	12.7	28.7
	2010	954 472	8.4	25.6	15.0	3.7	17.2	12.2	33.0
	2015	1 689 387	14.2	23.3	14.0	2.3	16.9	12.3	31.0
	2016	2 023 228	13.8	25.0	14.4	2.3	16.5	12.2	30.2
	2017	2 519 561	12.1	25.1	14.3	2.6	17.0	12.0	31.3
	2018	3 018 190	12.0	24.8	13.6	2.7	16.5	12.1	31.9
	2019	3 418 141	10.5	23.1	12.6	3.1	16.3	13.1	33.8
United Kingdom [29]	1970	54 503	2.2	31.8	26.6	6.8	13.9	9.9	35.3
(Pound Sterling)	1975	116 678	2.1	28.1	22.8	7.7	13.5	10.1	38.4
	1980	248 479	1.6	30.4	21.4	6.6	12.7	8.3	40.4
	1985	381 129	1.3	28.3	19.1	6.0	12.9	7.9	43.5
	1990	600 666	1.4	23.4	18.4	7.1	13.7	9.5	44.9
	1995	770 850	1.4	22.0	17.1	5.3	13.7	9.0	48.5
	2000	982 663	1.0	19.7	15.0	6.1	14.4	10.6	48.3
	2005	1 254 195	0.6	16.1	11.8	6.4	14.0	10.3	52.6
	2010	1 446 477	0.7	15.4	10.6	5.7	13.6	10.3	54.3
	2015	1 712 072	0.7	14.2	10.5	6.4	13.3	10.3	55.1
	2016	1 777 366	0.6	13.7	10.2	6.4	13.2	10.5	55.6
	2017	1 844 010	0.6	13.9	10.2	6.5	13.4	10.6	55.0
	2018	1 910 247	0.6	13.9	10.1	6.4	13.4	10.6	55.0
	2019	1 977 096	0.7	13.4	9.7	6.6	13.7	10.8	54.9
Oceania									
Australia [29]	1970	35 660	6.5	30.7	23.7	8.8	11.5	8.7	33.7
(Australian Dollar)	1975	78 503	5.6	28.2	19.9	9.0	11.3	8.2	37.7
	1980	144 358	5.9	28.9	18.5	8.2	10.0	7.9	39.2
	1985	243 740	4.5	28.3	16.8	7.0	12.0	9.0	39.1
	1990	381 559	3.5	22.9	13.7	7.3	13.2	9.1	44.1
	1995	484 462	3.7	21.9	13.9	6.5	13.7	9.3	45.0
	2000	643 948	3.8	20.3	12.0	5.6	13.1	9.1	48.0
	2005	917 416	3.0	20.5	10.7	7.3	12.6	8.7	48.0
	2010	1 323 757	2.4	20.4	7.9	7.9	11.7	8.1	49.5
	2015	1 543 894	2.6	15.5	6.5	8.5	11.7	8.0	53.7
	2016	1 642 459	2.9	17.0	6.2	8.1	11.3	7.7	52.9
	2017	1 724 162	2.6	17.7	6.2	8.2	11.0	7.5	52.9
	2018	1 826 425	2.3	19.2	6.0	7.9	10.7	7.3	52.6
	2019	1 858 891	2.0	19.8	6.1	7.7	10.6	7.2	52.8
Cook Islands [1,29,38]	1970	9 938 (t)	26.4	12.9	10.9	9.2	13.7	7.2	30.6
(New Zealand Dollar)	1975	14	18.2	7.2	6.4	4.5	25.2	8.2	36.8
	1980	24	11.6	4.8	4.4	3.9	32.7	7.7	39.3
	1985	49	5.1	5.4	5.2	3.2	29.1	8.9	48.2
	1990	100	6.5	6.8	4.0	1.6	24.8	8.4	51.8
	1995	160	5.1	5.6	2.6	1.7	24.8	9.5	53.3
	2000	186	7.4	5.5	3.2	2.5	32.9	11.5	40.1
	2005	248	4.9	5.7	3.6	3.3	32.3	10.5	43.4
	2010	304	3.4	5.2	2.6	2.7	30.8	10.9	47.0
	2015	386	3.2	4.7	2.4	6.6	29.5	13.6	42.3
	2016	397	3.0	5.1	2.4	2.5	32.4	14.2	42.9
	2017	434	3.3	5.1	2.6	3.5	32.2	15.0	40.8

Table 3. Gross Value Added by Kind of Economic Activity: Individual Countries or Areas

Major area, region and country	Year	Gross Value Added (at current prices) Million	Percentage Distributtion						
			Agriculture, hunting, forestry, fishing A-B	Mining, Manufacturing, Utilities C-E	Of which: Manufacturing D	Construction F	Wholesale, retail trade, restaurants and hotels G-H	Transport, storage and communication I	Other Activities J-P
	2018	459	3.1	4.7	2.5	3.1	33.8	15.2	40.2
	2019	513	2.7	4.3	2.3	4.6	34.7	13.5	40.2
Fiji [29]	1970	209	24.5	11.6	10.9	5.6	6.3	5.9	46.0
(Fiji Dollar)	1975	588	23.2	13.3	12.5	7.1	7.3	7.5	41.5
	1980	1 039	20.0	13.8	12.9	6.2	8.1	7.9	44.0
	1985	1 365	16.4	12.0	10.1	4.1	8.0	9.2	50.3
	1990	2 093	16.7	14.6	12.3	2.8	10.9	9.6	45.3
	1995	2 853	16.4	14.9	12.7	2.9	10.9	9.1	45.8
	2000	3 575	14.7	15.3	13.4	2.4	12.1	12.5	43.0
	2005	4 680	12.8	14.9	13.2	3.0	15.8	14.2	39.3
	2010	5 396	10.2	17.0	13.8	2.9	18.1	12.2	39.6
	2015	7 709	10.0	16.3	13.4	3.0	17.1	14.4	39.2
	2016	8 407	13.1	16.8	13.4	3.1	16.1	14.3	36.7
	2017	8 931	13.0	16.2	12.9	3.2	17.2	13.4	36.9
	2018	9 271	13.4	16.0	13.0	3.4	17.5	12.3	37.5
	2019	9 606	13.2	16.3	13.1	3.2	16.9	13.3	37.0
French Polynesia [1,38]	1970	24 228	8.6	7.9	6.1	5.3	14.7	9.3	54.2
(CFP Franc)	1975	50 808	5.8	7.7	6.5	8.5	14.7	9.3	54.0
	1980	109 282	5.8	8.3	7.3	8.8	14.5	9.2	53.4
	1985	255 929	4.7	10.7	0.6	10.4	14.0	8.9	51.5
	1990	323 791	5.0	10.7	8.6	4.9	14.9	9.5	55.0
	1995	368 727	5.2	8.6	6.1	4.0	15.5	9.8	57.0
	2000	433 614	5.1	9.1	6.5	4.9	15.2	9.7	56.1
	2005	491 585	3.4	7.9	5.7	4.7	15.7	10.1	58.1
	2010	494 717	2.5	7.8	5.1	4.5	13.1	9.7	62.4
	2015	514 858	3.6	8.6	5.7	3.5	13.5	12.1	58.8
	2016	531 806	3.6	8.5	5.8	3.4	14.3	12.6	57.6
	2017	546 854	3.6	8.4	5.5	3.6	13.7	12.1	58.6
	2018	560 620	3.6	8.5	5.7	3.5	13.8	12.3	58.3
	2019	576 761	3.6	8.5	5.7	3.5	14.0	12.3	58.2
Kiribati [1,10,41]	1970	15	14.8	48.5	...	3.6	12.4	2.5	18.1
(Australian Dollar)	1975	52	12.3	56.8	...	2.2	11.9	3.5	13.3
	1980	24	53.7	7.7	5.8	7.0	14.6	8.4	8.6
	1985	41	44.0	6.8	5.0	2.6	9.1	8.3	29.2
	1990	44	24.8	11.5	9.6	2.5	14.0	11.8	35.4
	1995	72	26.9	7.4	6.3	1.7	11.5	10.0	42.5
	2000	117	23.6	6.0	4.8	8.2	9.8	11.7	40.7
	2005	137	21.8	5.6	5.1	3.7	5.9	14.0	49.1
	2010	169	24.2	6.9	5.6	5.0	7.2	10.9	45.8
	2015	221	22.6	5.5	4.0	10.2	7.1	7.7	46.9
	2016	253	25.4	5.4	4.0	10.4	8.1	6.7	44.1
	2017	266	28.6	5.1	4.0	7.8	6.4	7.8	44.4
	2018	281	27.3	5.0	3.8	8.2	7.2	7.4	45.0
	2019	298	27.1	5.1	3.9	8.8	7.2	7.3	44.5
Marshall Islands [1,42]	1970	7 810 (t)	9.7	0.4	0.8	12.2	25.9	-3.7	55.5
(US Dollar)	1975	16	9.7	0.4	0.8	12.2	25.9	-3.7	55.5
	1980	25	9.7	0.4	0.8	12.2	25.9	-3.7	55.5
	1985	41	9.7	0.4	0.8	12.2	25.9	-3.7	55.5
	1990	73	9.6	0.6	0.8	11.7	24.8	-2.1	55.3
	1995	113	10.5	3.7	1.8	10.2	18.3	7.1	50.2
	2000	105	10.4	5.0	1.1	6.4	19.1	9.8	49.3
	2005	130	9.0	3.4	2.2	6.6	19.0	9.4	52.6
	2010	161	15.4	5.3	1.8	7.1	16.8	8.0	47.3
	2015	180	14.4	5.2	1.0	5.1	16.5	11.1	47.7
	2016	196	15.8	8.3	2.0	5.5	15.4	10.2	44.7
	2017	210	16.4	7.5	1.8	6.0	14.8	10.3	45.0
	2018	209	16.1	8.1	4.3	5.4	14.5	7.5	48.4
	2019	233	16.1	8.0	2.6	5.6	14.9	9.4	46.0
Micronesia (FS of)	1970	20	24.5	3.4	1.4	4.1	13.2	7.1	47.9
(US Dollar)	1975	47	24.5	3.4	1.4	4.1	13.2	7.1	47.9
	1980	66	24.5	3.4	1.4	4.1	13.2	7.1	47.9
	1985	104	24.5	3.4	1.4	4.1	13.2	7.1	47.9
	1990	152	24.5	3.4	1.4	4.1	13.1	7.1	47.9
	1995	213	24.9	2.7	1.5	4.4	13.0	7.2	47.8
	2000	222	25.4	4.6	1.7	4.1	13.8	7.2	44.9
	2005	232	24.2	2.6	0.6	3.0	15.2	7.1	47.8

Table 3. Gross Value Added by Kind of Economic Activity: Individual Countries or Areas

Major area, region and country	Year	Gross Value Added (at current prices) Million	Percentage Distributtion						
			Agriculture, hunting, forestry, fishing A-B	Mining, Manufacturing, Utilities C-E	Of which: Manufacturing D	Construction F	Wholesale, retail trade, restaurants and hotels G-H	Transport, storage and communication I	Other Activities J-P
	2010	275	26.7	1.7	0.5	6.1	15.4	6.1	44.0
	2015	298	27.8	3.7	0.4	2.8	14.7	6.0	45.0
	2016	313	28.8	3.8	0.6	2.6	14.8	6.5	43.4
	2017	344	29.5	3.3	0.6	2.4	14.0	6.1	44.7
	2018	378	23.9	3.3	0.5	1.9	12.5	5.7	52.7
	2019	390	27.4	3.5	0.6	2.3	13.8	6.1	47.0
Nauru [20]	1970	15	5.6	34.2	1.6	3.3	14.7	16.4	25.7
(Australian Dollar)	1975	28	6.4	24.2	1.8	3.8	17.0	18.9	29.7
	1980	39	5.6	33.8	1.6	3.3	14.9	16.5	25.9
	1985	51	6.0	29.3	1.7	3.6	15.8	17.6	27.6
	1990	68	6.5	23.0	1.9	3.9	17.3	19.2	30.1
	1995	51	6.4	24.0	1.9	3.8	17.0	19.2	29.6
	2000	40	5.3	36.1	1.7	2.9	13.8	17.3	24.5
	2005	34	7.8	-9.8	3.5	3.3	19.5	23.8	55.4
	2010	67	4.2	40.2	14.5	3.4	11.0	12.9	28.3
	2015	137	2.4	37.9	23.3	2.8	19.3	18.9	18.7
	2016	157	2.4	33.5	19.7	3.0	22.7	19.0	19.3
	2017	166	2.4	32.1	18.3	3.1	23.2	19.8	19.4
	2018	183	2.4	34.5	20.4	3.0	21.8	19.2	19.1
	2019	189	2.4	33.4	19.5	3.0	22.6	19.4	19.2
New Caledonia [7,38,46]	1970	38 204	4.3	33.9	32.3	3.9	34.4	3.1	20.4
(CFP Franc)	1975	63 643	3.0	34.6	32.0	13.5	20.3	4.1	24.6
	1980	90 848	3.0	24.2	21.7	9.1	21.3	3.7	38.6
	1985	139 650	1.8	22.5	20.2	3.4	23.8	3.4	45.0
	1990	250 426	2.0	19.3	16.7	5.7	23.0	5.6	44.5
	1995	329 293	1.8	16.2	14.7	5.7	22.2	6.3	47.7
	2000	410 014	2.4	16.9	14.9	9.1	12.3	7.3	52.1
	2005	550 894	1.7	17.8	16.0	8.9	12.4	7.5	51.8
	2010	778 708	1.5	17.5	15.9	10.9	12.2	7.3	50.7
	2015	868 689	2.1	11.6	9.5	12.3	11.9	7.5	54.5
	2016	893 710	1.9	12.3	10.4	12.5	12.0	7.3	54.0
	2017	920 152	2.0	12.7	10.7	12.3	12.0	7.3	53.9
	2018	946 293	2.0	12.2	10.2	12.3	12.0	7.4	54.1
	2019	969 444	2.0	12.4	10.4	12.4	12.0	7.3	54.0
New Zealand [29]	1970	5 604	12.3	28.1	25.0	6.9	15.5	8.8	28.3
(New Zealand Dollar)	1975	11 246	10.0	26.5	23.6	8.3	14.1	8.7	32.4
	1980	23 820	10.1	29.5	25.1	5.5	13.6	9.2	32.2
	1985	47 611	7.4	28.4	23.4	5.7	14.3	8.9	35.3
	1990	70 694	6.4	24.2	19.2	4.4	13.3	9.9	41.8
	1995	89 119	7.0	23.3	19.1	4.5	13.1	10.4	41.8
	2000	111 635	8.3	20.7	16.6	4.6	12.8	9.1	44.5
	2005	151 150	4.9	20.0	15.7	5.8	12.8	9.0	47.5
	2010	187 434	7.1	17.4	11.8	5.6	12.0	7.8	50.1
	2015	232 910	4.9	16.6	12.3	6.6	12.5	8.2	51.1
	2016	246 832	6.1	15.3	11.1	6.8	12.7	7.7	51.4
	2017	264 321	6.4	15.3	11.2	7.0	12.7	7.5	51.1
	2018	274 694	5.8	15.7	11.5	6.8	12.7	7.8	51.2
	2019	287 016	6.1	15.4	11.3	6.9	12.7	7.7	51.2
Palau [1,29]	1970	11	17.1	2.5	0.4	22.8	14.5	4.1	39.1
(US Dollar)	1975	17	17.1	2.5	0.4	22.8	14.5	4.1	39.1
	1980	28	16.9	2.4	0.4	22.8	14.4	4.0	39.3
	1985	48	16.7	2.4	0.4	23.0	14.3	4.0	39.5
	1990	96	21.6	3.4	0.6	19.8	16.8	5.9	32.4
	1995	121	8.1	3.1	0.9	8.0	28.2	8.9	43.7
	2000	146	5.4	5.4	1.6	8.5	29.2	8.7	42.8
	2005	167	4.2	3.0	0.9	12.3	22.6	10.2	47.8
	2010	168	4.2	5.2	0.9	5.7	24.0	11.2	49.7
	2015	250	3.3	3.9	1.1	5.0	32.8	11.4	43.6
	2016	267	3.3	5.2	1.1	5.1	32.4	11.6	42.4
	2017	256	3.6	3.5	1.1	5.7	31.4	11.7	44.2
	2018	259	3.5	3.7	1.1	5.8	30.2	10.6	46.3
	2019	255	3.4	4.3	1.2	6.1	27.9	9.7	48.6
Papua New Guinea [29]	1970	1 130	19.8	2.7	2.1	8.6	27.2	14.5	27.2
(Kina)	1975	2 156	15.4	13.7	2.8	2.9	26.2	12.8	29.0
	1980	3 197	19.1	14.0	3.7	2.8	19.7	8.4	36.0
	1985	4 225	18.5	12.2	3.8	2.2	18.8	7.6	40.7

Table 3. Gross Value Added by Kind of Economic Activity: Individual Countries or Areas

Major area, region and country	Year	Gross Value Added (at current prices) Million	Percentage Distributtion						
			Agriculture, hunting, forestry, fishing A-B	Mining, Manufacturing, Utilities C-E	Of which: Manufacturing D	Construction F	Wholesale, retail trade, restaurants and hotels G-H	Transport, storage and communication I	Other Activities J-P
	1990	5 036	17.3	16.2	3.4	3.0	19.7	10.1	33.7
	1995	9 402	21.8	20.7	3.2	2.3	18.5	8.5	28.1
	2000	13 942	23.2	27.6	3.1	3.7	7.7	4.9	32.9
	2005	21 819	22.5	28.7	2.6	5.5	14.5	3.9	24.9
	2010	37 559	20.2	24.5	2.5	9.7	13.4	4.7	27.4
	2015	57 459	18.3	28.2	1.9	8.2	12.0	4.1	29.2
	2016	62 454	18.6	27.9	2.0	8.2	12.0	4.0	29.2
	2017	69 267	18.5	31.1	2.0	7.0	11.6	3.9	27.9
	2018	75 867	17.8	32.0	1.8	6.6	11.6	3.9	28.1
	2019	80 793	18.4	28.9	2.0	7.8	12.0	4.0	28.9
Samoa [26,29,51]	1970	30	24.7	16.3	13.5	4.1	15.8	10.2	29.0
(Tala)	1975	54	24.7	16.3	13.5	4.1	15.8	10.2	29.0
	1980	106	24.7	16.3	13.5	4.1	15.8	10.2	29.0
	1985	197	24.7	16.3	13.5	4.1	15.8	10.2	29.0
	1990	267	24.5	16.2	13.4	4.1	15.9	10.2	29.1
	1995	497	22.3	15.9	13.0	4.3	16.6	10.8	30.2
	2000	786	18.3	15.3	12.4	4.3	20.7	11.6	29.7
	2005	1 202	13.7	15.9	13.0	6.5	21.2	14.6	28.1
	2010	1 720	9.1	11.6	9.6	6.5	31.8	11.9	29.1
	2015	2 015	8.9	10.8	8.1	7.3	31.3	12.1	29.6
	2016	2 107	10.1	10.7	8.1	6.3	31.9	11.9	29.1
	2017	2 106	10.3	10.2	7.3	5.7	32.8	11.3	29.6
	2018	2 157	9.4	8.4	5.7	6.2	35.0	10.8	30.2
	2019	2 237	10.1	8.9	6.1	6.8	34.8	10.4	29.0
Solomon Islands [1]	1970	26	51.6	4.2	3.8	4.2	10.2	5.3	24.5
(Solomon Islands Dollar)	1975	44	51.6	4.2	3.8	4.2	10.2	5.3	24.5
	1980	107	51.4	4.3	3.8	4.2	10.1	5.3	24.8
	1985	213	50.4	4.1	3.8	4.2	10.4	5.1	25.8
	1990	459	45.5	5.2	3.7	2.6	7.8	4.7	34.1
	1995	1 176	44.7	10.7	7.1	3.7	9.2	6.8	25.0
	2000	1 648	34.7	10.2	8.0	2.5	11.5	8.7	32.3
	2005	3 186	30.4	6.0	5.2	1.5	13.2	8.8	40.0
	2010	5 824	28.7	10.6	8.0	2.8	17.9	7.7	32.3
	2015	8 956	26.0	9.9	7.2	4.7	22.1	5.6	31.8
	2016	9 488	26.9	9.6	7.2	5.4	22.4	5.1	30.6
	2017	10 370	25.4	10.8	9.2	5.7	21.7	5.3	31.0
	2018	11 061	26.1	10.1	7.9	5.3	22.0	5.3	31.2
	2019	11 369	26.1	10.2	8.1	5.5	22.0	5.3	30.9
Tonga [54]	1970	13	47.6	7.2	5.8	3.4	12.7	4.5	24.7
(Pa'anga)	1975	28	50.0	6.7	5.2	3.8	13.3	3.8	22.4
	1980	61	45.6	7.3	6.0	3.9	14.6	6.6	22.1
	1985	88	37.8	8.2	5.7	6.7	13.5	8.0	25.9
	1990	175	34.7	8.0	6.0	5.7	14.0	9.1	28.5
	1995	230	23.9	11.3	8.7	10.3	10.9	7.3	36.3
	2000	294	22.4	12.1	10.1	8.6	10.6	7.3	39.0
	2005	435	20.7	11.6	8.5	7.8	13.0	6.0	40.9
	2010	623	18.7	10.7	6.8	9.8	13.2	6.9	40.7
	2015	728	19.7	10.9	7.0	7.2	14.1	7.8	40.3
	2016	789	19.6	10.8	7.1	8.0	14.8	7.0	39.7
	2017	853	20.0	10.7	7.1	8.8	15.2	7.2	38.0
	2018	890	20.6	10.9	7.1	7.7	15.9	6.9	38.0
	2019	977	23.4	9.7	6.2	8.3	15.0	6.8	36.8
Tuvalu [44]	1970	2 153 (t)	15.6	4.4	2.0	13.3	9.5	8.3	48.9
(Australian Dollar)	1975	2 743 (t)	15.5	4.4	2.0	13.3	9.6	8.3	48.9
	1980	3 550 (t)	15.0	4.3	1.9	13.0	9.7	8.4	49.6
	1985	5 034 (t)	10.8	3.4	1.5	10.2	10.8	9.4	55.4
	1990	11	25.6	3.6	1.6	10.9	8.6	7.5	43.8
	1995	14	24.0	3.5	1.6	10.5	8.9	7.7	45.4
	2000	22	20.4	0.8	0.8	6.6	12.4	10.0	49.8
	2005	27	22.2	2.9	0.9	5.4	9.4	9.4	50.6
	2010	33	27.3	0.2	1.1	5.4	8.8	6.8	51.5
	2015	45	21.4	1.9	0.9	10.8	8.6	6.2	51.1
	2016	51	20.7	2.9	0.9	12.5	8.2	6.6	49.1
	2017	54	20.0	3.1	0.8	14.8	9.2	6.2	46.7
	2018	59	21.9	1.4	0.9	11.1	9.1	6.5	50.0
	2019	65	21.4	1.9	0.9	11.5	8.9	6.4	49.8

Table 3. Gross Value Added by Kind of Economic Activity: Individual Countries or Areas

Major area, region and country	Year	Gross Value Added (at current prices) Million	Percentage Distributtion						
			Agriculture, hunting, forestry, fishing A-B	Mining, Manufacturing, Utilities C-E	Of which: Manufacturing D	Construction F	Wholesale, retail trade, restaurants and hotels G-H	Transport, storage and communication I	Other Activities J-P
Vanuatu [1,29]	1970	3 634	31.6	5.7	4.0	1.9	18.1	10.8	31.9
(Vatu)	1975	5 267	31.6	5.7	4.0	1.9	18.1	10.8	31.9
	1980	8 024	31.6	5.7	4.0	1.9	18.1	10.8	31.9
	1985	14 749	32.6	4.8	3.2	1.1	17.2	8.1	36.2
	1990	19 521	23.9	7.3	5.3	2.7	18.5	10.6	37.0
	1995	28 938	30.5	6.5	4.7	2.6	18.9	9.5	32.0
	2000	34 111	25.6	6.6	4.8	5.9	21.5	8.7	31.7
	2005	39 869	24.1	6.1	4.1	2.4	19.8	11.9	35.8
	2010	64 125	21.9	7.1	5.1	5.9	21.5	10.9	32.5
	2015	77 527	23.1	5.6	3.5	5.9	23.6	8.5	33.4
	2016	82 124	22.2	5.4	3.4	5.7	24.8	8.9	32.9
	2017	87 673	23.1	5.1	3.1	5.9	24.5	9.9	31.4
	2018	91 811	23.3	5.0	3.0	6.1	24.1	9.8	31.7
	2019	95 866	22.9	5.2	3.2	5.9	24.5	9.5	32.0

Notes for Table 3. Gross Value Added by Kind of Economic Activity: Individual Countries or Areas

1/ Gross Value Added
1970, 1975, 1980, 1985, 1990, 1995, 2000, 2005, 2010, 2015-2019
FISIM has not been allocated to intermediate consumption by economic activity.

2/ Gross Value Added
1990, 1995, 2000, 2005, 2010
FISIM has not been allocated to intermediate consumption by economic activity.

3/ Gross Value Added
2005, 2010, 2015-2019
FISIM has not been allocated to intermediate consumption by economic activity.

4/ Gross Value Added
1990, 1995, 2000, 2005, 2010, 2015-2019
FISIM has not been allocated to intermediate consumption by economic activity.

5/ Gross Value Added
2010, 2015-2019
FISIM has not been allocated to intermediate consumption by economic activity.

6/ Gross Value Added
1970, 1975, 1980, 1985, 1990, 1995, 2000, 2005
FISIM has not been allocated to intermediate consumption by economic activity.

7/ Gross Value Added
2000, 2005, 2010, 2015-2019
FISIM has not been allocated to intermediate consumption by economic activity.

8/ Gross Value Added
1970, 1975, 1980, 1985, 1990, 1995, 2000
Refers to Gross Domestic Product.

9/ Gross Value Added
1970, 1975, 1980, 1985, 1990, 1995, 2000, 2005, 2010, 2015-2019
Statistical discrepancy is pro rata distributed to the components of value added.

10/ Gross Value Added
1970, 1975, 1980, 1985, 1990, 1995, 2000, 2005, 2010, 2015-2019
At factor cost.

11/ Gross Value Added
2005, 2010, 2015-2017
FISIM has not been allocated to intermediate consumption by economic activity.

12/ Gross Value Added
1970, 1975, 1980, 1985, 2005, 2010, 2015-2019
FISIM has not been allocated to intermediate consumption by economic activity.

13/ Gross Value Added
2010
FISIM has not been allocated to intermediate consumption by economic activity.

14/ (a) Gross Value Added
1970, 1975, 1980, 1985, 1990, 1995, 2010
FISIM has not been allocated to intermediate consumption by economic activity.

(b) Construction
1970, 1975, 1980, 1985, 1990, 1995, 2000, 2005, 2010, 2015-2019
Refers to Buildings and public works.

(c) Wholesale, retail trade, restaurants and hotels
1970, 1975, 1980, 1985, 1990, 1995, 2000, 2005, 2010, 2015-2019
Refers to trade only.

15/ Gross Value Added
1970, 1975, 1980, 1985, 1990
FISIM has not been allocated to intermediate consumption by economic activity.

16/ Gross Value Added
1970, 1975, 1980, 1985, 1990, 1995
At factor cost.
1980, 1985, 1990, 1995, 2000, 2005, 2010, 2015-2019
FISIM has not been allocated to intermediate consumption by economic activity.

17/ Gross Value Added
1990, 1995, 2000, 2005
Statistical discrepancy is pro rata distributed to the components of value added.

18/ (a) Gross Value Added
1970, 1975, 1980, 1985
Refers to Gross Domestic Product.

(b) Wholesale, retail trade, restaurants and hotels
1970, 1975, 1980, 1985
Restaurants and Hotels are included in Other activities.

(c) Other Activities
1970, 1975, 1980, 1985
Includes Restaurants and hotels.

19/ (a) Gross Value Added
1970, 1975, 1980, 1985, 1990, 1995, 2000
Does not incorporate value added generated by binational hydroelectric plants.

(b) Mining, Manufacturing, Utilities
1970, 1975, 1980, 1985, 1990, 1995, 2000
Does not incorporate value added generated by binational hydroelectric plants.

20/ Gross Value Added
1970, 1975, 1980, 1985, 1990, 1995, 2000, 2005, 2010, 2015-2019
At producers' prices.

21/ Gross Value Added
1970, 1975, 1980, 1985
At factor cost.
1970, 1975, 1980, 1985
FISIM has not been allocated to intermediate consumption by economic activity.

22/ Gross Value Added
1985, 1990, 1995, 2000, 2005, 2010, 2015-2019
FISIM has not been allocated to intermediate consumption by economic activity.

23/ Gross Value Added
1970, 1990, 1995, 2000
FISIM has not been allocated to intermediate consumption by economic activity.
1990, 1995, 2000, 2005, 2010, 2015-2019
At producers' prices.

24/ Gross Value Added
1970, 1975, 1980, 1985, 1990, 1995, 2000, 2005, 2010, 2015-2019
Value added refers to GDP.

25/ (a) Gross Value Added
1995
FISIM has not been allocated to intermediate consumption by economic activity.

(b) Of which: Manufacturing
1990, 1995, 2000, 2005, 2010, 2015-2019
Includes Mining and quarrying.

26/ (a) Gross Value Added
2010, 2015-2019
Refers to Gross Domestic Product.

(b) Agriculture, hunting, forestry, fishing
Mining, Manufacturing, Utilities
Of which: Manufacturing
Construction
Wholesale, retail trade, restaurants and hotels
Transport, storage and communication
Other Activities
2010, 2015-2019
Includes Taxes less subsidies on production and imports.

27/ Gross Value Added
1990, 1995
FISIM has not been allocated to intermediate consumption by economic activity.

28/ (a) Agriculture, hunting, forestry, fishing
2015-2019
Excludes irrigation canals and landscaping care

(b) Mining, Manufacturing, Utilities
2015-2019
Excludes publishing activities, includes irrigation canals

(c) Of which: Manufacturing
2015-2019
Excludes recycling and publishing activities

(d) Wholesale, retail trade, restaurants and hotels
2015-2019
Excludes repair of personal and household goods

(e) Transport, storage and communication
2015-2019
Excludes travel agencies, includes publishing activities, computer and related activities and radio/TV activities

(f) Other Activities
2015-2019
Excludes computer and related activities and radio/TV activities, includes travel agencies and landscaping care

29/ (a) Agriculture, hunting, forestry, fishing
1970, 1975, 1980, 1985, 1990, 1995, 2000, 2005, 2010, 2015-2019
Excludes irrigation canals and landscaping care

(b) Mining, Manufacturing, Utilities
1970, 1975, 1980, 1985, 1990, 1995, 2000, 2005, 2010, 2015-2019
Excludes publishing activities, includes irrigation canals

(c) Of which: Manufacturing
1970, 1975, 1980, 1985, 1990, 1995, 2000, 2005, 2010, 2015-2019
Excludes recycling and publishing activities

(d) Wholesale, retail trade, restaurants and hotels
1970, 1975, 1980, 1985, 1990, 1995, 2000, 2005, 2010, 2015-2019
Excludes repair of personal and household goods

(e) Transport, storage and communication
1970, 1975, 1980, 1985, 1990, 1995, 2000, 2005, 2010, 2015-2019
Excludes travel agencies, includes publishing activities, computer and related activities and radio/TV activities

(f) Other Activities
1970, 1975, 1980, 1985, 1990, 1995, 2000, 2005, 2010, 2015-2019
Excludes computer and related activities and radio/TV activities, includes travel agencies and landscaping care

30/ Agriculture, hunting, forestry, fishing
1970, 1975, 1980, 1985, 1990, 1995, 2000, 2005, 2010, 2015-2019
Includes Mining and quarrying.

31/ Of which: Manufacturing
1970, 1975, 1980, 1985, 1990, 1995, 2000
Includes Mining and quarrying.

32/ Of which: Manufacturing
1970, 1975, 1980, 1985
Includes Mining and quarrying.

33/ Of which: Manufacturing
1970, 1975, 1980, 1985, 1990, 1995, 2000, 2005
Includes Mining and quarrying.

34/ Agriculture, hunting, forestry, fishing
2005, 2010, 2015-2019
Includes Mining and quarrying.

35/ (a) Agriculture, hunting, forestry, fishing
1970, 1975, 1980, 1985, 1990, 1995, 2000, 2005, 2010, 2015-2019
Excludes hunting and forestry.
1970, 1975, 1980, 1985, 1990, 1995, 2000, 2005, 2010, 2015-2019
Includes Mining and quarrying.

(b) Mining, Manufacturing, Utilities
1970, 1975, 1980, 1985, 1990, 1995, 2000, 2005, 2010, 2015-2019
Excludes mining and quarrying.
1970, 1975, 1980, 1985, 1990, 1995, 2000, 2005, 2010, 2015-2019
Includes waste management.

(c) Wholesale, retail trade, restaurants and hotels
1970, 1975, 1980, 1985, 1990, 1995, 2000, 2005, 2010, 2015-2019
Excludes repair of motor vehicles and motorcycles, personal and household goods.

(d) Other Activities

1970, 1975, 1980, 1985, 1990, 1995, 2000, 2005, 2010, 2015-2019

Excludes waste management.

1970, 1975, 1980, 1985, 1990, 1995, 2000, 2005, 2010, 2015-2019

Includes repair of motor vehicles and motorcycles, personal and household goods.

36/ Mining, Manufacturing, Utilities

1970, 1975, 1980, 1985, 1990, 1995, 2000, 2005, 2010, 2015-2019

Excludes mining and quarrying.

37/ (a) Agriculture, hunting, forestry, fishing

1970, 1975, 1980, 1985, 1990

Agricultural services and related activities such as cotton ginning and pressing are included in Manufacturing.

(b) Mining, Manufacturing, Utilities

1970, 1975, 1980, 1985, 1990

Agricultural services and related activities such as cotton ginning and pressing are included in Manufacturing.

1970, 1975, 1980, 1985, 1990

Gas distribution is included in Wholesale and retail trade.

(c) Of which: Manufacturing

1970, 1975, 1980, 1985, 1990

Agricultural services and related activities such as cotton ginning and pressing are included in Manufacturing.

1970, 1975, 1980, 1985, 1990

Distribution of petroleum products is included in Wholesale and retail trade.

(d) Wholesale, retail trade, restaurants and hotels

1970, 1975, 1980, 1985, 1990

Distribution of petroleum products is included in Wholesale and retail trade.

1970, 1975, 1980, 1985, 1990

Gas distribution is included in Wholesale and retail trade.

38/ Of which: Manufacturing

1970, 1975, 1980, 1985, 1990, 1995, 2000, 2005, 2010, 2015-2019

Includes Mining and quarrying.

39/ Of which: Manufacturing

1990, 1995

Includes Mining and quarrying.

40/ Of which: Manufacturing

1990, 1995, 2000, 2005, 2010, 2015-2019

Includes Mining and quarrying, and Electricity, gas and water supply.

41/ Of which: Manufacturing

1980, 1985, 1990

Includes Mining and quarrying.

42/ Of which: Manufacturing

1970, 1975, 1980, 1985, 1990, 1995

Includes Mining and quarrying.

43/ Construction

1970, 1975, 1980, 1985, 1990, 1995, 2000, 2005, 2010, 2015-2019

Includes Mining and quarrying.

44/ Construction

2010, 2015-2019

Includes Electricity, gas and water supply.

45/ Wholesale, retail trade, restaurants and hotels
1970, 1975, 1980, 1985, 1990, 1995, 2000, 2005, 2010, 2015-2019
Excludes repair of motor vehicles and motorcycles, personal and household goods.

46/ (a) Wholesale, retail trade, restaurants and hotels
1970, 1975, 1980, 1985, 1990, 1995, 2000, 2005, 2010, 2015-2019
Restaurants and Hotels are included in "Other activities".

(b) Other Activities
1970, 1975, 1980, 1985, 1990, 1995, 2000, 2005, 2010, 2015-2019
Includes Restaurants and hotels.

47/ Gross Value Added
Agriculture, hunting, forestry, fishing
Mining, Manufacturing, Utilities
Of which: Manufacturing
Construction
Wholesale, retail trade, restaurants and hotels
Transport, storage and communication
Other Activities
1970, 1975, 1980, 1985, 1990
Refers to data compiled according to the 1968 SNA.

48/ Gross Value Added
Agriculture, hunting, forestry, fishing
Mining, Manufacturing, Utilities
Of which: Manufacturing
Construction
Wholesale, retail trade, restaurants and hotels
Transport, storage and communication
Other Activities
1970, 1975, 1980, 1985, 1990, 1995, 2000
Refers to data compiled according to the 1968 SNA.

49/ Agriculture, hunting, forestry, fishing
Mining, Manufacturing, Utilities
Of which: Manufacturing
Construction
Wholesale, retail trade, restaurants and hotels
Transport, storage and communication
Other Activities
1970, 1975, 1980, 1985, 1990, 1995, 2000, 2005, 2010, 2015-2019
Includes Taxes less subsidies on production and imports.

50/ Agriculture, hunting, forestry, fishing
Mining, Manufacturing, Utilities
Of which: Manufacturing
Construction
Wholesale, retail trade, restaurants and hotels
Transport, storage and communication
Other Activities
1970, 1975, 1980, 1985, 1990, 1995, 2000, 2005, 2010, 2015-2019
At producers' prices.

51/ Agriculture, hunting, forestry, fishing
Mining, Manufacturing, Utilities
Of which: Manufacturing
Construction
Wholesale, retail trade, restaurants and hotels
Transport, storage and communication
Other Activities
1970, 1975, 1980, 1985, 1990, 1995, 2000, 2005
At producers' prices.

52/ Gross Value Added
Agriculture, hunting, forestry, fishing
Mining, Manufacturing, Utilities
Of which: Manufacturing
Construction
Wholesale, retail trade, restaurants and hotels
Transport, storage and communication
Other Activities
2010-2019
The Government of Ukraine has advised the United Nations that it is not in a position to provide statistical data concerning the Autonomous Republic of Crimea and the city of Sevastopol.

53/ (a) Agriculture, hunting, forestry, fishing
2010, 2015-2019
Excludes irrigation canals and landscaping care

(b) Mining, Manufacturing, Utilities
2010, 2015-2019
Excludes publishing activities, includes irrigation canals

(c) Of which: Manufacturing
2010, 2015-2019
Excludes recycling and publishing activities

(d) Wholesale, retail trade, restaurants and hotels
2010, 2015-2019
Excludes repair of personal and household goods

(e) Transport, storage and communication
2010, 2015-2019
Excludes travel agencies, includes publishing activities, computer and related activities and radio/TV activities

(f) Other Activities
2010, 2015-2019
Excludes computer and related activities and radio/TV activities, includes travel agencies and landscaping care

54/ (a) Agriculture, hunting, forestry, fishing
1995, 2000, 2005, 2010, 2015-2019
Excludes irrigation canals and landscaping care

(b) Mining, Manufacturing, Utilities
1995, 2000, 2005, 2010, 2015-2019
Excludes publishing activities, includes irrigation canals

(c) Of which: Manufacturing
1995, 2000, 2005, 2010, 2015-2019
Excludes recycling and publishing activities

(d) Wholesale, retail trade, restaurants and hotels
1995, 2000, 2005, 2010, 2015-2019
Excludes repair of personal and household goods

(e) Transport, storage and communication
1995, 2000, 2005, 2010, 2015-2019
Excludes travel agencies, includes publishing activities, computer and related activities and radio/TV activities

(f) Other Activities
1995, 2000, 2005, 2010, 2015-2019
Excludes computer and related activities and radio/TV activities, includes travel agencies and landscaping care

55/ (a) Agriculture, hunting, forestry, fishing
1990, 1995, 2000, 2005, 2010, 2015-2019
Excludes irrigation canals and landscaping care

(b) Mining, Manufacturing, Utilities
1990, 1995, 2000, 2005, 2010, 2015-2019
Excludes publishing activities, includes irrigation canals

(c) Of which: Manufacturing
1990, 1995, 2000, 2005, 2010, 2015-2019
Excludes recycling and publishing activities

(d) Wholesale, retail trade, restaurants and hotels
1990, 1995, 2000, 2005, 2010, 2015-2019
Excludes repair of personal and household goods

(e) Transport, storage and communication
1990, 1995, 2000, 2005, 2010, 2015-2019
Excludes travel agencies, includes publishing activities, computer and related activities and radio/TV activities

(f) Other Activities
1990, 1995, 2000, 2005, 2010, 2015-2019
Excludes computer and related activities and radio/TV activities, includes travel agencies and landscaping care

56/ (a) Agriculture, hunting, forestry, fishing
2000, 2005, 2010, 2015-2019
Excludes irrigation canals and landscaping care

(b) Mining, Manufacturing, Utilities
2000, 2005, 2010, 2015-2019
Excludes publishing activities, includes irrigation canals

(c) Of which: Manufacturing
2000, 2005, 2010, 2015-2019
Excludes recycling and publishing activities

(d) Wholesale, retail trade, restaurants and hotels
2000, 2005, 2010, 2015-2019
Excludes repair of personal and household goods

(e) Transport, storage and communication
2000, 2005, 2010, 2015-2019
Excludes travel agencies, includes publishing activities, computer and related activities and radio/TV activities

(f) Other Activities
2000, 2005, 2010, 2015-2019
Excludes computer and related activities and radio/TV activities, includes travel agencies and landscaping care

57/ (a) Agriculture, hunting, forestry, fishing
2016-2019
Excludes irrigation canals and landscaping care

(b) Mining, Manufacturing, Utilities
2016-2019
Excludes publishing activities, includes irrigation canals

(c) Of which: Manufacturing
2016-2019
Excludes recycling and publishing activities

(d) Wholesale, retail trade, restaurants and hotels
2016-2019
Excludes repair of personal and household goods

(e) Transport, storage and communication
2016-2019
Excludes travel agencies, includes publishing activities, computer and related activities and radio/TV activities

(f) Other Activities
2016-2019
Excludes computer and related activities and radio/TV activities, includes travel agencies and landscaping care

58/ (a) Agriculture, hunting, forestry, fishing
1980, 1985, 1990, 1995, 2000, 2005, 2010, 2015-2019
Excludes irrigation canals and landscaping care

(b) Mining, Manufacturing, Utilities
1980, 1985, 1990, 1995, 2000, 2005, 2010, 2015-2019
Excludes publishing activities, includes irrigation canals

(c) Of which: Manufacturing
1980, 1985, 1990, 1995, 2000, 2005, 2010, 2015-2019
Excludes recycling and publishing activities

(d) Wholesale, retail trade, restaurants and hotels
1980, 1985, 1990, 1995, 2000, 2005, 2010, 2015-2019
Excludes repair of personal and household goods

(e) Transport, storage and communication
1980, 1985, 1990, 1995, 2000, 2005, 2010, 2015-2019
Excludes travel agencies, includes publishing activities, computer and related activities and radio/TV activities

(f) Other Activities
1980, 1985, 1990, 1995, 2000, 2005, 2010, 2015-2019
Excludes computer and related activities and radio/TV activities, includes travel agencies and landscaping care

C. Growth Rates of Main National Accounts Aggregates at 2015 Prices

Description of Analysis in Tables 4, 5 and 6

C. Economic development expressed in rates of growth in real terms of gross domestic product and its components.

Tables 4 to 6 reflect trends in economic development expressed as rates of real growth of GDP and its components for the world, developed, developing and transition economies, as well as for individual countries or areas during the period 1970 - 2019.

The growth rates of GDP and its components for the regional and economic groupings are obtained from the sum of the GDPs and their components for the countries of a specific regional and economic grouping.

The data shown in these tables are computed as geometric mean of annual growth rates expressed as percentages for the years and periods indicated. Table 4 presents growth rates of total GDP and Tables 5 and 6 show growth rates of the components of GDP by expenditure and by kind of economic activity, respectively.

The first column of the three tables lists the economic and regional groupings as well as individual countries presented alphabetically by region. The next column in each table highlights the base year weights in 2015 of GDP, representing for individual countries' and sub-regions' weights of their GDP as a percentage of the region GDP and those for the regions and economic development groupings, as a percentage of the world GDP. In Tables 5 and 6, the third column presents, respectively, the shares of each expenditure and industry component as a percentage of GDP in 2015. The next four columns of the tables contain the average growth rates of GDP during the periods 1970-1979, 1980-1989, 1990-1999 and 2000-2009. The remaining columns show the annual rates of growth over the preceding year starting from 2014 through 2019.

Table 5 includes the rates of growth of each expenditure component of GDP as follows: (a) household final consumption expenditure; (b) general government final consumption expenditure; (c) gross fixed capital formation; (d) exports of goods and services; and (e) imports of goods and services.

Table 6 lists the average rates of growth of each economic activity component of GDP: (a) agriculture, hunting, forestry and fishing, (b) mining, manufacturing and utilities, (c) manufacturing, (d) construction, (e) wholesale and retail trade, restaurants and hotels (f) transport, storage and communication and (g) other activities.

Shown in following graphs are the average annual growth rates of real GDP over each of the last four decades as well as over the last five years, GDP in 2015 US dollars and the real GDP index with 1970=100. Each graph displays data by geographic region.

Figure 5. Average annual growth of real GDP by region

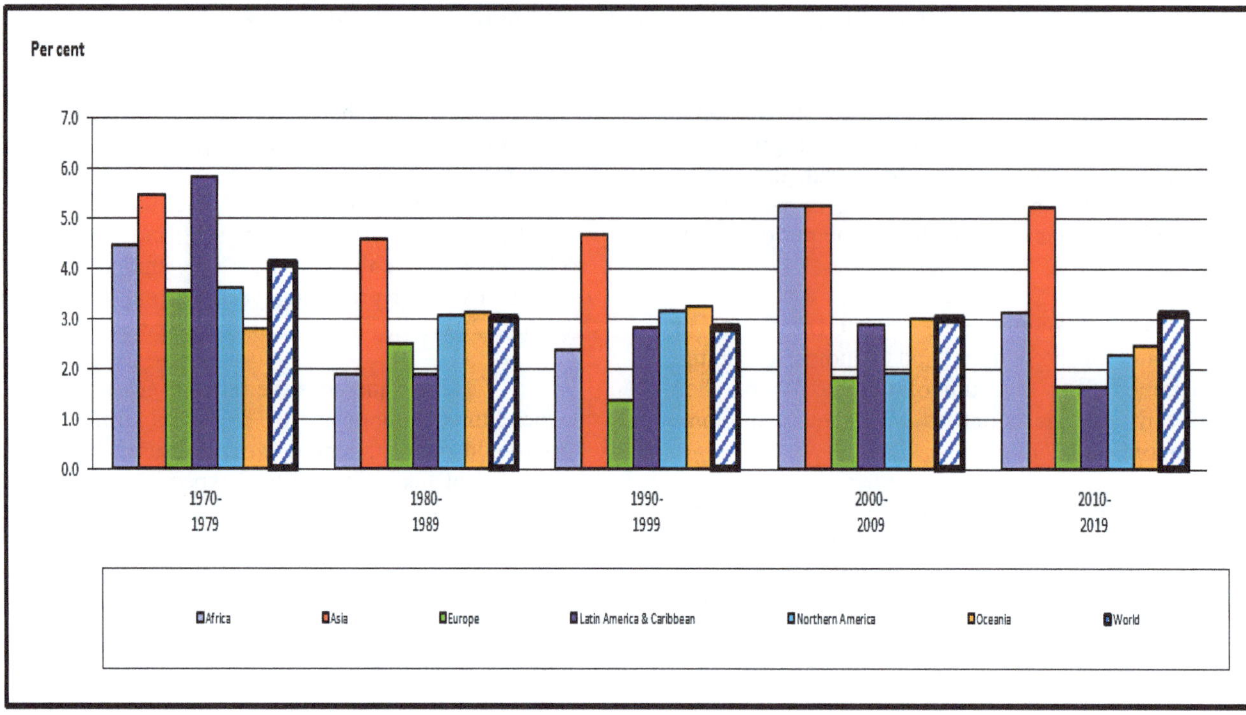

Figure 6. Index of real gross domestic product by region

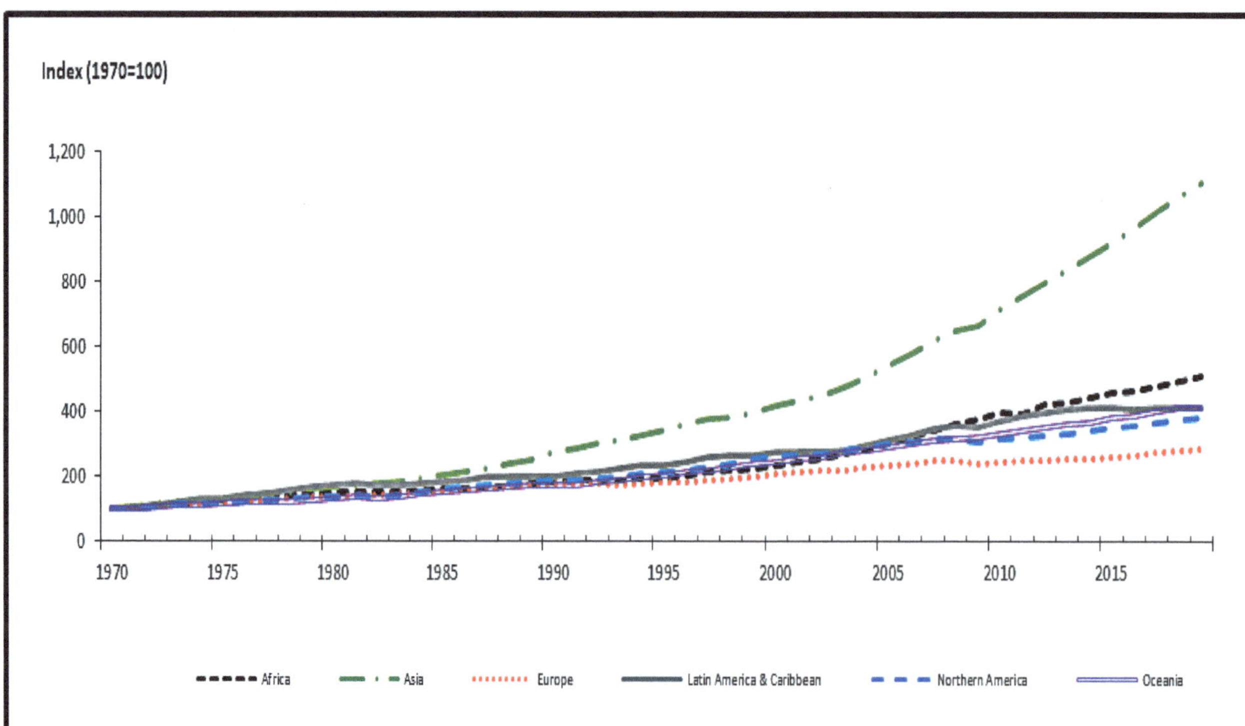

Figure 7. Real gross domestic product by region

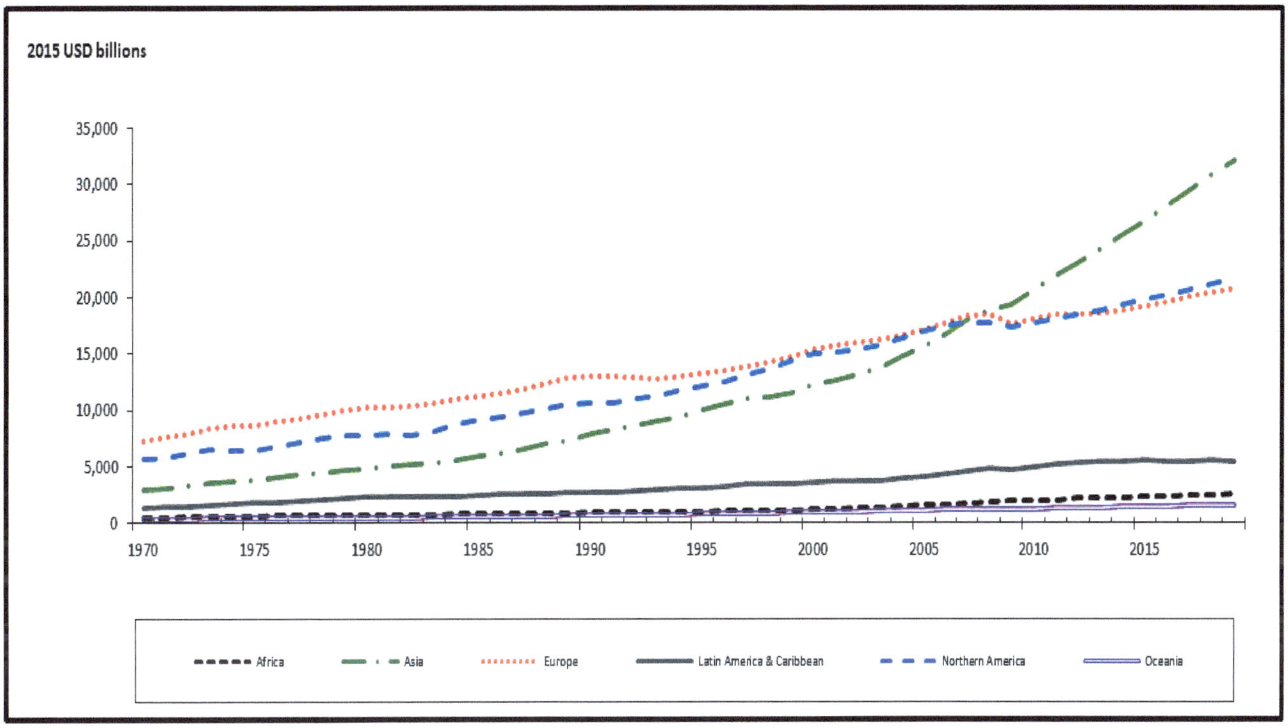

Table 4. Annual Average Rate of Growth of Gross Domestic Product by Major Area, Region and Country

Major area, region and country	Base year weights as percentage of total for world or region in 2015	Average rates of growth				Annual rate of change (percentage)					
		1970-1979	1980-1989	1990-1999	2000-2009	2014	2015	2016	2017	2018	2019
World	**100.0**	**4.1**	**3.1**	**2.8**	**2.8**	**3.0**	**3.1**	**2.7**	**3.4**	**3.1**	**2.4**
Developed economies	**58.0**	**3.6**	**3.1**	**2.5**	**1.4**	**2.0**	**2.5**	**1.7**	**2.5**	**2.3**	**1.7**
Developing economies	**39.3**	**5.8**	**3.2**	**5.0**	**5.8**	**4.7**	**4.4**	**4.3**	**4.7**	**4.3**	**3.5**
Transition economies	**2.7**	**4.9**	**3.9**	**-5.3**	**5.4**	**1.1**	**-1.2**	**0.9**	**2.4**	**3.0**	**2.2**
Africa	**3.1**	**4.5**	**1.7**	**2.3**	**5.4**	**3.2**	**2.8**	**1.8**	**3.3**	**3.3**	**3.0**
Northern Africa	*31.5*	*6.7*	*2.1*	*3.2*	*4.9*	*-1.1*	*1.8*	*3.2*	*4.9*	*4.1*	*3.7*
Algeria	7.2	6.4	3.0	1.6	3.9	3.8	3.7	3.2	1.3	1.2	0.8
Egypt	13.7	6.1	7.4	4.9	4.9	2.9	4.4	4.3	4.2	5.3	5.6
Libya	0.8	8.1	-3.5	1.3	5.7	-50.1	-45.5	-16.1	64.0	17.9	9.9
Morocco	4.4	5.4	3.8	2.5	5.6	4.0	4.9	3.2	5.8	3.8	3.6
Sudan	3.6	...	...	...	...	7.0	4.0	3.6	4.7	2.8	1.3
Sudan (Former)	...	3.8	2.1	5.4	...	...	...	...	...	...	...
Tunisia	1.9	7.3	3.2	4.8	4.3	2.9	1.2	1.2	1.9	2.7	1.0
Sub-Saharan Africa	68.5	3.4	1.5	1.7	5.8	5.3	3.3	1.1	2.6	2.9	2.7
Eastern Africa	*13.5*	*3.0*	*2.8*	*2.8*	*5.9*	*6.8*	*5.9*	*5.0*	*5.6*	*6.0*	*5.0*
Burundi	0.1	3.2	4.3	-1.8	3.1	4.2	-0.4	3.2	4.2	1.6	1.0
Comoros	0.0	4.4	2.9	1.9	0.7	3.9	2.0	2.8	5.6	3.8	3.2
Djibouti	0.1	1.6	0.4	1.4	5.8	7.1	7.7	6.7	5.4	8.4	7.7
Eritrea	0.1	...	...	10.0	-1.4	30.9	-20.6	7.4	-10.0	13.0	3.8
Ethiopia	2.7	...	...	2.4	8.2	10.3	10.4	7.6	9.5	6.9	8.3
Ethiopia (Former)	...	2.3	2.0	...	...	...	...	...	...	...	...
Kenya	2.8	5.2	4.3	2.0	3.9	5.4	5.7	5.9	4.8	6.3	5.4
Madagascar	0.5	1.0	0.4	1.4	2.8	3.3	3.1	4.0	3.9	3.2	4.4
Malawi	0.3	6.8	1.2	2.4	4.6	6.2	3.3	2.7	5.2	3.9	5.2
Mauritius	0.5	7.6	6.0	4.8	4.0	3.7	3.6	3.8	3.8	3.8	3.6
Mozambique	0.7	3.9	-0.7	6.8	8.2	7.4	6.7	3.8	3.7	3.4	2.3
Rwanda	0.4	5.1	2.3	1.7	8.3	6.2	8.9	6.0	4.0	8.6	9.4
Seychelles	0.1	9.2	3.1	4.9	1.6	4.5	4.9	4.6	4.4	3.8	4.7
Somalia	0.1	3.3	1.7	-3.3	2.9	3.7	2.7	2.9	1.4	2.8	2.9
South Sudan	0.3	...	...	...	...	30.3	7.9	-7.0	-3.7	3.8	0.9
U.R. of Tanzania: Mainland	2.0	3.7	2.3	4.0	6.6	6.7	6.2	6.9	6.8	7.0	7.0
Uganda	1.1	-1.6	3.9	7.2	7.8	4.5	5.7	2.6	4.5	7.7	6.7
Zambia	0.9	0.8	1.4	1.2	7.1	4.7	2.9	3.8	3.5	4.0	1.4
Zanzibar	0.1	...	...	6.4	6.4	6.4	6.3	5.7	7.7	7.1	7.1
Zimbabwe	0.9	1.9	4.1	1.5	1.4	2.4	1.8	0.8	4.7	4.8	-8.1
Middle Africa	*10.3*	*1.5*	*2.3*	*-0.1*	*7.1*	*5.3*	*2.0*	*-1.2*	*0.5*	*0.3*	*0.8*
Angola	5.0	0.2	2.8	1.0	9.2	4.8	0.9	-2.6	-0.1	-2.0	-1.5
Cameroon	1.3	5.8	1.6	1.5	4.0	5.9	5.7	4.6	3.5	4.1	3.9
Central African Republic	0.1	1.0	1.1	2.0	1.3	0.1	4.3	4.8	4.5	3.8	3.0
Chad	0.5	-1.7	4.5	2.8	11.0	3.8	4.6	-2.7	-2.4	2.3	3.0
Congo	0.5	4.6	5.5	0.8	4.8	6.0	-3.2	-10.2	-4.6	-6.2	-0.9
D.R. of the Congo	1.6	0.2	1.7	-5.5	4.4	9.5	6.9	2.4	3.7	5.8	4.4
Equatorial Guinea	0.6	2.2	3.3	21.6	18.1	0.4	-9.1	-8.8	-5.7	-6.4	-5.6
Gabon	0.6	8.2	1.4	1.8	0.5	4.3	3.9	2.1	0.5	1.2	3.6
Sao Tome and Principe	0.0	7.0	-1.4	1.6	5.1	6.5	3.9	4.2	3.8	2.9	1.3
Southern Africa	*15.1*	*3.1*	*1.9*	*1.8*	*3.5*	*2.1*	*1.2*	*0.6*	*1.4*	*1.0*	*0.3*
Botswana	0.6	15.1	12.7	5.2	3.6	4.1	-1.7	4.3	2.9	4.5	3.0
Eswatini	0.2	9.5	6.3	3.1	3.5	0.9	2.3	1.3	2.0	2.4	1.1
Lesotho	0.1	7.6	3.6	3.9	4.0	2.9	2.7	5.0	-1.3	-0.5	1.5
Namibia	0.5	3.2	1.1	3.7	4.4	5.8	4.5	-0.3	-0.3	0.7	-1.1
South Africa	13.7	3.0	1.7	1.6	3.5	1.8	1.2	0.4	1.4	0.8	0.2
Western Africa	*29.6*	*4.7*	*0.4*	*1.9*	*6.8*	*6.5*	*3.7*	*0.4*	*2.6*	*3.2*	*3.4*
Benin	0.5	3.2	3.3	4.9	4.1	13.1	13.0	3.3	5.7	6.7	6.9
Burkina Faso	0.5	4.5	3.9	5.6	5.7	4.3	3.9	6.0	6.2	6.7	5.7
Cabo Verde	0.1	0.2	5.8	6.7	5.6	0.6	1.0	4.7	3.7	4.5	5.7
Côte d'Ivoire	2.0	6.7	1.9	3.0	1.0	14.8	14.9	7.2	7.4	6.9	6.2
Gambia	0.1	2.5	4.5	2.8	3.4	-1.4	4.1	1.9	4.8	7.7	6.1
Ghana	2.1	0.7	2.0	4.4	5.4	2.9	2.2	3.4	8.1	6.3	6.5
Guinea	0.4	3.0	3.0	4.3	2.7	3.7	3.8	10.8	10.3	6.2	5.6
Guinea-Bissau	0.0	3.0	2.8	2.1	2.2	1.0	6.1	6.3	5.9	3.4	4.5
Liberia	0.1	3.1	-0.2	0.3	4.3	5.2	9.3	-0.5	2.5	1.2	-2.3
Mali	0.6	5.0	3.8	12.1	8.9	7.8	7.5	8.9	6.7	6.8	6.6
Mauritania	0.3	2.9	1.4	3.1	3.9	4.3	5.4	1.3	3.5	2.1	5.9

Table 4. Annual Average Rate of Growth of Gross Domestic Product by Major Area, Region and Country

Major area, region and country	Base year weights as percentage of total for world or region in 2015	Average rates of growth				Annual rate of change (percentage)					
		1970-1979	1980-1989	1990-1999	2000-2009	2014	2015	2016	2017	2018	2019
Niger	0.4	1.7	-1.3	2.9	4.5	7.5	4.3	5.7	5.0	7.0	5.8
Nigeria	21.4	5.3	-0.3	1.2	7.9	6.3	2.7	-1.6	0.8	1.9	2.2
Senegal	0.8	2.3	3.0	3.6	4.1	4.1	6.4	6.4	7.4	6.4	5.2
Sierra Leone	0.2	1.9	2.6	-8.8	9.3	4.6	-20.5	6.3	3.8	3.4	5.5
Togo	0.2	3.4	0.9	1.1	1.8	11.3	11.1	10.9	4.3	4.9	5.3
Americas	**33.7**	**4.1**	**3.0**	**3.3**	**1.9**	**2.2**	**2.3**	**1.0**	**2.1**	**2.4**	**1.6**
Latin America and the Caribbean	**7.3**	**5.8**	**1.5**	**3.1**	**2.8**	**0.9**	**0.1**	**-1.2**	**1.0**	**0.5**	**-0.6**
Caribbean	*1.4*	*4.6*	*3.2*	*2.5*	*2.5*	*1.4*	*2.5*	*1.1*	*0.6*	*1.2*	*2.1*
Anguilla	0.0	3.8	7.3	5.0	4.4	5.1	3.1	-2.5	-6.3	8.4	5.4
Antigua and Barbuda	0.0	3.6	6.3	3.4	2.5	3.8	3.8	5.5	3.1	7.0	3.4
Aruba	0.0	9.1	11.2	5.4	-0.2	0.3	5.7	2.1	2.0	0.9	-0.7
Bahamas	0.0	2.4	3.6	2.4	0.6	1.1	0.2	1.4	3.1	3.0	1.2
Barbados	0.0	2.9	1.4	0.9	1.0	-0.1	2.4	2.5	0.5	-0.6	-0.1
British Virgin Islands	0.0	3.2	5.9	18.0	0.0	1.7	0.8	7.3	0.7	2.8	2.6
Cayman Islands	0.0	9.4	9.3	6.8	1.3	2.7	2.8	3.2	3.1	4.1	3.2
Cuba	0.3	5.4	4.9	-2.2	5.5	1.0	4.4	0.5	1.8	2.2	2.0
Curaçao	0.0	...	...	...	...	-1.1	0.3	-1.0	-1.7	-2.2	-3.4
Dominica	0.0	3.5	4.9	2.0	2.6	4.4	-2.7	2.6	-6.8	2.3	3.6
Dominican Republic	0.3	7.0	3.3	6.1	4.5	7.1	6.9	6.7	4.7	7.0	5.1
Former Netherlands Antilles	...	8.2	-0.1	1.6	1.5	...	...	...	...	...	...
Grenada	0.0	6.5	5.6	3.5	2.0	7.4	6.4	3.7	4.4	4.1	2.0
Haiti	0.0	4.5	-0.6	-0.1	0.7	2.8	1.2	1.5	1.2	1.5	-0.9
Jamaica	0.1	-0.2	2.1	1.5	0.8	0.7	0.9	1.4	1.0	1.9	0.9
Montserrat	0.0	3.4	3.4	-10.1	1.7	1.6	1.2	1.3	-3.8	4.0	5.9
Puerto Rico	0.4	4.6	3.5	4.3	0.2	-1.2	-1.0	-1.3	-2.9	-4.7	1.2
Saint Kitts and Nevis	0.0	5.2	5.8	3.9	2.4	6.3	1.0	2.8	-2.0	2.9	2.5
Saint Lucia	0.0	6.3	7.3	2.9	2.3	1.3	0.1	3.4	3.5	2.6	1.7
Sint Maarten (Dutch part)	0.0	...	...	...	...	1.6	0.5	0.4	-8.4	-8.5	5.0
St. Vincent and the Grenadines	0.0	2.5	5.0	3.3	3.6	1.2	1.3	1.9	1.0	2.2	0.3
Trinidad and Tobago	0.1	4.7	-2.8	4.2	6.3	-0.9	1.5	-5.6	-3.0	0.1	-1.2
Turks and Caicos Islands	0.0	10.7	10.7	9.9	5.6	8.7	11.3	7.3	-2.5	5.6	5.3
Central America	*5.5*	*6.2*	*1.4*	*3.6*	*1.5*	*3.0*	*3.4*	*3.1*	*2.4*	*2.2*	*0.2*
Belize	0.0	3.9	4.3	3.7	3.8	3.6	2.8	0.1	1.9	2.1	0.3
Costa Rica	0.2	6.2	2.3	5.0	4.2	3.5	3.6	4.2	3.9	2.7	2.1
El Salvador	0.1	4.6	-0.4	4.9	1.9	1.4	2.4	2.5	2.2	2.4	2.4
Guatemala	0.2	5.9	0.6	4.2	3.4	4.4	4.1	2.7	3.0	3.2	3.8
Honduras	0.1	5.9	2.7	3.0	4.2	3.1	3.8	3.9	4.8	3.7	2.7
Mexico	4.6	6.4	1.5	3.4	1.1	2.8	3.3	2.9	2.1	2.1	-0.3
Nicaragua	0.1	0.0	-1.5	3.3	2.8	4.8	4.8	4.6	4.6	-4.0	-3.9
Panama	0.2	4.5	1.8	5.3	5.9	5.1	5.7	5.0	5.6	3.6	3.0
South America	*14.8*	*5.8*	*1.3*	*3.0*	*3.4*	*0.2*	*-1.3*	*-3.0*	*0.4*	*-0.2*	*-1.2*
Argentina	2.5	2.7	-1.1	4.8	2.7	-2.5	2.7	-2.1	2.7	-2.5	-2.2
Bolivia (Plurinational State of)	0.1	4.5	-0.3	3.9	3.8	5.5	4.9	4.3	4.2	4.2	2.2
Brazil	7.1	8.6	2.3	2.3	3.2	0.5	-3.5	-3.3	1.3	1.3	1.1
Chile	1.0	2.0	2.8	6.6	3.9	1.8	2.3	1.7	1.2	3.9	1.1
Colombia	1.2	5.7	3.3	2.6	4.0	4.5	3.0	2.1	1.4	2.5	3.3
Ecuador	0.4	7.3	2.5	2.1	4.2	3.8	0.1	-1.2	2.4	1.3	0.1
Guyana	0.0	1.8	-3.4	5.6	8.1	1.7	0.7	3.8	3.7	4.4	5.4
Paraguay [1]	0.1	8.5	3.1	2.1	4.8	4.9	3.1	4.3	5.0	3.4	0.2
Peru	0.8	3.4	-0.6	4.0	5.3	2.4	3.3	4.0	2.5	4.0	2.2
Suriname	0.0	3.9	1.5	0.8	4.8	0.3	-3.4	-5.6	1.8	2.6	0.3
Uruguay	0.2	2.7	0.4	3.7	2.5	3.2	0.4	1.7	2.6	1.6	0.2
Venezuela (Bolivarian Republic of)	1.4	4.8	0.0	1.9	3.7	-3.9	-6.2	-17.0	-15.7	-19.6	-35.0
Northern America	**26.4**	**3.6**	**3.4**	**3.3**	**1.7**	**2.6**	**2.9**	**1.7**	**2.4**	**3.0**	**2.1**
Bermuda	0.0	3.5	1.0	2.5	2.8	-3.7	0.8	-0.7	3.6	0.1	2.4
Canada	6.2	4.2	2.9	2.6	1.7	2.9	0.7	1.0	3.0	2.4	1.9
Greenland	0.0	6.4	2.5	1.2	2.9	4.7	-2.5	4.7	0.5	3.2	2.8
United States	72.1	3.5	3.5	3.4	1.6	2.5	3.1	1.7	2.3	3.0	2.2
Asia	**35.6**	**5.5**	**4.8**	**4.2**	**5.2**	**4.9**	**4.8**	**5.0**	**5.1**	**4.5**	**3.9**
Central Asia	*1.2*	*...*	*...*	*-4.0*	*7.8*	*5.6*	*3.5*	*3.2*	*4.7*	*4.8*	*4.7*
Kazakhstan	0.7	...	...	-5.0	8.4	4.2	1.2	1.1	4.1	4.1	4.5

Table 4. Annual Average Rate of Growth of Gross Domestic Product by Major Area, Region and Country

Major area, region and country	Base year weights as percentage of total for world or region in 2015	Average rates of growth				Annual rate of change (percentage)					
		1970-1979	1980-1989	1990-1999	2000-2009	2014	2015	2016	2017	2018	2019
Kyrgyzstan	0.0	...	...	-5.0	4.6	4.0	3.9	4.3	4.7	3.8	4.5
Tajikistan	0.0	...	...	-11.0	8.2	6.7	6.0	6.9	12.7	7.1	7.5
Turkmenistan	0.1	...	...	-3.2	7.5	10.3	6.5	6.2	6.5	6.2	3.0
Uzbekistan	0.3	...	...	-0.6	6.8	7.2	7.4	6.1	4.5	5.4	5.6
Eastern Asia	*66.8*	*5.3*	*5.9*	*4.3*	*5.3*	*5.0*	*4.8*	*4.7*	*5.3*	*4.8*	*4.4*
China	41.4	6.0	9.9	10.6	10.5	7.4	7.0	6.8	6.9	6.7	6.1
China, Hong Kong SAR	1.2	8.9	7.0	3.5	3.8	2.8	2.4	2.2	3.8	2.8	-1.2
China, Macao SAR	0.2	7.9	7.5	2.3	9.8	-1.2	-21.6	-0.7	9.9	5.4	-4.7
D.P.R. of Korea	0.1	7.6	2.7	-3.1	1.4	1.0	-1.1	3.9	-3.5	-4.1	0.4
Japan	16.4	4.6	4.5	1.1	0.3	0.4	1.2	0.5	2.2	0.3	0.7
Mongolia	0.0	5.7	6.2	-0.2	6.5	7.9	2.4	2.0	5.4	7.0	4.9
Republic of Korea	5.5	10.6	10.0	6.9	4.4	3.2	2.8	2.9	3.2	2.9	2.0
South-Eastern Asia	*9.2*	*7.1*	*5.2*	*4.9*	*5.0*	*4.6*	*4.7*	*4.8*	*5.3*	*5.1*	*4.2*
Brunei Darussalam	0.0	11.2	-3.1	2.2	1.2	-2.5	-0.4	-2.5	1.3	0.1	3.9
Cambodia	0.1	-7.3	5.9	6.6	8.2	7.1	7.0	6.9	7.0	7.7	6.8
Indonesia	3.2	7.8	6.0	4.1	5.1	5.0	4.9	5.0	5.1	5.2	5.0
Lao People's DR	0.1	3.0	6.0	6.2	7.2	7.6	7.3	7.0	6.9	6.2	4.7
Malaysia	1.1	9.7	5.5	6.9	4.3	6.0	5.1	4.4	5.8	4.8	4.3
Myanmar	0.2	3.9	0.9	7.2	12.2	7.5	6.4	5.8	6.4	6.8	2.9
Philippines	1.1	6.0	1.5	2.7	4.4	6.1	6.1	6.9	6.7	6.2	5.9
Singapore	1.2	8.6	7.5	6.9	4.9	3.9	3.0	3.2	4.0	3.4	0.7
Thailand	1.5	7.0	7.5	4.5	4.3	1.0	3.1	3.4	4.0	4.1	2.4
Timor-Leste	0.0	...	...	0.1	4.0	4.5	2.9	3.4	-4.1	-1.1	18.7
Viet Nam	0.7	4.7	5.6	7.7	6.8	6.0	6.7	6.2	6.8	7.1	7.0
Southern Asia	*11.7*	*2.7*	*4.3*	*4.9*	*5.8*	*6.6*	*6.2*	*8.4*	*6.4*	*4.6*	*3.1*
Afghanistan	0.1	0.1	-1.3	-4.7	11.3	3.1	-1.4	1.7	2.7	1.6	4.0
Bangladesh	0.7	0.8	3.5	4.6	5.8	6.1	6.6	7.1	7.3	7.9	8.2
Bhutan	0.0	3.9	10.1	5.0	8.4	4.0	6.6	8.1	4.7	3.0	3.8
India	8.0	2.6	5.6	5.8	6.5	7.4	8.0	8.3	7.0	6.1	4.2
Iran (Islamic Republic of)	1.5	3.0	1.0	3.3	4.3	4.6	-1.3	13.4	3.8	-5.4	-6.5
Maldives	0.0	4.7	11.0	7.1	4.5	7.3	2.9	6.3	7.2	8.1	7.0
Nepal	0.1	2.6	4.7	4.9	3.9	6.0	3.3	0.6	8.2	6.7	7.0
Pakistan	1.0	4.3	6.4	3.9	4.5	4.7	4.7	5.5	5.6	5.8	3.3
Sri Lanka	0.3	4.1	4.0	5.2	4.9	5.0	5.0	4.5	3.6	3.3	2.3
Western Asia	*11.1*	*7.6*	*0.2*	*3.6*	*4.1*	*3.3*	*3.8*	*3.2*	*2.4*	*2.2*	*1.3*
Armenia	0.0	...	...	-4.8	8.8	3.6	3.2	0.2	7.5	5.2	7.6
Azerbaijan	0.2	...	...	-6.8	15.9	2.8	1.0	-3.1	0.2	1.5	2.2
Bahrain	0.1	8.1	-0.6	4.5	5.5	4.4	2.9	3.6	3.9	1.8	1.8
Cyprus	0.1	3.4	6.1	4.6	3.5	-1.9	3.4	6.7	4.4	4.1	3.2
Georgia	0.1	...	...	-10.5	6.3	4.4	3.0	2.9	4.8	4.8	5.1
Iraq	0.6	11.8	-1.1	4.0	2.1	0.2	4.7	13.8	-3.8	0.9	4.4
Israel	1.1	5.7	3.4	5.8	2.9	3.8	2.3	4.0	3.6	3.4	3.5
Jordan	0.1	6.0	2.2	4.8	6.7	3.4	2.5	2.0	2.1	1.9	2.0
Kuwait	0.4	-0.1	0.4	6.1	5.4	0.5	0.6	2.9	-4.7	1.2	0.4
Lebanon	0.2	-2.9	-5.0	7.3	5.5	2.5	0.2	1.5	0.9	-1.9	-5.6
Oman	0.3	11.3	8.3	4.4	3.1	1.5	4.6	5.1	0.3	0.9	-0.8
Qatar	0.6	6.4	1.3	6.5	12.6	4.0	3.7	2.1	1.6	1.5	-0.2
Saudi Arabia	2.4	11.2	-3.6	2.2	3.2	3.7	4.1	1.7	-0.7	2.4	0.3
State of Palestine	0.1	8.0	2.0	9.9	4.4	-0.2	3.7	8.9	1.4	1.2	0.9
Syrian Arab Republic	0.1	9.7	0.6	6.5	5.1	-14.7	-6.1	-4.0	-1.5	2.7	4.8
Turkey	3.2	4.8	4.8	3.3	3.5	4.9	6.1	3.3	7.5	3.0	0.9
United Arab Emirates	1.3	13.0	-1.5	4.7	4.1	4.3	5.1	3.1	2.4	1.2	1.7
Yemen	0.1	...	...	6.8	4.7	-10.6	-30.5	-14.6	-10.0	-1.3	2.1
Yemen Arab Republic (Former)	...	8.9	5.1	...	...	...	...	...	...	...	...
Yemen Democratic (Former)	...	1.9	4.1	...	...	...	...	...	...	...	...
Europe	**25.6**	**3.6**	**2.6**	**1.4**	**1.6**	**1.7**	**1.9**	**1.8**	**2.5**	**2.1**	**1.5**
Eastern Europe	*13.7*	*5.3*	*3.4*	*-3.3*	*4.5*	*1.4*	*0.3*	*1.5*	*3.2*	*3.5*	*2.5*
Belarus	0.3	...	...	-2.0	7.3	1.7	-3.8	-2.5	2.5	3.1	1.2
Bulgaria	0.3	7.1	3.8	-2.9	4.9	1.9	4.0	3.8	3.5	3.1	3.4
Czechia	1.0	...	...	0.1	3.3	2.3	5.4	2.5	5.2	3.2	2.3
Czechoslovakia (Former)	...	4.7	1.8	...	...	...	...	...	...	...	...
Hungary	0.7	5.3	1.7	-0.2	2.2	4.2	3.8	2.1	4.3	5.4	4.6
Poland	2.5	5.9	1.0	3.6	3.9	3.4	4.2	3.1	4.8	5.4	4.5
Republic of Moldova	0.0	...	...	-11.3	4.9	5.0	-0.3	4.4	4.7	4.3	3.5
Romania	0.9	10.0	1.4	-1.6	5.2	3.4	3.9	4.8	7.1	4.4	4.1
Russian Federation	7.1	...	...	-5.3	4.9	0.7	-2.0	0.3	1.8	2.5	1.3

Table 4. Annual Average Rate of Growth of Gross Domestic Product by Major Area, Region and Country

Major area, region and country	Base year weights as percentage of total for world or region in 2015	Average rates of growth				Annual rate of change (percentage)					
		1970-1979	1980-1989	1990-1999	2000-2009	2014	2015	2016	2017	2018	2019
Slovakia	0.5	...	...	0.8	4.9	2.6	4.8	2.1	3.0	3.8	2.3
Ukraine [2]	0.5	...	...	-9.5	4.3	-6.6	-9.8	2.4	2.5	3.4	3.2
USSR (Former)	...	4.8	4.3	...	...	...	...	...	...	...	...
Northern Europe	*24.8*	*2.8*	*3.0*	*2.5*	*1.6*	*2.8*	*3.6*	*1.9*	*2.5*	*1.9*	*1.7*
Denmark	1.6	2.5	2.2	2.6	0.6	1.6	2.3	3.2	2.8	2.2	2.8
Estonia	0.1	...	...	-1.6	3.5	3.0	1.8	3.2	5.5	4.4	5.0
Finland	1.2	3.6	3.4	1.9	1.6	-0.4	0.5	2.8	3.3	1.5	1.1
Iceland	0.1	6.4	2.9	2.5	3.3	2.1	4.7	6.6	4.5	3.8	1.9
Ireland	1.5	4.9	3.1	6.7	3.0	8.6	25.2	2.0	9.1	8.5	5.6
Latvia	0.1	...	...	-5.4	4.7	1.1	4.0	2.4	3.3	4.0	2.1
Lithuania	0.2	...	...	-3.9	4.7	3.5	2.0	2.5	4.3	3.9	4.3
Norway	2.0	4.7	2.6	3.7	1.7	2.0	2.0	1.1	2.3	1.3	1.2
Sweden	2.6	2.0	2.4	1.8	1.8	2.7	4.5	2.1	2.6	2.0	1.3
United Kingdom	15.3	2.6	3.2	2.5	1.5	2.9	2.4	1.7	1.7	1.3	1.3
Southern Europe	*18.9*	*4.1*	*2.4*	*1.7*	*1.2*	*0.6*	*1.9*	*1.9*	*2.3*	*1.7*	*1.2*
Albania	0.1	4.0	2.6	0.8	5.8	1.8	2.2	3.3	3.8	4.1	2.2
Andorra	0.0	3.8	2.8	2.9	3.2	2.5	1.4	3.7	0.3	1.6	1.8
Bosnia and Herzegovina	0.1	...	...	12.5	3.9	1.2	3.1	3.1	3.2	3.7	2.7
Croatia	0.3	...	...	-2.1	3.0	-0.1	2.4	3.5	3.1	2.7	2.9
Greece	1.0	5.0	0.8	2.3	2.6	0.7	-0.4	-0.5	1.3	1.6	1.9
Italy	9.6	3.8	2.4	1.4	0.2	0.0	0.8	1.3	1.7	0.9	0.3
Kosovo	0.0	...	...	-8.5	4.9	1.2	4.1	4.1	4.2	3.8	4.9
Malta	0.1	10.2	3.6	5.1	1.9	9.0	10.9	5.8	6.5	7.3	4.7
Montenegro	0.0	...	...	-4.6	3.4	1.8	3.4	2.9	4.7	5.1	4.1
North Macedonia	0.1	...	...	-0.6	2.9	3.6	3.9	2.8	1.1	2.7	3.6
Portugal	1.0	4.8	3.2	2.8	0.6	0.8	1.8	2.0	3.5	2.8	2.2
San Marino	0.0	3.8	2.4	5.9	1.3	-0.9	-6.2	2.5	0.6	1.3	1.1
Serbia [3]	0.2	...	...	-7.2	5.1	-1.6	1.8	3.3	2.1	4.5	4.2
Slovenia	0.2	...	...	1.5	2.9	2.8	2.2	3.2	4.8	4.4	3.2
Spain	6.2	3.8	2.8	2.5	2.3	1.4	3.8	3.0	3.0	2.4	2.0
Yugoslavia (Former)	...	6.2	1.0	...	...	...	...	...	...	...	...
Western Europe	*42.6*	*3.1*	*2.1*	*2.0*	*1.0*	*1.7*	*1.5*	*1.8*	*2.4*	*1.8*	*1.1*
Austria	2.0	3.8	2.0	2.5	1.5	0.7	1.0	2.0	2.4	2.6	1.4
Belgium	2.4	3.2	1.9	2.1	1.6	1.6	2.0	1.3	1.6	1.8	1.7
France	12.7	3.9	2.4	1.9	1.2	1.0	1.1	1.1	2.3	1.8	1.5
Germany	17.5	3.1	2.0	1.8	0.5	2.2	1.5	2.2	2.6	1.3	0.6
Liechtenstein	0.0	3.0	4.6	4.8	0.9	3.0	0.0	2.3	3.2	3.9	0.6
Luxembourg	0.3	2.8	4.9	4.6	2.5	4.3	4.3	4.6	1.8	3.1	2.3
Monaco	0.0	3.9	2.4	1.9	1.7	7.2	4.9	3.5	-3.5	6.0	7.6
Netherlands	4.0	3.1	2.0	3.2	1.4	1.4	2.0	2.2	2.9	2.4	1.7
Switzerland	3.7	0.9	2.1	0.9	1.7	2.4	1.7	2.0	1.6	3.0	1.1
Oceania	**2.0**	**2.8**	**3.2**	**3.7**	**3.1**	**2.6**	**3.0**	**2.5**	**3.1**	**2.2**	**0.2**
Australia and New Zealand	*96.9*	*2.8*	*3.2*	*3.7*	*3.1*	*2.4*	*3.0*	*2.5*	*3.1*	*2.2*	*0.0*
Australia	84.9	2.9	3.4	3.7	3.2	2.2	2.8	2.3	2.9	2.2	-0.3
New Zealand	12.1	2.2	1.8	3.1	2.9	3.6	4.2	3.8	4.0	2.8	2.2
Melanesia	*2.5*	*2.5*	*2.8*	*3.9*	*2.9*	*11.2*	*4.6*	*4.3*	*3.4*	*0.8*	*4.4*
Fiji	0.3	5.7	2.1	2.5	1.4	27.5	4.7	2.5	5.4	3.5	0.5
New Caledonia	0.6	1.7	5.0	2.0	3.3	1.8	0.6	2.1	1.6	1.6	1.6
Papua New Guinea	1.5	1.7	1.8	5.4	3.0	13.5	6.6	5.5	3.5	-0.3	6.5
Solomon Islands	0.1	9.1	2.4	3.8	4.3	1.0	1.4	5.9	5.3	3.9	1.2
Vanuatu	0.1	7.7	5.9	3.4	3.5	2.3	0.2	3.5	4.4	2.9	2.8
Micronesia	*0.1*	*2.6*	*2.2*	*0.6*	*0.1*	*2.9*	*5.6*	*1.0*	*1.2*	*5.9*	*2.0*
Kiribati	0.0	2.6	0.5	1.9	0.4	-0.6	10.3	1.1	4.9	2.3	2.3
Marshall Islands	0.0	6.6	6.8	0.5	1.6	-0.7	-0.6	1.8	4.5	20.0	5.3
Micronesia (FS of)	0.0	6.6	4.1	1.9	0.0	-2.3	4.6	0.9	2.7	0.2	1.2
Nauru	0.0	0.3	-2.8	-11.5	-1.0	36.5	2.8	3.6	-5.5	5.7	1.0
Palau	0.0	0.1	3.6	3.3	-0.5	4.4	9.5	-0.4	-2.4	5.1	0.3
Polynesia	*0.5*	*4.8*	*5.1*	*1.9*	*1.2*	*1.1*	*2.5*	*2.8*	*2.4*	*2.3*	*2.4*
Cook Islands	0.0	0.3	3.9	1.7	2.0	5.4	5.7	4.9	9.5	5.7	4.8
French Polynesia	0.4	5.6	5.9	1.9	1.0	0.6	1.8	2.3	2.4	2.5	2.4
Samoa	0.1	3.7	0.3	2.1	3.2	2.6	6.7	3.7	-0.6	0.7	2.3
Tonga	0.0	2.4	5.0	2.5	-0.2	2.0	1.2	6.6	3.3	0.3	0.7
Tuvalu	0.0	-1.7	5.3	3.6	1.3	1.2	9.2	5.9	5.9	7.0	6.3

Notes for Table 4. Annual Average Rate of Growth of Gross Domestic Product by Major Area, Region and Country

1/ Paraguay

1970-2001

Does not incorporate export of binational hydroelectric power at market prices.

2/ Ukraine

2010-2019

The Government of Ukraine has advised the United Nations that it is not in a position to provide statistical data concerning the Autonomous Republic of Crimea and the city of Sevastopol.

3/ Serbia

1990-1998

Includes data for Kosovo and Metohija

Table 5.A. Average Rates of Growth of Gross Domestic Product by Expenditure - Household Final Consumption Expenditure

Major area, region and country	Base year weights as percentage of total for world or region in 2015	Base year share as percentage of total GDP in 2015	Average rates of growth 1970-1979	1980-1989	1990-1999	2000-2009	Annual rate of change (percentage) 2014	2015	2016	2017	2018	2019
World	**100.0**	**57.2**	**4.1**	**3.1**	**3.0**	**2.9**	**2.7**	**2.9**	**2.8**	**3.1**	**3.0**	**2.4**
Developed economies	**61.6**	**60.7**	**3.8**	**3.1**	**2.7**	**1.8**	**2.0**	**2.8**	**2.4**	**2.3**	**2.1**	**1.7**
Developing economies	**35.8**	**52.1**	**5.3**	**3.4**	**4.5**	**5.2**	**4.1**	**3.9**	**3.9**	**4.5**	**4.5**	**3.4**
Transition economies	**2.6**	**54.5**	**4.9**	**2.2**	**-3.1**	**8.1**	**0.3**	**-5.4**	**-0.1**	**3.5**	**3.9**	**3.8**
Africa	**3.7**	**69.4**	**4.0**	**2.6**	**2.5**	**6.6**	**3.1**	**2.7**	**1.6**	**3.5**	**3.4**	**2.2**
Northern Africa	*31.1*	*68.3*	*6.2*	*4.8*	*3.3*	*5.1*	*3.6*	*2.1*	*4.8*	*6.8*	*2.7*	*1.5*
Algeria	4.2	41.0	8.5	2.5	-0.4	5.0	4.4	3.9	3.3	1.8	2.8	2.1
Egypt	16.3	82.4	4.6	7.9	3.8	5.2	5.7	3.7	5.2	8.9	2.5	1.0
Libya	0.4	37.4	8.7	1.6	4.4	6.6	-50.1	-45.5	-16.1	64.0	17.9	9.9
Morocco	3.6	57.5	4.1	4.9	2.9	5.2	5.0	2.4	3.7	4.3	3.6	2.8
Sudan	4.6	87.1	...	...	...	...	14.0	2.1	8.6	3.9	1.3	0.7
Sudan (Former)	...	...	6.5	2.1	5.2	...	...	...	...	...	...	...
Tunisia	1.9	71.3	7.8	3.5	4.1	4.7	4.1	3.2	3.1	2.4	2.1	2.5
Sub-Saharan Africa	68.9	69.8	3.2	1.7	2.1	7.4	2.9	3.0	0.2	1.9	3.8	2.5
Eastern Africa	*14.5*	*74.5*	*2.9*	*3.1*	*3.4*	*6.7*	*3.7*	*5.5*	*1.1*	*4.2*	*5.1*	*10.2*
Burundi	0.2	90.5	2.9	3.3	-2.4	2.1	4.8	-2.9	-0.5	5.0	3.5	2.0
Comoros	0.1	93.3	4.4	3.0	4.0	3.0	2.3	1.7	0.2	5.3	1.3	2.5
Djibouti	0.1	61.0	0.5	2.4	2.9	4.7	9.3	10.5	11.3	10.6	10.8	10.9
Eritrea	0.1	65.0	...	...	6.7	1.3	7.1	-19.9	24.8	-25.0	24.5	11.3
Ethiopia	2.7	69.0	...	...	3.9	11.0	5.0	5.0	2.3	8.7	10.6	31.0
Ethiopia (Former)	...	...	2.7	0.8	...	...	...	...	...	...	...	...
Kenya	3.1	78.8	4.6	4.1	3.5	3.7	4.2	5.2	4.7	7.4	6.5	5.0
Madagascar	0.5	73.3	0.5	-1.4	1.9	2.6	-2.6	3.0	3.8	1.2	3.7	3.0
Malawi	0.3	83.9	5.4	3.1	3.9	4.7	6.2	3.3	2.7	5.2	3.9	5.2
Mauritius	0.5	74.7	6.0	5.9	4.8	5.1	2.6	2.9	3.0	3.2	3.2	3.3
Mozambique	0.6	64.6	3.9	-0.4	4.0	8.1	6.0	1.7	6.8	0.6	4.9	4.7
Rwanda	0.4	80.8	3.8	1.9	-1.0	6.5	6.4	12.0	4.2	-1.1	9.1	2.4
Seychelles	0.0	53.9	9.1	-0.7	5.6	9.6	4.5	5.0	1.5	11.1	8.0	3.6
Somalia	0.1	72.6	2.0	2.3	-3.3	3.4	4.1	2.7	3.1	3.3	3.0	3.2
South Sudan	0.8	188.9	...	...	...	...	-0.9	3.3	-7.0	-6.1	-0.5	-0.7
U.R. of Tanzania: Mainland	1.9	63.9	4.2	8.1	5.7	6.1	5.3	6.3	1.1	4.8	5.6	3.1
Uganda	1.2	78.0	-1.6	3.8	7.7	6.3	7.5	6.5	-3.4	3.4	4.0	12.3
Zambia	0.7	51.6	1.2	3.5	0.6	5.1	0.9	0.1	1.0	-3.1	-4.3	9.8
Zanzibar	0.0	63.9	...	...	9.5	4.7	4.2	3.5	-0.8	8.2	6.5	4.7
Zimbabwe	1.1	89.5	3.5	3.4	1.7	7.4	-2.6	19.1	-10.5	1.4	-6.7	0.6
Middle Africa	*8.4*	*56.6*	*1.4*	*3.0*	*-0.9*	*6.6*	*7.8*	*4.6*	*4.0*	*1.8*	*-0.5*	*1.4*
Angola	3.8	52.7	0.0	2.8	-2.1	11.8	12.7	3.0	5.9	2.9	-3.4	-1.5
Cameroon	1.4	70.7	6.6	0.5	1.9	3.7	5.3	5.3	3.3	4.3	4.7	5.0
Central African Republic	0.1	82.4	3.2	3.0	1.3	3.0	2.5	1.9	8.9	0.7	13.3	5.8
Chad	0.5	71.9	1.9	8.6	3.1	4.0	-12.2	11.5	1.3	-8.1	-0.7	1.9
Congo	0.3	38.1	4.3	5.9	1.8	6.6	7.7	5.5	-2.0	-9.4	4.6	-10.0
D.R. of the Congo	1.7	69.9	-0.6	4.0	-3.9	3.4	7.8	6.7	2.4	2.3	1.9	5.8
Equatorial Guinea	0.3	38.9	2.2	3.3	19.2	8.2	3.6	1.9	2.8	3.4	-7.5	3.4
Gabon	0.3	37.8	7.5	2.9	-1.8	3.3	5.5	4.1	3.1	-0.3	0.7	0.9
Sao Tome and Principe	0.0	80.4	10.6	2.0	-1.0	6.3	7.5	-11.4	3.2	7.9	5.5	2.4
Southern Africa	*13.0*	*59.9*	*3.5*	*2.9*	*2.5*	*4.1*	*0.9*	*2.4*	*1.0*	*2.0*	*1.7*	*1.1*
Botswana	0.5	52.0	11.1	5.5	5.0	7.6	0.8	4.0	2.2	6.5	4.1	3.5
Eswatini	0.2	66.9	10.7	4.3	6.5	3.5	1.3	-1.1	-1.9	5.6	2.7	-9.1
Lesotho	0.1	80.0	9.4	4.0	2.9	2.4	-1.3	7.5	0.7	1.6	-8.4	0.7
Namibia	0.5	68.5	3.8	4.3	4.1	6.6	3.3	13.7	11.3	-5.5	-1.3	4.3
South Africa	11.8	59.8	3.3	2.8	2.3	3.9	0.8	1.9	0.6	2.1	1.8	1.0
Western Africa	*33.0*	*77.3*	*3.8*	*-0.4*	*2.2*	*9.8*	*2.3*	*1.8*	*-1.5*	*0.9*	*5.1*	*-0.3*
Benin	0.5	75.2	3.0	1.4	5.1	3.6	12.8	9.4	1.9	3.5	3.5	6.9
Burkina Faso	0.5	71.5	3.7	1.5	6.3	4.2	1.3	3.7	4.3	3.5	3.9	5.8
Cabo Verde	0.1	65.2	0.1	5.1	7.2	5.2	1.2	3.2	2.5	7.1	1.5	5.9
Côte d'Ivoire	1.0	65.2	6.5	4.5	2.7	3.1	16.6	21.1	11.4	7.4	9.1	4.6
Gambia	0.1	81.7	6.2	1.2	1.8	5.3	0.5	0.9	0.6	9.5	8.1	3.5
Ghana	2.3	74.9	0.4	1.7	6.1	5.8	8.5	2.5	-0.6	1.7	9.4	4.2
Guinea	0.5	85.8	3.0	2.3	5.6	1.1	-2.2	4.5	4.7	7.3	1.4	4.4
Guinea-Bissau	0.1	85.3	4.7	10.5	1.7	2.7	2.5	11.1	14.7	6.2	2.1	6.3
Liberia	0.1	62.5	3.3	-1.8	-2.1	5.2	54.6	-6.4	-1.7	9.1	9.8	-2.8
Mali	0.7	80.5	8.0	0.7	12.6	8.7	11.1	15.9	10.3	0.6	5.8	5.5
Mauritania	0.2	63.9	6.4	1.0	1.6	4.2	3.0	4.3	4.3	2.7	2.7	2.5
Niger	0.4	67.4	0.3	0.3	3.8	4.4	3.6	7.1	9.9	5.8	5.9	6.6
Nigeria	24.3	79.0	4.1	-1.5	1.4	11.9	0.6	-0.3	-4.0	-0.4	4.6	-2.4
Senegal	0.8	72.6	3.2	2.3	2.7	4.8	5.2	4.4	5.3	4.9	4.3	3.0
Sierra Leone	0.3	102.3	3.5	1.8	-8.8	9.2	-15.1	0.3	10.1	-0.3	-6.8	13.6
Togo	0.3	79.2	1.2	3.5	3.3	2.4	12.4	11.9	11.0	3.3	8.6	7.4

Table 5.A. Average Rates of Growth of Gross Domestic Product by Expenditure - Household Final Consumption Expenditure

Major area, region and country	Base year weights as percentage of total for world or region in 2015	Base year share as percentage of total GDP in 2015	Average rates of growth				Annual rate of change (percentage)					
			1970-1979	1980-1989	1990-1999	2000-2009	2014	2015	2016	2017	2018	2019
Americas	**39.6**	**67.1**	**4.1**	**3.0**	**3.4**	**2.4**	**2.5**	**2.6**	**1.7**	**2.4**	**2.3**	**1.6**
Latin America and the Caribbean	**8.8**	**68.6**	**5.8**	**1.2**	**3.4**	**3.4**	**1.0**	**-1.0**	**-1.8**	**1.2**	**1.0**	**-1.4**
Caribbean	*1.3*	*63.0*	*4.6*	*2.7*	*2.8*	*2.6*	*1.3*	*2.3*	*2.1*	*1.5*	*3.0*	*3.8*
Anguilla	0.0	78.7	3.9	8.0	11.2	4.8	5.2	2.3	3.3	-28.1	36.3	34.2
Antigua and Barbuda	0.0	68.1	-2.2	3.7	3.9	1.7	-28.3	-2.3	14.8	16.4	-5.1	-0.8
Aruba	0.0	62.0	9.1	11.2	5.5	1.6	0.5	-4.4	-0.1	-0.1	0.0	-0.5
Bahamas	0.0	62.5	3.6	8.4	3.8	0.0	4.7	0.0	0.6	7.9	1.9	-3.6
Barbados	0.0	77.0	-3.0	1.7	4.4	-0.4	-1.8	1.5	-1.0	2.9	1.3	0.6
British Virgin Islands	0.0	34.8	-1.9	4.4	16.9	-1.4	2.3	0.6	7.2	0.8	2.7	2.6
Cayman Islands	0.0	54.0	9.4	9.7	6.8	1.3	2.5	2.5	4.4	1.8	3.8	3.4
Cuba	0.3	55.7	5.4	5.2	-2.5	3.6	4.6	7.4	4.1	1.7	2.2	4.0
Curaçao	0.0	66.0	...	...	...	...	-10.3	3.9	-0.2	0.7	1.4	-12.2
Dominica	0.0	78.5	8.6	2.4	0.8	4.8	5.2	-0.9	2.2	-4.8	13.2	-3.7
Dominican Republic	0.3	70.9	5.9	2.0	6.3	6.0	5.3	6.4	6.0	4.4	5.7	4.6
Former Netherlands Antilles	...	...	8.2	-2.3	0.8	3.4	...	...	...	...	...	...
Grenada	0.0	67.3	6.5	2.3	2.9	4.9	3.5	7.6	5.2	2.8	2.2	8.0
Haiti	0.0	96.1	4.6	-0.9	3.9	0.5	2.3	0.9	1.2	2.7	1.2	-0.2
Jamaica	0.1	81.1	0.2	3.9	4.3	1.2	-0.8	-0.1	-0.2	1.2	1.0	1.0
Montserrat	0.0	86.9	3.5	-4.5	-11.3	1.9	-16.7	6.6	4.9	-7.6	5.6	6.3
Puerto Rico	0.4	59.6	4.2	3.1	4.4	1.4	-3.1	-2.6	-2.8	-0.8	0.9	5.6
Saint Kitts and Nevis	0.0	66.4	6.8	2.2	5.1	1.3	3.4	2.2	7.8	1.0	3.1	3.5
Saint Lucia	0.0	68.9	7.0	4.2	1.8	1.2	3.5	-7.0	9.7	-4.1	-1.3	-2.7
Sint Maarten (Dutch part)	0.0	61.2	...	...	...	...	8.0	-4.0	2.1	4.2	4.0	2.9
St. Vincent and the Grenadines	0.0	80.3	3.2	3.2	2.5	6.7	4.5	0.2	3.4	-1.9	3.8	3.3
Trinidad and Tobago	0.1	57.0	7.9	-5.1	3.0	2.6	1.9	0.0	4.6	-2.7	8.0	5.2
Turks and Caicos Islands	0.0	41.2	10.6	10.8	4.8	7.4	21.7	12.6	2.7	0.0	5.4	4.6
Central America	*5.5*	*66.4*	*5.6*	*1.3*	*3.2*	*1.9*	*2.5*	*3.0*	*3.9*	*3.2*	*2.4*	*0.9*
Belize	0.0	71.2	3.2	2.2	5.7	2.2	0.8	5.0	4.9	-4.5	-3.0	0.3
Costa Rica	0.2	65.0	5.0	1.5	4.2	4.1	4.2	4.6	4.0	3.6	2.0	1.6
El Salvador	0.1	85.1	4.0	-0.8	5.3	1.9	1.1	2.8	2.0	1.7	4.0	2.6
Guatemala	0.3	84.3	5.4	1.0	4.2	3.7	4.5	5.1	4.1	3.2	3.5	4.3
Honduras	0.1	77.5	5.0	2.6	2.8	4.7	2.6	3.9	4.0	4.5	4.7	4.1
Mexico	4.5	65.6	5.9	1.3	2.9	1.6	2.1	2.7	3.7	3.2	2.3	0.4
Nicaragua	0.1	70.5	-0.3	-3.2	6.7	3.2	4.2	5.3	5.7	2.7	-4.5	-2.5
Panama	0.2	51.5	4.1	3.3	6.4	5.1	7.4	2.8	7.1	2.7	3.2	3.4
South America	*15.5*	*69.9*	*6.0*	*1.0*	*3.6*	*4.0*	*0.5*	*-2.6*	*-4.1*	*0.3*	*0.3*	*-2.8*
Argentina	2.5	65.9	2.5	-1.1	5.4	2.6	-4.4	3.7	-0.8	4.0	-2.4	-6.4
Bolivia (Plurinational State of)	0.1	68.4	3.4	0.8	3.6	3.2	5.4	5.2	3.4	4.7	4.3	3.7
Brazil	6.8	64.0	8.5	1.5	3.7	3.6	2.3	-4.9	-3.8	2.0	4.3	1.8
Chile	0.9	63.4	0.8	2.1	7.5	4.9	2.7	2.1	2.7	3.4	3.7	1.1
Colombia	1.2	68.5	5.7	2.6	1.8	3.7	4.3	3.1	1.6	2.1	3.0	4.6
Ecuador	0.4	61.4	6.4	1.8	1.9	4.6	2.7	-0.1	-2.4	3.7	2.1	1.5
Guyana	0.0	76.1	0.4	-2.4	1.8	11.5	-10.0	-7.1	-13.8	10.7	2.9	9.9
Paraguay	0.1	64.8	6.4	2.8	4.2	3.2	5.6	3.5	3.6	4.5	4.3	0.8
Peru	0.7	65.3	1.8	0.2	3.1	4.7	4.2	4.0	3.7	2.6	3.7	3.0
Suriname	0.0	36.8	4.4	-2.8	-5.3	-0.3	1.0	-3.9	-5.5	1.9	2.5	0.3
Uruguay	0.2	66.8	1.1	0.6	5.8	1.7	3.0	-0.5	0.1	4.6	1.5	0.5
Venezuela (Bolivarian Republic of)	2.5	121.3	7.5	1.1	1.4	6.4	-3.4	-8.9	-17.4	-14.4	-17.7	-34.1
Northern America	**30.8**	**66.7**	**3.7**	**3.6**	**3.4**	**2.2**	**2.9**	**3.7**	**2.7**	**2.7**	**2.7**	**2.4**
Bermuda	0.0	48.3	3.1	2.9	1.4	1.8	-1.9	1.4	2.3	2.4	-1.9	0.3
Canada	5.3	57.8	4.6	2.7	2.4	3.1	2.6	2.3	2.1	3.7	2.5	1.7
Greenland	0.0	39.5	2.8	-5.6	5.0	2.7	0.8	0.0	1.5	1.3	1.1	1.3
United States	72.5	67.4	3.6	3.6	3.5	2.1	3.0	3.8	2.8	2.6	2.7	2.4
Asia	**29.9**	**48.0**	**5.2**	**4.8**	**3.9**	**4.4**	**4.2**	**4.7**	**5.0**	**5.0**	**4.7**	**4.2**
Central Asia	*1.3*	*52.4*	...	...	*-5.6*	*7.0*	*4.4*	*4.0*	*3.7*	*2.8*	*5.7*	*5.7*
Kazakhstan	0.8	53.7	...	...	-7.4	8.6	1.4	1.8	1.2	1.5	6.1	5.8
Kyrgyzstan	0.0	90.5	...	...	-9.0	6.8	3.0	-0.9	-0.6	6.2	5.0	1.6
Tajikistan	0.1	82.5	...	...	-10.0	11.9	1.8	-15.0	6.4	5.4	-1.6	3.4
Turkmenistan	0.0	11.7	...	...	1.6	-3.3	27.2	16.2	-4.0	10.7	7.0	1.1
Uzbekistan	0.4	61.4	...	...	-3.2	5.0	10.7	11.8	9.4	3.9	5.9	6.7
Eastern Asia	*61.4*	*44.1*	*5.3*	*5.3*	*3.9*	*3.9*	*3.7*	*4.6*	*4.8*	*4.9*	*5.1*	*3.9*
China	32.6	37.8	4.3	9.0	9.1	8.7	7.2	8.3	8.5	7.3	8.1	6.4
China, Hong Kong SAR	1.6	66.4	9.7	6.9	4.1	2.8	3.3	4.8	2.0	5.5	5.3	-1.1
China, Macao SAR	0.1	26.1	7.9	7.2	4.2	5.5	5.9	2.1	-0.8	2.2	4.2	2.9
D.P.R. of Korea	...	...	...	...	...	...	...	...	...	...	...	...
Japan	19.4	56.6	5.1	4.0	1.5	0.7	-0.9	-0.2	-0.3	1.3	0.0	0.1

Table 5.A. Average Rates of Growth of Gross Domestic Product by Expenditure - Household Final Consumption Expenditure

Major area, region and country	Base year weights as percentage of total for world or region in 2015	Base year share as percentage of total GDP in 2015	Average rates of growth				Annual rate of change (percentage)					
			1970-1979	1980-1989	1990-1999	2000-2009	2014	2015	2016	2017	2018	2019
Mongolia	0.1	59.1	5.5	5.8	-1.9	7.9	6.3	8.1	-2.6	5.4	12.4	10.9
Republic of Korea	5.6	48.5	7.6	8.4	5.9	3.5	2.0	2.2	2.6	2.8	3.2	1.7
South-Eastern Asia	*10.8*	*56.1*	*6.0*	*4.7*	*5.2*	*4.8*	*4.8*	*5.2*	*5.2*	*5.1*	*5.5*	*5.4*
Brunei Darussalam	0.0	19.8	-4.9	2.9	3.5	4.9	-3.7	5.2	-1.3	4.7	2.2	5.9
Cambodia	0.1	76.8	-7.3	5.9	4.2	7.3	4.5	5.9	6.7	4.6	4.6	5.5
Indonesia	3.9	57.5	8.1	5.4	6.5	4.3	5.3	4.8	5.0	5.0	5.1	5.2
Lao People's DR	0.1	71.2	3.0	6.5	5.3	6.3	4.7	4.5	4.5	6.2	5.1	5.3
Malaysia	1.3	54.0	9.0	4.1	4.8	6.6	7.0	6.0	5.9	6.9	8.0	7.6
Myanmar	0.3	53.3	3.1	0.9	4.1	11.2	8.1	2.4	5.3	5.3	0.4	3.6
Philippines	1.7	73.8	4.7	2.7	3.7	4.4	5.6	6.3	7.1	5.9	5.6	5.8
Singapore	0.9	37.2	7.0	6.0	6.0	4.1	3.6	5.2	3.2	3.0	4.2	3.7
Thailand	1.6	51.0	6.3	5.5	3.9	4.1	0.8	2.3	2.9	3.0	4.6	3.1
Timor-Leste	0.0	58.2	...	...	1.9	0.5	5.6	-1.3	4.5	3.1	1.7	3.6
Viet Nam	1.0	68.0	4.7	5.6	4.9	6.6	6.1	9.3	7.3	7.4	7.3	7.4
Southern Asia	*14.9*	*61.0*	*3.3*	*3.8*	*4.2*	*5.1*	*5.5*	*5.8*	*7.1*	*6.5*	*5.5*	*4.6*
Afghanistan	0.1	80.0	2.1	-1.3	-1.3	9.7	-0.2	2.5	-0.8	-6.6	27.1	13.1
Bangladesh	1.1	72.4	-2.5	3.7	2.2	4.2	4.0	5.8	3.0	7.4	11.0	3.9
Bhutan	0.0	49.8	4.2	6.4	5.6	7.5	3.2	4.5	6.3	10.6	8.1	8.3
India	9.9	59.0	2.7	4.2	4.8	5.4	6.4	7.9	8.1	7.0	7.2	4.8
Iran (Islamic Republic of)	1.5	50.3	10.6	1.6	2.3	5.8	2.0	-3.5	3.8	2.5	-12.4	3.5
Maldives	0.0	41.1	7.0	8.2	6.1	7.3	6.3	22.1	12.9	13.1	10.6	5.5
Nepal	0.1	79.9	1.8	4.4	4.1	4.2	4.2	2.9	-0.7	2.6	3.3	5.5
Pakistan	1.7	79.0	5.3	4.5	4.9	3.7	5.6	2.9	7.6	8.5	6.8	4.1
Sri Lanka	0.4	67.4	5.0	4.8	5.3	4.7	3.7	7.5	7.4	3.6	3.7	2.9
Western Asia	*11.6*	*50.0*	*6.5*	*3.7*	*3.6*	*5.2*	*5.0*	*3.1*	*3.7*	*3.5*	*1.1*	*3.9*
Armenia	0.1	78.1	...	...	2.5	6.9	1.0	-7.7	-1.0	12.7	7.4	10.3
Azerbaijan	0.2	56.7	...	...	-3.6	12.4	8.4	10.3	1.7	0.2	2.6	1.5
Bahrain	0.1	45.5	4.7	0.5	2.7	6.2	-0.4	2.6	-0.1	1.3	-1.9	-0.7
Cyprus	0.1	67.9	4.1	6.1	5.8	4.3	0.2	2.8	4.4	4.5	3.3	3.0
Georgia	0.1	76.5	...	...	-6.7	6.1	5.7	3.8	-5.7	7.4	5.8	9.0
Iraq	0.8	59.1	1.4	10.9	4.1	17.9	10.5	28.4	15.4	-11.9	-8.3	7.4
Israel	1.3	54.5	6.4	5.7	6.6	3.3	4.1	4.1	6.3	3.4	3.7	3.9
Jordan	0.2	80.4	7.6	2.4	4.0	5.9	-2.7	1.4	-1.2	4.3	2.4	-1.4
Kuwait	0.4	41.5	10.2	1.9	4.7	5.1	4.9	3.4	1.1	3.5	5.4	4.9
Lebanon	0.4	90.8	-3.5	-3.6	5.7	5.1	4.4	2.2	0.6	0.1	-1.3	-7.4
Oman	0.2	38.6	11.2	1.2	5.3	7.8	4.0	3.7	5.4	8.7	2.1	0.9
Qatar	0.3	22.3	5.4	2.2	-1.1	16.9	8.0	7.6	7.0	4.4	-10.8	3.8
Saudi Arabia	2.1	40.3	11.6	6.5	0.9	7.7	6.1	6.8	0.9	3.2	1.9	4.5
State of Palestine	0.1	88.4	7.8	3.1	8.8	4.4	1.7	3.5	9.9	-1.1	1.1	4.2
Syrian Arab Republic	0.1	59.8	9.6	2.2	3.3	5.1	0.6	-4.6	-2.0	-1.1	4.0	5.7
Turkey	4.0	60.0	5.0	2.0	3.4	2.9	3.1	5.3	3.8	5.9	0.5	1.6
United Arab Emirates	1.0	35.4	17.5	8.8	5.3	3.7	12.3	-19.1	1.6	9.4	6.1	13.4
Yemen	0.2	90.8	...	...	5.5	7.9	-1.9	-19.1	-2.7	-1.7	3.1	8.4
Yemen Arab Republic (Former)	...	...	10.1	3.3	...	...	...	...	...	...	...	...
Yemen Democratic (Former)	...	...	4.2	3.8	...	...	...	...	...	...	...	...
Europe	**24.8**	**55.3**	**3.7**	**2.3**	**1.8**	**1.9**	**1.2**	**1.4**	**2.2**	**2.1**	**1.9**	**1.6**
Eastern Europe	*13.4*	*54.2*	*5.1*	*2.0*	*-0.4*	*6.6*	*0.6*	*-3.4*	*1.4*	*4.6*	*4.2*	*3.8*
Belarus	0.3	52.9	...	...	-0.9	11.1	4.2	-2.3	-4.2	4.7	8.0	4.6
Bulgaria	0.3	61.9	7.0	3.0	-5.3	6.1	2.9	3.8	3.5	3.8	4.3	5.8
Czechia	0.8	47.2	...	...	0.8	3.1	1.4	3.9	3.8	4.0	3.5	3.1
Czechoslovakia (Former)	...	...	4.9	2.0	...	...	...	...	...	...	...	...
Hungary	0.6	49.1	3.9	1.0	0.4	2.2	2.4	3.8	4.7	5.0	5.1	4.5
Poland	2.6	58.6	5.8	0.4	5.4	3.8	2.5	3.7	4.0	4.7	4.5	3.9
Republic of Moldova	0.1	87.4	...	...	-9.7	6.4	5.5	-2.4	2.9	5.3	3.9	3.7
Romania	1.0	61.8	8.6	1.2	-0.7	8.4	4.6	5.9	8.0	10.1	7.3	6.0
Russian Federation	6.7	51.9	...	...	-1.8	8.8	-0.2	-7.6	-1.4	3.2	2.9	2.4
Slovakia	0.5	54.0	...	...	-1.1	4.9	1.9	2.8	3.9	4.5	4.1	2.3
Ukraine [1]	0.6	67.8	...	...	-7.8	9.2	-8.1	-19.6	2.7	9.3	9.3	12.0
USSR (Former)	...	...	4.7	2.6	...	...	...	...	...	...	...	...
Northern Europe	*25.6*	*57.0*	*2.6*	*3.3*	*2.6*	*2.1*	*2.2*	*3.0*	*3.2*	*1.5*	*1.7*	*1.1*
Denmark	1.3	47.1	2.4	1.5	2.1	1.4	0.9	2.3	2.4	2.3	2.7	1.4
Estonia	0.1	51.3	...	...	-1.0	4.9	3.6	5.0	4.5	2.9	4.6	3.3
Finland	1.2	54.5	3.3	4.0	1.4	2.5	0.6	1.6	2.4	1.0	1.8	0.8
Iceland	0.1	50.0	6.5	3.0	3.2	1.1	3.2	4.5	7.2	8.1	4.8	1.6
Ireland	0.9	32.9	4.5	2.0	5.0	3.3	2.5	3.1	5.1	2.2	2.6	3.2
Latvia	0.2	59.7	...	...	-8.3	4.6	0.6	2.2	2.4	3.0	2.6	2.2
Lithuania	0.2	62.5	...	...	-1.9	5.4	3.7	4.1	4.1	3.5	3.7	3.4
Norway	1.6	43.5	3.8	1.9	3.2	3.3	2.1	2.7	1.1	2.2	1.9	1.5
Sweden	2.2	46.0	1.9	2.0	1.1	2.1	2.9	3.9	2.3	2.6	1.9	1.3
United Kingdom	17.8	64.3	2.5	3.9	3.0	1.8	2.3	3.0	3.4	1.1	1.4	0.9

Table 5.A. Average Rates of Growth of Gross Domestic Product by Expenditure - Household Final Consumption Expenditure

Major area, region and country	Base year weights as percentage of total for world or region in 2015	Base year share as percentage of total GDP in 2015	Average rates of growth				Annual rate of change (percentage)					
			1970-1979	1980-1989	1990-1999	2000-2009	2014	2015	2016	2017	2018	2019
Southern Europe	*20.8*	*60.9*	*4.1*	*2.4*	*1.8*	*1.3*	*0.8*	*2.0*	*1.8*	*2.1*	*1.5*	*1.0*
Albania	0.1	80.7	3.9	3.1	1.0	6.8	2.8	1.2	2.1	2.4	3.3	3.3
Andorra	0.0	58.5	3.8	2.2	2.6	2.7	3.2	-0.1	3.2	0.6	1.2	0.4
Bosnia and Herzegovina	0.1	81.6	...	...	12.8	4.4	1.9	1.6	2.2	1.1	2.3	2.7
Croatia	0.3	59.1	...	...	-2.1	3.1	-2.4	0.4	3.1	3.1	3.2	3.5
Greece	1.3	68.5	5.8	2.1	2.7	3.2	0.0	-0.3	-0.5	1.9	2.3	1.9
Italy	10.5	60.8	3.7	2.7	1.6	0.4	0.2	1.8	1.2	1.5	0.9	0.4
Kosovo	0.1	85.5	...	...	-9.0	4.1	9.7	6.6	6.6	1.8	4.8	0.3
Malta	0.0	48.3	8.5	4.0	5.7	1.7	2.6	5.0	2.6	3.3	7.8	2.9
Montenegro	0.0	79.2	...	...	-4.5	4.3	2.9	2.2	5.4	3.9	4.6	3.1
North Macedonia	0.1	68.8	...	...	1.8	3.4	2.2	4.4	3.9	2.1	3.4	3.5
Portugal	1.2	65.6	4.3	2.4	3.2	1.0	2.4	2.0	2.6	2.1	2.6	2.4
San Marino	0.0	40.4	3.7	2.3	1.0	0.2	-0.8	-8.2	-1.4	-2.3	-0.9	-0.5
Serbia	0.3	71.9	...	...	-8.0	5.2	-0.1	-0.6	1.9	2.2	3.1	3.6
Slovenia	0.2	54.0	...	...	2.8	2.9	1.6	2.0	4.4	1.9	3.6	4.8
Spain	6.6	58.5	4.1	2.3	2.3	2.3	1.7	2.9	2.7	3.0	1.8	0.9
Yugoslavia (Former)	...	...	6.1	0.1	...	...	...	...	...	...	...	...
Western Europe	*40.2*	*52.2*	*3.6*	*1.9*	*1.9*	*1.0*	*0.9*	*1.8*	*2.0*	*1.6*	*1.3*	*1.5*
Austria	1.9	52.7	4.2	2.1	2.0	1.5	0.3	0.5	1.5	1.9	1.1	0.8
Belgium	2.2	51.3	4.2	1.9	1.9	1.2	0.6	1.6	1.6	1.9	1.9	1.5
France	12.4	54.0	4.0	2.4	1.7	1.8	0.8	1.5	1.8	1.5	0.9	1.5
Germany	16.7	53.0	3.6	1.9	1.8	0.3	1.1	1.9	2.4	1.5	1.5	1.6
Liechtenstein	0.0	52.2	4.0	4.1	5.2	0.6	1.5	0.8	1.9	2.7	1.7	0.9
Luxembourg	0.2	30.1	4.2	2.8	2.8	2.1	4.1	1.8	3.4	2.1	3.3	2.8
Monaco	0.0	54.0	3.9	2.5	1.6	2.0	6.5	4.4	3.9	-4.0	5.8	7.3
Netherlands	3.2	45.0	3.7	0.8	3.3	0.6	0.4	2.0	1.1	2.1	2.2	1.5
Switzerland	3.5	52.2	1.9	1.6	1.3	1.5	1.0	2.5	1.6	1.2	0.8	1.4
Oceania	**2.0**	**58.2**	**3.1**	**3.1**	**3.5**	**3.7**	**2.1**	**3.5**	**2.9**	**2.9**	**2.2**	**-1.8**
Australia and New Zealand	*96.8*	*58.1*	*3.1*	*3.1*	*3.5*	*3.7*	*2.4*	*2.8*	*2.7*	*3.0*	*1.9*	*-2.2*
Australia	85.0	58.2	3.4	3.2	3.6	3.8	2.3	2.7	2.3	2.8	1.8	-3.0
New Zealand	11.9	57.2	1.5	2.2	2.9	3.5	3.2	3.5	6.2	4.4	3.1	3.2
Melanesia	*2.5*	*57.9*	*3.4*	*3.4*	*5.1*	*4.1*	*-13.7*	*35.1*	*7.9*	*-1.8*	*12.1*	*9.3*
Fiji	0.3	58.7	7.5	3.0	3.6	3.3	-4.8	2.9	10.7	1.2	0.7	4.2
New Caledonia	0.7	65.0	2.4	4.4	4.1	3.3	-0.1	4.5	3.3	3.0	2.6	2.7
Papua New Guinea	1.4	54.6	1.8	0.6	9.6	6.2	-26.9	79.1	9.5	-4.9	20.4	13.6
Solomon Islands	0.1	58.8	3.1	15.3	-3.9	0.2	4.6	1.1	6.2	3.3	6.7	7.4
Vanuatu	0.1	65.9	7.7	5.7	4.1	2.4	4.4	1.0	8.7	-1.9	3.3	-0.2
Micronesia	*0.1*	*78.8*	*2.9*	*3.0*	*-0.6*	*0.5*	*3.6*	*6.0*	*2.3*	*2.5*	*0.2*	*0.6*
Kiribati	0.0	105.1	3.2	2.8	-3.8	-0.1	3.3	11.6	0.8	3.8	-4.0	1.3
Marshall Islands	0.0	73.0	6.5	7.2	-0.6	0.7	0.5	1.0	6.4	9.0	-0.8	4.8
Micronesia (FS of)	0.0	70.4	6.6	4.1	1.9	0.7	-5.8	7.4	-2.8	4.4	0.4	0.5
Nauru	0.0	105.1	0.8	-0.6	-16.4	-1.5	41.8	4.0	3.3	-6.5	-0.8	0.0
Palau	0.0	66.4	0.1	3.7	5.4	0.9	1.9	4.2	6.2	-0.2	5.4	-2.6
Polynesia	*0.6*	*69.7*	*3.6*	*4.0*	*1.5*	*2.8*	*0.8*	*3.2*	*2.9*	*1.9*	*2.2*	*2.4*
Cook Islands	0.0	33.7	1.0	4.0	-1.2	-2.4	7.1	3.8	5.7	2.2	4.3	4.6
French Polynesia	0.4	65.3	3.8	4.7	1.3	2.9	0.2	1.8	2.9	2.2	2.1	2.7
Samoa	0.1	93.8	3.7	0.0	2.9	4.2	2.8	6.9	3.5	-0.6	0.7	2.2
Tonga	0.0	101.0	3.4	5.7	2.2	0.3	2.0	7.6	6.5	1.0	4.2	0.7
Tuvalu	0.0	139.0	-1.7	4.5	-0.2	25.7	-9.7	23.3	-45.9	41.2	14.8	-6.8

Notes for Table 5.A. Average Rate of Growth of Gross Domestic Product by Expenditure - Household Final Consumption Expenditure

1/ Ukraine

2010-2019

The Government of Ukraine has advised the United Nations that it is not in a position to provide statistical data concerning the Autonomous Republic of Crimea and the city of Sevastopol.

Table 5.B. Average Rates of Growth of Gross Domestic Product by Expenditure - General Government Final Consumption Expenditure

Major area, region and country	Base year weights as percentage of total for world or region in 2015	Base year share as percentage of total GDP in 2015	Average rates of growth 1970-1979	1980-1989	1990-1999	2000-2009	Annual rate of change (percentage) 2014	2015	2016	2017	2018	2019
World	**100.0**	**16.7**	**3.7**	**2.8**	**1.9**	**3.1**	**2.0**	**2.4**	**2.4**	**2.3**	**3.0**	**2.9**
Developed economies	**61.5**	**17.7**	**2.9**	**2.4**	**1.6**	**2.2**	**0.5**	**1.6**	**1.9**	**1.0**	**1.5**	**2.2**
Developing economies	**35.7**	**15.1**	**7.4**	**3.8**	**4.4**	**5.8**	**4.5**	**4.4**	**3.6**	**4.6**	**5.6**	**3.9**
Transition economies	**2.8**	**17.0**	**7.2**	**4.7**	**-3.1**	**2.2**	**4.3**	**-6.2**	**-0.8**	**3.5**	**1.3**	**3.0**
Africa	**2.6**	**14.1**	**4.9**	**2.4**	**1.3**	**5.5**	**-5.1**	**-0.7**	**-2.2**	**0.4**	**5.9**	**3.6**
Northern Africa	*35.7*	*16.0*	*7.3*	*1.9*	*1.6*	*3.5*	*-14.0*	*-3.8*	*-1.8*	*3.0*	*3.6*	*2.9*
Algeria	10.9	21.6	11.1	1.1	4.2	4.7	1.1	3.1	1.3	2.8	2.3	1.9
Egypt	11.4	11.8	4.5	5.4	5.0	4.1	7.4	3.6	1.4	-8.0	1.7	2.8
Libya	3.2	59.1	8.5	-2.5	-1.8	1.2	-55.4	-44.6	-30.4	33.7	14.6	2.1
Morocco	6.0	19.3	12.3	5.3	3.4	4.5	3.8	3.7	2.5	3.2	4.0	6.3
Sudan	1.6	6.3	...	...	...	...	-1.6	8.0	-11.5	49.8	8.4	2.5
Sudan (Former)	...	...	-0.5	2.9	-9.0	...	...	...	...	...	...	...
Tunisia	2.6	19.5	6.8	5.1	4.2	5.1	2.7	4.4	2.5	0.3	0.2	1.0
Sub-Saharan Africa	64.3	13.3	3.4	2.7	1.0	6.8	1.0	1.2	-2.5	-1.1	7.3	4.0
Eastern Africa	*13.5*	*14.1*	*6.0*	*2.2*	*2.3*	*5.2*	*12.6*	*8.6*	*8.4*	*4.6*	*4.2*	*4.0*
Burundi	0.2	18.4	3.9	6.1	-3.5	12.1	0.2	-3.7	3.7	8.0	6.7	3.7
Comoros	0.0	10.6	4.4	3.8	-4.0	3.2	20.1	-1.6	28.3	6.4	0.3	2.7
Djibouti	0.1	19.7	5.1	2.4	0.6	0.9	9.9	4.9	25.0	3.4	10.7	12.7
Eritrea	0.1	19.9	...	...	16.7	-7.1	-10.7	-6.5	13.3	4.7	17.6	4.2
Ethiopia	1.7	9.0	...	...	6.0	1.7	18.0	3.8	13.3	8.3	3.6	12.1
Ethiopia (Former)	...	...	6.7	0.9	...	...	...	...	...	...	...	...
Kenya	2.8	14.1	9.1	1.7	6.7	4.0	1.7	11.5	5.6	3.9	5.6	4.9
Madagascar	0.5	15.1	2.4	0.6	-1.0	2.2	2.9	0.5	-0.3	13.9	-36.6	0.0
Malawi	0.2	9.2	9.9	5.1	-0.2	8.5	6.2	3.3	2.7	5.2	3.9	5.2
Mauritius	0.5	14.9	5.1	3.2	4.5	3.0	4.6	3.1	2.9	1.6	4.2	2.7
Mozambique	1.3	25.9	4.2	0.5	3.5	10.7	18.3	8.3	20.2	3.2	-5.8	5.5
Rwanda	0.4	13.8	11.8	6.7	-2.8	8.7	20.7	5.1	9.2	7.3	5.0	17.6
Seychelles	0.1	20.3	9.3	3.6	5.5	0.0	4.5	5.0	1.5	11.1	8.0	3.6
Somalia	0.0	8.7	14.3	-0.8	-3.2	1.8	2.7	2.6	2.6	2.6	2.6	2.6
South Sudan	1.3	64.6	...	...	...	...	44.6	22.1	11.7	2.8	0.8	16.4
U.R. of Tanzania: Mainland	1.4	9.9	6.8	2.6	-4.0	10.9	6.1	9.6	3.2	1.1	2.0	2.3
Uganda	0.6	8.4	-1.7	3.4	6.9	4.5	12.8	3.6	-9.2	6.6	31.6	-4.4
Zambia	1.0	15.1	2.2	-2.1	-2.8	16.4	20.3	4.9	8.2	-9.5	-6.1	14.2
Zanzibar	0.0	9.9	...	...	-5.5	11.7	4.5	6.9	-3.5	1.1	2.2	2.5
Zimbabwe	1.2	18.9	11.8	6.8	-3.7	-3.1	19.8	15.9	13.1	14.5	27.2	-21.0
Middle Africa	*11.3*	*15.5*	*-1.0*	*2.6*	*-0.3*	*4.7*	*-7.1*	*-5.2*	*-8.9*	*-7.2*	*1.7*	*0.2*
Angola	5.8	16.4	0.8	4.5	3.8	3.5	-14.1	-8.8	-10.5	0.3	-1.7	-1.8
Cameroon	1.2	12.3	5.7	2.0	1.3	5.6	4.3	4.7	3.2	-1.6	3.9	3.8
Central African Republic	0.1	14.8	-1.8	-0.3	0.5	-5.0	-12.8	1.9	2.8	2.6	3.3	11.8
Chad	0.3	7.3	-14.1	14.2	2.7	10.2	-12.4	-0.4	1.6	-4.7	-3.2	2.4
Congo	0.7	20.4	6.8	4.4	-3.4	4.3	8.3	-10.6	-13.8	-16.8	-4.7	-1.3
D.R. of the Congo	1.7	14.4	-4.6	0.2	-18.1	10.2	4.9	2.6	-16.6	-43.3	8.4	8.3
Equatorial Guinea	0.9	21.9	2.2	3.1	7.0	15.8	-1.0	-0.7	-5.4	0.4	25.2	-2.3
Gabon	0.7	14.8	8.2	1.0	3.7	4.3	1.6	-7.3	-0.5	-3.6	-7.0	1.1
Sao Tome and Principe	0.0	25.2	-1.8	-0.8	2.5	11.6	7.0	-11.4	3.3	7.8	5.5	2.4
Southern Africa	*22.2*	*20.8*	*5.2*	*3.7*	*0.8*	*4.7*	*2.2*	*0.0*	*2.3*	*0.1*	*1.8*	*1.4*
Botswana [1]	0.9	20.6	14.6	16.7	5.8	1.4	10.8	2.5	2.3	1.5	3.7	3.2
Eswatini	0.3	21.9	12.6	2.4	9.7	8.4	4.9	16.3	7.5	2.9	-4.7	-3.5
Lesotho	0.2	34.4	15.9	2.3	5.6	4.5	5.9	-0.9	6.9	-4.5	0.7	-2.0
Namibia	0.9	27.4	3.6	4.7	4.1	4.3	4.4	12.1	1.1	-2.1	-0.1	0.4
South Africa	19.8	20.5	5.1	3.5	0.4	4.8	1.7	-0.8	2.2	0.2	1.9	1.5
Western Africa	*17.3*	*8.3*	*6.4*	*0.8*	*2.1*	*13.9*	*-1.8*	*1.6*	*-12.8*	*-4.2*	*22.8*	*9.4*
Benin	0.4	11.4	-1.4	-0.1	5.4	8.7	-0.2	9.8	-6.3	7.0	6.0	4.1
Burkina Faso	0.6	15.9	10.2	2.4	1.6	6.9	6.2	11.8	10.6	13.3	0.6	14.0
Cabo Verde	0.1	18.9	1.1	9.3	6.4	6.4	5.2	3.8	6.6	7.7	2.2	4.8
Côte d'Ivoire	1.3	9.3	9.3	0.5	1.4	1.1	11.0	3.1	5.9	15.2	4.4	4.3
Gambia	0.0	8.3	6.2	1.2	1.8	2.1	-6.7	0.7	4.0	-6.1	11.8	6.8
Ghana	1.5	9.7	5.4	-0.7	3.6	-2.7	7.6	-8.5	6.1	-10.8	1.8	5.4
Guinea	0.5	19.5	3.0	2.6	6.0	14.2	0.4	15.8	0.5	7.3	-0.2	5.6
Guinea-Bissau	0.0	15.5	4.3	-7.4	4.4	1.7	28.0	12.2	-2.8	18.7	0.3	3.7
Liberia	0.2	24.5	3.8	-4.3	5.5	15.8	4.6	14.3	-3.2	2.9	-4.4	4.1
Mali	0.6	16.2	-8.2	21.7	10.1	8.3	6.5	12.6	7.7	4.9	4.0	6.8
Mauritania	0.3	14.6	10.4	-1.4	5.4	2.4	4.6	6.0	2.7	5.3	4.5	5.5
Niger	0.5	16.7	2.3	-0.3	-1.4	3.5	25.9	4.9	-3.7	5.6	7.5	0.5
Nigeria	10.1	6.7	8.7	2.4	1.8	32.9	-7.0	-0.4	-24.9	-12.4	39.9	15.0
Senegal	0.8	14.3	4.8	3.3	0.4	3.6	3.5	5.7	4.2	4.1	3.8	10.0
Sierra Leone	0.1	10.2	1.7	0.3	-2.9	7.2	-19.3	24.2	17.9	-4.8	250.2	-42.3
Togo	0.2	15.0	10.6	-2.4	-1.5	1.6	16.6	19.5	3.7	-3.4	16.2	5.0

Table 5.B. Average Rates of Growth of Gross Domestic Product by Expenditure - General Government Final Consumption Expenditure

Major area, region and country	Base year weights as percentage of total for world or region in 2015	Base year share as percentage of total GDP in 2015	Average rates of growth				Annual rate of change (percentage)					
			1970-1979	1980-1989	1990-1999	2000-2009	2014	2015	2016	2017	2018	2019
Americas	**30.5**	**15.1**	**2.1**	**2.6**	**1.2**	**2.5**	**0.0**	**1.5**	**1.3**	**0.7**	**1.4**	**1.2**
Latin America and the Caribbean	**7.0**	**16.0**	**6.7**	**2.1**	**2.0**	**3.1**	**2.0**	**1.2**	**0.0**	**0.5**	**0.6**	**-0.9**
Caribbean	*1.4*	*15.9*	*5.2*	*3.9*	*1.3*	*4.3*	*1.2*	*-0.8*	*0.0*	*2.1*	*1.4*	*3.3*
Anguilla	0.0	16.8	4.0	5.8	6.2	5.6	-2.2	17.1	-5.4	9.2	-9.7	-6.0
Antigua and Barbuda	0.0	16.2	3.5	6.1	6.1	3.9	0.9	0.8	1.5	5.1	6.1	-4.7
Aruba	0.0	17.0	9.1	11.2	5.1	1.8	-8.1	4.5	-0.1	3.5	-0.9	-1.1
Bahamas	0.0	12.3	0.3	1.1	1.4	0.3	-4.4	9.6	-2.3	17.2	0.2	13.5
Barbados	0.0	13.6	-3.8	2.4	7.9	4.9	-6.1	-2.4	0.7	-2.0	-2.9	-2.5
British Virgin Islands	0.0	8.4	2.7	11.4	14.7	-2.1	2.8	0.3	7.2	0.9	2.7	2.6
Cayman Islands	0.0	9.3	9.5	7.7	7.5	1.2	2.8	1.0	6.4	2.4	4.2	4.3
Cuba [2]	0.7	32.2	5.4	4.8	-0.9	6.2	-1.0	0.0	-0.2	2.2	1.3	0.5
Curaçao	0.0	15.6	...	...	...	...	10.5	-0.8	0.3	4.8	0.3	-12.1
Dominica	0.0	21.3	4.0	2.0	2.6	1.4	7.7	1.5	-8.3	18.0	16.9	-11.4
Dominican Republic	0.2	10.3	2.4	3.3	8.3	5.0	4.3	6.9	1.9	0.8	2.8	6.3
Former Netherlands Antilles	...	...	7.7	-1.0	1.4	-1.8	...	...	...	...	...	...
Grenada	0.0	12.6	6.1	6.7	-0.6	5.3	-1.4	-9.6	2.1	-1.5	6.3	6.7
Haiti	0.0	2.0	2.9	-0.5	2.4	4.3	2.9	0.6	1.0	2.8	1.7	-16.5
Jamaica	0.1	13.8	8.0	0.3	3.0	1.5	-0.4	-0.1	1.3	0.7	-0.2	1.8
Montserrat	0.0	47.7	1.3	5.5	3.1	2.1	-2.2	-4.4	6.7	-5.2	3.3	6.9
Puerto Rico	0.2	8.8	5.2	5.0	2.7	1.4	7.4	-10.5	-3.8	3.1	-1.8	10.2
Saint Kitts and Nevis	0.0	19.3	5.7	3.6	6.0	10.9	4.1	2.7	1.9	5.6	4.2	3.7
Saint Lucia	0.0	12.3	4.5	6.3	4.3	7.0	5.6	-7.9	4.1	-0.4	-2.0	-3.4
Sint Maarten (Dutch part)	0.0	16.8	...	...	...	...	10.0	-1.6	-0.1	4.9	2.3	3.1
St. Vincent and the Grenadines	0.0	22.0	3.0	4.1	3.6	6.7	-2.3	7.6	-5.8	0.4	2.7	1.6
Trinidad and Tobago	0.1	14.0	9.8	0.9	-0.3	5.5	-0.4	-0.7	5.8	-3.2	8.0	5.4
Turks and Caicos Islands	0.0	21.3	10.7	10.6	2.0	8.9	5.4	10.0	9.2	-3.3	5.6	5.6
Central America	*4.6*	*12.5*	*8.4*	*2.5*	*2.2*	*1.4*	*2.5*	*2.1*	*2.6*	*1.0*	*3.0*	*-0.5*
Belize	0.0	15.6	4.7	3.5	4.1	4.8	5.1	5.8	8.3	0.6	7.2	0.3
Costa Rica	0.3	17.5	7.4	0.5	2.2	3.0	2.9	2.4	2.4	3.1	0.5	4.9
El Salvador	0.1	16.5	6.6	2.6	2.7	1.7	0.0	2.1	-1.0	0.1	0.2	-0.2
Guatemala	0.2	11.1	5.2	2.7	4.7	4.1	3.6	0.9	-3.1	1.9	6.1	3.5
Honduras	0.1	14.3	5.5	3.5	1.3	6.3	-2.6	2.1	4.4	1.4	1.9	0.6
Mexico	3.8	12.3	8.7	2.7	2.3	1.0	2.6	1.9	2.6	0.7	3.0	-1.4
Nicaragua	0.0	14.1	9.6	2.0	-4.4	2.5	6.0	5.6	8.2	1.6	-1.5	1.2
Panama	0.1	10.3	6.5	1.6	1.8	4.5	1.7	7.6	10.1	6.4	7.7	4.5
South America	*17.0*	*17.3*	*6.5*	*1.9*	*2.1*	*3.5*	*2.0*	*1.1*	*-0.7*	*0.2*	*-0.2*	*-1.3*
Argentina	3.1	18.1	3.8	-0.3	5.6	3.1	2.9	6.9	-0.5	2.7	-3.3	-1.5
Bolivia (Plurinational State of) [3]	0.2	17.5	8.8	-2.0	3.6	3.5	6.7	9.2	1.6	4.9	5.1	3.8
Brazil	9.3	19.8	8.5	2.9	0.9	3.1	0.8	-1.4	0.2	-0.7	0.4	-0.4
Chile	0.8	13.0	4.1	0.1	3.8	4.5	3.8	4.8	7.2	4.6	4.3	-0.3
Colombia	1.1	14.8	6.5	4.3	10.7	3.8	4.7	4.9	1.8	3.6	7.0	4.3
Ecuador	0.4	14.4	11.0	1.4	0.1	4.4	6.7	2.1	-0.2	3.2	3.5	-2.4
Guyana	0.0	17.0	6.8	-9.3	12.6	7.3	8.1	0.8	6.9	2.1	15.0	4.8
Paraguay	0.1	11.6	4.3	4.7	4.1	2.4	9.9	5.4	1.5	2.1	3.0	6.5
Peru	0.6	13.0	3.5	-3.2	4.8	4.9	6.5	8.0	5.2	3.3	2.7	4.5
Suriname	0.0	12.9	3.1	5.4	-10.8	3.8	-0.8	-2.6	-5.8	1.6	2.7	0.2
Uruguay	0.2	13.8	3.9	1.8	2.5	1.5	2.5	2.2	2.9	-0.7	0.8	0.8
Venezuela (Bolivarian Republic of)	1.2	12.9	3.3	1.9	-1.1	7.1	0.6	-3.2	-21.7	-13.0	-17.1	-34.7
Northern America	**23.5**	**14.8**	**1.2**	**2.7**	**1.0**	**2.3**	**-0.6**	**1.5**	**1.8**	**0.7**	**1.7**	**1.8**
Bermuda	0.0	12.5	3.5	2.7	0.7	5.4	-8.0	-0.2	-0.5	-2.2	-0.3	1.6
Canada	8.5	20.9	3.4	2.1	0.3	2.6	0.6	1.4	1.8	2.1	2.9	2.0
Greenland	0.0	44.2	6.8	2.6	1.5	2.5	-0.2	-0.6	1.8	2.3	1.8	2.0
United States	68.3	14.3	0.9	2.8	1.1	2.3	-0.8	1.6	1.8	0.6	1.5	1.8
Asia	**33.8**	**15.8**	**6.9**	**4.5**	**4.6**	**5.1**	**5.0**	**4.9**	**4.4**	**4.8**	**5.5**	**4.6**
Central Asia	*0.9*	*12.2*	...	...	*-5.6*	*5.6*	*8.8*	*4.0*	*2.8*	*2.6*	*-5.4*	*10.4*
Kazakhstan	0.5	11.6	...	...	-6.6	7.2	9.8	2.4	2.3	2.1	-14.1	15.5
Kyrgyzstan	0.0	17.8	...	...	-9.6	0.8	-0.5	0.9	1.5	1.3	1.3	0.5
Tajikistan	0.0	15.0	...	...	-11.4	3.5	4.1	3.3	3.9	15.2	7.3	8.7
Turkmenistan	0.1	9.0	...	...	0.1	3.0	9.5	6.1	6.7	6.2	6.1	3.1
Uzbekistan	0.3	14.3	...	...	-2.5	4.8	8.4	6.7	2.7	1.5	4.8	6.1
Eastern Asia	*70.7*	*16.8*	*5.9*	*4.8*	*5.5*	*5.0*	*4.8*	*5.6*	*6.0*	*4.8*	*5.8*	*5.1*
China	42.4	16.2	9.3	9.0	12.3	9.0	7.3	8.2	8.5	7.3	8.1	6.4
China, Hong Kong SAR	0.7	9.6	7.8	6.5	4.7	2.1	3.1	3.4	3.4	2.8	4.2	5.1
China, Macao SAR	0.1	9.6	7.9	13.0	5.9	6.8	6.4	4.2	4.5	-0.1	3.5	3.9
D.P.R. of Korea	...	...	...	...	...	...	...	...	...	...	...	...
Japan	20.5	19.8	5.3	3.5	2.9	1.4	0.5	1.5	1.4	0.2	0.9	1.9

Table 5.B. Average Rates of Growth of Gross Domestic Product by Expenditure - General Government Final Consumption Expenditure

Major area, region and country	Base year weights as percentage of total for world or region in 2015	Base year share as percentage of total GDP in 2015	Average rates of growth				Annual rate of change (percentage)					
			1970-1979	1980-1989	1990-1999	2000-2009	2014	2015	2016	2017	2018	2019
Mongolia	0.0	13.5	4.0	6.4	-11.8	1.8	12.2	-4.7	10.6	-1.8	-5.7	21.2
Republic of Korea	5.2	15.1	5.8	5.9	4.5	6.0	4.3	3.8	4.4	3.9	5.3	6.6
South-Eastern Asia	*6.8*	*11.7*	*9.0*	*4.0*	*3.8*	*6.6*	*2.7*	*5.1*	*2.4*	*3.0*	*4.7*	*4.7*
Brunei Darussalam	0.1	25.1	13.0	3.9	1.8	4.4	1.9	-3.6	-6.5	7.4	1.6	1.8
Cambodia	0.0	5.4	-7.2	11.5	7.7	11.5	2.4	4.4	5.7	6.5	6.5	5.8
Indonesia	2.0	9.7	12.0	5.2	0.1	8.9	1.2	5.3	-0.1	2.1	4.8	3.2
Lao People's DR	0.1	15.1	2.8	5.4	6.4	15.4	-3.1	5.0	-0.3	-1.3	1.1	-0.2
Malaysia	0.9	13.1	9.7	3.9	5.7	8.2	4.4	4.5	1.1	5.7	3.2	2.0
Myanmar	0.3	21.7	3.1	0.9	4.1	11.2	6.9	6.4	0.9	2.2	4.8	2.6
Philippines	0.8	10.9	7.3	0.7	2.0	3.3	3.3	7.6	9.0	6.2	13.0	10.5
Singapore	0.7	10.2	6.9	6.0	8.0	4.0	0.6	8.9	3.8	3.1	2.9	2.8
Thailand	1.6	17.1	9.5	4.7	6.6	5.4	2.8	2.5	2.2	0.1	1.8	6.0
Timor-Leste	0.0	58.8	...	...	1.9	3.5	11.8	3.6	-1.2	-5.8	-0.3	3.2
Viet Nam	0.3	6.3	4.7	5.9	6.1	7.6	7.0	7.0	7.5	7.3	6.3	5.8
Southern Asia	*7.8*	*10.5*	*9.5*	*2.6*	*4.6*	*5.5*	*6.4*	*7.2*	*5.8*	*9.2*	*6.4*	*3.2*
Afghanistan	0.1	22.2	7.5	-1.3	-1.3	20.5	2.6	4.9	5.2	-6.8	-9.6	26.0
Bangladesh	0.2	5.4	18.5	3.9	4.6	8.1	7.9	8.8	8.4	7.8	15.4	9.0
Bhutan	0.0	18.3	3.6	4.6	5.6	8.2	2.4	10.8	4.2	4.4	3.0	14.0
India	5.3	10.4	4.5	7.2	6.4	6.2	7.6	7.5	6.1	11.8	10.1	1.5
Iran (Islamic Republic of)	1.2	12.7	14.8	-4.1	2.3	2.1	4.2	4.8	3.7	3.9	-13.1	3.6
Maldives	0.0	18.2	2.8	12.3	9.0	10.2	8.8	7.4	4.3	-10.0	12.0	11.1
Nepal	0.1	10.9	3.5	9.5	5.2	5.7	10.0	7.4	-0.4	10.5	13.6	7.8
Pakistan	0.7	11.0	5.9	11.7	-0.1	7.8	1.5	8.1	8.2	5.3	8.6	10.0
Sri Lanka	0.2	9.0	3.3	4.8	5.5	7.1	6.0	10.2	2.3	-6.0	-5.1	9.6
Western Asia	*13.8*	*19.7*	*8.5*	*4.8*	*1.9*	*4.8*	*6.2*	*0.2*	*-3.6*	*2.6*	*4.4*	*1.8*
Armenia	0.0	13.1	...	...	-13.1	7.2	-1.2	4.7	-2.4	-2.1	-3.0	12.5
Azerbaijan	0.2	12.4	...	...	-12.0	7.9	3.7	1.3	6.9	1.3	1.3	2.0
Bahrain	0.1	17.6	8.9	6.6	2.6	7.9	4.0	3.7	-1.2	11.0	0.6	-5.2
Cyprus	0.1	16.4	5.7	7.2	3.2	4.9	-7.5	0.5	-0.9	2.1	3.5	11.3
Georgia	0.1	14.3	...	...	-17.9	19.5	9.0	4.4	10.9	1.1	1.6	14.3
Iraq	0.8	19.8	3.1	5.0	5.1	8.2	4.6	0.6	11.4	-13.7	5.0	-1.1
Israel	1.6	22.5	3.2	-0.2	1.8	1.9	3.9	2.7	4.4	3.4	4.0	3.6
Jordan	0.2	17.8	7.6	2.8	6.2	9.6	0.4	2.4	-4.4	2.8	3.7	-1.7
Kuwait	0.7	24.2	9.5	4.4	1.9	6.6	-0.8	-1.5	0.6	2.0	6.3	4.8
Lebanon	0.1	12.5	7.5	-1.1	-4.2	4.4	13.8	10.9	14.2	9.9	6.7	-6.2
Oman	0.5	28.4	11.7	11.6	2.3	6.5	6.5	-4.0	-9.7	0.8	2.6	0.3
Qatar	0.8	20.2	6.2	2.8	2.1	10.1	8.9	1.5	-10.9	-6.1	1.8	-1.5
Saudi Arabia	4.6	30.0	16.0	6.9	0.6	3.8	12.0	-1.8	-17.6	3.3	6.0	-3.5
State of Palestine	0.1	25.0	2.3	2.3	10.2	5.3	5.0	6.4	2.6	-13.7	7.3	-6.1
Syrian Arab Republic	0.1	12.1	13.6	-1.2	1.8	8.5	1.2	1.0	0.7	2.0	3.0	5.6
Turkey	2.8	13.8	7.2	8.9	4.7	5.0	3.1	3.9	9.5	5.0	6.6	4.4
United Arab Emirates	1.1	12.4	13.8	4.6	4.7	5.0	0.5	-3.0	-1.1	11.7	-5.0	14.3
Yemen	0.1	18.2	...	...	6.2	4.9	4.5	-19.9	-4.1	-0.5	2.7	8.2
Yemen Arab Republic (Former)	...	...	12.0	11.0	...	...	...	...	...	...	...	...
Yemen Democratic (Former)	...	...	2.6	10.0	...	...	...	...	...	...	...	...
Europe	**30.8**	**20.1**	**4.5**	**2.3**	**1.3**	**2.1**	**1.5**	**0.7**	**1.5**	**1.3**	**1.2**	**2.2**
Eastern Europe	*12.2*	*17.9*	*7.2*	*4.4*	*-1.6*	*2.0*	*3.7*	*-4.2*	*-0.2*	*3.4*	*2.5*	*3.2*
Belarus	0.2	14.9	...	...	-3.0	0.4	-1.8	-0.6	0.4	-0.9	-0.4	0.4
Bulgaria	0.2	16.1	7.3	5.3	-7.5	1.7	-0.1	1.8	2.2	4.3	5.3	5.5
Czechia	0.9	18.9	...	...	-1.2	2.4	1.0	1.8	2.5	1.8	3.8	2.3
Czechoslovakia (Former)	...	...	7.0	4.2	...	...	...	...	...	...	...	...
Hungary	0.6	19.7	5.2	1.9	-1.4	2.0	5.2	1.9	0.7	2.5	1.7	3.5
Poland	2.2	18.1	6.2	1.2	3.8	3.7	4.0	2.4	1.9	2.7	3.5	6.2
Republic of Moldova	0.0	14.5	...	...	-6.5	3.8	-2.1	-1.4	0.6	1.1	-0.2	-3.5
Romania	0.6	13.7	10.6	-0.1	4.6	-1.2	3.5	-0.3	2.2	4.2	2.1	6.4
Russian Federation	6.4	18.1	...	...	-2.7	1.7	4.4	-9.1	-1.9	4.0	2.5	2.4
Slovakia	0.4	18.6	...	...	-1.9	3.6	3.8	5.3	1.9	1.0	0.2	4.7
Ukraine [4]	0.4	18.9	...	...	-3.8	2.1	1.1	1.7	-0.5	5.2	0.1	-4.9
USSR (Former) [5]	...	...	7.2	5.3	...	...	...	...	...	...	...	...
Northern Europe	*25.5*	*20.7*	*3.1*	*1.1*	*2.0*	*2.4*	*1.9*	*1.9*	*1.5*	*0.9*	*1.0*	*3.0*
Denmark	2.0	25.5	3.4	0.7	2.3	1.9	1.9	1.7	0.2	0.9	0.3	1.2
Estonia	0.1	20.0	...	...	4.4	3.0	1.3	3.0	2.4	1.1	0.7	3.0
Finland	1.5	24.4	5.3	3.6	0.8	1.7	-0.1	1.3	0.9	0.1	1.6	1.1
Iceland	0.1	23.3	7.5	5.2	2.6	3.5	1.3	1.1	1.9	3.7	3.9	4.1
Ireland	0.9	12.5	6.2	-0.5	4.1	4.0	3.4	2.7	4.2	3.9	5.7	5.8
Latvia	0.1	18.2	...	...	1.6	2.1	3.5	2.7	2.5	3.4	1.6	2.6
Lithuania	0.2	17.2	...	...	-3.9	1.9	0.3	0.2	0.1	-0.3	0.2	0.1
Norway	2.3	23.2	5.3	2.4	3.3	2.6	2.7	2.4	2.3	1.9	1.4	1.7
Sweden	3.4	25.7	3.3	1.5	1.2	0.9	1.2	2.2	3.7	0.1	0.8	0.1
United Kingdom	14.8	19.5	2.5	0.7	2.1	2.9	2.0	1.8	1.0	0.7	0.6	4.1

Table 5.B. Average Rates of Growth of Gross Domestic Product by Expenditure - General Government Final Consumption Expenditure

Major area, region and country	Base year weights as percentage of total for world or region in 2015	Base year share as percentage of total GDP in 2015	Average rates of growth				Annual rate of change (percentage)					
			1970-1979	1980-1989	1990-1999	2000-2009	2014	2015	2016	2017	2018	2019
Southern Europe	*18.0*	*19.2*	*4.7*	*3.1*	*0.9*	*2.6*	*-0.5*	*0.5*	*0.7*	*0.4*	*0.9*	*1.0*
Albania	0.0	11.1	3.9	1.9	20.7	2.9	6.4	-1.1	4.7	3.2	0.7	3.1
Andorra	0.0	19.5	7.0	4.6	3.3	5.7	1.2	0.6	1.5	-2.0	1.8	3.0
Bosnia and Herzegovina	0.1	22.0	...	...	13.3	3.0	1.5	0.1	0.0	1.4	1.0	0.9
Croatia	0.3	20.1	...	...	-0.9	2.7	1.8	-0.9	0.5	2.2	1.3	3.3
Greece	1.0	20.4	6.9	1.5	1.2	3.4	-0.6	1.6	-0.2	-0.1	-4.2	1.2
Italy	9.1	19.1	3.8	2.9	0.0	1.2	-0.6	-0.6	0.7	-0.1	0.2	-0.2
Kosovo	0.0	15.4	...	...	-9.0	-2.9	-2.5	-6.5	-6.3	-0.6	8.9	9.6
Malta	0.0	17.5	9.0	5.2	8.2	2.1	6.6	3.7	-3.1	2.1	12.2	12.9
Montenegro	0.0	19.2	...	...	-4.2	9.8	1.4	1.9	0.8	-1.4	6.3	1.0
North Macedonia	0.0	17.0	...	...	-0.6	1.9	3.0	3.9	-4.9	-2.6	2.0	4.5
Portugal	0.9	17.9	8.4	5.1	3.2	1.9	-0.6	0.8	0.8	0.2	0.6	0.7
San Marino	0.0	20.0	4.8	4.0	1.6	3.4	-0.1	-3.9	0.9	1.7	-3.3	-0.2
Serbia	0.2	16.4	...	...	-5.8	4.0	0.9	-3.7	0.0	2.9	3.8	2.0
Slovenia	0.2	18.8	...	...	2.6	3.0	-0.2	2.3	2.4	0.4	3.0	1.7
Spain	6.0	19.5	5.6	4.9	2.9	5.1	-0.7	2.0	1.0	1.0	2.6	2.3
Yugoslavia (Former)	...	...	6.8	-0.8	...	...	...	...	...	...	...	...
Western Europe	*44.3*	*20.9*	*4.4*	*1.8*	*2.0*	*1.8*	*1.4*	*1.5*	*2.3*	*1.3*	*1.2*	*2.1*
Austria	2.0	19.8	3.6	1.6	2.8	1.8	0.8	0.9	1.8	0.9	1.2	1.5
Belgium	2.8	23.6	4.3	1.2	1.6	1.9	1.2	0.3	0.5	0.2	1.2	1.7
France	15.0	23.8	5.0	2.8	1.6	1.7	1.3	1.0	1.4	1.4	0.9	1.7
Germany	17.1	19.7	4.4	0.7	2.5	1.3	1.7	2.9	4.0	1.6	1.2	2.7
Liechtenstein	0.0	11.4	4.4	6.0	4.8	0.6	2.7	-1.0	0.6	2.2	1.8	0.5
Luxembourg	0.2	16.5	3.0	4.1	4.1	3.7	1.9	1.6	1.0	4.7	4.1	4.8
Monaco	0.0	23.8	6.0	2.5	2.7	2.6	7.3	3.5	3.1	-3.9	4.4	6.7
Netherlands	5.0	25.0	3.7	2.1	2.2	3.5	0.6	-0.1	1.3	0.9	1.7	1.6
Switzerland	2.1	11.4	2.2	3.4	0.9	1.5	2.2	0.6	0.4	0.6	0.9	0.9
Oceania	**2.2**	**18.8**	**3.9**	**3.3**	**2.7**	**3.3**	**2.6**	**3.8**	**4.4**	**3.8**	**4.0**	**5.5**
Australia and New Zealand	*96.2*	*18.6*	*3.9*	*3.3*	*2.8*	*3.3*	*2.5*	*4.2*	*4.7*	*3.6*	*4.8*	*6.2*
Australia	84.3	18.7	4.0	3.6	3.0	3.2	2.4	4.3	5.0	3.7	5.0	6.6
New Zealand	11.9	18.6	3.5	1.8	1.5	3.8	3.2	3.5	2.3	3.0	3.9	3.2
Melanesia	*2.9*	*21.7*	*4.3*	*2.6*	*0.2*	*4.1*	*6.1*	*-7.4*	*-3.5*	*10.5*	*-25.5*	*-24.8*
Fiji	0.3	20.1	9.1	2.7	1.3	1.2	3.4	5.7	0.8	2.9	2.1	1.9
New Caledonia	0.8	24.0	17.3	4.9	0.3	3.0	-1.3	3.3	2.3	2.4	2.2	1.8
Papua New Guinea	1.6	20.9	0.1	-0.4	0.6	5.7	10.9	-14.8	-8.2	17.0	-46.8	-64.2
Solomon Islands	0.1	29.9	10.7	13.5	-3.1	7.9	-6.8	1.6	10.1	0.7	7.3	7.9
Vanuatu	0.0	15.8	7.7	3.7	-3.4	1.8	-3.7	16.9	-1.4	19.5	4.5	-5.2
Micronesia	*0.2*	*42.7*	*2.4*	*2.9*	*-0.9*	*0.2*	*1.1*	*6.5*	*1.6*	*1.6*	*1.6*	*1.5*
Kiribati	0.0	40.4	-0.2	2.6	-3.8	-0.1	3.3	11.6	0.8	3.8	-4.0	1.3
Marshall Islands	0.0	56.7	6.5	5.1	1.4	2.1	-1.7	7.3	6.0	1.6	5.6	4.4
Micronesia (FS of)	0.1	48.9	6.6	4.1	1.9	0.7	-5.8	7.4	-2.8	4.4	0.4	0.5
Nauru	0.0	40.4	-2.5	-0.8	-16.4	-1.5	41.8	4.0	3.3	-6.5	-0.8	0.0
Palau	0.0	28.7	0.1	3.7	1.5	-2.0	1.4	1.3	4.1	-0.9	4.4	0.3
Polynesia	*0.7*	*29.5*	*3.7*	*4.4*	*1.2*	*2.8*	*-0.9*	*2.7*	*3.4*	*1.7*	*2.3*	*3.2*
Cook Islands	0.0	32.3	3.9	3.3	-2.5	2.1	5.6	5.4	5.1	3.2	4.1	4.7
French Polynesia	0.6	31.1	3.8	4.7	1.3	3.1	-1.6	1.7	3.4	1.8	2.2	2.8
Samoa	0.1	18.9	4.0	1.5	0.6	1.8	0.7	6.9	4.3	-1.1	0.8	2.3
Tonga	0.0	21.3	2.1	8.4	2.6	0.9	-0.3	3.1	-1.4	2.4	1.1	9.7
Tuvalu	0.0	95.5	-1.7	4.2	8.0	-4.3	13.3	28.5	4.8	1.3	10.7	5.5

Notes for Table 5.B. Average Rates of Growth of Gross Domestic Product by Expenditure - General Government Final Consumption Expenditure

1/ Botswana
2001-2009, 2013-2019
Excludes individual consumption of general government.

2/ Cuba
1996-2009, 2013-2019
Includes NPISH final consumption expenditure.

3/ Bolivia (Plurinational State of)
1996-2009, 2013-2019
Excludes individual consumption of general government.

4/ Ukraine
2010-2019
The Government of Ukraine has advised the United Nations that it is not in a position to provide statistical data concerning the Autonomous Republic of Crimea and the city of Sevastopol.

5/ USSR (Former)
1970-1990
Government final consumption expenditure includes net exports and net income from abroad.

Table 5.C. Average Rates of Growth of Gross Domestic Product by Expenditure - Gross Fixed Capital Formation

Major area, region and country	Base year weights as percentage of total for world or region in 2015	Base year share as percentage of total GDP in 2015	Average rates of growth				Annual rate of change (percentage)					
			1970-1979	1980-1989	1990-1999	2000-2009	2014	2015	2016	2017	2018	2019
World	**100.0**	**25.0**	**4.2**	**2.8**	**2.7**	**3.3**	**3.8**	**3.5**	**2.9**	**4.2**	**4.3**	**2.8**
Developed economies	**48.4**	**20.9**	**3.2**	**3.6**	**2.8**	**0.2**	**3.5**	**3.1**	**2.0**	**3.6**	**3.3**	**2.9**
Developing economies	**49.2**	**31.3**	**8.4**	**0.8**	**6.2**	**8.6**	**4.4**	**4.5**	**3.8**	**4.6**	**5.4**	**2.6**
Transition economies	**2.4**	**21.5**	**3.5**	**1.5**	**-16.3**	**9.3**	**-0.8**	**-6.7**	**1.6**	**5.8**	**3.7**	**6.2**
Africa	**2.7**	**22.2**	**6.7**	**-3.6**	**2.9**	**5.9**	**4.7**	**3.2**	**0.8**	**0.6**	**6.3**	**5.9**
Northern Africa	*32.4*	*22.9*	*9.5*	*-1.3*	*2.6*	*6.5*	*-0.8*	*2.7*	*5.1*	*2.7*	*6.8*	*5.2*
Algeria	13.6	42.3	10.4	-0.9	-0.4	8.0	6.4	5.7	3.5	3.4	3.1	1.0
Egypt	8.4	13.7	17.7	6.8	7.3	5.2	-1.2	9.3	9.8	5.8	15.7	12.9
Libya	1.3	37.6	7.8	-7.3	-3.1	4.3	-28.2	-36.3	-20.2	28.2	19.0	6.1
Morocco	5.6	28.4	8.3	2.7	4.2	7.8	-0.7	1.4	10.1	-0.4	1.3	3.3
Sudan	1.8	11.3	...	...	...	...	-2.8	3.9	1.9	-19.4	1.7	1.5
Sudan (Former)	...	...	4.8	-7.4	25.4	...	...	...	...	...	...	...
Tunisia	1.7	19.8	10.8	-2.1	4.6	3.6	-2.9	-0.5	1.1	0.3	2.0	1.1
Sub-Saharan Africa	67.6	21.9	5.7	-4.8	3.0	5.6	7.6	3.4	-1.3	-0.4	6.0	6.2
Eastern Africa	*16.8*	*27.6*	*-0.3*	*-0.7*	*2.6*	*10.1*	*12.7*	*10.6*	*3.2*	*10.5*	*9.5*	*13.6*
Burundi	0.1	12.3	15.4	0.8	9.7	13.8	7.7	-12.3	5.2	3.3	24.9	4.6
Comoros	0.0	13.5	4.4	-1.1	-1.6	1.9	-0.5	-0.5	-11.4	1.2	23.9	8.6
Djibouti	0.1	29.7	3.5	4.0	-6.3	30.1	17.9	17.5	1.3	-0.4	5.8	2.2
Eritrea	0.0	10.3	...	...	15.5	-5.9	-10.5	10.3	-23.1	7.4	-63.7	47.7
Ethiopia	4.8	39.2	...	...	-0.8	14.1	25.4	23.6	9.7	16.4	4.2	25.3
Ethiopia (Former)	...	...	-0.8	6.8	...	...	...	...	...	...	...	...
Kenya	2.7	21.6	3.1	-0.7	3.1	8.0	14.2	6.6	-9.2	8.3	1.3	2.4
Madagascar	0.4	19.0	3.3	0.4	-1.9	12.7	-1.1	1.1	11.5	-1.8	10.7	12.8
Malawi	0.2	12.6	15.4	-4.4	0.5	10.5	6.2	3.3	2.7	5.2	3.9	5.2
Mauritius	0.4	17.4	15.4	7.3	4.8	5.3	-5.9	-5.4	3.7	4.7	10.9	8.2
Mozambique	1.0	31.3	3.9	-5.9	6.9	6.9	12.4	-16.8	-9.4	-5.8	84.0	3.1
Rwanda	0.4	24.0	14.9	9.2	1.7	14.3	4.8	18.8	9.0	-10.2	5.9	32.0
Seychelles	0.1	36.9	9.2	4.4	6.4	-6.0	4.5	5.0	1.5	0.4	-5.0	2.8
Somalia	0.1	20.0	3.3	3.3	-4.6	1.8	2.7	2.6	2.6	2.6	2.6	2.6
South Sudan	0.3	21.4	...	...	...	...	2.8	2.7	-27.3	5.5	15.4	-0.2
U.R. of Tanzania: Mainland	3.0	32.8	4.2	-3.7	-0.1	11.9	7.2	7.2	15.5	15.2	15.1	15.4
Uganda	1.2	24.4	-1.6	6.9	8.6	11.2	1.3	6.5	0.7	4.7	11.3	6.7
Zambia	1.6	39.1	-11.0	-10.8	6.1	10.5	20.2	27.7	-5.7	12.9	-7.1	5.0
Zanzibar	0.1	31.9	...	...	-3.5	13.1	3.9	2.1	8.6	16.7	17.8	16.7
Zimbabwe	0.4	10.0	-1.5	1.9	0.0	-3.3	12.7	5.5	0.5	4.2	4.6	-7.8
Middle Africa	*12.9*	*28.0*	*2.5*	*-2.7*	*9.3*	*10.8*	*4.9*	*-3.7*	*-7.8*	*-13.7*	*-0.9*	*-3.8*
Angola	6.4	28.2	0.2	-6.7	18.2	10.0	3.3	-2.3	-7.7	-20.9	-5.8	-3.1
Cameroon	1.4	23.0	6.9	0.0	2.9	6.2	13.0	2.5	4.8	4.0	7.2	5.2
Central African Republic	0.1	20.6	-4.2	5.6	-0.9	-0.7	232.1	4.7	7.1	20.6	4.5	-9.0
Chad	0.4	16.9	-2.3	1.2	2.7	22.5	-9.3	0.4	-33.4	26.6	5.6	5.8
Congo	1.8	80.5	5.5	-5.7	1.3	13.0	16.6	19.9	-12.8	-49.5	-25.0	2.1
D.R. of the Congo	1.4	19.4	4.8	1.8	-12.7	17.4	5.4	-9.4	1.2	31.1	8.6	-12.9
Equatorial Guinea	0.6	24.5	2.2	2.6	41.9	19.0	-9.6	-39.2	-43.7	-11.2	16.3	-30.8
Gabon	0.8	29.2	12.5	-3.0	2.1	4.0	7.8	-14.3	3.8	-19.2	4.8	2.6
Sao Tome and Principe	0.0	35.4	11.9	3.6	5.1	5.1	-5.1	32.3	-9.3	3.2	-19.4	-15.3
Southern Africa	*14.4*	*21.2*	*3.7*	*-1.0*	*1.8*	*7.7*	*1.7*	*2.5*	*-4.1*	*-0.1*	*-0.4*	*-0.6*
Botswana	1.0	34.0	7.3	12.8	3.9	6.4	1.5	8.8	3.6	-8.8	8.1	6.4
Eswatini	0.1	12.5	21.7	9.3	-3.4	-0.8	3.1	5.6	8.1	-1.0	34.3	-35.4
Lesotho	0.1	27.7	25.2	3.5	2.9	-0.6	4.8	4.3	-6.2	2.7	2.5	19.2
Namibia	0.7	31.0	2.6	-5.7	7.1	11.9	22.4	-5.6	-26.8	-10.6	3.0	-0.2
South Africa	12.5	20.3	3.5	-1.5	1.7	7.9	0.7	2.5	-3.5	1.0	-1.4	-0.9
Western Africa	*23.4*	*17.6*	*8.0*	*-7.1*	*1.6*	*1.2*	*9.8*	*3.4*	*0.8*	*-1.9*	*10.0*	*7.7*
Benin	0.5	20.5	3.9	-6.5	6.5	4.3	1.2	0.7	0.3	25.3	16.2	10.4
Burkina Faso	0.4	19.2	18.7	5.2	4.1	8.8	-12.9	16.1	13.3	9.0	22.5	17.2
Cabo Verde	0.1	28.8	0.4	5.8	6.8	9.8	14.9	-15.8	19.7	6.1	16.1	-6.1
Côte d'Ivoire	2.1	23.7	10.8	-10.1	9.0	3.9	29.5	25.0	3.2	5.8	11.0	11.9
Gambia	0.1	20.3	3.2	7.9	2.7	1.1	2.0	33.1	33.5	-1.2	2.0	19.5
Ghana	2.8	29.2	-3.5	3.6	-1.4	2.3	-1.1	-2.7	12.2	1.0	13.2	-10.0
Guinea	0.4	24.0	2.9	6.2	1.3	11.3	5.0	8.8	137.0	-44.6	-14.6	-17.6
Guinea-Bissau	0.0	5.5	-1.0	-1.1	-11.4	1.9	2.1	6.6	-3.4	38.1	8.6	-18.9
Liberia	0.2	40.8	6.2	-9.2	17.7	15.0	-58.2	96.5	-1.9	-11.9	-13.6	-4.3
Mali	0.4	16.7	9.8	5.6	8.7	11.8	6.7	19.3	10.7	-3.2	8.4	16.8
Mauritania	0.4	34.3	2.0	-2.9	4.0	8.2	2.7	-9.0	-6.0	-17.6	31.9	4.4
Niger	0.6	32.4	8.2	-11.1	0.9	14.0	9.9	13.4	-14.0	9.2	11.4	11.4
Nigeria	14.3	14.8	9.1	-8.1	1.5	-0.2	13.4	0.6	-6.8	-2.8	9.7	11.8
Senegal	0.8	23.2	2.6	3.3	6.4	5.7	7.9	5.8	15.1	15.4	8.4	6.2
Sierra Leone	0.1	15.4	1.9	-2.7	-13.3	10.9	-5.3	-15.2	8.4	4.3	-33.7	3.5
Togo	0.2	23.2	17.5	-3.7	-7.5	4.2	12.6	12.9	13.8	-21.9	8.0	2.5

Table 5.C. Average Rates of Growth of Gross Domestic Product by Expenditure - Gross Fixed Capital Formation

Major area, region and country	Base year weights as percentage of total for world or region in 2015	Base year share as percentage of total GDP in 2015	Average rates of growth				Annual rate of change (percentage)					
			1970-1979	1980-1989	1990-1999	2000-2009	2014	2015	2016	2017	2018	2019
Americas	**28.0**	**20.7**	**5.3**	**2.2**	**5.0**	**0.8**	**2.8**	**0.8**	**-1.0**	**2.2**	**3.9**	**1.2**
Latin America and the Caribbean	**6.1**	**20.9**	**7.8**	**-2.7**	**4.7**	**3.8**	**-3.4**	**-5.8**	**-9.2**	**-2.8**	**1.4**	**-2.8**
Caribbean	*1.0*	*14.8*	*2.2*	*3.8*	*3.6*	*0.6*	*4.1*	*4.4*	*5.9*	*1.5*	*14.3*	*1.7*
Anguilla	0.0	25.2	3.8	6.2	5.7	0.7	33.0	5.3	-19.5	-2.8	130.6	-56.1
Antigua and Barbuda	0.0	24.5	7.4	10.6	4.4	5.5	9.3	1.4	7.2	3.6	70.0	-6.4
Aruba	0.0	20.1	9.1	11.2	6.2	4.0	-2.9	-5.1	5.6	1.5	0.3	-0.1
Bahamas	0.1	23.9	2.7	11.5	6.6	0.3	12.3	-18.8	5.5	9.1	-5.4	6.3
Barbados	0.0	16.7	3.0	-0.6	6.0	-1.9	-2.2	3.9	-2.3	-30.3	-5.2	-7.2
British Virgin Islands	0.0	23.9	-3.8	4.1	17.9	-0.1	1.7	0.7	7.3	0.7	2.8	2.6
Cayman Islands	0.0	13.7	9.6	9.6	7.0	1.2	3.6	-0.3	5.7	4.9	15.5	8.6
Cuba	0.1	8.6	5.4	5.1	-9.6	5.3	-2.7	15.6	6.5	3.3	6.3	5.6
Curaçao	0.0	21.9	...	...	...	...	-0.3	-10.6	4.9	5.5	-1.6	-11.1
Dominica	0.0	13.3	0.1	3.3	-2.3	2.3	12.6	-13.7	17.2	3.5	99.7	-31.9
Dominican Republic	0.3	23.3	11.5	3.2	9.6	1.2	9.3	18.9	12.3	-0.3	13.3	8.1
Former Netherlands Antilles	...	...	9.0	5.1	1.3	3.0	...	...	...	...	...	...
Grenada	0.0	17.7	14.6	9.2	5.1	-3.1	-2.0	3.3	11.8	24.0	19.4	-13.2
Haiti	0.1	32.4	13.0	-0.9	5.5	1.6	2.0	3.6	1.1	0.9	2.3	2.0
Jamaica	0.1	21.2	-8.9	7.6	1.2	-0.5	3.0	-4.8	0.1	4.6	5.7	1.9
Montserrat	0.0	16.4	3.8	15.5	-13.9	-5.5	8.2	-40.5	45.1	-7.5	-4.1	13.4
Puerto Rico	0.2	8.5	-2.9	4.6	8.0	-3.2	-6.1	-4.4	-4.4	7.2	62.0	-2.2
Saint Kitts and Nevis	0.0	30.7	5.9	10.8	-0.9	0.5	11.6	5.6	5.8	5.4	8.0	7.3
Saint Lucia	0.0	20.4	8.5	9.1	5.8	4.2	-14.3	3.8	12.0	9.1	1.2	2.2
Sint Maarten (Dutch part)	0.0	14.0	...	...	...	...	70.3	-2.7	0.6	11.0	16.4	19.1
St. Vincent and the Grenadines	0.0	25.3	2.9	2.8	3.8	4.2	2.5	0.3	12.7	-7.6	-0.1	-24.3
Trinidad and Tobago	0.1	20.6	14.6	-12.1	2.8	10.0	20.7	-5.8	9.2	-7.0	-26.2	-23.4
Turks and Caicos Islands	0.0	16.4	12.6	12.8	12.3	12.0	2.0	14.7	7.5	-3.6	6.3	5.2
Central America	*6.0*	*22.6*	*7.4*	*-2.5*	*6.4*	*1.6*	*3.3*	*5.1*	*1.1*	*-0.5*	*1.0*	*-4.6*
Belize	0.0	20.6	4.7	6.8	3.8	-1.8	5.7	24.7	7.2	-12.0	0.5	0.3
Costa Rica	0.2	18.6	10.6	0.8	7.7	4.4	3.3	3.0	4.8	-2.5	3.0	-6.4
El Salvador	0.1	15.7	9.5	1.2	8.6	-0.4	-6.4	9.0	3.6	3.6	6.7	9.6
Guatemala	0.2	14.5	7.8	-1.7	9.5	1.1	4.3	-1.5	-1.7	4.0	4.6	7.2
Honduras	0.1	23.7	7.2	-0.3	8.8	1.3	0.6	12.3	-7.4	11.2	5.7	-5.9
Mexico	5.0	22.5	7.6	-2.7	5.9	1.4	3.1	5.0	1.0	-1.6	0.9	-5.1
Nicaragua	0.1	29.3	-10.5	-0.5	9.5	-0.2	3.3	17.0	1.4	2.1	-20.1	-26.0
Panama	0.4	39.4	1.5	-12.4	21.4	7.8	8.7	6.5	2.1	7.6	0.7	-2.6
South America	*14.9*	*20.9*	*8.3*	*-3.2*	*4.1*	*5.0*	*-5.9*	*-10.1*	*-14.4*	*-4.2*	*0.6*	*-2.3*
Argentina	1.9	15.6	3.1	-6.7	10.2	3.3	-6.8	3.5	-5.8	12.2	-5.7	-15.9
Bolivia (Plurinational State of)	0.1	21.4	6.8	-1.5	9.3	3.1	9.9	5.0	3.4	11.8	3.2	-3.5
Brazil	6.1	17.8	9.9	-1.6	3.2	3.1	-4.2	-13.9	-12.1	-2.6	3.9	2.2
Chile	1.1	23.8	-1.0	4.5	7.5	7.2	-4.8	-0.3	-1.3	-3.1	4.8	4.2
Colombia	1.3	23.4	4.3	2.2	-1.0	10.6	9.2	2.8	-2.9	1.9	1.5	4.6
Ecuador	0.5	26.6	7.4	-2.5	-0.8	8.1	2.3	-6.2	-8.9	5.3	2.0	-3.4
Guyana	0.0	23.5	5.3	-1.9	4.5	9.2	54.4	-17.5	33.4	6.8	-0.7	18.3
Paraguay	0.1	19.4	17.3	0.1	-2.4	4.0	7.1	-2.1	2.0	5.9	6.9	-1.5
Peru	0.8	23.1	6.3	-4.6	6.7	8.6	-2.0	-7.2	-4.5	1.3	4.7	2.9
Suriname	0.0	42.1	5.9	-1.4	18.7	5.8	3.2	-4.1	-6.0	2.3	2.4	0.2
Uruguay	0.2	19.8	8.4	-7.2	8.8	3.9	2.4	-9.2	-1.6	-15.7	-2.7	1.4
Venezuela (Bolivarian Republic of)	2.6	39.5	10.1	-6.2	3.9	7.1	-16.9	-20.4	-45.1	-45.3	-19.6	-35.0
Northern America	**21.8**	**20.7**	**4.5**	**3.9**	**5.1**	**0.1**	**4.8**	**2.8**	**1.3**	**3.5**	**4.5**	**2.1**
Bermuda	0.0	11.9	4.2	3.3	4.7	0.3	9.3	1.5	11.2	10.5	-2.7	12.1
Canada	7.1	23.9	5.1	3.8	2.4	3.0	2.3	-5.2	-4.7	3.3	1.8	0.3
Greenland	0.0	24.0	3.5	-1.6	3.7	5.2	-19.1	5.9	14.0	-4.4	13.1	7.2
United States	71.0	20.4	4.4	3.9	5.4	-0.2	5.1	3.7	1.8	3.5	4.8	2.3
Asia	**46.8**	**32.8**	**6.2**	**5.1**	**3.5**	**7.0**	**5.5**	**5.7**	**5.2**	**5.5**	**5.3**	**3.0**
Central Asia	*1.0*	*26.3*	...	...	*-12.0*	*13.2*	*7.2*	*6.0*	*4.8*	*8.3*	*12.0*	*16.3*
Kazakhstan	0.5	22.9	...	...	-17.4	15.2	4.4	4.2	3.0	4.5	5.4	11.9
Kyrgyzstan	0.0	33.0	...	...	-9.2	8.3	17.4	3.9	7.9	9.2	6.9	2.3
Tajikistan	0.0	28.2	...	...	-12.5	9.5	19.7	24.4	20.3	3.8	15.8	13.0
Turkmenistan	0.2	49.1	...	...	-0.2	10.9	9.2	5.0	7.6	6.1	6.0	3.3
Uzbekistan	0.2	23.3	...	...	1.6	11.7	9.8	9.4	4.1	19.4	29.9	33.9
Eastern Asia	*72.1*	*35.5*	*5.1*	*6.0*	*3.8*	*6.4*	*5.8*	*6.4*	*5.8*	*5.6*	*5.3*	*3.9*
China	53.1	42.1	7.5	6.8	14.7	14.2	6.8	7.9	7.3	5.9	7.1	5.1
China, Hong Kong SAR	0.8	22.4	11.9	4.1	4.4	1.7	-0.1	-3.2	-0.1	3.1	1.7	-12.3
China, Macao SAR	0.1	24.6	7.9	9.0	2.0	15.0	37.1	5.4	-11.9	-2.5	-10.4	-20.1
D.P.R. of Korea	...	...	...	...	...	...	...	...	...	...	...	...
Japan	11.9	23.8	3.9	5.4	-0.5	-2.2	3.1	1.6	-0.3	3.0	0.6	1.3

Table 5.C. Average Rates of Growth of Gross Domestic Product by Expenditure - Gross Fixed Capital Formation

Major area, region and country	Base year weights as percentage of total for world or region in 2015	Base year share as percentage of total GDP in 2015	Average rates of growth				Annual rate of change (percentage)					
			1970-1979	1980-1989	1990-1999	2000-2009	2014	2015	2016	2017	2018	2019
Mongolia	0.0	21.2	6.1	8.0	13.1	3.0	-21.3	-28.9	-3.1	35.6	21.3	24.5
Republic of Korea	4.9	29.0	17.7	11.7	4.8	3.1	3.1	5.4	6.6	9.8	-2.2	-2.8
South-Eastern Asia	*7.9*	*27.9*	*10.7*	*6.2*	*1.8*	*5.8*	*3.9*	*5.8*	*6.0*	*5.8*	*5.4*	*3.6*
Brunei Darussalam	0.1	35.0	13.2	7.9	2.3	7.1	-31.3	6.5	-11.2	8.1	28.3	-4.4
Cambodia	0.0	21.4	-7.3	2.7	17.6	11.6	9.1	10.6	10.1	6.1	6.1	6.9
Indonesia	3.2	32.8	14.6	7.6	1.3	7.1	4.4	5.0	4.5	6.2	6.6	4.4
Lao People's DR	0.1	31.6	2.9	16.8	7.5	15.0	11.0	9.4	7.0	3.0	6.5	5.5
Malaysia	0.9	25.9	15.2	4.8	4.1	2.8	4.8	3.6	2.6	6.1	1.4	-2.1
Myanmar	0.2	32.5	8.8	-1.1	13.2	23.5	12.4	8.4	2.9	2.4	2.6	2.6
Philippines [1]	0.7	22.0	11.0	-0.5	1.7	2.6	7.2	16.9	26.1	9.4	12.9	1.5
Singapore	1.0	27.2	9.7	5.6	8.8	3.6	4.2	2.0	1.5	4.2	-3.4	-0.2
Thailand	1.1	24.5	6.7	9.0	-3.4	4.9	-2.2	4.4	2.9	1.8	3.8	2.2
Timor-Leste	0.0	35.5	...	...	1.9	7.8	6.1	-3.6	15.3	-16.7	-1.5	-10.4
Viet Nam	0.5	24.7	4.7	4.1	16.1	11.3	9.3	9.4	9.9	10.2	8.7	18.1
Southern Asia	*9.9*	*27.6*	*6.3*	*2.3*	*5.8*	*9.6*	*4.3*	*4.3*	*6.0*	*7.8*	*7.6*	*-1.2*
Afghanistan	0.0	13.7	8.6	-1.3	-5.6	11.4	-24.7	3.6	-0.7	17.7	4.5	-17.7
Bangladesh	0.6	28.9	11.5	2.1	8.3	8.2	9.9	7.1	8.9	10.1	10.5	8.4
Bhutan	0.0	55.7	4.3	7.6	10.7	7.9	27.5	12.9	10.2	-0.8	-6.3	-0.9
India	7.4	30.2	4.7	5.7	7.0	10.9	3.7	6.1	7.1	8.0	8.9	-1.7
Iran (Islamic Republic of)	1.0	22.7	8.2	-3.5	4.5	8.2	7.8	-12.0	-3.7	1.4	-3.8	-2.2
Maldives	0.0	33.0	7.1	11.1	8.9	12.6	22.8	17.8	2.8	7.5	29.1	-2.7
Nepal	0.1	28.0	13.5	6.0	6.9	4.3	11.4	19.6	-12.3	44.3	18.1	5.0
Pakistan	0.4	14.1	4.1	5.2	1.5	3.9	2.5	15.8	7.5	10.3	7.1	-8.9
Sri Lanka	0.2	26.0	7.5	-1.1	6.2	6.6	-2.8	2.5	7.8	6.1	-1.3	4.1
Western Asia	*9.2*	*27.2*	*12.1*	*-0.2*	*3.3*	*8.9*	*5.9*	*2.3*	*-0.5*	*1.7*	*1.3*	*-2.5*
Armenia	0.0	20.6	...	...	-14.5	15.4	-2.2	2.5	-11.4	9.7	4.8	4.4
Azerbaijan	0.2	27.8	...	...	-0.1	15.8	8.3	-8.2	-13.5	0.3	-1.2	4.0
Bahrain	0.1	24.0	9.4	1.2	0.3	11.0	5.9	-8.5	10.8	10.6	9.5	0.0
Cyprus	0.0	13.1	3.1	3.6	-0.7	5.0	-10.9	-0.2	48.9	24.1	-6.6	0.1
Georgia	0.0	24.4	...	...	-9.6	0.5	27.0	16.1	7.3	3.4	1.9	19.2
Iraq	0.5	27.6	18.7	-1.2	-15.3	16.8	5.7	20.4	-36.6	-2.6	-12.2	19.4
Israel	0.7	19.2	3.6	1.5	8.9	1.0	0.5	0.0	12.9	4.3	4.8	1.0
Jordan	0.1	21.8	16.7	-0.7	3.6	11.1	10.6	5.8	2.6	3.8	-2.1	-2.1
Kuwait	0.3	25.5	13.8	-5.4	5.0	15.4	9.8	15.3	8.9	1.0	4.7	-5.0
Lebanon	0.1	21.7	-1.1	1.7	2.6	9.7	-5.2	-3.5	10.7	-1.3	-1.8	-6.3
Oman	0.2	28.1	11.2	-0.2	6.4	15.1	2.4	-1.2	16.5	-4.3	-5.3	-3.8
Qatar	0.7	37.1	4.3	-1.8	6.2	26.3	11.3	1.6	22.5	1.3	3.8	2.0
Saudi Arabia	2.2	29.9	20.8	-2.8	3.1	12.0	7.5	3.7	-14.0	0.7	-2.1	4.0
State of Palestine	0.0	23.7	19.7	0.4	11.5	0.2	-5.3	14.3	10.9	6.9	2.5	-1.9
Syrian Arab Republic	0.0	19.2	15.2	-5.3	5.4	7.4	0.3	-0.1	0.3	4.3	8.0	10.2
Turkey	2.9	29.6	4.5	9.6	3.2	4.8	4.9	9.3	2.2	8.3	-0.3	-12.4
United Arab Emirates	1.0	23.4	18.9	-3.7	2.0	10.5	10.9	4.3	8.8	-17.3	3.6	0.0
Yemen	0.1	16.7	...	...	13.9	12.1	-3.6	-84.9	-22.7	41.1	181.8	13.3
Yemen Arab Republic (Former)	...	...	21.6	-6.0	...	...	...	...	...	...	...	...
Yemen Democratic (Former)	...	...	4.4	-2.7	...	...	...	...	...	...	...	...
Europe	**20.6**	**20.1**	**2.4**	**2.3**	**-0.3**	**1.3**	**2.2**	**3.3**	**3.3**	**3.9**	**2.8**	**4.7**
Eastern Europe	*14.5*	*21.3*	*3.7*	*1.7*	*-11.7*	*6.9*	*0.7*	*-3.3*	*-2.0*	*5.4*	*4.0*	*5.2*
Belarus	0.4	28.7	...	...	-5.6	15.3	-5.7	-15.5	-14.5	5.5	4.4	11.1
Bulgaria	0.3	20.9	6.7	4.1	4.3	11.7	3.5	2.7	-6.6	3.2	5.4	2.2
Czechia	1.3	26.7	...	...	1.7	3.4	3.3	9.7	-3.0	4.9	10.0	2.2
Czechoslovakia (Former)	...	...	4.6	2.1	...	...	...	...	...	...	...	...
Hungary	0.7	22.3	5.7	-0.4	3.0	2.2	12.2	4.9	-10.6	19.7	16.4	12.2
Poland	2.5	20.1	5.7	-0.2	9.6	4.0	10.0	6.1	-8.2	4.0	9.4	7.2
Republic of Moldova	0.0	24.3	...	...	-16.0	7.8	15.9	-4.8	-0.9	8.0	14.5	12.4
Romania	1.1	24.8	13.6	-0.6	0.6	10.1	3.2	7.6	-0.2	3.6	-1.2	18.0
Russian Federation	7.2	20.4	...	...	-17.9	9.1	-1.8	-10.6	1.3	4.7	0.1	1.4
Slovakia	0.5	23.8	...	...	-1.0	3.0	2.8	21.6	-9.3	3.5	2.6	5.8
Ukraine [2]	0.3	13.6	...	...	-18.7	2.5	-23.9	-9.3	20.6	15.8	16.7	14.3
USSR (Former)	...	...	3.2	1.9	...	...	...	...	...	...	...	...
Northern Europe	*23.9*	*19.3*	*1.6*	*4.4*	*2.1*	*1.0*	*5.6*	*6.6*	*8.3*	*3.2*	*0.7*	*8.7*
Denmark	1.6	20.0	1.7	3.7	3.7	0.6	3.0	5.4	7.8	4.1	4.7	2.8
Estonia	0.1	24.3	...	...	-2.8	4.5	-2.7	-3.2	5.1	7.8	3.9	11.1
Finland	1.3	21.3	1.3	5.2	0.0	0.9	-1.8	0.5	9.0	4.8	3.9	-1.0
Iceland	0.1	19.4	6.4	0.5	3.8	-3.6	15.9	21.3	17.8	10.8	-1.1	-6.3
Ireland	1.8	24.1	7.1	-0.4	8.0	2.2	18.5	50.4	50.6	0.0	-6.3	74.9
Latvia	0.2	21.9	...	...	-7.4	5.5	0.6	-2.0	-8.2	11.4	11.8	2.1
Lithuania	0.2	19.7	...	...	-2.7	5.2	5.7	4.9	3.4	8.9	10.0	6.2
Norway	2.4	23.8	4.7	1.0	4.6	3.9	-0.3	-4.0	3.9	2.6	2.8	6.1
Sweden	3.1	23.8	0.3	4.5	-0.4	1.9	6.0	6.9	4.0	5.5	1.4	-1.0
United Kingdom	13.1	17.2	1.1	5.2	2.1	0.2	7.0	5.3	4.4	2.8	0.4	1.5

Table 5.C. Average Rates of Growth of Gross Domestic Product by Expenditure - Gross Fixed Capital Formation

Major area, region and country	Base year weights as percentage of total for world or region in 2015	Base year share as percentage of total GDP in 2015	Average rates of growth				Annual rate of change (percentage)					
			1970-1979	1980-1989	1990-1999	2000-2009	2014	2015	2016	2017	2018	2019
Southern Europe	*16.0*	*17.1*	*2.8*	*2.0*	*1.9*	*0.7*	*0.2*	*3.3*	*3.2*	*5.2*	*4.2*	*2.3*
Albania	0.1	24.4	4.2	2.8	-4.6	7.9	-4.5	3.5	2.4	6.0	2.4	-4.1
Andorra	0.0	18.0	1.6	4.1	2.5	1.9	4.9	2.8	3.4	4.3	5.9	4.0
Bosnia and Herzegovina	0.1	18.2	...	...	16.4	4.3	11.5	-3.5	5.4	7.8	8.1	3.8
Croatia	0.3	19.5	...	...	3.8	6.8	-2.8	3.8	6.5	5.1	4.1	7.1
Greece	0.5	10.8	4.9	-1.5	4.2	2.2	-3.2	0.2	2.3	8.1	-6.6	-4.6
Italy	8.1	17.0	2.2	2.0	0.9	-0.1	-2.1	1.8	4.1	3.2	3.2	1.6
Kosovo	0.0	25.8	...	...	-9.1	3.6	-3.3	12.1	7.3	5.7	6.1	6.8
Malta	0.1	24.9	8.5	6.6	5.6	0.3	7.1	55.6	-0.2	-7.1	-1.8	6.2
Montenegro	0.0	20.1	...	...	-3.9	14.9	-2.5	11.9	38.4	18.7	14.7	-1.7
North Macedonia	0.1	23.9	...	...	-3.5	4.9	4.0	10.5	9.9	13.6	-7.3	6.6
Portugal	0.8	15.6	3.2	2.4	5.3	-1.6	2.3	5.9	2.5	11.5	6.2	5.4
San Marino	0.0	17.3	3.3	0.7	7.8	1.7	-15.9	-4.8	13.5	9.0	3.9	3.5
Serbia	0.2	17.0	...	...	-6.8	10.8	-3.4	16.9	-4.5	6.6	17.5	17.2
Slovenia	0.2	18.7	...	...	6.0	2.1	-0.1	-1.2	-3.6	10.2	9.6	5.8
Spain	5.6	18.0	1.7	5.2	2.8	1.5	4.1	4.9	2.4	6.8	6.1	2.7
Yugoslavia (Former)	...	...	8.6	-7.4	...	...	...	...	...	...	...	...
Western Europe	*45.6*	*21.5*	*1.7*	*2.0*	*1.8*	*0.3*	*1.7*	*3.8*	*2.3*	*3.4*	*3.1*	*3.2*
Austria	2.3	23.3	3.9	1.6	2.4	0.1	-0.4	2.3	4.3	4.1	3.9	4.0
Belgium	2.8	23.0	1.9	1.6	1.3	1.7	5.4	3.7	4.2	1.4	3.4	3.4
France	13.6	21.5	2.7	2.4	1.2	1.1	0.0	1.0	2.7	4.7	3.2	4.2
Germany	17.6	20.2	1.5	1.3	1.8	-0.8	3.2	1.7	3.8	2.5	3.5	2.5
Liechtenstein	0.0	25.2	2.1	6.2	4.7	0.2	3.1	0.5	3.2	5.2	1.7	0.8
Luxembourg	0.3	18.5	1.5	4.0	5.3	0.2	9.3	-5.0	3.2	2.4	-3.2	3.9
Monaco	0.0	21.5	2.9	1.8	0.6	2.0	6.1	3.3	5.0	-0.5	7.9	11.0
Netherlands	4.4	22.1	0.0	2.7	4.3	0.8	-2.4	29.0	-7.3	4.2	3.6	4.6
Switzerland	4.6	25.0	0.0	3.6	0.9	1.1	2.6	2.1	2.9	3.6	0.8	1.2
Oceania	**1.9**	**24.7**	**2.6**	**4.2**	**5.4**	**6.4**	**-2.6**	**-3.6**	**0.3**	**5.2**	**-0.9**	**-2.1**
Australia and New Zealand	*97.9*	*25.0*	*2.8*	*4.3*	*5.5*	*6.4*	*-2.5*	*-2.9*	*0.3*	*5.2*	*-0.9*	*-2.1*
Australia	86.8	25.3	3.0	4.0	5.6	6.8	-3.7	-3.6	0.0	5.0	-1.5	-2.8
New Zealand	11.2	22.9	1.5	6.4	4.7	3.4	8.3	3.6	2.8	6.9	3.7	2.5
Melanesia	*1.6*	*16.0*	*-4.0*	*1.0*	*1.1*	*6.7*	*-5.7*	*-35.4*	*-1.0*	*2.1*	*-1.0*	*0.2*
Fiji	0.2	17.3	7.3	-5.1	-0.1	-0.7	-34.0	13.0	-2.6	12.7	4.9	5.0
New Caledonia	0.8	34.9	-5.9	4.4	1.1	9.7	-5.7	0.6	-2.0	-3.1	-3.7	-2.8
Papua New Guinea	0.4	7.5	-7.9	1.5	1.4	6.3	0.0	-67.7	3.5	5.0	1.6	3.6
Solomon Islands	0.0	15.2	13.1	-1.3	0.7	9.7	-10.6	15.4	12.4	1.2	-33.1	3.9
Vanuatu	0.1	32.9	7.7	5.4	5.0	8.2	9.3	33.9	-21.9	16.3	15.3	-10.2
Micronesia	*0.1*	*31.3*	*8.3*	*2.1*	*-3.2*	*-1.4*	*8.5*	*6.3*	*3.1*	*4.6*	*-3.7*	*3.7*
Kiribati	0.0	45.3	14.1	1.7	-3.8	-0.1	3.3	11.6	0.8	3.8	-4.0	1.3
Marshall Islands	0.0	18.7	7.9	13.8	-4.5	8.4	-17.7	-2.5	18.9	14.8	-3.7	9.5
Micronesia (FS of)	0.0	29.8	6.6	4.1	1.9	0.7	-5.8	7.4	-2.8	4.4	0.4	0.5
Nauru	0.0	45.3	11.5	-1.7	-16.4	-1.5	41.8	4.0	3.3	-6.5	-0.8	0.0
Palau	0.0	27.3	0.1	3.5	4.2	-9.7	42.3	5.6	5.5	7.2	-9.3	8.9
Polynesia	*0.3*	*18.5*	*6.3*	*4.0*	*0.2*	*0.8*	*-1.1*	*9.0*	*-0.4*	*8.4*	*1.4*	*0.1*
Cook Islands	0.0	11.0	6.8	4.0	-1.2	-2.4	7.1	3.8	5.7	2.2	4.3	4.6
French Polynesia	0.3	19.9	6.7	4.2	0.2	0.8	-2.4	8.8	-2.8	9.0	4.4	-1.3
Samoa	0.0	9.0	3.6	2.4	-3.3	-1.6	2.6	6.9	3.6	-0.6	0.7	2.2
Tonga	0.0	23.3	5.5	3.1	6.1	3.7	8.2	6.5	17.3	16.1	-27.4	13.9
Tuvalu	0.0	27.0	-1.7	4.4	-0.5	5.7	42.4	519.6	36.4	-32.4	35.0	7.5

Notes for Table 5.C. Average Rates of Growth of Gross Domestic Product by Expenditure - Gross Fixed Capital Formation

1/ Philippines

1970-2009, 2013-2019

Includes intellectual property products.

2/ Ukraine

2010-2019

The Government of Ukraine has advised the United Nations that it is not in a position to provide statistical data concerning the Autonomous Republic of Crimea and the city of Sevastopol.

Table 5.D. Average Rates of Growth of Gross Domestic Product by Expenditure - Exports of goods and Services

Major area, region and country	Base year weights as percentage of total for world or region in 2015	Base year share as percentage of total GDP in 2015	Average rates of growth				Annual rate of change (percentage)					
			1970-1979	1980-1989	1990-1999	2000-2009	2014	2015	2016	2017	2018	2019
World	**100.0**	**28.4**	**6.5**	**3.7**	**6.3**	**4.0**	**3.8**	**2.9**	**2.2**	**5.4**	**4.4**	**0.9**
Developed economies	**55.0**	**26.9**	**6.3**	**4.6**	**6.2**	**2.5**	**4.3**	**4.5**	**2.7**	**4.9**	**3.5**	**1.6**
Developing economies	**41.9**	**30.3**	**7.0**	**2.0**	**7.4**	**6.3**	**3.5**	**0.8**	**1.5**	**6.1**	**5.4**	**0.0**
Transition economies	**3.1**	**32.0**	**4.8**	**4.4**	**-0.1**	**5.3**	**-0.6**	**2.0**	**3.4**	**5.5**	**5.5**	**0.8**
Africa	**2.3**	**21.5**	**5.7**	**-2.8**	**2.4**	**4.4**	**-7.3**	**-2.3**	**-0.3**	**13.6**	**5.7**	**3.3**
Northern Africa	*29.1*	*19.9*	*6.9*	*-4.7*	*0.8*	*4.6*	*-28.8*	*-6.5*	*-1.6*	*30.3*	*11.8*	*2.1*
Algeria	7.7	23.2	2.5	4.3	2.8	0.3	0.2	0.6	6.9	-4.4	-3.7	-6.1
Egypt	8.4	13.2	6.5	4.2	4.1	7.2	-13.9	-3.4	-18.1	64.1	27.7	-2.2
Libya	1.3	37.1	7.6	-7.2	-0.9	5.0	-78.8	-57.7	0.9	275.0	18.0	14.0
Morocco	7.1	34.8	4.5	5.7	4.3	6.5	8.4	5.4	7.8	9.2	5.5	8.1
Sudan	1.1	6.5	...	...	...	...	-7.3	-11.1	-3.0	11.0	6.1	1.9
Sudan (Former)	...	...	-2.1	-6.6	11.9	...	...	...	...	...	...	...
Tunisia	3.5	40.1	10.8	5.4	5.0	3.2	-1.5	-5.3	0.2	4.6	4.4	3.1
Sub-Saharan Africa	70.9	22.3	2.6	2.3	4.9	4.3	6.9	-0.4	0.2	6.9	2.7	3.9
Eastern Africa	*13.2*	*21.0*	*1.8*	*2.1*	*5.6*	*7.3*	*8.3*	*2.3*	*-3.7*	*6.7*	*6.2*	*4.9*
Burundi	0.0	6.3	0.0	1.2	-3.6	6.0	-3.3	-19.9	7.0	18.7	22.7	14.2
Comoros	0.0	10.1	5.8	8.5	1.8	-7.8	3.9	7.5	9.6	13.8	24.0	-1.8
Djibouti	0.7	140.6	2.3	1.2	-6.5	15.0	6.9	-1.2	-25.6	54.4	4.3	6.2
Eritrea	0.1	31.5	...	...	-1.2	1.3	214.9	-11.8	-31.1	27.8	8.0	-14.1
Ethiopia	1.2	9.4	...	...	5.7	11.8	2.8	-11.2	-8.1	7.7	11.8	17.7
Ethiopia (Former)	...	...	3.1	-3.3	...	...	...	...	...	...	...	...
Kenya	2.1	16.6	1.9	3.1	1.6	5.0	10.3	6.2	-2.2	-6.2	3.9	-0.2
Madagascar	0.6	28.4	-1.1	-0.3	3.5	2.3	39.4	-0.6	-1.0	45.4	2.4	10.9
Malawi	0.3	23.8	2.9	-1.2	5.6	10.2	6.2	3.3	2.7	5.2	3.9	5.2
Mauritius	1.1	48.8	8.1	8.8	5.3	1.9	6.6	1.8	-3.5	-1.0	2.3	0.5
Mozambique	1.0	31.1	3.8	-0.3	14.7	20.0	24.1	-6.7	-6.1	3.9	47.9	-10.7
Rwanda	0.2	13.1	10.4	3.0	-2.2	14.0	7.2	6.3	12.9	43.0	10.6	19.9
Seychelles	0.2	79.3	9.3	3.9	4.1	6.9	4.5	5.0	1.5	8.7	9.5	-1.6
Somalia	0.0	0.3	-2.0	-9.3	0.9	2.6	2.9	2.2	2.4	2.5	2.4	2.4
South Sudan	0.5	38.5	...	...	...	...	62.4	-1.3	-16.7	-8.7	5.7	8.3
U.R. of Tanzania: Mainland	1.6	17.1	-1.7	8.0	10.9	11.3	8.5	1.3	0.0	-4.1	-1.1	18.2
Uganda	1.0	19.3	-1.4	6.0	12.3	16.8	-16.5	16.1	-6.9	11.6	10.3	-7.4
Zambia	1.6	37.8	-0.2	-3.3	4.3	9.1	-3.2	-1.4	-5.4	5.0	10.0	-0.3
Zanzibar	0.0	17.1	...	...	8.8	12.1	1.1	0.6	1.0	-0.1	4.9	15.4
Zimbabwe	0.8	19.2	-0.7	5.9	18.3	-11.8	3.9	48.4	21.0	4.8	-29.3	21.4
Middle Africa	*15.0*	*31.3*	*5.0*	*5.4*	*7.4*	*6.2*	*2.8*	*-5.1*	*-9.7*	*11.0*	*-0.8*	*2.7*
Angola	6.9	29.8	0.2	7.4	10.4	7.7	0.7	-14.7	-18.4	24.5	-7.6	0.8
Cameroon	1.4	22.3	13.1	1.6	8.0	1.2	5.3	6.4	-0.6	-1.6	2.3	12.9
Central African Republic	0.1	17.1	-2.9	4.8	1.4	-5.1	13.7	10.0	-8.2	22.9	14.7	-2.2
Chad	0.6	26.8	-1.3	8.5	2.8	17.0	-27.2	74.1	-8.7	-13.9	6.2	15.6
Congo	1.0	43.2	9.5	6.6	5.1	0.9	6.7	-4.5	4.9	14.4	11.4	-3.6
D.R. of the Congo	2.1	27.7	9.4	7.1	3.8	6.0	21.4	4.1	-1.0	6.7	14.9	1.5
Equatorial Guinea	1.5	56.7	2.2	3.8	41.6	16.7	0.5	-6.4	-9.0	-3.8	-10.3	-1.5
Gabon	1.3	46.0	8.1	3.1	2.4	-1.4	0.4	8.7	0.4	-3.7	0.8	8.8
Sao Tome and Principe	0.0	11.8	12.5	-1.1	12.1	-0.7	61.6	16.6	3.9	-14.4	6.1	-1.9
Southern Africa	*22.0*	*31.4*	*1.3*	*1.9*	*5.0*	*1.4*	*3.9*	*0.6*	*1.3*	*-1.7*	*3.4*	*-3.4*
Botswana	1.4	49.8	24.7	13.5	5.0	-2.1	3.7	-18.3	13.1	-16.2	7.2	-16.6
Eswatini	0.4	43.0	5.0	1.8	5.7	3.2	11.7	-1.1	3.7	4.6	-2.5	5.0
Lesotho	0.2	42.7	13.3	2.6	10.5	10.6	-10.0	18.5	11.7	-0.1	11.0	-13.0
Namibia	0.8	35.6	2.9	-0.2	5.8	4.9	10.7	-12.0	-0.7	2.2	16.4	-2.2
South Africa	19.2	30.2	0.9	1.5	4.9	1.4	3.6	2.9	0.4	-0.7	2.6	-2.5
Western Africa	*20.8*	*15.1*	*4.0*	*1.3*	*2.7*	*4.6*	*12.7*	*0.3*	*8.6*	*13.1*	*2.2*	*10.5*
Benin	0.6	24.7	7.5	-5.1	9.0	5.6	43.9	-7.6	13.5	7.0	5.0	-12.0
Burkina Faso	0.6	26.1	8.4	-0.9	3.7	10.2	6.6	1.5	2.6	8.5	12.8	-5.5
Cabo Verde	0.1	44.9	0.6	8.0	8.5	1.9	-1.2	14.8	4.4	6.1	31.0	0.0
Côte d'Ivoire	2.5	27.4	4.0	2.1	5.2	2.1	4.8	7.3	-6.8	10.0	0.2	13.3
Gambia	0.1	19.6	-2.9	11.7	3.3	-11.4	10.9	-3.8	-12.8	9.6	8.0	14.2
Ghana	3.2	32.0	-4.6	2.3	9.0	1.2	-5.8	-0.3	14.8	16.5	10.3	6.7
Guinea	0.4	21.5	3.1	3.8	0.0	3.5	6.6	5.5	24.9	158.2	8.6	-1.8
Guinea-Bissau	0.1	27.5	10.1	7.3	13.2	7.4	11.8	8.0	-6.9	-8.1	19.3	14.6
Liberia	0.2	28.8	-1.1	-1.1	-1.5	-5.2	9.0	5.3	0.8	2.8	0.8	-8.8
Mali	0.6	24.0	3.6	-2.3	18.6	9.0	-6.6	4.2	3.3	17.2	-7.4	20.1
Mauritania	0.4	30.2	-1.4	7.0	2.5	6.0	2.7	2.6	-1.0	14.8	4.7	-7.1
Niger	0.3	14.3	4.2	1.0	1.4	5.0	-0.5	-9.0	-6.1	5.9	2.2	5.6
Nigeria	10.6	10.7	6.9	0.7	0.6	6.6	24.1	0.1	11.5	8.2	-0.9	15.0
Senegal	0.8	22.7	1.5	4.1	2.7	2.7	5.0	9.4	4.1	8.2	9.6	15.8
Sierra Leone	0.2	19.2	-1.8	-7.2	-7.3	12.7	60.5	-55.8	23.6	23.3	-34.9	32.2
Togo	0.3	28.7	2.9	1.0	1.6	2.5	-7.6	-1.4	7.2	-0.7	-3.2	-0.4

Table 5.D. Average Rates of Growth of Gross Domestic Product by Expenditure - Exports of goods and Services

Major area, region and country	Base year weights as percentage of total for world or region in 2015	Base year share as percentage of total GDP in 2015	Average rates of growth				Annual rate of change (percentage)					
			1970-1979	1980-1989	1990-1999	2000-2009	2014	2015	2016	2017	2018	2019
Americas	**18.5**	**15.6**	**6.4**	**5.0**	**7.2**	**2.3**	**3.6**	**2.0**	**0.9**	**3.3**	**3.2**	**0.1**
Latin America and the Caribbean	**5.5**	**21.4**	**7.0**	**4.7**	**7.1**	**3.3**	**1.2**	**4.6**	**1.9**	**3.1**	**3.3**	**0.1**
Caribbean	*3.8*	*42.7*	*5.4*	*4.1*	*2.3*	*2.9*	*-2.0*	*4.0*	*-1.1*	*-2.0*	*1.1*	*-1.9*
Anguilla	0.0	62.9	3.6	11.0	3.7	4.7	24.3	4.9	0.8	41.7	-18.5	3.2
Antigua and Barbuda	0.0	43.7	6.9	7.8	1.3	-0.2	6.4	-4.0	0.7	-4.2	1.4	9.2
Aruba	0.1	73.5	9.1	11.2	4.9	-1.0	3.2	0.0	-1.3	2.9	5.8	-1.4
Bahamas	0.1	37.9	0.3	-0.4	0.8	1.1	-2.9	0.2	2.1	1.7	10.4	3.5
Barbados	0.0	40.1	7.3	-1.9	6.8	1.9	-1.2	3.7	6.1	-1.6	3.2	2.1
British Virgin Islands	0.0	111.9	13.2	11.1	18.3	0.7	1.4	0.9	7.3	0.7	2.8	2.6
Cayman Islands	0.1	64.3	9.4	7.4	5.8	1.3	3.1	3.1	1.3	6.2	2.8	3.4
Cuba	0.4	17.1	5.4	4.1	1.0	9.6	-2.8	-0.1	-19.7	0.0	-2.4	-5.3
Curaçao	0.1	62.5	...	...	...	...	3.6	-13.2	-9.2	-5.6	9.1	-7.5
Dominica	0.0	47.3	-1.6	12.9	3.5	-1.4	41.1	-12.2	-3.3	-14.4	-26.6	35.0
Dominican Republic	0.4	23.8	11.3	3.5	7.5	-0.2	8.7	3.1	7.5	4.9	6.1	1.5
Former Netherlands Antilles	...	...	8.5	-3.1	0.6	2.2	...	...	...	...	...	...
Grenada	0.0	50.8	6.7	3.7	7.2	-4.8	8.1	-1.0	1.0	9.6	7.9	0.1
Haiti	0.0	20.0	8.9	-2.5	5.0	5.6	4.5	3.6	0.7	-1.2	2.0	-0.3
Jamaica	0.1	29.9	0.6	4.8	0.4	-0.3	1.0	4.8	2.7	5.1	8.2	3.6
Montserrat	0.0	27.2	3.5	13.7	-1.3	-5.3	-9.3	-3.9	9.2	-6.8	3.7	7.3
Puerto Rico	2.0	75.3	6.0	5.2	1.5	2.7	-2.1	3.8	3.1	-4.5	-0.6	-3.4
Saint Kitts and Nevis	0.0	37.7	5.0	3.5	3.9	-2.1	1.3	2.5	-1.7	5.2	4.2	2.3
Saint Lucia	0.0	40.1	7.4	8.4	3.4	1.4	1.2	-1.3	-5.3	9.1	7.7	1.2
Sint Maarten (Dutch part)	0.0	114.4	...	...	...	...	3.2	-1.7	-2.6	-23.1	-4.1	-5.7
St. Vincent and the Grenadines	0.0	37.8	3.0	8.2	-0.4	-3.5	32.4	11.4	6.4	-7.2	5.2	5.2
Trinidad and Tobago	0.3	50.0	1.1	1.2	3.4	7.0	-20.7	20.8	-20.5	-4.0	-1.9	-4.3
Turks and Caicos Islands	0.0	77.5	10.7	10.8	11.1	4.3	7.8	11.2	7.6	-2.7	5.6	5.4
Central America	*12.2*	*34.4*	*7.4*	*5.4*	*11.4*	*2.1*	*5.8*	*7.3*	*3.2*	*4.2*	*5.4*	*1.5*
Belize	0.0	58.8	2.9	9.0	3.6	4.8	-1.4	-0.8	-9.7	6.0	7.5	0.3
Costa Rica	0.4	30.8	7.2	6.3	9.2	3.8	5.0	2.6	9.4	4.0	4.7	2.6
El Salvador	0.2	29.5	7.5	-5.6	11.9	1.8	-0.6	3.3	0.2	3.4	2.2	6.5
Guatemala	0.3	19.8	6.7	-3.0	5.8	1.4	6.9	2.8	2.4	1.5	-0.3	-0.2
Honduras	0.2	45.2	5.8	0.9	0.6	3.0	3.4	2.9	0.9	6.1	0.7	2.3
Mexico	10.3	34.6	8.6	8.1	13.4	1.6	7.0	8.4	3.6	4.2	5.9	1.4
Nicaragua	0.1	40.1	6.7	-2.8	8.6	7.4	6.4	-1.0	4.6	9.7	-2.6	7.3
Panama	0.7	47.7	4.4	2.0	0.3	7.0	-7.1	0.9	-4.3	5.0	5.1	-0.1
South America	*13.8*	*14.5*	*7.7*	*4.6*	*6.6*	*4.3*	*-1.6*	*2.4*	*1.6*	*3.3*	*1.8*	*-0.7*
Argentina	1.8	10.7	5.9	3.8	7.1	4.0	-7.0	-2.8	5.3	1.7	-0.7	9.4
Bolivia (Plurinational State of)	0.3	30.9	3.7	1.8	3.5	6.1	10.9	-5.9	-5.7	-5.0	5.2	-1.8
Brazil	5.9	12.9	8.6	8.5	6.7	5.8	-1.1	6.8	0.9	4.9	4.0	-2.5
Chile	1.8	29.4	9.8	5.9	9.7	4.3	0.3	-1.7	0.5	-1.5	5.0	-2.3
Colombia	1.2	15.7	6.4	4.9	5.5	3.9	-0.3	1.7	-0.2	2.6	0.9	3.1
Ecuador	0.5	21.3	19.0	4.2	6.4	4.0	6.2	-0.6	1.4	0.7	1.2	5.2
Guyana	0.0	43.1	2.4	-2.7	9.1	9.8	-13.4	-1.2	14.9	1.8	2.1	2.0
Paraguay [1]	0.3	33.0	13.6	6.8	1.5	7.7	-2.5	0.1	9.5	8.3	1.8	-5.1
Peru	1.0	21.3	4.1	-0.2	8.1	6.8	-3.8	4.3	11.8	8.8	3.9	0.5
Suriname	0.1	50.3	4.3	-5.1	9.7	3.5	-0.8	-3.9	-4.9	1.5	2.5	0.4
Uruguay	0.3	22.5	7.6	3.9	5.7	6.8	3.5	-0.6	-0.2	6.9	-4.8	1.2
Venezuela (Bolivarian Republic of)	0.7	7.7	9.0	1.3	4.0	-3.1	-4.7	-0.9	-11.7	0.0	-22.8	-28.9
Northern America	**13.0**	**14.0**	**6.1**	**5.1**	**7.3**	**1.9**	**4.6**	**0.9**	**0.5**	**3.5**	**3.1**	**0.1**
Bermuda	0.1	50.0	3.3	0.8	1.8	3.2	-3.0	-2.2	0.1	0.7	6.7	0.4
Canada	12.6	31.8	4.1	5.1	8.4	-1.4	6.3	3.4	1.4	1.4	3.7	1.3
Greenland	0.0	37.6	13.3	4.1	-5.3	0.5	11.8	-9.9	15.2	-5.4	4.2	4.3
United States	57.5	12.4	6.8	5.2	7.0	2.8	4.2	0.4	0.3	3.9	3.0	-0.1
Asia	**38.7**	**30.8**	**7.9**	**3.9**	**7.4**	**6.7**	**4.9**	**0.6**	**1.6**	**6.2**	**5.5**	**-0.3**
Central Asia	*1.2*	*30.0*	...	...	*-5.9*	*5.1*	*-0.4*	*-0.6*	*0.7*	*6.4*	*8.2*	*5.9*
Kazakhstan	0.6	28.5	...	...	-4.6	4.0	-2.5	-4.1	-4.5	8.0	9.6	2.2
Kyrgyzstan	0.0	35.2	...	...	-9.3	5.6	-6.2	-5.6	-3.8	6.1	-2.7	19.8
Tajikistan	0.0	10.3	...	...	-10.8	7.8	0.0	0.0	0.0	5.3	1.7	2.3
Turkmenistan	0.3	74.1	...	...	-10.3	4.4	9.6	6.2	6.6	6.3	6.1	3.1
Uzbekistan	0.2	15.3	...	...	-3.3	14.6	-7.5	2.3	11.1	1.3	9.3	23.9
Eastern Asia	*58.3*	*26.9*	*10.2*	*8.9*	*9.3*	*8.1*	*6.7*	*0.2*	*0.2*	*6.7*	*3.8*	*0.6*
China	28.7	21.4	15.0	15.7	18.1	12.2	9.1	0.2	-0.7	8.2	4.2	2.6
China, Hong Kong SAR	7.4	195.9	8.3	12.6	7.9	6.6	1.0	-1.4	0.7	5.8	3.7	-5.6
China, Macao SAR	0.4	77.9	7.9	7.8	1.7	9.8	-4.5	-26.6	-1.9	16.8	9.8	-3.6
D.P.R. of Korea	0.0	5.9	7.6	4.4	-10.2	5.1	1.0	-1.1	3.9	-3.5	-4.1	0.4
Japan	9.4	17.6	8.6	5.6	3.8	2.6	9.3	2.9	1.7	6.8	3.4	-1.6

Table 5.D. Average Rates of Growth of Gross Domestic Product by Expenditure - Exports of goods and Services

Major area, region and country	Base year weights as percentage of total for world or region in 2015	Base year share as percentage of total GDP in 2015	Average rates of growth				Annual rate of change (percentage)					
			1970-1979	1980-1989	1990-1999	2000-2009	2014	2015	2016	2017	2018	2019
Mongolia	0.1	45.6	6.0	8.4	10.7	11.3	53.2	0.1	13.8	14.8	24.0	9.9
Republic of Korea	7.7	43.0	24.0	12.0	14.5	9.3	2.1	0.2	2.4	2.5	4.0	1.7
South-Eastern Asia	*18.4*	*61.2*	*9.6*	*7.0*	*9.7*	*5.6*	*4.2*	*3.7*	*2.9*	*8.9*	*7.6*	*0.2*
Brunei Darussalam	0.1	52.2	11.7	-4.4	2.7	-1.2	-0.1	-9.9	-1.9	-5.3	5.7	14.9
Cambodia	0.1	61.7	-7.5	15.8	36.4	12.9	11.3	7.2	8.6	5.3	5.3	7.8
Indonesia	2.2	21.2	9.1	2.5	4.5	5.6	1.1	-2.1	-1.7	8.9	6.5	-0.9
Lao People's DR	0.1	34.0	2.8	18.9	20.7	4.5	7.0	6.7	10.5	11.0	9.4	10.3
Malaysia	2.5	69.4	11.0	10.1	12.0	3.0	5.0	0.3	1.3	8.7	1.9	-1.3
Myanmar [2]	0.2	23.0	2.1	3.2	14.0	2.3	16.7	6.8	13.5	12.0	11.3	12.3
Philippines	1.0	28.4	6.7	3.7	7.2	2.9	12.6	8.5	11.6	19.7	13.4	3.2
Singapore	6.7	178.4	12.1	10.1	10.4	7.2	3.6	5.0	0.0	6.2	8.1	-1.6
Thailand	3.4	68.7	9.7	13.8	10.6	5.4	0.3	1.6	2.8	5.4	4.2	-2.6
Timor-Leste	0.0	3.0	...	...	-8.4	5.6	-22.5	-28.3	8.5	-39.1	16.6	1247.5
Viet Nam	2.1	89.8	4.7	4.7	15.6	10.4	11.6	12.6	13.9	16.7	14.3	6.7
Southern Asia	*7.2*	*18.9*	*-1.3*	*7.6*	*5.9*	*8.7*	*2.5*	*-3.2*	*9.0*	*3.8*	*7.3*	*-8.7*
Afghanistan	0.0	16.2	18.2	-1.4	6.7	13.6	26.5	-9.2	-13.9	43.2	-24.7	-21.2
Bangladesh	0.4	17.2	3.7	8.7	12.1	10.1	3.2	-2.8	2.2	-2.3	8.1	10.9
Bhutan	0.0	34.4	3.8	19.6	6.2	13.5	-5.3	-3.2	-5.3	6.5	4.6	0.3
India	5.2	19.8	8.0	4.6	11.7	13.4	1.8	-5.6	5.0	4.6	12.3	-6.6
Iran (Islamic Republic of)	0.9	19.7	-3.0	9.6	1.4	1.5	7.2	12.1	41.3	1.8	-12.8	-37.7
Maldives	0.0	78.4	6.0	10.7	7.5	7.5	9.1	-9.9	8.9	7.4	10.1	6.1
Nepal	0.0	11.6	13.2	4.6	14.8	-2.7	18.8	6.8	-13.7	11.3	6.2	4.7
Pakistan	0.3	10.6	-0.8	8.5	3.3	6.5	-1.5	-6.3	-1.6	-0.6	10.4	13.2
Sri Lanka	0.2	21.0	0.6	5.4	8.0	1.2	4.3	4.7	-0.7	7.6	0.5	7.1
Western Asia	*15.0*	*41.7*	*9.6*	*-2.2*	*4.6*	*3.2*	*0.8*	*0.8*	*1.8*	*2.0*	*8.6*	*-0.6*
Armenia	0.0	29.7	...	...	-8.4	6.5	6.4	4.9	19.1	18.7	2.9	13.2
Azerbaijan	0.2	37.8	...	...	-7.3	25.1	-4.5	7.6	11.4	-2.2	5.3	0.6
Bahrain	0.3	82.9	6.1	0.8	5.1	2.7	-4.1	-0.8	-2.8	3.7	3.3	-0.2
Cyprus	0.2	70.3	7.5	9.4	5.0	0.4	6.2	9.9	7.2	8.7	4.6	2.0
Georgia	0.1	40.9	...	...	-18.1	9.4	0.2	4.2	8.7	11.7	10.1	8.3
Iraq	0.7	36.7	15.2	2.9	1.1	-5.6	-0.4	-14.0	-7.9	17.4	29.8	-4.9
Israel	1.1	31.2	9.2	4.9	8.8	2.4	0.6	-2.9	0.9	4.1	5.6	4.1
Jordan	0.2	36.5	23.9	5.4	0.7	7.0	6.2	-7.4	0.9	2.9	3.1	12.7
Kuwait	0.7	53.8	-0.9	-0.6	6.4	3.7	1.4	-0.9	2.5	-4.8	-4.8	-2.0
Lebanon	0.1	23.1	3.9	-7.6	4.6	9.9	-7.0	10.2	-1.5	3.9	-4.7	-1.5
Oman	0.4	47.4	10.9	11.1	6.1	-0.2	-16.1	1.8	1.1	-1.1	4.4	5.4
Qatar	1.1	57.1	7.2	-2.4	8.6	8.8	0.4	-1.4	-3.9	0.7	4.6	0.3
Saudi Arabia	2.6	33.3	13.0	-8.3	1.2	1.0	-1.9	0.7	8.0	-3.1	6.8	-5.7
State of Palestine	0.0	16.1	13.6	1.3	12.0	1.9	9.6	-3.2	-1.6	13.9	2.5	1.7
Syrian Arab Republic	0.1	32.1	2.2	6.0	9.9	1.2	2.2	-12.0	-3.3	2.1	8.9	9.6
Turkey	2.6	24.5	4.6	17.7	9.4	5.9	7.1	3.2	-1.7	12.4	9.0	4.9
United Arab Emirates	4.4	100.9	11.1	-4.2	6.9	9.3	1.8	5.2	3.4	-2.5	11.5	-2.9
Yemen	0.0	7.0	...	...	20.0	-13.8	-4.1	-68.4	-64.6	-2.6	49.2	25.9
Yemen Arab Republic (Former)	...	...	31.4	0.4	...	...	...	...	...	...	...	...
Yemen Democratic (Former)	...	...	2.4	-2.6	...	...	...	...	...	...	...	...
Europe	**39.0**	**43.2**	**6.1**	**4.2**	**5.6**	**2.9**	**3.4**	**5.8**	**3.5**	**5.3**	**3.7**	**2.4**
Eastern Europe	*14.0*	*44.0*	*11.3*	*0.5*	*3.9*	*6.5*	*3.4*	*4.6*	*5.5*	*6.5*	*5.2*	*1.8*
Belarus	0.4	58.0	...	...	-7.2	5.5	4.6	2.1	2.6	7.5	3.8	0.3
Bulgaria	0.4	64.0	7.0	1.4	-3.8	7.1	3.1	6.4	8.6	5.8	1.7	1.9
Czechia	1.8	80.6	...	...	7.7	9.1	8.7	6.0	4.3	7.2	3.7	1.3
Czechoslovakia (Former)	...	...	...	...	...	...	...	...	...	...	...	...
Hungary	1.3	87.6	9.1	4.1	10.1	8.9	9.2	7.4	3.8	6.5	5.0	5.8
Poland	2.8	49.1	6.2	3.0	9.0	6.9	6.7	8.0	9.3	9.6	6.9	5.1
Republic of Moldova	0.0	31.9	...	...	-5.7	8.9	0.9	2.6	9.8	10.9	7.2	4.1
Romania	0.9	41.0	36.4	1.0	5.6	11.3	8.0	4.6	16.0	7.6	6.2	4.6
Russian Federation	4.7	28.6	...	...	12.1	6.0	0.5	3.7	3.2	5.0	5.5	-2.1
Slovakia	1.0	92.0	...	...	12.2	10.0	3.7	6.6	5.0	3.6	5.2	0.8
Ukraine [3]	0.6	52.6	...	...	-7.9	0.6	-14.2	-13.2	-1.8	3.8	-1.0	0.7
USSR (Former)	...	...	...	...	...	...	...	...	...	...	...	...
Northern Europe	*22.2*	*38.7*	*5.1*	*4.1*	*6.4*	*2.6*	*3.2*	*8.7*	*3.1*	*5.9*	*4.6*	*4.9*
Denmark	2.0	55.4	4.6	5.1	4.7	2.7	3.1	3.6	4.1	4.8	3.2	5.0
Estonia	0.2	76.9	...	...	5.8	5.9	2.6	-1.5	4.8	4.1	4.0	6.2
Finland	1.0	35.4	5.8	2.9	8.8	2.4	-2.0	0.4	3.9	8.6	1.7	7.7
Iceland	0.1	51.8	6.2	2.8	2.4	6.0	3.2	9.1	10.9	5.4	1.7	-5.0
Ireland	4.3	122.0	7.5	8.5	14.7	5.1	14.6	39.2	4.2	9.2	11.1	10.5
Latvia	0.2	60.3	...	...	-3.0	6.9	6.2	3.0	4.0	6.4	4.3	2.1
Lithuania	0.3	68.8	...	...	-3.4	9.9	-1.8	2.4	4.9	13.5	6.8	9.5
Norway	1.8	37.8	6.0	4.9	5.4	0.2	3.4	4.3	1.1	1.7	-0.2	1.5
Sweden	2.7	43.8	4.3	4.6	7.4	2.5	4.4	5.8	2.4	4.1	4.2	3.3
United Kingdom	9.6	27.3	5.0	3.3	5.8	2.2	0.2	2.8	2.7	5.4	3.0	2.8

Table 5.D. Average Rates of Growth of Gross Domestic Product by Expenditure - Exports of goods and Services

Major area, region and country	Base year weights as percentage of total for world or region in 2015	Base year share as percentage of total GDP in 2015	Average rates of growth				Annual rate of change (percentage)					
			1970-1979	1980-1989	1990-1999	2000-2009	2014	2015	2016	2017	2018	2019
Southern Europe	*14.5*	*33.2*	*7.6*	*4.6*	*5.7*	*1.0*	*3.9*	*4.8*	*3.6*	*6.1*	*3.0*	*2.2*
Albania	0.0	27.3	3.7	-0.4	6.9	11.8	1.2	1.0	11.3	13.2	4.1	6.1
Andorra	0.0	33.6	5.2	4.6	9.0	0.8	4.1	1.9	4.5	4.1	1.6	1.1
Bosnia and Herzegovina	0.1	35.5	...	...	20.2	3.9	4.2	9.8	9.4	11.7	6.1	0.1
Croatia	0.3	46.4	...	...	-6.3	3.1	7.4	10.3	7.0	6.8	3.7	4.6
Greece	0.8	32.2	14.5	1.9	8.3	1.1	8.2	5.0	-0.4	8.5	9.1	4.8
Italy	6.6	29.7	8.0	4.4	4.7	-0.1	2.6	4.3	1.9	5.4	2.2	1.0
Kosovo	0.0	21.9	...	...	-9.6	4.0	-7.4	-10.7	2.4	16.8	3.8	17.2
Malta	0.2	153.8	10.3	1.9	3.1	5.4	4.1	15.5	4.5	4.8	3.4	2.5
Montenegro	0.0	42.1	...	...	-4.1	12.0	-0.7	5.7	5.9	1.8	6.9	5.4
North Macedonia	0.1	48.7	...	...	2.2	1.9	16.5	8.5	9.1	8.3	15.6	8.3
Portugal	1.0	40.6	4.5	7.7	4.7	2.4	4.3	6.3	4.4	8.4	4.1	3.5
San Marino	0.0	174.5	3.8	2.5	2.3	1.5	-3.2	-4.1	2.0	-1.1	0.8	2.2
Serbia [4]	0.2	45.2	...	...	-3.4	14.4	4.3	9.3	12.0	8.2	7.5	7.7
Slovenia	0.4	77.1	...	...	-1.4	6.0	6.0	4.7	6.2	11.1	6.3	4.1
Spain	4.8	33.6	7.6	5.5	10.0	1.6	4.5	4.3	5.4	5.5	2.3	2.3
Yugoslavia (Former)	...	...	4.8	4.4	...	...	...	...	...	...	...	...
Western Europe	*49.3*	*50.0*	*5.6*	*4.5*	*5.6*	*2.8*	*3.4*	*5.2*	*3.0*	*4.3*	*3.1*	*1.4*
Austria	2.4	53.1	7.0	4.5	4.9	3.0	2.9	3.0	3.0	4.9	5.5	2.9
Belgium	4.3	77.8	5.3	4.5	4.7	2.0	5.2	3.7	6.2	5.5	0.6	1.0
France	9.0	30.6	7.8	4.1	6.7	1.2	3.3	4.6	1.8	4.4	4.4	1.9
Germany	19.0	46.9	5.1	4.6	5.5	4.0	4.8	5.4	2.5	4.7	2.3	1.0
Liechtenstein	0.0	62.4	6.3	7.6	7.1	1.9	-5.7	2.5	6.8	1.2	4.4	-0.6
Luxembourg	1.5	221.2	3.6	6.1	7.5	4.5	16.4	4.7	2.6	0.7	0.5	0.8
Monaco	0.0	30.6	6.9	2.8	4.4	0.1	8.3	8.1	2.3	-1.3	8.6	7.8
Netherlands	7.6	82.7	5.6	4.4	6.7	2.5	4.5	7.4	1.7	6.5	4.3	2.7
Switzerland	5.3	62.4	4.1	5.0	3.2	2.8	-6.2	4.1	6.5	-0.3	3.4	-0.2
Oceania	**1.5**	**21.0**	**4.4**	**5.2**	**7.0**	**2.5**	**7.0**	**6.8**	**4.8**	**4.1**	**3.6**	**-1.0**
Australia and New Zealand	*93.7*	*20.3*	*4.3*	*5.4*	*7.2*	*2.6*	*6.4*	*6.7*	*4.8*	*4.0*	*3.8*	*-1.2*
Australia	77.7	19.3	4.4	5.9	7.5	2.5	6.8	6.8	5.5	4.1	4.0	-1.9
New Zealand	16.0	27.9	3.8	3.6	5.8	2.7	4.6	6.3	1.6	3.6	2.8	2.3
Melanesia	*5.6*	*46.8*	*6.1*	*3.3*	*4.7*	*1.9*	*18.6*	*8.2*	*4.0*	*5.9*	*0.9*	*1.4*
Fiji	0.7	48.8	4.9	3.9	1.6	-0.5	-2.7	-2.3	-1.8	4.1	7.7	3.3
New Caledonia	0.5	18.0	-1.9	3.8	0.0	-1.1	20.3	-2.6	0.4	-0.3	1.6	3.9
Papua New Guinea	4.1	57.9	10.8	3.3	6.6	2.7	25.5	11.9	5.4	6.8	-0.9	1.5
Solomon Islands	0.2	50.3	18.8	-6.3	9.5	3.9	4.2	10.2	-3.8	14.2	12.6	-13.5
Vanuatu	0.1	44.3	7.7	3.0	0.1	7.2	-0.7	4.9	19.5	-1.1	3.5	1.5
Micronesia	*0.1*	*36.0*	*3.5*	*1.3*	*-0.2*	*1.8*	*2.5*	*11.1*	*-0.4*	*-4.1*	*-4.3*	*-4.2*
Kiribati	0.0	15.6	4.3	-1.6	2.5	1.9	10.9	28.3	24.7	-14.3	-36.7	-1.2
Marshall Islands	0.0	49.1	5.3	3.6	2.0	0.3	1.4	8.2	-8.8	8.9	8.6	2.6
Micronesia (FS of)	0.0	26.2	6.6	4.1	0.7	2.2	-13.7	5.1	1.9	1.8	0.4	1.3
Nauru	0.0	15.6	1.9	-4.9	-11.0	0.5	52.3	19.6	27.8	-22.8	-34.6	-2.5
Palau	0.1	58.6	0.1	3.6	-3.7	2.5	9.7	12.7	-3.9	-9.3	-5.4	-13.1
Polynesia	*0.5*	*23.8*	*-0.3*	*6.6*	*6.0*	*-2.5*	*4.5*	*3.1*	*6.2*	*4.2*	*5.6*	*0.2*
Cook Islands	0.1	84.5	0.1	-2.3	2.1	3.7	0.1	0.2	13.1	6.3	6.5	5.2
French Polynesia	0.3	19.6	-1.1	8.6	7.5	-4.4	6.1	1.9	4.4	5.4	6.7	-1.2
Samoa	0.1	33.0	3.2	4.0	4.6	3.4	3.6	10.0	1.3	-0.1	1.1	1.8
Tonga	0.0	17.0	-1.0	4.3	-4.5	-2.2	1.9	7.9	27.2	-5.8	1.3	-3.3
Tuvalu	0.0	10.5	-2.1	-1.7	2.4	23.2	-5.5	27.4	4.8	1.4	10.6	5.5

Notes for Table 5.D. Average Rates of Growth of Gross Domestic Product by Expenditure - Exports of goods and Services

1/ Paraguay

1970-2001

Does not incorporate export of binational hydroelectric power at market prices.

2/ Myanmar

1970-1996

Country used official exchange rates rather than market exchange rates in compiling imports and exports data.

3/ Ukraine

2010-2019

The Government of Ukraine has advised the United Nations that it is not in a position to provide statistical data concerning the Autonomous Republic of Crimea and the city of Sevastopol.

4/ Serbia

1990-2009, 2013-2019

Includes exports of goods and services to Montenegro.

Table 5.E. Average Rates of Growth of Gross Domestic Product by Expenditure - Imports of goods and services

Major area, region and country	Base year weights as percentage of total for world or region in 2015	Base year share as percentage of total GDP in 2015	Average rates of growth				Annual rate of change (percentage)					
			1970-1979	1980-1989	1990-1999	2000-2009	2014	2015	2016	2017	2018	2019
World	**100.0**	**28.0**	**6.3**	**4.0**	**6.0**	**4.4**	**3.1**	**1.9**	**1.6**	**5.9**	**4.7**	**1.2**
Developed economies	**55.5**	**26.8**	**5.5**	**5.1**	**6.2**	**2.5**	**4.6**	**5.6**	**3.2**	**4.7**	**3.7**	**3.2**
Developing economies	**41.9**	**29.8**	**8.1**	**1.7**	**7.3**	**7.4**	**2.1**	**-1.3**	**-0.5**	**7.1**	**6.0**	**-1.7**
Transition economies	**2.6**	**26.9**	**7.8**	**1.6**	**-6.9**	**8.8**	**-6.0**	**-15.7**	**0.1**	**12.7**	**5.2**	**4.9**
Africa	**3.2**	**28.5**	**6.7**	**-4.0**	**3.8**	**8.0**	**-2.1**	**-2.6**	**-3.4**	**7.6**	**8.1**	**2.8**
Northern Africa	*32.9*	*29.8*	*8.6*	*-1.1*	*0.8*	*7.4*	*-8.3*	*-2.5*	*-0.9*	*16.9*	*7.3*	*-3.3*
Algeria	9.2	36.5	10.6	-1.4	-1.9	10.6	8.4	6.4	-2.8	-7.1	-3.8	-6.9
Egypt	10.4	21.7	8.8	1.9	1.3	7.2	-0.1	-0.3	-4.1	49.1	13.8	-8.9
Libya	1.9	71.2	8.1	-6.5	-4.1	10.0	-50.2	-40.0	-24.2	46.5	17.5	5.5
Morocco	6.5	42.4	5.8	3.6	3.5	8.0	3.6	-2.0	11.1	3.8	7.3	5.5
Sudan	1.5	12.1	...	...	...	...	-35.5	8.6	2.0	10.3	2.4	1.1
Sudan (Former)	...	...	5.1	-12.6	6.4	...	...	...	...	...	...	...
Tunisia	3.3	50.9	11.5	1.8	3.2	2.9	0.9	-2.6	2.8	3.5	1.7	2.6
Sub-Saharan Africa	67.1	28.0	5.7	-6.0	5.9	8.3	1.3	-2.6	-4.6	2.8	8.7	6.3
Eastern Africa	*18.1*	*38.2*	*1.9*	*1.3*	*6.4*	*10.7*	*4.9*	*7.5*	*-3.4*	*1.7*	*6.2*	*5.2*
Burundi	0.1	28.9	8.7	-1.3	-2.7	10.8	-0.5	-14.4	-4.1	13.9	4.4	36.2
Comoros	0.0	27.7	4.5	5.4	0.1	7.5	3.0	-3.4	-2.1	6.0	11.5	1.0
Djibouti	0.5	139.5	3.2	4.9	-4.5	17.4	-22.7	-6.3	6.6	55.8	15.9	24.4
Eritrea	0.1	26.6	...	...	9.8	-2.1	27.9	6.4	-11.4	-3.3	11.6	3.6
Ethiopia	2.9	30.3	...	...	7.5	19.0	20.2	21.9	0.0	-7.5	2.2	18.5
Ethiopia (Former)	...	...	7.1	-0.1	...	...	...	...	...	...	...	...
Kenya	2.7	27.6	0.7	-0.7	7.9	8.3	10.6	1.2	-3.4	8.6	2.5	-2.0
Madagascar	0.6	32.8	0.5	-9.3	1.8	7.9	7.0	6.5	4.8	23.7	11.1	4.6
Malawi	0.4	39.5	0.4	-1.6	4.0	12.5	6.2	3.3	2.7	5.2	3.9	5.2
Mauritius	1.0	58.8	9.3	8.6	4.9	1.5	3.7	8.5	2.6	2.2	0.4	1.7
Mozambique	1.5	62.8	3.8	-0.3	5.7	11.7	11.8	-17.3	8.0	-12.9	43.4	0.0
Rwanda	0.4	32.0	10.6	7.3	-8.1	7.6	14.5	23.0	7.6	5.8	8.1	18.0
Seychelles	0.2	86.1	9.3	2.6	6.9	6.9	4.5	5.0	1.5	11.7	8.7	-1.4
Somalia	0.0	1.7	2.8	-4.2	-6.7	1.4	2.8	2.3	2.4	2.5	2.4	2.5
South Sudan	2.1	213.5	...	...	...	...	-0.2	4.0	-0.1	-1.8	-2.5	-0.1
U.R. of Tanzania: Mainland	1.7	23.7	3.6	6.6	6.0	15.6	3.3	-5.2	-8.9	-7.1	16.7	-1.4
Uganda	1.2	30.5	-1.6	5.1	8.6	9.3	-2.6	13.9	-24.2	6.9	11.6	1.0
Zambia	1.5	48.0	-6.7	-4.9	13.1	9.4	-5.6	17.9	-18.5	0.4	2.3	-4.8
Zanzibar	0.0	23.7	...	...	4.2	13.3	-2.0	-7.9	-14.8	-3.3	12.0	1.4
Zimbabwe	1.1	37.6	-0.2	5.2	19.7	-3.9	0.4	80.6	-3.3	3.2	-25.3	17.2
Middle Africa	*12.4*	*34.4*	*2.7*	*0.5*	*11.0*	*8.2*	*-1.0*	*-12.8*	*-14.8*	*3.5*	*-3.6*	*0.4*
Angola	5.8	33.1	0.4	0.0	13.4	8.4	-5.2	-23.9	-24.7	11.2	-16.0	0.0
Cameroon	1.3	27.6	13.8	-4.6	8.9	4.5	8.6	-0.3	-1.5	-0.6	8.1	14.9
Central African Republic	0.1	36.1	-0.9	4.0	0.1	-1.4	58.9	10.3	5.2	16.1	22.3	8.2
Chad	0.5	25.6	0.8	14.6	2.3	9.9	-31.5	21.2	-1.2	3.1	3.5	9.7
Congo	1.4	80.9	8.2	-0.9	9.6	6.9	15.9	24.1	-9.0	-21.3	5.1	-7.8
D.R. of the Congo	1.8	31.6	8.0	10.7	3.7	12.8	8.7	-6.5	-5.7	9.3	7.4	-8.5
Equatorial Guinea	0.8	42.2	2.2	2.9	49.6	12.2	-5.6	-15.5	-16.3	8.3	7.4	1.9
Gabon	0.6	27.9	11.4	1.0	-0.2	4.6	7.9	-9.3	0.2	-14.8	-1.0	3.9
Sao Tome and Principe	0.0	55.4	18.7	5.1	3.4	6.8	18.1	-7.2	-5.0	1.4	-2.8	-5.5
Southern Africa	*18.0*	*33.9*	*0.3*	*0.5*	*5.6*	*5.5*	*0.7*	*4.9*	*-3.5*	*-1.0*	*3.8*	*0.0*
Botswana	1.2	56.1	13.9	9.9	3.3	3.5	3.5	2.8	-5.4	-21.1	11.8	6.7
Eswatini	0.3	40.8	11.0	-2.0	6.3	3.6	0.3	2.8	8.2	7.1	4.7	-7.8
Lesotho	0.3	86.4	17.2	3.5	4.1	3.6	-1.0	7.5	1.3	-0.1	0.9	-3.5
Namibia	1.1	62.0	3.2	0.6	5.3	11.0	17.1	-0.4	-0.2	-8.6	3.9	3.2
South Africa	15.1	31.5	-0.6	0.0	5.9	5.4	-0.6	5.4	-3.9	1.0	3.3	-0.5
Western Africa	*18.7*	*18.0*	*8.7*	*-11.5*	*3.1*	*9.1*	*0.7*	*-9.9*	*-0.1*	*7.0*	*21.8*	*14.4*
Benin	0.6	32.0	7.3	-8.2	7.6	5.7	20.3	-4.9	3.3	14.3	4.8	-7.0
Burkina Faso	0.6	33.0	11.0	-0.3	1.1	6.3	-8.9	11.2	7.3	10.1	16.5	10.1
Cabo Verde	0.1	59.2	0.4	5.8	8.0	5.9	11.0	1.8	7.4	14.7	16.1	0.9
Côte d'Ivoire	1.8	25.4	6.0	-2.9	7.6	3.8	0.6	17.1	0.5	11.2	12.7	1.5
Gambia	0.1	33.3	7.8	3.1	1.3	-4.2	23.5	6.3	1.5	19.1	-5.2	10.3
Ghana	3.2	43.6	-5.0	-2.3	11.0	0.7	-14.4	7.9	-1.1	7.9	4.6	1.7
Guinea	0.7	50.9	3.0	3.6	1.5	5.0	-5.0	13.2	65.2	18.2	-5.8	-11.1
Guinea-Bissau	0.1	32.5	6.8	0.7	0.3	6.3	33.5	14.0	14.6	10.4	-4.5	19.2
Liberia	0.2	56.6	3.6	-10.6	7.2	7.2	-12.9	26.2	-3.4	-0.2	-7.7	-7.0
Mali	0.8	39.6	11.3	-1.4	13.6	10.9	8.3	33.2	12.1	-13.5	-4.4	27.2
Mauritania	0.4	47.2	9.1	1.5	2.3	10.2	-15.0	-7.1	-3.1	10.8	2.9	-4.4
Niger	0.4	30.5	6.2	-2.4	0.2	9.7	5.0	7.4	-14.4	11.6	7.3	10.3
Nigeria	8.1	10.8	10.1	-14.3	1.6	11.9	6.0	-26.8	-9.0	4.8	49.2	27.3
Senegal	1.0	35.4	4.1	2.4	3.4	4.3	4.3	7.7	6.7	16.7	7.6	5.5
Sierra Leone	0.3	47.1	2.6	-9.8	-7.8	7.9	-1.3	-18.3	23.9	6.3	-11.5	16.5
Togo	0.4	45.4	9.9	-0.1	0.7	2.0	-5.3	12.3	16.5	-11.4	5.8	6.0

Table 5.E. Average Rates of Growth of Gross Domestic Product by Expenditure - Imports of goods and services

Major area, region and country	Base year weights as percentage of total for world or region in 2015	Base year share as percentage of total GDP in 2015	Average rates of growth				Annual rate of change (percentage)					
			1970-1979	1980-1989	1990-1999	2000-2009	2014	2015	2016	2017	2018	2019
Americas	**23.1**	**19.2**	**5.4**	**4.2**	**8.7**	**2.6**	**1.3**	**0.9**	**-2.3**	**3.8**	**4.1**	**-0.1**
Latin America and the Caribbean	**7.2**	**27.7**	**5.6**	**-0.8**	**9.1**	**4.7**	**-4.5**	**-6.2**	**-10.4**	**1.6**	**4.4**	**-2.7**
Caribbean	*2.6*	*36.8*	*4.7*	*3.0*	*3.0*	*2.5*	*-0.9*	*2.4*	*0.1*	*-0.3*	*8.3*	*1.6*
Anguilla	0.0	83.5	3.7	10.2	9.1	3.6	26.7	6.9	-0.3	12.8	22.3	-15.0
Antigua and Barbuda	0.0	51.2	4.6	6.6	2.7	1.6	1.2	-10.5	6.3	6.1	12.2	-1.4
Aruba	0.0	74.1	9.1	11.2	5.9	2.8	-1.5	-3.0	-0.1	1.2	3.4	-2.3
Bahamas	0.1	38.3	0.6	3.6	4.7	-0.1	12.7	-6.3	3.9	9.2	-3.9	1.0
Barbados	0.0	47.4	0.9	-2.4	8.5	-0.4	-0.1	9.9	4.5	-7.0	3.7	2.2
British Virgin Islands	0.0	77.0	3.7	9.0	16.9	-0.2	1.8	0.7	7.3	0.7	2.8	2.6
Cayman Islands	0.0	41.4	9.4	8.7	5.6	1.3	3.8	1.1	3.3	8.2	6.2	5.9
Cuba	0.3	14.5	5.4	4.7	-6.5	5.0	-1.5	10.1	-10.6	-1.6	-2.0	-1.4
Curaçao	0.1	77.5	...	...	...	...	-5.0	-8.9	-5.4	3.9	10.6	-18.8
Dominica	0.0	60.5	5.9	2.7	0.4	2.5	39.1	-9.6	-3.1	1.0	29.4	-13.0
Dominican Republic	0.4	28.4	8.1	-0.8	9.7	0.8	4.8	11.0	8.1	-3.0	8.5	5.8
Former Netherlands Antilles	...	...	8.5	-3.3	0.0	3.7	...	...	...	...	...	...
Grenada	0.0	50.0	8.3	2.4	4.9	-0.7	-5.7	0.8	2.2	13.3	11.5	0.9
Haiti	0.1	50.5	12.3	-2.7	12.4	2.1	2.6	2.2	0.8	2.0	1.5	-1.0
Jamaica	0.1	46.2	0.2	7.8	4.5	0.3	-0.1	-2.0	-0.3	5.8	6.0	4.2
Montserrat	0.0	81.6	3.1	2.4	-6.0	-3.3	-18.3	-7.6	16.7	-9.6	3.6	8.5
Puerto Rico	1.1	52.4	2.9	4.7	2.6	3.0	-3.1	-1.5	-1.6	0.5	16.5	3.5
Saint Kitts and Nevis	0.0	54.2	6.3	3.9	2.1	1.0	1.0	6.8	7.2	4.2	5.6	4.9
Saint Lucia	0.0	41.7	7.6	6.4	3.6	0.8	-1.8	-12.8	9.8	-0.1	1.2	-5.5
Sint Maarten (Dutch part)	0.0	106.4	...	...	...	...	13.6	-4.9	-1.8	-11.7	0.8	-0.8
St. Vincent and the Grenadines	0.0	54.3	3.6	3.3	1.6	5.5	9.3	-2.2	14.0	-7.5	5.6	-2.8
Trinidad and Tobago	0.2	41.7	14.0	-4.2	2.5	4.7	-8.6	13.2	1.9	-8.1	-11.7	-11.7
Turks and Caicos Islands	0.0	56.6	10.6	10.9	5.6	9.9	11.8	12.6	5.4	-1.8	5.7	5.0
Central America	*10.8*	*37.5*	*7.4*	*-0.2*	*11.1*	*1.7*	*4.9*	*5.6*	*2.4*	*5.9*	*5.1*	*-0.8*
Belize	0.0	66.3	4.3	6.8	5.6	-0.9	3.5	9.6	1.6	-0.6	-4.3	0.3
Costa Rica	0.4	31.7	7.3	3.1	7.8	2.8	5.0	4.5	8.9	3.7	0.1	0.4
El Salvador	0.2	47.1	8.3	-2.0	11.1	1.0	-2.5	4.7	-0.5	1.4	5.5	3.8
Guatemala	0.4	30.1	5.7	-2.6	10.3	1.5	3.4	3.6	0.9	2.9	3.9	5.6
Honduras	0.3	62.1	5.2	-0.6	4.2	2.4	3.4	8.5	-1.6	7.2	2.2	-2.8
Mexico	8.8	36.6	8.8	-0.1	12.4	1.5	5.9	5.9	2.8	6.4	5.9	-0.9
Nicaragua	0.2	58.1	0.7	-3.9	11.7	4.1	3.1	12.0	4.1	3.9	-14.0	-6.0
Panama	0.6	52.3	3.3	0.0	2.5	5.7	-3.9	-0.1	-4.8	4.3	4.1	-3.3
South America	*17.9*	*23.1*	*5.2*	*-2.3*	*9.9*	*6.9*	*-9.0*	*-13.1*	*-19.8*	*-1.4*	*3.1*	*-5.1*
Argentina	1.6	11.8	6.7	-8.5	20.1	1.9	-11.5	4.7	5.8	15.4	-4.7	-18.7
Bolivia (Plurinational State of)	0.3	37.1	3.9	2.2	5.7	3.9	15.1	-5.4	-4.2	5.6	1.9	1.5
Brazil	5.2	14.1	9.1	-1.3	10.9	5.3	-1.9	-14.2	-10.3	6.7	8.3	1.1
Chile	1.5	29.6	3.5	1.3	10.7	7.5	-6.5	-1.1	0.9	4.6	7.9	-2.3
Colombia	1.4	22.7	5.3	0.5	8.0	8.0	7.8	-1.1	-3.5	1.0	5.8	9.2
Ecuador	0.5	24.0	11.4	-2.1	1.6	9.2	4.8	-8.2	-9.6	12.2	4.4	1.6
Guyana	0.1	61.0	4.1	-2.5	5.7	12.0	-6.3	-16.4	-6.0	18.1	1.2	12.7
Paraguay	0.2	31.5	13.1	2.6	3.8	5.0	2.9	-2.6	1.1	12.0	8.9	-3.4
Peru	0.9	23.9	-0.5	-4.3	8.5	7.5	-1.0	1.0	1.6	7.1	3.3	1.3
Suriname	0.0	42.4	5.2	-9.0	11.5	1.2	3.0	-4.8	-5.5	2.2	2.3	0.3
Uruguay	0.3	22.9	4.9	-1.2	11.6	4.2	0.8	-7.3	-6.2	0.5	-2.0	0.2
Venezuela (Bolivarian Republic of)	6.0	84.0	3.8	-2.5	8.8	8.6	-18.5	-23.1	-50.1	-34.7	-8.8	-32.6
Northern America	**15.9**	**16.8**	**5.3**	**6.9**	**8.5**	**1.7**	**4.6**	**4.4**	**1.4**	**4.6**	**4.0**	**1.0**
Bermuda	0.0	23.3	3.0	3.7	2.1	-1.9	1.6	-4.0	4.0	4.7	4.1	4.3
Canada	11.0	34.3	6.4	5.5	6.9	1.6	2.5	0.8	0.1	4.6	3.4	0.4
Greenland	0.0	45.5	4.7	-2.8	-0.9	2.1	-11.5	1.7	11.0	-3.1	5.7	4.4
United States	57.6	15.3	5.1	7.3	8.9	1.7	5.0	5.2	1.7	4.7	4.1	1.1
Asia	**36.2**	**28.4**	**9.6**	**5.2**	**5.5**	**7.0**	**4.6**	**0.2**	**1.7**	**7.6**	**5.9**	**-1.6**
Central Asia	*1.1*	*25.9*	...	...	*-12.2*	*4.4*	*-0.4*	*-1.6*	*-0.3*	*4.8*	*11.6*	*11.7*
Kazakhstan	0.6	24.5	...	...	-14.0	2.8	-4.0	-0.1	-2.0	1.0	6.6	11.6
Kyrgyzstan	0.1	75.8	...	...	-13.8	8.4	1.6	-13.2	-1.1	7.4	7.4	2.9
Tajikistan	0.0	42.3	...	...	-11.2	12.9	1.0	0.0	0.0	5.3	1.7	2.3
Turkmenistan	0.2	44.2	...	...	-5.9	0.6	10.1	6.8	6.0	6.5	6.2	3.0
Uzbekistan	0.2	15.1	...	...	-9.5	16.5	0.3	-11.2	-2.2	15.5	38.5	24.9
Eastern Asia	*56.2*	*23.9*	*8.9*	*7.9*	*7.1*	*6.7*	*6.3*	*0.5*	*2.0*	*6.3*	*5.3*	*-1.5*
China	26.4	18.1	16.5	9.6	17.5	14.3	8.7	0.6	3.6	7.3	7.6	-0.9
China, Hong Kong SAR	7.9	193.5	10.0	11.6	8.5	5.9	1.0	-1.8	0.9	6.6	4.5	-6.8
China, Macao SAR	0.2	38.7	7.9	8.9	2.8	6.3	12.5	1.1	-10.4	7.9	7.4	-1.7
D.P.R. of Korea	0.0	11.1	7.6	5.7	-7.6	2.6	1.1	-1.1	3.9	-3.5	-4.1	0.4
Japan	10.4	18.0	7.0	6.1	2.8	1.0	8.3	0.8	-1.6	3.4	3.4	-0.7

Table 5.E. Average Rates of Growth of Gross Domestic Product by Expenditure - Imports of goods and services

Major area, region and country	Base year weights as percentage of total for world or region in 2015	Base year share as percentage of total GDP in 2015	Average rates of growth				Annual rate of change (percentage)					
			1970-1979	1980-1989	1990-1999	2000-2009	2014	2015	2016	2017	2018	2019
Mongolia	0.1	44.6	6.4	10.4	3.0	9.2	6.8	-11.4	12.7	24.8	30.9	19.1
Republic of Korea	7.0	36.1	18.3	10.2	9.4	6.6	1.3	2.1	5.2	8.9	1.7	-0.6
South-Eastern Asia	*18.2*	*55.8*	*9.8*	*6.4*	*7.8*	*5.7*	*2.9*	*3.4*	*3.4*	*9.8*	*8.7*	*-0.9*
Brunei Darussalam	0.1	37.7	7.2	4.2	3.2	4.5	-22.9	-8.9	-10.8	1.3	28.1	13.8
Cambodia	0.2	66.1	-7.2	3.6	26.0	12.4	10.1	6.5	8.6	4.1	4.1	6.0
Indonesia	2.4	20.8	17.8	2.5	3.5	5.9	2.1	-6.2	-2.4	8.1	11.9	-7.7
Lao People's DR	0.1	51.8	2.8	20.6	13.4	10.3	2.5	4.0	4.6	5.0	4.5	4.7
Malaysia	2.5	61.9	12.0	8.1	10.1	3.5	4.0	0.8	1.4	10.2	1.5	-2.5
Myanmar [1]	0.3	30.9	3.2	-4.7	4.2	2.8	21.9	3.5	10.0	-2.2	-7.7	-0.2
Philippines	1.3	34.3	7.2	3.5	7.0	2.3	9.9	14.6	20.2	18.1	16.0	2.1
Singapore	6.1	151.1	10.3	9.2	10.2	6.4	2.8	3.4	0.2	7.5	7.3	-1.7
Thailand	3.0	57.2	7.1	10.2	5.0	5.2	-5.3	0.0	-1.0	6.2	8.6	-4.4
Timor-Leste	0.0	56.9	...	...	1.9	2.8	11.6	-7.6	8.2	-8.7	2.8	22.7
Viet Nam	2.3	89.0	4.7	4.6	15.3	11.8	12.8	18.1	15.3	17.5	12.8	8.3
Southern Asia	*9.1*	*22.0*	*8.2*	*-0.6*	*2.8*	*10.8*	*0.4*	*-6.1*	*4.5*	*15.9*	*7.2*	*-8.4*
Afghanistan	0.1	33.2	17.6	-1.4	13.1	9.7	-15.0	-3.1	-8.6	0.7	33.9	15.0
Bangladesh	0.7	25.7	-12.8	5.1	6.4	6.9	1.2	3.2	-7.1	2.9	27.0	-2.0
Bhutan	0.0	67.8	4.2	10.5	10.5	11.4	0.0	17.2	-9.3	-0.9	8.2	-3.9
India	6.3	22.1	6.2	6.3	14.0	14.6	0.9	-5.9	4.4	17.4	8.6	-9.0
Iran (Islamic Republic of)	1.0	19.3	12.1	-3.4	-5.1	8.3	-4.5	-20.2	6.1	13.4	-19.9	-30.4
Maldives	0.0	71.2	10.0	10.1	8.5	10.9	10.5	1.0	9.7	8.2	12.8	0.3
Nepal	0.1	41.5	11.0	6.9	9.5	3.9	21.0	9.6	2.8	27.2	10.5	7.8
Pakistan	0.6	17.1	7.5	2.6	2.6	4.8	0.3	-1.6	16.0	21.2	15.8	5.8
Sri Lanka	0.3	28.5	0.8	2.6	8.1	2.8	9.6	10.6	7.9	7.1	1.8	-5.8
Western Asia	*15.5*	*39.5*	*12.1*	*3.5*	*4.2*	*7.5*	*3.9*	*-0.6*	*-2.9*	*4.6*	*3.0*	*0.9*
Armenia	0.1	41.9	...	...	-3.6	6.8	-1.0	-15.1	7.6	24.6	12.9	7.8
Azerbaijan	0.2	34.8	...	...	-3.9	23.1	0.8	21.3	5.2	-1.7	4.0	1.2
Bahrain	0.3	71.7	6.7	-0.1	2.6	3.8	-7.4	-5.7	-3.2	7.6	5.7	-7.0
Cyprus	0.2	67.7	6.5	7.2	3.7	1.9	7.6	8.1	9.0	12.8	2.4	1.5
Georgia	0.1	57.9	...	...	-12.8	8.8	14.5	7.2	2.4	8.1	10.3	6.9
Iraq	0.8	37.3	14.1	16.1	4.4	-1.1	9.8	13.2	-14.6	-4.9	4.2	6.8
Israel	1.1	28.2	5.6	4.1	9.0	0.9	2.2	-0.1	10.0	4.9	6.4	3.6
Jordan	0.3	58.8	18.6	3.1	0.0	8.5	0.2	-3.6	-3.9	6.4	1.6	0.9
Kuwait	0.7	44.9	18.4	-1.4	1.7	7.9	7.9	6.8	4.2	9.2	-0.9	-0.5
Lebanon	0.3	48.7	3.1	-3.5	-1.1	8.0	0.2	8.5	5.9	2.1	1.1	-9.0
Oman	0.4	44.0	11.1	-1.1	6.3	9.8	-26.9	3.4	-10.2	15.9	-3.4	-0.4
Qatar	0.8	36.6	5.8	-4.0	3.5	19.7	6.4	-9.2	4.9	-2.8	1.2	2.1
Saudi Arabia	3.3	38.8	17.9	2.1	-0.9	11.8	6.6	1.5	-20.3	0.4	2.6	1.4
State of Palestine	0.1	54.7	11.6	2.6	10.3	2.6	4.0	10.3	2.0	1.3	4.5	1.4
Syrian Arab Republic	0.1	32.5	10.3	1.2	1.2	5.4	2.2	2.0	2.5	6.0	8.5	10.8
Turkey	3.0	26.6	3.1	7.6	8.6	4.6	0.3	0.7	3.0	10.6	-6.4	-5.3
United Arab Emirates	3.5	74.4	14.0	1.6	6.0	14.0	9.9	-5.7	2.7	3.0	10.9	3.6
Yemen	0.1	28.6	...	...	16.4	6.0	-6.1	-43.8	-1.6	15.7	29.6	28.3
Yemen Arab Republic (Former)	...	...	21.3	-4.0	...	...	...	...	...	...	...	...
Yemen Democratic (Former)	...	...	6.1	4.1	...	...	...	...	...	...	...	...
Europe	**36.0**	**39.3**	**5.4**	**4.3**	**5.0**	**3.1**	**3.4**	**5.0**	**4.2**	**5.3**	**3.7**	**3.6**
Eastern Europe	*13.5*	*38.6*	*7.4*	*1.2*	*1.1*	*8.6*	*0.4*	*-6.1*	*3.6*	*10.9*	*5.5*	*3.7*
Belarus	0.4	57.9	...	...	-10.2	9.1	2.0	-10.6	-1.4	11.1	7.3	5.2
Bulgaria	0.4	63.0	6.5	1.5	-6.6	9.8	5.2	4.8	5.2	7.4	5.7	2.4
Czechia	1.9	74.6	...	...	8.1	8.5	10.0	6.8	2.8	6.3	5.8	1.4
Czechoslovakia (Former)	...	...	...	...	...	...	...	...	...	...	...	...
Hungary	1.3	79.6	6.5	1.7	12.7	7.4	11.0	6.0	3.4	8.5	7.0	7.5
Poland	2.9	46.3	5.6	0.9	16.1	5.4	9.9	6.9	7.9	10.2	7.4	3.3
Republic of Moldova	0.1	57.4	...	...	-2.3	8.4	3.1	-5.8	2.8	11.0	9.7	5.1
Romania	1.0	41.6	36.8	-0.9	2.2	16.0	8.7	8.0	16.5	10.8	9.1	8.0
Russian Federation	3.7	20.6	...	...	2.9	12.1	-7.3	-25.0	-3.7	17.3	2.6	2.2
Slovakia	1.0	88.9	...	...	5.4	8.6	4.5	8.5	4.8	3.9	4.9	2.1
Ukraine [2]	0.7	55.2	...	...	-12.1	4.5	-22.1	-16.7	9.3	12.6	3.0	6.3
USSR (Former)	...	...	...	...	...	...	...	...	...	...	...	...
Northern Europe	*23.1*	*36.6*	*4.1*	*5.2*	*5.6*	*3.0*	*4.7*	*8.4*	*6.4*	*3.0*	*3.4*	*8.1*
Denmark	2.0	48.6	4.0	4.2	4.9	4.1	3.9	4.6	3.7	4.2	4.8	2.4
Estonia	0.2	73.0	...	...	5.6	6.4	3.0	-1.9	6.5	3.0	5.7	3.7
Finland	1.1	36.0	4.0	4.5	4.3	3.5	-0.9	2.0	5.7	4.2	5.4	3.3
Iceland	0.1	44.7	6.9	2.3	4.8	-0.7	9.8	13.8	14.5	12.3	0.8	-9.9
Ireland	3.6	93.2	7.8	5.1	13.1	4.8	14.7	32.4	18.9	1.1	4.0	32.4
Latvia	0.2	62.0	...	...	-6.6	5.7	2.9	1.6	3.6	8.6	6.4	3.0
Lithuania	0.4	69.8	...	...	-1.3	9.3	-1.7	9.4	4.0	11.1	6.0	6.3
Norway	1.6	32.1	3.0	2.4	5.1	3.5	2.0	1.9	2.7	1.9	1.9	5.2
Sweden	2.7	40.0	2.6	4.2	5.0	1.9	6.4	6.1	4.5	4.7	3.8	1.1
United Kingdom	11.2	28.7	4.5	6.2	5.6	2.4	3.3	5.4	3.9	2.6	2.7	3.3

Table 5.E. Average Rates of Growth of Gross Domestic Product by Expenditure - Imports of goods and services

Major area, region and country	Base year weights as percentage of total for world or region in 2015	Base year share as percentage of total GDP in 2015	Average rates of growth				Annual rate of change (percentage)					
			1970-1979	1980-1989	1990-1999	2000-2009	2014	2015	2016	2017	2018	2019
Southern Europe	*14.8*	*30.9*	*5.6*	*5.2*	*5.5*	*1.7*	*5.1*	*6.2*	*3.7*	*6.7*	*4.5*	*1.1*
Albania	0.1	44.5	4.2	1.8	18.2	9.3	4.3	-2.9	6.9	8.4	2.4	2.7
Andorra	0.0	30.6	4.2	5.0	7.0	0.1	7.3	2.1	1.4	5.9	4.4	0.1
Bosnia and Herzegovina	0.1	53.8	...	...	13.8	3.0	7.6	1.7	7.2	7.7	3.7	1.4
Croatia	0.3	46.2	...	...	-3.9	5.0	3.2	9.4	6.5	8.4	7.5	4.8
Greece	0.9	33.2	7.8	4.6	7.5	1.7	6.7	7.9	2.2	7.4	8.0	3.0
Italy	6.5	26.7	4.6	4.9	3.9	0.7	3.5	6.5	3.9	6.1	3.5	-0.6
Kosovo	0.0	50.4	...	...	-9.8	-1.2	7.0	2.2	6.4	5.4	9.0	5.6
Malta	0.2	144.2	8.2	3.1	3.5	5.0	0.2	18.1	1.6	-0.5	3.0	3.0
Montenegro	0.0	60.6	...	...	-3.8	14.5	1.6	4.4	15.3	8.4	9.2	2.4
North Macedonia	0.1	65.0	...	...	3.1	4.0	14.1	9.9	11.1	5.2	9.1	9.0
Portugal	1.1	39.9	4.4	6.3	7.8	1.7	7.9	8.0	5.0	8.1	5.0	4.7
San Marino	0.0	146.9	3.8	2.5	1.1	1.1	-4.4	-6.0	2.9	0.0	0.6	1.9
Serbia [3]	0.3	52.2	...	...	-10.0	16.8	5.1	4.0	7.0	11.1	10.8	10.7
Slovenia	0.4	69.1	...	...	2.1	5.3	4.2	4.3	6.3	10.7	7.2	4.4
Spain	4.8	30.6	6.7	8.7	9.0	2.1	6.8	5.1	2.6	6.8	4.2	0.7
Yugoslavia (Former)	...	...	7.8	1.6	...	...	...	...	...	...	...	...
Western Europe	*48.6*	*44.8*	*5.7*	*3.9*	*5.3*	*2.6*	*3.3*	*6.6*	*3.4*	*4.5*	*3.1*	*2.2*
Austria	2.5	49.3	7.1	3.4	4.3	2.4	3.0	3.6	3.7	5.3	5.0	2.4
Belgium	4.7	76.4	6.0	4.0	4.5	1.9	5.5	3.9	7.5	5.2	1.3	0.8
France	10.1	31.2	7.2	4.2	5.1	2.2	4.9	5.9	2.9	4.5	3.1	2.5
Germany	17.5	39.3	5.6	3.3	5.9	2.9	3.9	5.8	4.5	5.3	3.6	2.6
Liechtenstein	0.0	50.7	6.8	7.7	7.2	1.7	-6.8	3.1	5.6	0.7	1.3	-0.5
Luxembourg	1.4	187.2	3.5	5.1	7.1	4.7	19.5	3.4	1.6	0.6	-0.3	0.9
Monaco	0.0	31.2	7.1	2.3	2.9	1.0	8.6	6.0	2.4	0.1	8.5	7.5
Netherlands	7.6	75.2	4.7	3.7	7.0	2.5	3.3	14.5	-2.0	6.2	4.7	3.2
Switzerland	4.7	50.7	4.5	5.1	3.2	2.6	-7.3	4.8	5.3	-0.9	0.4	-0.1
Oceania	**1.6**	**22.9**	**2.8**	**5.8**	**7.3**	**7.5**	**1.1**	**0.4**	**4.8**	**6.9**	**0.9**	**23.7**
Australia and New Zealand	*94.0*	*22.2*	*3.2*	*6.3*	*7.9*	*7.8*	*1.9*	*0.2*	*4.9*	*7.3*	*0.8*	*25.0*
Australia	79.9	21.5	3.3	6.5	8.4	8.4	1.0	-0.1	4.8	7.3	0.2	-7.3
New Zealand	14.2	26.9	3.1	5.5	5.8	4.1	7.4	2.3	5.2	7.2	3.9	200.1
Melanesia	*4.8*	*43.9*	*0.1*	*2.0*	*3.3*	*4.7*	*-11.9*	*2.6*	*4.5*	*0.4*	*2.6*	*1.7*
Fiji	0.7	52.4	7.7	5.1	1.3	0.9	-11.1	-6.3	-0.8	6.2	9.5	5.0
New Caledonia	1.1	41.7	-4.4	3.1	2.8	4.2	-4.8	4.2	-0.6	-1.1	-1.3	-0.7
Papua New Guinea	2.7	41.5	-0.3	-0.7	6.1	6.6	-15.7	2.9	8.1	-0.9	1.8	1.7
Solomon Islands	0.2	60.2	12.1	9.4	-3.1	5.3	-1.6	13.6	4.5	3.2	2.8	5.0
Vanuatu	0.1	64.5	7.7	4.7	-0.1	6.8	0.2	26.2	2.3	3.3	10.4	-4.2
Micronesia	*0.3*	*87.4*	*5.0*	*3.4*	*-3.6*	*-0.1*	*2.3*	*8.8*	*3.2*	*1.7*	*-4.3*	*1.5*
Kiribati	0.1	106.7	6.7	3.5	-9.1	-0.3	8.4	15.1	4.0	-0.4	-15.0	-0.1
Marshall Islands	0.1	93.6	6.8	8.3	-2.3	1.7	-9.2	9.9	7.0	10.7	3.1	6.9
Micronesia (FS of)	0.1	77.2	6.6	4.1	1.6	2.0	-12.9	10.3	-6.0	5.8	0.6	-0.1
Nauru	0.0	106.7	4.3	0.1	-21.1	-1.7	48.8	7.3	6.5	-10.3	-12.2	-1.4
Palau	0.1	76.0	0.1	3.6	4.4	-4.0	11.6	2.5	8.3	-1.5	-3.6	0.6
Polynesia	*0.8*	*41.4*	*1.7*	*2.9*	*1.5*	*2.1*	*-0.6*	*7.5*	*2.6*	*5.8*	*3.4*	*0.6*
Cook Islands	0.0	55.6	2.0	0.4	-2.9	-0.5	-1.5	0.5	6.4	2.8	4.1	2.5
French Polynesia	0.6	36.0	1.0	2.9	2.1	2.2	-0.3	4.9	1.6	7.7	4.2	-0.4
Samoa	0.1	54.7	3.6	2.6	2.2	3.2	2.8	9.1	2.1	-0.4	1.0	1.9
Tonga	0.1	64.5	3.4	5.6	-0.7	0.9	-8.4	22.6	16.9	3.5	-1.4	4.8
Tuvalu	0.0	172.0	-1.8	2.5	2.7	9.5	-3.3	59.1	-31.8	12.2	21.7	-4.0

Notes for Table 5.E. Average Rates of Growth of Gross Domestic Product by Expenditure - Imports of goods and services

1/ Myanmar

1970-1996

Country used official exchange rates rather than market exchange rates in compiling imports and exports data.

2/ Ukraine

2010-2019

The Government of Ukraine has advised the United Nations that it is not in a position to provide statistical data concerning the Autonomous Republic of Crimea and the city of Sevastopol.

3/ Serbia

1990-2009, 2013-2019

Includes imports of goods and services from Montenegro.

Table 6.A. Average Rates of Growth of Gross Domestic Product by Kind of Economic Activity - Agriculture, Hunting, Forestry and Fishing

Major area, region and country	Base year weights as percentage of total for world or region in 2015	Base year share as percentage of total GDP in 2015	Average rates of growth				Annual rate of change (percentage)					
			1970-1979	1980-1989	1990-1999	2000-2009	2014	2015	2016	2017	2018	2019
World	**100.0**	**4.4**	**2.2**	**3.3**	**2.0**	**3.0**	**3.0**	**2.4**	**2.2**	**3.5**	**2.5**	**2.5**
Developed economies	**17.4**	**1.3**	**1.3**	**2.2**	**0.6**	**0.9**	**2.5**	**1.2**	**1.1**	**-0.1**	**1.1**	**0.4**
Developing economies	**78.7**	**8.8**	**2.3**	**3.8**	**3.1**	**3.5**	**3.0**	**2.6**	**2.4**	**4.4**	**2.9**	**3.0**
Transition economies	**3.9**	**6.7**	**6.3**	**2.6**	**-4.8**	**3.5**	**3.1**	**2.9**	**3.8**	**1.0**	**1.0**	**1.3**
Africa	**11.3**	**16.2**	**1.6**	**2.8**	**2.9**	**5.6**	**4.9**	**3.9**	**2.4**	**4.9**	**3.1**	**1.8**
Northern Africa	*27.8*	*14.0*	*2.2*	*3.0*	*4.2*	*4.8*	*3.3*	*3.0*	*-0.7*	*6.6*	*3.1*	*1.5*
Algeria	5.4	12.1	2.4	3.9	4.5	7.1	2.5	6.0	1.8	0.6	3.5	2.7
Egypt [1]	10.1	11.3	2.4	3.2	3.2	3.6	3.0	3.1	3.1	3.2	3.1	3.1
Libya	0.0	0.9	5.2	1.7	1.6	4.7	-52.3	-48.9	-21.7	59.3	30.6	7.5
Morocco	3.6	14.3	1.0	4.8	-0.6	8.4	-4.6	2.4	-9.2	25.9	-2.0	-4.1
Sudan	7.5	32.0	...	...	...	...	9.6	0.2	-2.2	7.9	4.0	1.2
Sudan (Former)	...	...	1.8	0.7	10.4	...	...	...	...	...	...	...
Tunisia [1]	1.2	10.9	5.3	0.1	3.7	2.8	4.8	12.3	-8.5	1.8	11.3	0.8
Sub-Saharan Africa	72.2	17.3	1.4	2.7	2.3	5.9	5.5	4.2	3.6	4.2	3.1	2.0
Eastern Africa	*21.6*	*26.7*	*2.0*	*2.7*	*2.4*	*3.5*	*5.3*	*4.2*	*3.1*	*4.5*	*4.3*	*3.5*
Burundi	0.3	37.5	1.6	3.0	-1.2	-1.1	-3.2	-1.5	2.7	2.1	1.1	2.0
Comoros	0.1	31.7	4.4	3.9	1.9	-0.7	1.8	1.0	5.0	9.7	4.9	4.3
Djibouti	0.0	1.3	0.2	2.8	2.8	3.7	-1.8	1.3	-4.4	35.2	15.3	5.4
Eritrea	0.1	17.2	...	...	9.1	-1.0	30.8	-18.1	10.1	-12.4	14.1	4.1
Ethiopia	6.3	38.8	...	...	2.0	6.6	5.4	6.4	2.3	6.7	3.5	3.8
Ethiopia (Former)	...	...	0.9	0.1	...	...	...	...	...	...	...	...
Kenya [2]	5.4	32.2	4.1	4.1	1.8	2.1	4.4	5.3	4.7	1.6	6.0	3.6
Madagascar	0.8	27.0	0.4	2.1	1.9	2.4	1.6	-1.5	1.3	1.3	0.4	5.9
Malawi [2]	0.5	32.4	5.6	1.6	5.1	1.5	6.3	-1.0	-0.1	6.1	0.6	3.9
Mauritius [3]	0.1	3.6	6.9	3.2	-2.3	2.1	3.7	0.3	3.7	-0.2	-1.3	3.9
Mozambique [2]	1.0	25.9	3.9	0.8	3.6	7.8	3.7	3.0	4.2	4.0	3.4	1.2
Rwanda [2]	0.6	26.3	7.0	0.8	-0.5	5.5	6.7	5.0	3.9	4.8	6.1	5.0
Seychelles [2]	0.0	2.4	7.0	-2.8	10.3	-2.5	-7.1	-4.0	0.9	3.3	14.1	2.9
Somalia	0.2	60.2	1.4	3.3	-5.1	2.9	4.6	2.1	3.1	3.3	2.8	3.1
South Sudan	0.1	4.2	...	...	...	...	35.0	-8.7	-11.9	-29.4	-11.8	35.6
U.R. of Tanzania: Mainland [2]	3.5	29.2	1.9	3.8	4.2	4.5	6.9	5.4	4.8	5.9	5.3	4.4
Uganda [2]	1.7	25.8	-1.6	3.3	4.3	3.0	2.7	4.0	-0.3	4.5	5.0	5.0
Zambia [4]	0.3	5.3	-1.3	6.3	2.9	-1.6	1.1	-7.7	3.7	9.8	-21.2	7.7
Zanzibar [5]	0.1	24.2	...	...	5.0	5.1	0.2	5.3	3.8	7.9	3.7	2.7
Zimbabwe	0.5	9.3	2.5	2.8	2.8	-5.5	23.0	-5.2	-3.9	10.0	18.3	-16.4
Middle Africa	*7.7*	*12.0*	*1.6*	*1.7*	*0.5*	*4.1*	*9.0*	*6.8*	*6.1*	*2.2*	*1.4*	*1.8*
Angola	3.0	9.1	0.3	0.6	-4.0	8.1	15.9	11.2	3.9	0.5	-1.6	-1.5
Cameroon [2]	1.3	16.1	5.5	1.5	1.5	2.7	6.2	5.3	5.0	3.2	5.1	2.9
Central African Republic	0.1	32.5	2.3	2.3	3.4	1.1	-1.4	0.6	5.0	3.2	3.4	3.9
Chad	0.9	29.5	-1.7	3.3	4.1	7.5	7.5	3.1	20.7	3.1	4.0	4.6
Congo	0.2	6.3	2.2	3.0	-1.6	4.5	-0.5	-5.0	-0.2	15.0	-4.2	3.5
D.R. of the Congo	1.9	19.7	1.6	2.5	2.0	1.3	4.7	4.7	3.3	1.6	1.6	3.1
Equatorial Guinea	0.1	1.9	2.2	2.7	5.6	-2.4	7.2	11.8	5.4	-2.7	-0.6	-5.6
Gabon	0.2	4.7	8.1	0.8	2.7	1.8	9.7	8.3	11.6	12.2	9.5	11.1
Sao Tome and Principe	0.0	12.2	7.0	-0.5	4.1	3.5	4.8	3.2	2.0	1.5	-3.5	-1.0
Southern Africa	*2.3*	*2.6*	*3.9*	*2.6*	*0.5*	*2.1*	*5.4*	*-5.9*	*-8.0*	*17.2*	*-4.0*	*-6.0*
Botswana	0.1	2.4	9.5	1.0	1.0	3.7	-0.3	0.3	0.6	1.9	2.6	-0.1
Eswatini [2]	0.1	9.8	8.1	2.3	1.8	2.7	-6.7	3.4	-8.5	-4.9	7.8	-2.1
Lesotho [2]	0.0	4.2	5.3	-0.7	1.2	-0.9	-15.5	1.2	53.0	-8.9	-20.0	-1.0
Namibia [2]	0.2	6.7	3.0	1.3	1.4	0.5	4.7	-13.3	0.7	7.0	-1.9	-2.6
South Africa	1.9	2.3	3.5	2.9	0.3	2.3	6.8	-5.9	-10.1	21.1	-4.8	-6.9
Western Africa	*40.7*	*22.0*	*0.6*	*3.1*	*3.1*	*8.3*	*4.9*	*4.4*	*4.0*	*3.8*	*3.2*	*1.5*
Benin [6]	0.8	28.7	3.6	6.7	5.6	4.4	15.9	36.3	9.0	7.6	7.3	5.2
Burkina Faso [2]	0.7	24.9	0.5	4.9	7.9	2.5	4.4	-3.2	4.2	-0.2	13.3	1.7
Cabo Verde [2]	0.0	10.0	-0.8	3.7	1.8	0.1	-0.2	8.1	-4.5	-12.2	-18.5	-7.3
Côte d'Ivoire	2.3	19.0	4.4	4.8	1.5	0.0	18.1	4.9	-4.0	3.7	4.6	4.7
Gambia [2]	0.1	24.3	-1.4	-0.3	2.9	3.2	-12.4	4.0	-0.2	-4.4	6.0	-10.0
Ghana [2]	2.8	22.1	1.1	0.6	3.4	4.7	0.9	2.3	2.9	6.1	4.8	4.6
Guinea	0.5	20.1	3.0	2.6	4.6	2.1	4.5	6.1	6.0	8.6	7.1	7.2
Guinea-Bissau	0.1	49.0	0.3	8.0	2.9	2.8	-6.5	2.9	5.3	-0.3	0.7	-0.3
Liberia	0.4	69.5	4.5	0.0	3.5	3.4	5.1	0.0	-22.8	-1.1	-0.2	0.4
Mali	1.4	39.8	4.0	2.6	9.0	9.3	11.8	8.3	11.0	3.5	7.7	6.6
Mauritania [2]	0.4	23.0	-3.0	0.8	1.4	0.8	-3.9	10.3	5.4	-2.9	0.7	2.8
Niger [2]	0.9	34.9	-3.9	1.2	4.9	5.5	8.5	1.9	17.4	5.4	7.1	5.1
Nigeria [2]	28.5	20.9	-0.1	3.5	3.5	10.9	4.3	3.7	4.1	3.4	2.1	0.2
Senegal [2]	0.7	16.0	1.6	2.1	2.3	2.3	2.2	10.6	5.4	11.5	7.9	4.2
Sierra Leone	0.7	60.5	2.7	3.7	-8.5	11.1	0.8	3.5	3.9	4.5	3.9	5.6
Togo	0.3	24.2	1.3	4.7	3.8	8.1	-0.2	10.5	12.4	7.8	3.4	3.3

Table 6.A. Average Rates of Growth of Gross Domestic Product by Kind of Economic Activity - Agriculture, Hunting, Forestry and Fishing

Major area, region and country	Base year weights as percentage of total for world or region in 2015	Base year share as percentage of total GDP in 2015	Average rates of growth				Annual rate of change (percentage)					
			1970-1979	1980-1989	1990-1999	2000-2009	2014	2015	2016	2017	2018	2019
Americas	**14.8**	**1.9**	**1.9**	**2.8**	**2.3**	**2.3**	**1.1**	**4.0**	**0.8**	**2.3**	**1.4**	**1.4**
Latin America and the Caribbean	**8.1**	**5.2**	**3.2**	**1.9**	**2.5**	**2.4**	**2.0**	**1.7**	**-2.7**	**5.7**	**-0.6**	**1.8**
Caribbean	*2.4*	*3.3*	*3.2*	*2.5*	*-1.8*	*0.5*	*1.4*	*1.4*	*4.8*	*1.3*	*1.7*	*1.9*
Anguilla	0.0	2.3	4.0	5.1	-1.5	1.8	1.7	6.2	36.3	-30.6	-31.2	75.0
Antigua and Barbuda	0.0	1.8	0.4	-1.2	1.3	0.7	-17.0	2.6	3.7	15.0	0.7	1.4
Aruba [2,7]	0.0	0.0	9.1	11.2	2.3	0.8	-2.0	0.1	0.5	-1.0	3.5	-1.4
Bahamas [2]	0.0	0.9	2.4	2.6	0.9	-0.3	-6.0	0.7	5.2	-5.3	-10.6	-11.9
Barbados [2]	0.0	1.5	-1.7	-3.5	-1.1	-2.8	-2.5	0.4	-1.0	-3.3	14.8	-6.3
British Virgin Islands [2]	0.0	0.1	1.5	2.9	8.3	-1.7	4.6	-0.5	8.5	-5.9	0.7	1.4
Cayman Islands [2]	0.0	0.4	9.4	9.3	6.8	3.9	8.2	2.2	2.6	2.5	1.1	3.3
Cuba	0.7	3.9	5.4	5.2	-5.5	-0.1	2.2	2.5	5.8	-1.4	2.6	2.3
Curaçao [8]	0.0	0.5	...	...	...	...	-36.0	73.6	-8.5	-1.7	-4.8	-1.6
Dominica	0.0	16.5	1.4	3.4	-1.6	-0.7	-0.2	-2.8	9.3	-19.1	-27.4	14.9
Dominican Republic [2]	0.8	5.9	3.3	1.4	2.3	3.7	2.5	2.3	5.6	5.8	5.5	4.1
Former Netherlands Antilles [9]	...	...	8.2	-0.2	1.4	0.1	...	...	...	...	...	...
Grenada	0.0	8.6	5.6	-0.2	-1.1	-1.2	38.6	33.9	-10.5	-15.4	3.0	-4.8
Haiti	0.3	17.3	1.6	-0.9	-1.1	-0.4	-1.5	-5.4	3.1	0.8	1.0	-1.2
Jamaica	0.2	7.2	1.5	-0.3	4.1	0.2	-0.5	0.0	12.9	-3.5	4.1	0.4
Montserrat	0.0	1.4	1.8	-3.1	-17.8	-2.1	43.2	-28.2	22.0	-12.0	-2.5	-8.9
Puerto Rico [10]	0.2	0.8	3.9	2.1	-2.7	-1.2	1.2	-3.3	-3.8	-1.3	-17.6	-2.5
Saint Kitts and Nevis	0.0	1.1	4.9	-0.5	0.4	3.2	0.6	-1.9	-8.8	26.6	3.7	16.2
Saint Lucia [2]	0.0	2.5	6.2	7.8	-5.6	-2.7	-8.6	2.4	2.4	-2.9	1.7	-0.8
Sint Maarten (Dutch part)	0.0	0.1	...	...	...	...	40.3	-10.3	-5.6	-3.1	-10.0	4.2
St. Vincent and the Grenadines	0.0	7.3	1.0	9.0	-3.6	2.4	2.8	-3.5	6.5	4.5	2.8	-1.0
Trinidad and Tobago [2]	0.1	1.1	-1.2	0.9	-0.1	-7.3	3.0	35.9	-7.3	7.9	-9.6	-3.3
Turks and Caicos Islands	0.0	0.6	10.7	10.7	6.8	-1.2	33.0	1.2	-3.5	0.0	-8.5	-3.2
Central America	*11.5*	*4.1*	*3.3*	*0.3*	*1.8*	*1.9*	*3.3*	*1.5*	*3.5*	*3.7*	*2.2*	*1.7*
Belize	0.0	14.7	3.6	2.6	5.7	3.1	2.4	-12.5	-21.7	9.8	-3.9	-0.7
Costa Rica [2]	0.6	5.4	2.9	3.2	5.5	1.8	1.5	-2.7	5.2	3.7	1.8	-1.2
El Salvador [2]	0.3	6.1	4.9	-9.5	-3.0	1.1	5.9	-3.5	6.3	-3.8	-3.3	2.2
Guatemala [2]	1.3	10.6	5.0	1.0	2.8	3.0	1.6	2.6	2.4	3.1	2.4	2.3
Honduras	0.5	12.6	2.8	2.9	1.6	2.9	2.8	2.6	4.8	10.3	2.7	-1.0
Mexico [2]	8.0	3.4	3.0	0.8	1.6	1.6	3.8	2.1	3.5	3.4	2.4	1.9
Nicaragua	0.4	17.8	2.6	-0.8	3.8	3.4	2.1	-0.7	4.8	9.2	0.9	2.6
Panama	0.3	2.9	2.0	3.1	2.7	1.8	1.9	0.1	0.7	1.1	2.6	4.9
South America	*40.9*	*5.8*	*3.1*	*2.5*	*3.1*	*2.6*	*1.7*	*1.8*	*-4.8*	*6.5*	*-1.6*	*1.8*
Argentina	7.1	6.1	2.9	0.5	3.3	-0.4	3.1	7.5	-4.7	3.0	-14.3	19.7
Bolivia (Plurinational State of)	0.7	12.6	4.5	1.4	2.9	3.1	3.8	5.1	3.1	7.6	6.9	5.3
Brazil [2]	16.6	5.0	4.2	3.2	3.8	3.5	2.8	3.3	-5.2	14.2	1.4	1.3
Chile [2]	1.9	4.0	2.1	5.7	4.5	5.9	0.2	6.0	2.6	2.2	1.6	-1.5
Colombia [2]	3.7	6.6	4.6	2.7	1.1	2.0	2.9	4.3	2.7	5.6	2.4	2.0
Ecuador [2]	2.0	10.2	0.3	5.2	4.1	3.7	7.6	2.9	0.9	5.5	0.1	1.8
Guyana [3]	0.2	27.0	0.9	-1.2	8.8	13.4	7.7	3.3	-11.1	12.7	6.6	-0.5
Paraguay [2]	0.7	10.2	6.5	4.2	2.6	4.4	4.0	-0.5	3.1	6.0	5.3	-1.5
Peru [2,11]	2.9	7.7	0.1	3.2	5.0	3.3	-1.1	4.0	1.7	3.0	9.6	0.9
Suriname	0.1	10.0	4.7	0.6	-1.0	3.9	3.6	4.2	1.4	12.4	-1.6	-2.2
Uruguay	0.7	6.7	-1.0	0.2	2.7	1.5	0.3	-1.2	2.5	-5.7	6.0	-3.8
Venezuela (Bolivarian Republic of)	4.2	6.3	3.1	2.4	1.7	2.4	-4.6	-15.3	-24.4	-14.0	-18.1	-36.2
Northern America	**6.7**	**1.1**	**0.3**	**4.0**	**2.0**	**2.2**	**0.0**	**6.8**	**5.0**	**-1.5**	**3.8**	**0.9**
Bermuda [2]	0.0	0.2	3.5	1.0	3.3	-3.0	-33.7	2.1	45.0	-4.9	-8.5	8.0
Canada [2]	6.2	2.0	0.2	2.4	0.9	1.1	-6.7	4.4	4.1	2.3	1.9	5.8
Greenland [2]	0.1	17.6	6.4	2.5	1.2	0.9	19.1	-20.3	17.0	4.4	-4.0	5.5
United States [2,12]	38.9	1.0	0.3	4.4	2.2	2.4	1.1	7.3	5.1	-2.1	4.2	0.1
Asia	**62.2**	**7.5**	**2.0**	**4.0**	**2.6**	**3.2**	**2.7**	**2.4**	**2.9**	**4.0**	**3.2**	**3.3**
Central Asia	*2.0*	*13.4*	...	...	*-3.4*	*5.2*	*5.0*	*6.4*	*5.3*	*2.4*	*2.1*	*2.1*
Kazakhstan [5]	0.4	5.0	...	...	-7.2	5.5	1.3	3.5	5.4	3.2	3.8	-0.1
Kyrgyzstan [5]	0.0	15.4	...	...	0.4	2.7	-0.5	6.2	2.9	2.2	2.6	2.6
Tajikistan	0.1	24.7	...	...	-7.5	8.9	9.2	3.4	5.2	8.3	7.8	7.1
Turkmenistan	0.2	9.4	...	...	-6.2	-1.4	8.0	19.3	-0.8	7.4	8.0	1.5
Uzbekistan [5]	1.3	33.6	...	...	0.5	6.1	6.0	6.1	6.2	1.2	0.3	2.5
Eastern Asia	*53.5*	*6.0*	*2.1*	*4.8*	*3.0*	*3.5*	*3.8*	*3.4*	*2.6*	*3.9*	*3.5*	*3.4*
China [12]	48.8	8.7	2.4	6.1	4.0	4.2	4.2	4.0	3.5	4.1	3.6	3.7
China, Hong Kong SAR [7,13]	0.0	0.1	8.6	-5.4	-6.0	-4.2	-6.0	-6.8	-2.0	-5.1	-1.8	-0.4
China, Macao SAR	...	...	...	...	...	...	...	...	...	...	...	...
D.P.R. of Korea	0.2	21.6	7.6	2.7	-0.8	1.9	1.2	-0.8	2.5	-1.3	-1.8	1.4
Japan [2,10]	2.5	1.1	0.5	1.2	-2.0	-2.2	-3.1	-4.5	-7.3	0.9	1.5	-2.6

Table 6.A. Average Rates of Growth of Gross Domestic Product by Kind of Economic Activity - Agriculture, Hunting, Forestry and Fishing

Major area, region and country	Base year weights as percentage of total for world or region in 2015	Base year share as percentage of total GDP in 2015	Average rates of growth 1970-1979	1980-1989	1990-1999	2000-2009	Annual rate of change (percentage) 2014	2015	2016	2017	2018	2019
Mongolia [2]	0.1	14.5	5.7	3.1	0.3	2.9	13.7	10.7	6.2	1.8	4.5	8.4
Republic of Korea [2]	1.5	2.2	4.3	5.0	2.2	1.9	5.1	-0.2	-5.6	2.3	0.2	2.3
South-Eastern Asia	*13.4*	*11.0*	*4.0*	*3.6*	*2.6*	*3.6*	*2.8*	*1.2*	*0.9*	*3.6*	*3.1*	*2.3*
Brunei Darussalam [2]	0.0	1.1	1.4	3.3	3.6	3.2	4.7	6.4	-3.6	-1.6	-1.6	-1.4
Cambodia	0.2	28.2	-7.3	6.5	4.1	5.2	0.3	0.2	1.2	1.8	1.2	-0.7
Indonesia [2]	5.9	13.9	3.7	3.6	2.3	3.5	4.2	3.8	3.4	3.9	3.9	3.6
Lao People's DR [2]	0.1	19.7	3.0	5.4	4.6	3.3	4.1	3.6	2.8	2.9	1.3	-0.9
Malaysia [2,10]	1.3	8.4	7.7	4.2	0.2	3.0	2.0	1.4	-3.7	5.9	0.1	2.0
Myanmar [10]	0.9	26.7	3.9	0.8	5.9	8.4	3.1	1.4	-1.5	0.1	1.6	0.1
Philippines [2,12]	1.5	10.3	4.0	1.2	1.9	3.2	1.7	0.1	-1.2	4.0	0.9	1.5
Singapore [2,8]	0.0	0.0	2.9	-4.5	-3.3	-3.8	3.3	-0.5	1.7	-0.9	-0.1	5.1
Thailand [2,10]	1.8	8.9	4.2	4.6	3.5	2.4	-0.3	-6.5	-1.3	3.7	5.1	0.2
Timor-Leste [5]	0.0	17.8	...	...	5.3	2.7	-1.3	-4.4	-1.3	-3.0	2.9	2.5
Viet Nam [2,14]	1.7	18.9	4.7	5.8	4.4	3.7	3.4	2.4	1.4	2.9	3.8	2.0
Southern Asia	*25.3*	*17.1*	*0.8*	*3.2*	*2.8*	*2.5*	*1.0*	*1.2*	*5.3*	*5.0*	*2.8*	*3.1*
Afghanistan [15]	0.2	27.3	0.6	-2.7	-1.3	5.4	5.1	-12.1	5.3	9.3	-5.9	20.8
Bangladesh	1.5	15.3	-0.3	1.6	2.6	3.6	4.4	3.3	2.8	3.0	4.2	3.9
Bhutan	0.0	15.1	3.9	5.6	1.3	0.7	2.1	4.7	4.2	2.9	4.4	3.8
India [2]	17.6	17.7	0.3	3.4	2.7	2.3	-0.2	0.6	6.8	5.9	2.4	3.1
Iran (Islamic Republic of)	2.1	10.6	5.7	4.4	2.5	2.4	5.4	4.6	4.2	3.2	4.6	4.4
Maldives [2]	0.0	6.3	2.1	5.3	2.2	1.3	-0.3	-0.4	1.5	8.3	4.8	5.0
Nepal	0.3	31.7	0.8	4.4	2.1	3.5	4.5	1.1	0.2	5.2	2.8	5.1
Pakistan [2]	3.2	25.1	1.9	4.1	4.3	2.9	2.5	2.1	0.2	2.2	3.9	0.8
Sri Lanka [2]	0.3	8.8	2.8	1.3	2.3	2.4	4.6	4.7	-3.7	-0.4	6.5	0.6
Western Asia	*5.7*	*3.9*	*2.3*	*2.0*	*1.5*	*1.6*	*-0.5*	*0.3*	*-1.1*	*1.8*	*2.8*	*5.7*
Armenia [5]	0.1	18.9	...	...	-2.5	7.2	6.1	13.2	-5.0	-5.1	-6.9	-2.6
Azerbaijan [5]	0.2	6.7	...	...	-6.8	5.5	-2.6	6.6	2.6	4.2	4.6	7.3
Bahrain [10]	0.0	0.3	8.2	4.9	4.9	2.6	11.4	-3.1	6.9	-0.9	3.8	2.1
Cyprus [2]	0.0	2.1	-2.4	2.7	1.6	-4.1	-15.1	2.2	16.2	0.7	3.0	1.4
Georgia [5]	0.1	8.8	...	...	-9.2	-0.1	-0.9	-0.1	-2.8	-7.7	13.8	-1.1
Iraq	0.4	4.2	1.7	4.2	2.6	-1.5	-2.0	-36.9	-0.3	-16.0	12.8	38.8
Israel [2]	0.2	1.3	3.5	-3.3	1.0	4.7	-4.3	-6.5	5.1	1.5	-2.6	1.3
Jordan [2]	0.1	4.9	3.6	1.1	-3.8	9.3	7.5	5.0	3.8	4.8	3.2	2.5
Kuwait	0.0	0.5	0.0	17.4	-2.1	2.7	7.3	-5.1	0.5	6.2	-0.4	-2.7
Lebanon [2]	0.1	3.6	-3.1	-5.9	12.8	-0.1	15.5	-13.3	6.3	13.4	-4.0	29.1
Oman	0.1	1.9	11.8	7.8	5.2	1.8	1.8	32.6	8.3	8.7	28.3	1.9
Qatar [2,10]	0.0	0.2	3.8	0.5	1.2	4.1	25.1	7.7	9.0	8.2	8.3	1.8
Saudi Arabia [2]	0.9	2.6	5.9	11.8	1.9	1.4	2.5	0.6	0.6	0.5	0.3	1.3
State of Palestine [2]	0.1	8.7	8.0	2.0	6.9	6.8	2.7	-4.0	10.4	-6.0	1.6	0.0
Syrian Arab Republic [12]	0.2	20.7	7.5	-2.1	5.4	2.0	-6.0	3.5	-0.4	-1.2	12.0	8.4
Turkey [2]	3.0	7.8	1.7	0.5	1.0	1.4	0.5	9.3	-2.6	4.9	2.1	3.7
United Arab Emirates	0.1	0.7	14.6	10.5	9.4	-3.4	-0.2	1.3	3.4	3.3	5.4	2.7
Yemen	0.2	18.2	...	...	6.1	5.9	-15.6	-18.7	-10.2	-7.9	-3.1	2.6
Yemen Arab Republic (Former)	...	...	3.6	3.2	...	...	...	...	...	...	...	...
Yemen Democratic (Former)	...	...	-4.3	6.8	...	...	...	...	...	...	...	...
Europe	**10.3**	**1.9**	**3.3**	**2.0**	**-0.9**	**1.2**	**5.2**	**-0.5**	**-0.5**	**1.2**	**0.0**	**1.2**
Eastern Europe	*30.6*	*4.3*	*6.4*	*2.5*	*-3.7*	*2.7*	*4.3*	*-1.9*	*3.9*	*1.4*	*0.1*	*0.7*
Belarus [5]	1.1	7.2	...	...	-4.6	4.9	2.5	-2.4	3.8	4.3	-3.4	3.1
Bulgaria [2]	0.6	4.7	6.8	-1.5	-1.9	-1.7	7.0	-7.9	7.7	9.0	-2.0	3.6
Czechia [5]	1.3	2.5	...	...	5.6	1.7	7.0	6.7	5.3	-3.8	4.0	5.4
Czechoslovakia (Former)	...	...	-0.1	3.7	...	...	...	...	...	...	...	...
Hungary [2]	1.4	4.5	3.0	2.4	-2.8	4.0	14.9	-0.2	12.6	-6.6	4.1	0.4
Poland [2]	3.5	2.7	6.0	1.8	2.8	3.1	1.1	-9.4	2.1	0.9	-9.1	0.1
Republic of Moldova [5]	0.3	13.2	...	...	-10.9	-0.2	8.6	-13.3	18.4	8.6	2.6	-4.3
Romania [2]	2.3	4.8	5.8	0.3	-2.2	1.5	5.0	-11.1	4.2	14.5	10.8	-3.2
Russian Federation	16.1	4.3	...	...	-5.3	2.7	3.3	2.4	2.3	1.5	-2.0	0.6
Slovakia [5]	0.7	2.9	...	...	-6.0	12.2	27.0	-14.9	9.8	-10.3	9.3	7.9
Ukraine [5,16]	3.4	14.2	...	...	-7.1	3.0	2.3	-4.4	6.3	-2.3	8.0	1.3
USSR (Former)	...	...	7.0	2.9	...	...	...	...	...	...	...	...
Northern Europe	*14.3*	*1.1*	*1.0*	*1.8*	*-2.2*	*0.6*	*10.9*	*-0.3*	*-4.1*	*5.4*	*-4.4*	*7.9*
Denmark [2]	0.9	1.1	3.5	3.7	4.3	-2.8	17.1	-12.5	-15.3	14.0	-4.8	22.1
Estonia [5]	0.2	3.3	...	...	-0.5	1.9	12.3	2.8	-23.8	1.8	-29.4	54.2
Finland [2]	1.6	2.6	0.3	-1.5	-1.0	1.5	6.9	3.6	2.2	2.1	-2.3	1.2
Iceland [2]	0.3	5.9	5.3	1.5	-1.5	0.2	-1.3	4.5	-0.2	0.2	-1.2	17.2
Ireland [2]	0.8	1.0	1.6	2.6	-2.0	-3.9	26.7	5.6	9.9	5.6	-12.1	28.4
Latvia [5]	0.3	4.0	...	...	-8.5	3.8	8.0	2.7	-4.3	1.8	-3.6	12.3
Lithuania [5]	0.4	3.8	...	...	-21.1	0.7	3.9	4.9	-3.9	0.0	-10.4	9.6
Norway [2]	1.8	1.7	0.4	0.6	3.1	3.8	6.9	-5.5	-6.0	4.2	0.2	4.4
Sweden [2]	2.2	1.6	-0.8	2.3	-1.9	2.7	6.5	2.4	-1.7	6.1	-7.0	2.5
United Kingdom [2]	5.8	0.7	1.6	2.5	0.6	-0.3	13.6	0.0	-6.0	6.3	-3.3	6.3

Table 6.A. Average Rates of Growth of Gross Domestic Product by Kind of Economic Activity - Agriculture, Hunting, Forestry and Fishing

Major area, region and country	Base year weights as percentage of total for world or region in 2015	Base year share as percentage of total GDP in 2015	Average rates of growth				Annual rate of change (percentage)					
			1970-1979	1980-1989	1990-1999	2000-2009	2014	2015	2016	2017	2018	2019
Southern Europe	*28.3*	*2.9*	*1.3*	*1.2*	*2.0*	*-0.2*	*-1.2*	*3.9*	*1.5*	*-2.5*	*4.1*	*-0.9*
Albania [2]	0.7	22.5	3.9	2.1	4.0	3.3	2.0	0.8	2.0	0.8	1.2	1.4
Andorra [2]	0.0	0.6	3.8	2.7	-2.5	0.9	-5.9	-3.1	5.4	7.6	-0.8	1.2
Bosnia and Herzegovina [5]	0.3	7.3	...	...	7.9	4.7	-12.7	9.2	7.6	-8.1	9.0	-2.0
Croatia [5]	0.5	3.6	...	...	-3.2	1.7	-13.7	2.4	6.4	-2.5	2.2	1.2
Greece [2]	2.3	4.4	1.5	0.5	1.9	-2.2	5.1	-2.4	-7.4	13.1	-1.4	5.1
Italy [2]	11.6	2.3	0.1	1.7	2.9	-0.6	-2.3	4.7	-0.1	-3.8	1.8	-1.7
Kosovo [5]	0.2	12.6	...	...	-7.1	7.3	0.8	-4.1	3.1	2.7	-10.6	8.0
Malta [2]	0.0	1.2	3.7	3.5	1.6	-1.4	3.6	5.2	19.2	-31.3	18.8	-4.3
Montenegro [5]	0.1	9.8	...	...	-4.4	2.4	1.8	2.1	3.9	-3.1	3.3	-2.2
North Macedonia [5]	0.3	11.1	...	...	0.8	3.3	3.1	1.9	-0.4	-12.5	7.4	3.8
Portugal [2]	1.3	2.4	2.3	0.5	0.5	-0.2	0.0	5.1	-1.2	2.0	-1.1	3.4
San Marino [2]	0.0	0.0	3.8	2.4	6.4	-2.6	-45.9	-26.9	-30.4	51.2	-18.8	-1.5
Serbia [5]	0.8	8.1	...	...	-6.6	1.9	2.0	2.2	7.5	-11.4	15.1	-1.6
Slovenia [5]	0.3	2.4	...	...	-0.4	0.0	2.0	13.1	-1.4	-5.1	23.7	-3.2
Spain [2]	10.0	3.0	2.6	1.7	2.7	-0.2	-1.3	4.7	4.8	-3.7	7.5	-2.3
Yugoslavia (Former)	...	...	2.0	0.1	...	...	...	...	...	...	...	...
Western Europe	*26.7*	*1.2*	*2.2*	*2.0*	*-0.1*	*1.4*	*10.4*	*-3.5*	*-5.8*	*2.8*	*-1.9*	*0.7*
Austria [2]	1.3	1.3	1.5	-0.1	1.2	1.0	2.8	2.1	2.2	5.3	3.5	-0.8
Belgium [2]	1.0	0.8	0.5	2.5	2.7	0.6	0.2	18.8	-7.1	4.3	-15.2	-1.7
France [2]	12.0	1.8	2.8	2.6	1.9	1.1	14.7	0.1	-12.4	8.2	4.3	-0.7
Germany [2]	7.0	0.8	1.2	1.8	-3.5	2.5	9.7	-13.8	-1.8	-3.6	-14.2	3.7
Liechtenstein [2]	0.0	0.1	3.0	3.4	-19.6	-2.3	8.8	-10.3	7.1	20.5	6.0	-5.4
Luxembourg [2]	0.0	0.2	0.5	1.4	3.1	-8.9	17.4	1.9	-10.7	-5.0	-1.9	3.2
Monaco	...	...	...	...	...	...	...	...	...	...	...	...
Netherlands [2]	4.0	1.9	9.1	5.3	1.9	1.4	4.6	2.1	2.2	0.5	-1.3	1.4
Switzerland [2]	1.3	0.6	0.7	-2.1	-1.0	-0.2	11.0	-9.4	0.9	-3.1	7.8	1.9
Oceania	**1.4**	**3.2**	**2.4**	**3.0**	**3.3**	**1.3**	**2.4**	**-4.9**	**6.9**	**-2.6**	**-5.3**	**-4.6**
Australia and New Zealand	*87.8*	*2.9*	*2.3*	*3.1*	*3.3*	*1.4*	*2.1*	*-5.3*	*7.6*	*-3.3*	*-6.6*	*-5.7*
Australia [2]	69.4	2.6	3.0	3.4	3.6	1.7	1.4	-7.4	9.6	-2.7	-10.1	-8.0
New Zealand [2]	18.4	4.9	0.1	2.0	2.1	0.0	5.3	3.5	0.2	-6.1	8.5	2.1
Melanesia	*11.1*	*13.9*	*3.0*	*2.0*	*4.1*	*1.5*	*4.4*	*-2.2*	*2.2*	*3.1*	*4.7*	*2.6*
Fiji [2]	0.9	10.0	3.1	2.4	0.4	-0.4	13.7	2.9	-10.8	8.3	6.4	1.3
New Caledonia	0.4	2.1	-2.7	-0.9	2.8	-2.4	5.3	7.3	12.3	10.7	8.4	8.8
Papua New Guinea [2]	8.8	18.3	2.7	2.1	4.8	1.6	3.4	-2.6	2.7	2.4	4.6	2.1
Solomon Islands	0.7	26.0	9.1	1.1	2.5	4.6	6.7	1.8	5.7	3.6	3.7	4.4
Vanuatu [2]	0.4	23.1	7.7	2.2	4.9	2.0	4.2	-15.8	5.1	0.4	0.9	5.6
Micronesia	*0.4*	*15.7*	*5.8*	*2.1*	*0.8*	*0.2*	*3.7*	*5.8*	*0.1*	*3.3*	*0.7*	*2.8*
Kiribati [1]	0.1	22.6	8.8	-0.5	1.4	-0.5	5.9	2.7	11.4	9.0	0.3	6.9
Marshall Islands	0.1	14.4	6.6	6.8	0.7	2.4	-1.5	0.5	-2.4	5.3	4.2	2.3
Micronesia (FS of)	0.2	27.8	6.6	4.1	1.7	0.3	5.6	9.5	-4.8	-0.9	0.1	1.8
Nauru [10]	0.0	2.4	1.1	-1.6	-14.9	-5.5	9.5	31.4	-4.8	-7.4	10.3	-1.2
Palau [2]	0.0	3.3	0.1	3.7	3.0	-1.0	-5.9	-3.7	7.7	10.8	-5.2	-5.6
Polynesia	*0.8*	*5.2*	*1.7*	*3.1*	*0.9*	*-3.5*	*2.0*	*-2.1*	*-4.8*	*2.3*	*-1.7*	*2.4*
Cook Islands [2]	0.0	3.2	-7.2	-3.6	6.0	-4.7	-1.4	-2.2	-3.1	3.2	-2.5	-3.0
French Polynesia	0.4	3.6	1.7	4.4	1.4	-3.8	2.5	-3.8	-11.5	2.1	2.8	2.3
Samoa [2,17]	0.2	8.9	3.7	0.3	-1.1	-3.4	0.7	1.9	7.1	7.1	-12.4	2.4
Tonga [18]	0.2	19.7	0.8	6.1	2.2	-2.8	2.5	-1.7	-1.3	-2.5	0.4	3.6
Tuvalu	0.0	21.4	-1.5	10.4	0.0	1.5	-0.5	-1.8	2.9	0.8	0.6	1.4

Notes for Table 6.A. Average Rates of Growth of Gross Domestic Product by Kind of Economic Activity - Agriculture, Hunting, Forestry and Fishing

1/ 1970-2019
At factor cost.

2/ 1970-2019
Excludes irrigation canals and landscaping care

3/ 2006-2019
Excludes irrigation canals and landscaping care

4/ 2010-2019
Excludes irrigation canals and landscaping care

5/ 1990-2019
Excludes irrigation canals and landscaping care

6/ 2015-2019
Excludes irrigation canals and landscaping care

7/ 1970-2019
Includes Mining and quarrying.

8/ 2005-2019
Includes Mining and quarrying.

9/ 1970-2009
Includes Mining and quarrying.

10/ 1970-2019
At producers' prices.

11/ 1970-2001
At producers' prices.

12/ 1970-2019
Includes Taxes less subsidies on production and imports.

13/ 1970-2019
Excludes hunting and forestry.

14/ 1970-2009
At producers' prices.

15/ 2016-2019
Excludes irrigation canals and landscaping care

16/ 2010-2019
The Government of Ukraine has advised the United Nations that it is not in a position to provide statistical data concerning the Autonomous Republic of Crimea and the city of Sevastopol.

17/ (a) 1970-2008
At producers' prices.

(b) 2009-2019
Includes Taxes less subsidies on production and imports.

18/ 1994-2019
Excludes irrigation canals and landscaping care

Table 6.B. Average Rates of Growth of Gross Domestic Product by Kind of Economic Activity - Mining, Manufacturing and Utilities

Major area, region and country	Base year weights as percentage of total for world or region in 2015	Base year share as percentage of total GDP in 2015	Average rates of growth				Annual rate of change (percentage)					
			1970-1979	1980-1989	1990-1999	2000-2009	2014	2015	2016	2017	2018	2019
World	**100.0**	**22.3**	**4.0**	**2.5**	**2.6**	**2.6**	**3.2**	**3.1**	**2.8**	**3.6**	**3.5**	**2.7**
Developed economies	**46.1**	**17.7**	**3.1**	**2.4**	**2.0**	**0.3**	**2.5**	**2.6**	**0.6**	**3.2**	**2.7**	**1.6**
Developing economies	**50.9**	**28.8**	**6.1**	**2.0**	**5.3**	**5.6**	**4.3**	**3.9**	**4.9**	**4.1**	**4.1**	**3.8**
Transition economies	**3.0**	**26.0**	**5.3**	**5.3**	**-6.7**	**3.8**	**-2.4**	**-1.5**	**2.5**	**2.0**	**3.1**	**2.3**
Africa	**3.1**	**22.8**	**5.5**	**-0.8**	**1.1**	**3.1**	**-1.8**	**-0.6**	**-0.8**	**3.3**	**3.3**	**1.9**
Northern Africa	*38.1*	*27.0*	*6.9*	*-1.7*	*2.2*	*3.4*	*-8.3*	*-3.5*	*0.6*	*3.1*	*4.7*	*1.2*
Algeria	8.1	25.7	3.9	2.3	1.9	0.9	0.1	1.0	6.9	-1.1	-4.4	-3.1
Egypt [1]	20.1	31.4	9.5	6.1	3.7	5.0	1.4	0.4	-1.0	0.8	5.7	1.6
Libya	1.9	65.6	7.3	-5.7	1.0	2.9	-53.1	-48.9	-22.8	60.8	31.3	7.0
Morocco	4.1	23.3	5.8	3.1	2.8	4.1	8.9	2.2	4.3	4.3	6.5	4.2
Sudan	2.1	12.6	...	...	...	...	-0.8	8.4	7.0	3.0	2.6	0.4
Sudan (Former)	...	...	2.9	3.0	10.6	...	...	...	...	...	...	...
Tunisia [1]	1.8	22.0	5.7	2.9	3.1	2.4	-0.9	-1.1	-0.7	-0.5	0.2	-1.1
Sub-Saharan Africa	61.9	20.8	3.9	0.0	0.0	2.9	2.9	1.3	-1.7	3.4	2.5	2.4
Eastern Africa	*8.2*	*14.2*	*3.9*	*2.2*	*2.0*	*6.4*	*6.0*	*4.0*	*5.1*	*6.0*	*6.1*	*3.2*
Burundi	0.1	12.7	5.8	4.7	-3.4	0.9	10.1	-3.5	2.0	8.8	2.5	4.5
Comoros	0.0	8.9	4.4	3.6	3.0	0.3	1.1	8.4	-5.3	-0.7	3.0	0.2
Djibouti	0.0	7.8	1.2	3.1	-1.7	4.8	18.9	10.1	7.4	11.3	10.0	7.0
Eritrea	0.1	15.5	...	...	12.5	-6.6	34.7	-18.9	9.7	-11.9	13.8	4.1
Ethiopia	0.7	5.9	...	...	0.2	6.9	13.0	12.1	16.5	19.5	6.9	6.6
Ethiopia (Former)	...	...	3.5	3.8	...	...	...	...	...	...	...	...
Kenya [2]	1.6	13.2	9.6	3.9	1.0	3.5	3.9	5.0	4.5	2.1	4.9	3.9
Madagascar	0.3	13.2	2.3	-1.6	1.7	2.2	7.0	6.7	4.8	5.8	2.0	6.8
Malawi [2]	0.2	13.2	6.4	3.5	0.9	7.0	5.0	3.5	1.1	2.0	3.5	5.2
Mauritius [3]	0.4	17.3	8.1	9.7	5.4	1.4	1.9	0.4	0.7	1.7	0.9	1.0
Mozambique [2]	0.5	18.3	3.8	-3.1	9.5	11.3	8.0	11.2	6.9	11.1	4.6	-1.1
Rwanda [2]	0.2	10.9	3.4	4.2	-0.7	5.9	-5.0	5.4	8.0	8.9	10.8	8.4
Seychelles [2]	0.0	10.3	9.8	4.4	24.5	-2.0	-5.0	8.9	-1.2	3.5	11.3	2.0
Somalia	0.0	3.2	3.5	-3.1	1.2	3.3	5.8	2.6	3.9	4.1	3.6	3.9
South Sudan	0.5	38.6	...	...	...	...	25.0	-13.2	-4.6	8.0	18.0	-4.3
U.R. of Tanzania: Mainland [2]	1.3	14.6	3.7	-1.3	6.0	8.1	8.8	7.2	9.5	6.8	6.0	9.5
Uganda [2]	0.7	14.2	-1.6	4.5	12.0	5.6	5.8	10.1	2.0	2.6	7.5	10.1
Zambia [4]	1.0	24.8	1.5	-0.8	-2.8	9.8	1.2	2.1	3.2	4.9	5.8	-2.4
Zanzibar [5]	0.0	10.9	...	...	6.1	3.7	7.6	10.3	8.7	9.5	0.8	19.5
Zimbabwe	0.8	22.6	1.8	3.2	0.2	-0.5	-3.4	-0.4	1.3	2.3	3.3	-6.5
Middle Africa	*15.0*	*32.6*	*1.4*	*2.5*	*-0.7*	*5.8*	*1.8*	*7.6*	*-0.8*	*-0.6*	*-1.0*	*1.9*
Angola	6.7	29.1	0.2	3.4	2.6	9.1	-5.0	12.1	0.3	-3.7	-6.6	3.5
Cameroon [2]	1.3	22.2	6.2	4.9	0.1	2.4	5.1	9.8	2.0	-0.7	1.9	5.1
Central African Republic	0.1	21.4	0.0	1.4	0.4	3.2	-14.8	11.9	3.2	1.6	1.2	2.0
Chad	0.7	28.3	-1.7	3.8	3.2	31.4	9.5	36.0	-15.3	-4.9	2.7	0.3
Congo	0.7	30.5	16.3	10.1	5.1	0.4	2.2	-9.9	-6.4	18.2	4.7	6.1
D.R. of the Congo	3.1	43.9	-1.0	1.4	-10.3	2.7	16.2	7.2	2.3	6.0	12.2	1.6
Equatorial Guinea	1.3	49.7	2.2	0.5	47.9	17.4	1.5	-9.2	-7.9	-5.2	-11.7	-8.6
Gabon	1.2	45.6	8.1	1.2	0.3	-4.6	3.3	3.2	0.4	-3.6	-5.6	-2.1
Sao Tome and Principe	0.0	8.8	7.0	-1.4	1.5	4.8	-2.9	4.7	8.8	3.4	1.8	1.0
Southern Africa	*15.7*	*25.1*	*1.5*	*1.3*	*0.6*	*1.0*	*-0.5*	*-0.1*	*-0.8*	*1.1*	*0.6*	*-1.3*
Botswana	0.7	25.9	21.2	16.5	2.1	-1.4	-1.4	-13.1	0.0	-4.9	6.3	-1.0
Eswatini [2]	0.3	34.3	10.0	14.2	2.7	2.9	1.3	-2.1	0.8	3.2	-0.2	1.3
Lesotho [2]	0.1	31.9	6.7	6.8	11.7	8.0	-4.3	3.7	7.3	-0.9	7.7	-0.1
Namibia [2]	0.5	24.0	3.1	0.7	2.1	3.9	-0.5	-1.5	2.6	2.9	7.8	-3.3
South Africa	14.1	25.0	1.3	0.9	0.4	1.0	-0.5	0.7	-1.1	1.4	0.0	-1.3
Western Africa	*23.0*	*17.4*	*7.3*	*-2.4*	*-0.5*	*1.9*	*4.8*	*-2.3*	*-5.3*	*6.8*	*4.5*	*4.8*
Benin [6]	0.3	12.8	1.1	19.2	9.3	-1.0	8.7	3.3	1.0	-0.2	4.0	12.0
Burkina Faso [2]	0.5	23.1	1.5	-1.1	2.2	7.5	12.5	2.8	4.0	7.7	3.8	2.5
Cabo Verde [2]	0.0	11.7	0.4	7.9	6.9	1.9	5.8	10.5	0.3	6.6	12.2	4.5
Côte d'Ivoire	1.4	16.2	8.3	-3.9	5.7	3.1	0.2	9.0	5.3	26.6	7.4	7.2
Gambia [2]	0.0	9.4	-5.0	4.6	2.2	3.9	8.4	3.0	-3.8	-6.5	3.5	6.6
Ghana [2]	2.3	25.3	-2.1	0.6	-1.5	3.8	1.7	-1.6	2.9	19.7	13.7	9.6
Guinea	0.4	22.7	3.0	2.7	4.2	1.1	8.8	-4.2	26.3	17.4	11.3	26.5
Guinea-Bissau	0.0	11.9	2.8	0.5	1.4	1.3	2.2	8.8	5.5	4.5	5.3	7.4
Liberia	0.0	8.4	0.7	-3.3	-45.7	35.9	5.1	-3.2	-0.4	6.0	1.4	-10.2
Mali	0.4	14.7	-0.3	4.6	14.6	8.2	-1.8	-3.9	2.4	20.4	18.4	11.2
Mauritania [2]	0.2	18.7	-2.1	5.8	4.9	1.6	-0.3	3.3	-4.7	6.8	-5.7	6.6
Niger [2]	0.4	19.6	12.6	0.7	-1.9	2.8	-0.5	-3.4	-3.7	6.2	3.2	9.5
Nigeria [2]	16.3	16.7	8.7	-3.0	-1.2	1.4	5.7	-3.4	-9.4	2.4	1.8	2.3
Senegal [2]	0.8	23.9	3.7	5.0	2.2	2.8	1.2	9.1	3.3	6.0	7.0	4.1
Sierra Leone	0.0	3.5	-4.4	-0.5	-8.6	4.6	14.9	-81.7	33.8	-7.9	-1.4	12.5
Togo	0.2	17.9	5.5	1.3	0.4	1.3	8.4	21.9	21.3	2.6	3.6	5.6

Table 6.B. Average Rates of Growth of Gross Domestic Product by Kind of Economic Activity - Mining, Manufacturing and Utilities

Major area, region and country	Base year weights as percentage of total for world or region in 2015	Base year share as percentage of total GDP in 2015	Average rates of growth				Annual rate of change (percentage)					
			1970-1979	1980-1989	1990-1999	2000-2009	2014	2015	2016	2017	2018	2019
Americas	**25.4**	**16.5**	**3.2**	**2.2**	**3.0**	**1.1**	**1.8**	**1.3**	**0.0**	**1.2**	**2.4**	**1.8**
Latin America and the Caribbean	**6.6**	**21.5**	**5.6**	**1.4**	**3.0**	**1.5**	**-0.5**	**-1.0**	**2.6**	**-2.1**	**-2.0**	**-1.7**
Caribbean	*2.3*	*27.7*	*5.3*	*2.8*	*3.1*	*1.4*	*1.6*	*1.8*	*-0.9*	*-2.2*	*-2.6*	*1.5*
Anguilla	0.0	7.1	3.9	6.5	9.8	8.1	6.4	2.3	2.5	-16.3	7.9	10.9
Antigua and Barbuda	0.0	8.7	1.8	8.6	2.1	4.5	0.9	1.4	4.0	1.8	8.0	3.9
Aruba [2]	0.0	8.7	9.1	11.2	7.1	-0.2	-1.0	29.7	2.4	0.0	2.1	-0.8
Bahamas [2]	0.0	6.2	2.4	3.4	3.4	1.3	26.4	20.6	-1.2	-11.9	-9.2	-3.5
Barbados [2]	0.0	9.1	6.6	0.2	0.9	-1.8	-1.8	3.8	-1.3	1.6	0.4	-4.3
British Virgin Islands [2]	0.0	4.3	2.2	13.5	19.4	0.3	6.8	3.2	5.9	-15.8	1.1	0.6
Cayman Islands [2]	0.0	3.6	9.4	10.1	6.7	2.3	2.0	-1.5	5.0	2.7	3.4	2.3
Cuba	0.4	17.1	5.4	4.7	-1.1	2.7	-3.1	5.8	-4.6	-0.9	-0.8	-0.8
Curaçao	0.0	13.8	...	...	...	...	11.9	-1.5	-4.2	-2.3	-11.9	3.9
Dominica	0.0	10.8	4.7	7.1	3.1	0.4	-1.2	-1.0	-2.9	-19.0	-10.9	18.7
Dominican Republic [2]	0.3	19.6	9.6	2.5	6.2	1.3	9.5	0.7	7.7	1.3	4.4	3.1
Former Netherlands Antilles	...	...	8.0	-1.0	0.5	0.6	...	...	...	...	...	...
Grenada	0.0	8.1	6.0	9.6	6.6	1.2	1.0	4.0	3.9	1.9	7.1	4.8
Haiti	0.0	9.3	7.0	-3.7	-5.8	0.7	7.2	-0.2	1.6	1.1	1.1	0.8
Jamaica	0.0	14.5	-0.4	2.3	-1.2	-1.6	-0.6	1.7	1.4	0.7	5.5	-0.8
Montserrat	0.0	6.5	4.8	1.5	-17.4	4.5	2.3	14.1	10.4	6.3	12.8	6.8
Puerto Rico [7]	1.3	50.1	5.4	3.2	4.0	0.4	1.4	1.0	-1.0	-3.9	-5.6	2.5
Saint Kitts and Nevis	0.0	9.0	5.0	1.7	3.7	2.6	2.0	0.5	-8.2	-1.7	7.8	2.4
Saint Lucia [2]	0.0	7.4	6.6	8.7	3.6	2.6	1.4	1.2	2.5	1.9	3.6	5.0
Sint Maarten (Dutch part)	0.0	4.4	...	...	...	...	-1.3	-15.1	-7.7	5.8	-14.4	4.8
St. Vincent and the Grenadines	0.0	10.1	5.0	6.2	2.3	1.4	3.5	2.3	0.1	1.0	3.4	-9.0
Trinidad and Tobago [2]	0.2	33.8	4.2	-2.6	3.8	9.0	-1.9	-0.5	-7.6	-0.4	-1.8	-2.4
Turks and Caicos Islands	0.0	5.9	10.7	10.7	9.1	3.5	6.5	2.9	3.8	-6.4	2.8	3.7
Central America	*7.5*	*23.0*	*7.2*	*2.1*	*3.4*	*-0.2*	*2.8*	*1.0*	*0.3*	*0.3*	*0.7*	*0.0*
Belize	0.0	12.5	6.0	2.5	2.9	7.8	-3.7	-7.3	-1.1	2.9	0.0	-10.0
Costa Rica [2]	0.2	15.8	8.1	2.4	4.4	1.3	1.2	-2.5	4.6	3.2	2.1	1.8
El Salvador [2]	0.1	22.3	2.9	1.3	6.1	0.8	1.6	0.2	0.3	3.1	3.2	1.1
Guatemala [2]	0.3	19.0	6.8	-0.4	4.1	2.3	7.1	3.2	1.9	0.3	0.8	2.7
Honduras	0.1	21.2	7.6	3.6	4.0	3.7	2.8	4.4	3.4	4.0	4.1	2.1
Mexico [2]	6.6	24.2	7.5	2.2	3.2	-0.4	2.6	0.9	-0.1	-0.1	0.5	-0.4
Nicaragua	0.1	21.9	-2.7	-2.5	3.8	3.5	7.5	2.2	3.7	1.1	1.1	1.1
Panama	0.1	10.4	4.0	0.5	4.4	2.6	6.9	6.7	5.3	5.2	1.7	7.8
South America	*16.3*	*20.2*	*5.1*	*0.9*	*2.8*	*2.3*	*-2.1*	*-2.2*	*4.2*	*-3.1*	*-3.1*	*-3.0*
Argentina	3.0	22.1	2.4	-1.5	4.9	2.5	-3.7	1.2	-5.1	1.4	-3.8	-4.9
Bolivia (Plurinational State of)	0.2	27.3	4.9	-1.3	3.6	5.0	4.9	2.3	3.5	1.9	2.1	-0.1
Brazil [2]	6.4	16.8	9.3	1.2	1.7	2.2	-3.0	-5.7	-2.7	2.4	-0.8	0.9
Chile [2]	1.4	25.4	2.0	3.3	6.5	1.1	1.1	0.0	-1.2	0.4	5.4	-0.8
Colombia [2]	1.5	23.5	5.8	5.1	2.0	3.0	1.7	0.7	1.1	-2.2	0.9	1.9
Ecuador [2]	0.5	22.3	12.9	4.2	1.7	3.9	3.2	-0.4	0.2	1.7	-1.6	1.9
Guyana [3]	0.0	18.2	-2.7	-9.2	7.1	-4.0	-7.1	7.1	26.5	-5.0	3.0	11.4
Paraguay [2,8]	0.3	30.8	8.0	2.3	1.2	4.9	2.6	4.3	6.4	3.5	3.7	-4.3
Peru [2,9]	1.1	25.6	5.4	-2.3	3.9	5.4	-0.9	3.4	5.8	2.0	2.4	-0.6
Suriname	0.0	17.9	2.6	-2.5	-2.1	4.6	-7.1	-3.0	2.1	25.0	3.4	-3.9
Uruguay	0.2	17.5	3.4	-0.6	0.6	2.7	5.5	2.8	2.2	-3.0	1.8	0.0
Venezuela (Bolivarian Republic of)	1.8	22.7	0.4	0.8	2.4	0.5	-5.5	-4.7	51.5	-27.4	-25.0	-28.1
Northern America	**18.8**	**15.2**	**2.5**	**2.5**	**3.1**	**1.0**	**2.7**	**2.2**	**-1.0**	**2.4**	**4.0**	**3.0**
Bermuda [2,10]	0.0	2.1	3.5	1.0	3.0	-2.1	-2.9	-3.9	-16.7	3.2	5.1	-3.1
Canada [2]	6.4	17.8	3.2	2.3	3.0	-1.3	4.9	-0.7	-0.2	4.7	4.0	-0.3
Greenland [2]	0.0	8.1	6.4	2.5	1.3	-0.2	34.1	-7.8	12.3	-35.6	42.5	2.4
United States [2,11]	67.5	15.0	2.4	2.5	3.1	1.2	2.4	2.4	-1.0	2.2	4.0	3.4
Asia	**48.5**	**29.7**	**5.7**	**3.8**	**4.8**	**5.5**	**5.2**	**4.7**	**4.8**	**5.1**	**4.6**	**4.3**
Central Asia	*1.0*	*26.8*	...	...	*-3.5*	*7.2*	*2.5*	*0.2*	*3.8*	*7.3*	*5.6*	*4.9*
Kazakhstan [5]	0.6	26.2	...	...	-2.7	7.4	0.8	-1.5	-0.5	7.8	4.4	4.1
Kyrgyzstan [5]	0.0	18.3	...	...	-7.8	-0.4	-1.1	-3.9	5.2	9.3	5.1	6.9
Tajikistan	0.0	15.0	...	...	-12.2	1.5	7.9	11.8	23.1	46.3	-7.4	18.6
Turkmenistan	0.2	48.1	...	...	-1.1	12.1	5.5	0.0	12.5	4.7	5.4	4.1
Uzbekistan [5]	0.2	20.0	...	...	-3.8	4.8	4.8	5.3	5.5	5.8	11.1	6.6
Eastern Asia	*70.1*	*30.8*	*5.6*	*5.7*	*5.3*	*6.4*	*5.7*	*4.6*	*4.2*	*5.7*	*4.9*	*4.6*
China [11]	48.7	34.1	8.9	10.2	14.3	11.3	6.7	5.7	5.7	6.2	6.1	5.7
China, Hong Kong SAR [10,12]	0.1	2.6	8.7	5.5	-5.0	-1.4	0.3	-2.1	-0.7	0.7	0.6	0.0
China, Macao SAR	0.0	1.7	7.9	6.8	-4.3	-10.9	17.4	12.3	0.1	12.8	-5.7	2.1
D.P.R. of Korea	0.1	37.2	7.6	2.7	-6.5	1.5	0.6	-4.4	8.1	-7.7	-9.7	-1.5
Japan [2,7]	13.3	23.6	4.5	4.1	0.6	-0.4	2.8	2.9	-0.3	4.9	1.8	2.4

Table 6.B. Average Rates of Growth of Gross Domestic Product by Kind of Economic Activity - Mining, Manufacturing and Utilities

Major area, region and country	Base year weights as percentage of total for world or region in 2015	Base year share as percentage of total GDP in 2015	Average rates of growth				Annual rate of change (percentage)					
			1970-1979	1980-1989	1990-1999	2000-2009	2014	2015	2016	2017	2018	2019
Mongolia [2]	0.0	29.2	5.7	7.0	0.4	6.1	15.2	11.2	0.1	-0.4	8.2	2.5
Republic of Korea [2]	5.5	31.9	15.2	11.6	8.5	5.4	3.1	1.7	2.0	3.9	2.8	1.5
South-Eastern Asia	*9.2*	*29.6*	*8.7*	*5.1*	*6.0*	*3.8*	*3.7*	*2.8*	*4.0*	*4.7*	*4.4*	*3.3*
Brunei Darussalam [2]	0.1	57.8	9.6	-5.2	2.8	-1.3	-3.5	-0.2	-2.8	1.2	-0.6	3.4
Cambodia	0.0	19.0	-7.3	6.5	12.2	9.1	7.4	9.7	7.1	7.6	9.6	7.6
Indonesia [2]	3.3	30.8	9.3	5.6	5.6	3.2	3.4	2.0	3.4	3.2	3.8	3.2
Lao People's DR [2]	0.0	24.7	2.9	5.6	12.6	12.3	6.5	4.2	12.9	10.2	4.2	7.5
Malaysia [2,7]	1.3	34.2	8.0	7.0	7.3	2.1	5.2	4.8	3.9	4.4	3.2	2.6
Myanmar [7]	0.2	28.0	3.3	1.0	11.0	19.6	10.1	6.9	8.5	8.4	8.3	8.5
Philippines [2,11]	0.9	24.1	6.9	1.1	2.6	3.3	7.9	5.4	7.2	7.5	4.9	4.2
Singapore [2,10]	0.8	20.6	10.8	6.7	6.5	3.4	2.7	-4.7	3.6	9.7	6.5	-1.3
Thailand [2,7]	1.7	33.4	10.8	9.8	6.5	5.0	0.2	1.9	2.3	2.3	3.0	2.0
Timor-Leste [5]	0.0	1.1	...	...	-13.1	-6.9	7.6	31.2	14.9	33.6	1.0	951.4
Viet Nam [2,13]	0.7	30.9	4.7	5.7	13.4	7.2	6.3	9.4	7.1	7.8	8.8	8.9
Southern Asia	*8.3*	*22.0*	*-0.1*	*7.8*	*4.2*	*5.9*	*7.3*	*9.2*	*11.9*	*6.1*	*5.8*	*8.5*
Afghanistan [14]	0.0	6.9	4.8	0.5	-8.9	2.6	-2.7	-1.9	3.1	11.0	27.3	-5.5
Bangladesh	0.5	20.4	2.1	2.4	6.9	7.7	8.2	10.0	11.9	10.7	12.7	13.4
Bhutan	0.0	27.7	5.0	34.3	4.7	13.6	2.4	7.0	3.5	0.5	-2.9	1.9
India [2]	5.6	22.1	4.6	7.9	5.6	7.2	8.1	11.9	8.4	6.8	4.5	8.0
Iran (Islamic Republic of)	1.4	27.0	-2.7	8.6	1.8	3.0	6.4	1.7	30.9	3.2	8.8	11.5
Maldives [2]	0.0	4.0	7.2	11.4	9.4	4.9	2.5	5.7	14.4	11.3	7.9	4.5
Nepal	0.0	7.8	3.7	8.0	9.6	2.0	5.8	0.6	-7.7	12.4	9.3	7.6
Pakistan [2]	0.6	18.0	5.0	8.7	4.4	6.2	4.3	4.9	4.6	3.9	4.4	2.8
Sri Lanka [2]	0.2	21.1	6.0	4.9	7.3	4.4	2.6	4.0	4.8	4.8	2.6	2.2
Western Asia	*11.4*	*31.0*	*8.0*	*-2.3*	*3.3*	*2.1*	*2.0*	*4.0*	*4.1*	*0.2*	*1.7*	*-0.2*
Armenia [5]	0.0	17.9	...	...	-10.7	5.3	-1.1	5.2	8.0	12.4	4.8	8.3
Azerbaijan [5]	0.2	35.9	...	...	-10.9	20.0	-2.1	1.0	0.5	-4.3	1.0	1.7
Bahrain [7]	0.1	33.2	7.7	-5.1	6.3	1.0	4.5	1.5	2.3	-0.7	0.1	4.5
Cyprus [2]	0.0	7.6	5.0	4.7	1.4	1.0	-1.5	9.0	12.9	2.2	4.7	2.3
Georgia [5]	0.0	13.9	...	...	-13.8	5.5	2.2	-5.9	4.5	3.6	3.4	2.3
Iraq	0.8	38.6	11.3	-2.0	5.1	-0.7	3.5	19.1	23.7	-3.8	-1.5	4.0
Israel [2]	0.6	16.6	2.2	4.3	4.7	1.0	2.3	0.5	-3.2	2.5	2.3	0.6
Jordan [2]	0.1	24.7	5.9	4.8	6.7	8.0	3.8	2.9	0.8	2.1	1.4	1.7
Kuwait	0.8	46.2	-1.3	0.6	5.6	1.7	-0.5	-1.6	3.9	-6.8	0.1	-1.6
Lebanon [2]	0.1	11.7	-3.0	-4.4	9.4	4.6	-4.1	-4.0	-2.5	-2.4	-1.8	-2.0
Oman	0.4	43.2	11.3	9.9	3.3	0.6	-1.3	4.6	3.8	-1.5	3.6	2.0
Qatar [2,7]	1.0	45.5	6.6	-0.3	8.2	8.7	0.2	0.3	-0.6	-0.4	0.7	-1.7
Saudi Arabia [2]	3.3	38.7	10.6	-5.9	2.2	1.4	2.8	5.1	2.9	-2.3	3.2	-3.2
State of Palestine [2]	0.0	13.6	8.0	2.2	5.1	4.3	-6.5	-5.3	12.3	14.5	-1.8	-0.2
Syrian Arab Republic [11]	0.1	26.6	4.8	5.9	10.7	1.6	-0.6	-4.7	-2.4	2.9	8.9	10.3
Turkey [2]	2.2	22.4	6.8	6.9	3.8	3.3	5.2	5.1	4.5	9.3	1.4	-0.7
United Arab Emirates	1.6	34.2	12.3	-5.9	1.7	1.0	1.3	6.0	3.2	-0.8	1.6	3.1
Yemen	0.1	15.8	...	...	9.8	-2.5	-12.6	-55.6	-11.3	-13.1	1.3	1.6
Yemen Arab Republic (Former)	...	...	13.9	11.5	...	...	...	...	...	...	...	...
Yemen Democratic (Former)	...	...	-2.0	3.5	...	...	...	...	...	...	...	...
Europe	**21.6**	**20.0**	**3.6**	**2.5**	**0.4**	**0.2**	**1.4**	**2.5**	**2.5**	**3.1**	**1.9**	**0.1**
Eastern Europe	*17.9*	*26.5*	*5.8*	*4.1*	*-4.7*	*3.3*	*-0.1*	*0.7*	*2.8*	*2.5*	*3.4*	*3.7*
Belarus [5]	0.4	28.7	...	...	-1.4	7.7	1.7	-6.1	-0.6	6.0	5.2	0.9
Bulgaria [2]	0.3	23.1	7.4	6.1	-4.4	4.2	4.3	3.7	6.6	3.5	-1.2	1.8
Czechia [5]	1.6	31.9	...	...	-2.5	4.2	2.9	5.3	3.0	7.6	1.6	2.3
Czechoslovakia (Former)	...	...	5.3	0.6	...	...	...	...	...	...	...	...
Hungary [2]	0.8	27.1	6.5	1.6	1.9	1.3	6.3	7.9	1.8	2.4	3.0	39.2
Poland [2]	3.2	26.0	6.0	2.2	7.1	4.4	4.6	3.8	4.2	2.4	5.6	4.4
Republic of Moldova [5]	0.0	17.8	...	...	-13.0	0.7	8.0	3.3	2.8	3.2	4.4	3.0
Romania [2]	1.2	27.4	11.3	-1.7	-2.5	5.3	4.7	4.9	5.3	8.8	4.7	-2.6
Russian Federation	9.3	26.1	...	...	-6.8	2.7	-3.3	-1.4	2.3	0.9	2.6	1.9
Slovakia [5]	0.6	26.1	...	...	-5.8	5.6	16.0	8.0	-0.9	0.6	8.6	1.2
Ukraine [5,15]	0.5	23.3	...	...	-10.5	2.9	-10.9	-14.6	1.6	-0.5	1.7	-0.5
USSR (Former)	...	...	5.2	5.4	...	...	...	...	...	...	...	...
Northern Europe	*22.3*	*18.1*	*2.5*	*2.8*	*2.5*	*-0.8*	*1.8*	*7.7*	*0.9*	*2.9*	*2.0*	*-0.1*
Denmark [2]	1.4	18.1	2.5	3.6	2.6	-1.7	0.1	-0.6	5.0	5.7	1.8	3.7
Estonia [5]	0.1	21.2	...	...	-3.8	2.5	5.5	0.2	4.5	7.4	6.8	-3.0
Finland [2]	1.2	20.5	4.1	3.7	4.5	1.2	-0.3	-0.2	3.6	8.7	-2.0	3.7
Iceland [2]	0.1	17.0	6.8	1.2	2.1	2.4	2.8	3.3	-0.9	-0.4	3.1	1.4
Ireland [2]	3.1	39.3	5.6	4.9	10.9	1.5	10.1	82.8	-1.6	3.5	10.9	3.3
Latvia [5]	0.1	15.7	...	...	-8.5	1.5	-4.5	7.3	3.8	4.7	0.1	1.2
Lithuania [5]	0.2	22.2	...	...	-8.6	5.2	3.7	1.8	3.5	5.2	3.0	3.6
Norway [2]	2.8	28.5	7.2	4.7	4.9	-0.7	1.6	1.4	-0.2	3.5	-2.1	-2.5
Sweden [2]	2.4	18.7	1.7	2.4	4.7	-0.3	-0.1	4.7	1.4	1.7	2.4	-1.4
United Kingdom [2]	10.8	14.2	1.9	2.4	1.3	-1.4	1.5	0.3	0.9	1.7	1.0	-1.2

Table 6.B. Average Rates of Growth of Gross Domestic Product by Kind of Economic Activity - Mining, Manufacturing and Utilities

Major area, region and country	Base year weights as percentage of total for world or region in 2015	Base year share as percentage of total GDP in 2015	Average rates of growth				Annual rate of change (percentage)					
			1970-1979	1980-1989	1990-1999	2000-2009	2014	2015	2016	2017	2018	2019
Southern Europe	*16.9*	*17.9*	*5.3*	*2.5*	*1.2*	*-0.7*	*-0.1*	*1.8*	*3.3*	*3.6*	*1.7*	*0.3*
Albania [2]	0.0	14.6	4.0	2.3	-10.5	3.5	-0.2	1.8	1.5	-1.4	16.4	-3.0
Andorra [2]	0.0	5.4	3.8	2.8	1.7	2.3	0.3	-0.2	5.4	0.0	2.0	1.7
Bosnia and Herzegovina [5]	0.1	21.9	...	...	12.0	5.3	0.6	3.8	5.2	5.4	4.0	-2.0
Croatia [5]	0.2	20.8	...	...	-4.0	1.2	3.0	2.3	5.7	1.6	-0.5	0.9
Greece [2]	0.7	14.2	7.3	1.4	1.6	1.1	-4.2	-1.4	0.5	3.7	0.4	0.9
Italy [2]	9.0	18.9	5.1	2.4	1.0	-1.7	-0.8	1.3	3.2	3.4	2.1	-0.7
Kosovo [5]	0.0	20.8	...	...	-10.3	8.2	0.1	5.8	1.8	2.9	2.4	5.2
Malta [2]	0.0	9.4	15.9	2.0	3.0	-3.9	-1.2	-2.7	1.4	7.2	8.7	2.1
Montenegro [5]	0.0	12.8	...	...	-4.7	-3.4	-0.8	1.0	-2.9	-0.1	17.7	-1.2
North Macedonia [5]	0.0	19.3	...	...	-4.5	2.6	11.5	4.9	-3.0	1.4	4.1	3.1
Portugal [2]	0.9	18.3	5.4	3.5	2.6	-0.5	2.3	2.5	1.1	3.9	4.5	-0.8
San Marino [2]	0.0	30.7	3.8	2.4	6.1	-3.1	-2.9	0.2	3.1	0.8	13.8	-0.8
Serbia [5]	0.3	26.4	...	...	-7.0	2.3	-7.9	4.5	2.1	2.6	0.9	0.4
Slovenia [5]	0.3	27.0	...	...	-0.3	2.6	3.9	1.7	5.1	7.0	2.8	6.0
Spain [2]	5.1	16.4	5.1	2.2	2.3	0.3	1.3	2.9	4.1	3.7	0.6	1.7
Yugoslavia (Former)	...	...	6.0	4.2	...	...	...	...	...	...	...	...
Western Europe	*42.9*	*20.0*	*2.5*	*1.4*	*1.0*	*0.0*	*2.5*	*1.0*	*2.8*	*3.3*	*1.4*	*-1.5*
Austria [2]	2.2	22.0	3.8	1.9	2.4	0.9	0.7	0.7	3.9	4.0	4.9	1.0
Belgium [2]	2.0	16.8	4.5	2.7	1.9	0.1	3.3	2.6	-1.1	1.0	-1.6	2.2
France [2]	9.0	14.3	3.9	1.3	2.2	0.0	0.4	0.4	0.3	1.1	0.6	0.1
Germany [2]	22.4	25.5	2.1	1.3	0.0	-0.4	4.6	1.6	4.5	3.9	0.6	-3.6
Liechtenstein [2]	0.1	39.1	2.9	2.7	11.1	2.0	0.5	-0.5	3.0	8.0	-3.9	4.4
Luxembourg [2]	0.1	6.7	0.7	4.1	3.1	-3.7	-6.3	12.1	12.1	-0.4	3.0	1.3
Monaco [7]	0.0	4.9	3.9	2.4	1.9	-0.9	-18.7	8.9	-16.8	-0.1	-6.0	-10.0
Netherlands [2]	3.2	16.0	3.1	1.2	2.0	0.4	-0.3	-1.1	0.6	3.1	1.9	-0.1
Switzerland [2]	4.0	20.1	0.8	0.8	1.4	1.1	-0.1	-0.3	2.6	5.0	6.1	2.6
Oceania	**1.3**	**15.7**	**3.0**	**3.1**	**2.5**	**1.6**	**4.0**	**3.2**	**0.9**	**3.4**	**2.1**	**2.8**
Australia and New Zealand	*96.2*	*15.6*	*3.0*	*3.1*	*2.4*	*1.7*	*3.2*	*2.5*	*0.5*	*3.3*	*2.4*	*2.1*
Australia [2]	83.6	15.5	3.0	3.4	2.5	1.8	3.3	2.6	0.6	3.5	2.5	1.9
New Zealand [2]	12.6	16.6	3.2	1.7	1.8	0.8	2.2	2.2	0.4	2.1	1.9	3.5
Melanesia	*3.5*	*22.0*	*1.3*	*2.4*	*7.4*	*-0.2*	*42.8*	*25.1*	*11.8*	*6.4*	*-6.3*	*20.5*
Fiji [2]	0.3	16.3	4.5	2.0	4.2	1.1	12.3	7.4	6.7	3.2	3.9	5.6
New Caledonia	0.4	11.6	-2.0	7.7	-2.3	-0.7	25.6	-16.6	0.6	-1.5	2.7	3.4
Papua New Guinea [2]	2.7	28.2	2.7	-1.7	11.9	-0.4	58.4	40.0	14.3	7.8	-8.6	24.8
Solomon Islands	0.1	9.9	9.0	3.7	15.0	4.1	-18.0	-8.8	2.9	13.1	3.8	8.8
Vanuatu [2]	0.0	5.6	7.7	9.6	1.0	0.4	-0.3	-3.8	7.1	3.1	2.5	3.5
Micronesia	*0.0*	*7.9*	*3.5*	*-2.3*	*0.0*	*-0.2*	*-2.4*	*27.9*	*-4.5*	*-3.4*	*21.8*	*9.8*
Kiribati [1]	0.0	5.5	5.8	-0.4	-0.9	1.3	-0.5	4.4	3.6	0.7	2.5	2.4
Marshall Islands	0.0	5.2	6.6	6.6	9.8	3.0	-11.5	-4.2	16.7	9.8	88.4	36.2
Micronesia (FS of)	0.0	3.7	6.6	4.1	2.1	-5.3	-4.4	1.8	13.3	3.9	1.7	3.5
Nauru	0.0	37.9	-1.2	-5.3	-5.1	3.1	1.9	60.9	-13.8	-6.4	13.6	-3.4
Palau [2]	0.0	3.9	0.1	4.0	7.6	-2.3	-1.3	27.8	-15.1	-24.2	6.7	13.6
Polynesia	*0.3*	*8.8*	*2.4*	*4.2*	*0.0*	*-0.3*	*0.6*	*4.5*	*4.1*	*0.3*	*0.7*	*2.8*
Cook Islands [2]	0.0	4.7	-9.7	-10.9	2.1	2.0	-2.6	-3.7	10.4	9.6	12.0	1.4
French Polynesia	0.2	8.6	4.0	6.1	-0.2	-0.4	0.4	6.2	3.6	1.4	3.5	2.1
Samoa [2, 16]	0.0	10.8	3.7	0.3	1.2	-0.5	1.3	-1.5	4.9	-8.3	-15.7	10.4
Tonga [17]	0.0	10.9	4.3	1.4	-0.3	0.0	1.8	2.4	6.3	3.8	0.4	-2.0
Tuvalu	0.0	1.9	-1.5	7.8	5.6	4.1	4.2	8.4	-1.4	-4.1	0.8	-1.6

Notes for Table 6.B. Average Rates of Growth of Gross Domestic Product by Kind of Economic Activity - Mining, Manufacturing and Utilities

1/ 1970-2019
At factor cost.

2/ 1970-2019
Excludes publishing activities, includes irrigation canals

3/ 2006-2019
Excludes publishing activities, includes irrigation canals

4/ 2010-2019
Excludes publishing activities, includes irrigation canals

5/ 1990-2019
Excludes publishing activities, includes irrigation canals

6/ 2015-2019
Excludes publishing activities, includes irrigation canals

7/ 1970-2019
At producers' prices.

8/ 1970-2001
Does not incorporate value added generated by binational hydroelectric plants.

9/ 1970-2001
At producers' prices.

10/ 1970-2019
Excludes mining and quarrying.

11/ 1970-2019
Includes Taxes less subsidies on production and imports.

12/ 1970-2019
Includes waste management.

13/ 1970-2009
At producers' prices.

14/ 2016-2019
Excludes publishing activities, includes irrigation canals

15/ 2010-2019
The Government of Ukraine has advised the United Nations that it is not in a position to provide statistical data concerning the Autonomous Republic of Crimea and the city of Sevastopol.

16/ (a) 1970-2008
At producers' prices.

(b) 2009-2019
Includes Taxes less subsidies on production and imports.

17/ 1994-2019
Excludes publishing activities, includes irrigation canals

Table 6.C. Average Rates of Growth of Gross Domestic Product by Kind of Economic Activity - Manufacturing

Major area, region and country	Base year weights as percentage of total for world or region in 2015	Base year share as percentage of total GDP in 2015	Average rates of growth				Annual rate of change (percentage)					
			1970-1979	1980-1989	1990-1999	2000-2009	2014	2015	2016	2017	2018	2019
World	**100.0**	**17.1**	**3.8**	**2.9**	**2.1**	**4.0**	**3.6**	**3.4**	**2.4**	**4.3**	**3.8**	**2.6**
Developed economies	**47.7**	**14.1**	**3.2**	**2.6**	**2.0**	**0.2**	**2.5**	**2.8**	**0.7**	**3.4**	**2.8**	**1.0**
Developing economies	**50.2**	**21.7**	**6.6**	**3.3**	**3.9**	**11.5**	**5.0**	**4.3**	**4.1**	**5.3**	**4.8**	**3.9**
Transition economies	**2.2**	**14.3**	**5.3**	**5.4**	**-6.9**	**3.6**	**-2.1**	**-1.7**	**3.6**	**2.8**	**2.5**	**2.8**
Africa	**2.0**	**11.2**	**4.9**	**1.3**	**0.5**	**3.4**	**4.5**	**2.4**	**1.7**	**3.2**	**4.2**	**2.4**
Northern Africa	*36.1*	*12.6*	*5.6*	*5.8*	*4.3*	*4.3*	*3.8*	*3.5*	*1.6*	*2.5*	*4.7*	*2.8*
Algeria	3.0	4.6	8.7	4.4	-1.9	4.0	3.1	4.6	3.6	4.4	3.6	3.7
Egypt [1]	21.5	16.5	3.2	7.4	6.1	4.6	4.8	3.1	0.8	2.1	4.8	3.1
Libya	0.2	3.7	11.0	6.0	2.6	4.4	-53.0	-50.1	-24.6	64.1	32.4	6.6
Morocco	6.6	18.2	5.7	3.5	2.6	3.2	13.1	7.6	2.2	2.0	6.1	3.4
Sudan	2.2	6.5	...	...	...	...	-0.6	10.2	8.2	3.4	2.8	0.4
Sudan (Former)	...	...	2.8	2.6	6.7	...	...	...	...	...	...	...
Tunisia [1]	2.7	16.2	12.0	6.4	5.7	3.1	0.9	0.0	0.6	1.2	1.2	-1.0
Sub-Saharan Africa	63.9	10.5	4.8	0.1	-1.2	2.9	4.8	1.8	1.7	3.5	3.9	2.1
Eastern Africa	*10.0*	*8.5*	*5.0*	*3.0*	*2.4*	*4.0*	*4.5*	*6.0*	*5.4*	*5.8*	*4.8*	*4.1*
Burundi	0.1	11.6	5.8	4.7	-3.4	1.0	11.4	-3.3	2.0	7.5	2.1	3.8
Comoros	0.0	7.5	4.4	4.4	2.1	0.7	-0.9	14.6	-3.4	-0.7	3.8	2.3
Djibouti	0.0	2.9	1.4	0.2	-2.4	4.9	49.8	4.3	7.6	14.8	9.7	6.9
Eritrea	0.0	6.0	...	...	11.8	-8.1	34.5	-18.9	9.7	-11.9	13.8	4.1
Ethiopia	1.1	4.7	...	...	-0.4	7.0	16.6	18.2	18.4	24.7	6.8	7.7
Ethiopia (Former)	...	...	3.5	3.5	...	...	...	...	...	...	...	...
Kenya [2]	2.4	10.0	10.6	4.7	1.3	3.0	2.5	3.6	3.1	0.7	4.3	3.2
Madagascar	0.4	8.9	2.3	-1.6	2.0	2.7	2.5	2.8	5.6	4.3	4.8	4.6
Malawi [2]	0.2	10.8	6.2	3.4	0.5	7.7	6.3	3.8	1.3	2.0	3.5	5.2
Mauritius [3]	0.6	14.7	8.1	9.9	5.2	1.0	1.8	0.1	0.3	1.5	0.7	0.7
Mozambique [2]	0.5	9.3	3.8	-3.1	7.3	9.1	4.6	7.6	3.6	2.6	1.8	1.4
Rwanda [2]	0.2	7.6	3.9	2.7	2.2	8.0	-12.6	8.3	6.7	6.5	13.5	11.2
Seychelles [2]	0.0	7.1	10.1	3.9	23.2	-3.2	-6.3	7.4	1.7	4.7	13.0	1.7
Somalia	0.0	2.5	3.0	-3.4	0.5	3.3	4.7	2.1	3.1	3.3	2.8	3.1
South Sudan	0.1	2.2	...	...	...	...	6.7	24.4	-3.8	11.2	-22.9	4.2
U.R. of Tanzania: Mainland [2]	1.5	8.6	4.5	-1.2	4.3	8.5	10.0	7.1	10.8	8.2	8.3	5.8
Uganda [2]	0.9	9.8	-1.6	4.7	13.1	6.1	4.5	10.2	0.7	0.1	3.5	7.1
Zambia [4]	0.6	7.9	1.8	3.8	0.2	5.1	6.5	5.6	1.8	4.4	4.1	2.4
Zanzibar [5]	0.0	8.4	...	...	6.3	2.6	9.1	10.9	8.0	8.6	-1.6	25.0
Zimbabwe	1.0	13.3	3.5	3.1	0.3	-2.6	-5.1	0.2	0.6	1.3	1.3	-4.9
Middle Africa	*9.5*	*10.2*	*-0.7*	*1.6*	*-6.5*	*5.3*	*-1.9*	*6.4*	*8.7*	*2.5*	*-0.4*	*0.7*
Angola	2.8	6.0	0.1	-3.1	-1.4	11.0	-10.1	12.3	11.8	1.4	0.6	-3.3
Cameroon [2]	1.8	15.9	6.0	6.1	-0.9	3.6	1.1	3.1	5.0	6.5	3.6	4.3
Central African Republic	0.1	20.4	3.7	0.7	0.8	5.7	-12.5	14.2	4.2	1.0	1.0	2.1
Chad	0.4	9.5	-1.7	3.8	3.2	9.3	-25.2	14.8	11.5	-8.4	0.6	0.9
Congo	0.4	8.4	0.8	6.6	-4.5	9.6	-2.4	-17.5	5.4	-7.0	-16.2	-6.0
D.R. of the Congo	2.6	18.4	-1.4	1.8	-9.9	-2.0	9.9	13.7	8.6	2.4	-0.8	6.1
Equatorial Guinea	1.0	17.8	2.2	0.4	33.0	30.9	0.9	-10.2	5.4	9.4	-10.2	-12.0
Gabon	0.4	6.7	8.4	1.6	6.2	4.7	9.8	1.1	13.7	0.3	11.7	8.4
Sao Tome and Principe	0.0	6.5	7.0	-1.4	1.5	4.6	-3.6	3.3	11.4	1.0	-1.5	1.6
Southern Africa	*17.0*	*13.4*	*4.9*	*1.9*	*0.8*	*2.2*	*0.4*	*-0.3*	*1.3*	*-0.1*	*1.1*	*-0.5*
Botswana	0.3	6.4	23.1	10.3	7.1	4.2	0.5	3.2	1.6	2.2	3.4	2.8
Eswatini [2]	0.5	33.2	14.3	15.7	2.7	2.9	4.7	1.8	1.5	3.2	-0.4	1.4
Lesotho [2]	0.1	16.9	5.4	10.5	7.1	6.8	-11.4	15.2	17.9	-5.8	9.6	-0.4
Namibia [2]	0.5	12.4	3.4	3.4	2.3	5.5	2.7	-3.1	10.2	-1.0	1.0	3.5
South Africa	15.4	13.4	4.9	1.7	0.6	2.0	0.3	-0.4	0.8	-0.2	1.0	-0.8
Western Africa	*27.4*	*10.2*	*9.1*	*-2.5*	*-1.4*	*2.1*	*10.4*	*0.1*	*-1.7*	*5.3*	*6.8*	*3.4*
Benin [6]	0.5	10.9	1.0	23.0	5.3	-1.1	8.8	-4.9	6.4	-0.6	3.8	11.3
Burkina Faso [2]	0.6	12.8	4.0	1.4	3.6	5.3	13.1	6.5	2.6	-4.3	-1.0	3.7
Cabo Verde [2]	0.0	7.5	0.4	7.5	6.6	0.0	7.6	2.5	-0.5	7.3	14.4	3.4
Côte d'Ivoire	2.0	11.7	6.2	5.9	4.4	1.4	3.8	4.0	-3.8	47.7	29.1	4.8
Gambia [2]	0.0	7.0	-5.1	4.3	1.9	2.7	3.3	2.6	-7.0	-7.9	0.3	5.0
Ghana [2]	2.3	12.4	-1.9	0.4	-3.5	3.1	-2.6	3.7	7.9	9.5	4.1	6.3
Guinea	0.4	13.2	3.0	2.7	4.3	1.1	7.1	10.0	8.7	10.9	65.4	28.3
Guinea-Bissau	0.0	11.2	2.8	0.5	1.8	1.2	0.3	9.1	6.1	2.8	2.6	9.9
Liberia	0.1	5.6	8.5	0.7	-47.8	39.2	5.1	-0.1	-4.8	5.0	-1.6	-13.1
Mali	0.7	13.8	-0.3	4.6	13.9	8.9	-3.2	-4.1	1.9	20.7	19.5	11.5
Mauritania [2]	0.2	8.3	4.3	7.1	5.1	1.6	-12.9	17.5	-8.4	27.4	-3.1	-1.0
Niger [2]	0.3	7.2	12.6	0.9	0.7	2.8	1.3	1.8	5.5	7.4	2.9	4.5
Nigeria [2]	18.9	9.5	12.7	-4.2	-2.8	1.8	14.7	-1.5	-4.3	-0.2	2.1	0.8
Senegal [2]	1.2	19.1	3.6	5.2	2.5	2.6	-0.4	6.1	5.9	5.1	5.8	3.8
Sierra Leone	0.0	1.8	4.0	-4.3	-8.5	6.1	-7.1	0.4	4.8	4.9	3.2	4.5
Togo	0.3	13.6	5.0	1.9	-0.1	1.3	12.1	14.8	26.7	3.8	2.4	5.8

Table 6.C. Average Rates of Growth of Gross Domestic Product by Kind of Economic Activity - Manufacturing

Major area, region and country	Base year weights as percentage of total for world or region in 2015	Base year share as percentage of total GDP in 2015	Average rates of growth				Annual rate of change (percentage)					
			1970-1979	1980-1989	1990-1999	2000-2009	2014	2015	2016	2017	2018	2019
Americas	**25.0**	**12.4**	**3.6**	**2.4**	**3.4**	**0.9**	**1.0**	**0.6**	**-1.4**	**2.1**	**3.1**	**1.0**
Latin America and the Caribbean	**6.3**	**15.6**	**6.2**	**1.2**	**2.6**	**1.4**	**-1.3**	**-1.5**	**-3.3**	**0.9**	**-0.1**	**-1.8**
Caribbean	*2.6*	*23.9*	*6.3*	*3.0*	*3.0*	*1.7*	*-0.4*	*2.7*	*-0.5*	*-3.1*	*-2.6*	*0.9*
Anguilla	0.0	2.3	3.8	4.2	11.0	9.1	16.5	1.3	-5.5	-3.5	12.3	2.3
Antigua and Barbuda	0.0	3.1	-1.0	4.7	-0.1	4.4	3.9	1.5	6.4	-2.4	6.6	-6.2
Aruba [2]	0.0	3.9	9.1	11.2	12.2	0.3	5.5	9.6	4.8	8.3	-3.8	0.5
Bahamas [2]	0.0	2.8	2.4	4.2	4.1	-1.1	6.3	-11.2	38.1	-8.3	-27.6	-0.1
Barbados [2]	0.0	6.2	6.9	-0.5	0.1	-3.1	-4.3	4.8	-1.3	1.6	0.5	-3.4
British Virgin Islands [2,7]	0.0	2.3	0.7	10.8	25.9	-1.7	9.6	8.2	8.7	-11.4	4.4	3.6
Cayman Islands [2]	0.0	0.9	9.5	7.7	4.8	2.3	3.3	2.1	8.1	2.4	6.7	4.5
Cuba	0.4	15.1	5.4	4.5	-1.6	3.3	-3.6	6.3	-5.2	-1.1	-0.9	-1.0
Curaçao	0.0	11.8	...	...	...	...	-2.4	27.7	-5.5	-3.4	-13.9	6.0
Dominica	0.0	4.7	6.5	7.3	1.1	-2.1	-6.8	-9.5	-20.6	-18.8	-11.6	8.0
Dominican Republic [2]	0.3	15.8	7.0	2.8	6.9	2.0	5.3	4.4	3.2	2.7	6.2	2.5
Former Netherlands Antilles	...	...	7.7	-3.7	-0.9	0.6	...	...	...	...	...	...
Grenada	0.0	4.0	5.5	11.7	6.0	-0.7	1.6	3.7	4.5	2.7	9.4	6.9
Haiti	0.0	8.0	7.7	-3.6	-5.9	0.9	7.5	-0.3	1.6	1.0	1.2	0.8
Jamaica	0.0	9.1	-1.1	3.0	-3.2	-1.2	-0.8	2.0	1.9	1.9	0.9	1.8
Montserrat	0.0	1.8	7.2	-0.4	-19.9	6.0	-3.1	-0.9	46.8	5.9	8.8	1.1
Puerto Rico [8]	1.6	48.1	7.5	3.1	3.9	1.1	-0.6	1.4	-0.1	-5.1	-5.3	1.2
Saint Kitts and Nevis	0.0	7.5	4.9	1.1	3.1	2.4	2.0	0.1	-10.6	-2.1	7.9	1.4
Saint Lucia [2]	0.0	3.4	6.4	8.8	-0.9	2.5	0.0	0.7	3.2	1.3	6.6	8.6
Sint Maarten (Dutch part)	0.0	1.0	...	...	...	...	-0.1	-1.4	-9.3	-14.2	-0.8	1.8
St. Vincent and the Grenadines	0.0	5.7	5.4	5.7	0.8	-0.8	6.0	1.9	-3.2	1.6	6.9	-20.0
Trinidad and Tobago [2]	0.1	15.8	1.7	-1.5	6.9	10.6	-2.5	2.2	-2.2	-1.8	0.2	-2.9
Turks and Caicos Islands	0.0	0.8	10.7	10.7	9.1	-2.5	7.0	-3.2	-1.0	-0.7	-2.9	-3.0
Central America	*7.5*	*17.4*	*6.9*	*1.5*	*3.9*	*-0.5*	*3.9*	*2.8*	*1.7*	*3.0*	*1.9*	*0.4*
Belize	0.0	8.1	5.4	1.4	1.4	8.4	-7.5	-14.7	-7.5	1.2	2.4	1.0
Costa Rica [2]	0.2	12.4	8.2	2.1	4.1	0.9	0.8	-5.1	4.5	3.3	2.5	1.9
El Salvador [2]	0.1	18.0	2.4	1.7	5.3	-0.2	2.4	4.4	1.9	1.0	1.8	1.0
Guatemala [2]	0.3	15.2	6.3	-0.4	2.8	2.2	3.4	3.7	3.0	2.9	3.2	3.1
Honduras	0.1	18.1	7.6	3.2	3.8	3.7	3.0	3.9	3.0	3.9	3.8	2.1
Mexico [2]	6.6	18.3	7.1	1.6	4.0	-0.8	4.0	3.0	1.6	3.0	1.8	0.2
Nicaragua	0.1	15.7	0.9	-2.9	3.3	3.4	7.6	2.5	3.7	2.9	0.5	0.2
Panama	0.1	6.6	3.4	-0.7	3.9	0.5	3.5	3.4	1.1	2.6	1.0	-1.1
South America	*15.1*	*14.0*	*5.9*	*0.8*	*2.0*	*2.3*	*-3.7*	*-4.2*	*-6.4*	*0.5*	*-0.7*	*-3.6*
Argentina	3.0	16.9	2.2	-1.9	4.6	2.9	-5.1	0.8	-5.6	2.6	-5.0	-6.3
Bolivia (Plurinational State of)	0.1	12.5	5.8	-1.6	3.7	4.2	4.0	4.6	6.2	3.3	5.5	3.2
Brazil [2]	6.2	12.2	9.3	1.2	1.4	1.9	-4.7	-8.5	-4.8	2.3	1.5	0.1
Chile [2]	0.9	12.8	0.6	2.8	4.5	2.1	-0.7	0.2	-1.1	1.1	5.2	0.6
Colombia [2]	1.2	13.7	6.5	2.8	0.1	3.5	2.9	2.0	3.2	-1.8	1.8	1.6
Ecuador [2]	0.5	15.6	7.1	3.0	1.4	3.1	0.2	-0.8	-0.9	3.6	0.6	-0.1
Guyana [3]	0.0	6.3	7.4	-5.5	6.8	0.5	5.8	1.0	-16.2	1.5	2.2	14.7
Paraguay [2]	0.2	21.0	7.8	2.1	1.0	0.4	7.0	5.2	4.6	6.2	1.4	0.1
Peru [2,9]	0.9	15.1	3.0	-1.4	3.3	4.9	-1.1	-0.9	-0.1	0.6	5.7	-1.7
Suriname	0.0	11.0	2.8	-3.5	-4.1	3.8	-8.2	1.1	7.2	21.5	4.3	-4.5
Uruguay	0.2	14.6	3.4	-0.9	-0.2	4.3	4.2	4.9	0.7	-3.5	1.9	-1.1
Venezuela (Bolivarian Republic of)	1.8	17.7	5.5	1.4	1.0	1.1	-7.1	-7.4	-29.7	-12.8	-16.7	-37.2
Northern America	**18.7**	**11.6**	**2.8**	**2.9**	**3.6**	**0.7**	**1.8**	**1.3**	**-0.7**	**2.5**	**4.2**	**1.8**
Bermuda [2]	0.0	0.5	3.5	1.0	2.6	-5.2	-0.3	-3.4	2.4	6.4	-2.5	2.0
Canada [2]	5.1	10.7	4.5	3.0	3.4	-2.6	3.0	0.6	0.0	1.9	2.9	-0.2
Greenland [2]	0.0	4.2	6.4	2.5	1.3	-4.7	45.7	-9.5	18.7	-58.4	92.4	-1.7
United States [2,10]	69.7	11.7	2.7	2.9	3.7	1.0	1.7	1.4	-0.8	2.6	4.2	2.0
Asia	**50.1**	**23.4**	**5.6**	**5.6**	**2.7**	**10.9**	**5.6**	**5.1**	**4.4**	**5.8**	**4.9**	**4.4**
Central Asia	*0.8*	*16.1*	...	...	*-4.0*	*6.7*	*4.3*	*1.5*	*7.1*	*6.2*	*5.2*	*6.5*
Kazakhstan [5]	0.3	10.8	...	...	-3.0	6.1	1.6	0.2	1.8	6.1	4.5	5.8
Kyrgyzstan [5]	0.0	15.4	...	...	-7.6	-0.3	-2.9	-6.2	5.8	6.7	5.1	8.3
Tajikistan [11]	0.0	15.0	...	...	-12.2	1.5	7.9	11.8	23.1	46.3	-7.4	18.6
Turkmenistan [12]	0.3	45.4	...	...	-1.5	12.1	5.5	0.0	12.5	4.7	5.4	4.1
Uzbekistan [5]	0.2	14.7	...	...	-3.8	4.8	8.0	5.9	6.7	4.2	7.9	9.4
Eastern Asia	*77.3*	*26.8*	*5.2*	*5.2*	*1.6*	*13.4*	*5.7*	*5.0*	*4.1*	*5.7*	*5.0*	*4.6*
China [13]	53.1	29.4	...	...	...	...	6.6	5.8	5.6	6.2	6.1	5.6
China, Hong Kong SAR	0.1	1.1	8.6	4.7	-9.2	-4.5	-0.4	-1.5	-0.4	0.4	1.3	0.4
China, Macao SAR [14]	0.0	0.8	7.9	6.8	-5.2	-13.2	12.9	14.6	-6.9	7.7	5.8	2.0
D.P.R. of Korea	0.1	20.4	7.6	2.7	-7.5	1.1	0.8	-3.4	4.8	-6.9	-9.1	-1.1
Japan [2,8]	14.9	20.9	4.5	4.5	0.4	-0.2	3.0	4.1	-0.5	4.5	1.8	2.6

Table 6.C. Average Rates of Growth of Gross Domestic Product by Kind of Economic Activity - Manufacturing

Major area, region and country	Base year weights as percentage of total for world or region in 2015	Base year share as percentage of total GDP in 2015	Average rates of growth				Annual rate of change (percentage)					
			1970-1979	1980-1989	1990-1999	2000-2009	2014	2015	2016	2017	2018	2019
Mongolia [2]	0.0	8.3	5.7	7.0	-2.6	8.3	4.2	2.6	-0.8	19.9	15.7	11.0
Republic of Korea [2]	6.4	29.0	18.2	12.3	8.7	5.5	3.2	1.7	2.3	3.7	3.3	1.3
South-Eastern Asia	*8.5*	*21.6*	*9.5*	*7.2*	*6.3*	*4.5*	*4.2*	*3.3*	*4.6*	*6.1*	*5.3*	*3.5*
Brunei Darussalam [2]	0.0	14.3	14.8	-3.7	3.2	-0.4	-6.8	2.4	-0.7	9.0	-0.6	2.1
Cambodia	0.0	17.0	-7.3	6.6	12.4	8.8	6.6	9.2	6.5	7.0	9.2	6.6
Indonesia [2]	3.0	21.7	13.8	12.3	6.9	4.4	4.6	4.3	4.3	4.3	4.3	3.8
Lao People's DR [2]	0.0	9.2	3.0	7.7	12.6	9.4	9.8	4.4	3.1	4.4	6.2	6.7
Malaysia [2,8]	1.1	22.6	12.7	8.6	9.1	2.7	6.1	4.8	4.4	6.0	5.0	3.8
Myanmar [8]	0.2	21.3	3.1	0.4	8.4	22.1	9.7	9.6	9.8	9.9	9.7	9.8
Philippines [2,10]	1.0	20.0	6.3	0.7	2.3	2.9	8.3	5.7	7.1	8.4	4.9	3.8
Singapore [2]	0.9	19.2	11.0	6.7	6.5	3.3	2.7	-5.1	3.7	10.4	7.0	-1.4
Thailand [2,8]	1.8	27.4	10.9	9.3	6.0	4.9	0.0	1.5	2.2	3.0	3.8	2.1
Timor-Leste [5]	0.0	1.0	...	...	0.5	-2.8	10.3	36.3	17.2	37.1	2.8	11.0
Viet Nam [2,15]	0.4	15.2	4.7	4.7	11.2	10.7	7.4	10.6	11.9	14.4	13.0	11.3
Southern Asia	*7.6*	*16.0*	*4.8*	*6.6*	*5.6*	*7.8*	*7.6*	*9.7*	*7.6*	*6.7*	*6.0*	*7.5*
Afghanistan [16]	0.0	4.2	4.8	0.5	-8.9	1.4	-9.8	-8.0	-7.3	-3.4	68.5	-9.6
Bangladesh	0.5	17.4	2.0	2.0	6.7	7.7	8.8	10.3	11.7	11.0	13.4	14.2
Bhutan	0.0	8.6	5.0	20.4	7.4	9.2	9.2	4.4	2.4	6.5	3.7	4.2
India [2]	5.5	17.1	4.5	7.7	5.8	8.2	7.9	13.1	7.9	6.6	5.7	8.2
Iran (Islamic Republic of)	0.8	12.5	8.9	3.8	5.6	7.8	8.0	-4.6	6.9	5.3	2.1	3.5
Maldives [2]	0.0	2.2	7.2	11.5	8.8	2.0	-1.1	7.2	8.4	13.0	11.4	2.2
Nepal	0.0	6.0	3.0	7.9	10.2	0.6	6.3	0.4	-8.0	9.7	0.2	0.0
Pakistan [2]	0.6	13.5	4.9	8.5	4.1	7.6	5.6	3.9	3.7	5.8	5.4	-0.3
Sri Lanka [2]	0.2	17.5	5.9	4.2	7.7	3.7	2.5	5.0	3.0	4.2	3.6	1.9
Western Asia	*5.9*	*12.6*	*5.9*	*5.6*	*4.0*	*4.1*	*4.1*	*3.9*	*2.9*	*5.8*	*1.2*	*-0.9*
Armenia [5]	0.0	10.1	...	...	-16.4	6.7	6.0	-5.5	11.1	11.8	11.2	8.7
Azerbaijan [5]	0.0	5.4	...	...	-10.9	7.1	3.7	2.9	-1.2	-1.1	6.4	11.5
Bahrain [8]	0.1	17.5	4.5	11.2	5.7	7.3	4.9	3.2	5.2	1.1	1.9	2.7
Cyprus [2]	0.0	4.8	5.8	4.5	0.2	-0.4	0.4	7.2	15.0	12.6	5.6	-1.4
Georgia [5,17]	0.0	10.0	...	...	-17.1	6.8	3.8	-12.6	3.7	1.7	4.1	1.9
Iraq	0.1	2.2	13.4	1.3	1.3	-0.8	-22.2	-16.5	3.7	31.7	-16.8	5.2
Israel [2,14]	0.6	14.6	1.6	5.7	4.6	0.3	2.2	0.3	-4.6	3.1	1.8	0.1
Jordan [2]	0.1	20.5	3.8	3.7	7.8	9.5	1.6	1.4	1.4	1.0	1.4	1.2
Kuwait	0.1	6.1	9.5	1.6	5.6	5.6	-13.2	-5.7	19.9	6.9	-5.6	-1.9
Lebanon [2]	0.1	8.7	-3.9	-4.4	9.7	4.8	-5.0	-4.7	-5.7	-1.8	-3.8	-0.9
Oman	0.1	9.4	9.9	25.0	3.0	13.5	-2.6	4.2	3.0	3.2	9.8	4.5
Qatar [2,8]	0.2	8.6	9.5	7.8	1.9	10.0	4.2	4.4	0.4	1.0	6.1	-1.9
Saudi Arabia [2]	1.4	12.7	6.1	6.1	3.5	6.3	9.5	6.6	3.2	1.3	2.1	-1.6
State of Palestine [2]	0.0	10.9	8.0	2.2	4.1	3.9	-9.1	-9.4	15.1	17.2	0.3	-0.5
Syrian Arab Republic [10]	0.0	4.7	4.0	3.6	12.7	24.8	-1.7	-4.2	-2.3	2.7	9.0	10.3
Turkey [2]	2.4	18.9	6.7	7.0	4.0	3.7	5.6	5.9	4.0	9.3	1.1	-2.3
United Arab Emirates	0.5	8.8	24.1	8.1	8.9	2.9	3.8	5.6	4.9	8.2	-0.9	2.2
Yemen	0.0	10.4	...	...	14.9	4.8	-6.6	-26.1	-8.8	-7.9	-4.3	3.4
Yemen Arab Republic (Former)	...	...	13.7	10.7	...	...	...	...	...	...	...	...
Yemen Democratic (Former)	...	...	-2.0	3.5	...	...	...	...	...	...	...	...
Europe	**22.1**	**15.7**	**3.5**	**2.2**	**0.5**	**0.2**	**2.6**	**3.3**	**2.5**	**3.6**	**2.1**	**-0.1**
Eastern Europe	*15.0*	*17.4*	*5.9*	*4.1*	*-4.3*	*4.5*	*1.5*	*2.3*	*3.4*	*3.3*	*3.4*	*2.2*
Belarus [5]	0.4	23.8	...	...	-0.9	10.2	0.2	-6.5	-0.2	6.9	5.2	1.2
Bulgaria [2]	0.2	15.4	7.4	6.1	-4.6	5.4	6.2	5.5	6.2	5.8	1.1	1.8
Czechia [5]	1.7	26.6	...	...	2.2	5.7	3.6	7.6	4.6	8.7	2.0	3.1
Czechoslovakia (Former)	...	...	5.3	0.6	...	...	...	...	...	...	...	...
Hungary [2]	0.9	24.0	6.6	2.2	3.9	2.3	7.1	8.7	0.3	3.4	3.3	2.6
Poland [2]	3.1	19.7	6.0	2.3	9.2	7.8	8.3	7.8	4.9	2.1	6.6	5.1
Republic of Moldova [5]	0.0	13.7	...	...	-13.6	0.6	8.4	4.3	3.4	4.0	3.6	4.3
Romania [2]	1.3	22.3	11.3	-2.2	-4.0	5.8	6.5	4.5	6.4	7.9	2.7	-2.6
Russian Federation	6.3	13.9	...	...	-6.8	2.8	-3.8	-1.8	2.8	1.2	1.6	1.9
Slovakia [5]	0.6	21.7	...	...	-1.9	8.6	19.6	11.9	-0.8	1.7	11.7	-1.8
Ukraine [5,18]	0.4	14.0	...	...	-11.7	4.2	-8.6	-15.2	3.7	4.0	1.1	1.0
USSR (Former)	...	...	5.2	5.4	...	...	...	...	...	...	...	...
Northern Europe	*20.7*	*13.2*	*2.0*	*2.1*	*1.8*	*-0.5*	*2.8*	*9.8*	*0.7*	*3.5*	*3.2*	*0.7*
Denmark [2]	1.4	14.3	2.4	1.6	2.3	-1.2	1.3	-0.5	6.0	9.4	2.4	5.9
Estonia [5]	0.1	15.9	...	...	-1.1	2.7	5.6	2.4	4.3	3.9	8.8	1.9
Finland [2]	1.3	17.0	3.7	3.6	5.1	1.1	-0.9	0.4	4.9	8.9	-2.6	4.9
Iceland [2]	0.1	11.8	6.7	0.4	1.9	1.3	3.0	5.9	-0.8	-1.9	2.2	1.4
Ireland [2]	3.8	37.5	5.6	4.9	11.4	1.4	10.5	91.4	-1.6	3.5	11.4	3.2
Latvia [5]	0.1	11.9	...	...	-9.9	0.7	-2.9	4.4	1.7	6.7	7.6	2.1
Lithuania [5]	0.3	19.1	...	...	-9.4	5.7	4.3	3.1	3.2	5.6	3.8	4.0
Norway [2]	1.0	7.7	1.8	-0.2	1.3	1.2	3.0	-4.7	-4.3	0.3	0.9	3.2
Sweden [2]	2.5	15.3	1.3	2.1	5.1	-0.4	-0.6	5.2	2.2	2.7	3.1	-0.6
United Kingdom [2]	10.2	10.5	1.8	2.1	0.6	-1.2	2.8	-0.5	0.3	2.3	1.1	-1.7

Table 6.C. Average Rates of Growth of Gross Domestic Product by Kind of Economic Activity - Manufacturing

Major area, region and country	Base year weights as percentage of total for world or region in 2015	Base year share as percentage of total GDP in 2015	Average rates of growth				Annual rate of change (percentage)					
			1970-1979	1980-1989	1990-1999	2000-2009	2014	2015	2016	2017	2018	2019
Southern Europe	*17.3*	*14.4*	*6.0*	*2.4*	*1.3*	*-1.1*	*1.0*	*3.2*	*2.6*	*4.4*	*1.4*	*0.2*
Albania [2]	0.0	6.5	4.0	2.3	-9.3	7.9	9.4	5.0	4.5	12.4	6.3	5.3
Andorra [2]	0.0	4.2	3.8	2.8	2.1	2.6	-1.8	2.2	4.7	0.6	-2.2	4.4
Bosnia and Herzegovina [5]	0.1	13.7	...	...	11.3	5.6	4.3	6.4	5.4	8.3	1.8	-0.1
Croatia [5]	0.2	15.6	...	...	-5.4	1.2	3.9	4.2	6.5	2.5	-0.8	0.0
Greece [2]	0.6	9.4	6.8	0.5	0.6	1.0	2.4	1.8	-4.0	4.9	1.9	3.8
Italy [2]	9.8	16.0	6.4	2.3	1.2	-1.8	0.2	2.5	3.0	3.5	1.7	-0.7
Kosovo [5]	0.0	13.2	...	...	-10.9	5.6	-1.3	4.8	2.8	3.0	4.2	5.3
Malta [2]	0.0	8.5	16.3	1.5	2.9	-4.0	-1.3	-4.3	1.3	8.3	8.8	1.4
Montenegro [5]	0.0	4.9	...	...	-4.7	-6.7	-2.1	6.0	-4.1	9.5	9.0	-1.0
North Macedonia [5]	0.0	13.5	...	...	-5.9	2.6	21.5	5.0	-1.5	1.6	4.5	-0.1
Portugal [2]	0.9	13.9	5.3	3.2	2.0	-1.2	2.7	2.8	2.1	6.0	3.6	0.0
San Marino [19]	0.0	30.7	3.8	2.4	6.1	-3.1	-2.9	0.2	3.1	0.8	13.8	-0.8
Serbia [5]	0.2	17.7	...	...	-6.7	2.3	-6.4	3.1	3.0	4.5	1.5	0.2
Slovenia [5]	0.3	23.1	...	...	-0.3	2.7	4.5	2.8	5.6	7.8	2.8	7.5
Spain [2]	5.0	12.4	5.1	2.2	2.5	-0.5	2.1	4.6	2.3	5.7	0.0	1.2
Yugoslavia (Former)	...	...	6.2	4.9	...	...	...	...	...	...	...	...
Western Europe	*47.0*	*17.2*	*2.4*	*1.5*	*0.9*	*0.0*	*3.6*	*1.0*	*3.0*	*3.5*	*1.5*	*-1.4*
Austria [2]	2.4	18.7	3.7	2.4	2.3	1.1	2.2	0.9	4.4	3.7	5.3	0.7
Belgium [2]	2.2	14.2	3.7	2.8	1.7	0.0	3.1	2.7	-1.6	1.5	-0.3	1.9
France [2]	9.4	11.7	3.5	1.2	2.3	0.3	1.6	0.7	0.9	2.2	0.0	0.2
Germany [2]	25.3	22.6	2.1	1.4	-0.2	-0.7	5.0	1.1	3.9	3.5	0.7	-3.5
Liechtenstein [2]	0.1	37.6	2.9	2.7	11.9	2.2	0.7	-0.9	3.6	8.4	-4.1	4.5
Luxembourg [2]	0.1	5.1	1.4	5.1	2.9	-4.4	-8.7	14.7	17.7	-1.5	-0.9	0.8
Monaco [8]	0.0	4.9	3.9	2.4	1.9	-0.9	-18.7	8.9	-16.8	-0.1	-6.0	-10.0
Netherlands [2]	3.1	12.0	2.5	2.6	2.6	0.5	2.4	0.7	2.2	6.1	4.0	0.8
Switzerland [2]	4.5	18.0	0.8	0.8	1.3	1.7	1.8	0.7	4.4	4.8	5.5	2.6
Oceania	**0.8**	**7.2**	**2.1**	**1.6**	**1.9**	**0.6**	**-0.7**	**-1.6**	**0.3**	**2.2**	**-0.2**	**-0.5**
Australia and New Zealand	*97.8*	*7.2*	*2.1*	*1.5*	*1.9*	*0.6*	*-1.0*	*-1.4*	*0.2*	*2.2*	*-0.2*	*-0.6*
Australia [2]	77.4	6.5	2.0	1.6	1.9	0.8	-1.6	-2.4	-0.4	2.0	-0.7	-1.6
New Zealand [2]	20.4	12.3	2.6	0.9	2.1	-0.1	1.6	2.5	2.6	2.9	1.8	3.3
Melanesia	*1.8*	*5.1*	*-0.2*	*5.7*	*0.9*	*0.8*	*14.6*	*-12.2*	*1.9*	*0.1*	*-1.3*	*0.9*
Fiji [2]	0.5	13.4	4.5	1.6	4.4	0.4	16.5	5.9	6.0	1.4	1.5	2.9
New Caledonia [14]	0.8	9.5	-2.6	8.1	-2.6	-0.9	26.6	-20.7	-2.7	-5.0	-1.4	-0.6
Papua New Guinea [2]	0.4	1.9	2.9	1.5	5.5	3.2	-0.9	-12.9	3.8	3.7	-6.7	-2.6
Solomon Islands	0.1	7.2	9.0	3.7	6.9	10.7	-11.6	-12.4	11.6	18.0	5.7	11.7
Vanuatu [2]	0.0	3.5	7.7	11.0	0.9	-2.1	0.8	-4.5	2.9	2.0	3.9	3.0
Micronesia	*0.0*	*3.6*	*5.6*	*1.4*	*-1.2*	*3.3*	*-11.3*	*49.1*	*-6.7*	*-5.2*	*14.3*	*0.9*
Kiribati [20]	0.0	4.0	...	-0.4	-1.2	1.1	-0.6	3.6	2.4	3.5	1.9	2.6
Marshall Islands	0.0	1.0	6.6	6.9	3.8	2.8	-22.9	1.5	25.9	-14.2	72.6	23.1
Micronesia (FS of)	0.0	0.4	6.6	4.1	2.6	-15.0	0.8	13.4	41.7	4.6	1.0	11.3
Nauru [8]	0.0	23.3	1.1	-1.6	-14.3	31.1	-16.8	88.7	-15.8	-8.6	16.5	-4.2
Palau [2]	0.0	1.1	0.1	3.8	0.2	-6.2	1.0	10.8	7.1	-1.0	0.9	2.5
Polynesia	*0.4*	*5.9*	*2.3*	*3.4*	*-1.2*	*-1.4*	*-5.0*	*6.7*	*5.3*	*-2.9*	*0.4*	*3.1*
Cook Islands [2,14]	0.0	2.4	-9.5	-14.0	-0.4	1.5	-3.3	2.5	6.4	10.8	11.4	3.0
French Polynesia [14]	0.3	5.7	4.2	5.3	-1.6	-1.6	-5.1	9.6	4.7	-1.3	4.6	2.3
Samoa [2,21]	0.1	8.1	3.7	0.3	1.0	-0.9	-6.8	-2.5	6.8	-12.6	-20.3	12.4
Tonga [22]	0.0	7.0	3.9	1.6	-1.3	-1.3	0.9	3.0	7.4	1.5	-0.8	-4.8
Tuvalu	0.0	0.9	-1.5	7.8	-0.3	4.4	10.6	12.2	2.9	-7.9	2.1	-1.1

Notes for Table 6.C. Average Rates of Growth of Gross Domestic Product by Kind of Economic Activity - Manufacturing

1/ 1970-2019
At factor cost.

2/ 1970-2019
Excludes recycling and publishing activities

3/ 2006-2019
Excludes recycling and publishing activities

4/ 2010-2019
Excludes recycling and publishing activities

5/ 1990-2019
Excludes recycling and publishing activities

6/ 2015-2019
Excludes recycling and publishing activities

7/ 1970-2009
Includes Mining and quarrying.

8/ 1970-2019
At producers' prices.

9/ 1970-2001
At producers' prices.

10/ 1970-2019
Includes Taxes less subsidies on production and imports.

11/ 1990-2019
Includes Mining and quarrying, and Electricity, gas and water supply.

12/ 1990-2019
Includes Mining and quarrying.

13/ 2005-2019
Includes Taxes less subsidies on production and imports.

14/ 1970-2019
Includes Mining and quarrying.

15/ 1970-2009
At producers' prices.

16/ 2016-2019
Excludes recycling and publishing activities

17/ 1990-1995
Includes Mining and quarrying.

18/ 2010-2019
The Government of Ukraine has advised the United Nations that it is not in a position to provide statistical data concerning the Autonomous Republic of Crimea and the city of Sevastopol.

19/ 1970-2019
Includes Mining and quarrying, and Electricity, gas and water supply. Excludes recycling and publishing activities

20/ (a) 1978-2019
At factor cost.

(b) 1980-1990
Includes Mining and quarrying.

21/ (a) 1970-2008
At producers' prices.

(b) 2009-2019
Includes Taxes less subsidies on production and imports.

22/ 1994-2019
Excludes recycling and publishing activities

Table 6.D. Average Rates of Growth of Gross Domestic Product by Kind of Economic Activity - Construction

Major area, region and country	Base year weights as percentage of total for world or region in 2015	Base year share as percentage of total GDP in 2015	Average rates of growth				Annual rate of change (percentage)					
			1970-1979	1980-1989	1990-1999	2000-2009	2014	2015	2016	2017	2018	2019
World	**100.0**	**5.7**	**2.1**	**1.9**	**0.6**	**1.5**	**3.6**	**3.0**	**3.1**	**3.2**	**2.8**	**2.0**
Developed economies	**49.8**	**4.9**	**1.0**	**1.8**	**0.4**	**-1.3**	**2.0**	**2.3**	**1.9**	**3.3**	**2.0**	**1.1**
Developing economies	**47.0**	**6.7**	**7.5**	**1.0**	**4.3**	**7.2**	**5.8**	**4.0**	**4.5**	**3.1**	**3.6**	**2.7**
Transition economies	**3.2**	**7.1**	**6.3**	**5.8**	**-13.0**	**7.8**	**-0.8**	**-0.4**	**1.2**	**1.8**	**3.6**	**4.6**
Africa	**3.2**	**5.9**	**4.4**	**-0.1**	**2.6**	**9.1**	**6.2**	**5.4**	**4.2**	**5.4**	**4.7**	**4.8**
Northern Africa	*34.3*	*6.3*	*7.9*	*2.3*	*2.8*	*7.4*	*3.7*	*5.6*	*7.2*	*6.2*	*6.3*	*5.6*
Algeria	14.2	11.6	7.9	2.1	2.0	8.7	6.9	4.8	5.1	4.6	5.3	3.9
Egypt [1]	11.9	4.8	9.5	4.5	3.3	5.4	7.4	9.8	11.2	9.5	10.0	9.6
Libya	0.2	1.5	7.0	-3.1	2.4	9.2	-52.4	-50.0	-25.6	65.4	32.1	6.8
Morocco	4.3	6.2	8.5	1.0	1.0	7.1	4.5	4.3	2.9	6.2	1.4	1.6
Sudan	2.3	3.6	...	...	...	...	-12.6	5.8	13.1	0.4	1.4	1.7
Sudan (Former)	...	...	3.6	2.1	6.2	...	...	...	...	...	...	...
Tunisia [1]	1.4	4.6	4.8	1.3	5.7	5.0	3.6	-3.1	1.0	-1.5	0.5	-0.4
Sub-Saharan Africa	65.7	5.7	2.9	-1.6	2.4	10.3	7.6	5.3	2.6	4.9	3.9	4.3
Eastern Africa	*17.7*	*7.9*	*-0.1*	*0.4*	*3.4*	*10.0*	*11.3*	*15.6*	*13.9*	*12.0*	*11.6*	*11.5*
Burundi	0.1	3.7	11.3	4.7	-3.4	8.5	-3.2	-3.4	2.0	3.0	0.5	1.8
Comoros	0.0	1.9	4.5	-7.2	7.9	5.5	3.5	-7.0	-5.5	-40.1	-14.8	-4.2
Djibouti	0.1	4.3	3.2	4.4	-3.7	9.1	-9.1	10.1	3.8	19.3	105.5	12.0
Eritrea	0.2	15.7	...	...	21.0	3.1	35.4	-19.1	9.6	-11.8	13.8	4.1
Ethiopia	5.2	11.6	...	...	3.5	12.1	23.9	31.6	25.0	20.7	15.7	15.0
Ethiopia (Former)	...	...	-0.1	1.3	...	...	...	...	...	...	...	...
Kenya	2.4	5.2	3.6	1.5	1.6	4.9	13.1	13.8	9.9	8.4	6.9	6.4
Madagascar	0.6	6.7	2.3	-1.6	4.0	13.5	3.2	9.7	6.0	6.8	7.9	10.3
Malawi	0.1	3.2	7.1	-0.8	3.4	7.1	4.8	3.5	3.4	4.4	4.8	5.4
Mauritius	0.4	4.4	6.8	5.2	5.4	6.6	-8.5	-4.9	0.0	7.5	9.5	8.5
Mozambique	0.2	2.1	3.8	-3.1	13.2	9.9	15.1	9.2	2.6	-3.2	-0.5	2.2
Rwanda	0.5	8.3	5.5	2.9	1.0	11.7	9.9	15.5	4.9	-10.0	4.8	32.9
Seychelles	0.0	3.7	10.1	-5.6	24.4	8.1	14.1	3.5	-2.2	-3.1	9.4	8.2
Somalia	0.0	4.2	0.4	0.2	0.0	3.1	4.6	2.1	3.1	3.3	2.8	3.1
South Sudan	0.3	6.4	...	...	...	...	26.9	-3.8	-10.0	-11.3	-20.5	-6.5
U.R. of Tanzania: Mainland	4.0	12.1	1.0	0.2	7.8	10.3	2.5	12.9	14.5	15.1	13.7	14.1
Uganda	1.4	8.0	-1.6	6.1	13.1	13.1	8.1	4.1	5.6	3.4	12.4	16.9
Zambia	1.6	10.6	-3.8	-2.9	-2.6	12.8	10.6	18.0	10.2	6.4	2.4	-5.0
Zanzibar	0.1	9.2	...	...	4.4	21.1	6.2	9.1	6.5	0.8	4.1	3.1
Zimbabwe	0.3	2.4	-2.6	0.8	-0.4	3.2	6.9	4.0	1.5	3.9	2.0	-6.2
Middle Africa	*16.4*	*9.3*	*1.2*	*0.3*	*2.0*	*15.1*	*2.5*	*-4.0*	*-5.2*	*0.3*	*-2.8*	*-2.7*
Angola	11.5	12.9	0.1	1.0	3.5	12.8	2.9	-1.3	2.5	2.5	0.0	-3.2
Cameroon	1.1	5.2	5.7	-5.7	-3.1	19.9	7.5	8.4	10.4	8.9	7.6	5.8
Central African Republic	0.0	1.5	1.5	8.4	-5.6	4.5	-22.1	35.5	-12.6	7.6	19.2	3.9
Chad	0.3	3.4	-1.7	9.3	-0.5	14.3	-2.7	-43.8	-4.9	22.7	-16.4	6.8
Congo	1.7	19.4	5.7	-10.1	3.1	17.8	18.3	6.5	-49.3	-23.3	-72.1	-48.3
D.R. of the Congo	0.2	0.9	-1.3	0.0	-12.8	11.1	1.2	-6.4	-19.6	31.4	10.1	35.1
Equatorial Guinea	0.9	9.3	2.3	3.4	31.2	38.6	-8.6	-32.6	-39.1	-25.4	-10.0	-26.4
Gabon	0.6	6.3	8.1	1.1	0.2	7.7	-10.8	-3.7	-1.1	-21.3	0.0	-8.0
Sao Tome and Principe	0.0	6.9	7.0	-1.4	1.3	4.0	15.6	4.4	1.6	2.1	-0.8	-2.5
Southern Africa	*10.4*	*4.3*	*2.3*	*-1.0*	*-0.8*	*8.8*	*4.5*	*2.9*	*-0.5*	*-1.0*	*-1.0*	*-2.7*
Botswana	0.7	7.3	13.7	8.8	4.2	5.3	3.7	4.0	4.2	3.5	3.7	3.0
Eswatini	0.1	3.1	17.1	-1.2	7.7	1.5	0.0	9.4	20.0	-9.9	-0.3	2.6
Lesotho	0.1	5.7	10.1	9.3	7.0	-2.8	-5.6	4.4	-14.9	-3.4	-4.2	10.5
Namibia	0.5	6.0	2.7	-8.2	5.6	9.5	40.8	22.7	-41.1	-23.1	-8.7	-7.9
South Africa	9.0	4.1	1.9	-1.2	-1.5	9.3	3.5	1.8	1.2	-0.6	-1.2	-3.3
Western Africa	*21.3*	*4.2*	*6.5*	*-4.6*	*4.8*	*8.5*	*11.2*	*6.7*	*0.9*	*4.5*	*3.0*	*4.1*
Benin	0.4	5.0	3.3	4.6	5.6	4.3	-9.1	5.4	0.6	2.2	7.0	17.4
Burkina Faso	0.3	3.7	-0.8	0.8	8.5	8.6	1.8	28.1	12.6	-5.6	-3.2	4.2
Cabo Verde	0.1	9.1	0.2	7.4	4.0	7.7	7.4	-14.0	6.0	10.0	3.9	10.6
Côte d'Ivoire	1.6	4.9	10.1	2.7	11.7	4.0	39.0	24.4	34.3	24.2	6.5	23.8
Gambia	0.1	9.4	5.6	6.0	2.4	-1.6	11.5	54.7	44.4	-1.4	1.8	15.0
Ghana	3.2	9.3	-0.9	-1.5	9.2	12.0	-0.4	9.5	8.4	5.1	1.1	-4.4
Guinea	0.4	5.9	3.0	2.7	4.7	5.9	3.0	-3.1	2.9	0.9	0.2	1.4
Guinea-Bissau	0.0	1.0	2.7	0.3	-23.6	15.5	8.0	-23.7	-17.8	119.0	2.8	-10.9
Liberia	0.0	2.1	6.3	-2.1	-26.1	39.9	5.1	-18.4	25.4	10.1	14.3	0.4
Mali	0.4	4.6	-0.3	4.5	17.3	9.1	24.2	2.7	12.6	8.1	2.6	6.9
Mauritania	0.3	6.6	1.4	2.9	-0.3	3.5	0.9	4.4	-9.0	-1.3	14.1	-3.5
Niger	0.2	3.5	12.6	-1.7	-0.1	6.4	5.3	5.2	5.6	9.7	19.3	1.5
Nigeria	13.8	3.7	7.8	-6.9	4.0	8.9	13.0	4.4	-5.9	1.0	2.3	1.8
Senegal	0.3	2.5	3.2	3.6	8.0	6.3	11.1	15.5	5.6	15.9	11.5	7.1
Sierra Leone	0.0	1.1	2.8	0.6	-8.4	9.5	-7.6	5.1	6.7	5.1	-6.5	4.7
Togo [2]	0.1	2.3	7.0	-0.4	1.8	2.1	54.8	14.1	48.0	9.9	-10.4	15.0

Table 6.D. Average Rates of Growth of Gross Domestic Product by Kind of Economic Activity - Construction

Major area, region and country	Base year weights as percentage of total for world or region in 2015	Base year share as percentage of total GDP in 2015	Average rates of growth				Annual rate of change (percentage)					
			1970-1979	1980-1989	1990-1999	2000-2009	2014	2015	2016	2017	2018	2019
Americas	**28.3**	**4.7**	**1.5**	**1.4**	**2.1**	**-1.4**	**1.5**	**1.7**	**0.9**	**1.6**	**2.4**	**-1.0**
Latin America and the Caribbean	**8.3**	**6.8**	**6.8**	**-1.4**	**2.9**	**3.1**	**0.4**	**-2.6**	**-3.1**	**-2.5**	**1.6**	**-3.6**
Caribbean	*1.7*	*5.9*	*2.6*	*3.8*	*0.0*	*1.8*	*4.7*	*9.2*	*4.3*	*4.2*	*8.5*	*5.0*
Anguilla	0.0	8.7	3.8	9.1	2.3	3.3	38.9	7.2	-23.0	-2.7	157.1	-54.5
Antigua and Barbuda	0.0	10.0	3.6	9.8	5.0	5.5	7.1	3.9	19.2	20.1	27.1	6.6
Aruba	0.0	5.0	9.1	11.2	4.0	-1.9	2.9	11.8	8.3	-3.3	2.5	0.0
Bahamas	0.1	6.6	2.4	4.1	-8.1	0.0	3.8	-23.0	14.3	13.7	-7.8	12.6
Barbados	0.0	6.4	-0.3	1.9	2.1	3.2	1.4	-1.2	-2.6	2.1	-6.4	-1.9
British Virgin Islands	0.0	2.4	-8.0	9.8	22.6	0.3	12.7	12.2	-9.8	27.2	18.6	11.5
Cayman Islands	0.0	3.8	9.6	8.8	5.8	-2.2	2.6	7.6	4.1	2.4	7.8	4.9
Cuba	0.4	5.4	5.4	5.8	-10.1	5.6	-2.3	17.0	4.7	9.0	9.3	7.3
Curaçao	0.0	6.4	...	...	...	...	-22.0	46.6	1.4	0.1	-6.5	-1.0
Dominica	0.0	3.9	5.5	1.5	2.4	1.2	9.2	-19.0	35.6	-4.9	98.3	-6.3
Dominican Republic	0.6	11.0	10.8	6.5	8.3	1.4	14.6	19.7	9.5	4.1	12.2	7.4
Former Netherlands Antilles	...	...	8.0	-3.0	-0.6	2.2	...	...	...	...	...	...
Grenada	0.0	6.2	7.7	4.7	5.6	-1.3	-4.7	7.0	13.1	29.1	12.2	-0.6
Haiti	0.2	25.4	13.7	3.6	-1.8	1.9	7.9	2.3	0.2	0.9	2.1	0.2
Jamaica	0.1	7.6	-6.9	6.0	-0.7	0.3	1.7	1.4	0.4	1.0	3.3	-0.6
Montserrat	0.0	5.8	2.8	16.6	-12.4	-3.6	4.9	-39.3	33.6	-40.6	8.5	50.5
Puerto Rico [3]	0.1	1.0	-8.1	2.5	7.0	-3.6	-8.2	-12.6	-16.1	-9.8	29.6	1.0
Saint Kitts and Nevis	0.0	17.1	4.6	10.0	4.9	-2.0	14.8	7.7	7.8	6.8	-8.8	2.0
Saint Lucia	0.0	5.2	9.2	9.8	6.7	3.7	-0.9	16.2	-0.8	7.8	-13.2	-0.3
Sint Maarten (Dutch part)	0.0	5.4	...	...	...	...	-4.7	-16.5	-3.3	12.1	-18.7	6.6
St. Vincent and the Grenadines	0.0	7.9	2.6	5.5	4.6	4.7	-11.7	8.7	-0.8	6.3	2.5	-2.1
Trinidad and Tobago	0.1	6.3	14.3	-9.2	5.0	6.0	1.3	-2.7	-4.2	-3.8	-0.1	-5.4
Turks and Caicos Islands	0.0	5.2	10.7	10.7	10.3	4.3	5.2	33.3	9.1	33.8	7.2	16.9
Central America	*9.0*	*7.8*	*6.5*	*-1.7*	*3.2*	*1.7*	*3.5*	*3.6*	*2.3*	*0.5*	*1.3*	*-5.2*
Belize	0.0	3.8	7.1	6.9	1.0	-1.7	6.6	18.7	11.7	-3.8	-6.5	-18.4
Costa Rica	0.2	5.3	11.5	-1.7	4.8	8.0	2.1	9.4	-3.4	-2.1	8.0	-10.7
El Salvador	0.1	5.6	8.6	-1.7	8.9	2.6	-0.4	-2.9	2.4	5.9	6.4	9.1
Guatemala	0.3	5.2	14.3	-3.2	6.7	2.9	7.5	1.6	-0.3	3.0	5.1	8.3
Honduras	0.1	5.3	5.4	2.0	2.2	-1.1	-9.6	2.3	6.2	8.5	6.9	-0.4
Mexico	7.4	7.7	6.4	-1.6	2.8	1.4	2.8	2.4	2.0	-0.6	0.8	-6.2
Nicaragua	0.1	6.5	-11.7	-0.3	5.1	-5.9	1.8	25.4	-1.4	8.6	-15.6	-38.1
Panama	0.8	18.3	4.6	-16.8	24.9	8.7	13.9	13.9	8.0	8.3	3.3	0.1
South America	*18.6*	*6.5*	*7.3*	*-1.9*	*3.2*	*3.9*	*-1.2*	*-6.2*	*-6.4*	*-4.8*	*0.9*	*-3.8*
Argentina	2.6	5.4	2.8	-5.6	7.5	3.0	-2.0	3.0	-11.2	10.5	1.4	-5.5
Bolivia (Plurinational State of)	0.1	3.6	4.9	-3.8	6.3	3.3	7.8	5.4	7.8	5.0	3.5	1.9
Brazil	7.7	5.7	9.3	1.2	2.5	2.4	-2.1	-9.0	-10.0	-9.2	5.8	-1.2
Chile	1.4	7.2	-3.3	3.6	5.3	4.5	-1.9	4.3	3.4	-3.8	3.0	4.9
Colombia	1.8	7.9	4.2	4.0	-2.0	8.5	8.9	6.3	3.6	-2.0	-0.4	-1.3
Ecuador	1.0	12.1	5.2	-2.5	-2.3	8.0	4.7	-0.8	-5.8	-4.4	0.6	-5.2
Guyana	0.0	8.0	0.6	-1.3	6.2	9.9	-2.0	-5.0	5.7	4.9	2.9	3.1
Paraguay	0.2	6.5	19.6	0.9	0.0	3.0	11.0	2.0	8.7	3.5	1.6	-0.9
Peru [4]	1.2	7.6	3.5	-0.9	7.4	8.0	1.8	-5.4	-2.6	2.4	5.4	1.6
Suriname	0.0	10.1	6.0	-2.9	-1.1	7.1	19.7	16.6	-16.8	2.5	18.9	4.0
Uruguay	0.4	10.5	9.0	-5.9	6.6	1.0	0.7	-6.1	-2.6	-2.1	-2.8	-2.0
Venezuela (Bolivarian Republic of)	2.1	7.8	11.8	-8.9	3.0	5.7	-7.0	-22.4	-7.5	-16.7	-21.8	-33.5
Northern America	**20.0**	**4.1**	**0.5**	**2.1**	**2.0**	**-2.7**	**2.0**	**3.5**	**2.6**	**3.2**	**2.7**	**0.0**
Bermuda [5]	0.0	3.3	3.5	1.0	4.0	0.5	-4.0	0.7	10.5	4.6	14.0	9.6
Canada	10.2	8.0	3.3	2.3	-0.7	3.5	2.6	-2.3	-4.8	3.7	2.0	-0.2
Greenland	0.0	9.5	6.4	2.5	1.2	10.0	-18.2	28.8	7.2	16.1	4.7	9.2
United States [6]	60.5	3.8	0.3	2.1	2.2	-3.3	1.9	4.6	3.8	3.1	2.8	0.0
Asia	**42.5**	**6.6**	**5.1**	**2.8**	**1.3**	**4.9**	**6.7**	**4.7**	**5.6**	**4.1**	**3.3**	**3.6**
Central Asia	*1.2*	*6.8*	...	...	*-9.6*	*15.1*	*8.3*	*7.4*	*8.9*	*4.7*	*4.7*	*12.4*
Kazakhstan	0.6	6.3	...	...	-15.2	17.5	4.6	4.4	7.4	2.8	4.6	13.2
Kyrgyzstan	0.0	9.2	...	...	-16.2	11.8	27.1	16.3	9.3	7.9	7.8	10.6
Tajikistan	0.1	12.5	...	...	-6.4	14.2	24.9	21.2	21.8	17.4	-36.7	-3.3
Turkmenistan	0.2	9.7	...	...	10.5	12.5	5.6	-0.1	12.5	4.7	5.4	4.1
Uzbekistan	0.3	5.9	...	...	-2.9	10.3	17.6	18.8	7.2	6.0	14.3	19.0
Eastern Asia	*64.6*	*6.3*	*4.0*	*3.6*	*0.7*	*3.5*	*7.7*	*5.7*	*6.3*	*3.8*	*3.0*	*4.1*
China [6]	44.5	6.9	4.4	9.6	10.9	12.6	9.6	7.3	7.7	3.9	4.8	5.6
China, Hong Kong SAR	0.8	4.6	9.0	3.9	3.9	-4.0	13.0	5.4	5.1	-1.3	3.3	-6.0
China, Macao SAR	0.2	8.8	7.9	8.1	-2.8	25.3	37.4	11.2	-21.8	-29.5	-14.7	-22.2
D.P.R. of Korea	0.1	9.0	7.6	2.7	-6.9	1.5	1.4	4.8	1.2	-4.4	-4.4	2.9
Japan [3]	14.1	5.6	3.4	2.5	-2.1	-3.9	3.9	0.9	1.5	3.4	-1.0	1.7

Table 6.D. Average Rates of Growth of Gross Domestic Product by Kind of Economic Activity - Construction

Major area, region and country	Base year weights as percentage of total for world or region in 2015	Base year share as percentage of total GDP in 2015	Average rates of growth				Annual rate of change (percentage)					
			1970-1979	1980-1989	1990-1999	2000-2009	2014	2015	2016	2017	2018	2019
Mongolia	0.0	4.6	5.7	7.3	-8.7	4.2	-4.3	-0.2	-4.9	11.4	4.7	5.8
Republic of Korea	4.2	5.3	11.3	8.0	1.9	2.2	1.5	6.2	9.8	5.9	-2.8	-2.5
South-Eastern Asia	*9.6*	*6.9*	*11.5*	*3.1*	*3.5*	*6.0*	*7.0*	*8.3*	*6.4*	*5.2*	*6.6*	*5.7*
Brunei Darussalam	0.0	2.4	14.3	0.0	-1.4	5.1	-22.0	4.8	-6.6	9.3	6.0	-0.5
Cambodia	0.1	10.4	-7.3	4.8	11.4	11.8	20.0	19.2	21.8	18.0	17.3	18.7
Indonesia	5.1	10.5	16.4	5.4	4.2	7.0	7.0	6.4	5.2	6.8	6.1	5.8
Lao People's DR	0.0	6.3	3.0	6.8	5.0	9.8	11.4	20.7	8.4	18.0	22.6	-5.1
Malaysia [3]	0.8	4.8	11.2	1.6	7.1	2.6	11.7	8.4	7.4	6.7	4.2	0.1
Myanmar [3]	0.2	5.9	6.5	4.4	13.2	20.3	10.9	7.1	9.7	8.1	8.7	8.9
Philippines [6]	1.2	6.8	13.6	-3.9	0.5	3.8	7.2	11.6	12.1	5.1	14.9	7.7
Singapore	0.9	5.1	5.1	3.0	10.6	4.7	8.8	6.0	-1.1	-5.4	-3.5	2.8
Thailand [3]	0.6	2.8	5.1	9.7	-2.9	3.3	-2.4	17.1	7.9	-2.8	2.7	4.5
Timor-Leste	0.0	17.2	...	...	-0.3	-2.0	-11.8	21.7	7.2	-30.7	5.8	-6.7
Viet Nam [7]	0.6	6.0	4.7	5.6	10.4	9.7	6.9	10.8	10.0	8.7	9.2	9.1
Southern Asia	*12.0*	*7.1*	*5.7*	*0.6*	*4.6*	*8.7*	*4.0*	*0.9*	*4.0*	*5.0*	*4.9*	*3.9*
Afghanistan	0.0	3.9	15.0	2.4	2.8	12.5	-1.2	-0.6	-9.7	2.1	2.0	-1.4
Bangladesh	0.8	7.4	0.0	8.4	7.7	7.7	8.1	8.6	8.6	8.8	9.9	10.2
Bhutan	0.0	16.8	5.1	16.1	20.5	6.0	6.5	10.6	13.6	6.2	-8.0	4.0
India	9.0	7.9	2.0	4.1	4.9	9.7	4.3	3.6	5.9	5.0	6.1	5.0
Iran (Islamic Republic of)	1.4	6.1	11.1	-5.9	3.2	7.1	-0.9	-17.0	-13.1	1.2	-7.8	-7.5
Maldives	0.0	8.1	11.3	6.7	11.8	11.5	28.5	27.2	5.6	14.1	20.5	-0.3
Nepal	0.1	7.1	2.2	9.1	6.1	3.1	9.1	2.9	-4.4	12.4	10.0	8.1
Pakistan	0.3	2.1	6.4	4.8	2.3	4.2	6.0	7.3	13.7	9.0	8.2	-7.6
Sri Lanka	0.4	8.2	2.7	3.3	6.2	5.8	10.6	-2.5	8.3	4.4	-2.5	4.0
Western Asia	*12.6*	*7.7*	*10.4*	*-1.7*	*3.2*	*7.6*	*4.4*	*1.0*	*2.7*	*3.9*	*0.4*	*-2.5*
Armenia	0.1	10.3	...	...	-13.3	14.4	-4.5	-3.1	-14.1	2.8	0.6	3.7
Azerbaijan	0.4	13.0	...	...	8.0	22.6	8.8	-13.4	-22.6	0.4	-8.8	-6.1
Bahrain [3]	0.1	7.5	14.4	5.0	-3.1	19.5	6.5	5.9	5.7	1.8	5.6	0.0
Cyprus	0.0	4.0	3.0	-0.4	-0.4	5.6	-13.4	-5.7	22.3	19.7	24.7	13.4
Georgia	0.1	7.6	...	...	-22.5	14.4	22.5	23.0	10.7	5.8	-7.2	4.4
Iraq	0.6	6.4	28.1	-6.5	7.1	16.8	-4.6	-35.4	-9.0	-32.1	24.3	-2.5
Israel	0.9	6.0	1.8	-1.1	6.9	-0.2	3.2	0.9	6.8	6.7	4.9	6.1
Jordan	0.1	3.4	10.5	-5.5	7.2	9.1	6.6	-1.2	0.9	-1.2	-0.4	-0.4
Kuwait	0.2	2.5	17.2	-10.6	10.5	5.3	0.5	-6.2	-10.9	24.7	2.0	-7.0
Lebanon	0.1	5.3	-4.3	-4.4	12.4	5.1	1.0	-7.8	14.8	-5.2	-10.0	4.9
Oman	0.3	7.4	10.7	-2.9	4.3	25.1	6.6	8.9	12.5	-2.5	-7.7	-4.5
Qatar [3]	1.0	9.9	2.8	-1.2	7.7	26.9	22.9	20.4	28.5	17.5	4.5	-1.9
Saudi Arabia	2.5	6.7	21.3	-6.1	2.5	5.6	6.7	4.1	-3.2	-3.3	-3.5	4.6
State of Palestine	0.0	5.6	8.0	2.2	17.1	3.3	-37.3	-4.4	17.3	4.9	12.5	-2.5
Syrian Arab Republic [6]	0.0	3.4	17.1	-7.0	6.2	6.2	-0.1	-4.8	-2.5	3.0	8.9	10.3
Turkey	4.1	9.2	1.8	6.5	1.7	5.8	4.8	4.9	5.1	9.4	-1.9	-8.6
United Arab Emirates	2.0	9.7	16.1	-0.5	3.8	10.8	3.2	3.8	-1.9	2.6	2.4	-2.6
Yemen	0.1	4.3	...	...	3.6	12.0	-26.0	-32.6	-11.4	-14.8	0.0	3.1
Yemen Arab Republic (Former)	...	...	17.5	-1.5	...	...	...	...	...	...	...	...
Yemen Democratic (Former)	...	...	31.6	2.8	...	...	...	...	...	...	...	...
Europe	**23.2**	**5.5**	**1.3**	**2.1**	**-1.7**	**0.8**	**1.4**	**1.7**	**1.8**	**2.8**	**2.6**	**2.7**
Eastern Europe	*17.2*	*6.9*	*6.2*	*5.3*	*-9.0*	*5.7*	*0.6*	*1.3*	*-1.1*	*2.2*	*5.1*	*1.9*
Belarus	0.5	9.0	...	...	-8.5	14.2	-1.3	-10.2	-15.8	-4.6	4.8	3.1
Bulgaria	0.2	4.4	7.4	6.1	-0.3	8.3	-3.4	4.3	-7.3	4.5	1.4	3.4
Czechia	1.0	5.7	...	...	-7.9	2.7	5.1	2.1	-3.7	0.8	0.2	-2.4
Czechoslovakia (Former)	...	...	4.5	1.7	...	...	...	...	...	...	...	...
Hungary	0.5	4.2	6.4	0.3	0.4	0.4	8.5	6.4	-15.1	21.3	15.1	13.0
Poland	3.6	8.0	6.0	2.0	11.1	1.9	9.0	7.2	-8.1	6.5	11.8	-4.1
Republic of Moldova	0.1	8.3	...	...	-21.8	8.6	10.9	0.6	-4.1	5.1	17.5	15.2
Romania	1.1	6.7	7.7	-0.5	0.7	12.6	4.1	6.5	12.3	-8.0	-1.0	17.3
Russian Federation	9.4	7.2	...	...	-12.1	7.1	-2.8	-0.7	1.6	0.5	3.8	2.0
Slovakia	0.7	7.8	...	...	-7.1	8.7	7.5	0.7	-0.5	10.1	-2.4	-4.7
Ukraine [8]	0.2	2.3	...	...	-21.3	-2.8	-19.7	-18.4	15.1	25.6	8.4	23.0
USSR (Former)	...	...	6.5	6.5	...	...	...	...	...	...	...	...
Northern Europe	*27.1*	*6.0*	*-0.1*	*3.7*	*-0.7*	*0.6*	*7.1*	*4.2*	*3.9*	*5.8*	*1.7*	*2.1*
Denmark	1.4	5.0	-2.1	1.4	1.3	-0.4	2.9	10.6	8.4	4.1	7.3	0.6
Estonia	0.1	6.1	...	...	-0.2	3.3	-6.1	0.4	12.0	9.4	12.6	-8.2
Finland	1.4	6.5	1.5	2.7	-3.2	0.6	-3.3	2.9	4.8	2.2	2.1	-3.9
Iceland	0.1	5.4	1.6	2.0	1.3	-2.5	10.2	12.5	28.0	10.3	7.2	-0.1
Ireland	0.6	2.0	5.6	4.9	8.8	-0.2	6.8	6.6	10.7	13.3	11.8	7.5
Latvia	0.2	6.1	...	...	-16.9	5.5	-2.6	-0.4	-9.6	14.6	12.5	2.2
Lithuania	0.3	7.4	...	...	-9.6	7.2	13.2	-0.3	-6.9	6.0	9.6	8.0
Norway	2.3	6.4	2.6	2.3	1.9	2.6	1.9	1.9	3.8	3.2	3.8	3.8
Sweden	2.9	6.2	0.8	1.7	-0.7	2.8	3.4	6.6	-0.3	6.8	3.3	5.1
United Kingdom	17.9	6.4	-0.5	4.5	-0.7	0.1	9.9	3.8	4.1	6.1	0.0	1.8

Table 6.D. Average Rates of Growth of Gross Domestic Product by Kind of Economic Activity - Construction

Major area, region and country	Base year weights as percentage of total for world or region in 2015	Base year share as percentage of total GDP in 2015	Average rates of growth				Annual rate of change (percentage)					
			1970-1979	1980-1989	1990-1999	2000-2009	2014	2015	2016	2017	2018	2019
Southern Europe	*16.4*	*4.8*	*0.5*	*1.2*	*0.0*	*0.9*	*-5.3*	*1.3*	*2.4*	*0.9*	*2.8*	*3.5*
Albania	0.1	10.1	4.0	4.3	9.2	9.7	-13.3	6.2	2.5	6.6	2.5	-3.4
Andorra	0.0	5.8	3.8	2.8	3.8	3.6	-4.0	-0.4	5.4	5.6	13.8	-7.0
Bosnia and Herzegovina	0.1	4.7	...	...	11.1	3.0	7.8	3.2	2.6	3.9	2.9	5.8
Croatia	0.2	5.0	...	...	-4.6	7.6	-2.8	2.7	2.8	2.6	4.5	8.0
Greece	0.4	2.2	3.2	0.1	1.7	1.3	-21.3	3.1	12.7	-32.5	1.0	1.5
Italy	7.6	4.3	-0.2	0.5	-1.1	0.6	-7.7	-2.4	0.6	0.8	1.2	1.8
Kosovo	0.0	8.4	...	...	-12.6	-1.7	-6.1	15.8	4.5	8.6	9.3	3.5
Malta	0.0	3.9	8.1	0.9	1.6	-1.0	0.2	6.6	-2.0	9.1	6.2	11.6
Montenegro	0.0	4.5	...	...	-4.6	12.2	2.2	4.7	32.0	24.5	10.9	12.6
North Macedonia	0.1	8.1	...	...	-2.9	3.4	5.1	8.0	-2.8	1.6	-11.9	5.9
Portugal	0.8	4.1	3.4	3.4	2.6	-3.4	-8.3	0.0	1.8	5.3	3.6	5.1
San Marino	0.0	3.7	3.8	2.4	5.8	2.3	-12.0	-20.4	8.3	0.4	7.1	0.9
Serbia	0.2	4.5	...	...	-8.9	11.8	1.4	17.3	6.1	5.4	12.4	33.7
Slovenia	0.2	5.4	...	...	1.2	3.5	9.8	-3.2	-3.3	7.1	8.1	7.1
Spain	6.7	5.8	0.2	3.1	0.8	1.3	-1.3	5.4	3.9	2.0	4.1	4.3
Yugoslavia (Former)	...	...	5.3	-4.1	...	...	...	...	...	...	...	...
Western Europe	*39.3*	*5.0*	*0.8*	*0.2*	*-0.6*	*-0.7*	*1.0*	*0.3*	*1.3*	*1.6*	*2.1*	*3.0*
Austria	2.3	6.2	3.2	-0.6	2.9	-0.6	-2.3	-2.5	-0.1	3.3	1.8	2.7
Belgium	2.3	5.2	2.3	-1.3	1.1	2.6	2.2	3.8	0.1	1.5	5.1	4.2
France	12.7	5.5	2.0	0.6	-1.2	0.8	-2.7	-0.6	-1.0	2.2	0.9	2.6
Germany	14.7	4.6	0.7	-0.7	-0.4	-3.0	4.0	-0.1	1.9	0.1	1.7	3.5
Liechtenstein	0.0	4.0	3.0	6.0	-4.2	1.2	2.6	3.5	0.7	12.0	-1.7	1.7
Luxembourg	0.3	5.5	2.1	2.8	3.7	2.8	12.2	0.2	4.0	2.5	11.2	2.0
Monaco [3]	0.1	12.7	3.9	2.4	1.9	1.3	6.9	72.2	20.9	-48.7	17.1	12.5
Netherlands	3.1	4.3	-4.1	0.7	0.7	0.7	3.2	6.9	8.6	7.5	4.8	5.1
Switzerland	3.7	5.1	0.8	3.0	-2.9	0.5	1.6	-1.2	1.1	0.7	3.0	0.2
Oceania	**2.8**	**8.3**	**1.7**	**2.5**	**4.2**	**6.9**	**-1.4**	**-1.1**	**-1.8**	**4.9**	**-0.2**	**-3.9**
Australia and New Zealand	*97.1*	*8.3*	*1.5*	*2.5*	*4.2*	*6.9*	*-1.5*	*-1.0*	*-2.0*	*5.1*	*-0.2*	*-4.0*
Australia	87.7	8.5	1.8	2.6	4.3	7.3	-2.4	-1.8	-3.0	5.0	-0.7	-4.6
New Zealand	9.5	6.6	-0.1	2.4	3.8	4.1	8.8	7.1	7.4	6.0	3.8	0.9
Melanesia	*2.6*	*8.5*	*7.3*	*0.3*	*4.3*	*8.7*	*0.8*	*-5.3*	*4.2*	*-4.4*	*0.9*	*-0.6*
Fiji	0.1	3.0	2.6	-6.1	1.2	1.6	27.7	4.0	10.1	9.7	7.4	9.1
New Caledonia	0.9	12.3	13.2	-2.7	6.7	5.9	-7.4	3.3	7.2	2.9	2.0	1.6
Papua New Guinea	1.5	8.2	2.7	5.7	3.2	12.7	3.8	-11.7	1.9	-10.6	-0.9	-3.5
Solomon Islands	0.0	4.7	9.1	2.4	-1.9	3.5	16.2	11.7	11.4	4.6	9.2	8.4
Vanuatu	0.0	5.9	7.7	9.7	-0.6	4.7	9.7	101.6	2.0	10.4	6.9	-1.5
Micronesia	*0.0*	*5.0*	*4.7*	*2.4*	*0.1*	*0.9*	*-13.0*	*14.5*	*11.6*	*-3.5*	*2.8*	*2.6*
Kiribati [1]	0.0	10.2	8.4	-8.2	8.3	0.9	-2.6	30.1	14.9	-22.1	11.1	1.3
Marshall Islands	0.0	5.1	6.6	7.0	-2.3	3.1	-13.9	-3.9	15.9	15.9	8.5	13.4
Micronesia (FS of)	0.0	2.8	6.6	4.1	1.1	1.3	-40.1	-12.3	0.3	1.8	-16.5	-14.8
Nauru [3]	0.0	2.8	1.1	-1.6	-15.2	-1.7	55.9	-10.3	8.8	-4.1	3.0	2.2
Palau	0.0	5.0	0.2	3.5	11.1	-1.3	7.4	51.5	12.0	4.5	0.5	2.6
Polynesia	*0.2*	*4.3*	*8.9*	*-0.2*	*1.6*	*0.3*	*5.6*	*1.2*	*-2.7*	*7.2*	*-1.7*	*7.7*
Cook Islands	0.0	6.6	-9.2	-2.5	7.2	5.9	-0.1	90.3	-40.4	38.9	-1.1	27.4
French Polynesia	0.1	3.5	10.6	0.2	1.1	-0.7	5.3	-9.3	0.4	8.5	-0.3	2.3
Samoa [9]	0.1	7.3	3.7	0.3	1.6	7.8	2.1	26.5	-12.9	-12.1	12.6	14.2
Tonga	0.0	7.2	8.2	-4.7	6.1	1.0	18.5	-5.1	22.8	18.0	-32.4	16.2
Tuvalu	0.0	10.8	-1.5	7.8	0.4	11.4	-8.4	45.1	24.9	25.5	31.5	27.3

Notes for Table 6.D. Average Rates of Growth of Gross Domestic Product by Kind of Economic Activity - Construction

1/ 1970-2019
At factor cost.

2/ 1970-2019
Refers to Buildings and public works

3/ 1970-2019
At producers' prices.

4/ 1970-2001
At producers' prices.

5/ 1970-2019
Includes Mining and quarrying.

6/ 1970-2019
Includes Taxes less subsidies on production and imports.

7/ 1970-2009
At producers' prices.

8/ 2010-2019
The Government of Ukraine has advised the United Nations that it is not in a position to provide statistical data concerning the Autonomous Republic of Crimea and the city of Sevastopol.

9/ (a) 1970-2008
At producers' prices.

(b) 2009-2019
Includes Taxes less subsidies on production and imports.

Table 6.E. Average Rates of Growth of Gross Domestic Product by Kind of Economic Activity - Wholesale, retail trade, restaurants and hotels

Major area, region and country	Base year weights as percentage of total for world or region in 2015	Base year share as percentage of total GDP in 2015	Average rates of growth				Annual rate of change (percentage)					
			1970-1979	1980-1989	1990-1999	2000-2009	2014	2015	2016	2017	2018	2019
World	**100.0**	**14.4**	**4.5**	**3.6**	**3.5**	**2.5**	**3.2**	**3.4**	**2.3**	**3.7**	**2.7**	**2.3**
Developed economies	**58.3**	**14.5**	**4.1**	**3.8**	**3.5**	**0.9**	**2.1**	**3.5**	**1.9**	**2.5**	**1.3**	**1.0**
Developing economies	**38.8**	**14.1**	**6.0**	**3.7**	**4.3**	**5.9**	**5.0**	**3.7**	**3.2**	**5.5**	**4.6**	**4.0**
Transition economies	**3.0**	**16.6**	**5.6**	**-1.3**	**-3.2**	**8.1**	**2.9**	**-1.8**	**-0.2**	**2.9**	**3.2**	**2.5**
Africa	**3.5**	**16.5**	**4.2**	**3.0**	**2.5**	**6.4**	**5.2**	**3.6**	**1.6**	**2.2**	**2.9**	**2.1**
Northern Africa	*28.9*	*14.8*	*7.7*	*4.5*	*4.0*	*4.3*	*1.8*	*3.8*	*2.6*	*3.9*	*5.4*	*3.5*
Algeria	6.8	15.4	6.8	3.7	1.5	8.1	9.8	4.8	1.8	3.3	2.6	2.2
Egypt [1]	13.6	15.3	9.4	7.3	4.4	2.5	0.2	5.9	0.2	5.1	7.8	3.9
Libya	0.2	4.7	7.8	-1.7	1.3	10.5	-50.5	-46.8	-19.1	54.5	28.0	8.8
Morocco	2.8	11.2	5.1	3.6	2.4	4.1	2.6	1.1	4.8	6.3	4.3	4.9
Sudan	4.0	17.5	...	...	...	...	4.2	4.8	11.3	-2.1	2.9	3.1
Sudan (Former)	...	...	6.5	2.2	7.3	...	...	...	...	...	...	...
Tunisia [1]	1.6	14.5	12.5	3.4	4.3	4.5	2.0	-3.5	2.4	3.2	3.3	3.0
Sub-Saharan Africa	71.1	17.2	3.1	2.3	1.6	7.6	6.7	3.5	1.2	1.6	1.8	1.6
Eastern Africa	*12.6*	*15.7*	*2.3*	*2.2*	*3.1*	*6.1*	*8.1*	*7.2*	*5.1*	*5.8*	*6.6*	*5.2*
Burundi	0.1	7.2	1.9	5.6	-1.2	1.9	-1.9	-6.6	-2.8	13.5	1.4	4.0
Comoros	0.1	21.0	4.5	3.1	4.2	1.8	2.0	0.2	2.0	7.1	5.1	3.0
Djibouti	0.2	32.4	1.5	2.8	0.1	8.8	9.5	3.0	9.8	5.4	3.7	8.4
Eritrea	0.1	11.5	...	...	8.3	-0.5	35.7	-17.8	8.4	-11.6	14.0	3.9
Ethiopia	3.2	20.0	...	...	1.6	10.6	19.5	16.0	10.0	5.4	10.6	11.3
Ethiopia (Former)	...	...	1.8	2.7	...	...	...	...	...	...	...	...
Kenya [2]	1.5	8.9	1.9	4.1	2.8	4.8	3.1	5.0	4.9	6.9	8.3	7.2
Madagascar	0.5	16.6	1.0	0.0	1.1	2.1	5.3	1.4	6.2	-2.4	-6.1	4.1
Malawi [2]	0.3	20.3	7.2	0.1	2.1	6.2	6.2	4.9	2.7	4.9	4.1	4.3
Mauritius [3]	0.5	18.5	8.2	6.9	6.0	3.9	4.2	5.2	5.6	3.7	3.8	2.0
Mozambique [2]	0.6	14.3	3.9	-1.9	5.1	9.1	8.6	8.3	-1.2	-2.2	2.0	0.1
Rwanda [2]	0.3	12.4	4.8	2.0	-1.2	12.5	8.8	11.8	6.8	3.5	15.6	14.4
Seychelles [2]	0.1	23.0	9.6	3.4	-9.3	2.2	0.4	4.2	3.6	5.7	1.3	4.8
Somalia	0.0	10.6	5.7	0.4	0.2	3.1	4.6	2.1	3.1	3.3	2.8	3.1
South Sudan	0.2	10.9	...	...	...	...	36.8	49.6	-19.9	-17.1	-4.2	4.4
U.R. of Tanzania: Mainland [2]	1.4	11.8	1.2	2.7	3.9	7.0	8.9	3.3	5.6	5.6	5.8	5.1
Uganda [2]	1.1	17.4	-1.6	4.0	9.0	8.3	0.4	4.6	1.3	23.8	8.0	3.4
Zambia [4]	1.4	25.4	5.2	5.6	3.5	6.9	3.5	1.3	0.1	1.1	3.2	0.5
Zanzibar [5]	0.1	22.9	...	...	8.6	3.9	3.1	6.1	10.5	11.8	14.4	11.2
Zimbabwe	1.0	21.1	1.9	-0.1	2.5	0.0	2.5	3.8	6.8	7.6	4.5	-8.7
Middle Africa	*11.0*	*17.4*	*1.8*	*2.8*	*-1.4*	*8.8*	*11.4*	*-4.2*	*-1.7*	*0.5*	*1.1*	*-0.1*
Angola	6.7	21.2	0.2	3.5	-2.5	11.4	15.3	-8.3	-4.8	1.4	-0.4	-2.6
Cameroon [2]	1.7	21.2	5.7	0.6	2.3	5.3	5.5	3.3	5.7	4.6	5.0	5.0
Central African Republic	0.1	17.7	-1.2	-0.5	-1.0	1.0	36.4	8.8	10.3	7.1	4.1	7.2
Chad	0.5	15.7	-1.7	4.2	2.7	5.2	3.8	2.4	-14.0	-8.0	1.5	1.6
Congo	0.4	12.6	4.4	6.3	-3.2	7.9	9.0	-0.2	13.7	-21.9	-4.1	-4.1
D.R. of the Congo [6]	1.1	11.3	3.6	3.1	-3.8	6.8	4.8	10.8	7.7	3.5	1.8	4.0
Equatorial Guinea	0.3	8.7	2.3	3.1	4.3	13.5	-2.4	-13.4	-11.0	-12.5	9.8	0.1
Gabon	0.2	5.6	8.3	1.7	1.4	0.3	3.4	-0.7	-0.4	-0.3	6.1	1.7
Sao Tome and Principe	0.0	31.4	7.0	-1.2	0.6	6.5	5.4	2.4	5.1	3.6	0.6	1.0
Southern Africa	*13.0*	*15.1*	*2.8*	*2.3*	*2.3*	*3.7*	*2.2*	*1.9*	*2.3*	*0.0*	*0.6*	*0.2*
Botswana	0.6	18.0	16.3	0.7	14.6	7.8	10.7	-3.9	13.4	9.0	3.6	4.1
Eswatini [2]	0.2	15.3	4.0	4.5	5.8	3.8	0.6	5.9	3.5	-2.9	2.5	1.0
Lesotho [2]	0.1	12.7	7.3	4.4	4.8	3.9	-0.8	-5.0	2.6	-2.6	-10.0	8.9
Namibia [2]	0.4	14.3	3.3	1.6	5.8	6.2	12.3	6.5	1.9	-6.1	-4.5	-3.4
South Africa	11.7	15.0	2.7	2.3	1.9	3.5	1.4	2.1	1.7	-0.3	0.6	0.0
Western Africa	*34.4*	*18.8*	*4.5*	*2.1*	*1.9*	*10.4*	*6.4*	*5.6*	*0.3*	*0.9*	*0.5*	*1.0*
Benin [7]	0.5	17.9	3.2	3.7	2.9	3.1	8.1	43.1	4.7	2.4	4.8	6.9
Burkina Faso [2]	0.4	13.8	7.0	1.1	-0.4	7.8	-0.9	5.1	0.1	6.8	6.0	5.2
Cabo Verde [2]	0.1	16.9	0.3	4.3	4.1	8.1	-1.9	-11.2	5.0	11.8	7.3	5.8
Côte d'Ivoire	1.6	14.1	6.2	-0.8	-2.5	-0.2	21.3	12.6	4.4	13.0	4.4	5.2
Gambia [2]	0.1	35.0	7.1	7.0	3.6	-0.8	0.9	-0.3	-4.3	16.0	10.0	8.4
Ghana [2]	2.0	15.9	-1.0	4.0	7.8	6.0	1.9	1.4	0.3	8.1	2.9	4.3
Guinea	0.5	23.2	3.0	3.0	3.5	1.2	0.7	5.0	5.6	5.6	-2.4	2.9
Guinea-Bissau	0.1	18.5	11.7	4.5	1.3	0.4	2.8	6.1	11.0	4.1	4.8	7.1
Liberia	0.0	5.6	3.9	-2.7	12.2	-11.5	5.1	6.9	20.5	1.1	-4.6	-7.9
Mali	0.4	13.3	4.5	-0.6	12.5	8.9	3.2	17.1	6.9	-1.8	2.1	3.9
Mauritania [2]	0.2	15.9	7.7	4.2	7.0	4.3	11.0	4.4	-0.8	11.4	2.8	7.0
Niger [2]	0.4	16.4	3.5	-2.0	1.1	3.5	3.5	5.4	3.9	6.2	5.7	5.8
Nigeria [2]	27.1	20.1	4.7	2.9	1.9	13.2	6.5	5.0	-0.5	-1.1	-0.5	-0.2
Senegal [2]	0.7	16.0	1.4	2.2	2.6	3.0	4.8	6.9	5.9	8.3	6.3	5.2
Sierra Leone	0.1	9.7	1.5	5.9	-8.5	8.8	-4.6	-0.8	4.8	4.9	1.9	1.0
Togo [8]	0.1	8.2	2.7	-0.4	2.6	4.5	-4.0	-4.1	18.3	5.2	5.8	6.5

Table 6.E. Average Rates of Growth of Gross Domestic Product by Kind of Economic Activity - Wholesale, retail trade, restaurants and hotels

Major area, region and country	Base year weights as percentage of total for world or region in 2015	Base year share as percentage of total GDP in 2015	Average rates of growth				Annual rate of change (percentage)					
			1970-1979	1980-1989	1990-1999	2000-2009	2014	2015	2016	2017	2018	2019
Americas	**36.8**	**15.4**	**4.4**	**4.1**	**4.3**	**1.2**	**2.2**	**2.6**	**-0.1**	**2.3**	**1.4**	**0.0**
Latin America and the Caribbean	**8.7**	**18.1**	**5.6**	**1.0**	**2.7**	**2.8**	**-0.2**	**-1.3**	**-3.8**	**1.9**	**0.4**	**-1.8**
Caribbean	*1.6*	*18.6*	*4.0*	*3.0*	*1.6*	*2.6*	*3.3*	*4.4*	*1.3*	*1.1*	*1.8*	*1.9*
Anguilla	0.0	26.0	3.7	8.0	4.7	2.1	6.1	2.2	3.4	-15.9	-3.6	37.4
Antigua and Barbuda	0.0	26.2	5.0	7.0	2.9	1.0	4.8	2.2	4.0	-1.0	3.3	4.8
Aruba [2]	0.0	27.0	9.1	11.2	4.8	-3.4	1.4	6.0	1.1	2.8	0.7	-0.8
Bahamas [2]	0.1	23.6	2.4	4.3	0.6	1.6	0.2	7.3	-1.1	-2.4	9.1	3.1
Barbados [2]	0.0	23.5	4.9	1.9	1.1	0.2	-0.6	6.0	5.4	1.4	1.3	-0.8
British Virgin Islands [2]	0.0	18.7	14.3	2.2	15.9	-1.1	-3.7	0.6	-5.6	-0.9	-2.2	-2.4
Cayman Islands [2]	0.0	11.9	9.4	11.3	5.9	0.8	3.0	1.4	3.3	4.1	6.3	3.6
Cuba	0.5	24.0	5.4	4.0	-3.9	4.4	3.2	6.3	1.0	2.5	0.7	2.7
Curaçao	0.0	16.0	...	...	...	...	-3.6	14.7	-4.4	-3.5	2.2	-5.6
Dominica	0.0	13.4	2.2	5.8	3.8	3.5	6.1	-7.1	-2.3	-13.4	27.1	5.1
Dominican Republic [2]	0.3	19.5	7.4	3.5	8.1	3.1	7.6	7.6	6.8	4.6	6.8	2.0
Former Netherlands Antilles	...	...	8.2	3.3	0.1	1.3	...	...	...	...	...	...
Grenada	0.0	13.9	6.5	3.8	4.6	-0.3	16.9	5.6	2.4	7.4	8.4	1.1
Haiti	0.1	26.4	5.7	0.1	1.5	1.6	4.2	2.7	0.7	1.1	0.9	-1.0
Jamaica	0.1	23.3	-3.4	2.5	1.9	0.9	1.0	0.9	0.7	1.5	1.2	2.1
Montserrat	0.0	10.0	2.4	1.1	-15.2	1.3	1.8	15.8	-1.2	-6.1	6.9	2.9
Puerto Rico [9]	0.3	9.5	3.2	3.7	5.0	1.7	1.6	-3.1	0.0	0.7	-3.2	0.1
Saint Kitts and Nevis	0.0	16.4	6.2	11.6	3.1	1.9	3.0	2.5	2.9	-2.4	4.8	5.8
Saint Lucia [2]	0.0	34.0	6.4	5.4	2.4	2.2	6.7	-3.8	3.1	7.6	4.8	0.7
Sint Maarten (Dutch part)	0.0	25.6	...	...	...	...	8.3	6.7	1.2	-11.9	-6.3	4.7
St. Vincent and the Grenadines	0.0	15.3	2.0	5.9	7.1	4.1	0.0	-2.3	1.1	-2.5	6.0	-2.2
Trinidad and Tobago [2]	0.2	25.7	3.5	-4.0	5.4	2.3	1.1	5.0	-6.6	-9.9	-2.0	2.2
Turks and Caicos Islands	0.0	43.6	10.7	10.7	8.4	5.8	7.8	10.8	16.4	-7.5	6.3	5.4
Central America	*7.4*	*21.3*	*6.1*	*0.5*	*3.9*	*0.9*	*3.3*	*4.5*	*3.1*	*3.6*	*2.7*	*0.5*
Belize	0.0	23.9	2.6	3.0	3.8	2.2	3.8	5.3	14.8	6.3	4.0	1.6
Costa Rica [2]	0.2	13.6	5.5	1.3	2.7	3.2	4.8	4.4	4.1	2.5	1.9	0.1
El Salvador [2]	0.1	16.1	5.6	4.0	3.4	1.0	3.6	1.1	1.7	1.5	2.1	2.0
Guatemala [2]	0.3	22.5	5.3	-0.5	4.4	2.5	3.8	4.2	3.2	3.2	3.0	4.0
Honduras	0.1	17.5	6.9	-1.1	3.4	1.9	2.1	3.1	3.2	3.6	4.4	2.8
Mexico [2]	6.3	21.6	6.3	0.5	3.9	0.5	3.4	4.6	3.0	3.6	2.8	0.3
Nicaragua	0.0	16.2	-2.8	-2.6	4.4	2.7	3.7	5.6	5.1	7.0	-13.7	-5.9
Panama	0.3	24.4	4.6	-1.4	5.5	7.1	1.1	3.2	3.8	3.4	2.9	1.8
South America	*14.5*	*16.8*	*5.6*	*1.0*	*2.2*	*3.8*	*-2.0*	*-4.6*	*-7.8*	*1.0*	*-1.1*	*-3.7*
Argentina	2.7	18.6	2.6	-2.6	5.1	2.7	-6.3	3.3	-2.7	2.2	-3.8	-6.9
Bolivia (Plurinational State of)	0.1	10.6	3.5	2.3	3.3	3.0	3.9	4.3	4.4	5.1	5.0	3.8
Brazil [2]	6.4	15.7	9.4	3.1	2.1	3.2	0.8	-7.2	-6.1	2.6	1.6	0.5
Chile [2]	0.7	12.4	2.4	2.2	7.6	5.3	2.8	2.2	1.7	3.0	3.8	0.0
Colombia [2]	0.9	13.0	6.1	2.4	-0.2	5.0	5.0	3.2	3.7	1.8	2.8	5.0
Ecuador [2]	0.3	13.4	5.8	1.5	0.3	3.7	3.3	-1.1	-3.5	5.5	2.3	-0.4
Guyana [3]	0.0	8.2	1.8	-3.9	3.9	5.8	-1.0	-11.9	2.0	6.4	4.0	5.0
Paraguay [2]	0.1	13.9	8.8	2.7	1.2	3.0	7.3	-0.2	2.4	9.8	2.0	4.6
Peru [2,10]	0.8	16.5	2.5	0.1	3.8	3.4	2.7	3.1	2.8	1.3	2.8	3.4
Suriname	0.0	25.0	5.2	-4.4	0.6	8.9	-1.6	-10.8	-26.7	-21.9	-2.6	5.7
Uruguay	0.2	14.3	2.8	-0.6	6.1	1.3	-0.6	-4.0	-2.8	6.2	-1.3	-2.1
Venezuela (Bolivarian Republic of)	2.3	27.5	4.7	-0.4	-0.5	5.8	-10.2	-12.8	-31.8	-11.0	-16.9	-37.5
Northern America	**28.2**	**14.7**	**4.0**	**5.2**	**4.7**	**0.8**	**2.9**	**3.9**	**1.1**	**2.5**	**1.6**	**0.5**
Bermuda [2]	0.0	10.1	3.5	1.0	2.0	-2.3	-5.8	-0.9	0.2	12.3	-4.6	2.4
Canada [2]	4.8	12.5	5.1	3.8	2.8	2.6	2.5	-1.0	2.0	2.7	2.4	1.4
Greenland [2]	0.0	11.9	6.4	2.5	1.2	1.8	-1.0	6.7	-1.1	1.1	0.2	0.1
United States [2,11]	71.7	14.9	3.9	5.3	4.8	0.7	3.0	4.2	1.0	2.4	1.6	0.4
Asia	**34.3**	**13.5**	**7.7**	**5.5**	**4.5**	**4.6**	**4.7**	**4.4**	**4.6**	**6.0**	**4.4**	**4.7**
Central Asia	*1.2*	*14.6*	*...*	*...*	*-3.5*	*8.8*	*8.6*	*2.9*	*0.4*	*3.2*	*6.5*	*6.2*
Kazakhstan [5]	0.9	19.1	...	...	-3.0	8.5	8.0	0.8	-1.6	3.2	7.1	6.8
Kyrgyzstan [5]	0.0	22.6	...	...	-6.9	10.8	8.7	7.3	8.2	7.2	5.8	5.1
Tajikistan	0.0	16.7	...	...	-11.5	11.6	6.2	3.5	6.6	-3.9	-2.0	0.1
Turkmenistan	0.0	3.8	...	...	-11.3	6.3	22.4	16.2	-2.9	9.9	7.2	1.3
Uzbekistan [5]	0.2	8.4	...	...	1.6	10.3	10.4	11.3	9.2	2.0	5.4	5.0
Eastern Asia	*65.8*	*13.2*	*8.1*	*5.8*	*4.5*	*4.0*	*4.1*	*4.0*	*4.7*	*5.7*	*3.7*	*4.4*
China [11,12]	36.4	11.6	6.1	14.3	9.1	12.2	9.6	6.7	7.7	7.9	6.7	7.4
China, Hong Kong SAR [12]	2.2	26.1	8.8	9.5	3.1	5.3	1.4	-1.2	0.6	3.9	4.4	-6.6
China, Macao SAR	0.1	14.5	7.9	7.1	-1.6	11.8	2.8	-7.4	10.6	13.9	7.8	10.7
D.P.R. of Korea	...	...	...	...	...	...	...	...	...	...	...	...
Japan [2,9]	20.3	16.4	8.2	4.0	3.1	-0.6	-3.1	0.9	0.8	2.6	-2.1	-0.2

Table 6.E. Average Rates of Growth of Gross Domestic Product by Kind of Economic Activity - Wholesale, retail trade, restaurants and hotels

Major area, region and country	Base year weights as percentage of total for world or region in 2015	Base year share as percentage of total GDP in 2015	Average rates of growth				Annual rate of change (percentage)					
			1970-1979	1980-1989	1990-1999	2000-2009	2014	2015	2016	2017	2018	2019
Mongolia [2]	0.0	13.6	5.6	28.1	-1.9	6.3	1.9	-7.7	-2.5	6.9	2.5	7.1
Republic of Korea [2]	4.0	10.5	8.5	9.2	5.6	2.0	1.0	3.3	2.7	1.8	2.9	1.1
South-Eastern Asia	*12.1*	*17.9*	*6.5*	*5.7*	*4.6*	*5.4*	*4.7*	*5.3*	*5.4*	*5.9*	*6.7*	*5.5*
Brunei Darussalam [2]	0.0	6.0	38.8	0.9	-0.3	4.4	-1.6	0.4	-3.2	1.1	2.5	7.3
Cambodia	0.1	15.2	-7.2	3.9	5.0	7.5	7.7	5.7	5.2	6.1	6.4	4.9
Indonesia [2]	4.0	16.8	7.9	6.4	4.1	5.7	5.3	2.9	4.2	4.6	5.1	4.8
Lao People's DR [2]	0.1	17.0	3.0	6.9	11.8	10.0	13.0	9.9	5.1	5.1	10.2	4.3
Malaysia [2,9]	1.6	18.9	10.7	4.0	8.6	6.6	8.5	6.9	6.5	7.3	8.4	7.2
Myanmar [6,9]	0.3	19.1	3.4	-0.1	6.3	11.4	5.7	6.6	7.6	7.9	7.9	7.8
Philippines [2,11]	1.6	19.9	5.0	3.0	3.9	4.9	5.7	7.1	7.8	7.4	5.9	7.9
Singapore [2]	1.5	18.6	7.2	5.9	6.6	6.0	3.6	3.3	1.1	1.5	2.8	-2.3
Thailand [2,9]	2.1	18.7	6.2	7.7	2.9	2.9	0.0	7.9	7.0	8.0	10.6	6.7
Timor-Leste [5]	0.0	18.3	...	...	-1.6	5.4	2.8	2.5	6.5	-6.9	-9.6	13.9
Viet Nam [2,13]	0.8	15.4	4.7	5.6	6.7	7.9	7.0	7.0	7.8	8.5	8.0	8.2
Southern Asia	*10.4*	*12.6*	*5.6*	*5.5*	*5.3*	*6.3*	*7.0*	*6.5*	*8.2*	*8.5*	*7.1*	*7.6*
Afghanistan [14]	0.1	11.3	1.0	0.3	-19.1	19.0	0.4	3.9	-3.7	0.6	7.9	0.5
Bangladesh	0.8	14.2	3.0	3.1	5.2	6.8	6.7	6.4	6.5	7.4	7.4	8.1
Bhutan	0.0	10.4	3.8	0.7	6.8	10.8	14.2	13.2	12.2	11.2	10.2	11.2
India [2]	6.3	11.4	4.1	6.2	7.8	7.2	9.8	11.1	10.1	10.0	8.5	9.9
Iran (Islamic Republic of)	1.5	13.2	9.2	3.8	3.4	6.2	0.5	-6.1	6.2	4.7	1.0	1.3
Maldives [2]	0.0	35.4	5.8	17.8	7.0	1.4	6.6	-2.7	6.4	8.1	9.0	9.5
Nepal	0.1	16.7	0.8	3.8	6.2	0.3	10.4	2.5	-3.0	11.4	12.3	10.7
Pakistan [2]	1.4	19.3	4.9	7.6	3.5	4.3	4.8	2.6	4.7	7.5	6.6	3.1
Sri Lanka [2]	0.3	13.4	5.8	6.3	6.0	4.1	3.0	5.1	2.7	4.0	4.8	2.0
Western Asia	*10.5*	*13.0*	*8.8*	*2.9*	*4.2*	*5.8*	*5.5*	*3.9*	*0.1*	*6.2*	*3.2*	*2.8*
Armenia [5]	0.0	13.3	...	...	3.2	11.1	4.6	-7.1	4.7	21.0	10.5	11.2
Azerbaijan [5]	0.2	13.4	...	...	-6.4	13.7	11.4	11.5	1.6	3.3	3.9	4.2
Bahrain [9]	0.1	7.1	7.6	3.8	0.8	11.8	3.9	2.4	2.6	8.9	-0.3	1.7
Cyprus [2]	0.1	16.9	5.4	9.8	5.2	2.8	1.2	2.4	10.0	9.0	4.9	4.0
Georgia [5]	0.1	17.0	...	...	-2.6	7.3	0.8	0.2	1.4	7.8	6.7	8.8
Iraq	0.5	10.9	15.8	0.6	5.0	5.8	-0.5	2.0	-11.5	0.4	3.8	7.3
Israel [2]	0.9	11.9	6.1	1.9	5.5	5.8	5.8	2.4	4.7	5.6	3.2	4.5
Jordan [2]	0.1	10.7	6.9	-3.5	2.5	5.8	3.7	0.5	1.2	1.5	1.3	1.0
Kuwait	0.2	4.9	11.7	-2.2	6.1	3.6	6.0	-6.5	-1.0	-0.3	1.8	-0.4
Lebanon [2]	0.2	18.7	-3.1	-5.2	10.7	4.9	-0.5	0.9	-6.7	3.5	-5.7	-2.7
Oman	0.2	9.1	10.8	7.4	6.3	6.2	2.2	6.0	4.8	3.8	-5.5	-6.0
Qatar [2,9]	0.4	9.5	7.9	-1.1	6.4	19.0	12.4	5.3	-9.7	-0.9	0.4	1.3
Saudi Arabia [2]	2.1	11.4	20.1	2.1	4.3	10.9	6.0	2.8	-1.6	0.6	1.0	6.3
State of Palestine [2]	0.1	24.6	8.0	2.2	7.6	2.4	-0.7	8.9	8.0	8.0	5.3	0.0
Syrian Arab Republic [11]	0.1	22.5	9.9	0.5	4.2	9.2	0.8	-6.3	-3.5	-2.6	3.9	4.4
Turkey [2]	3.5	16.2	7.1	6.8	3.1	2.3	7.7	7.0	1.3	11.3	6.2	1.4
United Arab Emirates	1.5	14.7	12.0	1.3	5.1	5.5	4.9	6.1	4.1	9.4	1.9	1.5
Yemen	0.1	19.0	...	...	5.8	9.0	-9.9	-26.7	-10.1	-7.7	-0.5	0.7
Yemen Arab Republic (Former)	...	...	11.3	4.0	...	...	...	...	...	...	...	...
Yemen Democratic (Former)	...	...	-2.1	3.2	...	...	...	...	...	...	...	...
Europe	**23.7**	**14.2**	**3.6**	**2.0**	**1.9**	**2.0**	**2.6**	**3.2**	**2.7**	**2.5**	**2.0**	**2.3**
Eastern Europe	*15.7*	*16.4*	*5.5*	*0.3*	*0.1*	*6.2*	*1.9*	*-0.2*	*0.8*	*4.1*	*3.4*	*2.5*
Belarus [5]	0.3	15.0	...	...	-0.9	10.6	6.8	-2.3	-6.9	3.9	6.1	0.3
Bulgaria [2]	0.3	16.4	7.0	4.4	-0.8	5.5	-1.4	6.8	0.8	5.6	5.3	0.4
Czechia [5]	0.9	12.9	...	...	-0.1	3.2	6.8	9.3	-0.2	6.6	3.6	2.9
Czechoslovakia (Former)	...	...	6.6	4.8	...	...	...	...	...	...	...	...
Hungary [2]	0.5	12.0	5.3	-0.1	-3.2	1.2	6.9	3.9	0.8	7.8	10.0	6.4
Poland [2]	3.3	18.8	6.0	2.6	13.5	3.4	0.0	4.0	5.1	6.5	5.1	5.3
Republic of Moldova [5]	0.0	17.0	...	...	-4.8	4.6	5.8	0.3	6.9	8.9	5.9	6.8
Romania [2]	0.8	12.0	10.2	2.0	-2.9	6.9	9.0	12.6	3.8	8.9	5.4	3.2
Russian Federation	8.7	17.3	...	...	-1.9	8.0	3.0	-2.7	-0.9	2.3	2.0	1.2
Slovakia [5]	0.4	12.4	...	...	9.5	5.6	-5.4	-3.4	-0.1	3.1	0.4	-1.9
Ukraine [5,15]	0.5	16.9	...	...	-12.5	9.5	-13.6	-14.8	4.4	2.7	4.7	3.8
USSR (Former)	...	...	5.2	-0.7	...	...	...	...	...	...	...	...
Northern Europe	*22.0*	*12.7*	*2.1*	*3.3*	*3.0*	*1.8*	*3.9*	*4.0*	*3.6*	*2.4*	*2.6*	*3.7*
Denmark [2]	1.6	14.6	2.2	1.3	3.7	0.7	3.6	4.7	3.8	3.7	1.9	4.3
Estonia [5]	0.1	13.8	...	...	-0.2	2.1	3.7	0.5	4.6	5.7	8.7	6.8
Finland [2]	0.9	11.0	3.4	4.2	0.0	3.0	-1.6	-1.4	4.7	4.4	0.3	1.4
Iceland [2]	0.1	12.2	4.5	3.5	3.6	1.1	11.1	11.2	8.4	7.7	5.1	-1.3
Ireland [2]	1.1	9.7	4.3	2.2	3.9	0.7	6.8	7.1	6.2	4.4	3.5	3.4
Latvia [5]	0.2	16.6	...	...	1.2	7.6	3.1	7.2	4.5	3.2	4.4	4.7
Lithuania [5]	0.3	19.6	...	...	6.7	4.8	2.7	4.0	4.0	3.6	4.5	7.6
Norway [2]	1.3	9.2	2.8	0.6	4.9	3.0	5.3	3.9	2.8	1.9	1.1	3.2
Sweden [2]	2.3	12.5	2.0	2.4	2.9	3.5	6.2	4.7	5.3	3.1	2.3	2.4
United Kingdom [2]	14.2	13.3	1.9	3.8	2.9	1.5	3.7	3.9	3.0	1.8	2.8	4.0

Table 6.E. Average Rates of Growth of Gross Domestic Product by Kind of Economic Activity - Wholesale, retail trade, restaurants and hotels

Major area, region and country	Base year weights as percentage of total for world or region in 2015	Base year share as percentage of total GDP in 2015	Average rates of growth				Annual rate of change (percentage)					
			1970-1979	1980-1989	1990-1999	2000-2009	2014	2015	2016	2017	2018	2019
Southern Europe	*22.4*	*16.8*	*4.5*	*1.5*	*1.8*	*1.0*	*1.9*	*4.7*	*3.3*	*2.8*	*1.1*	*1.5*
Albania [2]	0.1	14.3	4.1	2.9	4.8	1.9	3.7	-0.7	3.4	4.0	4.9	2.7
Andorra [2]	0.0	24.4	3.8	2.8	2.3	2.6	0.1	0.6	3.7	3.9	2.2	0.3
Bosnia and Herzegovina [5]	0.1	18.1	...	...	15.9	6.6	1.6	3.4	4.1	6.9	5.2	5.8
Croatia [5]	0.3	18.3	...	...	-5.2	5.3	0.5	6.1	4.1	5.1	4.3	4.1
Greece [2]	1.3	18.5	5.7	2.4	1.4	1.4	-0.8	6.1	-2.1	1.6	2.2	1.7
Italy [2]	10.3	15.2	3.8	1.9	1.9	0.0	2.8	3.7	2.7	2.4	0.5	0.3
Kosovo [5]	0.0	16.3	...	...	-8.8	4.9	7.8	3.6	4.2	4.3	7.2	4.5
Malta [2]	0.1	16.3	9.9	3.3	4.1	-1.5	5.7	13.7	-0.7	4.8	6.3	3.6
Montenegro [5]	0.0	23.9	...	...	-4.4	10.0	2.4	8.4	1.9	6.4	5.6	5.9
North Macedonia [5]	0.1	16.6	...	...	21.2	5.0	3.2	4.2	8.3	7.2	2.7	3.3
Portugal [2]	1.4	19.8	3.6	0.7	1.9	0.4	3.6	2.3	3.7	2.7	2.4	4.5
San Marino [2]	0.0	13.6	3.8	2.4	5.9	-0.6	-4.1	-17.8	7.1	4.6	-2.2	0.0
Serbia [5]	0.2	14.8	...	...	-7.2	10.9	-1.5	2.8	3.9	5.5	6.6	6.2
Slovenia [5]	0.2	14.1	...	...	1.6	3.5	3.1	4.8	4.9	5.8	6.0	2.6
Spain [2]	8.3	18.6	4.6	2.1	1.9	1.8	0.8	6.1	4.7	3.0	1.0	2.1
Yugoslavia (Former)	...	...	8.2	-5.4	...	...	...	...	...	...	...	...
Western Europe	*40.0*	*13.2*	*3.1*	*2.2*	*1.9*	*1.4*	*2.5*	*3.4*	*2.7*	*1.7*	*1.7*	*1.9*
Austria [2]	2.4	17.3	4.6	2.9	2.7	1.5	1.4	1.4	1.6	1.3	3.2	1.5
Belgium [2]	2.3	13.8	2.2	0.0	0.4	2.3	0.3	2.0	1.8	-3.4	1.7	1.3
France [2]	11.7	13.1	3.9	2.7	2.0	0.8	1.2	3.9	2.2	1.9	2.4	1.7
Germany [2]	13.9	11.2	3.0	2.0	2.0	1.4	3.5	2.3	3.3	2.9	1.6	2.8
Liechtenstein [2]	0.0	5.7	3.0	4.2	-9.1	3.3	2.2	0.1	0.1	33.7	30.2	-19.0
Luxembourg [2]	0.3	11.8	6.0	4.1	3.7	1.0	1.8	-11.5	5.5	-3.5	-3.9	2.0
Monaco [9]	0.1	22.2	3.9	2.4	1.9	1.8	5.6	4.7	-3.7	7.8	8.7	5.9
Netherlands [2]	4.3	15.4	3.6	2.7	4.2	0.5	3.0	3.5	3.4	3.0	3.5	2.7
Switzerland [2]	4.9	17.7	0.9	2.5	-0.4	3.4	3.9	7.8	2.5	-0.9	-1.9	-0.9
Oceania	**1.6**	**11.8**	**1.6**	**2.5**	**4.1**	**3.1**	**3.5**	**3.2**	**3.0**	**2.5**	**1.4**	**-2.4**
Australia and New Zealand	*96.5*	*11.8*	*1.6*	*2.5*	*4.4*	*3.0*	*3.5*	*3.4*	*3.0*	*2.6*	*1.4*	*-2.6*
Australia [2]	83.9	11.7	1.9	2.7	4.6	3.2	3.4	3.5	2.7	2.2	1.0	-3.2
New Zealand [2]	12.6	12.5	0.2	1.3	3.1	2.1	4.5	2.9	4.4	5.2	3.6	1.3
Melanesia	*2.8*	*13.1*	*1.2*	*3.8*	*-1.5*	*7.5*	*3.3*	*-2.1*	*1.7*	*2.0*	*2.3*	*1.2*
Fiji [2]	0.4	17.1	5.6	3.6	3.3	2.7	17.3	4.3	2.2	3.0	0.0	1.7
New Caledonia [6]	0.6	11.9	-3.8	5.3	-5.6	4.3	1.8	0.2	1.0	0.8	0.8	0.9
Papua New Guinea [2]	1.5	12.0	3.1	3.1	-1.0	11.5	1.1	-4.8	1.5	1.7	3.3	0.5
Solomon Islands	0.2	22.1	9.2	2.4	4.6	6.0	3.1	1.1	4.7	6.1	4.0	4.9
Vanuatu [2]	0.1	23.6	7.7	5.4	4.3	2.9	4.2	0.5	2.7	3.3	1.5	4.1
Micronesia	*0.1*	*18.8*	*2.2*	*2.8*	*-0.4*	*-1.0*	*7.8*	*5.8*	*3.4*	*-2.3*	*3.5*	*-0.7*
Kiribati [1]	0.0	7.1	-2.9	-2.2	1.7	-0.1	-12.8	76.3	28.7	-20.2	12.5	7.0
Marshall Islands	0.0	16.5	6.6	7.0	-3.2	0.5	2.3	-3.3	0.1	4.9	19.9	8.0
Micronesia (FS of)	0.0	14.7	6.6	4.1	1.5	-1.2	-2.9	5.3	8.5	4.6	-1.6	2.7
Nauru [9]	0.0	19.3	1.1	-1.6	-14.8	-3.6	60.8	-19.7	16.3	-4.5	1.2	3.7
Palau [2]	0.1	32.8	0.1	3.5	3.0	-1.4	7.4	12.1	-5.0	-5.2	-0.7	-10.2
Polynesia	*0.6*	*16.4*	*5.7*	*4.5*	*2.2*	*1.4*	*1.2*	*2.7*	*8.4*	*-0.1*	*4.7*	*3.3*
Cook Islands [2]	0.0	29.5	9.5	0.6	4.3	2.1	7.2	1.7	13.1	8.1	8.1	8.7
French Polynesia	0.4	13.5	6.3	5.8	1.7	0.1	0.9	2.1	7.5	-1.5	3.1	3.3
Samoa [2,16]	0.2	31.3	3.7	0.3	4.2	5.6	1.2	4.3	8.2	0.0	7.3	2.2
Tonga [17]	0.0	14.1	3.0	5.2	1.7	1.9	-3.4	3.6	15.2	3.9	6.5	-0.4
Tuvalu	0.0	8.6	-1.9	2.1	0.2	-5.4	6.8	6.3	-2.5	6.9	3.5	2.5

Notes for Table 6.E. Average Rates of Growth of Gross Domestic Product by Kind of Economic Activity - Wholesale, retail trade, restaurants and hotels

1/ 1970-2019
At factor cost.

2/ 1970-2019
Excludes repair of personal and household goods

3/ 2006-2019
Excludes repair of personal and household goods

4/ 2010-2019
Excludes repair of personal and household goods

5/ 1990-2019
Excludes repair of personal and household goods

6/ 1970-2019
Restaurants and Hotels are included in "Other activities".

7/ 2015-2019
Excludes repair of personal and household goods

8/ 1970-2019
Refers to trade only

9/ 1970-2019
At producers' prices.

10/ 1970-2001
At producers' prices.

11/ 1970-2019
Includes Taxes less subsidies on production and imports.

12/ 1970-2019
Excludes repair of motor vehicles and motorcycles, personal and household goods.

13/ 1970-2009
At producers' prices.

14/ 2016-2019
Excludes repair of personal and household goods

15/ 2010-2019
The Government of Ukraine has advised the United Nations that it is not in a position to provide statistical data concerning the Autonomous Republic of Crimea and the city of Sevastopol.

16/ (a) 1970-2008
At producers' prices.

(b) 2009-2019
Includes Taxes less subsidies on production and imports.

17/ 1994-2019
Excludes repair of personal and household goods

Table 6.F. Average Rates of Growth of Gross Domestic Product by Kind of Economic Activity - Transport, storage and communication

Major area, region and country	Base year weights as percentage of total for world or region in 2015	Base year share as percentage of total GDP in 2015	Average rates of growth				Annual rate of change (percentage)					
			1970-1979	1980-1989	1990-1999	2000-2009	2014	2015	2016	2017	2018	2019
World	**100.0**	**8.6**	**4.5**	**3.6**	**4.0**	**3.8**	**3.5**	**4.2**	**3.8**	**5.2**	**4.9**	**4.1**
Developed economies	**65.8**	**9.8**	**3.6**	**3.6**	**4.2**	**2.7**	**2.6**	**4.4**	**4.0**	**5.0**	**5.0**	**4.1**
Developing economies	**31.6**	**6.9**	**8.2**	**4.2**	**6.0**	**6.8**	**5.4**	**4.1**	**3.9**	**5.6**	**5.0**	**4.4**
Transition economies	**2.6**	**8.6**	**8.0**	**2.1**	**-8.0**	**5.6**	**3.3**	**-0.3**	**0.6**	**4.0**	**3.1**	**2.8**
Africa	**3.5**	**9.7**	**5.9**	**2.4**	**3.5**	**9.8**	**6.4**	**5.0**	**3.3**	**3.3**	**5.7**	**5.8**
Northern Africa	*29.5*	*8.9*	*10.7*	*4.5*	*3.5*	*8.0*	*5.0*	*2.4*	*3.6*	*7.0*	*4.4*	*4.6*
Algeria	7.7	10.4	11.5	3.7	1.1	6.4	6.2	6.1	3.8	3.9	5.1	3.7
Egypt [1]	12.3	8.2	18.5	8.4	3.9	8.2	5.5	4.8	6.4	9.6	3.9	6.0
Libya	0.2	3.4	8.1	-0.5	3.0	12.3	-50.3	-46.7	-18.8	54.2	27.6	9.0
Morocco	2.8	6.6	6.9	3.7	6.6	7.3	-1.9	1.2	5.3	2.1	5.5	5.0
Sudan	4.2	10.7	...	...	...	...	21.0	-2.7	-5.3	7.3	3.2	3.3
Sudan (Former)	...	...	6.3	1.1	2.8	...	...	...	...	...	...	...
Tunisia [1]	2.2	11.6	7.6	4.3	7.7	6.9	3.6	-0.8	4.5	4.6	3.1	0.4
Sub-Saharan Africa	70.5	10.1	4.3	1.3	3.6	10.9	7.0	6.1	3.2	1.7	6.2	6.3
Eastern Africa	*11.7*	*8.6*	*2.5*	*2.6*	*4.1*	*8.0*	*8.4*	*7.1*	*6.4*	*7.0*	*8.8*	*7.6*
Burundi	0.1	4.9	10.8	5.6	-1.2	10.9	51.8	8.6	-6.2	7.8	3.4	1.6
Comoros	0.0	8.3	4.5	5.1	4.4	-1.2	4.8	1.7	3.4	3.0	-2.9	-2.2
Djibouti	0.3	24.8	1.2	3.3	5.7	3.0	9.3	3.7	7.6	0.0	-0.8	8.8
Eritrea	0.1	12.3	...	...	9.0	-0.5	35.2	-18.3	8.9	-11.7	13.9	3.9
Ethiopia	1.2	4.4	...	...	1.6	10.4	12.7	13.3	13.7	15.1	6.4	21.0
Ethiopia (Former)	...	...	4.5	5.7	...	...	...	...	...	...	...	...
Kenya [2]	2.9	10.2	4.2	5.5	2.0	8.4	8.5	7.8	7.7	8.6	9.5	8.1
Madagascar	0.4	8.5	1.0	0.0	2.2	2.4	1.1	-1.2	1.6	15.8	1.3	6.6
Malawi [2]	0.2	7.9	7.3	0.2	1.5	7.5	9.1	7.0	4.9	6.3	6.3	6.2
Mauritius [3]	0.5	10.6	7.9	6.0	7.4	8.4	4.6	5.2	5.0	4.6	4.6	4.4
Mozambique [2]	0.8	11.6	3.8	-1.7	8.9	7.8	13.7	1.5	1.3	4.6	4.8	4.2
Rwanda [2]	0.3	7.1	4.2	2.5	7.8	15.8	4.7	11.8	8.1	14.0	18.0	11.6
Seychelles [2]	0.1	19.2	9.1	-0.1	33.4	2.0	16.9	6.5	8.8	7.2	2.4	3.4
Somalia	0.1	9.4	0.8	3.8	2.9	3.0	4.6	2.1	3.1	3.3	2.8	3.1
South Sudan	0.3	10.6	...	...	...	...	44.3	57.0	-0.1	-11.4	-3.0	0.8
U.R. of Tanzania: Mainland [2]	2.0	10.0	3.6	0.2	4.8	7.8	9.0	5.8	5.0	6.6	11.3	8.4
Uganda [2]	0.8	6.9	-1.6	3.6	9.2	15.6	-0.1	11.0	11.7	9.7	14.9	3.2
Zambia [4]	0.7	7.3	2.6	2.9	2.6	16.2	7.1	1.5	7.6	-3.6	23.5	9.1
Zanzibar [5]	0.0	7.2	...	...	6.7	13.3	15.9	-1.2	-1.4	7.0	7.4	5.0
Zimbabwe	1.0	11.7	-1.2	2.2	4.5	3.4	1.1	4.9	1.1	5.1	2.6	-6.9
Middle Africa	*7.4*	*6.9*	*1.3*	*2.2*	*-1.4*	*8.5*	*6.7*	*6.0*	*-0.2*	*3.4*	*-1.3*	*1.3*
Angola	2.9	5.3	0.1	2.1	-2.5	9.1	9.1	4.7	-0.6	1.8	-0.1	-2.9
Cameroon [2]	1.1	8.5	5.7	0.6	2.1	4.9	4.2	4.5	3.3	4.7	2.2	4.8
Central African Republic	0.0	3.3	-0.4	2.9	9.4	0.7	11.6	24.7	-6.1	2.3	5.2	0.4
Chad	0.4	6.9	-1.7	4.5	2.5	16.0	9.6	3.4	-10.0	-11.0	2.2	2.2
Congo	0.4	7.8	3.9	3.3	-3.0	8.0	5.7	9.1	-13.7	1.7	-9.2	-7.1
D.R. of the Congo	1.8	10.9	-0.3	3.1	-3.4	10.6	6.0	9.7	2.4	3.7	-1.4	4.7
Equatorial Guinea	0.4	6.2	2.0	1.2	2.6	12.2	-2.1	-3.9	-1.1	-5.6	-2.2	5.1
Gabon	0.4	6.0	8.3	1.8	3.3	3.1	8.3	12.7	5.9	30.9	-12.9	6.5
Sao Tome and Principe	0.0	11.6	7.0	-1.2	0.6	8.9	8.3	5.4	0.7	5.6	6.6	3.9
Southern Africa	*14.4*	*9.8*	*5.5*	*1.7*	*4.7*	*5.3*	*3.8*	*1.7*	*1.4*	*1.4*	*1.6*	*-0.1*
Botswana	0.4	6.5	12.6	23.0	11.3	6.7	9.8	4.5	6.6	4.7	6.4	5.2
Eswatini [2]	0.1	4.6	5.9	5.7	3.7	2.9	9.2	2.8	6.7	4.0	4.5	5.0
Lesotho [2]	0.1	5.9	7.3	4.7	4.6	9.3	11.7	6.7	9.9	-4.1	-1.5	3.0
Namibia [2]	0.2	5.0	2.9	2.0	6.3	12.5	7.5	16.9	4.8	-1.4	-3.1	0.7
South Africa	13.6	10.2	5.6	1.5	4.6	5.2	3.5	1.4	1.1	1.4	1.6	-0.4
Western Africa	*37.0*	*11.9*	*6.4*	*-0.9*	*5.0*	*19.1*	*7.9*	*7.5*	*3.5*	*-0.2*	*8.7*	*9.1*
Benin [6]	0.6	11.5	3.2	3.8	2.9	5.2	15.0	16.6	4.3	6.8	5.8	4.7
Burkina Faso [2]	0.2	4.4	7.0	0.6	12.4	10.4	6.0	-5.8	8.5	8.6	-2.6	2.9
Cabo Verde [2]	0.1	15.2	1.0	7.7	12.8	4.4	-6.3	2.7	0.0	2.2	-4.1	5.8
Côte d'Ivoire	2.7	13.8	8.1	-3.4	2.8	2.3	22.2	28.8	18.6	-7.6	3.8	6.3
Gambia [2]	0.0	6.9	7.9	10.5	4.1	9.4	2.8	-3.9	4.6	18.4	17.6	3.0
Ghana [2]	1.7	8.2	3.4	7.2	6.8	6.3	10.8	4.9	2.3	7.6	4.3	16.4
Guinea	0.2	5.4	3.0	3.0	4.0	1.6	1.8	13.5	11.5	11.5	5.1	9.3
Guinea-Bissau	0.0	5.0	11.7	4.4	4.7	4.5	8.4	13.5	4.1	5.8	6.0	5.8
Liberia	0.1	6.1	5.6	-1.2	-8.3	2.8	5.1	6.9	20.5	1.1	-4.6	-7.9
Mali	0.3	5.8	4.5	2.2	15.9	8.2	17.3	9.1	12.8	0.8	2.0	4.1
Mauritania [2]	0.2	6.7	5.9	1.4	8.0	13.9	29.8	2.6	9.1	-0.9	4.2	10.3
Niger [2]	0.2	4.9	3.5	-1.7	4.4	3.5	5.8	6.2	9.7	6.1	6.9	5.1
Nigeria [2]	29.5	12.9	7.6	-2.0	5.5	24.9	6.7	6.1	1.8	-0.6	10.1	9.3
Senegal [2]	0.7	9.6	1.5	3.8	4.8	11.5	3.2	1.6	2.0	8.0	1.0	3.9
Sierra Leone	0.1	4.2	4.3	-2.2	-8.6	15.9	-2.8	1.7	5.3	5.2	4.0	6.7
Togo	0.3	14.5	2.7	-0.4	2.6	7.2	14.8	24.8	7.6	8.9	6.7	4.6

Table 6.F. Average Rates of Growth of Gross Domestic Product by Kind of Economic Activity - Transport, storage and communication

Major area, region and country	Base year weights as percentage of total for world or region in 2015	Base year share as percentage of total GDP in 2015	Average rates of growth 1970-1979	1980-1989	1990-1999	2000-2009	Annual rate of change (percentage) 2014	2015	2016	2017	2018	2019
Americas	**37.7**	**9.4**	**4.9**	**3.6**	**4.8**	**3.4**	**3.2**	**6.6**	**5.4**	**5.4**	**5.7**	**4.9**
Latin America and the Caribbean	**6.4**	**8.0**	**7.9**	**2.4**	**3.9**	**4.0**	**3.2**	**2.3**	**0.4**	**2.2**	**2.0**	**0.0**
Caribbean	*1.1*	*7.4*	*5.5*	*4.4*	*3.7*	*4.6*	*5.3*	*4.2*	*3.2*	*-1.8*	*4.0*	*2.6*
Anguilla	0.0	10.3	3.8	6.9	8.8	6.3	5.3	6.6	-12.2	-10.2	3.1	-4.3
Antigua and Barbuda	0.0	11.9	5.6	8.5	5.5	-0.2	-0.4	8.4	2.8	1.1	7.0	3.8
Aruba [2]	0.0	8.7	9.1	11.2	4.4	0.4	-3.6	14.5	0.2	-2.4	4.6	-1.6
Bahamas [2]	0.0	10.4	2.4	4.0	1.8	0.5	12.4	-0.4	-1.0	-11.4	-2.9	-10.7
Barbados [2]	0.0	12.3	2.3	3.7	3.0	2.5	3.5	0.6	9.5	-1.8	-2.6	3.0
British Virgin Islands [2]	0.0	8.4	7.4	10.4	19.9	-1.1	3.9	-0.6	14.1	-1.5	2.5	3.5
Cayman Islands [2]	0.0	6.6	9.3	9.9	7.1	1.7	1.6	2.1	2.3	2.0	2.4	2.1
Cuba	0.3	8.7	5.4	5.2	-0.6	5.7	4.3	6.5	3.4	3.6	6.4	4.8
Curaçao	0.0	11.9	...	...	...	...	6.4	-4.7	-6.3	-2.3	-1.4	-3.7
Dominica	0.0	15.6	5.6	8.6	5.9	2.7	2.9	-4.1	-5.8	-1.2	0.4	6.3
Dominican Republic [2]	0.3	10.0	7.7	4.1	10.5	11.8	6.4	5.9	6.3	4.6	7.5	2.4
Former Netherlands Antilles	...	...	8.6	-6.8	-0.3	3.1	...	...	...	...	...	...
Grenada	0.0	11.7	6.5	9.2	7.0	1.5	8.7	-2.3	3.8	5.1	8.5	7.0
Haiti	0.0	13.4	8.4	9.3	1.3	3.2	3.0	3.3	0.4	1.0	1.0	-1.0
Jamaica	0.0	7.9	1.9	4.7	6.7	1.8	0.8	1.0	0.7	1.0	1.4	0.8
Montserrat	0.0	7.6	4.4	5.9	-6.5	-0.5	0.2	18.5	-5.7	7.6	6.9	10.0
Puerto Rico [7]	0.2	3.6	6.1	5.0	6.4	1.1	7.6	2.7	6.3	-23.6	-4.1	4.7
Saint Kitts and Nevis	0.0	11.6	4.2	8.9	4.6	6.2	8.8	12.7	0.3	4.3	4.8	3.5
Saint Lucia [2]	0.0	9.3	7.0	10.6	4.2	2.5	6.3	4.2	-7.2	-0.7	8.3	17.9
Sint Maarten (Dutch part)	0.0	12.5	...	...	...	...	9.4	5.2	1.4	-15.6	-3.6	4.3
St. Vincent and the Grenadines	0.0	13.4	3.8	7.6	5.1	6.2	-0.1	-1.9	-1.0	-3.5	1.0	6.6
Trinidad and Tobago [2]	0.1	6.0	3.7	2.7	7.1	5.3	3.1	-1.8	-11.3	0.4	2.3	-1.4
Turks and Caicos Islands	0.0	10.6	10.7	10.7	9.8	1.5	5.7	10.4	12.1	1.1	8.0	6.3
Central America	*5.0*	*8.8*	*10.6*	*1.6*	*4.4*	*2.9*	*3.5*	*6.9*	*6.7*	*5.3*	*3.8*	*0.1*
Belize	0.0	9.5	7.8	12.5	7.3	4.2	0.1	1.2	8.3	2.2	5.1	4.1
Costa Rica [2]	0.2	9.3	11.2	4.4	1.2	8.0	6.3	8.2	3.7	10.6	4.5	4.4
El Salvador [2]	0.1	8.7	0.3	2.1	6.2	2.4	-4.8	6.0	6.8	-0.8	0.6	2.6
Guatemala [2]	0.2	7.9	8.2	1.8	6.0	12.1	2.7	5.4	3.6	4.2	4.1	3.1
Honduras	0.1	7.4	4.1	5.3	3.1	10.2	4.4	4.2	3.6	3.3	3.5	3.1
Mexico [2]	4.1	8.7	11.1	1.5	4.4	2.1	3.7	7.2	7.4	4.9	3.8	-0.7
Nicaragua	0.0	5.8	-0.9	-3.4	4.0	6.2	4.3	7.7	7.1	5.8	-4.2	-7.7
Panama	0.3	12.3	10.9	1.6	5.5	8.4	1.9	2.7	1.8	11.4	5.6	6.3
South America	*10.9*	*7.7*	*7.1*	*2.6*	*3.7*	*4.4*	*2.9*	*0.2*	*-2.8*	*1.1*	*0.8*	*-0.3*
Argentina	1.5	6.4	2.0	1.3	7.3	5.7	0.8	3.0	3.4	2.3	-2.8	-0.7
Bolivia (Plurinational State of)	0.1	10.8	11.3	4.2	5.5	3.9	5.0	5.3	5.7	5.2	4.4	1.6
Brazil [2]	5.2	7.8	9.4	3.2	2.6	3.3	3.1	-2.9	-4.0	1.2	1.9	0.9
Chile [2]	0.9	9.1	3.1	3.8	8.8	4.5	2.9	5.5	3.8	2.0	3.3	1.8
Colombia [2]	1.0	8.9	7.8	2.5	3.6	4.8	5.0	2.8	-0.1	1.2	2.7	3.4
Ecuador [2]	0.3	7.3	10.1	3.1	3.3	5.8	3.5	2.6	0.6	0.4	4.4	1.3
Guyana [3]	0.0	6.2	3.2	0.9	5.0	5.4	6.1	2.2	1.1	1.3	4.1	4.7
Paraguay [2]	0.1	7.9	9.6	3.7	5.5	5.4	4.1	4.3	2.7	6.7	3.0	3.2
Peru [2,8]	0.7	9.6	2.5	0.1	3.8	4.6	4.9	6.2	6.1	5.8	5.4	3.8
Suriname	0.0	12.0	3.0	0.8	4.9	8.5	4.4	2.8	1.7	-3.7	-9.3	2.0
Uruguay	0.1	6.2	2.7	1.5	9.7	8.8	7.4	4.8	8.1	9.4	6.8	3.5
Venezuela (Bolivarian Republic of)	0.9	6.6	7.3	0.8	1.5	8.6	0.7	-0.9	-27.2	-12.9	-17.7	-36.7
Northern America	**31.3**	**9.8**	**4.3**	**3.9**	**4.9**	**3.3**	**3.3**	**7.6**	**6.4**	**6.0**	**6.4**	**5.8**
Bermuda [2]	0.0	4.8	3.5	1.0	2.6	0.5	-6.2	-3.2	-3.2	6.8	-2.1	0.4
Canada [2]	4.8	7.6	5.7	3.7	3.6	2.0	4.8	2.4	3.0	5.0	2.8	2.1
Greenland [2]	0.0	11.9	6.4	2.5	1.2	4.8	8.0	-0.1	6.9	-4.2	4.0	2.1
United States [2,9]	78.2	10.0	4.2	3.9	5.0	3.4	3.2	7.9	6.6	6.1	6.6	6.0
Asia	**30.1**	**7.1**	**4.1**	**5.1**	**4.9**	**5.2**	**4.8**	**3.2**	**3.6**	**5.7**	**4.8**	**4.3**
Central Asia	*1.7*	*10.7*	...	...	*-7.4*	*9.3*	*7.7*	*5.8*	*2.8*	*6.5*	*4.2*	*4.7*
Kazakhstan [5]	1.1	11.8	...	...	-8.7	9.3	7.4	5.4	3.0	4.5	4.5	5.2
Kyrgyzstan [5]	0.0	8.9	...	...	-11.3	13.2	5.5	2.0	-4.8	-3.0	1.2	3.3
Tajikistan	0.1	14.0	...	...	-10.8	21.3	1.1	-3.8	-5.5	9.6	-29.9	-10.1
Turkmenistan	0.1	5.9	...	...	-9.4	3.9	22.4	16.2	-2.9	9.9	7.2	1.3
Uzbekistan [5]	0.4	10.0	...	...	-0.6	9.3	6.6	6.0	5.5	11.2	6.7	5.6
Eastern Asia	*60.1*	*6.3*	*2.6*	*5.5*	*4.9*	*4.0*	*3.9*	*2.0*	*3.3*	*5.5*	*5.1*	*4.0*
China [9]	26.4	4.4	6.8	10.1	10.6	8.9	6.9	4.4	6.9	9.6	8.3	7.1
China, Hong Kong SAR	1.6	9.9	9.0	9.7	3.1	4.2	3.2	3.6	3.4	4.5	3.1	0.7
China, Macao SAR	0.1	3.7	7.9	7.5	9.6	-1.6	19.6	4.7	6.7	2.1	7.8	5.5
D.P.R. of Korea	...	...	...	...	...	...	...	...	...	...	...	...
Japan [2,7]	24.0	10.2	1.7	4.4	2.9	1.2	1.4	-0.7	-0.8	1.6	1.5	0.6

Table 6.F. Average Rates of Growth of Gross Domestic Product by Kind of Economic Activity - Transport, storage and communication

Major area, region and country	Base year weights as percentage of total for world or region in 2015	Base year share as percentage of total GDP in 2015	Average rates of growth 1970-1979	1980-1989	1990-1999	2000-2009	Annual rate of change (percentage) 2014	2015	2016	2017	2018	2019
Mongolia [2]	0.0	8.0	5.6	27.2	-1.2	15.4	11.7	2.9	6.6	14.0	7.6	4.7
Republic of Korea [2]	6.1	8.4	12.2	8.4	9.8	5.7	1.5	1.7	3.1	2.9	4.2	2.4
South-Eastern Asia	*10.9*	*8.4*	*9.2*	*7.1*	*6.6*	*7.9*	*6.8*	*6.8*	*6.1*	*7.3*	*4.4*	*6.2*
Brunei Darussalam [2]	0.0	3.8	23.5	13.4	3.5	3.9	-1.7	-1.3	-6.8	5.0	-1.6	3.7
Cambodia	0.1	8.6	-7.3	5.5	8.5	7.7	7.7	8.0	7.7	8.0	7.5	8.9
Indonesia [2]	4.0	8.8	14.5	7.5	4.2	12.8	8.8	8.3	8.2	9.1	7.0	8.1
Lao People's DR [2]	0.0	3.4	3.2	7.8	7.3	8.8	9.0	13.4	6.0	5.4	7.5	5.9
Malaysia [2,7]	1.4	9.0	12.6	7.4	8.9	5.7	8.1	8.0	7.1	7.7	7.6	6.7
Myanmar [7]	0.5	13.6	2.7	3.3	11.2	18.2	12.0	9.7	8.3	9.2	8.8	8.8
Philippines [2,9]	1.0	6.4	5.0	3.6	4.5	7.6	6.5	8.0	5.3	4.0	5.4	6.7
Singapore [2]	1.8	11.5	14.4	8.6	8.1	4.5	3.7	1.5	3.1	5.8	2.3	2.1
Thailand [2,7]	1.7	8.1	6.6	7.8	6.8	6.2	4.0	6.6	3.1	5.8	-5.4	2.8
Timor-Leste [5]	0.0	2.3	...	...	-0.3	44.7	-47.2	68.4	13.5	-3.5	3.8	33.3
Viet Nam [2,7]	0.4	3.8	4.7	5.4	6.9	8.6	6.1	5.9	6.8	7.8	7.8	8.7
Southern Asia	*13.2*	*8.4*	*7.6*	*3.5*	*6.9*	*8.7*	*6.2*	*5.0*	*4.5*	*4.4*	*4.8*	*5.0*
Afghanistan [11]	0.1	10.8	6.2	-0.7	-1.3	15.1	-3.6	-3.7	-2.7	-4.1	-8.9	-3.0
Bangladesh	1.2	11.6	1.7	4.9	4.6	7.7	6.0	6.0	6.1	6.8	6.6	7.2
Bhutan	0.0	9.7	4.1	12.8	9.3	7.8	9.0	8.9	8.5	13.3	10.9	10.9
India [2]	7.2	6.8	6.1	7.2	8.0	10.3	8.8	8.9	3.5	3.3	6.2	6.1
Iran (Islamic Republic of)	2.3	10.8	14.7	-3.4	8.1	9.2	1.6	-6.1	6.7	7.1	2.0	2.2
Maldives [2]	0.0	11.2	5.8	1.4	12.4	5.1	5.5	43.5	8.6	1.9	3.7	6.7
Nepal	0.1	8.4	8.6	3.5	8.5	6.4	5.2	6.2	2.0	6.5	4.6	5.9
Pakistan [2]	1.7	12.4	5.5	6.1	5.3	4.3	4.2	5.2	5.1	4.6	2.6	3.7
Sri Lanka [2]	0.5	13.6	4.6	3.6	4.9	8.2	4.5	5.4	5.6	3.5	2.5	2.3
Western Asia	*14.1*	*9.2*	*9.8*	*3.1*	*4.6*	*6.3*	*5.9*	*4.0*	*2.4*	*6.0*	*3.7*	*3.0*
Armenia [5]	0.0	6.5	...	...	-8.2	10.3	14.7	-3.7	10.6	9.2	7.2	10.7
Azerbaijan [5]	0.2	8.7	...	...	-10.6	15.0	11.1	6.1	-1.7	7.6	8.4	4.0
Bahrain [7]	0.1	7.6	15.2	4.2	4.0	11.5	6.0	6.8	3.1	12.9	8.3	-4.8
Cyprus [2]	0.1	12.7	7.0	8.8	5.0	3.9	1.4	3.0	12.7	10.0	3.6	4.5
Georgia [5]	0.1	9.3	...	...	-6.6	6.5	4.3	5.8	-6.5	10.8	4.1	10.0
Iraq	1.0	10.6	19.0	-1.6	4.0	-8.4	6.1	4.5	8.7	5.6	5.0	3.3
Israel [2]	1.8	12.1	2.1	5.3	4.6	5.7	7.6	6.6	6.9	3.9	5.7	5.5
Jordan [2]	0.2	9.3	6.2	6.4	5.4	5.8	1.7	2.9	2.9	2.7	3.2	3.2
Kuwait	0.5	6.4	9.3	0.8	10.5	21.2	2.5	0.5	2.5	-14.5	6.2	-5.6
Lebanon [2]	0.2	6.4	-3.5	-5.1	5.3	8.5	5.0	4.7	-3.8	-0.1	-3.5	-3.0
Oman	0.2	5.7	9.9	8.5	9.6	15.7	9.4	5.3	-0.6	11.3	-4.0	0.0
Qatar [2,7]	0.5	5.2	6.9	2.1	11.1	27.5	9.3	6.8	4.2	-0.2	3.0	1.8
Saudi Arabia [2]	2.2	6.3	11.5	2.8	2.9	14.9	6.2	5.8	2.7	2.2	2.1	5.6
State of Palestine [2]	0.0	6.8	8.0	2.1	15.0	2.7	3.9	8.4	-1.1	-4.5	1.7	-3.5
Syrian Arab Republic [9]	0.1	9.5	7.5	5.0	8.6	4.9	-0.5	-5.8	-3.4	-2.9	4.0	4.4
Turkey [2]	4.9	12.0	9.4	5.1	5.1	4.3	4.8	5.4	1.5	11.1	4.2	2.3
United Arab Emirates	1.9	9.7	15.1	3.5	6.7	10.4	8.6	2.4	-0.3	7.2	2.3	2.3
Yemen	0.2	13.8	...	...	3.6	10.9	-5.2	-33.8	-13.0	-10.9	-0.4	1.8
Yemen Arab Republic (Former)	...	...	10.4	6.2	...	...	...	...	...	...	...	...
Yemen Democratic (Former)	...	...	9.1	4.3	...	...	...	...	...	...	...	...
Europe	**26.9**	**9.6**	**4.3**	**2.8**	**2.5**	**2.7**	**2.1**	**1.9**	**2.1**	**4.6**	**4.1**	**3.0**
Eastern Europe	*13.3*	*9.4*	*7.3*	*1.6*	*-3.9*	*4.2*	*2.7*	*1.3*	*3.1*	*6.4*	*4.7*	*3.2*
Belarus [5]	0.3	11.1	...	...	-6.7	4.8	3.9	-2.1	2.9	6.7	8.1	3.6
Bulgaria [2]	0.3	11.4	7.0	4.5	2.4	7.1	4.3	6.0	8.5	0.4	5.3	0.4
Czechia [5]	1.1	10.9	...	...	1.4	2.2	0.7	6.7	3.6	9.7	8.3	2.7
Czechoslovakia (Former)	...	...	4.4	-2.2	...	...	...	...	...	...	...	...
Hungary [2]	0.7	11.3	5.4	2.6	-0.9	3.5	3.7	1.2	5.0	6.2	8.2	8.1
Poland [2]	2.7	10.5	6.0	2.9	12.3	3.4	2.4	2.2	5.9	11.4	7.9	4.8
Republic of Moldova [5]	0.0	10.8	...	...	-17.9	8.2	3.8	4.7	5.2	4.4	3.6	4.1
Romania [2]	1.2	13.1	8.3	1.5	-1.7	7.3	4.3	11.3	14.2	12.3	4.5	3.2
Russian Federation	5.7	7.7	...	...	-7.1	4.5	3.1	-2.6	-1.0	2.4	2.0	1.1
Slovakia [5]	0.6	11.8	...	...	7.0	0.9	10.7	11.1	-2.1	3.9	1.3	7.7
Ukraine [5,12]	0.6	12.3	...	...	-15.5	7.0	-7.2	-1.7	4.3	5.7	3.0	5.0
USSR (Former)	...	...	8.1	2.0	...	...	...	...	...	...	...	...
Northern Europe	*27.6*	*10.8*	*2.5*	*3.4*	*4.4*	*2.3*	*2.5*	*4.5*	*2.1*	*4.6*	*5.4*	*3.8*
Denmark [2]	1.7	10.5	1.2	3.1	3.8	1.1	-2.8	3.9	6.6	2.3	3.4	-0.4
Estonia [5]	0.2	14.1	...	...	-1.5	3.6	3.9	0.0	2.5	12.2	11.6	18.2
Finland [2]	1.3	10.5	4.0	3.5	3.4	1.2	0.1	-0.5	1.5	3.6	4.0	1.5
Iceland [2]	0.1	11.2	5.8	4.3	5.9	1.0	4.0	10.3	15.3	5.6	4.3	-0.2
Ireland [2]	2.0	12.0	4.3	2.2	3.8	6.6	10.9	14.4	8.1	23.2	22.6	15.5
Latvia [5]	0.2	14.0	...	...	-1.6	3.8	-3.3	1.6	2.8	7.2	5.9	-1.4
Lithuania [5]	0.3	15.1	...	...	2.8	5.6	4.0	-0.4	5.8	9.4	6.8	4.1
Norway [2]	2.0	9.7	4.6	2.3	4.0	1.5	-0.3	1.3	-0.6	1.2	2.7	2.3
Sweden [2]	3.6	13.3	4.4	2.9	2.2	3.3	5.4	6.6	-2.8	3.2	5.4	0.3
United Kingdom [2]	16.2	10.3	1.9	3.8	5.2	2.1	2.2	4.0	2.3	3.0	3.4	3.2

Table 6.F. Average Rates of Growth of Gross Domestic Product by Kind of Economic Activity - Transport, storage and communication

Major area, region and country	Base year weights as percentage of total for world or region in 2015	Base year share as percentage of total GDP in 2015	Average rates of growth				Annual rate of change (percentage)					
			1970-1979	1980-1989	1990-1999	2000-2009	2014	2015	2016	2017	2018	2019
Southern Europe	*17.5*	*8.9*	*5.4*	*3.2*	*3.3*	*2.2*	*1.0*	*0.4*	*1.8*	*5.3*	*2.2*	*3.0*
Albania [2]	0.0	6.9	4.1	2.1	4.3	13.6	0.4	7.0	5.9	4.7	-0.9	6.4
Andorra [2]	0.0	5.7	3.8	2.9	3.9	4.7	6.3	5.9	9.6	-0.2	0.1	3.0
Bosnia and Herzegovina [5]	0.1	9.7	...	...	17.0	5.8	3.4	2.3	1.8	3.9	2.5	8.7
Croatia [5]	0.2	8.9	...	...	-4.0	4.8	-2.3	2.0	4.2	5.1	4.3	4.1
Greece [2]	1.0	9.2	7.5	3.8	5.5	5.2	-2.1	-14.5	-3.2	12.1	4.8	4.9
Italy [2]	9.1	9.1	5.6	3.8	4.2	1.8	-0.7	-0.7	3.5	3.6	-0.3	1.6
Kosovo [5]	0.0	6.7	...	...	-8.0	0.6	20.7	7.0	3.3	3.0	4.4	4.7
Malta [2]	0.1	12.9	15.3	2.6	7.9	1.3	12.5	17.9	9.5	6.2	5.2	4.4
Montenegro [5]	0.0	9.5	...	...	-4.5	2.9	1.0	4.0	0.6	4.6	4.9	4.0
North Macedonia [5]	0.0	7.9	...	...	1.0	5.0	3.2	4.2	8.3	7.2	2.7	3.3
Portugal [2]	0.9	8.3	5.1	4.2	3.5	2.8	-2.4	0.8	-0.1	5.6	4.0	4.9
San Marino [2]	0.0	5.6	3.8	2.4	5.8	2.1	121.4	-12.2	15.6	1.4	9.3	1.5
Serbia [5]	0.2	10.2	...	...	-9.3	9.1	1.7	3.4	3.0	4.0	5.4	7.0
Slovenia [5]	0.2	10.3	...	...	0.7	4.9	4.5	5.1	3.9	9.0	5.6	7.0
Spain [2]	5.6	8.5	4.6	2.1	2.1	1.6	5.0	4.7	-0.3	6.9	5.2	4.0
Yugoslavia (Former)	...	...	7.4	4.4	...	...	...	...	...	...	...	...
Western Europe	*41.6*	*9.3*	*3.0*	*3.1*	*3.6*	*2.7*	*2.1*	*0.9*	*1.8*	*3.8*	*3.9*	*2.4*
Austria [2]	1.9	9.2	5.9	2.9	3.7	1.2	2.0	0.7	1.8	1.4	3.1	1.6
Belgium [2]	2.5	9.8	1.7	2.1	1.9	2.0	2.7	4.1	0.9	2.9	4.6	0.2
France [2]	12.7	9.6	4.1	5.3	4.9	2.6	2.2	0.5	2.5	4.5	1.8	3.6
Germany [2]	16.7	9.1	3.0	2.0	3.5	3.4	1.5	0.6	1.3	3.6	5.7	2.1
Liechtenstein [2]	0.0	3.5	3.0	4.5	-5.9	1.6	2.1	4.3	2.1	-9.0	22.3	-5.6
Luxembourg [2]	0.3	11.0	5.9	9.8	10.5	4.7	8.8	18.3	15.0	3.6	9.6	5.9
Monaco [7]	0.0	8.0	3.9	2.4	1.9	2.2	-0.5	1.8	3.4	9.8	-0.7	6.8
Netherlands [2]	4.0	9.7	3.6	2.7	5.0	2.8	3.2	2.1	2.2	5.4	2.9	2.0
Switzerland [2]	3.4	8.4	0.9	2.8	0.7	1.3	2.6	-0.4	1.0	1.7	3.2	1.7
Oceania	**1.8**	**8.0**	**4.9**	**4.1**	**5.0**	**3.7**	**3.0**	**3.9**	**2.7**	**3.5**	**2.3**	**-2.8**
Australia and New Zealand	*97.3*	*8.1*	*4.9*	*4.1*	*5.0*	*3.8*	*2.9*	*3.9*	*2.7*	*3.6*	*2.3*	*-3.0*
Australia [2]	85.1	8.0	5.1	4.1	4.9	3.9	2.3	3.5	3.1	3.6	2.2	-3.8
New Zealand [2]	12.2	8.2	3.5	3.6	6.0	2.9	7.7	6.3	0.0	2.9	2.5	2.8
Melanesia	*1.9*	*6.2*	*4.0*	*3.9*	*3.3*	*3.7*	*5.1*	*5.0*	*2.2*	*3.0*	*2.3*	*2.9*
Fiji [2]	0.5	14.4	8.0	5.8	4.6	1.7	18.4	1.3	-1.8	3.7	0.1	0.7
New Caledonia	0.6	7.5	2.9	7.2	5.0	3.9	-2.4	8.8	3.1	3.7	3.6	3.3
Papua New Guinea [2]	0.8	4.1	3.1	2.2	1.7	4.5	3.8	5.9	3.3	1.8	3.0	3.6
Solomon Islands	0.1	5.6	9.1	3.3	5.4	5.3	0.4	-4.8	9.2	1.8	2.1	4.4
Vanuatu [2]	0.1	8.5	7.7	4.0	1.3	5.7	0.9	1.8	3.9	8.4	-2.9	5.6
Micronesia	*0.1*	*9.9*	*2.1*	*-0.1*	*-0.6*	*-0.2*	*7.5*	*2.4*	*3.8*	*2.4*	*20.2*	*10.4*
Kiribati [1]	0.0	7.7	6.9	-0.8	5.0	1.4	-2.9	-10.6	-4.1	17.8	-4.7	3.0
Marshall Islands	0.0	11.1	...	...	...	1.0	9.8	4.0	1.8	5.3	26.5	10.7
Micronesia (FS of)	0.0	6.0	6.6	4.1	1.6	-1.9	-10.2	2.3	13.8	2.5	1.3	1.6
Nauru [7]	0.0	18.9	1.1	-1.6	-14.4	-10.2	42.5	2.1	2.6	-4.7	5.4	0.9
Palau [2]	0.0	11.4	0.1	4.0	1.0	4.3	7.1	8.8	3.1	-1.2	51.2	21.0
Polynesia	*0.7*	*11.9*	*5.1*	*5.7*	*2.4*	*1.6*	*2.9*	*5.5*	*6.1*	*-1.0*	*3.2*	*2.9*
Cook Islands [2]	0.0	13.6	-0.9	5.9	5.4	5.7	6.8	11.5	14.2	6.5	9.4	5.4
French Polynesia	0.5	12.1	5.6	6.5	1.7	1.1	2.5	3.7	6.5	-1.7	3.9	2.9
Samoa [2,13]	0.1	12.1	3.7	0.3	4.5	4.5	7.5	13.8	2.5	-3.3	-4.7	1.9
Tonga [14]	0.0	7.8	6.8	5.2	8.2	-2.4	-6.0	9.6	-0.5	11.4	4.6	1.5
Tuvalu	0.0	6.2	-1.9	2.1	34.3	-1.4	-2.7	21.2	10.0	5.6	12.1	9.2

Notes for Table 6.F. Average Rates of Growth of Gross Domestic Product by Kind of Economic Activity - Transport, storage and communication

1/ 1970-2019
At factor cost.

2/ 1970-2019
Excludes travel agencies, includes publishing activities, computer and related activities and radio/TV activities

3/ 2006-2019
Excludes travel agencies, includes publishing activities, computer and related activities and radio/TV activities

4/ 2010-2019
Excludes travel agencies, includes publishing activities, computer and related activities and radio/TV activities

5/ 1990-2019
Excludes travel agencies, includes publishing activities, computer and related activities and radio/TV activities

6/ 2015-2019
Excludes travel agencies, includes publishing activities, computer and related activities and radio/TV activities

7/ 1970-2019
At producers' prices.

8/ 1970-2001
At producers' prices.

9/ 1970-2019
Includes Taxes less subsidies on production and imports.

10/ 1970-2009
At producers' prices.

11/ 2016-2019
Excludes travel agencies, includes publishing activities, computer and related activities and radio/TV activities

12/ 2010-2019
The Government of Ukraine has advised the United Nations that it is not in a position to provide statistical data concerning the Autonomous Republic of Crimea and the city of Sevastopol.

13/ (a) 1970-2008
At producers' prices.

(b) 2009-2019
Includes Taxes less subsidies on production and imports.

14/ 1994-2019
Excludes travel agencies, includes publishing activities, computer and related activities and radio/TV activities

Table 6.G. Average Rates of Growth of Gross Domestic Product by Kind of Economic Activity - Other Activities

Major area, region and country	Base year weights as percentage of total for world or region in 2015	Base year share as percentage of total GDP in 2015	Average rates of growth				Annual rate of change (percentage)					
			1970-1979	1980-1989	1990-1999	2000-2009	2014	2015	2016	2017	2018	2019
World	**100.0**	**44.6**	**4.1**	**3.2**	**2.6**	**2.8**	**2.8**	**2.9**	**2.5**	**2.8**	**3.2**	**3.0**
Developed economies	**67.3**	**51.8**	**3.7**	**3.0**	**2.2**	**1.7**	**1.8**	**1.8**	**1.5**	**1.8**	**2.1**	**1.8**
Developing economies	**30.7**	**34.7**	**6.7**	**4.3**	**5.0**	**6.3**	**5.3**	**5.7**	**5.0**	**5.1**	**5.3**	**5.4**
Transition economies	**2.0**	**35.0**	**1.9**	**4.7**	**-1.8**	**4.7**	**0.6**	**-0.7**	**0.1**	**1.9**	**2.5**	**1.9**
Africa	**2.0**	**28.9**	**5.6**	**3.7**	**2.6**	**5.3**	**4.3**	**3.5**	**1.8**	**2.7**	**2.2**	**2.6**
Northern Africa	*32.1*	*28.9*	*8.6*	*4.9*	*3.4*	*5.0*	*1.9*	*3.1*	*3.8*	*3.8*	*3.4*	*3.8*
Algeria	6.2	24.8	9.1	3.7	1.7	4.6	5.0	4.0	2.4	1.6	3.3	2.7
Egypt [1]	14.6	29.0	9.8	8.9	4.5	4.9	5.5	4.5	4.6	4.1	3.0	4.3
Libya	0.5	23.8	9.5	0.4	1.6	5.1	-48.7	-44.2	-13.8	47.8	24.2	10.5
Morocco	5.4	38.4	7.1	5.8	3.1	5.3	3.4	3.1	3.8	3.3	4.2	5.5
Sudan	3.1	23.5	...	...	...	...	8.5	10.3	6.7	2.3	1.7	0.4
Sudan (Former)	...	...	6.3	5.0	3.8	...	...	...	...	...	...	...
Tunisia [1]	2.3	36.5	4.5	3.1	6.3	5.6	3.2	2.9	2.9	3.1	1.8	2.0
Sub-Saharan Africa	67.9	28.9	4.6	3.2	2.1	5.4	5.5	3.6	0.9	2.2	1.6	2.0
Eastern Africa	*12.2*	*26.8*	*5.1*	*3.6*	*2.1*	*5.9*	*7.3*	*5.7*	*4.9*	*7.2*	*2.5*	*4.9*
Burundi	0.1	34.1	2.5	5.6	-1.3	8.4	9.1	2.8	2.8	5.4	4.4	4.4
Comoros	0.0	28.2	4.5	3.7	2.2	1.3	5.5	4.9	3.2	4.7	3.2	4.8
Djibouti	0.1	29.4	1.7	3.0	1.0	3.3	2.9	13.8	4.9	5.1	5.5	7.3
Eritrea	0.1	27.8	...	...	10.6	-1.0	35.2	-18.3	8.9	-11.7	13.9	3.9
Ethiopia	1.8	19.3	...	...	2.7	8.8	7.0	5.9	6.0	7.5	7.2	7.9
Ethiopia (Former)	...	...	6.5	3.9	...	...	...	...	...	...	...	...
Kenya [2]	2.8	30.2	7.2	5.6	0.1	2.8	6.5	6.3	6.4	4.7	5.2	5.9
Madagascar	0.5	28.1	1.6	0.5	0.5	2.6	2.2	2.2	4.1	4.9	2.0	2.3
Malawi [2]	0.2	23.0	9.2	2.7	2.2	4.0	4.6	4.5	5.3	5.0	5.5	5.5
Mauritius [3]	0.7	45.7	7.9	4.1	6.4	6.6	5.4	4.3	4.2	4.0	4.1	3.9
Mozambique [2]	0.6	27.7	3.9	-1.9	3.3	7.9	9.1	9.5	4.6	2.2	2.5	3.3
Rwanda [2]	0.4	35.0	3.8	4.7	10.0	8.0	7.0	9.4	7.2	4.9	6.1	5.4
Seychelles [2]	0.1	41.4	9.0	-0.1	15.3	2.6	2.8	4.2	5.1	2.6	3.9	7.8
Somalia	0.0	12.5	8.2	0.6	1.5	3.6	13.8	6.3	9.6	10.0	8.7	9.6
South Sudan	0.3	29.4	...	...	...	...	36.7	27.4	-6.3	-6.9	-7.1	8.0
U.R. of Tanzania: Mainland [2]	1.5	22.4	8.4	2.3	2.3	6.6	9.7	8.3	7.2	4.5	4.3	5.4
Uganda [2]	1.0	27.6	-1.6	3.9	6.7	7.0	7.8	2.9	1.6	6.8	11.0	6.6
Zambia [4]	0.8	26.8	4.8	2.1	2.0	7.0	7.5	3.3	4.3	41.1	-21.6	1.4
Zanzibar [5]	0.0	25.6	...	...	6.3	5.9	11.3	7.7	3.2	3.5	6.1	7.1
Zimbabwe	0.9	32.9	3.4	5.1	1.4	6.8	1.3	1.1	1.6	3.4	-0.8	-4.2
Middle Africa	*7.9*	*21.9*	*1.2*	*2.0*	*-1.5*	*5.5*	*3.5*	*-0.2*	*-2.6*	*0.9*	*3.6*	*-1.2*
Angola	4.1	22.3	0.2	1.6	-2.5	5.4	2.5	-1.4	-6.7	1.5	3.8	-5.2
Cameroon [2]	1.2	26.9	5.7	1.1	2.1	5.2	4.4	3.1	4.8	4.0	4.7	2.5
Central African Republic	0.1	23.6	1.4	4.1	1.9	-3.3	-13.1	-2.7	1.8	5.9	4.1	-27.7
Chad	0.3	16.2	-1.7	4.1	-0.6	14.2	-2.6	-11.7	-2.6	-11.0	-0.4	4.0
Congo	0.4	23.3	2.8	5.1	-1.7	3.6	5.3	-7.0	-6.8	-3.3	-2.4	-2.6
D.R. of the Congo [6]	0.7	13.3	1.0	3.1	-4.0	3.9	9.9	6.5	3.3	1.2	3.4	8.6
Equatorial Guinea	0.5	24.2	2.4	7.1	5.9	16.2	2.7	1.5	-2.8	-0.1	4.2	0.6
Gabon	0.7	31.8	8.3	1.9	4.1	4.3	5.7	3.1	4.9	-0.5	4.4	3.2
Sao Tome and Principe	0.0	29.0	7.0	-1.2	0.5	3.4	6.0	2.6	5.2	5.0	3.8	3.7
Southern Africa	*21.1*	*43.1*	*3.8*	*3.4*	*2.2*	*4.4*	*2.9*	*1.8*	*1.5*	*1.4*	*1.6*	*2.0*
Botswana	0.8	39.9	14.4	15.1	6.6	5.0	3.7	3.9	3.0	2.9	4.1	4.5
Eswatini [2]	0.2	32.9	9.4	2.4	2.8	5.3	2.8	5.3	1.6	5.4	3.1	3.4
Lesotho [2]	0.1	39.6	7.3	5.1	2.9	5.2	11.4	5.3	2.6	0.3	3.1	-1.6
Namibia [2]	0.7	44.0	3.6	5.0	2.9	4.2	5.5	6.5	1.6	1.5	-0.3	1.8
South Africa	19.3	43.3	3.7	3.2	2.1	4.4	2.8	1.4	1.4	1.3	1.5	1.9
Western Africa	*26.6*	*25.6*	*9.2*	*3.5*	*3.9*	*6.2*	*7.6*	*5.4*	*-0.3*	*0.8*	*0.6*	*1.6*
Benin [7]	0.4	24.1	3.2	3.5	1.6	7.2	13.0	21.5	-1.5	7.3	6.3	4.2
Burkina Faso [2]	0.5	30.2	6.7	6.3	3.4	6.4	8.2	5.5	10.1	5.7	4.0	10.3
Cabo Verde [2]	0.1	37.2	0.3	7.8	9.8	5.7	3.9	3.4	6.6	-2.9	7.0	6.6
Côte d'Ivoire	2.1	31.1	8.8	-3.2	8.7	0.7	14.5	17.0	4.7	12.2	4.8	5.2
Gambia [2]	0.0	15.0	4.0	3.4	3.0	3.2	1.7	1.8	-0.3	-0.5	5.4	17.6
Ghana [2]	1.3	19.1	2.8	6.3	7.6	6.2	6.0	3.4	4.9	-2.1	1.9	6.1
Guinea	0.3	22.6	3.0	3.0	3.2	4.0	1.3	12.4	3.5	3.2	3.7	4.1
Guinea-Bissau	0.0	14.6	11.7	4.6	0.9	4.1	13.0	4.6	3.2	11.9	2.3	6.2
Liberia	0.0	8.3	7.3	1.2	-8.4	-0.2	5.1	6.9	20.5	1.1	-4.6	-7.9
Mali	0.4	21.8	4.5	1.5	10.7	8.2	9.4	8.2	8.1	3.9	4.8	5.6
Mauritania [2]	0.3	29.1	16.1	-0.6	1.6	0.8	0.8	5.9	3.7	3.3	5.4	7.9
Niger [2]	0.3	20.6	3.5	-1.1	3.4	3.2	13.4	7.9	1.9	1.8	5.6	7.4
Nigeria [2]	19.7	25.8	11.4	4.6	3.5	7.1	7.2	4.0	-2.5	-1.0	-1.0	-0.3
Senegal [2]	0.8	32.0	2.2	3.5	3.7	3.8	4.4	2.3	10.1	4.0	6.0	5.7
Sierra Leone	0.1	21.0	4.8	3.3	-8.4	4.6	6.7	6.3	4.9	5.5	5.0	4.2
Togo	0.2	33.0	2.7	-0.4	2.1	3.8	11.0	23.4	15.8	2.4	8.5	5.6

Table 6.G. Average Rates of Growth of Gross Domestic Product by Kind of Economic Activity - Other Activities

Major area, region and country	Base year weights as percentage of total for world or region in 2015	Base year share as percentage of total GDP in 2015	Average rates of growth				Annual rate of change (percentage)					
			1970-1979	1980-1989	1990-1999	2000-2009	2014	2015	2016	2017	2018	2019
Americas	**40.3**	**52.2**	**3.7**	**2.8**	**2.4**	**2.0**	**2.2**	**1.9**	**1.3**	**1.7**	**2.3**	**1.9**
Latin America and the Caribbean	**6.3**	**40.4**	**6.3**	**2.5**	**2.9**	**3.0**	**1.7**	**1.0**	**0.2**	**0.9**	**1.4**	**0.5**
Caribbean	*1.0*	*37.0*	*4.9*	*4.4*	*3.2*	*3.1*	*0.4*	*0.0*	*1.6*	*1.1*	*0.3*	*1.6*
Anguilla	0.0	45.7	4.0	6.9	5.3	5.7	-1.4	3.7	-6.7	-1.0	-1.6	9.3
Antigua and Barbuda	0.0	41.3	3.0	4.2	3.6	2.5	4.5	3.7	3.9	2.8	4.6	3.2
Aruba [2]	0.0	50.6	9.1	11.2	6.0	0.8	-0.1	0.9	2.9	2.3	0.4	-0.5
Bahamas [2]	0.0	52.2	2.4	3.0	3.5	0.2	2.5	1.6	3.8	5.1	-0.6	0.2
Barbados [2]	0.0	47.3	1.7	2.0	0.9	1.8	-0.9	1.3	0.5	0.6	-0.6	0.7
British Virgin Islands [2]	0.0	66.1	2.7	8.0	19.6	0.4	1.8	1.0	11.2	1.3	3.8	3.8
Cayman Islands [2]	0.0	73.7	9.4	9.6	7.1	1.2	1.9	2.8	2.6	3.2	2.9	2.7
Cuba	0.3	40.9	5.5	5.9	0.3	8.7	1.3	0.4	0.8	1.4	1.9	1.2
Curaçao	0.0	51.4	...	...	...	...	-3.0	-6.4	0.5	-1.7	0.1	-4.8
Dominica	0.0	39.8	5.2	2.4	2.3	2.2	5.5	2.0	3.2	0.2	-18.8	3.8
Dominican Republic [2]	0.2	33.9	7.4	3.7	3.5	4.0	5.9	5.5	6.5	3.2	5.0	5.9
Former Netherlands Antilles	...	...	8.2	3.4	2.1	1.3	...	...	...	...	...	...
Grenada	0.0	51.5	6.6	5.9	3.6	4.6	2.4	3.8	2.4	2.6	-0.8	2.7
Haiti	0.0	8.3	6.5	-0.2	1.7	0.7	3.6	2.7	2.1	1.2	2.3	-1.9
Jamaica	0.0	39.5	3.1	2.1	3.0	1.8	0.5	0.5	0.6	0.8	0.7	1.7
Montserrat	0.0	68.7	2.6	2.2	-7.9	3.6	-1.6	1.5	-2.9	-2.5	1.9	5.2
Puerto Rico [8]	0.3	35.0	3.9	5.6	4.3	0.6	-3.7	-4.2	-1.3	-1.5	-4.7	-1.1
Saint Kitts and Nevis	0.0	44.8	5.0	4.4	4.0	3.8	4.0	-2.2	5.2	-0.1	3.7	2.4
Saint Lucia [2]	0.0	41.7	6.2	6.6	4.5	2.5	-1.7	0.4	4.0	1.6	2.0	1.2
Sint Maarten (Dutch part)	0.0	52.0	...	...	...	...	-1.3	-0.7	2.0	-6.4	-10.2	5.6
St. Vincent and the Grenadines	0.0	46.0	2.3	1.9	4.0	2.2	1.8	1.9	1.0	1.4	0.3	1.8
Trinidad and Tobago [2]	0.1	27.1	7.5	-2.3	2.3	4.0	0.3	0.9	1.3	1.8	0.4	2.3
Turks and Caicos Islands	0.0	34.1	10.7	10.7	9.7	8.0	1.7	5.2	-1.9	3.6	4.5	3.0
Central America	*3.6*	*35.1*	*5.5*	*2.6*	*3.2*	*2.5*	*2.3*	*3.5*	*3.5*	*2.5*	*2.7*	*1.3*
Belize	0.0	35.7	3.5	3.7	2.8	5.7	4.7	10.1	1.6	1.2	0.2	-11.4
Costa Rica [2]	0.2	50.5	5.0	2.2	5.1	5.1	4.1	4.5	4.8	4.2	2.9	3.9
El Salvador [2]	0.1	41.3	4.8	1.1	6.5	3.0	1.5	3.8	2.8	2.6	2.2	2.7
Guatemala [2]	0.2	34.9	5.3	1.8	4.5	3.9	4.4	4.6	2.8	3.3	3.5	4.0
Honduras	0.1	35.9	8.8	3.3	3.3	7.9	4.7	5.5	4.1	4.1	4.1	5.6
Mexico [2]	3.0	34.5	5.7	2.7	3.0	2.2	2.0	3.3	3.4	2.2	2.6	0.9
Nicaragua	0.0	31.8	-1.5	-0.9	1.8	3.4	6.0	4.4	5.2	3.7	-1.2	-4.0
Panama	0.1	31.7	6.5	2.2	4.8	4.5	5.3	5.2	5.7	4.2	4.7	3.2
South America	*11.0*	*42.9*	*6.7*	*2.3*	*2.8*	*3.1*	*1.6*	*0.3*	*-1.0*	*0.3*	*1.0*	*0.1*
Argentina	1.7	41.3	3.0	0.2	4.9	2.2	0.3	2.2	0.5	2.4	1.7	-1.6
Bolivia (Plurinational State of)	0.1	35.1	5.8	-2.2	5.4	2.4	6.0	7.0	6.0	4.7	5.7	4.2
Brazil [2]	5.9	49.0	9.4	3.1	2.1	2.9	0.7	-1.2	-0.7	0.2	1.4	1.5
Chile [2]	0.7	42.0	3.2	1.7	4.9	5.1	2.5	2.5	2.5	1.1	3.8	2.3
Colombia [2]	0.8	40.1	5.9	3.3	5.2	4.1	5.7	3.9	2.5	3.1	3.7	4.2
Ecuador [2]	0.2	34.7	7.0	3.9	1.8	3.8	4.4	1.8	-0.3	1.2	2.3	1.0
Guyana [3]	0.0	32.4	2.9	-0.5	2.0	11.1	3.4	2.8	2.9	2.1	2.3	3.8
Paraguay [2]	0.1	30.6	6.7	2.4	2.8	2.3	3.7	5.4	3.0	2.9	5.5	2.4
Peru [2,9]	0.4	33.0	2.8	0.2	3.7	2.9	5.7	5.1	4.0	2.8	4.3	4.0
Suriname	0.0	25.0	4.2	4.7	-1.4	2.7	3.2	-5.7	2.4	-13.6	6.6	3.9
Uruguay	0.2	44.8	1.8	2.4	1.9	0.8	3.3	1.5	0.3	-0.9	0.0	0.6
Venezuela (Bolivarian Republic of)	0.7	29.1	8.3	2.1	0.8	5.4	2.6	-3.2	-20.4	-13.2	-20.1	-35.4
Northern America	**34.0**	**55.1**	**3.3**	**2.8**	**2.3**	**1.8**	**2.3**	**2.0**	**1.5**	**1.8**	**2.5**	**2.2**
Bermuda [2]	0.0	79.5	3.5	1.0	2.4	4.3	-3.0	0.6	-0.8	2.4	0.3	0.6
Canada [2]	5.9	52.0	4.0	2.7	2.5	2.9	2.3	1.9	1.7	2.7	2.3	2.7
Greenland [2]	0.0	41.1	6.4	2.5	1.0	1.7	-0.8	-0.9	0.3	2.0	0.0	0.8
United States [2,10]	78.5	55.3	3.3	2.8	2.3	1.8	2.3	2.0	1.5	1.8	2.5	2.2
Asia	**29.1**	**35.5**	**6.5**	**4.9**	**4.3**	**5.5**	**5.1**	**6.0**	**5.4**	**5.2**	**5.4**	**5.7**
Central Asia	*0.9*	*27.7*	...	...	*-4.1*	*7.3*	*6.1*	*5.7*	*1.9*	*3.4*	*4.0*	*4.1*
Kazakhstan [5]	0.6	31.6	...	...	-5.1	8.8	3.8	3.7	1.6	1.3	1.8	2.4
Kyrgyzstan [5]	0.0	25.6	...	...	-2.7	2.3	0.7	0.9	1.6	2.1	0.9	0.9
Tajikistan	0.0	17.1	...	...	-11.4	5.3	-2.0	5.9	-6.5	2.2	26.9	15.8
Turkmenistan	0.1	23.0	...	...	-1.9	4.3	22.4	16.2	-2.9	9.9	7.2	1.3
Uzbekistan [5]	0.2	22.1	...	...	-0.4	4.6	8.9	8.3	6.0	7.1	8.3	9.5
Eastern Asia	*71.3*	*37.5*	*6.1*	*5.6*	*4.3*	*5.4*	*4.9*	*6.5*	*5.5*	*5.5*	*5.8*	*5.9*
China [10]	40.8	34.2	5.5	13.9	10.8	11.7	8.1	10.3	8.4	8.3	8.4	8.5
China, Hong Kong SAR [11]	1.8	56.7	9.0	7.1	5.8	3.5	2.9	2.9	2.9	3.3	2.5	2.1
China, Macao SAR	0.3	71.3	7.9	7.7	2.3	8.2	-2.5	-18.0	0.9	8.2	4.9	4.6
D.P.R. of Korea	0.1	32.2	7.6	2.7	1.1	0.6	1.3	0.8	0.6	0.5	0.9	0.9
Japan [2,8]	20.3	43.1	5.9	4.0	1.6	0.9	0.2	1.6	1.1	0.7	1.1	0.9

Table 6.G. Average Rates of Growth of Gross Domestic Product by Kind of Economic Activity - Other Activities

Major area, region and country	Base year weights as percentage of total for world or region in 2015	Base year share as percentage of total GDP in 2015	Average rates of growth				Annual rate of change (percentage)					
			1970-1979	1980-1989	1990-1999	2000-2009	2014	2015	2016	2017	2018	2019
Mongolia [2]	0.0	30.1	5.6	27.7	-2.3	4.7	10.8	5.9	1.1	5.3	4.6	5.6
Republic of Korea [2]	6.0	41.6	7.5	9.5	7.0	4.8	4.0	3.2	2.9	2.7	4.0	3.4
South-Eastern Asia	*6.8*	*26.2*	*6.8*	*6.4*	*4.6*	*5.4*	*4.9*	*5.2*	*5.2*	*5.0*	*3.9*	*5.1*
Brunei Darussalam [2]	0.0	28.9	16.9	5.6	3.4	3.9	1.4	-1.4	-0.6	0.7	0.6	2.6
Cambodia	0.0	18.6	-7.3	5.8	6.1	10.9	9.9	7.7	8.8	6.2	6.7	6.2
Indonesia [2]	1.7	19.1	8.3	6.9	2.5	6.0	5.4	6.6	5.7	4.9	5.9	6.9
Lao People's DR [2]	0.0	29.0	3.0	6.3	-0.1	6.1	4.6	5.8	4.1	3.9	4.0	8.8
Malaysia [2,8]	0.8	24.7	9.5	6.2	8.0	6.2	5.1	3.3	4.6	5.4	5.5	5.1
Myanmar [6,8]	0.0	6.6	5.2	4.5	5.7	11.2	10.1	8.7	9.3	9.8	8.4	9.7
Philippines [2,10]	1.0	32.5	5.0	3.4	3.2	5.2	6.1	6.5	8.0	7.2	7.6	6.8
Singapore [2]	1.4	44.1	6.1	10.4	5.9	5.0	4.6	5.3	3.4	3.8	4.1	2.9
Thailand [2,8]	1.2	28.2	7.9	6.0	4.3	4.4	2.8	3.2	3.8	3.9	-4.8	2.5
Timor-Leste [5]	0.0	43.2	...	...	0.7	8.5	14.1	3.4	4.9	7.9	-0.3	-2.7
Viet Nam [2,12]	0.5	24.9	4.7	5.7	10.0	6.3	5.7	6.0	6.5	6.7	6.3	6.4
Southern Asia	*10.3*	*32.7*	*8.3*	*1.4*	*6.0*	*6.5*	*7.9*	*7.2*	*7.5*	*6.0*	*6.9*	*7.2*
Afghanistan [13]	0.1	39.8	0.9	1.2	-3.1	26.1	12.6	3.6	5.9	-1.8	3.1	-1.0
Bangladesh	0.6	31.2	1.6	5.8	4.2	4.6	4.9	5.4	6.2	6.3	5.7	5.9
Bhutan	0.0	20.4	3.6	9.2	5.2	8.8	5.3	6.1	9.3	1.1	7.3	6.1
India [2]	7.2	34.1	4.3	7.1	8.0	7.5	10.0	9.0	8.9	6.5	7.8	8.5
Iran (Islamic Republic of)	1.4	32.3	13.7	-6.0	2.6	3.9	1.7	0.4	1.7	3.4	2.2	2.0
Maldives [2]	0.0	35.1	6.1	19.6	1.4	9.5	7.8	-4.5	6.2	6.1	6.8	6.8
Nepal	0.1	28.3	3.9	4.5	6.2	6.8	4.3	6.2	5.0	7.0	5.5	5.8
Pakistan [2]	0.6	23.1	6.7	6.7	4.9	6.4	4.4	5.2	6.8	6.8	7.9	6.3
Sri Lanka [2]	0.3	34.8	3.8	3.8	6.0	4.9	5.7	6.5	5.2	3.5	5.2	2.3
Western Asia	*10.8*	*35.1*	*7.2*	*2.8*	*3.3*	*5.2*	*3.9*	*2.8*	*3.5*	*2.8*	*2.7*	*2.9*
Armenia [5]	0.0	33.1	...	...	3.0	9.2	5.8	5.7	1.3	6.9	8.8	10.1
Azerbaijan [5]	0.1	22.2	...	...	-4.7	4.6	7.4	3.9	-4.5	3.2	2.0	3.6
Bahrain [8]	0.1	44.3	9.5	12.7	2.7	8.2	4.4	2.7	5.0	5.5	2.0	1.2
Cyprus [2]	0.1	56.7	4.3	7.3	7.3	4.2	-1.9	3.4	2.8	1.5	2.2	2.4
Georgia [5]	0.1	43.4	...	...	-13.7	6.3	4.6	4.8	5.3	5.0	5.8	5.0
Iraq	0.5	29.4	8.4	2.3	0.9	15.2	-8.5	-8.1	4.8	-2.2	2.4	2.0
Israel [2]	1.5	52.2	8.1	3.8	6.0	2.8	3.1	2.4	3.7	4.1	3.2	3.7
Jordan [2]	0.2	47.0	2.6	3.8	4.7	6.1	3.0	3.2	2.9	2.4	2.4	2.6
Kuwait	0.6	39.6	7.5	3.6	6.9	7.3	3.1	1.8	2.2	3.2	2.4	2.6
Lebanon [2]	0.3	54.3	-2.6	-5.0	6.4	4.2	3.7	1.4	4.1	0.7	0.6	-5.9
Oman	0.3	32.7	11.6	7.9	4.1	6.3	6.2	3.5	4.6	2.3	0.6	0.2
Qatar [2,8]	0.5	29.8	7.0	4.1	4.1	15.8	9.9	8.7	5.7	3.1	2.5	4.3
Saudi Arabia [2]	2.4	34.3	12.2	1.7	2.0	4.2	3.5	2.3	1.2	2.2	3.2	3.5
State of Palestine [2]	0.1	40.8	8.0	2.0	9.2	4.0	5.0	2.1	9.3	-8.0	-0.6	3.4
Syrian Arab Republic [10]	0.0	17.3	13.1	-0.8	3.9	10.4	-0.7	-5.6	-3.5	-2.9	4.1	4.4
Turkey [2]	2.7	32.4	4.4	2.7	2.5	3.6	5.7	5.1	5.2	4.5	4.2	3.8
United Arab Emirates	1.2	30.9	14.7	7.1	5.9	7.4	8.0	4.7	5.0	2.2	-0.7	0.7
Yemen	0.1	28.9	...	...	6.2	5.0	-6.1	-19.5	-24.3	-9.8	-2.7	3.0
Yemen Arab Republic (Former)	...	...	10.7	7.0	...	...	...	...	...	...	...	...
Yemen Democratic (Former)	...	...	3.9	6.6	...	...	...	...	...	...	...	...
Europe	**26.4**	**48.8**	**3.7**	**3.0**	**2.0**	**1.8**	**1.2**	**1.2**	**1.2**	**1.8**	**1.8**	**1.4**
Eastern Europe	*10.1*	*36.5*	*3.3*	*3.7*	*-0.6*	*3.8*	*0.3*	*0.1*	*1.1*	*2.5*	*3.0*	*2.3*
Belarus [5]	0.2	29.0	...	...	-3.5	3.7	-0.7	-0.6	-2.3	-2.2	-0.9	0.3
Bulgaria [2]	0.2	40.1	7.0	4.5	-5.3	4.8	2.5	3.2	2.1	4.7	6.3	-10.6
Czechia [5]	0.7	36.3	...	...	2.0	1.6	1.3	2.4	3.5	2.6	3.9	2.5
Czechoslovakia (Former)	...	...	4.9	2.4	...	...	...	...	...	...	...	...
Hungary [2]	0.5	40.8	5.5	5.0	0.4	2.0	1.1	2.0	2.8	3.9	4.6	1.8
Poland [2]	1.7	34.1	5.9	-0.1	-1.0	3.5	3.5	4.7	3.0	3.4	4.5	6.2
Republic of Moldova [5]	0.0	32.9	...	...	-7.5	5.2	1.6	0.6	2.0	0.3	1.2	2.1
Romania [2]	0.7	36.1	9.8	1.7	2.9	2.6	2.0	-0.6	1.1	6.6	2.7	4.1
Russian Federation	5.5	37.4	...	...	-1.2	4.6	-0.4	-1.9	-0.3	1.7	2.3	1.2
Slovakia [5]	0.4	38.9	...	...	4.8	2.9	-8.2	5.3	6.5	2.6	3.4	2.5
Ukraine [5,14]	0.3	31.0	...	...	-3.2	1.9	1.0	-3.0	-0.3	1.6	3.4	4.8
USSR (Former)	...	...	0.9	5.3	...	...	...	...	...	...	...	...
Northern Europe	*25.9*	*51.3*	*3.1*	*2.9*	*2.6*	*2.3*	*2.2*	*2.1*	*1.4*	*1.4*	*1.4*	*1.4*
Denmark [2]	1.6	50.7	3.3	1.5	1.3	1.2	1.8	2.0	1.6	1.2	1.5	2.7
Estonia [5]	0.1	41.6	...	...	-2.4	4.1	1.2	3.6	2.5	4.3	1.1	2.7
Finland [2]	1.2	48.9	4.2	3.7	1.5	1.0	-0.1	0.7	1.7	1.9	2.5	1.1
Iceland [2]	0.1	48.2	6.3	5.1	3.9	4.4	1.5	0.3	7.4	5.8	4.1	2.1
Ireland [2]	1.2	36.1	4.6	1.7	5.2	3.3	5.0	5.9	0.4	6.6	5.5	3.5
Latvia [5]	0.1	43.7	...	...	1.6	4.9	3.1	2.5	1.9	0.3	2.9	2.7
Lithuania [5]	0.1	31.9	...	...	0.8	3.4	1.6	2.5	2.5	1.8	2.5	2.8
Norway [2]	1.8	44.5	3.8	2.7	2.9	2.6	2.1	1.9	1.5	1.8	2.7	2.0
Sweden [2]	2.5	47.7	3.0	1.7	0.6	1.3	2.1	3.2	3.2	2.0	1.5	1.8
United Kingdom [2]	17.1	55.1	2.8	3.5	3.1	2.5	2.3	1.8	1.1	0.9	0.9	1.0

Table 6.G. Average Rates of Growth of Gross Domestic Product by Kind of Economic Activity - Other Activities

Major area, region and country	Base year weights as percentage of total for world or region in 2015	Base year share as percentage of total GDP in 2015	Average rates of growth				Annual rate of change (percentage)					
			1970-1979	1980-1989	1990-1999	2000-2009	2014	2015	2016	2017	2018	2019
Southern Europe	*18.8*	*48.8*	*4.0*	*3.4*	*1.5*	*2.0*	*0.6*	*0.8*	*0.8*	*1.5*	*1.6*	*1.1*
Albania [2]	0.0	31.5	4.1	2.9	2.6	4.6	6.6	3.6	4.3	7.3	2.8	3.0
Andorra [2]	0.0	58.1	3.8	2.9	4.4	3.3	3.7	2.2	2.0	-1.6	1.0	2.9
Bosnia and Herzegovina [5]	0.1	38.3	...	...	15.6	2.3	2.9	1.8	1.1	2.3	2.3	3.4
Croatia [5]	0.2	43.4	...	...	4.0	2.2	0.7	0.7	2.1	1.8	1.8	2.0
Greece [2]	1.1	51.5	5.5	2.6	2.3	3.3	2.6	0.6	-0.4	0.4	0.5	0.4
Italy [2]	9.8	50.2	3.5	3.4	1.0	0.7	0.5	0.3	0.0	0.6	0.8	0.3
Kosovo [5]	0.0	35.2	...	...	-9.1	2.8	-1.5	-1.9	1.2	4.2	7.0	5.0
Malta [2]	0.1	56.3	11.6	4.4	6.7	5.8	12.2	13.1	7.3	7.7	7.2	6.4
Montenegro [5]	0.0	39.4	...	...	-4.8	-2.0	2.9	2.4	0.9	3.7	3.1	4.7
North Macedonia [5]	0.0	37.1	...	...	2.4	0.9	4.2	5.3	2.3	0.3	2.5	2.3
Portugal [2]	1.0	47.1	3.5	3.9	3.2	1.7	-0.4	0.9	1.4	2.8	2.0	1.4
San Marino [2]	0.0	46.3	3.8	2.4	5.9	2.0	-4.5	-6.0	-0.2	0.3	-7.7	-0.5
Serbia [5]	0.1	35.9	...	...	-7.4	4.1	0.4	-1.3	1.7	2.4	2.1	2.5
Slovenia [5]	0.2	40.7	...	...	2.9	2.6	2.1	0.8	2.3	2.9	3.0	1.0
Spain [2]	6.2	47.7	4.6	4.2	2.2	4.3	0.4	1.6	1.9	2.7	2.7	2.0
Yugoslavia (Former)	...	...	7.6	1.2	...	...	...	...	...	...	...	...
Western Europe	*45.1*	*51.3*	*4.0*	*2.7*	*2.4*	*1.1*	*1.0*	*1.1*	*1.3*	*2.0*	*1.8*	*1.4*
Austria [2]	1.8	44.0	3.9	2.3	2.4	2.2	0.5	1.1	1.4	2.3	1.6	1.3
Belgium [2]	2.6	53.7	5.1	3.9	3.3	1.7	1.1	1.4	1.6	2.8	2.3	1.9
France [2]	14.5	55.8	3.9	2.2	1.6	1.4	1.1	0.6	1.2	2.0	2.1	1.4
Germany [2]	17.6	48.8	4.8	3.0	3.0	0.5	0.6	1.3	1.1	2.2	1.0	1.3
Liechtenstein [2]	0.0	47.6	3.1	6.0	5.8	1.7	2.0	2.6	1.8	-6.5	6.8	2.2
Luxembourg [2]	0.4	64.7	10.6	4.6	5.0	3.3	4.0	5.6	2.4	2.6	2.3	1.9
Monaco [8]	0.0	52.3	3.9	2.4	1.9	2.1	9.1	-1.5	3.3	4.3	4.5	8.9
Netherlands [2]	4.3	52.8	4.3	1.9	3.1	1.9	1.3	1.7	1.4	1.9	1.7	1.4
Switzerland [2]	3.9	48.0	0.9	2.7	1.3	1.5	2.8	0.7	2.0	1.2	3.6	1.1
Oceania	**2.3**	**53.0**	**4.0**	**3.9**	**3.8**	**3.1**	**2.5**	**3.5**	**3.3**	**3.1**	**3.7**	**1.6**
Australia and New Zealand	*97.8*	*53.4*	*4.0*	*4.0*	*3.9*	*3.2*	*2.5*	*3.5*	*3.3*	*3.1*	*3.7*	*1.5*
Australia [2]	86.3	53.7	4.0	4.3	4.0	3.1	2.5	3.6	3.2	3.0	3.8	1.5
New Zealand [2]	11.5	51.1	3.9	2.1	3.0	3.4	2.3	3.2	4.4	3.7	2.7	1.7
Melanesia	*1.7*	*36.4*	*4.7*	*2.5*	*3.7*	*2.9*	*2.5*	*0.5*	*3.0*	*2.3*	*4.3*	*2.3*
Fiji [2]	0.2	39.2	5.2	1.4	0.9	1.3	22.0	3.6	0.0	4.1	2.0	2.1
New Caledonia [6]	0.6	54.5	9.1	4.5	3.2	3.7	0.3	2.9	4.2	3.2	2.6	2.7
Papua New Guinea [2]	0.8	29.2	3.1	1.5	5.1	2.7	0.4	-2.4	2.4	1.2	6.1	1.7
Solomon Islands	0.0	31.8	9.1	4.9	3.5	2.5	3.5	7.8	10.3	2.9	7.1	6.8
Vanuatu [2]	0.0	33.4	7.7	6.9	1.0	3.3	1.7	3.1	2.7	0.7	1.7	4.9
Micronesia	*0.1*	*42.7*	*2.3*	*4.1*	*0.3*	*1.0*	*2.7*	*4.0*	*1.3*	*1.7*	*4.4*	*2.5*
Kiribati [1]	0.0	46.9	-7.8	21.0	4.1	2.4	1.6	5.0	2.6	6.0	-0.2	2.8
Marshall Islands	0.0	47.7	6.6	6.8	-0.6	2.2	1.5	2.9	1.2	3.1	13.3	6.4
Micronesia (FS of)	0.0	45.0	6.6	4.1	1.8	0.6	0.2	2.5	0.1	2.5	1.5	1.5
Nauru	0.0	18.7	1.1	-1.6	-14.9	-4.0	28.5	4.2	4.8	-6.6	6.1	1.1
Palau [2]	0.0	43.6	0.1	3.6	2.3	0.3	4.1	6.1	1.5	-1.9	4.1	0.2
Polynesia	*0.5*	*53.3*	*5.0*	*6.3*	*1.9*	*2.2*	*0.1*	*2.0*	*1.2*	*4.1*	*2.0*	*1.9*
Cook Islands [2]	0.0	42.3	2.3	8.9	2.7	2.8	-0.3	0.3	11.0	5.6	1.4	4.8
French Polynesia	0.4	58.8	5.3	6.7	1.7	2.1	-0.2	1.8	0.7	4.5	1.9	2.1
Samoa [2,15]	0.0	29.6	3.7	0.3	3.6	4.2	3.9	7.4	2.1	2.3	3.2	-2.2
Tonga [16]	0.0	40.3	3.9	5.2	3.3	0.4	0.6	-0.7	3.2	-0.6	1.7	1.2
Tuvalu	0.0	51.1	-1.9	2.1	4.9	2.2	2.5	5.5	1.5	2.3	3.2	2.5

Notes for Table 6.G. Average Rates of Growth of Gross Domestic Product by Kind of Economic Activity - Other Activities

1/ 1970-2019
At factor cost.

2/ 1970-2019
Excludes computer and related activities and radio/TV activities, includes travel agencies and landscaping care

3/ 2006-2019
Excludes computer and related activities and radio/TV activities, includes travel agencies and landscaping care

4/ 2010-2019
Excludes computer and related activities and radio/TV activities, includes travel agencies and landscaping care

5/ 1990-2019
Excludes computer and related activities and radio/TV activities, includes travel agencies and landscaping care

6/ 1970-2019
Includes Restaurants and hotels.

7/ 2015-2019
Excludes computer and related activities and radio/TV activities, includes travel agencies and landscaping care

8/ 1970-2019
At producers' prices.

9/ 1970-2001
At producers' prices.

10/ 1970-2019
Includes Taxes less subsidies on production and imports.

11/ (a) 1970-2019
Excludes waste management.

(b) 1970-2019
Includes repair of motor vehicles and motorcycles, personal and household goods.

12/ 1970-2009
At producers' prices.

13/ 2016-2019
Excludes repair of motor vehicles and motorcycles, personal and household goods.

14/ 2010-2019
The Government of Ukraine has advised the United Nations that it is not in a position to provide statistical data concerning the Autonomous Republic of Crimea and the city of Sevastopol.

15/ (a) 1970-2008
At producers' prices.

(b) 2009-2019
Includes Taxes less subsidies on production and imports.

16/ 1994-2019
Excludes computer and related activities and radio/TV activities, includes travel agencies and landscaping care

D. Implicit Price Deflators of Gross Domestic Product: Individual Countries or Areas (2015 = 100)

Description of Analysis in Table 7

D. Price development expressed in terms of indices of implicit price deflators of gross domestic product

This final section of the publication presents an analysis of economic development represented by the movements of prices and exchange rates in relation to economic growth for the years 1970, 1975, 1980, 1985, 1990, 1995, 2000, 2005, 2010 and 2015 through 2019.

In table 7, indices of GDP at current prices derived from GDP in national currency and US dollars are shown in columns 1 and 2. Column 3 shows the index of the volume of GDP in national currency. Column 4 presents indices of price deflators of GDP in national currency and column 5 includes indices of price deflators of GDP in US dollars. The price indices in columns 4 and 5 are obtained by dividing, respectively, the indices of GDP at current prices in national currencies and in US dollars shown in columns 1 and 2, by the volume indices presented in column 3. Column 6 provides an implied development in exchange rates derived either by dividing the GDP deflators in national currency (column 4) by the GDP deflators in US dollar listed in column 5, or by dividing the GDP indices in national currencies by the United States dollar indices listed in column 1 and 2, respectively.

To determine whether adjustments in exchange rates have been sufficient to reflect inflationary pressures in the economy, exchange rate movements in column 6 are compared with price changes in columns 4 and 5.

The data presented in the table reflect four different situations in countries. In the first group, the movement of exchange rates as calculated in column 6 is exactly the same as the movement of domestic prices reflected in the price indices presented in column 4. For these countries, there is no movement over time of the price index in terms of US dollars that is presented in column 5. In this case the growth of GDP in US dollars is not affected by domestic price changes as all domestic price changes have been eliminated through the movement of the exchange rate.

A second group of countries are those having fixed exchange rates. There is no movement of the exchange rates in column 6 i.e., the index always remains 100. In this case all domestic inflation is reflected in the growth of GDP in US dollar terms.

In a third group of countries, the exchange rate index in column 6 is not fixed but lags behind the movement of domestic prices as reflected in the price indices presented in column 4. For this group of countries, the price index in terms of US dollars as presented in column 5 is higher than 100 and the countries' domestic inflation thus affects the growth of GDP in US dollars, though not to the extent that this was the case for countries with a fixed exchange rate. Only some of the domestic inflation is eliminated from the growth of GDP in US dollars through the movement of the exchange rates.

There is a fourth group of countries where the exchange rates overreact to the movements of prices in the domestic economy. For these countries, the index of exchange rates in column 6 is much higher than the price index in terms of national currency in column 4. This case implies that the price index in terms of US dollars as shown in column 5 is lower than 100 and this has the effect that the growth of GDP in US dollars is lower than GDP in national currency.

Again, a note of caution is advised when using the price index information presented in the table. For one, the deflators shown may not be fully comparable between countries because a wide variety of methods had been applied to obtain the data on price movements. To cite an example, for some countries, explicit price indices were used directly in the calculations while for other countries implicit price indices were derived by dividing volume indices into indices of current price development of GDP. Likewise, even as the index numbers are shown for a common base year 2015 = 100, GDP data at constant prices used in the calculations actually have been compiled according to different original weight base periods.

Table 7. Implicit price deflators of Gross Domestic Product in US Dollars and National Currency (2015 = 100)

Major area, region and country	Year	GDP in Current Prices: National Currency (1)	GDP in Current Prices: US Dollars (2)	Gross Domestic Product at Constant Prices (3)	GDP Implicit Price Deflators (2015 = 100): National Currency (4)	GDP Implicit Price Deflators (2015 = 100): US Dollars (5)	Exchange Rates (6)
Africa							
Algeria (Algerian Dinar)	1970	0.2	3.1	21.0	0.7	14.8	4.9
	1975	0.4	9.4	26.6	1.4	35.2	3.9
	1980	1.0	25.5	36.9	2.6	69.0	3.8
	1985	1.7	34.9	46.7	3.7	74.7	5.0
	1990	3.3	37.2	48.5	6.8	76.7	8.9
	1995	12.0	25.3	49.1	24.4	51.5	47.3
	2000	24.6	32.9	58.2	42.3	56.6	74.7
	2005	45.2	62.2	74.9	60.4	83.0	72.8
	2010	71.8	97.1	84.9	84.5	114.4	73.9
	2015	100.0	100.0	100.0	100.0	100.0	100.0
	2016	104.8	96.4	103.2	101.5	93.4	108.7
	2017	112.9	102.5	104.5	108.0	98.0	110.2
	2018	122.4	105.7	105.8	115.7	99.9	115.8
	2019	122.2	103.1	106.6	114.6	96.7	118.5
Angola (Kwanza)	1970	0.0	3.3	22.9	0.0	14.3	0.0
	1975	0.0	3.6	25.8	0.0	13.8	0.0
	1980	0.0	6.2	24.0	0.0	25.7	0.0
	1985	0.0	7.9	26.2	0.0	30.0	0.0
	1990	0.0	11.8	30.5	0.0	38.6	0.0
	1995	0.0	5.7	25.7	0.0	22.2	0.0
	2000	0.9	10.5	34.5	2.5	30.4	8.4
	2005	23.1	31.8	53.6	43.1	59.4	72.6
	2010	55.2	72.1	80.2	68.9	90.0	76.5
	2015	100.0	100.0	100.0	100.0	100.0	100.0
	2016	118.6	87.0	97.4	121.8	89.3	136.3
	2017	145.2	105.1	97.3	149.3	108.0	138.2
	2018	183.7	87.2	95.3	192.7	91.5	210.6
	2019	222.3	73.2	93.9	236.7	77.9	303.9
Benin (CFA Franc BCEAO)	1970	1.3	2.8	11.3	11.7	25.0	46.7
	1975	2.1	5.9	13.1	16.3	45.1	36.2
	1980	4.7	13.0	16.4	28.5	79.8	35.7
	1985	7.5	9.9	21.2	35.5	46.7	75.9
	1990	8.1	17.5	23.8	33.8	73.5	46.0
	1995	17.4	20.6	30.4	57.2	67.8	84.4
	2000	27.2	22.6	38.9	69.9	58.1	120.3
	2005	37.6	42.2	47.1	79.9	89.6	89.2
	2010	51.3	61.3	56.9	90.2	107.7	83.7
	2015	100.0	100.0	100.0	100.0	100.0	100.0
	2016	104.0	103.9	103.3	100.7	100.5	100.2
	2017	109.5	111.6	109.2	100.3	102.2	98.1
	2018	117.7	125.3	116.5	101.0	107.6	93.9
	2019	125.3	126.6	124.5	100.7	101.7	99.0
Botswana (Pula)	1970	0.0	0.5	2.6	1.2	17.6	7.1
	1975	0.1	1.9	6.0	2.3	31.7	7.3
	1980	0.5	5.9	10.5	4.3	56.2	7.7
	1985	1.1	5.8	17.7	6.2	32.8	18.8
	1990	4.7	25.8	32.9	14.4	78.4	18.4

Table 7. Implicit price deflators of Gross Domestic Product in US Dollars and National Currency (2015 = 100)

Major area, region and country	Year	GDP in Current Prices: National Currency (1)	GDP in Current Prices: US Dollars (2)	Gross Domestic Product at Constant Prices (3)	GDP Implicit Price Deflators (2015 = 100): National Currency (4)	GDP Implicit Price Deflators (2015 = 100): US Dollars (5)	Exchange Rates (6)
	1995	9.0	32.8	41.2	21.8	79.7	27.4
	2000	20.2	40.1	53.0	38.1	75.7	50.4
	2005	34.7	68.9	63.4	54.8	108.7	50.5
	2010	59.5	88.7	79.2	75.1	112.0	67.1
	2015	100.0	100.0	100.0	100.0	100.0	100.0
	2016	116.8	108.5	104.3	112.0	104.0	107.6
	2017	123.3	120.7	107.3	114.9	112.5	102.2
	2018	130.3	129.4	112.1	116.2	115.4	100.7
	2019	135.1	127.2	115.5	117.0	110.1	106.2
Burkina Faso..	1970	2.0	4.3	12.3	16.3	34.9	46.7
(CFA Franc BCEAO)	1975	3.1	8.5	15.3	20.0	55.3	36.2
	1980	6.6	18.4	18.5	35.4	99.2	35.7
	1985	11.3	14.9	22.5	50.4	66.4	75.9
	1990	13.7	29.8	26.0	52.8	114.7	46.0
	1995	19.3	22.9	31.5	61.3	72.6	84.4
	2000	30.1	25.0	43.2	69.8	58.0	120.3
	2005	46.3	52.0	58.8	78.8	88.4	89.2
	2010	71.5	85.4	76.8	93.1	111.2	83.7
	2015	100.0	100.0	100.0	100.0	100.0	100.0
	2016	108.7	108.5	106.0	102.6	102.4	100.2
	2017	117.1	119.3	112.5	104.1	106.0	98.1
	2018	127.5	135.8	120.1	106.2	113.1	93.9
	2019	133.9	135.2	127.0	105.5	106.5	99.0
Burundi..	1970	0.5	8.7	36.8	1.3	23.7	5.6
(Burundi Franc)	1975	0.7	14.8	38.0	1.9	38.9	5.0
	1980	1.9	33.8	47.8	4.1	70.7	5.7
	1985	3.2	41.7	60.8	5.3	68.6	7.7
	1990	4.5	40.9	72.4	6.2	56.5	10.9
	1995	5.7	35.6	65.0	8.7	54.7	15.9
	2000	11.6	25.2	61.1	18.9	41.3	45.8
	2005	27.3	39.7	67.8	40.4	58.7	68.8
	2010	56.6	72.3	84.5	67.0	85.5	78.3
	2015	100.0	100.0	100.0	100.0	100.0	100.0
	2016	109.7	104.3	103.2	106.3	101.0	105.3
	2017	125.9	114.5	107.5	117.1	106.4	110.0
	2018	124.3	109.6	109.3	113.7	100.3	113.4
	2019	125.4	106.8	111.2	112.8	96.1	117.4
Cabo Verde..	1970	1.3	4.6	16.2	8.2	28.2	28.9
(Cabo Verde Escudo)	1975	2.2	8.4	15.1	14.3	55.7	25.7
	1980	4.1	10.1	17.4	23.5	58.2	40.4
	1985	9.0	9.8	24.0	37.7	40.9	92.2
	1990	15.5	21.9	29.0	53.2	75.6	70.4
	1995	27.0	35.0	37.4	72.2	93.4	77.3
	2000	46.2	38.4	55.9	82.7	68.7	120.4
	2005	61.8	69.3	72.7	85.0	95.3	89.2
	2010	87.3	104.3	92.9	94.0	112.3	83.7
	2015	100.0	100.0	100.0	100.0	100.0	100.0
	2016	104.5	104.2	104.7	99.8	99.5	100.3
	2017	109.1	110.9	108.6	100.5	102.1	98.4
	2018	115.8	123.2	113.5	102.0	108.5	94.0

Table 7. Implicit price deflators of Gross Domestic Product in US Dollars and National Currency (2015 = 100)

Major area, region and country	Year	GDP in Current Prices: National Currency (1)	GDP in Current Prices: US Dollars (2)	Gross Domestic Product at Constant Prices (3)	GDP Implicit Price Deflators (2015 = 100): National Currency (4)	GDP Implicit Price Deflators (2015 = 100): US Dollars (5)	Exchange Rates (6)
	2019	123.0	124.2	119.9	102.6	103.5	99.1
Cameroon	1970	2.0	4.3	22.3	8.9	19.1	46.7
(CFA Franc BEAC)	1975	4.3	11.7	26.6	16.0	44.1	36.2
	1980	11.7	32.6	41.4	28.2	78.9	35.7
	1985	23.6	31.1	57.2	41.2	54.3	75.9
	1990	19.1	41.5	44.7	42.6	92.7	46.0
	1995	26.3	31.2	42.7	61.6	73.0	84.4
	2000	39.1	32.5	53.0	73.9	61.4	120.3
	2005	51.8	58.1	65.6	78.9	88.5	89.2
	2010	70.8	84.6	77.9	90.9	108.6	83.7
	2015	100.0	100.0	100.0	100.0	100.0	100.0
	2016	105.8	105.6	104.6	101.1	100.9	100.2
	2017	111.2	113.3	108.4	102.6	104.5	98.1
	2018	117.5	125.2	112.8	104.2	111.0	93.9
	2019	124.5	125.7	117.1	106.3	107.4	99.0
Central African Republic	1970	7.6	16.3	84.2	9.0	19.3	46.7
(CFA Franc BEAC)	1975	11.8	32.6	82.6	14.3	39.5	36.2
	1980	24.5	68.6	87.9	27.9	78.1	35.7
	1985	40.5	53.4	94.6	42.9	56.5	75.9
	1990	40.9	89.0	95.9	42.7	92.7	46.0
	1995	58.1	68.9	105.5	55.0	65.3	84.4
	2000	67.9	56.5	116.9	58.1	48.3	120.3
	2005	74.3	83.4	114.3	65.0	72.9	89.2
	2010	105.7	126.3	137.5	76.9	91.8	83.7
	2015	100.0	100.0	100.0	100.0	100.0	100.0
	2016	107.9	107.7	104.8	103.0	102.8	100.2
	2017	120.0	122.3	109.5	109.6	111.7	98.1
	2018	123.0	131.1	113.6	108.3	115.3	93.9
	2019	129.8	131.0	117.0	110.9	112.0	99.0
Chad	1970	1.4	3.0	17.9	7.9	16.9	46.7
(CFA Franc BEAC)	1975	2.3	6.4	21.6	10.8	29.8	36.2
	1980	2.4	6.7	14.5	16.7	46.7	35.7
	1985	6.4	8.4	17.8	36.0	47.4	75.9
	1990	7.2	15.7	22.1	32.6	70.9	46.0
	1995	11.9	14.1	24.8	47.9	56.8	84.4
	2000	16.2	13.5	28.3	57.4	47.7	120.3
	2005	50.9	57.1	56.4	90.3	101.3	89.2
	2010	78.6	93.8	83.1	94.6	113.0	83.7
	2015	100.0	100.0	100.0	100.0	100.0	100.0
	2016	89.0	88.9	97.3	91.5	91.4	100.2
	2017	87.3	88.9	95.0	91.9	93.6	98.1
	2018	91.3	97.3	97.2	94.0	100.1	93.9
	2019	95.5	96.4	100.0	95.4	96.4	99.0
Comoros	1970	2.4	3.9	27.5	8.8	14.1	62.3
(Comoro Franc)	1975	5.7	11.8	34.6	16.6	34.3	48.3
	1980	12.8	26.8	43.7	29.2	61.3	47.6
	1985	25.2	24.8	53.7	46.8	46.2	101.3
	1990	32.5	52.9	56.7	57.2	93.2	61.4
	1995	42.2	50.0	63.4	66.6	79.0	84.4

Table 7. Implicit price deflators of Gross Domestic Product in US Dollars and National Currency (2015 = 100)

Major area, region and country	Year	GDP in Current Prices: National Currency (1)	GDP in Current Prices: US Dollars (2)	Gross Domestic Product at Constant Prices (3)	GDP Implicit Price Deflators (2015 = 100): National Currency (4)	GDP Implicit Price Deflators (2015 = 100): US Dollars (5)	Exchange Rates (6)
	2000	52.6	43.7	68.8	76.5	63.5	120.4
	2005	72.7	81.5	77.0	94.5	105.9	89.2
	2010	78.7	93.9	77.0	102.2	122.1	83.7
	2015	100.0	100.0	100.0	100.0	100.0	100.0
	2016	105.1	104.8	102.8	102.2	102.0	100.3
	2017	109.5	111.6	108.5	100.9	102.8	98.2
	2018	114.6	122.0	112.7	101.7	108.3	93.9
	2019	119.6	120.7	116.3	102.9	103.8	99.1
Congo..	1970	1.1	2.4	16.3	6.9	14.8	46.7
(CFA Franc BEAC)	1975	2.3	6.3	21.4	10.7	29.4	36.2
	1980	5.6	15.7	27.6	20.3	56.9	35.7
	1985	15.1	19.9	46.3	32.7	43.0	75.9
	1990	12.0	26.2	45.2	26.7	57.9	46.0
	1995	15.8	18.8	46.2	34.3	40.7	84.4
	2000	34.4	28.6	52.0	66.1	55.0	120.3
	2005	48.2	54.0	63.5	75.9	85.1	89.2
	2010	97.4	116.4	87.4	111.5	133.2	83.7
	2015	100.0	100.0	100.0	100.0	100.0	100.0
	2016	86.5	86.4	89.8	96.4	96.2	100.2
	2017	92.0	93.7	85.6	107.4	109.4	98.1
	2018	106.7	113.7	80.3	132.9	141.5	93.9
	2019	104.5	105.5	79.6	131.2	132.5	99.0
Côte d'Ivoire...	1970	1.5	3.3	19.9	7.7	16.5	46.7
(CFA Franc BCEAO)	1975	3.1	8.5	27.2	11.3	31.3	36.2
	1980	7.9	22.2	31.8	25.0	69.9	35.7
	1985	11.6	15.2	32.2	35.9	47.3	75.9
	1990	12.0	26.0	37.0	32.3	70.1	46.0
	1995	20.5	24.3	40.1	51.0	60.5	84.4
	2000	28.1	23.3	47.5	59.1	49.1	120.3
	2005	33.3	37.3	47.5	70.0	78.6	89.2
	2010	48.0	57.4	56.0	85.8	102.5	83.7
	2015	100.0	100.0	100.0	100.0	100.0	100.0
	2016	104.9	104.8	107.2	97.9	97.8	100.2
	2017	110.6	112.7	115.1	96.1	97.9	98.1
	2018	119.0	126.7	123.0	96.7	103.0	93.9
	2019	126.6	127.9	130.7	96.9	97.9	99.0
D.R. of the Congo.................................	1970	0.0	12.6	68.1	0.0	18.5	0.0
(Franc Congolais)	1975	0.0	25.7	76.6	0.0	33.6	0.0
	1980	0.0	41.2	71.0	0.0	58.1	0.0
	1985	0.0	19.8	77.8	0.0	25.5	0.0
	1990	0.0	39.1	77.5	0.0	50.4	0.0
	1995	0.0	23.6	53.2	0.0	44.3	0.0
	2000	1.3	22.0	43.6	3.1	50.5	6.1
	2005	16.1	31.6	52.5	30.7	60.1	51.2
	2010	55.6	56.9	68.8	80.9	82.6	97.8
	2015	100.0	100.0	100.0	100.0	100.0	100.0
	2016	116.1	106.4	102.4	113.3	103.9	109.1
	2017	157.0	99.3	106.2	147.8	93.5	158.1
	2018	217.9	124.3	112.3	193.9	110.7	175.2
	2019	222.1	124.8	117.3	189.3	106.4	177.9

Table 7. Implicit price deflators of Gross Domestic Product in US Dollars and National Currency (2015 = 100)

Major area, region and country	Year	GDP in Current Prices: National Currency (1)	GDP in Current Prices: US Dollars (2)	Gross Domestic Product at Constant Prices (3)	GDP Implicit Price Deflators (2015 = 100): National Currency (4)	GDP Implicit Price Deflators (2015 = 100): US Dollars (5)	Exchange Rates (6)
Djibouti	1970	3.5	2.9	21.2	16.6	13.7	120.6
(Djibouti Franc)	1975	6.9	6.9	26.3	26.3	26.3	100.0
	1980	12.3	12.3	25.6	48.1	48.1	100.0
	1985	14.5	14.5	27.2	53.4	53.4	100.0
	1990	18.7	18.7	28.2	66.2	66.2	100.0
	1995	20.8	20.8	31.2	66.7	66.7	100.0
	2000	22.3	22.3	32.3	69.1	69.1	100.0
	2005	29.0	29.0	37.9	76.5	76.5	100.0
	2010	50.9	50.9	59.9	84.9	84.9	100.0
	2015	100.0	100.0	100.0	100.0	100.0	100.0
	2016	107.1	107.1	106.7	100.4	100.4	100.0
	2017	113.1	113.1	112.4	100.7	100.7	100.0
	2018	119.5	119.5	121.9	98.1	98.1	100.0
	2019	129.5	129.5	131.3	98.6	98.6	100.0
Egypt	1970	0.1	2.6	8.9	1.6	28.9	5.7
(Egyptian Pound)	1975	0.2	4.0	10.3	2.0	38.6	5.1
	1980	0.6	6.3	16.6	3.5	38.1	9.1
	1985	1.7	7.5	25.8	6.5	29.1	22.4
	1990	4.0	11.3	33.4	12.0	33.9	35.4
	1995	9.1	20.7	42.0	21.7	49.3	44.1
	2000	13.6	30.1	54.1	25.1	55.6	45.1
	2005	22.3	29.7	64.9	34.4	45.8	75.1
	2010	49.4	67.5	87.6	56.4	77.1	73.1
	2015	100.0	100.0	100.0	100.0	100.0	100.0
	2016	110.9	85.1	104.3	106.2	81.5	130.3
	2017	142.0	61.4	108.7	130.6	56.5	231.2
	2018	181.6	78.6	114.5	158.6	68.7	231.0
	2019	217.8	99.9	120.8	180.2	82.6	218.0
Equatorial Guinea	1970	0.1	0.2	2.1	3.5	7.6	46.7
(CFA Franc BEAC)	1975	0.1	0.3	2.6	3.6	10.0	36.2
	1980	0.2	0.4	2.7	5.6	15.7	35.7
	1985	0.5	0.7	3.5	14.6	19.2	75.9
	1990	0.6	1.3	3.7	16.0	34.8	46.0
	1995	1.4	1.6	5.6	24.5	29.0	84.4
	2000	13.8	11.5	24.3	56.9	47.3	120.3
	2005	57.6	64.7	75.1	76.8	86.2	89.2
	2010	103.6	123.7	99.1	104.5	124.9	83.7
	2015	100.0	100.0	100.0	100.0	100.0	100.0
	2016	85.5	85.3	91.2	93.7	93.6	100.2
	2017	90.9	92.6	86.0	105.7	107.7	98.1
	2018	94.6	100.8	80.5	117.5	125.1	93.9
	2019	82.9	83.7	76.1	108.9	110.0	99.0
Eritrea	1990	4.9	16.5	36.4	13.5	45.3	29.8
(Nakfa)	1995	12.7	31.8	69.8	18.2	45.5	40.1
	2000	22.0	35.1	86.0	25.5	40.8	62.6
	2005	54.5	54.6	83.4	65.4	65.4	100.0
	2010	79.0	79.0	83.9	94.1	94.1	100.0
	2015	100.0	100.0	100.0	100.0	100.0	100.0
	2016	107.8	108.0	107.4	100.4	100.5	99.8

Table 7. Implicit price deflators of Gross Domestic Product in US Dollars and National Currency (2015 = 100)

Major area, region and country	Year	GDP in Current Prices: National Currency (1)	GDP in Current Prices: US Dollars (2)	Gross Domestic Product at Constant Prices (3)	GDP Implicit Price Deflators (2015 = 100): National Currency (4)	GDP Implicit Price Deflators (2015 = 100): US Dollars (5)	Exchange Rates (6)
	2017	92.7	94.6	96.6	96.0	97.9	98.0
	2018	97.7	99.6	109.2	89.4	91.2	98.0
	2019	96.5	98.4	113.4	85.1	86.8	98.0
Eswatini	1970	0.2	3.8	10.6	2.0	35.7	5.6
(Lilangeni)	1975	0.6	9.7	20.4	2.8	47.7	5.8
	1980	1.2	19.8	24.7	4.9	80.1	6.1
	1985	2.3	13.2	27.8	8.3	47.5	17.4
	1990	6.2	30.8	46.9	13.3	65.6	20.3
	1995	13.3	46.7	54.6	24.3	85.5	28.4
	2000	23.2	42.7	61.1	38.0	69.8	54.4
	2005	38.9	78.0	73.6	52.9	106.1	49.8
	2010	62.5	109.0	86.5	72.3	125.9	57.4
	2015	100.0	100.0	100.0	100.0	100.0	100.0
	2016	108.7	94.3	101.3	107.3	93.1	115.3
	2017	114.1	109.2	103.3	110.4	105.6	104.5
	2018	120.2	115.8	105.7	113.7	109.5	103.8
	2019	127.8	112.8	107.0	119.4	105.5	113.3
Ethiopia	1990	1.8	17.8	20.1	8.9	88.5	10.1
(Ethiopian Birr)	1995	3.6	12.0	21.1	17.0	56.9	29.9
	2000	5.1	12.7	26.4	19.3	48.2	39.9
	2005	8.1	19.3	36.1	22.5	53.5	42.1
	2010	29.2	41.7	60.4	48.3	69.0	70.0
	2015	100.0	100.0	100.0	100.0	100.0	100.0
	2016	120.8	114.4	107.6	112.3	106.4	105.6
	2017	141.2	121.7	117.8	119.9	103.4	116.0
	2018	169.5	127.2	125.9	134.7	101.0	133.3
	2019	207.7	147.0	136.3	152.4	107.9	141.3
Gabon	1970	1.3	2.9	24.0	5.6	11.9	46.7
(CFA Franc BEAC)	1975	6.9	19.0	53.9	12.8	35.3	36.2
	1980	13.5	37.7	50.0	26.9	75.4	35.7
	1985	24.5	32.3	56.5	43.4	57.1	75.9
	1990	19.3	42.0	59.8	32.3	70.2	46.0
	1995	32.4	38.4	69.7	46.5	55.1	84.4
	2000	47.5	39.5	69.4	68.5	56.9	120.3
	2005	59.4	66.6	72.9	81.6	91.5	89.2
	2010	83.6	99.9	77.5	107.9	128.9	83.7
	2015	100.0	100.0	100.0	100.0	100.0	100.0
	2016	97.7	97.6	102.1	95.7	95.6	100.2
	2017	101.9	103.9	102.6	99.4	101.2	98.1
	2018	111.0	118.2	103.9	106.9	113.8	93.9
	2019	116.4	117.5	107.7	108.1	109.1	99.0
Gambia	1970	0.6	11.6	26.1	2.2	44.5	4.9
(Dalasi)	1975	1.8	42.4	32.1	5.6	132.3	4.3
	1980	2.5	60.8	32.7	7.5	185.6	4.0
	1985	7.2	78.9	42.4	17.0	185.9	9.2
	1990	15.8	85.3	50.4	31.4	169.4	18.5
	1995	21.3	94.8	55.8	38.1	169.7	22.5
	2000	28.4	94.4	68.7	41.3	137.4	30.1
	2005	50.1	74.6	79.7	62.9	93.6	67.2

Table 7. Implicit price deflators of Gross Domestic Product in US Dollars and National Currency (2015 = 100)

Major area, region and country	Year	GDP in Current Prices		Gross Domestic Product at Constant Prices (3)	GDP Implicit Price Deflators (2015 = 100)		Exchange Rates (6)
		National Currency (1)	US Dollars (2)		National Currency (4)	US Dollars (5)	
	2010	73.8	112.0	98.0	75.3	114.3	65.9
	2015	100.0	100.0	100.0	100.0	100.0	100.0
	2016	109.9	106.5	101.9	107.8	104.4	103.2
	2017	119.7	109.2	106.9	112.0	102.2	109.6
	2018	137.7	121.5	115.1	119.6	105.6	113.3
	2019	156.4	132.3	122.0	128.2	108.4	118.3
Ghana..	1970	0.0	9.6	20.3	0.0	47.1	0.0
(Cedi)	1975	0.0	9.5	20.6	0.0	46.0	0.0
	1980	0.0	14.1	21.6	0.0	65.1	0.0
	1985	0.0	17.8	21.2	0.2	84.1	0.2
	1990	0.2	26.9	26.8	0.9	100.4	0.9
	1995	0.9	27.9	33.0	2.8	84.6	3.3
	2000	3.2	21.5	40.9	7.8	52.5	14.9
	2005	11.4	46.3	52.8	21.7	87.7	24.7
	2010	33.8	86.6	71.1	47.5	121.8	39.0
	2015	100.0	100.0	100.0	100.0	100.0	100.0
	2016	119.2	111.9	103.4	115.2	108.1	106.6
	2017	142.3	120.0	111.9	127.2	107.2	118.6
	2018	166.6	133.3	118.9	140.2	112.1	125.0
	2019	193.7	136.2	126.6	153.0	107.6	142.2
Guinea..	1970	0.1	8.7	21.8	0.6	39.8	1.4
(Guinea Franc)	1975	0.2	14.2	25.9	0.7	54.9	1.4
	1980	0.3	22.7	29.2	1.0	77.7	1.2
	1985	0.8	32.4	32.3	2.6	100.3	2.6
	1990	3.9	44.4	39.7	9.9	111.9	8.8
	1995	7.9	59.8	48.0	16.5	124.5	13.2
	2000	11.3	48.5	59.8	19.0	81.2	23.3
	2005	22.5	46.2	69.5	32.4	66.5	48.7
	2010	59.6	77.9	79.9	74.6	97.5	76.5
	2015	100.0	100.0	100.0	100.0	100.0	100.0
	2016	117.1	97.8	110.8	105.7	88.3	119.7
	2017	142.5	117.4	122.2	116.6	96.0	121.4
	2018	149.3	124.0	129.8	115.0	95.5	120.4
	2019	172.4	140.5	137.2	125.7	102.4	122.7
Guinea-Bissau..............................	1970	0.0	26.8	37.9	0.1	70.8	0.1
(CFA Franc BCEAO)	1975	0.0	48.5	44.1	0.1	109.8	0.1
	1980	0.0	44.8	41.7	0.1	107.4	0.1
	1985	0.2	39.6	45.9	0.4	86.3	0.4
	1990	3.8	58.2	55.5	6.9	104.9	6.5
	1995	35.9	76.4	64.5	55.6	118.4	47.0
	2000	41.7	34.6	66.6	62.6	52.0	120.3
	2005	49.9	56.0	72.2	69.2	77.6	89.2
	2010	67.9	81.1	85.1	79.8	95.3	83.7
	2015	100.0	100.0	100.0	100.0	100.0	100.0
	2016	112.7	112.6	106.3	106.1	105.9	100.2
	2017	126.5	128.9	112.6	112.4	114.5	98.1
	2018	123.9	132.0	116.3	106.5	113.5	93.9
	2019	125.0	126.2	121.6	102.8	103.8	99.0

Table 7. Implicit price deflators of Gross Domestic Product in US Dollars and National Currency (2015 = 100)

Major area, region and country	Year	GDP in Current Prices: National Currency (1)	GDP in Current Prices: US Dollars (2)	Gross Domestic Product at Constant Prices (3)	GDP Implicit Price Deflators (2015 = 100): National Currency (4)	GDP Implicit Price Deflators (2015 = 100): US Dollars (5)	Exchange Rates (6)
Kenya......	1970	0.3	3.9	16.4	1.7	24.0	7.3
(Kenyan Shilling)	1975	0.6	7.5	20.1	2.8	37.5	7.5
	1980	1.2	16.4	27.3	4.5	60.2	7.6
	1985	2.4	14.2	31.6	7.5	45.0	16.7
	1990	4.6	19.8	41.6	11.1	47.6	23.3
	1995	11.0	21.0	45.0	24.4	46.7	52.4
	2000	17.5	22.6	49.8	35.2	45.4	77.6
	2005	25.9	33.6	59.9	43.1	56.1	77.0
	2010	50.4	62.5	76.4	66.0	81.8	80.7
	2015	100.0	100.0	100.0	100.0	100.0	100.0
	2016	111.8	108.1	105.9	105.6	102.1	103.4
	2017	129.9	123.4	111.0	117.1	111.2	105.3
	2018	141.5	137.1	118.0	119.9	116.2	103.2
	2019	155.0	149.2	124.3	124.7	120.0	103.9
Lesotho......	1970	0.2	3.3	13.0	1.4	25.8	5.6
(Loti)	1975	0.4	6.8	17.2	2.3	39.8	5.8
	1980	1.1	17.5	24.4	4.4	71.4	6.1
	1985	2.0	11.7	26.2	7.8	44.7	17.5
	1990	5.0	24.8	35.8	14.0	69.3	20.3
	1995	10.7	37.7	43.5	24.6	86.5	28.4
	2000	18.8	34.7	53.3	35.4	65.1	54.4
	2005	30.6	61.5	61.4	49.9	100.2	49.8
	2010	54.9	95.7	80.8	67.9	118.4	57.4
	2015	100.0	100.0	100.0	100.0	100.0	100.0
	2016	105.2	91.3	105.0	100.2	86.9	115.3
	2017	105.9	101.3	103.7	102.1	97.7	104.5
	2018	112.6	108.5	103.2	109.1	105.2	103.8
	2019	117.5	103.7	104.8	112.1	99.0	113.3
Liberia......	1970	11.9	11.9	56.3	21.0	21.0	100.0
(US Dollar)	1975	23.3	23.3	63.3	36.8	36.8	100.0
	1980	35.0	35.0	69.5	50.4	50.4	100.0
	1985	40.3	40.3	64.0	63.0	63.0	100.0
	1990	22.3	22.3	33.3	67.0	67.0	100.0
	1995	7.8	7.8	9.3	84.0	84.0	100.0
	2000	24.2	24.2	43.9	55.0	55.0	100.0
	2005	26.5	26.5	35.4	74.8	74.8	100.0
	2010	48.4	48.4	69.0	70.1	70.1	100.0
	2015	100.0	100.0	100.0	100.0	100.0	100.0
	2016	103.3	103.3	99.5	103.8	103.8	100.0
	2017	103.5	103.5	102.0	101.5	101.5	100.0
	2018	102.8	102.8	103.2	99.6	99.6	100.0
	2019	96.7	96.7	100.9	95.9	95.9	100.0
Libya......	1970	5.8	22.5	290.8	2.0	7.7	25.9
(Libyan Dinar)	1975	16.6	77.3	389.5	4.3	19.8	21.4
	1980	46.3	216.2	590.5	7.8	36.6	21.4
	1985	36.3	169.2	492.2	7.4	34.4	21.4
	1990	36.1	176.0	445.1	8.1	39.5	20.5
	1995	48.5	160.2	480.4	10.1	33.3	30.3
	2000	80.8	217.8	513.4	15.7	42.4	37.1

Table 7. Implicit price deflators of Gross Domestic Product in US Dollars and National Currency (2015 = 100)

Major area, region and country	Year	GDP in Current Prices: National Currency (1)	GDP in Current Prices: US Dollars (2)	Gross Domestic Product at Constant Prices (3)	GDP Implicit Price Deflators (2015 = 100): National Currency (4)	GDP Implicit Price Deflators (2015 = 100): US Dollars (5)	Exchange Rates (6)
	2005	243.7	257.3	663.0	36.8	38.8	94.7
	2010	420.2	458.2	882.6	47.6	51.9	91.7
	2015	100.0	100.0	100.0	100.0	100.0	100.0
	2016	87.3	86.7	83.9	104.0	103.4	100.7
	2017	141.7	140.4	137.6	103.0	102.0	100.9
	2018	194.3	196.6	162.2	119.8	121.2	98.8
	2019	186.8	184.5	178.3	104.8	103.5	101.2
Madagascar (Malagasy Ariary)	1970	0.2	9.3	48.8	0.4	19.1	1.9
	1975	0.3	19.1	50.3	0.6	37.9	1.5
	1980	0.5	33.8	53.8	0.9	62.8	1.4
	1985	1.1	24.3	50.1	2.2	48.5	4.5
	1990	3.2	31.9	57.3	5.7	55.6	10.2
	1995	9.4	32.4	56.4	16.7	57.4	29.1
	2000	18.3	39.8	68.1	26.9	58.4	46.1
	2005	35.3	51.7	76.2	46.3	67.8	68.3
	2010	62.8	88.2	87.7	71.7	100.6	71.2
	2015	100.0	100.0	100.0	100.0	100.0	100.0
	2016	113.3	104.6	104.0	109.0	100.6	108.3
	2017	123.6	116.4	108.1	114.4	107.7	106.2
	2018	138.1	121.5	111.5	123.9	109.0	113.7
	2019	153.6	124.6	116.5	131.9	107.0	123.3
Malawi (Kwacha)	1970	0.0	9.0	17.6	0.1	51.1	0.2
	1975	0.0	17.2	25.7	0.1	66.9	0.2
	1980	0.1	34.8	34.9	0.2	99.6	0.2
	1985	0.1	31.5	35.8	0.3	88.0	0.3
	1990	0.3	49.2	40.8	0.7	120.8	0.5
	1995	1.2	38.5	43.2	2.7	89.0	3.1
	2000	5.8	49.0	51.2	11.4	95.7	11.9
	2005	13.5	56.8	57.6	23.4	98.7	23.7
	2010	32.6	108.2	82.3	39.6	131.5	30.1
	2015	100.0	100.0	100.0	100.0	100.0	100.0
	2016	118.7	82.6	102.7	115.6	80.4	143.7
	2017	144.3	98.7	108.0	133.5	91.4	146.2
	2018	163.7	111.6	112.2	145.8	99.5	146.6
	2019	186.0	125.9	118.1	157.5	106.6	147.7
Mali (CFA Franc BCEAO)	1970	1.1	2.4	4.5	25.3	54.1	46.7
	1975	1.9	5.4	5.3	36.5	100.7	36.2
	1980	4.5	12.6	6.7	67.4	188.6	35.7
	1985	7.3	9.6	7.7	95.2	125.4	75.9
	1990	9.6	20.9	9.6	100.0	217.3	46.0
	1995	18.3	21.7	16.6	110.0	130.4	84.4
	2000	27.1	22.6	28.1	96.6	80.3	120.3
	2005	42.5	47.7	40.7	104.5	117.2	89.2
	2010	68.3	81.5	67.3	101.4	121.2	83.7
	2015	100.0	100.0	100.0	100.0	100.0	100.0
	2016	107.4	107.2	108.9	98.6	98.5	100.2
	2017	115.2	117.3	116.2	99.1	101.0	98.1
	2018	122.4	130.4	124.1	98.6	105.0	93.9
	2019	131.8	133.1	132.3	99.6	100.6	99.0

Table 7. Implicit price deflators of Gross Domestic Product in US Dollars and National Currency (2015 = 100)

Major area, region and country	Year	GDP in Current Prices		Gross Domestic Product at Constant Prices (3)	GDP Implicit Price Deflators (2015 = 100)		Exchange Rates (6)
		National Currency (1)	US Dollars (2)		National Currency (4)	US Dollars (5)	
Mauritania (Ouguiya)	1970	1.3	7.4	29.9	4.2	24.8	17.1
	1975	2.3	17.4	35.7	6.4	48.6	13.3
	1980	4.3	30.1	38.9	10.9	77.4	14.1
	1985	5.9	24.8	38.7	15.2	64.0	23.7
	1990	9.2	37.1	43.6	21.1	85.2	24.8
	1995	15.4	38.4	50.9	30.2	75.5	40.0
	2000	21.2	28.9	55.3	38.4	52.2	73.6
	2005	38.9	47.6	67.6	57.6	70.4	81.8
	2010	77.6	91.3	80.3	96.6	113.7	85.0
	2015	100.0	100.0	100.0	100.0	100.0	100.0
	2016	112.6	103.8	101.3	111.2	102.5	108.5
	2017	120.8	109.6	104.8	115.3	104.6	110.2
	2018	125.6	114.3	107.0	117.4	106.8	109.9
	2019	139.2	123.1	113.4	122.8	108.6	113.0
Mauritius (Mauritius Rupee)	1970	0.3	1.8	10.8	2.6	16.3	15.8
	1975	0.9	5.2	14.8	6.0	34.9	17.2
	1980	2.3	10.4	18.7	12.2	55.5	21.9
	1985	4.3	9.8	23.5	18.5	42.0	44.1
	1990	9.9	23.4	33.9	29.2	69.0	42.4
	1995	18.1	36.5	42.9	42.3	85.2	49.6
	2000	31.2	41.6	56.2	55.5	74.1	74.9
	2005	48.8	57.9	66.4	73.5	87.3	84.1
	2010	75.1	85.6	83.6	89.9	102.3	87.8
	2015	100.0	100.0	100.0	100.0	100.0	100.0
	2016	106.1	104.6	103.8	102.1	100.8	101.4
	2017	111.5	113.4	107.8	103.5	105.2	98.4
	2018	117.4	121.3	111.9	105.0	108.4	96.8
	2019	122.7	121.3	115.8	106.0	104.7	101.2
Morocco (Moroccan Dirham)	1970	2.4	4.6	15.4	15.4	29.8	51.8
	1975	4.3	10.4	19.6	22.1	53.2	41.5
	1980	8.8	21.8	25.7	34.2	84.9	40.3
	1985	15.4	14.9	30.3	50.9	49.4	103.1
	1990	25.3	30.0	37.5	67.4	79.8	84.4
	1995	33.5	38.3	39.3	85.1	97.4	87.5
	2000	41.8	38.4	47.4	88.2	81.0	108.8
	2005	56.1	61.8	60.5	92.8	102.2	90.8
	2010	79.4	92.1	80.3	98.9	114.7	86.2
	2015	100.0	100.0	100.0	100.0	100.0	100.0
	2016	102.6	102.1	103.2	99.4	98.9	100.4
	2017	107.6	108.4	109.2	98.5	99.3	99.3
	2018	112.2	116.7	113.4	99.0	103.0	96.1
	2019	116.5	118.3	117.4	99.2	100.7	98.5
Mozambique (Metical)	1970	0.0	25.2	12.9	0.1	196.2	0.1
	1975	0.0	40.1	16.5	0.2	243.7	0.1
	1980	0.0	40.0	18.8	0.2	212.2	0.1
	1985	0.1	56.6	15.0	0.4	377.5	0.1
	1990	0.6	24.6	17.9	3.2	137.2	2.3
	1995	4.1	18.2	21.3	19.3	85.4	22.6
	2000	13.5	35.5	32.7	41.3	108.4	38.1

Table 7. Implicit price deflators of Gross Domestic Product in US Dollars and National Currency (2015 = 100)

Major area, region and country	Year	GDP in Current Prices: National Currency (1)	GDP in Current Prices: US Dollars (2)	Gross Domestic Product at Constant Prices (3)	GDP Implicit Price Deflators (2015 = 100): National Currency (4)	GDP Implicit Price Deflators (2015 = 100): US Dollars (5)	Exchange Rates (6)
	2005	30.9	53.6	49.3	62.7	108.6	57.7
	2010	59.1	69.6	70.8	83.5	98.3	84.9
	2015	100.0	100.0	100.0	100.0	100.0	100.0
	2016	118.0	74.8	103.8	113.7	72.1	157.7
	2017	131.8	82.9	107.7	122.4	76.9	159.0
	2018	140.4	93.1	111.4	126.0	83.5	150.9
	2019	150.0	95.9	114.0	131.6	84.1	156.4
Namibia (Namibian Dollar)	1970	0.3	5.4	21.7	1.4	24.7	5.6
	1975	0.6	9.9	26.6	2.1	37.4	5.7
	1980	1.3	21.5	30.7	4.2	70.0	6.0
	1985	2.5	14.2	30.4	8.1	46.9	17.3
	1990	5.0	24.7	34.5	14.4	71.6	20.1
	1995	9.8	35.0	41.7	23.6	84.0	28.2
	2000	18.3	34.0	49.5	37.0	68.7	53.9
	2005	31.2	63.2	63.0	49.5	100.3	49.4
	2010	56.9	100.1	77.6	73.3	129.0	56.8
	2015	100.0	100.0	100.0	100.0	100.0	100.0
	2016	108.0	94.6	99.7	108.3	94.9	114.2
	2017	116.8	113.0	99.5	117.4	113.6	103.3
	2018	122.6	119.4	100.2	122.4	119.2	102.7
	2019	123.0	109.7	99.0	124.3	110.8	112.2
Niger (CFA Franc BCEAO)	1970	2.8	5.9	36.6	7.5	16.1	46.7
	1975	4.5	12.3	32.1	13.9	38.4	36.2
	1980	13.3	37.2	41.5	32.1	89.8	35.7
	1985	16.0	21.1	36.2	44.3	58.4	75.9
	1990	16.7	36.4	36.6	45.8	99.4	46.0
	1995	20.8	24.6	39.4	52.8	62.6	84.4
	2000	28.7	23.8	46.1	62.1	51.6	120.3
	2005	41.4	46.5	57.5	72.0	80.8	89.2
	2010	66.0	78.9	74.0	89.2	106.6	83.7
	2015	100.0	100.0	100.0	100.0	100.0	100.0
	2016	106.7	106.5	105.7	100.9	100.8	100.2
	2017	113.5	115.6	111.0	102.3	104.2	98.1
	2018	124.6	132.7	118.7	104.9	111.8	93.9
	2019	132.5	133.8	125.7	105.5	106.5	99.0
Nigeria (Naira)	1970	0.0	5.9	17.6	0.1	33.8	0.4
	1975	0.1	19.8	25.5	0.2	77.7	0.3
	1980	0.1	49.3	28.6	0.5	172.6	0.3
	1985	0.2	42.5	24.6	0.8	172.7	0.5
	1990	0.5	12.4	31.1	1.7	40.0	4.2
	1995	3.3	10.2	31.4	10.4	32.6	31.9
	2000	7.4	14.0	36.4	20.4	38.5	52.8
	2005	24.3	35.6	55.6	43.7	64.1	68.2
	2010	57.4	73.5	78.3	73.3	93.9	78.1
	2015	100.0	100.0	100.0	100.0	100.0	100.0
	2016	107.8	81.8	98.4	109.5	83.2	131.7
	2017	120.7	76.0	99.2	121.7	76.6	158.9
	2018	135.7	85.3	101.1	134.2	84.4	159.1
	2019	153.0	95.9	103.3	148.1	92.9	159.5

Table 7. Implicit price deflators of Gross Domestic Product in US Dollars and National Currency (2015 = 100)

Major area, region and country	Year	GDP in Current Prices: National Currency (1)	GDP in Current Prices: US Dollars (2)	Gross Domestic Product at Constant Prices (3)	GDP Implicit Price Deflators (2015 = 100): National Currency (4)	GDP Implicit Price Deflators (2015 = 100): US Dollars (5)	Exchange Rates (6)
Rwanda	1970	0.4	2.7	12.4	3.0	21.5	13.9
(Rwanda Franc)	1975	0.9	7.1	12.9	7.0	54.9	12.8
	1980	1.9	15.5	21.2	8.7	73.3	11.9
	1985	3.0	21.2	24.1	12.4	88.1	14.0
	1990	3.3	28.5	25.4	13.0	112.2	11.6
	1995	5.2	14.4	16.3	32.1	88.3	36.4
	2000	13.1	24.2	32.0	40.9	75.6	54.1
	2005	26.6	34.4	47.3	56.3	72.7	77.4
	2010	58.0	71.8	70.4	82.4	101.9	80.9
	2015	100.0	100.0	100.0	100.0	100.0	100.0
	2016	111.3	101.9	106.0	105.0	96.2	109.2
	2017	125.1	108.4	110.2	113.5	98.4	115.3
	2018	134.9	112.9	119.6	112.7	94.4	119.4
	2019	151.4	121.4	130.9	115.6	92.7	124.7
Sao Tome and Principe	1970	0.0	11.1	26.6	0.1	41.8	0.1
(Dobra)	1975	0.0	18.0	32.4	0.1	55.4	0.1
	1980	0.0	24.4	48.2	0.1	50.7	0.2
	1985	0.0	24.7	44.0	0.1	56.2	0.2
	1990	0.2	35.6	41.4	0.6	86.2	0.6
	1995	2.0	31.0	44.4	4.5	69.8	6.4
	2000	8.2	22.8	48.1	17.1	47.4	36.1
	2005	19.0	39.7	60.1	31.5	66.0	47.8
	2010	52.0	62.0	80.0	64.9	77.5	83.7
	2015	100.0	100.0	100.0	100.0	100.0	100.0
	2016	109.5	109.2	104.2	105.1	104.8	100.3
	2017	117.1	119.0	108.2	108.2	110.0	98.4
	2018	122.6	130.5	111.4	110.1	117.2	93.9
	2019	131.3	132.5	112.8	116.4	117.5	99.1
Senegal	1970	3.2	6.9	25.3	12.8	27.4	46.7
(CFA Franc BCEAO)	1975	5.5	15.1	28.4	19.3	53.2	36.2
	1980	8.5	23.7	30.0	28.3	79.1	35.7
	1985	15.5	20.4	34.8	44.7	58.8	75.9
	1990	20.8	45.2	40.7	51.1	111.1	46.0
	1995	30.0	35.5	43.6	68.7	81.4	84.4
	2000	41.0	34.1	55.0	74.6	62.0	120.3
	2005	56.6	63.4	69.1	81.9	91.8	89.2
	2010	78.8	94.2	82.2	95.9	114.6	83.7
	2015	100.0	100.0	100.0	100.0	100.0	100.0
	2016	107.4	107.2	106.4	100.9	100.8	100.2
	2017	116.0	118.2	114.2	101.6	103.5	98.1
	2018	122.8	130.8	121.5	101.1	107.7	93.9
	2019	131.9	133.2	127.8	103.2	104.2	99.0
Seychelles	1970	0.7	1.6	13.8	4.9	11.8	41.7
(Seychelles Rupee)	1975	1.9	4.2	19.3	9.8	21.7	45.3
	1980	6.2	12.9	29.5	21.0	43.8	48.0
	1985	7.9	14.8	31.8	25.0	46.6	53.6
	1990	13.0	32.3	41.9	30.9	77.1	40.1
	1995	15.9	44.6	48.3	33.0	92.2	35.8
	2000	23.3	54.2	64.2	36.3	84.5	42.9

Table 7. Implicit price deflators of Gross Domestic Product in US Dollars and National Currency (2015 = 100)

Major area, region and country	Year	GDP in Current Prices: National Currency (1)	GDP in Current Prices: US Dollars (2)	Gross Domestic Product at Constant Prices (3)	GDP Implicit Price Deflators (2015 = 100): National Currency (4)	GDP Implicit Price Deflators (2015 = 100): US Dollars (5)	Exchange Rates (6)
	2005	27.6	66.7	63.6	43.4	105.0	41.3
	2010	63.8	70.4	78.7	81.1	89.4	90.6
	2015	100.0	100.0	100.0	100.0	100.0	100.0
	2016	103.6	103.6	104.6	99.1	99.1	100.0
	2017	113.4	110.7	109.1	103.9	101.4	102.5
	2018	120.3	115.1	113.2	106.2	101.7	104.5
	2019	130.0	123.3	118.6	109.6	104.0	105.4
Sierra Leone (Leone)	1970	0.0	10.7	47.8	0.0	22.4	0.0
	1975	0.0	17.7	51.9	0.0	34.0	0.0
	1980	0.0	31.4	58.4	0.0	53.7	0.0
	1985	0.0	32.4	65.9	0.0	49.2	0.1
	1990	0.6	20.7	76.3	0.8	27.1	3.0
	1995	4.1	27.7	59.1	7.0	46.9	14.9
	2000	8.3	20.3	34.7	24.1	58.4	41.2
	2005	22.1	38.9	63.1	35.0	61.6	56.9
	2010	47.5	60.7	81.4	58.4	74.6	78.3
	2015	100.0	100.0	100.0	100.0	100.0	100.0
	2016	112.6	90.9	106.3	105.9	85.5	123.8
	2017	127.9	88.0	110.4	115.9	79.8	145.3
	2018	150.1	96.2	114.2	131.5	84.2	156.1
	2019	172.1	97.0	120.5	142.8	80.5	177.3
Somalia (Somali Shilling)	1970	0.0	23.4	55.3	0.0	42.4	0.0
	1975	0.0	52.0	65.8	0.0	79.1	0.0
	1980	0.1	39.5	75.1	0.1	52.5	0.1
	1985	0.3	55.7	82.1	0.3	67.8	0.5
	1990	5.4	68.3	86.3	6.2	79.1	7.9
	1995	19.8	77.1	59.4	33.4	129.8	25.7
	2000	60.7	141.1	65.5	92.7	215.5	43.0
	2005	109.1	159.2	76.6	142.4	207.7	68.5
	2010	105.5	75.1	86.9	121.4	86.4	140.5
	2015	100.0	100.0	100.0	100.0	100.0	100.0
	2016	103.7	100.1	102.9	100.8	97.2	103.6
	2017	111.4	107.3	104.3	106.7	102.9	103.8
	2018	116.6	106.8	107.2	108.7	99.6	109.2
	2019	122.1	111.8	110.4	110.6	101.3	109.2
South Africa (Rand)	1970	0.3	5.9	32.9	1.0	17.9	5.6
	1975	0.7	12.1	39.4	1.8	30.8	5.8
	1980	1.6	26.4	45.8	3.5	57.7	6.1
	1985	3.3	18.8	49.0	6.7	38.3	17.5
	1990	7.5	36.8	53.3	14.0	69.0	20.3
	1995	14.1	49.6	55.6	25.4	89.2	28.4
	2000	23.7	43.6	63.8	37.2	68.4	54.4
	2005	40.5	81.2	77.0	52.6	105.5	49.8
	2010	67.9	118.3	89.7	75.7	131.9	57.4
	2015	100.0	100.0	100.0	100.0	100.0	100.0
	2016	107.6	93.4	100.4	107.2	93.0	115.3
	2017	114.9	110.0	101.8	112.9	108.0	104.5
	2018	120.3	116.0	102.6	117.3	113.0	103.8
	2019	125.4	110.7	102.8	122.0	107.7	113.2

Table 7. Implicit price deflators of Gross Domestic Product in US Dollars and National Currency (2015 = 100)

Major area, region and country	Year	GDP in Current Prices: National Currency (1)	GDP in Current Prices: US Dollars (2)	Gross Domestic Product at Constant Prices (3)	GDP Implicit Price Deflators (2015 = 100): National Currency (4)	GDP Implicit Price Deflators (2015 = 100): US Dollars (5)	Exchange Rates (6)
South Sudan	2010	127.9	226.9	111.5	114.8	203.5	56.4
(South Sudanese Pound)	2015	100.0	100.0	100.0	100.0	100.0	100.0
	2016	559.9	49.0	93.0	601.8	52.7	1142.7
	2017	1483.0	53.4	89.6	1655.0	59.5	2779.2
	2018	2465.8	71.3	93.0	2650.5	76.7	3457.5
	2019	2912.2	75.4	93.8	3103.3	80.3	3863.8
Sudan	2010	25.0	65.2	80.5	31.0	81.0	38.3
(Sudanese Pound)	2015	100.0	100.0	100.0	100.0	100.0	100.0
	2016	119.7	106.8	103.6	115.6	103.1	112.0
	2017	161.3	145.4	108.4	148.8	134.1	110.9
	2018	232.6	57.6	111.5	208.7	51.7	403.8
	2019	317.8	41.6	112.9	281.5	36.8	764.4
Togo	1970	2.7	5.8	28.7	9.4	20.1	46.7
(CFA Franc BCEAO)	1975	4.7	13.0	31.6	14.9	41.2	36.2
	1980	8.8	24.6	36.9	23.8	66.5	35.7
	1985	12.2	16.1	34.8	35.1	46.3	75.9
	1990	17.7	38.5	42.5	41.7	90.6	46.0
	1995	26.2	31.1	41.9	62.6	74.2	84.4
	2000	33.5	27.8	46.5	72.0	59.8	120.3
	2005	38.0	42.7	49.1	77.5	86.9	89.2
	2010	53.6	64.1	58.0	92.5	110.5	83.7
	2015	100.0	100.0	100.0	100.0	100.0	100.0
	2016	113.0	112.8	110.9	101.9	101.7	100.2
	2017	117.4	119.6	115.7	101.5	103.4	98.1
	2018	125.3	133.4	121.4	103.2	109.9	93.9
	2019	134.7	136.0	127.8	105.4	106.4	99.0
Tunisia	1970	1.0	3.7	13.3	7.4	27.6	26.8
(Tunisian Dinar)	1975	2.3	11.0	19.8	11.4	55.7	20.5
	1980	4.6	22.2	26.9	17.1	82.7	20.6
	1985	9.1	21.4	33.0	27.6	64.8	42.5
	1990	14.0	31.3	38.2	36.7	82.0	44.8
	1995	22.1	45.9	46.2	47.9	99.3	48.2
	2000	34.8	49.7	60.6	57.4	82.1	69.9
	2005	49.4	74.8	73.3	67.4	102.0	66.1
	2010	74.5	102.0	91.5	81.3	111.5	73.0
	2015	100.0	100.0	100.0	100.0	100.0	100.0
	2016	106.0	96.8	101.2	104.7	95.6	109.5
	2017	113.7	92.2	103.2	110.2	89.3	123.3
	2018	124.3	92.1	105.9	117.3	87.0	134.9
	2019	134.4	89.9	107.0	125.6	84.0	149.6
U.R. of Tanzania: Mainland	1970	0.0	4.9	14.1	0.1	34.6	0.4
(Tanzanian Shilling)	1975	0.0	9.8	17.6	0.2	55.8	0.4
	1980	0.1	18.7	20.2	0.4	92.7	0.4
	1985	0.2	23.4	21.4	1.0	109.4	0.9
	1990	1.3	13.8	25.8	5.2	53.3	9.8
	1995	4.4	15.2	31.4	14.0	48.4	28.9
	2000	10.5	26.1	38.6	27.2	67.7	40.2
	2005	20.5	36.2	54.2	37.9	66.8	56.7

Table 7. Implicit price deflators of Gross Domestic Product in US Dollars and National Currency (2015 = 100)

Major area, region and country	Year	GDP in Current Prices: National Currency (1)	GDP in Current Prices: US Dollars (2)	Gross Domestic Product at Constant Prices (3)	GDP Implicit Price Deflators (2015 = 100): National Currency (4)	GDP Implicit Price Deflators (2015 = 100): US Dollars (5)	Exchange Rates (6)
	2010	47.1	66.6	72.9	64.7	91.4	70.8
	2015	100.0	100.0	100.0	100.0	100.0	100.0
	2016	114.9	105.1	106.9	107.5	98.3	109.3
	2017	125.9	112.4	114.1	110.3	98.5	111.9
	2018	136.8	120.3	122.0	112.1	98.6	113.7
	2019	148.3	129.0	130.6	113.6	98.8	114.9
Uganda	1970	0.0	5.7	15.2	0.0	37.2	0.0
(Uganda Shilling)	1975	0.0	11.1	15.4	0.0	71.9	0.0
	1980	0.0	12.9	12.7	0.0	101.9	0.0
	1985	0.0	18.9	14.4	0.3	131.5	0.2
	1990	2.3	17.2	19.0	12.0	90.5	13.2
	1995	8.5	28.5	27.2	31.3	104.6	29.9
	2000	13.7	27.0	37.2	36.8	72.6	50.7
	2005	24.4	44.5	53.5	45.6	83.1	54.9
	2010	52.7	78.4	79.1	66.6	99.2	67.2
	2015	100.0	100.0	100.0	100.0	100.0	100.0
	2016	106.9	101.3	102.6	104.2	98.7	105.5
	2017	120.4	108.0	107.2	112.3	100.8	111.4
	2018	136.0	118.3	115.4	117.8	102.5	115.0
	2019	148.5	129.9	123.1	120.6	105.5	114.3
Zambia	1970	0.0	7.4	25.8	0.0	28.7	0.0
(Kwacha)	1975	0.0	12.7	29.3	0.0	43.5	0.0
	1980	0.0	20.7	28.9	0.0	71.7	0.0
	1985	0.0	13.3	30.0	0.0	44.3	0.0
	1990	0.1	18.2	32.8	0.2	55.4	0.4
	1995	1.8	18.3	31.8	5.8	57.5	10.0
	2000	6.2	17.3	37.9	16.4	45.5	36.0
	2005	20.7	39.9	51.2	40.3	78.0	51.7
	2010	54.0	97.2	77.8	69.4	124.9	55.6
	2015	100.0	100.0	100.0	100.0	100.0	100.0
	2016	122.9	102.8	103.8	118.4	99.1	119.5
	2017	136.8	124.0	107.4	127.3	115.5	110.3
	2018	156.8	129.5	111.7	140.4	115.9	121.2
	2019	165.3	110.7	113.4	145.8	97.6	149.3
Zanzibar	1990	1.1	11.5	22.7	5.0	50.8	9.8
(Tanzanian Shilling)	1995	4.5	15.7	29.5	15.3	53.2	28.9
	2000	10.1	25.2	41.0	24.6	61.3	40.2
	2005	21.0	37.0	57.6	36.4	64.2	56.7
	2010	49.0	69.3	75.0	65.4	92.4	70.8
	2015	100.0	100.0	100.0	100.0	100.0	100.0
	2016	116.6	106.6	105.7	110.3	100.9	109.3
	2017	136.9	122.3	113.9	120.2	107.4	111.9
	2018	155.7	136.9	122.0	127.6	112.3	113.7
	2019	175.3	152.6	130.6	134.3	116.8	114.9
Zimbabwe	1970	11.7	11.7	24.4	47.9	47.9	100.0
(US Dollar)	1975	27.2	27.2	30.7	88.4	88.4	100.0
	1980	41.4	41.4	32.1	129.0	129.0	100.0
	1985	43.7	43.7	39.5	110.6	110.6	100.0
	1990	67.9	67.9	49.4	137.6	137.6	100.0

Table 7. Implicit price deflators of Gross Domestic Product in US Dollars and National Currency (2015 = 100)

Major area, region and country	Year	GDP in Current Prices: National Currency (1)	GDP in Current Prices: US Dollars (2)	Gross Domestic Product at Constant Prices (3)	GDP Implicit Price Deflators (2015 = 100): National Currency (4)	GDP Implicit Price Deflators (2015 = 100): US Dollars (5)	Exchange Rates (6)
	1995	55.4	55.4	52.4	105.8	105.8	100.0
	2000	43.7	43.7	51.9	84.2	84.2	100.0
	2005	36.0	36.0	41.7	86.4	86.4	100.0
	2010	60.3	60.3	70.6	85.4	85.4	100.0
	2015	100.0	100.0	100.0	100.0	100.0	100.0
	2016	102.9	102.9	100.8	102.2	102.2	100.0
	2017	110.4	110.4	105.5	104.7	104.7	100.0
	2018	121.8	121.8	110.6	110.1	110.1	100.0
	2019	107.4	107.4	101.6	105.7	105.7	100.0
Latin America and the Caribbean							
Anguilla (East Caribbean Dollar)	1970	0.9	1.2	12.4	7.1	9.5	74.2
	1975	1.8	2.2	14.5	12.4	15.4	80.4
	1980	3.7	3.7	18.2	20.2	20.2	100.0
	1985	8.2	8.2	22.0	37.3	37.3	100.0
	1990	22.9	22.9	43.2	53.0	53.0	100.0
	1995	31.4	31.4	51.5	60.9	60.9	100.0
	2000	45.5	45.5	67.8	67.0	67.0	100.0
	2005	69.3	69.3	90.9	76.2	76.2	100.0
	2010	81.0	81.0	95.2	85.1	85.1	100.0
	2015	100.0	100.0	100.0	100.0	100.0	100.0
	2016	96.9	96.9	97.5	99.4	99.4	100.0
	2017	86.0	86.0	91.3	94.2	94.2	100.0
	2018	97.0	97.0	98.9	98.0	98.0	100.0
	2019	114.8	114.8	104.3	110.1	110.1	100.0
Antigua and Barbuda (East Caribbean Dollar)	1970	1.9	2.5	21.2	8.9	12.0	74.1
	1975	5.1	6.4	25.9	19.8	24.6	80.4
	1980	10.1	10.1	31.0	32.4	32.4	100.0
	1985	18.3	18.3	40.4	45.3	45.3	100.0
	1990	34.4	34.4	55.6	61.9	61.9	100.0
	1995	43.2	43.2	61.7	70.0	70.0	100.0
	2000	61.8	61.8	80.0	77.3	77.3	100.0
	2005	76.5	76.5	92.2	83.0	83.0	100.0
	2010	85.9	85.9	92.1	93.3	93.3	100.0
	2015	100.0	100.0	100.0	100.0	100.0	100.0
	2016	107.5	107.5	105.5	101.9	101.9	100.0
	2017	109.8	109.8	108.8	100.9	100.9	100.0
	2018	120.1	120.1	116.4	103.2	103.2	100.0
	2019	124.3	124.3	120.3	103.4	103.4	100.0
Argentina (Argentine Peso)	1970	0.0	5.3	38.2	0.0	13.8	0.0
	1975	0.0	8.0	44.0	0.0	18.2	0.0
	1980	0.0	12.7	49.2	0.0	25.8	0.0
	1985	0.0	14.8	44.5	0.0	33.3	0.0
	1990	1.3	23.8	44.0	2.9	54.0	5.3
	1995	4.7	43.4	58.6	8.0	74.0	10.8
	2000	5.2	47.8	66.5	7.8	71.8	10.8
	2005	9.8	31.1	73.2	13.4	42.5	31.4
	2010	27.9	66.1	92.9	30.0	71.2	42.2
	2015	100.0	100.0	100.0	100.0	100.0	100.0
	2016	138.2	86.5	97.9	141.1	88.3	159.8

Table 7. Implicit price deflators of Gross Domestic Product in US Dollars and National Currency (2015 = 100)

Major area, region and country	Year	GDP in Current Prices: National Currency (1)	GDP in Current Prices: US Dollars (2)	Gross Domestic Product at Constant Prices (3)	GDP Implicit Price Deflators (2015 = 100): National Currency (4)	GDP Implicit Price Deflators (2015 = 100): US Dollars (5)	Exchange Rates (6)
	2017	178.8	99.7	100.5	177.8	99.1	179.4
	2018	245.3	80.6	98.0	250.2	82.2	304.3
	2019	363.6	69.7	95.9	379.1	72.7	521.5
Aruba	1970	6.8	6.8	8.9	75.9	75.9	100.0
(Aruban Guilder)	1975	8.8	8.8	13.8	63.7	63.7	100.0
	1980	11.4	11.4	21.3	53.5	53.5	100.0
	1985	14.8	14.8	32.9	44.9	44.9	100.0
	1990	29.3	29.3	57.6	50.9	50.9	100.0
	1995	47.4	47.4	78.3	60.5	60.5	100.0
	2000	67.2	67.2	96.4	69.8	69.8	100.0
	2005	83.7	83.7	102.7	81.5	81.5	100.0
	2010	85.7	85.7	91.5	93.7	93.7	100.0
	2015	100.0	100.0	100.0	100.0	100.0	100.0
	2016	101.0	101.6	102.1	99.5	99.5	100.0
	2017	104.7	104.7	104.1	100.6	100.6	100.0
	2018	109.7	109.7	105.0	104.5	104.5	100.0
	2019	112.8	112.8	104.3	108.2	108.2	100.0
Bahamas	1970	6.5	6.5	39.8	16.4	16.4	100.2
(Bahamian Dollar)	1975	9.4	9.4	29.8	31.6	31.6	100.0
	1980	18.7	18.7	52.4	35.7	35.7	100.0
	1985	28.2	28.2	62.9	44.9	44.9	100.0
	1990	40.7	40.7	70.9	57.4	57.4	100.0
	1995	44.1	44.1	70.6	62.5	62.5	100.0
	2000	69.0	69.0	91.2	75.7	75.7	100.0
	2005	84.0	84.0	99.0	84.9	84.9	100.0
	2010	86.2	86.2	97.8	88.1	88.1	100.0
	2015	100.0	100.0	100.0	100.0	100.0	100.0
	2016	101.9	101.9	101.4	100.4	100.4	100.0
	2017	106.7	106.7	104.6	102.0	102.0	100.0
	2018	111.2	111.2	107.8	103.2	103.2	100.0
	2019	116.0	116.0	109.1	106.3	106.3	100.0
Barbados	1970	4.6	4.6	55.9	8.3	8.3	100.0
(Barbados Dollar)	1975	10.3	10.2	59.1	17.4	17.3	100.9
	1980	21.9	21.9	75.5	29.0	29.0	100.0
	1985	30.5	30.5	74.0	41.2	41.2	100.0
	1990	43.6	43.6	82.7	52.7	52.7	100.0
	1995	48.7	48.7	79.2	61.5	61.5	100.0
	2000	66.9	66.9	93.8	71.3	71.3	100.0
	2005	83.5	83.5	99.4	84.0	84.0	100.0
	2010	96.1	96.1	100.3	95.8	95.8	100.0
	2015	100.0	100.0	100.0	100.0	100.0	100.0
	2016	102.4	102.4	102.5	100.0	100.0	100.0
	2017	105.6	105.6	103.0	102.5	102.5	100.0
	2018	107.9	107.9	102.4	105.4	105.4	100.0
	2019	110.5	110.5	102.3	108.0	108.0	100.0
Belize	1970	1.3	1.6	16.4	8.2	9.9	83.3
(Belize Dollar)	1975	6.1	6.7	20.0	30.3	33.6	90.4
	1980	12.5	12.5	24.2	51.7	51.7	100.0
	1985	13.4	13.4	24.6	54.5	54.5	100.0

Table 7. Implicit price deflators of Gross Domestic Product in US Dollars and National Currency (2015 = 100)

Major area, region and country	Year	GDP in Current Prices: National Currency (1)	GDP in Current Prices: US Dollars (2)	Gross Domestic Product at Constant Prices (3)	GDP Implicit Price Deflators (2015 = 100): National Currency (4)	GDP Implicit Price Deflators (2015 = 100): US Dollars (5)	Exchange Rates (6)
	1990	26.0	26.0	39.4	66.0	66.0	100.0
	1995	36.0	36.0	46.0	78.3	78.3	100.0
	2000	48.3	48.3	61.6	78.4	78.4	100.0
	2005	63.9	63.9	78.8	81.1	81.1	100.0
	2010	79.9	79.9	88.7	90.0	90.0	100.0
	2015	100.0	100.0	100.0	100.0	100.0	100.0
	2016	103.0	103.0	100.1	102.9	102.9	100.0
	2017	106.5	106.5	102.0	104.5	104.5	100.0
	2018	108.6	108.6	104.1	104.3	104.3	100.0
	2019	109.0	109.0	104.4	104.5	104.5	100.0
Bolivia (Plurinational State of)	1970	0.0	3.1	24.4	0.0	12.6	0.0
(Boliviano)	1975	0.0	7.3	32.3	0.0	22.5	0.0
	1980	0.0	10.7	35.7	0.0	29.8	0.0
	1985	1.3	12.5	32.4	3.9	38.5	10.1
	1990	6.8	14.8	36.3	18.7	40.7	45.9
	1995	14.1	20.3	44.4	31.9	45.9	69.5
	2000	22.8	25.4	52.5	43.4	48.4	89.5
	2005	33.8	28.9	61.2	55.2	47.3	116.7
	2010	60.5	59.5	76.6	79.0	77.8	101.5
	2015	100.0	100.0	100.0	100.0	100.0	100.0
	2016	102.9	102.9	104.3	98.6	98.6	100.0
	2017	113.7	113.7	108.6	104.6	104.6	100.0
	2018	122.1	122.1	113.2	107.8	107.8	100.0
	2019	123.9	123.9	115.7	107.1	107.1	100.0
Brazil	1970	0.0	2.0	19.4	0.0	10.1	0.0
(Brazilian Real)	1975	0.0	6.0	31.3	0.0	19.2	0.0
	1980	0.0	10.6	44.3	0.0	23.9	0.0
	1985	0.0	10.4	47.2	0.0	22.0	0.0
	1990	0.0	22.6	51.8	0.0	43.6	0.0
	1995	11.9	43.2	59.9	19.9	72.0	27.6
	2000	19.9	36.2	66.2	30.1	54.7	55.0
	2005	36.2	49.5	75.9	47.7	65.2	73.2
	2010	64.8	122.6	94.5	68.6	129.7	52.9
	2015	100.0	100.0	100.0	100.0	100.0	100.0
	2016	104.6	99.6	96.7	108.1	103.0	104.9
	2017	109.8	114.5	98.0	112.0	116.8	95.9
	2018	114.9	104.6	99.3	115.7	105.4	109.8
	2019	121.0	102.5	100.4	120.5	102.1	118.0
British Virgin Islands	1970	1.0	1.0	6.3	15.6	15.6	100.0
(US Dollar)	1975	1.3	1.3	6.9	19.2	19.2	100.0
	1980	2.7	2.7	9.6	28.1	28.1	100.0
	1985	4.5	4.5	11.2	40.0	40.0	100.0
	1990	10.2	10.2	20.3	50.3	50.3	100.0
	1995	38.6	38.6	62.6	61.7	61.7	100.0
	2000	73.0	73.0	97.9	74.6	74.6	100.0
	2005	84.6	84.6	102.7	82.4	82.4	100.0
	2010	86.9	86.9	97.8	88.9	88.9	100.0
	2015	100.0	100.0	100.0	100.0	100.0	100.0
	2016	109.5	109.5	107.3	102.1	102.1	100.0
	2017	102.8	102.8	108.1	95.1	95.1	100.0

Table 7. Implicit price deflators of Gross Domestic Product in US Dollars and National Currency (2015 = 100)

Major area, region and country	Year	GDP in Current Prices: National Currency (1)	GDP in Current Prices: US Dollars (2)	Gross Domestic Product at Constant Prices (3)	GDP Implicit Price Deflators (2015 = 100): National Currency (4)	GDP Implicit Price Deflators (2015 = 100): US Dollars (5)	Exchange Rates (6)
	2018	106.3	106.3	111.1	95.7	95.7	100.0
	2019	110.4	110.4	114.0	96.9	96.9	100.0
Cayman Islands (Cayman Islands Dollar)	1970	0.7	0.6	7.4	8.8	8.8	100.9
	1975	2.0	2.0	11.4	17.5	17.2	101.6
	1980	4.8	4.7	18.3	26.4	25.9	101.6
	1985	11.6	11.5	27.8	41.9	41.2	101.6
	1990	26.0	25.6	46.1	56.5	55.6	101.6
	1995	36.3	35.7	55.7	65.2	64.1	101.6
	2000	63.8	62.7	83.9	76.0	74.8	101.6
	2005	85.2	83.8	94.1	90.5	89.1	101.6
	2010	88.3	89.4	91.3	96.7	97.9	98.8
	2015	100.0	100.0	100.0	100.0	100.0	100.0
	2016	104.3	104.3	103.2	101.0	101.0	100.0
	2017	109.4	109.4	106.4	102.8	102.8	100.0
	2018	117.2	115.3	110.8	105.7	104.0	101.6
	2019	127.9	125.8	114.4	111.8	110.0	101.6
Chile (Chilean Peso)	1970	0.0	4.0	17.3	0.0	23.0	0.0
	1975	0.0	3.3	15.5	0.2	21.3	0.8
	1980	0.8	12.6	22.2	3.4	56.7	6.0
	1985	1.9	7.8	21.4	8.9	36.3	24.6
	1990	6.7	14.3	29.7	22.5	48.3	46.6
	1995	18.7	30.8	45.0	41.5	68.5	60.7
	2000	26.5	32.1	55.1	48.1	58.3	82.5
	2005	43.1	50.4	68.7	62.8	73.4	85.6
	2010	69.9	89.6	82.6	84.6	108.5	78.0
	2015	100.0	100.0	100.0	100.0	100.0	100.0
	2016	106.3	102.7	101.7	104.5	100.9	103.5
	2017	112.7	113.6	102.9	109.5	110.4	99.2
	2018	119.9	122.3	107.0	112.0	114.3	98.0
	2019	124.4	115.7	108.1	115.0	107.1	107.5
Colombia (Colombian Peso)	1970	0.0	3.5	17.2	0.1	20.0	0.7
	1975	0.1	6.3	22.7	0.3	27.6	1.1
	1980	0.3	16.0	29.5	0.9	54.2	1.7
	1985	0.9	16.7	33.0	2.6	50.7	5.2
	1990	3.5	19.3	41.2	8.6	46.7	18.3
	1995	12.4	37.3	51.2	24.3	73.0	33.3
	2000	25.7	33.8	53.6	48.1	63.1	76.1
	2005	42.0	49.6	64.0	65.6	77.6	84.6
	2010	67.6	97.6	79.6	85.0	122.7	69.2
	2015	100.0	100.0	100.0	100.0	100.0	100.0
	2016	107.3	96.4	102.1	105.1	94.4	111.4
	2017	114.4	106.3	103.5	110.5	102.7	107.6
	2018	122.5	113.7	106.1	115.5	107.1	107.8
	2019	132.0	110.3	109.6	120.5	100.7	119.7
Costa Rica (Costa Rican Colon)	1970	0.0	2.3	15.5	0.2	14.7	1.2
	1975	0.1	4.6	20.8	0.4	21.9	1.6
	1980	0.2	11.2	26.9	0.7	41.8	1.6
	1985	0.9	9.1	27.2	3.2	33.4	9.4
	1990	2.3	13.3	34.1	6.7	38.9	17.1

Table 7. Implicit price deflators of Gross Domestic Product in US Dollars and National Currency (2015 = 100)

Major area, region and country	Year	GDP in Current Prices: National Currency (1)	GDP in Current Prices: US Dollars (2)	Gross Domestic Product at Constant Prices (3)	GDP Implicit Price Deflators (2015 = 100): National Currency (4)	GDP Implicit Price Deflators (2015 = 100): US Dollars (5)	Exchange Rates (6)
	1995	7.1	21.0	44.4	15.9	47.4	33.6
	2000	15.7	27.3	54.7	28.8	49.9	57.7
	2005	32.6	36.4	66.1	49.3	55.1	89.4
	2010	66.9	68.0	83.4	80.3	81.6	98.4
	2015	100.0	100.0	100.0	100.0	100.0	100.0
	2016	106.3	104.3	104.2	102.0	100.1	101.9
	2017	113.3	106.8	108.3	104.7	98.6	106.2
	2018	119.3	110.5	111.2	107.3	99.5	107.9
	2019	123.9	112.8	113.5	109.2	99.4	109.9
Cuba..	1970	6.5	6.5	26.5	24.6	24.6	100.1
(Cuban Peso)	1975	12.3	14.9	34.5	35.5	43.3	82.1
	1980	16.5	22.8	40.6	40.5	56.3	72.1
	1985	24.1	26.3	61.2	39.4	43.0	91.7
	1990	24.7	32.8	60.5	40.8	54.3	75.3
	1995	27.4	34.9	42.0	65.1	83.1	78.4
	2000	35.1	35.1	52.4	66.9	66.9	100.1
	2005	48.9	48.9	67.0	73.1	73.0	100.1
	2010	73.8	73.8	87.1	84.8	84.7	100.1
	2015	100.0	100.0	100.0	100.0	100.0	100.0
	2016	104.9	104.8	100.5	104.3	104.2	100.1
	2017	111.2	111.1	102.3	108.6	108.5	100.1
	2018	114.8	114.7	104.6	109.7	109.6	100.1
	2019	120.9	120.8	106.7	113.3	113.2	100.1
Curaçao..	2005	74.4	74.4	95.5	77.9	77.9	100.0
(Netherlands Antillian Guilder)	2010	93.6	93.6	101.2	92.5	92.5	100.0
	2015	100.0	100.0	100.0	100.0	100.0	100.0
	2016	99.1	99.1	99.0	100.0	100.0	100.0
	2017	98.9	98.9	97.3	101.6	101.6	100.0
	2018	99.2	99.2	95.2	104.3	104.3	100.0
	2019	98.4	98.4	91.9	107.0	107.0	100.0
Dominica..	1970	3.2	4.3	25.9	12.2	16.4	74.1
(East Caribbean Dollar)	1975	6.3	7.8	35.7	17.6	21.9	80.4
	1980	13.5	13.5	40.1	33.6	33.6	100.0
	1985	22.1	22.1	50.2	44.0	44.0	100.0
	1990	37.3	37.3	64.8	57.5	57.5	100.0
	1995	50.8	50.8	70.5	72.0	72.0	100.0
	2000	61.7	61.7	79.2	77.9	77.9	100.0
	2005	67.4	67.4	84.9	79.4	79.4	100.0
	2010	91.3	91.3	100.7	90.7	90.7	100.0
	2015	100.0	100.0	100.0	100.0	100.0	100.0
	2016	106.6	106.6	102.6	103.9	103.9	100.0
	2017	96.1	96.1	95.6	100.6	100.6	100.0
	2018	101.8	101.8	97.8	104.1	104.1	100.0
	2019	107.7	107.7	101.3	106.4	106.4	100.0
Dominican Republic................................	1970	0.1	2.6	10.7	0.5	24.3	2.2
(Dominican Peso)	1975	0.1	6.3	16.5	0.8	38.3	2.2
	1980	0.3	11.7	21.4	1.2	54.6	2.2
	1985	0.5	7.9	23.5	2.3	33.6	6.9
	1990	2.5	13.4	27.1	9.3	49.3	18.9

Table 7. Implicit price deflators of Gross Domestic Product in US Dollars and National Currency (2015 = 100)

Major area, region and country	Year	GDP in Current Prices: National Currency (1)	GDP in Current Prices: US Dollars (2)	Gross Domestic Product at Constant Prices (3)	GDP Implicit Price Deflators (2015 = 100): National Currency (4)	GDP Implicit Price Deflators (2015 = 100): US Dollars (5)	Exchange Rates (6)
	1995	6.7	22.1	35.0	19.1	63.3	30.2
	2000	12.3	33.7	48.8	25.1	69.0	36.4
	2005	33.8	49.9	58.0	58.2	86.0	67.7
	2010	61.9	74.7	78.6	78.7	95.0	82.8
	2015	100.0	100.0	100.0	100.0	100.0	100.0
	2016	108.8	106.4	106.7	102.0	99.7	102.3
	2017	118.6	112.4	111.6	106.3	100.7	105.5
	2018	132.1	120.2	119.4	110.6	100.7	109.9
	2019	142.3	125.0	125.5	113.4	99.6	113.9
Ecuador	1970	2.9	2.9	17.5	16.5	16.5	100.0
(US Dollar)	1975	7.8	7.8	27.4	28.4	28.4	100.0
	1980	18.0	18.0	34.0	52.9	52.9	100.0
	1985	17.3	17.3	38.4	44.9	44.9	100.0
	1990	15.3	15.3	44.0	34.9	34.9	100.0
	1995	24.6	24.6	50.9	48.3	48.3	100.0
	2000	18.4	18.4	53.8	34.3	34.3	100.0
	2005	41.8	41.8	68.1	61.4	61.4	100.0
	2010	70.1	70.1	80.5	87.0	87.0	100.0
	2015	100.0	100.0	100.0	100.0	100.0	100.0
	2016	100.7	100.7	98.8	101.9	101.9	100.0
	2017	105.0	105.0	101.1	103.9	103.9	100.0
	2018	108.3	108.3	102.4	105.8	105.8	100.0
	2019	108.2	108.2	102.5	105.6	105.6	100.0
El Salvador	1970	1.4	1.4	35.0	4.1	4.1	100.0
(US Dollar)	1975	2.5	2.5	45.7	5.5	5.5	100.0
	1980	5.0	5.0	48.1	10.4	10.4	100.0
	1985	8.1	8.1	43.8	18.4	18.4	100.0
	1990	20.6	20.6	48.0	42.8	42.8	100.0
	1995	38.1	38.1	64.8	58.7	58.7	100.0
	2000	50.3	50.3	75.3	66.8	66.8	100.0
	2005	62.7	62.7	84.6	74.1	74.1	100.0
	2010	78.7	78.7	90.8	86.7	86.7	100.0
	2015	100.0	100.0	100.0	100.0	100.0	100.0
	2016	103.2	103.2	102.5	100.7	100.7	100.0
	2017	106.6	106.6	104.8	101.6	101.6	100.0
	2018	111.4	111.4	107.4	103.8	103.8	100.0
	2019	115.3	115.3	110.0	104.9	104.9	100.0
Grenada	1970	1.4	1.9	16.7	8.5	11.5	74.1
(East Caribbean Dollar)	1975	4.1	5.1	22.9	17.8	22.2	80.4
	1900	8.8	8.8	29.3	30.1	30.1	100.0
	1985	13.6	13.6	36.2	37.6	37.6	100.0
	1990	23.7	23.7	50.2	47.1	47.1	100.0
	1995	27.9	27.9	52.4	53.3	53.3	100.0
	2000	52.2	52.2	72.0	72.5	72.5	100.0
	2005	69.7	69.7	89.8	77.6	77.6	100.0
	2010	77.3	77.3	85.9	90.1	90.1	100.0
	2015	100.0	100.0	100.0	100.0	100.0	100.0
	2016	106.5	106.5	103.7	102.6	102.6	100.0
	2017	112.9	112.9	108.3	104.2	104.2	100.0
	2018	117.2	117.2	112.8	103.9	103.9	100.0

Table 7. Implicit price deflators of Gross Domestic Product in US Dollars and National Currency (2015 = 100)

Major area, region and country	Year	GDP in Current Prices: National Currency (1)	GDP in Current Prices: US Dollars (2)	Gross Domestic Product at Constant Prices (3)	GDP Implicit Price Deflators (2015 = 100): National Currency (4)	GDP Implicit Price Deflators (2015 = 100): US Dollars (5)	Exchange Rates (6)
	2019	121.5	121.5	115.1	105.6	105.6	100.0
Guatemala (Quetzal)	1970	0.4	2.7	21.0	1.7	12.8	13.1
	1975	0.7	5.1	27.6	2.4	18.6	13.1
	1980	1.5	11.1	36.5	4.0	30.5	13.1
	1985	2.1	15.8	34.5	6.0	45.8	13.1
	1990	6.3	10.8	39.8	15.9	27.1	58.6
	1995	15.7	20.7	49.1	32.0	42.1	75.9
	2000	27.6	27.2	59.5	46.3	45.7	101.4
	2005	42.9	43.1	69.1	62.1	62.3	99.7
	2010	68.9	65.4	82.7	83.3	79.1	105.3
	2015	100.0	100.0	100.0	100.0	100.0	100.0
	2016	105.5	106.2	102.7	102.7	103.4	99.3
	2017	110.5	115.2	105.8	104.5	108.9	96.0
	2018	115.5	117.6	109.2	105.8	107.7	98.2
	2019	124.0	123.4	113.4	109.4	108.8	100.5
Guyana (Guyana Dollar)	1970	0.1	10.0	29.9	0.3	33.4	1.0
	1975	0.2	18.8	36.2	0.6	51.9	1.1
	1980	0.3	22.0	35.6	0.8	61.9	1.2
	1985	0.4	17.2	28.4	1.2	60.5	2.1
	1990	2.8	14.8	25.2	11.2	58.5	19.1
	1995	15.9	23.2	35.6	44.8	65.1	68.8
	2000	23.5	26.6	40.7	57.7	65.3	88.3
	2005	44.7	46.2	63.4	70.6	72.9	96.8
	2010	79.1	80.2	85.1	93.0	94.3	98.6
	2015	100.0	100.0	100.0	100.0	100.0	100.0
	2016	104.7	104.7	103.8	100.9	100.9	100.0
	2017	110.9	110.9	107.7	103.0	103.0	100.0
	2018	112.5	111.9	112.5	100.1	99.5	100.6
	2019	122.1	120.9	118.5	103.0	102.0	101.0
Haiti (Gourde)	1970	0.5	5.3	55.5	0.9	9.5	9.9
	1975	1.1	10.8	66.9	1.6	16.2	9.9
	1980	2.2	22.0	88.3	2.5	24.9	9.9
	1985	3.1	31.9	84.2	3.7	37.9	9.9
	1990	3.7	37.1	84.1	4.3	44.1	9.9
	1995	9.6	32.3	74.3	12.9	43.5	29.8
	2000	18.3	43.9	84.1	21.8	52.2	41.8
	2005	38.6	48.4	81.8	47.2	59.2	79.8
	2010	63.0	80.3	84.9	74.2	94.5	78.5
	2015	100.0	100.0	100.0	100.0	100.0	100.0
	2016	113.6	90.9	101.5	112.0	89.6	124.9
	2017	130.3	102.0	102.6	126.9	99.4	127.7
	2018	149.1	111.2	104.2	143.2	106.7	134.2
	2019	168.8	96.4	103.2	163.6	93.4	175.2
Honduras (Lempira)	1970	0.4	3.9	18.9	1.9	20.8	9.1
	1975	0.6	6.4	22.6	2.6	28.3	9.1
	1980	1.3	14.6	32.0	4.2	45.7	9.1
	1985	1.9	20.7	34.8	5.4	59.5	9.1
	1990	3.2	17.3	40.6	8.0	42.7	18.7
	1995	9.7	22.5	48.3	20.1	46.6	43.2

Table 7. Implicit price deflators of Gross Domestic Product in US Dollars and National Currency (2015 = 100)

Major area, region and country	Year	GDP in Current Prices: National Currency (1)	GDP in Current Prices: US Dollars (2)	Gross Domestic Product at Constant Prices (3)	GDP Implicit Price Deflators (2015 = 100): National Currency (4)	GDP Implicit Price Deflators (2015 = 100): US Dollars (5)	Exchange Rates (6)
	2000	23.2	34.3	56.1	41.3	61.1	67.6
	2005	39.9	46.5	70.4	56.7	66.0	85.8
	2010	65.0	75.5	84.1	77.3	89.8	86.1
	2015	100.0	100.0	100.0	100.0	100.0	100.0
	2016	107.7	103.5	103.9	103.7	99.6	104.1
	2017	118.0	110.3	108.9	108.4	101.2	107.0
	2018	124.7	114.5	113.0	110.4	101.4	108.9
	2019	133.6	119.6	115.9	115.2	103.2	111.7
Jamaica..	1970	0.1	12.2	67.3	0.1	18.2	0.7
(Jamaican Dollar)	1975	0.2	25.0	73.5	0.3	34.0	0.8
	1980	0.4	23.4	62.4	0.6	37.5	1.5
	1985	0.9	18.3	62.7	1.4	29.3	4.8
	1990	2.3	37.2	79.6	2.9	46.7	6.1
	1995	13.9	46.3	92.0	15.1	50.3	30.1
	2000	23.3	63.4	91.8	25.4	69.1	36.8
	2005	42.2	79.2	99.2	42.5	79.8	53.3
	2010	69.5	93.1	96.8	71.7	96.2	74.6
	2015	100.0	100.0	100.0	100.0	100.0	100.0
	2016	106.1	99.2	101.4	104.7	97.8	107.0
	2017	114.2	104.3	102.4	111.5	101.9	109.5
	2018	122.1	110.8	104.3	117.1	106.2	110.2
	2019	127.2	111.5	105.3	120.8	105.9	114.0
Mexico..	1970	0.0	3.9	23.2	0.0	16.7	0.1
(Mexican Peso)	1975	0.0	9.6	31.9	0.0	30.0	0.1
	1980	0.0	20.3	44.0	0.1	46.1	0.1
	1985	0.3	19.2	48.4	0.6	39.6	1.6
	1990	4.5	25.6	52.6	8.6	48.7	17.7
	1995	12.5	30.8	57.8	21.5	53.2	40.5
	2000	36.1	60.5	74.8	48.2	80.8	59.7
	2005	51.5	75.0	80.3	64.2	93.3	68.8
	2010	72.1	90.4	86.5	83.3	104.5	79.7
	2015	100.0	100.0	100.0	100.0	100.0	100.0
	2016	108.4	92.1	102.9	105.4	89.5	117.8
	2017	118.1	98.9	105.1	112.4	94.1	119.4
	2018	126.6	104.3	107.3	118.0	97.2	121.4
	2019	130.5	107.3	107.0	121.9	100.3	121.6
Montserrat..	1970	9.4	12.7	105.3	8.9	12.1	74.2
(East Caribbean Dollar)	1975	18.8	23.4	122.5	15.4	19.1	80.4
	1980	46.1	46.1	154.0	29.9	29.9	100.0
	1985	71.0	71.0	173.5	40.9	40.9	100.0
	1990	122.9	122.9	222.2	55.3	55.3	100.0
	1995	112.2	112.2	194.7	57.6	57.6	100.0
	2000	58.6	58.6	83.4	70.2	70.2	100.0
	2005	79.6	79.6	92.3	86.3	86.3	100.0
	2010	90.4	90.4	90.7	99.8	99.8	100.0
	2015	100.0	100.0	100.0	100.0	100.0	100.0
	2016	102.4	102.4	101.3	101.0	101.0	100.0
	2017	97.2	97.2	97.5	99.7	99.7	100.0
	2018	101.2	101.2	101.4	99.8	99.8	100.0
	2019	109.6	109.6	107.4	102.1	102.1	100.0

Table 7. Implicit price deflators of Gross Domestic Product in US Dollars and National Currency (2015 = 100)

Major area, region and country	Year	GDP in Current Prices		Gross Domestic Product at Constant Prices (3)	GDP Implicit Price Deflators (2015 = 100)		Exchange Rates (6)
		National Currency (1)	US Dollars (2)		National Currency (4)	US Dollars (5)	
Nicaragua..	1970	0.0	8.9	45.1	0.0	19.8	0.0
(Cordoba Oro)	1975	0.0	18.3	59.2	0.0	30.9	0.0
	1980	0.0	21.2	47.2	0.0	45.0	0.0
	1985	0.0	28.3	48.7	0.0	58.1	0.0
	1990	0.1	27.9	41.1	0.4	67.7	0.5
	1995	8.9	32.3	44.9	19.9	71.8	27.7
	2000	18.6	39.9	57.4	32.4	69.5	46.5
	2005	30.3	49.4	67.1	45.2	73.6	61.4
	2010	53.8	68.7	76.7	70.2	89.6	78.4
	2015	100.0	100.0	100.0	100.0	100.0	100.0
	2016	109.4	104.1	104.6	104.6	99.6	105.0
	2017	119.1	108.1	109.4	108.9	98.8	110.3
	2018	118.6	102.4	105.1	112.8	97.5	115.8
	2019	119.3	98.2	101.0	118.1	97.2	121.5
Panama..	1970	2.2	2.2	11.0	19.7	19.7	100.0
(Balboa)	1975	3.9	3.9	13.8	28.4	28.4	100.0
	1980	7.6	7.6	18.7	40.7	40.7	100.0
	1985	10.8	10.8	22.4	48.0	48.0	100.0
	1990	11.4	11.4	23.8	48.0	48.0	100.0
	1995	17.0	17.0	31.1	54.7	54.7	100.0
	2000	21.8	21.8	39.0	56.0	56.0	100.0
	2005	29.1	29.1	48.1	60.4	60.4	100.0
	2010	54.4	54.4	68.9	79.0	79.0	100.0
	2015	100.0	100.0	100.0	100.0	100.0	100.0
	2016	107.1	107.1	105.0	102.0	102.0	100.0
	2017	115.0	115.0	110.8	103.8	103.8	100.0
	2018	120.0	120.0	114.8	104.6	104.6	100.0
	2019	123.5	123.5	118.3	104.4	104.4	100.0
Paraguay..	1970	0.0	1.9	13.2	0.3	14.2	2.4
(Guarani)	1975	0.1	4.8	18.6	0.6	25.7	2.4
	1980	0.3	14.1	30.6	1.1	45.9	2.4
	1985	0.8	14.4	34.3	2.5	41.9	5.9
	1990	3.9	16.7	41.5	9.5	40.1	23.6
	1995	10.9	28.9	49.0	22.2	58.9	37.7
	2000	17.0	25.4	48.5	35.0	52.3	67.0
	2005	37.1	31.3	63.2	58.7	49.5	118.7
	2010	68.5	75.3	82.3	83.3	91.5	91.0
	2015	100.0	100.0	100.0	100.0	100.0	100.0
	2016	108.6	99.7	104.3	104.1	95.6	108.9
	2017	116.4	107.9	109.5	106.4	98.5	108.0
	2018	123.0	111.7	113.2	108.7	98.7	110.1
	2019	126.3	105.3	113.4	111.3	92.9	119.9
Peru..	1970	0.0	3.1	24.2	0.0	12.7	0.0
(Nuevo Sol)	1975	0.0	7.0	31.8	0.0	22.0	0.0
	1980	0.0	8.8	34.7	0.0	25.3	0.0
	1985	0.0	7.7	34.7	0.0	22.1	0.0
	1990	0.9	15.3	31.4	2.9	48.9	5.9
	1995	19.9	28.1	40.5	49.1	69.4	70.8
	2000	29.9	27.3	46.1	64.9	59.2	109.6

Table 7. Implicit price deflators of Gross Domestic Product in US Dollars and National Currency (2015 = 100)

Major area, region and country	Year	GDP in Current Prices: National Currency (1)	GDP in Current Prices: US Dollars (2)	Gross Domestic Product at Constant Prices (3)	GDP Implicit Price Deflators (2015 = 100): National Currency (4)	GDP Implicit Price Deflators (2015 = 100): US Dollars (5)	Exchange Rates (6)
	2005	41.5	40.1	56.8	73.1	70.6	103.5
	2010	69.0	77.7	79.2	87.1	98.2	88.7
	2015	100.0	100.0	100.0	100.0	100.0	100.0
	2016	107.2	101.1	104.0	103.1	97.3	106.0
	2017	113.8	111.2	106.6	106.8	104.3	102.4
	2018	120.7	117.0	110.8	109.0	105.6	103.2
	2019	125.3	119.5	113.2	110.7	105.6	104.8
Puerto Rico..	1970	4.9	4.9	31.4	15.8	15.8	100.0
(US Dollar)	1975	8.0	8.0	37.0	21.7	21.7	100.0
	1980	14.2	14.2	47.7	29.7	29.7	100.0
	1985	19.9	19.9	51.4	38.7	38.7	100.0
	1990	30.0	30.0	67.7	44.4	44.4	100.0
	1995	41.8	41.8	82.5	50.7	50.7	100.0
	2000	60.5	60.5	101.7	59.5	59.5	100.0
	2005	81.2	81.2	110.2	73.7	73.7	100.0
	2010	95.2	95.2	102.9	92.5	92.5	100.0
	2015	100.0	100.0	100.0	100.0	100.0	100.0
	2016	100.9	100.9	98.7	102.2	102.2	100.0
	2017	100.1	100.1	95.9	104.4	104.4	100.0
	2018	97.7	97.7	91.4	106.8	106.8	100.0
	2019	101.6	101.6	92.5	109.8	109.8	100.0
Saint Kitts and Nevis..............................	1970	2.0	2.7	15.6	12.8	17.3	74.1
(East Caribbean Dollar)	1975	4.4	5.5	19.6	22.6	28.2	80.4
	1980	7.4	7.4	26.8	27.7	27.7	100.0
	1985	12.0	12.0	32.7	36.8	36.8	100.0
	1990	23.5	23.5	46.6	50.5	50.5	100.0
	1995	34.0	34.0	56.5	60.1	60.1	100.0
	2000	45.6	45.6	72.2	63.2	63.2	100.0
	2005	59.3	59.3	84.5	70.1	70.1	100.0
	2010	82.3	82.3	88.8	92.8	92.8	100.0
	2015	100.0	100.0	100.0	100.0	100.0	100.0
	2016	105.2	105.2	102.8	102.3	102.3	100.0
	2017	108.0	108.0	100.8	107.1	107.1	100.0
	2018	109.5	109.5	103.7	105.5	105.5	100.0
	2019	113.8	113.8	106.3	107.1	107.1	100.0
Saint Lucia..	1970	1.7	2.3	19.3	8.8	11.8	74.1
(East Caribbean Dollar)	1975	4.3	5.3	23.3	18.3	22.8	80.4
	1980	10.0	10.0	31.4	31.9	31.9	100.0
	1985	16.5	16.5	40.3	40.9	40.9	100.0
	1990	30.8	30.8	61.0	50.5	50.5	100.0
	1995	40.9	40.9	67.9	60.2	60.2	100.0
	2000	51.8	51.8	78.5	65.9	65.9	100.0
	2005	61.9	61.9	84.3	73.5	73.5	100.0
	2010	82.2	82.2	96.5	85.2	85.2	100.0
	2015	100.0	100.0	100.0	100.0	100.0	100.0
	2016	103.2	103.2	103.4	99.7	99.7	100.0
	2017	110.6	110.6	107.0	103.3	103.3	100.0
	2018	114.3	114.3	109.9	104.0	104.0	100.0
	2019	117.4	117.4	111.8	105.0	105.0	100.0

Table 7. Implicit price deflators of Gross Domestic Product in US Dollars and National Currency (2015 = 100)

Major area, region and country	Year	GDP in Current Prices		Gross Domestic Product at Constant Prices (3)	GDP Implicit Price Deflators (2015 = 100)		Exchange Rates (6)
		National Currency (1)	US Dollars (2)		National Currency (4)	US Dollars (5)	
Sint Maarten (Dutch part)........................	2005	66.4	66.4	85.4	77.7	77.7	100.0
(Netherlands Antillian Guilder)	2010	84.1	84.1	95.1	88.4	88.4	100.0
	2015	100.0	100.0	100.0	100.0	100.0	100.0
	2016	100.5	100.5	100.4	100.1	100.1	100.0
	2017	95.1	95.1	92.0	103.4	103.4	100.0
	2018	89.5	89.5	84.2	106.3	106.3	100.0
	2019	94.6	94.6	88.4	107.0	107.0	100.0
St. Vincent and the Grenadines..............	1970	2.1	2.8	25.4	8.2	11.1	74.1
(East Caribbean Dollar)	1975	4.1	5.1	24.6	16.5	20.5	80.4
	1980	9.3	9.3	32.5	28.5	28.5	100.0
	1985	17.7	17.7	41.0	43.0	43.0	100.0
	1990	31.0	31.0	52.5	59.1	59.1	100.0
	1995	41.3	41.3	60.7	68.0	68.0	100.0
	2000	52.5	52.5	71.3	73.5	73.5	100.0
	2005	72.9	72.9	88.7	82.2	82.2	100.0
	2010	90.2	90.2	94.8	95.1	95.1	100.0
	2015	100.0	100.0	100.0	100.0	100.0	100.0
	2016	102.5	102.5	101.9	100.6	100.6	100.0
	2017	104.9	104.9	102.9	101.9	101.9	100.0
	2018	107.4	107.4	105.1	102.1	102.1	100.0
	2019	109.3	109.3	105.5	103.6	103.6	100.0
Suriname..	1970	0.0	7.4	37.2	0.0	20.0	0.1
(Surinam Dollar)	1975	0.0	13.3	44.0	0.0	30.3	0.1
	1980	0.0	22.7	48.1	0.0	47.3	0.1
	1985	0.0	25.0	53.0	0.0	47.2	0.1
	1990	0.0	15.7	52.6	0.1	29.8	0.2
	1995	2.3	17.6	52.4	4.4	33.7	13.0
	2000	9.4	24.2	57.6	16.2	41.9	38.7
	2005	36.6	45.8	73.6	49.8	62.2	80.0
	2010	73.3	91.2	92.3	79.4	98.9	80.4
	2015	100.0	100.0	100.0	100.0	100.0	100.0
	2016	119.1	65.4	94.4	126.2	69.2	182.3
	2017	147.2	67.2	96.1	153.2	69.9	219.2
	2018	158.1	72.4	98.6	160.3	73.4	218.4
	2019	168.6	77.2	98.8	170.5	78.1	218.3
Trinidad and Tobago..............................	1970	1.0	3.3	26.6	3.9	12.4	31.4
(Trinidad and Tobago Dollar)	1975	3.3	9.8	30.5	11.0	32.2	34.0
	1980	9.4	25.1	44.5	21.2	56.3	37.6
	1985	11.4	29.6	39.1	29.1	75.7	38.4
	1990	13.6	20.4	35.0	38.8	58.2	66.6
	1995	20.0	21.4	37.5	53.3	57.2	93.3
	2000	32.4	32.8	53.9	60.0	60.8	98.8
	2005	63.4	64.2	79.5	79.8	80.7	98.8
	2010	88.8	88.9	96.3	92.2	92.3	100.0
	2015	100.0	100.0	100.0	100.0	100.0	100.0
	2016	93.8	89.7	94.4	99.4	95.0	104.6
	2017	95.3	89.7	91.6	104.1	97.9	106.3
	2018	100.7	94.9	91.6	109.9	103.5	106.2
	2019	98.5	93.0	90.5	108.8	102.7	105.9

Table 7. Implicit price deflators of Gross Domestic Product in US Dollars and National Currency (2015 = 100)

Major area, region and country	Year	GDP in Current Prices: National Currency (1)	GDP in Current Prices: US Dollars (2)	Gross Domestic Product at Constant Prices (3)	GDP Implicit Price Deflators (2015 = 100): National Currency (4)	GDP Implicit Price Deflators (2015 = 100): US Dollars (5)	Exchange Rates (6)
Turks and Caicos Islands........................ (US Dollar)	1970	1.0	1.0	2.6	39.6	39.6	100.0
	1975	1.9	1.9	4.3	43.4	43.4	100.0
	1980	3.4	3.4	7.2	47.4	47.4	100.0
	1985	6.2	6.2	12.0	51.8	51.8	100.0
	1990	11.2	11.2	19.9	56.6	56.6	100.0
	1995	20.2	20.2	32.6	61.9	61.9	100.0
	2000	33.9	33.9	48.6	69.8	69.8	100.0
	2005	61.4	61.4	73.3	83.8	83.8	100.0
	2010	72.9	72.9	80.3	90.8	90.8	100.0
	2015	100.0	100.0	100.0	100.0	100.0	100.0
	2016	109.6	109.6	107.3	102.2	102.2	100.0
	2017	108.5	108.5	104.6	103.8	103.8	100.0
	2018	118.2	118.2	110.4	107.0	107.0	100.0
	2019	127.1	127.1	116.3	109.3	109.3	100.0
Uruguay.. (Peso Uruguayo)	1970	0.0	4.8	32.8	0.0	14.5	0.0
	1975	0.0	7.2	35.4	0.0	20.3	0.0
	1980	0.0	20.0	44.1	0.0	45.3	0.0
	1985	0.0	9.8	38.5	0.1	25.5	0.4
	1990	0.7	17.3	46.2	1.6	37.5	4.3
	1995	9.3	40.0	56.4	16.5	70.9	23.2
	2000	19.0	42.8	62.8	30.2	68.2	44.3
	2005	29.2	32.6	63.4	46.0	51.4	89.6
	2010	55.5	75.6	84.7	65.5	89.3	73.4
	2015	100.0	100.0	100.0	100.0	100.0	100.0
	2016	109.2	98.9	101.7	107.3	97.3	110.4
	2017	117.3	111.7	104.3	112.4	107.1	104.9
	2018	125.8	111.9	106.0	118.6	105.5	112.4
	2019	135.7	105.2	106.3	127.7	99.0	129.0
Venezuela (Bolivarian Republic of)......... (Bolivar Fuerte)	1970	0.0	4.0	37.3	0.0	10.8	0.0
	1975	0.0	9.3	47.5	0.0	19.7	0.0
	1980	0.0	20.1	55.9	0.0	36.0	0.0
	1985	0.0	17.4	52.3	0.0	33.3	0.0
	1990	0.0	13.7	59.5	0.1	23.0	0.3
	1995	0.2	21.8	70.4	0.3	30.9	1.0
	2000	1.3	34.0	73.1	1.8	46.6	3.9
	2005	5.0	42.3	82.9	6.1	51.0	11.9
	2010	16.9	114.4	99.5	17.0	115.0	14.7
	2015	100.0	100.0	100.0	100.0	100.0	100.0
	2016	349.5	83.8	83.0	421.3	101.0	416.9
	2017	2499.6	72.0	70.0	3572.9	102.9	3470.6
	2018	1315447.4	59.3	56.2	2339330.0	105.4	2219039.7
	2019	171059673.0	39.2	36.6	468006937.7	107.3	436155558.0
Northern America							
Bermuda.. (Bermudian Dollar)	1970	4.0	4.0	45.4	8.8	8.8	100.0
	1975	7.4	7.4	50.8	14.6	14.6	100.0
	1980	13.6	13.6	64.0	21.2	21.2	100.0
	1985	21.5	21.5	63.7	33.7	33.7	100.0
	1990	30.6	30.6	68.3	44.8	44.8	100.0

Table 7. Implicit price deflators of Gross Domestic Product in US Dollars and National Currency (2015 = 100)

Major area, region and country	Year	GDP in Current Prices: National Currency (1)	GDP in Current Prices: US Dollars (2)	Gross Domestic Product at Constant Prices (3)	GDP Implicit Price Deflators (2015 = 100): National Currency (4)	GDP Implicit Price Deflators (2015 = 100): US Dollars (5)	Exchange Rates (6)
	1995	38.4	38.4	73.0	52.6	52.6	100.0
	2000	52.3	52.3	87.8	59.6	59.6	100.0
	2005	73.2	73.2	99.8	73.3	73.3	100.0
	2010	99.7	99.7	113.4	87.9	87.9	100.0
	2015	100.0	100.0	100.0	100.0	100.0	100.0
	2016	103.7	103.7	99.3	104.4	104.4	100.0
	2017	107.3	107.3	102.9	104.3	104.3	100.0
	2018	109.2	109.2	103.0	105.9	105.9	100.0
	2019	110.6	110.6	105.5	104.8	104.8	100.0
Canada (Canadian Dollar)	1970	4.7	5.7	29.4	15.9	19.5	81.7
	1975	8.9	11.2	36.2	24.7	31.1	79.5
	1980	16.2	17.7	43.5	37.3	40.8	91.4
	1985	25.1	23.5	49.6	50.7	47.5	106.8
	1990	34.9	38.3	56.4	61.9	67.9	91.2
	1995	41.8	38.9	61.4	68.1	63.4	107.3
	2000	55.6	47.9	74.8	74.3	64.0	116.1
	2005	71.4	75.4	84.9	84.1	88.8	94.7
	2010	83.7	103.9	89.9	93.1	115.6	80.5
	2015	100.0	100.0	100.0	100.0	100.0	100.0
	2016	101.8	98.2	101.0	100.8	97.2	103.6
	2017	107.5	106.0	104.1	103.3	101.9	101.5
	2018	112.1	110.7	106.6	105.2	103.8	101.3
	2019	116.1	111.9	108.6	106.9	103.1	103.7
Greenland (Danish Krone)	1970	3.4	3.0	29.9	11.3	10.2	111.5
	1975	7.9	9.2	40.8	19.3	22.6	85.4
	1980	17.4	20.8	56.9	30.7	36.6	83.8
	1985	28.4	18.1	55.6	51.1	32.4	157.5
	1990	41.0	44.6	62.5	65.6	71.3	92.0
	1995	44.0	52.9	61.8	71.2	85.5	83.3
	2000	56.1	46.7	74.5	75.3	62.7	120.1
	2005	66.0	74.0	83.6	78.9	88.6	89.1
	2010	83.7	100.2	98.4	85.1	101.8	83.6
	2015	100.0	100.0	100.0	100.0	100.0	100.0
	2016	108.4	108.3	104.7	103.5	103.5	100.1
	2017	111.0	113.1	105.2	105.5	107.5	98.1
	2018	114.6	122.1	108.6	105.6	112.5	93.9
	2019	119.9	121.0	111.6	107.5	108.4	99.1
United States (US Dollar)	1970	5.9	5.9	28.4	20.7	20.7	100.0
	1975	9.2	9.2	32.4	28.5	28.5	100.0
	1980	15.7	15.7	38.8	40.4	40.4	100.0
	1985	23.8	23.8	45.6	52.2	52.2	100.0
	1990	32.7	32.7	53.7	60.9	60.9	100.0
	1995	41.9	41.9	61.0	68.7	68.7	100.0
	2000	56.2	56.2	75.3	74.6	74.6	100.0
	2005	71.5	71.5	85.5	83.6	83.6	100.0
	2010	82.2	82.2	89.5	91.9	91.9	100.0
	2015	100.0	100.0	100.0	100.0	100.0	100.0
	2016	102.8	102.8	101.7	101.0	101.0	100.0
	2017	107.2	107.2	104.1	102.9	102.9	100.0
	2018	113.0	113.0	107.2	105.4	105.4	100.0

Table 7. Implicit price deflators of Gross Domestic Product in US Dollars and National Currency (2015 = 100)

Major area, region and country	Year	GDP in Current Prices: National Currency (1)	GDP in Current Prices: US Dollars (2)	Gross Domestic Product at Constant Prices (3)	GDP Implicit Price Deflators (2015 = 100): National Currency (4)	GDP Implicit Price Deflators (2015 = 100): US Dollars (5)	Exchange Rates (6)
	2019	117.5	117.5	109.5	107.3	107.3	100.0
Asia							
Afghanistan (Afghani)	1970	0.0	9.3	55.9	0.0	16.5	0.1
	1975	0.0	12.4	53.0	0.0	23.4	0.1
	1980	0.0	19.5	54.7	0.0	35.7	0.1
	1985	0.0	17.8	60.5	0.0	29.4	0.1
	1990	0.0	19.0	46.5	0.0	40.9	0.1
	1995	0.2	14.7	33.9	0.6	43.5	1.4
	2000	13.8	17.9	28.6	48.4	62.5	77.5
	2005	26.9	33.2	51.3	52.5	64.8	80.9
	2010	59.7	78.5	78.8	75.7	99.7	76.0
	2015	100.0	100.0	100.0	100.0	100.0	100.0
	2016	107.0	96.4	101.7	105.3	94.8	111.0
	2017	110.7	99.5	104.3	106.1	95.4	111.3
	2018	113.3	96.1	106.0	106.9	90.7	117.9
	2019	121.5	95.5	110.3	110.1	86.6	127.1
Armenia (Armenian Dram)	1990	0.0	21.8	54.5	0.0	40.0	0.0
	1995	11.0	13.0	28.8	38.4	45.2	84.9
	2000	21.8	19.3	36.9	59.0	52.3	112.9
	2005	47.4	49.5	66.8	71.0	74.1	95.8
	2010	73.2	93.6	80.7	90.7	115.9	78.2
	2015	100.0	100.0	100.0	100.0	100.0	100.0
	2016	100.5	99.9	100.2	100.3	99.8	100.5
	2017	110.3	109.2	107.7	102.4	101.4	101.0
	2018	119.3	118.0	113.3	105.3	104.2	101.1
	2019	130.2	129.6	121.9	106.8	106.3	100.5
Azerbaijan (Azerbaijanian Manat)	1990	0.0	12.3	38.8	0.0	31.7	0.0
	1995	3.9	5.8	16.2	24.2	35.8	67.6
	2000	8.7	9.9	22.8	38.0	43.5	87.3
	2005	23.0	25.0	42.3	54.5	59.0	92.3
	2010	78.1	99.7	90.4	86.4	110.2	78.3
	2015	100.0	100.0	100.0	100.0	100.0	100.0
	2016	111.1	71.3	96.9	114.6	73.6	155.7
	2017	129.3	77.0	97.1	133.2	79.3	168.0
	2018	147.3	88.8	98.5	149.5	90.1	165.9
	2019	150.2	90.5	100.7	149.1	89.9	165.9
Bahrain (Bahraini Dinar)	1970	1.7	1.4	15.1	11.3	9.0	126.6
	1975	4.0	3.8	19.2	20.8	19.8	105.2
	1980	12.1	12.1	31.3	38.8	38.7	100.3
	1985	14.4	14.4	25.8	55.7	55.7	100.0
	1990	15.8	15.8	31.1	50.8	50.8	100.0
	1995	21.8	21.8	39.4	55.3	55.3	100.0
	2000	29.1	29.1	49.6	58.7	58.7	100.0
	2005	51.3	51.3	63.7	80.5	80.5	100.0
	2010	82.6	82.6	83.5	98.9	98.9	100.0
	2015	100.0	100.0	100.0	100.0	100.0	100.0
	2016	103.7	103.7	103.6	100.1	100.1	100.0
	2017	114.0	114.0	107.6	105.9	105.9	100.0

Table 7. Implicit price deflators of Gross Domestic Product in US Dollars and National Currency (2015 = 100)

Major area, region and country	Year	GDP in Current Prices: National Currency (1)	GDP in Current Prices: US Dollars (2)	Gross Domestic Product at Constant Prices (3)	GDP Implicit Price Deflators (2015 = 100): National Currency (4)	GDP Implicit Price Deflators (2015 = 100): US Dollars (5)	Exchange Rates (6)
	2018	121.0	121.0	109.5	110.5	110.5	100.0
	2019	123.9	123.9	111.5	111.1	111.1	100.0
Bangladesh (Taka)	1970	0.3	3.2	16.8	1.8	19.0	9.3
	1975	1.1	4.4	14.8	7.3	29.4	24.8
	1980	1.7	8.6	18.2	9.4	47.3	19.8
	1985	3.5	9.9	21.7	16.3	45.4	35.9
	1990	6.4	14.5	26.5	24.2	54.5	44.3
	1995	10.1	19.5	32.7	30.8	59.6	51.7
	2000	15.6	23.4	42.1	37.2	55.5	66.9
	2005	24.5	29.6	54.8	44.6	54.0	82.5
	2010	52.6	58.9	73.6	71.5	80.0	89.4
	2015	100.0	100.0	100.0	100.0	100.0	100.0
	2016	114.3	113.3	107.1	106.7	105.8	100.9
	2017	130.3	126.3	114.9	113.4	109.9	103.2
	2018	148.5	138.7	124.0	119.8	111.9	107.1
	2019	167.7	154.8	134.1	125.1	115.5	108.3
Bhutan (Ngultrum)	1970	0.4	3.1	5.1	7.1	60.4	11.7
	1975	0.6	4.3	5.5	10.3	79.2	13.1
	1980	0.8	6.4	7.6	10.4	84.6	12.3
	1985	1.7	8.6	10.5	15.8	81.9	19.3
	1990	3.7	13.7	20.0	18.6	68.2	27.3
	1995	7.3	14.4	24.1	30.3	59.9	50.5
	2000	15.4	21.9	33.8	45.4	64.8	70.1
	2005	28.1	40.9	49.5	56.8	82.6	68.7
	2010	56.4	79.1	77.9	72.4	101.6	71.3
	2015	100.0	100.0	100.0	100.0	100.0	100.0
	2016	112.9	107.8	108.1	104.4	99.7	104.7
	2017	124.1	122.3	113.2	109.7	108.1	101.5
	2018	130.2	122.1	116.6	111.7	104.7	106.6
	2019	140.5	128.0	121.0	116.1	105.8	109.8
Brunei Darussalam (Brunei Dollar)	1970	3.9	1.7	38.5	10.1	4.5	222.6
	1975	19.6	11.3	57.1	34.3	19.9	172.5
	1980	74.6	47.9	92.7	80.4	51.7	155.7
	1985	54.8	34.2	76.9	71.2	44.5	160.0
	1990	39.8	30.2	70.3	56.5	42.9	131.8
	1995	41.8	40.6	82.2	50.9	49.4	103.1
	2000	64.5	51.4	87.8	73.5	58.6	125.4
	2005	98.9	81.7	97.2	101.7	84.0	121.1
	2010	105.1	106.0	100.5	104.6	105.5	99.2
	2015	100.0	100.0	100.0	100.0	100.0	100.0
	2016	88.6	88.2	97.5	90.8	90.4	100.5
	2017	94.2	93.8	98.8	95.3	94.9	100.4
	2018	102.9	104.9	98.9	104.1	106.1	98.1
	2019	103.4	104.2	102.7	100.6	101.4	99.2
Cambodia (Riel)	1970	0.0	4.3	20.9	0.1	20.3	0.4
	1975	0.0	4.0	14.2	0.1	28.0	0.4
	1980	0.0	4.0	10.0	0.1	39.6	0.3
	1985	0.0	5.9	11.5	0.2	51.2	0.5
	1990	1.0	9.4	17.0	5.8	55.5	10.5

Table 7. Implicit price deflators of Gross Domestic Product in US Dollars and National Currency (2015 = 100)

Major area, region and country	Year	GDP in Current Prices: National Currency (1)	GDP in Current Prices: US Dollars (2)	Gross Domestic Product at Constant Prices (3)	GDP Implicit Price Deflators (2015 = 100): National Currency (4)	GDP Implicit Price Deflators (2015 = 100): US Dollars (5)	Exchange Rates (6)
	1995	11.0	18.3	23.2	47.6	79.1	60.3
	2000	19.2	20.3	32.7	58.6	62.0	94.4
	2005	35.1	34.9	51.2	68.5	68.1	100.6
	2010	64.1	62.3	70.7	90.6	88.1	102.9
	2015	100.0	100.0	100.0	100.0	100.0	100.0
	2016	110.6	110.9	106.9	103.5	103.8	99.8
	2017	122.3	122.9	114.4	107.0	107.4	99.6
	2018	135.6	136.1	123.1	110.1	110.6	99.6
	2019	149.8	150.1	131.5	113.9	114.1	99.8
China (Yuan Renminbi)	1970	0.3	0.8	2.1	15.8	40.0	39.5
	1975	0.4	1.5	2.8	15.8	52.9	29.9
	1980	0.7	2.8	3.8	17.4	72.2	24.1
	1985	1.3	2.8	6.4	20.8	44.1	47.2
	1990	2.7	3.6	9.3	29.4	38.3	76.8
	1995	8.9	6.6	16.6	53.7	40.0	134.1
	2000	14.6	11.0	25.1	58.0	43.6	132.9
	2005	27.2	20.7	40.1	67.9	51.6	131.6
	2010	59.8	55.0	68.3	87.6	80.6	108.7
	2015	100.0	100.0	100.0	100.0	100.0	100.0
	2016	108.4	101.6	106.8	101.4	95.0	106.7
	2017	120.8	111.3	114.3	105.7	97.4	108.5
	2018	133.4	125.6	122.0	109.4	103.0	106.2
	2019	143.8	129.7	129.4	111.1	100.2	110.9
China, Hong Kong SAR (Hong Kong Dollar)	1970	1.0	1.2	8.7	11.1	14.2	78.2
	1975	2.1	3.2	11.9	17.4	27.3	63.7
	1980	6.0	9.3	20.5	29.2	45.4	64.2
	1985	11.6	11.5	27.1	42.7	42.5	100.5
	1990	25.0	24.9	39.4	63.5	63.1	100.5
	1995	46.7	46.8	51.0	91.5	91.7	99.8
	2000	55.8	55.5	58.0	96.1	95.6	100.5
	2005	58.9	58.7	71.4	82.5	82.2	100.3
	2010	74.1	73.9	86.5	85.6	85.5	100.2
	2015	100.0	100.0	100.0	100.0	100.0	100.0
	2016	103.8	103.7	102.2	101.6	101.5	100.1
	2017	110.9	110.3	106.0	104.6	104.0	100.5
	2018	118.2	116.9	109.1	108.4	107.2	101.1
	2019	119.5	118.2	107.7	110.9	109.8	101.1
China, Macao SAR (Pataca)	1970	0.3	0.4	5.2	5.3	7.0	75.8
	1975	0.6	1.0	7.6	8.3	12.9	64.2
	1980	1.4	2.2	11.1	12.7	19.9	63.8
	1985	3.0	3.0	15.4	19.3	19.3	100.2
	1990	7.1	7.1	23.0	31.0	30.9	100.5
	1995	15.4	15.4	30.6	50.3	50.4	99.8
	2000	14.9	14.8	29.9	49.7	49.5	100.5
	2005	26.7	26.7	51.3	52.1	51.9	100.3
	2010	62.1	62.0	87.3	71.1	71.0	100.2
	2015	100.0	100.0	100.0	100.0	100.0	100.0
	2016	100.2	100.1	99.3	100.9	100.8	100.1
	2017	112.5	111.9	109.1	103.1	102.6	100.5
	2018	122.8	121.4	115.0	106.7	105.6	101.1

Table 7. Implicit price deflators of Gross Domestic Product in US Dollars and National Currency (2015 = 100)

Major area, region and country	Year	GDP in Current Prices: National Currency (1)	GDP in Current Prices: US Dollars (2)	Gross Domestic Product at Constant Prices (3)	GDP Implicit Price Deflators (2015 = 100): National Currency (4)	GDP Implicit Price Deflators (2015 = 100): US Dollars (5)	Exchange Rates (6)
	2019	120.0	118.7	109.6	109.5	108.3	101.1
Cyprus	1970	2.5	3.1	18.8	13.1	16.5	79.0
(Euro)	1975	2.8	4.0	15.7	17.8	25.4	69.9
	1980	8.2	12.2	26.9	30.4	45.5	66.9
	1985	15.9	13.7	35.3	45.1	38.8	116.1
	1990	27.5	31.7	49.5	55.5	64.0	86.8
	1995	43.1	50.2	63.8	67.5	78.7	85.7
	2000	59.4	50.4	78.3	75.9	64.3	117.9
	2005	83.1	94.5	95.4	87.1	99.1	87.9
	2010	108.9	130.0	108.8	100.1	119.5	83.7
	2015	100.0	100.0	100.0	100.0	100.0	100.0
	2016	105.9	105.6	106.7	99.2	98.9	100.3
	2017	112.4	114.5	111.4	100.9	102.8	98.2
	2018	118.6	126.3	115.9	102.3	108.9	93.9
	2019	123.1	124.2	119.7	102.9	103.8	99.1
D.P.R. of Korea	1970	0.7	30.3	46.7	1.5	64.7	2.4
(North Korean Won)	1975	1.2	49.6	76.7	1.5	64.7	2.4
	1980	1.4	60.7	93.7	1.5	64.7	2.4
	1985	1.7	74.2	112.4	1.5	66.0	2.3
	1990	1.8	90.3	113.7	1.6	79.4	2.0
	1995	0.6	29.8	90.3	0.7	33.0	2.0
	2000	1.3	65.1	86.1	1.5	75.6	2.0
	2005	102.9	80.0	97.5	105.5	82.0	128.5
	2010	80.3	85.6	97.0	82.7	88.3	93.7
	2015	100.0	100.0	100.0	100.0	100.0	100.0
	2016	103.3	103.1	103.9	99.4	99.3	100.2
	2017	106.8	106.6	100.3	106.6	106.4	100.2
	2018	104.8	107.4	96.1	109.0	111.8	97.5
	2019	100.3	100.3	96.4	104.0	104.0	100.0
Georgia	1990	0.0	59.4	113.3	0.0	52.4	0.0
(Lari)	1995	11.4	19.0	32.1	35.6	59.2	60.2
	2000	18.7	21.5	42.7	43.9	50.4	87.1
	2005	36.0	45.1	60.8	59.3	74.2	79.9
	2010	64.3	81.9	78.5	81.9	104.3	78.5
	2015	100.0	100.0	100.0	100.0	100.0	100.0
	2016	105.6	101.3	102.9	102.6	98.4	104.3
	2017	120.1	108.6	107.9	111.3	100.7	110.6
	2018	131.4	117.7	113.1	116.2	104.0	111.7
	2019	147.3	118.7	118.9	123.9	99.8	124.2
India	1970	0.3	2.9	9.6	3.5	30.4	11.7
(Indian Rupee)	1975	0.6	4.7	11.0	5.6	42.9	13.1
	1980	1.1	8.7	12.9	8.3	67.6	12.3
	1985	2.1	10.7	16.6	12.5	64.7	19.3
	1990	4.2	15.3	22.1	18.9	69.3	27.3
	1995	8.8	17.3	28.3	30.9	61.1	50.5
	2000	15.5	22.2	38.1	40.8	58.3	70.1
	2005	26.4	38.4	52.0	50.7	73.7	68.7
	2010	55.4	77.8	73.0	75.9	106.5	71.3
	2015	100.0	100.0	100.0	100.0	100.0	100.0

Table 7. Implicit price deflators of Gross Domestic Product in US Dollars and National Currency (2015 = 100)

Major area, region and country	Year	GDP in Current Prices: National Currency (1)	GDP in Current Prices: US Dollars (2)	Gross Domestic Product at Constant Prices (3)	GDP Implicit Price Deflators (2015 = 100): National Currency (4)	GDP Implicit Price Deflators (2015 = 100): US Dollars (5)	Exchange Rates (6)
	2016	111.8	106.7	108.3	103.2	98.6	104.7
	2017	124.2	122.3	115.9	107.1	105.5	101.5
	2018	137.8	129.2	123.0	112.0	105.1	106.6
	2019	147.9	134.7	128.2	115.4	105.1	109.8
Indonesia (Rupiah)	1970	0.0	1.2	7.7	0.4	15.8	2.7
	1975	0.1	4.1	11.3	1.1	36.7	3.1
	1980	0.5	9.8	16.5	2.8	59.7	4.7
	1985	1.0	11.9	21.7	4.5	54.6	8.3
	1990	2.1	15.5	30.4	7.1	51.2	13.8
	1995	4.6	27.5	44.2	10.4	62.1	16.8
	2000	12.8	20.4	45.9	28.0	44.5	62.9
	2005	25.6	35.4	57.8	44.3	61.2	72.5
	2010	59.6	87.7	76.4	77.9	114.8	67.9
	2015	100.0	100.0	100.0	100.0	100.0	100.0
	2016	107.6	108.3	105.0	102.4	103.1	99.4
	2017	117.9	118.0	110.4	106.8	106.9	99.9
	2018	128.7	121.1	116.1	110.9	104.3	106.3
	2019	137.4	130.0	121.9	112.7	106.7	105.7
Iran (Islamic Republic of) (Iranian Rial)	1970	0.0	2.8	37.2	0.0	7.5	0.3
	1975	0.0	13.3	54.9	0.1	24.1	0.2
	1980	0.1	24.3	38.0	0.2	64.0	0.2
	1985	0.1	19.4	46.4	0.3	41.8	0.7
	1990	0.3	24.5	47.3	0.7	51.8	1.4
	1995	1.7	29.1	54.6	3.2	53.3	5.9
	2000	5.6	28.4	65.9	8.5	43.0	19.8
	2005	17.8	57.6	84.0	21.2	68.5	30.9
	2010	44.1	124.8	102.2	43.2	122.2	35.3
	2015	100.0	100.0	100.0	100.0	100.0	100.0
	2016	115.2	108.1	113.4	101.6	95.4	106.6
	2017	134.2	117.2	117.7	114.1	99.6	114.5
	2018	165.4	117.4	111.3	148.6	105.5	140.9
	2019	222.2	153.5	104.0	213.6	147.5	144.8
Iraq (Iraqi Dinar)	1970	0.0	2.0	15.8	0.0	12.5	0.1
	1975	0.0	4.1	23.9	0.0	17.2	0.2
	1980	0.0	10.5	43.2	0.1	24.3	0.3
	1985	0.0	10.1	32.2	0.1	31.4	0.3
	1990	0.1	14.3	39.1	0.1	36.6	0.4
	1995	4.2	2.9	19.3	21.7	15.1	143.4
	2000	29.1	14.2	56.5	51.5	25.1	205.0
	2005	37.8	30.0	56.4	67.0	53.1	126.1
	2010	83.2	83.1	72.3	115.2	114.9	100.2
	2015	100.0	100.0	100.0	100.0	100.0	100.0
	2016	101.2	99.9	113.8	88.9	87.8	101.3
	2017	115.9	114.3	109.5	105.9	104.4	101.4
	2018	130.9	129.2	110.4	118.5	117.0	101.3
	2019	136.7	135.1	115.3	118.6	117.1	101.3
Israel (New Israeli Sheqel)	1970	0.0	2.0	14.1	0.0	14.3	0.0
	1975	0.0	4.8	20.3	0.0	23.8	0.0
	1980	0.0	8.0	23.5	0.0	34.0	0.1

Table 7. Implicit price deflators of Gross Domestic Product in US Dollars and National Currency (2015 = 100)

Major area, region and country	Year	GDP in Current Prices: National Currency (1)	GDP in Current Prices: US Dollars (2)	Gross Domestic Product at Constant Prices (3)	GDP Implicit Price Deflators (2015 = 100): National Currency (4)	GDP Implicit Price Deflators (2015 = 100): US Dollars (5)	Exchange Rates (6)
	1985	2.8	9.1	27.4	10.1	33.4	30.3
	1990	10.2	19.6	34.0	29.9	57.7	51.9
	1995	25.9	33.5	48.0	54.1	69.8	77.5
	2000	46.3	44.1	61.6	75.2	71.6	104.9
	2005	54.9	47.5	68.0	80.7	69.9	115.5
	2010	75.1	78.0	84.1	89.2	92.8	96.2
	2015	100.0	100.0	100.0	100.0	100.0	100.0
	2016	105.1	106.4	104.0	101.1	102.3	98.8
	2017	109.1	117.8	107.7	101.3	109.4	92.6
	2018	114.2	123.6	111.4	102.5	111.0	92.4
	2019	120.9	131.8	115.3	104.8	114.3	91.7
Japan (Yen)	1970	14.4	4.8	32.6	44.2	14.9	297.4
	1975	29.1	11.9	40.7	71.6	29.2	245.2
	1980	47.2	25.2	50.4	93.6	49.9	187.3
	1985	62.8	31.9	61.8	101.6	51.6	197.1
	1990	85.4	71.4	78.5	108.7	90.9	119.6
	1995	96.5	124.1	84.6	114.1	146.8	77.7
	2000	99.1	111.3	89.3	111.0	124.7	89.0
	2005	98.6	108.3	94.7	104.1	114.4	91.1
	2010	94.2	129.9	95.2	98.9	136.4	72.5
	2015	100.0	100.0	100.0	100.0	100.0	100.0
	2016	100.8	112.1	100.5	100.3	111.6	89.9
	2017	102.7	110.9	102.7	100.0	108.0	92.7
	2018	103.0	112.9	103.0	99.9	109.6	91.2
	2019	104.3	115.8	103.7	100.5	111.6	90.1
Jordan (Jordanian Dinar)	1970	0.8	1.6	13.2	6.1	12.0	50.3
	1975	1.5	3.3	13.0	11.3	25.1	45.0
	1980	4.5	10.7	24.8	18.2	43.3	42.0
	1985	7.6	13.7	30.8	24.7	44.4	55.6
	1990	10.0	10.7	30.1	33.4	35.7	93.5
	1995	17.7	18.0	40.7	43.6	44.2	98.6
	2000	22.6	22.6	47.6	47.4	47.5	99.9
	2005	33.6	33.6	64.9	51.8	51.9	99.9
	2010	70.3	70.3	87.4	80.5	80.5	100.0
	2015	100.0	100.0	100.0	100.0	100.0	100.0
	2016	103.4	103.4	102.0	101.4	101.4	100.0
	2017	107.3	107.3	104.1	103.1	103.1	100.0
	2018	111.3	111.3	106.1	104.8	104.8	100.0
	2019	115.3	115.3	108.2	106.6	106.6	100.0
Kazakhstan (Tenge)	1990	0.0	16.1	51.7	0.0	31.1	0.0
	1995	2.5	11.1	31.7	7.8	35.1	22.3
	2000	6.4	9.9	35.9	17.7	27.6	64.1
	2005	18.6	31.0	58.8	31.6	52.7	59.9
	2010	53.4	80.3	79.5	67.1	101.0	66.5
	2015	100.0	100.0	100.0	100.0	100.0	100.0
	2016	114.9	74.5	101.1	113.6	73.6	154.3
	2017	133.0	90.5	105.2	126.4	86.0	147.0
	2018	151.2	97.3	109.6	138.0	88.8	155.5
	2019	170.1	98.5	114.5	148.5	86.1	172.6

Table 7. Implicit price deflators of Gross Domestic Product in US Dollars and National Currency (2015 = 100)

Major area, region and country	Year	GDP in Current Prices: National Currency (1)	GDP in Current Prices: US Dollars (2)	Gross Domestic Product at Constant Prices (3)	GDP Implicit Price Deflators (2015 = 100): National Currency (4)	GDP Implicit Price Deflators (2015 = 100): US Dollars (5)	Exchange Rates (6)
Kuwait	1970	3.0	2.5	48.9	6.1	5.1	118.7
(Kuwaiti Dinar)	1975	10.1	10.5	38.8	26.0	27.0	96.4
	1980	22.5	25.0	39.2	57.4	63.9	89.8
	1985	18.7	18.7	30.5	61.3	61.4	100.0
	1990	15.5	16.1	29.9	51.7	53.9	95.9
	1995	23.0	23.2	47.5	48.4	48.8	99.2
	2000	33.6	32.9	53.5	62.8	61.6	102.0
	2005	68.4	70.5	79.0	86.7	89.3	97.1
	2010	96.0	100.7	83.7	114.7	120.4	95.3
	2015	100.0	100.0	100.0	100.0	100.0	100.0
	2016	95.9	95.5	102.9	93.2	92.8	100.4
	2017	106.2	105.3	98.1	108.3	107.4	100.8
	2018	123.2	122.8	99.3	124.1	123.6	100.4
	2019	118.6	117.5	99.7	118.9	117.8	100.9
Kyrgyzstan	1990	0.0	39.1	79.1	0.0	49.4	0.0
(Som)	1995	3.8	22.3	40.1	9.4	55.7	16.8
	2000	15.2	20.5	52.7	28.8	38.9	74.0
	2005	23.4	36.8	63.4	36.9	58.1	63.6
	2010	51.2	71.8	78.8	64.9	91.1	71.3
	2015	100.0	100.0	100.0	100.0	100.0	100.0
	2016	110.6	102.0	104.3	106.1	97.8	108.5
	2017	123.2	115.3	109.3	112.8	105.5	106.8
	2018	132.3	123.9	113.4	116.6	109.2	106.8
	2019	137.1	126.6	118.5	115.7	106.8	108.3
Lao People's DR	1970	0.0	0.8	7.3	0.0	11.4	0.0
(Kip)	1975	0.0	1.5	9.5	0.0	15.7	0.0
	1980	0.0	2.3	10.4	0.0	22.2	0.2
	1985	0.1	4.4	15.2	0.5	28.6	1.7
	1990	0.5	6.3	18.8	2.9	33.4	8.7
	1995	1.3	12.9	25.3	5.0	50.8	9.9
	2000	12.1	12.6	34.2	35.6	36.7	96.8
	2005	26.8	20.5	46.9	57.1	43.7	130.8
	2010	51.5	50.8	68.8	74.9	73.9	101.4
	2015	100.0	100.0	100.0	100.0	100.0	100.0
	2016	110.3	109.8	107.0	103.0	102.6	100.4
	2017	120.0	118.6	114.4	104.9	103.7	101.2
	2018	130.0	126.1	121.5	106.9	103.7	103.1
	2019	139.3	130.8	127.2	109.5	102.8	106.5
Lebanon	1970	0.0	4.0	43.2	0.0	9.2	0.2
(Lebanese Pound)	1975	0.0	8.7	39.5	0.0	22.1	0.2
	1980	0.0	10.9	34.2	0.1	31.9	0.2
	1985	0.0	4.6	47.9	0.1	9.5	1.1
	1990	2.7	5.9	27.2	10.0	21.7	46.1
	1995	24.8	23.0	48.4	51.2	47.6	107.6
	2000	33.4	33.4	52.0	64.2	64.2	100.0
	2005	43.0	43.0	62.9	68.4	68.4	100.0
	2010	77.0	77.0	90.7	84.9	84.9	100.0
	2015	100.0	100.0	100.0	100.0	100.0	100.0
	2016	102.5	102.5	101.5	101.0	101.0	100.0

Table 7. Implicit price deflators of Gross Domestic Product in US Dollars and National Currency (2015 = 100)

Major area, region and country	Year	GDP in Current Prices: National Currency (1)	GDP in Current Prices: US Dollars (2)	Gross Domestic Product at Constant Prices (3)	GDP Implicit Price Deflators (2015 = 100): National Currency (4)	GDP Implicit Price Deflators (2015 = 100): US Dollars (5)	Exchange Rates (6)
	2017	106.4	106.4	102.4	103.9	103.9	100.0
	2018	110.1	110.1	100.4	109.6	109.6	100.0
	2019	106.9	106.9	94.8	112.8	112.8	100.0
Malaysia	1970	1.0	1.3	5.7	17.8	22.6	78.4
(Malaysian Ringgit)	1975	1.9	3.1	9.3	20.4	33.3	61.3
	1980	4.5	8.1	14.0	32.4	58.1	55.7
	1985	6.6	10.4	17.9	36.7	57.7	63.6
	1990	10.1	14.6	24.8	40.9	59.0	69.3
	1995	18.9	29.5	38.9	48.5	75.7	64.1
	2000	30.3	31.1	49.2	61.5	63.3	97.3
	2005	46.2	47.6	62.0	74.5	76.8	97.0
	2010	69.8	84.6	77.2	90.4	109.6	82.5
	2015	100.0	100.0	100.0	100.0	100.0	100.0
	2016	106.2	100.0	104.4	101.7	95.7	106.2
	2017	116.6	105.9	110.5	105.5	95.8	110.1
	2018	123.0	119.0	115.8	106.2	102.8	103.3
	2019	128.4	121.0	120.8	106.3	100.2	106.1
Maldives	1970	0.3	1.0	4.6	6.9	22.3	30.9
(Rufiyaa)	1975	0.5	1.3	4.9	9.9	26.5	37.5
	1980	1.1	2.3	8.3	13.4	27.3	49.1
	1985	1.9	4.0	15.0	12.4	26.9	46.2
	1990	4.2	6.8	24.7	17.2	27.7	62.2
	1995	10.6	13.8	34.3	30.8	40.2	76.6
	2000	16.5	21.6	47.5	34.8	45.4	76.6
	2005	23.6	28.3	51.2	46.0	55.2	83.3
	2010	52.5	63.0	75.8	69.2	83.0	83.3
	2015	100.0	100.0	100.0	100.0	100.0	100.0
	2016	106.6	106.6	106.3	100.2	100.2	100.0
	2017	115.8	115.7	114.0	101.6	101.5	100.1
	2018	129.2	129.0	123.3	104.8	104.6	100.2
	2019	137.4	137.3	131.9	104.2	104.1	100.1
Mongolia	1970	0.0	1.7	11.2	0.3	15.4	1.8
(Tugrik)	1975	0.0	3.1	14.7	0.3	21.2	1.3
	1980	0.1	5.9	19.6	0.3	30.0	0.9
	1985	0.1	10.6	27.2	0.3	38.7	0.7
	1990	0.1	14.9	32.9	0.2	45.2	0.5
	1995	3.3	14.6	28.7	11.6	51.0	22.8
	2000	6.1	11.2	32.9	18.7	34.2	54.6
	2005	15.2	24.9	45.0	33.9	55.4	61.2
	2010	42.1	61.2	61.6	68.5	99.4	68.9
	2015	100.0	100.0	100.0	100.0	100.0	100.0
	2016	103.4	95.2	102.0	101.4	93.3	108.6
	2017	120.4	97.2	107.6	112.0	90.4	123.8
	2018	140.0	111.6	115.1	121.6	96.9	125.5
	2019	159.4	117.9	120.7	132.0	97.7	135.2
Myanmar	1970	0.0	4.3	6.7	0.3	63.9	0.4
(Kyat)	1975	0.0	6.3	7.6	0.5	82.7	0.5
	1980	0.1	9.8	10.1	0.5	96.5	0.6
	1985	0.1	10.6	12.3	0.6	86.4	0.7

Table 7. Implicit price deflators of Gross Domestic Product in US Dollars and National Currency (2015 = 100)

Major area, region and country	Year	GDP in Current Prices		Gross Domestic Product at Constant Prices (3)	GDP Implicit Price Deflators (2015 = 100)		Exchange Rates (6)
		National Currency (1)	US Dollars (2)		National Currency (4)	US Dollars (5)	
	1990	0.2	9.7	11.1	2.1	87.3	2.4
	1995	0.9	15.0	15.2	6.2	98.6	6.3
	2000	4.1	13.6	23.2	17.7	58.7	30.2
	2005	19.6	22.2	42.9	45.8	51.7	88.6
	2010	58.0	70.3	70.3	82.5	99.9	82.6
	2015	100.0	100.0	100.0	100.0	100.0	100.0
	2016	111.4	104.9	105.8	105.4	99.2	106.2
	2017	124.8	106.6	112.5	110.9	94.8	117.0
	2018	141.8	115.3	120.1	118.1	96.0	123.0
	2019	157.1	120.3	123.6	127.1	97.3	130.6
Nepal (Nepalese Rupee)	1970	0.5	5.0	17.2	2.9	29.1	9.9
	1975	0.8	7.8	18.8	4.4	41.3	10.7
	1980	1.2	10.0	21.1	5.6	47.5	11.7
	1985	2.3	13.2	26.8	8.7	49.1	17.8
	1990	5.2	18.2	33.6	15.5	54.2	28.7
	1995	11.0	21.8	43.2	25.6	50.4	50.7
	2000	19.1	27.5	54.7	35.0	50.4	69.4
	2005	27.7	39.7	65.1	42.5	61.0	69.7
	2010	56.0	78.3	80.9	69.2	96.7	71.5
	2015	100.0	100.0	100.0	100.0	100.0	100.0
	2016	105.8	100.9	100.6	105.2	100.3	104.9
	2017	125.6	123.0	108.9	115.3	113.0	102.1
	2018	142.9	134.4	116.2	123.1	115.7	106.4
	2019	162.4	147.7	124.3	130.7	118.8	110.0
Oman (Rial Omani)	1970	0.4	0.4	6.2	6.9	6.4	108.4
	1975	2.9	3.2	9.6	29.9	33.3	89.8
	1980	8.2	9.1	17.1	48.0	53.4	89.8
	1985	13.5	15.0	33.0	40.9	45.5	89.8
	1990	16.9	16.9	38.1	44.4	44.4	100.0
	1995	20.0	20.0	50.6	39.4	39.4	100.0
	2000	28.5	28.5	59.7	47.8	47.8	100.0
	2005	45.4	45.4	62.3	73.0	73.0	100.0
	2010	83.2	83.2	80.1	103.9	103.9	100.0
	2015	100.0	100.0	100.0	100.0	100.0	100.0
	2016	95.7	95.7	105.1	91.1	91.1	100.0
	2017	103.2	103.2	105.5	97.9	97.9	100.0
	2018	116.7	116.7	106.4	109.6	109.6	100.0
	2019	111.6	111.6	105.6	105.7	105.7	100.0
Pakistan (Pakistan Rupee)	1970	0.2	4.9	12.7	1.8	38.6	4.6
	1975	0.5	5.5	15.2	3.5	36.3	9.6
	1980	1.1	11.6	20.3	5.5	57.2	9.6
	1985	2.3	14.5	27.9	8.1	52.1	15.5
	1990	4.1	19.3	37.0	11.0	52.3	21.1
	1995	8.9	28.9	46.4	19.2	62.4	30.8
	2000	15.0	28.8	54.4	27.6	52.9	52.2
	2005	25.5	44.1	69.5	36.7	63.5	57.9
	2010	54.2	65.4	82.2	65.9	79.5	82.9
	2015	100.0	100.0	100.0	100.0	100.0	100.0
	2016	105.9	103.9	105.5	100.4	98.5	101.9
	2017	116.3	113.4	111.4	104.4	101.8	102.6

Table 7. Implicit price deflators of Gross Domestic Product in US Dollars and National Currency (2015 = 100)

Major area, region and country	Year	GDP in Current Prices: National Currency (1)	GDP in Current Prices: US Dollars (2)	Gross Domestic Product at Constant Prices (3)	GDP Implicit Price Deflators (2015 = 100): National Currency (4)	GDP Implicit Price Deflators (2015 = 100): US Dollars (5)	Exchange Rates (6)
	2018	126.1	106.4	117.9	107.0	90.3	118.5
	2019	140.5	96.2	121.8	115.3	79.0	146.0
Philippines	1970	0.3	2.5	16.9	1.9	15.0	13.0
(Philippine Peso)	1975	0.9	5.6	22.4	4.0	25.2	15.9
	1980	2.0	12.3	30.1	6.7	40.9	16.5
	1985	4.8	11.6	28.2	16.9	41.3	40.9
	1990	9.0	16.8	35.5	25.2	47.2	53.4
	1995	15.9	28.0	39.5	40.1	70.9	56.5
	2000	26.9	27.7	47.1	57.0	58.7	97.1
	2005	42.6	35.2	59.0	72.3	59.7	121.1
	2010	67.6	68.2	75.0	90.1	90.9	99.1
	2015	100.0	100.0	100.0	100.0	100.0	100.0
	2016	108.7	104.1	106.9	101.7	97.4	104.4
	2017	118.7	107.1	114.0	104.1	93.9	110.8
	2018	130.8	113.0	121.1	108.0	93.3	115.7
	2019	139.7	122.7	128.3	108.9	95.7	113.8
Qatar	1970	0.4	0.3	5.8	7.5	5.7	130.8
(Qatari Rial)	1975	1.6	1.5	8.8	18.7	17.3	108.0
	1980	4.9	4.8	10.0	48.5	48.3	100.5
	1985	3.8	3.8	9.5	40.1	40.1	100.0
	1990	4.6	4.6	11.6	39.2	39.2	100.0
	1995	5.0	5.0	13.0	38.6	38.6	100.0
	2000	11.0	11.0	22.2	49.5	49.5	100.0
	2005	27.5	27.5	32.8	83.9	83.9	100.0
	2010	77.4	77.4	75.1	103.0	103.0	100.0
	2015	100.0	100.0	100.0	100.0	100.0	100.0
	2016	93.8	93.8	102.1	91.9	91.9	100.0
	2017	103.2	103.2	103.7	99.5	99.5	100.0
	2018	118.3	118.3	105.3	112.4	112.4	100.0
	2019	113.4	113.4	105.1	107.9	107.9	100.0
Republic of Korea	1970	0.2	0.6	4.3	3.9	14.1	27.5
(Won)	1975	0.6	1.5	7.0	9.1	21.3	42.8
	1980	2.4	4.5	10.5	22.7	42.3	53.7
	1985	5.3	6.9	16.6	32.1	41.7	76.9
	1990	12.1	19.3	27.4	44.2	70.6	62.6
	1995	26.4	38.7	41.3	63.9	93.7	68.2
	2000	39.3	39.3	54.5	72.1	72.1	100.0
	2005	57.7	63.8	69.7	82.9	91.5	90.5
	2010	79.8	78.1	86.0	92.7	90.7	102.2
	2015	100.0	100.0	100.0	100.0	100.0	100.0
	2016	105.0	102.3	102.9	102.0	99.4	102.6
	2017	110.7	110.8	106.2	104.3	104.3	99.9
	2018	114.5	117.7	109.3	104.8	107.7	97.3
	2019	115.7	112.3	111.5	103.8	100.7	103.0
Saudi Arabia	1970	1.0	0.8	19.0	5.2	4.3	120.0
(Saudi Riyal)	1975	6.7	7.1	37.1	18.1	19.3	93.8
	1980	22.3	25.1	52.4	42.6	48.0	88.7
	1985	15.3	15.9	30.6	50.2	51.9	96.6
	1990	18.0	18.0	43.3	41.5	41.5	100.0

Table 7. Implicit price deflators of Gross Domestic Product in US Dollars and National Currency (2015 = 100)

Major area, region and country	Year	GDP in Current Prices		Gross Domestic Product at Constant Prices (3)	GDP Implicit Price Deflators (2015 = 100)		Exchange Rates (6)
		National Currency (1)	US Dollars (2)		National Currency (4)	US Dollars (5)	
	1995	21.9	21.9	51.5	42.5	42.5	100.0
	2000	29.0	29.0	55.9	51.8	51.8	100.0
	2005	50.2	50.2	68.0	73.8	73.8	99.9
	2010	80.7	80.7	77.8	103.7	103.7	100.0
	2015	100.0	100.0	100.0	100.0	100.0	100.0
	2016	98.6	98.6	101.7	97.0	97.0	100.0
	2017	105.2	105.2	100.9	104.3	104.3	100.0
	2018	120.2	120.2	103.4	116.3	116.3	100.0
	2019	121.2	121.2	103.7	116.9	116.9	100.0
Singapore..	1970	1.4	0.6	4.7	29.5	13.2	222.7
(Singapore Dollar)	1975	3.2	1.9	7.3	44.3	25.7	172.5
	1980	6.1	3.9	10.9	55.9	35.9	155.7
	1985	9.7	6.0	15.2	63.4	39.6	160.0
	1990	16.6	12.6	23.0	72.4	54.9	131.8
	1995	29.4	28.5	34.7	84.6	82.0	103.1
	2000	39.1	31.2	45.6	85.8	68.4	125.4
	2005	50.2	41.5	57.8	86.9	71.8	121.1
	2010	77.2	77.9	80.2	96.3	97.1	99.2
	2015	100.0	100.0	100.0	100.0	100.0	100.0
	2016	104.0	103.5	103.2	100.7	100.2	100.5
	2017	111.5	111.0	107.7	103.5	103.0	100.4
	2018	118.9	121.2	111.4	106.7	108.7	98.1
	2019	119.9	120.8	112.2	106.8	107.6	99.2
Sri Lanka..	1970	0.2	3.5	11.6	1.3	30.1	4.4
(Sri Lanka Rupee)	1975	0.3	5.6	13.4	2.2	41.8	5.2
	1980	0.7	6.1	17.7	4.2	34.3	12.2
	1985	1.7	8.5	22.7	7.5	37.5	20.0
	1990	3.4	11.6	26.8	12.8	43.4	29.5
	1995	7.2	19.0	35.0	20.5	54.3	37.7
	2000	13.5	23.7	44.7	30.1	53.1	56.7
	2005	25.6	34.7	54.4	47.1	63.7	74.0
	2010	58.6	70.4	74.2	79.0	94.9	83.2
	2015	100.0	100.0	100.0	100.0	100.0	100.0
	2016	109.5	102.2	104.5	104.8	97.8	107.2
	2017	121.7	108.5	108.2	112.5	100.2	112.2
	2018	131.2	109.7	111.8	117.3	98.1	119.6
	2019	137.1	104.2	114.4	119.9	91.1	131.6
State of Palestine..................................	1970	1.3	1.3	7.3	17.4	17.4	100.0
(US Dollar)	1975	4.1	4.1	11.5	36.0	36.0	100.0
	1980	7.7	7.7	16.7	46.0	46.0	100.0
	1985	7.2	7.2	17.1	42.1	42.1	100.0
	1990	13.9	13.9	23.8	58.3	58.3	100.0
	1995	23.5	23.5	38.8	60.6	60.6	100.0
	2000	30.9	30.9	50.9	60.6	60.6	100.0
	2005	36.7	36.7	62.6	58.6	58.6	100.0
	2010	69.3	69.3	79.3	87.4	87.4	100.0
	2015	100.0	100.0	100.0	100.0	100.0	100.0
	2016	110.3	110.3	108.9	101.3	101.3	100.0
	2017	115.4	115.4	110.4	104.5	104.5	100.0
	2018	116.5	116.5	111.8	104.2	104.2	100.0

Table 7. Implicit price deflators of Gross Domestic Product in US Dollars and National Currency (2015 = 100)

Major area, region and country	Year	GDP in Current Prices: National Currency (1)	GDP in Current Prices: US Dollars (2)	Gross Domestic Product at Constant Prices (3)	GDP Implicit Price Deflators (2015 = 100): National Currency (4)	GDP Implicit Price Deflators (2015 = 100): US Dollars (5)	Exchange Rates (6)
	2019	122.1	122.1	112.8	108.2	108.2	100.0
Syrian Arab Republic	1970	0.2	9.2	27.0	0.6	34.0	1.6
(Syrian Pound)	1975	0.5	27.8	50.4	0.9	55.2	1.6
	1980	1.1	68.9	69.7	1.6	98.8	1.6
	1985	1.8	52.6	80.5	2.3	65.4	3.5
	1990	5.9	58.5	76.6	7.7	76.3	10.1
	1995	12.6	70.9	113.2	11.1	62.7	17.8
	2000	20.0	103.0	135.4	14.8	76.1	19.4
	2005	33.3	148.8	173.1	19.2	85.9	22.4
	2010	61.7	316.7	219.9	28.1	144.0	19.5
	2015	100.0	100.0	100.0	100.0	100.0	100.0
	2016	125.9	64.8	96.0	131.1	67.5	194.2
	2017	145.2	69.9	94.6	153.6	73.9	207.8
	2018	156.9	85.7	97.1	161.6	88.2	183.1
	2019	201.6	106.8	101.8	198.0	104.9	188.8
Tajikistan	1990	0.0	36.1	90.4	0.0	40.0	0.0
(Somoni)	1995	0.1	15.5	34.4	0.4	45.1	0.9
	2000	3.7	11.0	34.4	10.7	31.9	33.7
	2005	14.9	29.4	54.6	27.3	53.9	50.6
	2010	51.0	71.8	74.8	68.3	96.1	71.1
	2015	100.0	100.0	100.0	100.0	100.0	100.0
	2016	112.5	88.5	106.9	105.2	82.8	127.1
	2017	133.1	95.9	120.6	110.4	79.6	138.7
	2018	146.8	98.9	129.2	113.7	76.5	148.5
	2019	164.1	106.1	138.8	118.2	76.4	154.6
Thailand	1970	1.1	1.8	8.6	12.9	21.3	60.7
(Baht)	1975	2.3	3.9	11.4	20.3	34.0	59.5
	1980	5.0	8.4	16.6	30.0	50.2	59.8
	1985	8.0	10.0	21.7	36.7	46.3	79.3
	1990	16.5	22.0	35.4	46.5	62.2	74.7
	1995	30.7	42.2	53.2	57.6	79.2	72.7
	2000	36.9	31.5	55.2	66.8	57.1	117.1
	2005	55.4	47.2	71.9	77.0	65.6	117.4
	2010	78.6	85.0	86.5	91.0	98.3	92.5
	2015	100.0	100.0	100.0	100.0	100.0	100.0
	2016	105.9	102.8	103.4	102.5	99.4	103.1
	2017	112.4	113.5	107.5	104.6	105.5	99.1
	2018	118.7	125.8	112.0	106.0	112.4	94.3
	2019	122.4	135.1	114.6	106.8	117.8	90.7
Timor-Leste	1990	12.7	12.7	45.5	28.0	28.0	100.0
(US Dollar)	1995	26.1	26.1	70.1	37.2	37.2	100.0
	2000	23.0	23.0	52.2	44.1	44.1	100.0
	2005	29.0	29.0	57.3	50.6	50.6	100.0
	2010	55.3	55.3	81.2	68.1	68.1	100.0
	2015	100.0	100.0	100.0	100.0	100.0	100.0
	2016	103.5	103.5	103.4	100.2	100.2	100.0
	2017	100.3	100.3	99.1	101.2	101.2	100.0
	2018	97.8	97.8	98.1	99.8	99.8	100.0
	2019	126.6	126.6	116.4	108.7	108.7	100.0

Table 7. Implicit price deflators of Gross Domestic Product in US Dollars and National Currency (2015 = 100)

Major area, region and country	Year	GDP in Current Prices: National Currency (1)	GDP in Current Prices: US Dollars (2)	Gross Domestic Product at Constant Prices (3)	GDP Implicit Price Deflators (2015 = 100): National Currency (4)	GDP Implicit Price Deflators (2015 = 100): US Dollars (5)	Exchange Rates (6)
Turkey	1970	0.0	2.9	13.5	0.0	21.6	0.0
(New Turkish Lira)	1975	0.0	7.4	17.8	0.0	41.7	0.0
	1980	0.0	11.0	20.0	0.0	54.7	0.0
	1985	0.0	10.7	25.4	0.0	42.2	0.0
	1990	0.0	24.0	33.3	0.1	72.1	0.1
	1995	0.5	27.0	39.0	1.2	69.2	1.7
	2000	7.3	31.7	47.9	15.2	66.3	23.0
	2005	28.9	58.6	60.8	47.6	96.4	49.4
	2010	49.7	89.9	71.1	69.9	126.5	55.3
	2015	100.0	100.0	100.0	100.0	100.0	100.0
	2016	111.7	100.6	103.3	108.1	97.4	111.0
	2017	133.3	99.4	111.1	120.0	89.5	134.1
	2018	159.9	90.1	114.4	139.8	78.7	177.5
	2019	183.8	88.1	115.4	159.2	76.3	208.6
Turkmenistan	1990	0.0	8.5	36.7	0.0	23.2	0.0
(Turkmenistan Manat)	1995	0.1	6.1	23.2	0.4	26.2	1.7
	2000	4.1	13.7	28.9	14.2	47.4	29.9
	2005	14.3	39.3	37.0	38.5	106.2	36.2
	2010	51.4	62.6	60.7	84.7	103.3	82.0
	2015	100.0	100.0	100.0	100.0	100.0	100.0
	2016	101.0	100.3	106.2	95.1	94.5	100.7
	2017	105.9	105.2	113.1	93.7	93.0	100.7
	2018	113.8	113.0	120.0	94.8	94.2	100.7
	2019	134.9	133.9	123.6	109.1	108.3	100.7
United Arab Emirates	1970	0.4	0.3	8.0	4.8	3.7	129.7
(UAE Dirham)	1975	4.5	4.2	14.7	30.6	28.4	107.9
	1980	12.5	12.3	30.5	40.8	40.4	100.9
	1985	11.5	11.5	27.9	41.2	41.2	100.0
	1990	14.3	14.3	31.3	45.8	45.8	100.0
	1995	18.6	18.6	38.8	47.9	47.9	100.0
	2000	29.5	29.5	53.2	55.5	55.5	100.0
	2005	51.1	51.1	69.0	74.0	74.0	100.0
	2010	80.9	80.9	77.7	104.1	104.1	100.0
	2015	100.0	100.0	100.0	100.0	100.0	100.0
	2016	99.7	99.7	103.1	96.7	96.7	100.0
	2017	107.7	107.7	105.5	102.1	102.1	100.0
	2018	117.9	117.9	106.8	110.4	110.4	100.0
	2019	117.6	117.6	108.6	108.3	108.3	100.0
Uzbekistan	1990	0.0	21.6	36.1	0.0	59.7	0.0
(Uzbekistan Sum)	1995	0.2	19.8	29.3	0.6	67.4	0.9
	2000	1.9	20.2	35.6	5.2	56.8	9.2
	2005	9.0	20.9	46.4	19.4	45.0	43.1
	2010	35.2	57.3	69.7	50.5	82.2	61.5
	2015	100.0	100.0	100.0	100.0	100.0	100.0
	2016	115.4	99.9	106.1	108.7	94.2	115.5
	2017	143.9	72.3	110.8	129.9	65.2	199.1
	2018	193.5	61.6	116.9	165.6	52.7	314.2
	2019	243.5	70.8	123.4	197.4	57.4	344.1

Table 7. Implicit price deflators of Gross Domestic Product in US Dollars and National Currency (2015 = 100)

Major area, region and country	Year	GDP in Current Prices		Gross Domestic Product at Constant Prices (3)	GDP Implicit Price Deflators (2015 = 100)		Exchange Rates (6)
		National Currency (1)	US Dollars (2)		National Currency (4)	US Dollars (5)	
Viet Nam (Dong)	1970	0.0	1.4	7.5	0.0	19.2	0.0
	1975	0.0	2.0	8.2	0.0	24.5	0.0
	1980	0.0	1.2	10.9	0.0	11.4	0.0
	1985	0.0	2.5	15.3	0.0	16.2	0.1
	1990	1.0	3.3	18.7	5.3	17.9	29.9
	1995	5.5	10.7	27.8	19.7	38.6	50.9
	2000	10.5	16.1	38.9	27.1	41.5	65.3
	2005	21.8	29.8	55.2	39.5	54.0	73.1
	2010	51.5	60.0	75.0	68.6	80.0	85.8
	2015	100.0	100.0	100.0	100.0	100.0	100.0
	2016	107.4	106.2	106.2	101.1	100.0	101.1
	2017	119.4	115.8	113.4	105.2	102.1	103.1
	2018	132.2	126.9	121.5	108.8	104.5	104.2
	2019	144.0	135.5	130.0	110.8	104.3	106.2
Yemen (Yemeni Rial)	1990	2.6	15.1	58.5	4.4	25.8	17.1
	1995	10.3	22.3	76.4	13.4	29.2	46.1
	2000	30.7	40.8	114.1	26.9	35.7	75.3
	2005	63.7	71.4	147.7	43.1	48.4	89.1
	2010	118.5	115.9	179.0	66.2	64.8	102.2
	2015	100.0	100.0	100.0	100.0	100.0	100.0
	2016	92.8	82.7	85.4	108.7	96.8	112.3
	2017	90.6	77.8	76.9	117.8	101.2	116.5
	2018	100.0	85.9	75.9	131.9	113.3	116.5
	2019	108.9	93.5	77.4	140.6	120.8	116.5
Europe							
Albania (Lek)	1970	0.8	19.9	27.9	2.8	71.4	4.0
	1975	0.9	22.9	33.9	2.7	67.6	4.0
	1980	1.0	18.8	41.0	2.5	45.9	5.6
	1985	1.1	20.4	45.4	2.5	45.0	5.6
	1990	1.1	18.8	46.3	2.4	40.7	6.0
	1995	15.5	21.0	41.6	37.2	50.5	73.6
	2000	34.9	30.6	53.2	65.7	57.6	114.1
	2005	56.1	70.7	70.8	79.2	99.9	79.3
	2010	86.4	104.7	91.5	94.4	114.5	82.5
	2015	100.0	100.0	100.0	100.0	100.0	100.0
	2016	102.7	104.2	103.3	99.4	100.8	98.6
	2017	108.1	114.3	107.2	100.8	106.6	94.6
	2018	114.0	133.0	111.6	102.2	119.2	85.7
	2019	117.0	134.2	114.1	102.6	117.6	87.2
Andorra (Euro)	1970	1.7	3.6	32.1	5.2	11.1	46.7
	1975	3.8	10.0	41.6	9.2	24.0	38.3
	1980	9.7	20.3	45.9	21.1	44.2	47.8
	1985	17.8	15.7	49.2	36.3	32.0	113.3
	1990	31.7	46.7	61.2	51.8	76.2	67.9
	1995	44.5	53.5	66.0	67.3	81.0	83.1
	2000	61.7	51.2	80.3	76.8	63.8	120.4
	2005	101.0	113.3	112.5	89.8	100.7	89.2
	2010	103.5	123.6	104.9	98.6	117.8	83.7

Table 7. Implicit price deflators of Gross Domestic Product in US Dollars and National Currency (2015 = 100)

Major area, region and country	Year	GDP in Current Prices: National Currency (1)	GDP in Current Prices: US Dollars (2)	Gross Domestic Product at Constant Prices (3)	GDP Implicit Price Deflators (2015 = 100): National Currency (4)	GDP Implicit Price Deflators (2015 = 100): US Dollars (5)	Exchange Rates (6)
	2015	100.0	100.0	100.0	100.0	100.0	100.0
	2016	104.1	103.8	103.7	100.3	100.1	100.3
	2017	105.6	107.6	104.1	101.5	103.4	98.2
	2018	108.4	115.4	105.7	102.5	109.2	93.9
	2019	112.1	113.1	107.7	104.1	105.0	99.1
Austria (Euro)	1970	8.4	4.0	35.4	23.8	11.4	209.6
	1975	14.7	10.5	42.9	34.3	24.4	140.4
	1980	22.4	21.5	50.4	44.4	42.6	104.3
	1985	30.3	18.2	54.3	55.9	33.5	166.8
	1990	40.0	43.6	63.0	63.4	69.2	91.6
	1995	51.3	63.1	70.3	73.0	89.8	81.3
	2000	62.0	51.5	81.5	76.2	63.3	120.4
	2005	73.8	82.8	88.9	83.0	93.1	89.2
	2010	85.9	102.6	94.9	90.6	108.2	83.7
	2015	100.0	100.0	100.0	100.0	100.0	100.0
	2016	103.9	103.6	102.0	101.8	101.6	100.3
	2017	107.3	109.3	104.4	102.7	104.6	98.2
	2018	111.9	119.2	107.1	104.5	111.3	93.9
	2019	115.5	116.6	108.7	106.3	107.3	99.1
Belarus (Belarussian Ruble)	1990	0.0	34.5	52.2	0.0	66.1	0.0
	1995	0.0	25.4	34.0	0.0	74.6	0.1
	2000	1.1	19.1	46.2	2.3	41.3	5.5
	2005	7.5	55.3	66.3	11.3	83.4	13.5
	2010	19.0	101.4	94.3	20.1	107.5	18.7
	2015	100.0	100.0	100.0	100.0	100.0	100.0
	2016	105.6	84.5	97.5	108.3	86.7	124.9
	2017	117.6	96.9	100.0	117.6	96.9	121.3
	2018	136.0	106.3	103.2	131.9	103.1	127.9
	2019	146.8	111.7	104.5	140.5	107.0	131.3
Belgium (Euro)	1970	7.9	5.8	37.3	21.3	15.5	137.5
	1975	14.4	14.2	44.5	32.3	31.9	101.1
	1980	22.1	27.4	52.0	42.4	52.8	80.4
	1985	30.5	18.7	54.5	55.9	34.2	163.2
	1990	40.8	44.4	63.5	64.3	70.0	91.9
	1995	50.5	62.3	68.7	73.5	90.7	81.0
	2000	61.5	51.1	79.1	77.8	64.6	120.4
	2005	74.4	83.4	87.1	85.4	95.8	89.2
	2010	87.1	104.1	93.8	93.0	111.0	83.7
	2015	100.0	100.0	100.0	100.0	100.0	100.0
	2016	103.2	102.9	101.3	101.9	101.7	100.3
	2017	106.8	108.8	102.9	103.8	105.7	98.2
	2018	110.5	117.7	104.8	105.5	112.3	93.9
	2019	114.3	115.4	106.6	107.2	108.2	99.1
Bosnia and Herzegovina (Convertible Marks)	1990	0.0	47.8	21.6	0.0	221.0	0.0
	1995	10.3	12.5	23.1	44.3	54.2	81.8
	2000	42.3	35.1	65.7	64.4	53.5	120.4
	2005	61.7	69.2	81.3	76.0	85.2	89.2
	2010	88.7	106.0	93.6	94.8	113.2	83.7
	2015	100.0	100.0	100.0	100.0	100.0	100.0

Table 7. Implicit price deflators of Gross Domestic Product in US Dollars and National Currency (2015 = 100)

Major area, region and country	Year	GDP in Current Prices: National Currency (1)	GDP in Current Prices: US Dollars (2)	Gross Domestic Product at Constant Prices (3)	GDP Implicit Price Deflators (2015 = 100): National Currency (4)	GDP Implicit Price Deflators (2015 = 100): US Dollars (5)	Exchange Rates (6)
	2016	104.6	104.3	103.1	101.4	101.1	100.3
	2017	109.7	111.5	106.4	103.1	104.8	98.4
	2018	117.0	124.5	110.4	106.0	112.8	94.0
	2019	123.2	124.4	113.4	108.7	109.7	99.1
Bulgaria (Bulgarian Lev)	1970	0.0	17.8	29.4	0.0	60.4	0.1
	1975	0.0	23.5	42.8	0.0	54.9	0.1
	1980	0.0	21.4	57.7	0.1	37.1	0.1
	1985	0.0	32.6	68.1	0.1	47.8	0.1
	1990	0.1	40.9	73.3	0.1	55.8	0.1
	1995	1.4	37.5	65.5	2.2	57.3	3.8
	2000	31.5	26.2	59.2	53.2	44.2	120.3
	2005	52.6	59.0	78.1	67.4	75.5	89.2
	2010	83.3	99.5	91.6	90.9	108.6	83.7
	2015	100.0	100.0	100.0	100.0	100.0	100.0
	2016	106.4	106.2	103.8	102.5	102.3	100.2
	2017	114.5	116.4	107.5	106.6	108.4	98.4
	2018	122.8	130.7	110.8	110.9	118.0	93.9
	2019	132.8	134.2	114.5	116.0	117.2	99.0
Croatia (Croatian Kuna)	1990	0.1	33.6	92.1	0.1	36.5	0.3
	1995	34.5	45.3	66.7	51.7	67.8	76.3
	2000	52.8	43.7	78.8	67.0	55.5	120.7
	2005	79.5	91.6	98.2	80.9	93.3	86.7
	2010	96.8	120.7	100.8	96.0	119.8	80.2
	2015	100.0	100.0	100.0	100.0	100.0	100.0
	2016	103.4	104.2	103.5	99.9	100.7	99.2
	2017	107.9	111.7	106.7	101.1	104.6	96.6
	2018	112.7	123.1	109.6	102.9	112.3	91.6
	2019	117.8	122.0	112.8	104.4	108.1	96.6
Czechia (Czech Koruna)	1990	15.8	21.7	63.9	24.7	33.9	73.0
	1995	34.5	32.0	61.6	56.0	51.9	107.9
	2000	51.6	32.9	67.2	76.8	49.0	156.9
	2005	71.0	72.9	81.3	87.3	89.7	97.4
	2010	86.3	111.2	91.9	93.9	120.9	77.6
	2015	100.0	100.0	100.0	100.0	100.0	100.0
	2016	103.7	104.4	102.5	101.1	101.8	99.4
	2017	110.5	116.3	107.8	102.5	107.8	95.0
	2018	116.9	132.4	111.3	105.1	119.0	88.3
	2019	124.3	133.3	113.9	109.2	117.1	93.2
Denmark (Danish Krone)	1970	6.3	5.6	43.8	14.3	12.9	111.5
	1975	11.4	13.4	47.6	24.0	28.1	85.4
	1980	19.7	23.5	54.3	36.3	43.3	83.8
	1985	32.6	20.7	62.1	52.5	33.3	157.5
	1990	42.0	45.7	66.7	62.9	68.4	92.0
	1995	50.9	61.1	74.9	68.0	81.6	83.3
	2000	65.2	54.2	86.9	75.0	62.4	120.1
	2005	77.9	87.4	92.8	83.9	94.1	89.1
	2010	88.9	106.4	93.8	94.8	113.4	83.6
	2015	100.0	100.0	100.0	100.0	100.0	100.0
	2016	103.5	103.5	103.2	100.3	100.2	100.1

Table 7. Implicit price deflators of Gross Domestic Product in US Dollars and National Currency (2015 = 100)

Major area, region and country	Year	GDP in Current Prices		Gross Domestic Product at Constant Prices (3)	GDP Implicit Price Deflators (2015 = 100)		Exchange Rates (6)
		National Currency (1)	US Dollars (2)		National Currency (4)	US Dollars (5)	
	2017	107.7	109.7	106.2	101.4	103.4	98.1
	2018	110.7	117.9	108.5	102.0	108.7	93.9
	2019	114.7	115.7	111.6	102.8	103.7	99.1
Estonia (Euro)	1990	0.2	24.5	63.7	0.4	38.5	1.0
	1995	13.8	19.4	44.7	30.8	43.4	70.9
	2000	29.7	24.7	60.6	49.1	40.8	120.3
	2005	54.5	61.2	86.3	63.2	70.9	89.2
	2010	71.5	85.4	84.9	84.2	100.6	83.7
	2015	100.0	100.0	100.0	100.0	100.0	100.0
	2016	105.5	105.3	103.2	102.3	102.0	100.3
	2017	114.8	116.9	108.9	105.5	107.4	98.2
	2018	124.8	132.9	113.6	109.9	117.0	93.9
	2019	135.3	136.5	119.3	113.4	114.5	99.1
Finland (Euro)	1970	3.8	4.8	33.6	11.2	14.3	78.3
	1975	8.6	12.5	41.7	20.6	30.0	68.6
	1980	15.9	22.9	48.7	32.7	46.9	69.6
	1985	27.6	23.8	56.1	49.1	42.5	115.6
	1990	43.0	60.3	66.5	64.7	90.7	71.3
	1995	46.6	57.2	65.1	71.6	87.9	81.5
	2000	64.5	53.6	83.6	77.2	64.1	120.4
	2005	77.9	87.4	95.1	81.9	91.8	89.2
	2010	89.0	106.3	99.6	89.3	106.7	83.7
	2015	100.0	100.0	100.0	100.0	100.0	100.0
	2016	102.9	102.6	102.8	100.1	99.8	100.3
	2017	106.9	108.9	106.2	100.7	102.5	98.2
	2018	110.5	117.7	107.8	102.6	109.2	93.9
	2019	113.8	114.9	109.0	104.4	105.4	99.1
France (Euro)	1970	5.7	6.1	37.3	15.3	16.3	93.9
	1975	10.7	14.8	45.1	23.8	32.8	72.5
	1980	20.5	28.8	53.3	38.5	54.0	71.4
	1985	34.5	22.7	57.7	59.8	39.3	151.9
	1990	47.9	52.1	68.1	70.4	76.4	92.1
	1995	55.4	65.7	72.6	76.3	90.4	84.4
	2000	67.3	55.9	83.9	80.2	66.6	120.4
	2005	80.3	90.1	91.2	88.1	98.7	89.2
	2010	90.8	108.4	95.0	95.5	114.1	83.7
	2015	100.0	100.0	100.0	100.0	100.0	100.0
	2016	101.6	101.4	101.1	100.5	100.3	100.3
	2017	104.5	106.4	103.4	101.0	102.9	98.2
	2018	107.4	114.3	105.3	102.0	108.6	93.9
	2019	110.3	111.4	106.9	103.3	104.2	99.1
Germany (Euro)	1970	13.3	6.4	41.7	32.0	15.4	207.5
	1975	20.4	14.6	47.0	43.4	31.1	139.5
	1980	29.2	28.3	55.4	52.7	51.1	103.1
	1985	36.4	21.8	59.3	61.4	36.8	166.9
	1990	48.4	52.8	69.8	69.3	75.7	91.6
	1995	62.6	77.0	76.9	81.4	100.1	81.3
	2000	69.7	57.9	84.5	82.5	68.6	120.4
	2005	75.6	84.8	86.7	87.2	97.8	89.2

Table 7. Implicit price deflators of Gross Domestic Product in US Dollars and National Currency (2015 = 100)

Major area, region and country	Year	GDP in Current Prices: National Currency (1)	GDP in Current Prices: US Dollars (2)	Gross Domestic Product at Constant Prices (3)	GDP Implicit Price Deflators (2015 = 100): National Currency (4)	GDP Implicit Price Deflators (2015 = 100): US Dollars (5)	Exchange Rates (6)
	2010	84.7	101.2	92.0	92.1	110.0	83.7
	2015	100.0	100.0	100.0	100.0	100.0	100.0
	2016	103.6	103.3	102.2	101.3	101.1	100.3
	2017	107.7	109.7	104.9	102.7	104.6	98.2
	2018	110.9	118.1	106.2	104.4	111.2	93.9
	2019	114.0	115.0	106.8	106.7	107.7	99.1
Greece (Euro)	1970	0.7	6.7	48.3	1.4	13.9	9.8
	1975	1.5	14.6	61.7	2.5	23.7	10.4
	1980	4.0	29.1	75.7	5.3	38.4	13.9
	1985	11.0	24.5	76.2	14.4	32.1	45.0
	1990	25.9	50.1	81.1	31.9	61.8	51.6
	1995	52.8	70.1	86.3	61.3	81.2	75.4
	2000	80.2	67.4	103.2	77.7	65.4	118.9
	2005	113.1	126.9	124.8	90.6	101.6	89.2
	2010	127.3	152.0	122.8	103.6	123.8	83.7
	2015	100.0	100.0	100.0	100.0	100.0	100.0
	2016	98.9	98.7	99.5	99.4	99.2	100.3
	2017	100.6	102.5	100.8	99.8	101.7	98.2
	2018	102.1	108.7	102.4	99.7	106.2	93.9
	2019	104.1	105.1	104.3	99.9	100.8	99.1
Hungary (Forint)	1970	1.1	5.1	40.1	2.7	12.7	21.5
	1975	1.6	10.1	54.4	2.9	18.6	15.7
	1980	2.4	20.4	63.8	3.7	31.9	11.6
	1985	3.4	19.0	69.6	4.9	27.2	17.9
	1990	6.7	29.7	71.4	9.4	41.6	22.6
	1995	16.7	37.1	63.4	26.4	58.6	45.0
	2000	38.1	37.8	73.2	52.1	51.6	101.0
	2005	64.5	90.3	90.8	71.1	99.5	71.4
	2010	78.5	105.5	90.2	87.0	116.9	74.4
	2015	100.0	100.0	100.0	100.0	100.0	100.0
	2016	103.5	102.7	102.1	101.4	100.6	100.8
	2017	112.3	114.3	106.5	105.4	107.3	98.2
	2018	124.1	128.3	112.3	110.5	114.2	96.7
	2019	136.0	130.7	117.5	115.8	111.3	104.1
Iceland (Iceland Krona)	1970	0.0	3.0	21.1	0.1	14.4	0.7
	1975	0.1	8.1	28.8	0.3	28.1	1.2
	1980	0.7	19.5	39.0	1.8	49.9	3.6
	1985	5.4	17.2	43.8	12.4	39.3	31.5
	1990	16.5	37.3	51.2	32.2	72.8	44.2
	1995	20.1	41.0	51.8	38.8	79.2	49.0
	2000	30.9	51.8	67.0	46.1	77.3	59.6
	2005	46.2	96.7	82.3	56.1	117.4	47.7
	2010	72.9	78.7	87.0	83.8	90.4	92.7
	2015	100.0	100.0	100.0	100.0	100.0	100.0
	2016	108.6	118.6	106.6	101.8	111.2	91.6
	2017	114.1	140.8	111.5	102.3	126.3	81.0
	2018	121.5	148.0	115.7	105.0	127.9	82.1
	2019	129.3	139.1	117.9	109.6	117.9	92.9

Table 7. Implicit price deflators of Gross Domestic Product in US Dollars and National Currency (2015 = 100)

Major area, region and country	Year	GDP in Current Prices: National Currency (1)	GDP in Current Prices: US Dollars (2)	Gross Domestic Product at Constant Prices (3)	GDP Implicit Price Deflators (2015 = 100): National Currency (4)	GDP Implicit Price Deflators (2015 = 100): US Dollars (5)	Exchange Rates (6)
Ireland (Euro)	1970	0.9	1.5	12.2	7.2	12.3	58.7
	1975	2.1	3.3	15.5	13.3	20.9	63.7
	1980	5.1	7.5	19.4	26.3	38.4	68.5
	1985	9.7	7.3	22.0	44.1	33.1	133.2
	1990	14.4	16.9	27.7	52.0	61.0	85.1
	1995	20.8	23.7	34.8	59.9	68.2	87.8
	2000	41.2	34.3	54.5	75.7	62.9	120.4
	2005	64.8	72.6	70.6	91.7	102.8	89.2
	2010	63.8	76.2	72.1	88.5	105.6	83.7
	2015	100.0	100.0	100.0	100.0	100.0	100.0
	2016	103.0	102.8	102.0	101.0	100.7	100.3
	2017	114.3	116.4	111.3	102.7	104.6	98.2
	2018	124.4	132.5	120.8	103.0	109.7	93.9
	2019	135.5	136.7	127.5	106.2	107.2	99.1
Italy (Euro)	1970	2.2	6.2	46.2	4.8	13.4	35.8
	1975	4.6	12.4	53.9	8.6	23.0	37.4
	1980	12.8	26.0	67.0	19.0	38.8	49.1
	1985	26.9	24.6	72.9	37.0	33.8	109.4
	1990	44.0	64.1	85.0	51.7	75.4	68.6
	1995	59.7	64.0	90.6	65.9	70.6	93.3
	2000	75.0	62.3	100.3	74.8	62.1	120.4
	2005	90.2	101.2	105.0	86.0	96.4	89.2
	2010	97.3	116.2	103.5	94.1	112.3	83.7
	2015	100.0	100.0	100.0	100.0	100.0	100.0
	2016	102.4	102.2	101.3	101.1	100.9	100.3
	2017	104.9	106.9	103.0	101.9	103.8	98.2
	2018	107.0	113.9	104.0	102.9	109.6	93.9
	2019	108.1	109.1	104.3	103.6	104.6	99.1
Kosovo (Euro)	1990	62.9	68.7	114.2	55.1	60.2	91.6
	1995	66.9	82.4	61.8	108.3	133.3	81.3
	2000	31.7	26.3	54.0	58.7	48.7	120.4
	2005	51.0	57.1	66.5	76.6	85.9	89.2
	2010	75.8	90.5	85.5	88.7	105.9	83.7
	2015	100.0	100.0	100.0	100.0	100.0	100.0
	2016	104.5	104.3	104.1	100.4	100.2	100.3
	2017	110.5	112.5	108.5	101.8	103.7	98.2
	2018	115.8	123.3	112.6	102.9	109.5	93.9
	2019	122.3	123.5	118.2	103.5	104.5	99.1
Latvia (Euro)	1990	0.4	35.4	90.5	0.4	39.2	1.1
	1995	16.5	19.8	44.9	36.8	44.2	83.3
	2000	27.9	29.2	57.8	48.3	50.4	95.7
	2005	55.5	62.3	85.8	64.7	72.6	89.1
	2010	73.4	87.7	83.8	87.6	104.6	83.7
	2015	100.0	100.0	100.0	100.0	100.0	100.0
	2016	103.3	103.0	102.4	100.9	100.6	100.3
	2017	109.8	111.8	105.7	103.9	105.8	98.2
	2018	118.7	126.3	110.0	107.9	114.9	93.9
	2019	124.0	125.2	112.2	110.5	111.6	99.1

Table 7. Implicit price deflators of Gross Domestic Product in US Dollars and National Currency (2015 = 100)

Major area, region and country	Year	GDP in Current Prices: National Currency (1)	GDP in Current Prices: US Dollars (2)	Gross Domestic Product at Constant Prices (3)	GDP Implicit Price Deflators (2015 = 100): National Currency (4)	GDP Implicit Price Deflators (2015 = 100): US Dollars (5)	Exchange Rates (6)
Liechtenstein	1970	8.0	1.8	26.1	30.7	6.8	454.4
(Swiss Franc)	1975	12.2	4.6	28.4	43.1	16.1	268.2
	1980	19.0	10.9	35.8	53.2	30.5	174.1
	1985	27.7	10.9	41.4	67.0	26.2	255.3
	1990	40.4	28.0	52.4	77.1	53.4	144.3
	1995	52.8	43.0	58.7	90.1	73.3	122.9
	2000	76.9	43.8	82.3	93.5	53.3	175.5
	2005	83.5	64.5	85.7	97.5	75.3	129.4
	2010	97.2	89.7	95.4	101.9	94.0	108.4
	2015	100.0	100.0	100.0	100.0	100.0	100.0
	2016	101.9	99.5	102.3	99.6	97.2	102.4
	2017	105.7	103.3	105.6	100.1	97.8	102.3
	2018	110.9	109.1	109.7	101.0	99.4	101.6
	2019	112.0	108.4	110.4	101.4	98.2	103.3
Lithuania	1990	0.1	24.7	74.5	0.1	33.1	0.4
(Euro)	1995	20.8	16.2	43.2	48.1	37.4	128.5
	2000	35.8	27.8	54.3	65.9	51.3	128.5
	2005	56.2	63.0	78.3	71.7	80.5	89.1
	2010	75.1	89.7	83.0	90.4	108.0	83.7
	2015	100.0	100.0	100.0	100.0	100.0	100.0
	2016	104.1	103.9	102.5	101.6	101.3	100.3
	2017	113.2	115.3	106.9	105.9	107.9	98.2
	2018	121.8	129.7	111.1	109.6	116.7	93.9
	2019	130.7	131.9	115.9	112.7	113.8	99.1
Luxembourg	1970	3.6	2.6	19.6	18.3	13.3	137.5
(Euro)	1975	5.7	5.6	22.6	25.0	24.7	101.1
	1980	8.7	10.8	25.3	34.3	42.6	80.4
	1985	13.4	8.2	28.6	46.8	28.7	163.2
	1990	21.0	22.9	41.1	51.3	55.8	91.9
	1995	30.3	37.4	49.8	60.8	75.0	81.0
	2000	44.3	36.8	66.5	66.6	55.4	120.4
	2005	57.7	64.7	76.9	75.0	84.1	89.2
	2010	77.2	92.2	86.8	88.9	106.2	83.7
	2015	100.0	100.0	100.0	100.0	100.0	100.0
	2016	105.4	105.1	104.6	100.8	100.5	100.3
	2017	109.1	111.1	106.5	102.5	104.4	98.2
	2018	115.3	122.8	109.8	105.1	111.9	93.9
	2019	122.0	123.1	112.3	108.6	109.7	99.1
Malta	1970	2.6	2.4	9.8	26.6	24.7	107.6
(Euro)	1975	4.6	4.6	14.6	31.3	31.5	99.4
	1980	10.8	12.1	25.1	42.8	48.0	89.2
	1985	13.1	10.8	27.3	47.8	39.5	121.2
	1990	20.2	24.6	36.9	54.8	66.7	82.1
	1995	31.5	34.5	48.1	65.4	71.7	91.2
	2000	42.8	37.8	61.8	69.3	61.2	113.2
	2005	53.3	59.7	68.5	77.9	87.2	89.3
	2010	68.3	81.6	75.7	90.3	107.9	83.7
	2015	100.0	100.0	100.0	100.0	100.0	100.0
	2016	107.4	107.1	105.8	101.5	101.2	100.3

Table 7. Implicit price deflators of Gross Domestic Product in US Dollars and National Currency (2015 = 100)

Major area, region and country	Year	GDP in Current Prices		Gross Domestic Product at Constant Prices (3)	GDP Implicit Price Deflators (2015 = 100)		Exchange Rates (6)
		National Currency (1)	US Dollars (2)		National Currency (4)	US Dollars (5)	
	2017	117.2	119.4	112.7	104.0	105.9	98.2
	2018	128.4	136.8	121.0	106.2	113.0	93.9
	2019	137.5	138.8	126.6	108.6	109.6	99.1
Monaco (Euro)	1970	4.3	4.5	28.1	15.2	16.2	93.9
	1975	8.0	11.0	33.9	23.6	32.5	72.5
	1980	15.3	21.4	40.1	38.2	53.5	71.4
	1985	25.7	16.9	43.4	59.3	39.0	151.9
	1990	35.7	38.8	51.2	69.8	75.8	92.1
	1995	41.3	49.0	54.6	75.7	89.7	84.4
	2000	50.1	41.7	63.1	79.5	66.0	120.4
	2005	59.9	67.1	68.6	87.3	97.9	89.2
	2010	71.7	85.7	75.1	95.5	114.1	83.7
	2015	100.0	100.0	100.0	100.0	100.0	100.0
	2016	103.6	103.3	103.5	100.2	99.9	100.3
	2017	100.9	102.8	99.8	101.0	102.9	98.2
	2018	107.9	114.9	105.8	102.0	108.6	93.9
	2019	117.5	118.6	113.8	103.2	104.2	99.1
Montenegro (Euro)	1990	48.5	53.0	88.1	55.1	60.1	91.6
	1995	24.4	30.0	44.3	55.0	67.7	81.3
	2000	29.4	24.5	66.1	44.5	37.0	120.4
	2005	50.1	56.2	75.9	66.0	74.0	89.2
	2010	85.5	102.1	91.4	93.6	111.7	83.7
	2015	100.0	100.0	100.0	100.0	100.0	100.0
	2016	108.2	107.9	102.9	105.1	104.8	100.3
	2017	117.6	119.8	107.8	109.1	111.2	98.2
	2018	127.6	135.9	113.3	112.6	119.9	93.9
	2019	135.5	136.7	117.9	114.9	116.0	99.1
Netherlands (Euro)	1970	9.1	5.0	35.8	25.3	13.9	182.2
	1975	16.7	13.2	42.3	39.5	31.1	127.3
	1980	25.5	25.5	48.7	52.4	52.3	100.1
	1985	31.4	18.8	51.5	61.0	36.5	167.2
	1990	38.1	41.6	60.7	62.8	68.5	91.6
	1995	47.8	59.1	68.0	70.2	86.9	80.8
	2000	65.5	54.4	84.2	77.8	64.7	120.4
	2005	79.8	89.5	90.0	88.7	99.5	89.2
	2010	92.6	110.6	96.3	96.2	114.8	83.7
	2015	100.0	100.0	100.0	100.0	100.0	100.0
	2016	102.7	102.4	102.2	100.5	100.2	100.3
	2017	107.0	109.0	105.2	101.7	103.6	98.2
	2018	112.2	119.4	107.6	104.2	111.0	93.9
	2019	117.4	118.5	109.5	107.3	108.3	99.1
North Macedonia (Denar)	1990	0.1	28.9	67.0	0.1	43.2	0.3
	1995	31.9	46.8	57.1	55.9	81.9	68.2
	2000	44.5	37.5	66.1	67.3	56.7	118.7
	2005	55.2	62.2	72.9	75.7	85.3	88.7
	2010	78.2	93.5	88.6	88.3	105.5	83.7
	2015	100.0	100.0	100.0	100.0	100.0	100.0
	2016	106.4	106.0	102.8	103.5	103.1	100.4
	2017	110.6	112.3	104.0	106.4	108.1	98.4

Table 7. Implicit price deflators of Gross Domestic Product in US Dollars and National Currency (2015 = 100)

Major area, region and country	Year	GDP in Current Prices: National Currency (1)	GDP in Current Prices: US Dollars (2)	Gross Domestic Product at Constant Prices (3)	GDP Implicit Price Deflators (2015 = 100): National Currency (4)	GDP Implicit Price Deflators (2015 = 100): US Dollars (5)	Exchange Rates (6)
	2018	117.7	125.5	106.8	110.2	117.5	93.8
	2019	124.8	126.1	110.6	112.9	114.1	98.9
Norway (Norwegian Krone)	1970	2.9	3.3	26.8	11.0	12.4	88.6
	1975	5.5	8.5	34.0	16.3	25.1	64.8
	1980	10.2	16.7	42.4	24.1	39.4	61.2
	1985	18.1	17.0	50.3	36.0	33.7	106.6
	1990	24.1	31.0	54.7	44.1	56.8	77.6
	1995	31.0	39.4	65.7	47.1	60.0	78.6
	2000	48.4	44.4	78.5	61.7	56.5	109.1
	2005	64.0	80.1	87.5	73.1	91.5	79.9
	2010	83.3	111.1	91.8	90.8	121.1	75.0
	2015	100.0	100.0	100.0	100.0	100.0	100.0
	2016	99.6	95.6	101.1	98.5	94.6	104.2
	2017	105.9	103.3	103.4	102.4	99.8	102.6
	2018	113.5	112.5	104.8	108.3	107.4	100.8
	2019	114.1	104.5	106.0	107.7	98.7	109.1
Poland (Zloty)	1970	0.0	5.9	26.6	0.0	22.2	0.1
	1975	0.0	10.2	35.4	0.0	28.9	0.1
	1980	0.0	12.4	42.1	0.0	29.4	0.1
	1985	0.1	15.3	41.7	0.1	36.8	0.4
	1990	3.5	13.8	40.9	8.5	33.8	25.2
	1995	19.2	29.8	45.5	42.1	65.4	64.3
	2000	41.6	36.0	58.9	70.5	61.2	115.3
	2005	55.0	64.1	68.4	80.3	93.6	85.8
	2010	80.3	100.4	86.5	92.9	116.2	80.0
	2015	100.0	100.0	100.0	100.0	100.0	100.0
	2016	103.5	98.9	103.1	100.3	95.9	104.6
	2017	110.5	110.2	108.1	102.2	101.9	100.3
	2018	117.8	122.9	113.9	103.4	107.9	95.8
	2019	127.0	124.7	119.1	106.7	104.7	101.9
Portugal (Euro)	1970	0.6	4.1	33.3	1.9	12.2	15.9
	1975	1.4	9.7	41.3	3.3	23.5	14.1
	1980	4.6	16.5	53.0	8.6	31.2	27.7
	1985	12.8	13.6	55.4	23.2	24.6	94.3
	1990	31.1	39.5	73.0	42.7	54.1	78.9
	1995	49.5	59.3	79.4	62.4	74.6	83.6
	2000	71.5	59.4	97.0	73.7	61.2	120.4
	2005	88.2	98.9	101.3	87.1	97.7	89.2
	2010	99.9	119.3	104.3	95.8	114.4	83.7
	2015	100.0	100.0	100.0	100.0	100.0	100.0
	2016	103.8	103.5	102.0	101.7	101.4	100.3
	2017	109.0	111.1	105.6	103.3	105.2	98.2
	2018	114.2	121.6	108.6	105.1	111.9	93.9
	2019	118.7	119.8	111.0	106.9	107.9	99.1
Republic of Moldova (Moldovan Leu)	1990	0.0	61.5	145.2	0.0	42.4	0.0
	1995	5.3	27.4	57.2	9.3	47.8	19.5
	2000	13.2	20.0	50.5	26.1	39.5	66.1
	2005	31.0	46.3	71.1	43.6	65.1	67.0
	2010	59.2	90.1	83.3	71.1	108.1	65.7

Table 7. Implicit price deflators of Gross Domestic Product in US Dollars and National Currency (2015 = 100)

Major area, region and country	Year	GDP in Current Prices		Gross Domestic Product at Constant Prices (3)	GDP Implicit Price Deflators (2015 = 100)		Exchange Rates (6)
		National Currency (1)	US Dollars (2)		National Currency (4)	US Dollars (5)	
	2015	100.0	100.0	100.0	100.0	100.0	100.0
	2016	110.3	104.2	104.4	105.7	99.8	105.9
	2017	122.7	124.8	109.3	112.3	114.2	98.3
	2018	132.1	147.9	114.0	115.8	129.8	89.3
	2019	144.1	154.4	117.9	122.2	130.9	93.4
Romania (New Leu)	1970	0.0	7.1	24.6	0.0	29.1	0.1
	1975	0.0	12.9	42.1	0.0	30.6	0.0
	1980	0.0	20.5	60.3	0.0	34.0	0.0
	1985	0.0	28.5	70.4	0.0	40.5	0.0
	1990	0.0	22.8	64.3	0.0	35.5	0.1
	1995	1.1	21.2	57.8	1.9	36.7	5.1
	2000	11.4	21.0	57.1	20.0	36.9	54.2
	2005	40.3	55.3	75.1	53.6	73.7	72.7
	2010	74.1	93.4	86.4	85.8	108.2	79.3
	2015	100.0	100.0	100.0	100.0	100.0	100.0
	2016	107.4	106.0	104.8	102.5	101.1	101.3
	2017	120.4	119.0	112.3	107.2	106.0	101.2
	2018	133.7	135.8	117.2	114.0	115.9	98.4
	2019	148.7	140.6	122.0	121.9	115.2	105.8
Russian Federation (Russian Ruble)	1990	0.0	42.0	85.5	0.0	49.1	0.0
	1995	1.7	29.4	53.1	3.3	55.5	5.9
	2000	8.8	19.1	57.5	15.4	33.3	46.2
	2005	26.2	56.5	77.4	33.9	73.0	46.4
	2010	56.2	112.7	92.1	61.0	122.4	49.8
	2015	100.0	100.0	100.0	100.0	100.0	100.0
	2016	103.0	93.6	100.3	102.7	93.4	110.0
	2017	110.5	115.5	102.1	108.3	113.1	95.7
	2018	125.6	122.1	104.7	120.0	116.7	102.8
	2019	131.6	123.9	106.1	124.1	116.8	106.2
San Marino (Euro)	1970	2.0	5.7	39.2	5.2	14.4	35.8
	1975	4.2	11.4	45.8	9.3	24.8	37.4
	1980	11.7	23.8	56.9	20.5	41.8	49.1
	1985	24.7	22.5	61.9	39.9	36.4	109.4
	1990	40.2	58.6	72.2	55.8	81.3	68.6
	1995	67.1	71.9	93.9	71.4	76.5	93.3
	2000	96.8	80.4	123.9	78.1	64.9	120.4
	2005	127.4	142.9	145.9	87.3	97.9	89.2
	2010	126.3	150.8	132.6	95.2	113.7	83.7
	2015	100.0	100.0	100.0	100.0	100.0	100.0
	2016	103.7	103.4	102.5	101.2	100.9	100.3
	2017	105.8	107.7	103.1	102.6	104.5	98.2
	2018	109.6	116.7	104.4	104.9	111.7	93.9
	2019	111.9	112.9	105.6	106.0	106.9	99.1
Serbia (Serbian Dinar)	1990	0.0	102.2	111.7	0.0	91.5	0.0
	1995	1.4	55.2	53.5	2.6	103.3	2.5
	2000	10.1	24.9	60.5	16.6	41.1	40.5
	2005	42.8	69.8	82.7	51.8	84.5	61.3
	2010	75.3	105.5	95.7	78.7	110.2	71.4
	2015	100.0	100.0	100.0	100.0	100.0	100.0

Table 7. Implicit price deflators of Gross Domestic Product in US Dollars and National Currency (2015 = 100)

Major area, region and country	Year	GDP in Current Prices: National Currency (1)	GDP in Current Prices: US Dollars (2)	Gross Domestic Product at Constant Prices (3)	GDP Implicit Price Deflators (2015 = 100): National Currency (4)	GDP Implicit Price Deflators (2015 = 100): US Dollars (5)	Exchange Rates (6)
	2016	104.9	102.6	103.3	101.5	99.3	102.3
	2017	110.3	111.4	105.5	104.6	105.6	99.0
	2018	117.6	127.7	110.3	106.6	115.8	92.1
	2019	125.6	129.8	114.9	109.2	112.9	96.7
Slovakia	1990	12.6	19.0	50.0	25.2	38.1	66.1
(Euro)	1995	24.8	22.7	45.7	54.3	49.6	109.4
	2000	39.7	23.4	54.3	73.2	43.2	169.5
	2005	63.3	55.4	69.3	91.3	79.9	114.2
	2010	85.5	102.1	88.1	97.0	115.9	83.7
	2015	100.0	100.0	100.0	100.0	100.0	100.0
	2016	101.6	101.3	102.1	99.5	99.2	100.3
	2017	106.0	107.9	105.2	100.7	102.6	98.2
	2018	112.2	119.5	109.2	102.7	109.4	93.9
	2019	117.7	118.8	111.7	105.3	106.3	99.1
Slovenia	1990	2.2	42.2	63.1	3.5	66.9	5.2
(Euro)	1995	27.2	49.6	61.3	44.4	80.9	54.9
	2000	48.5	47.1	74.9	64.8	62.8	103.0
	2005	74.9	84.0	89.3	83.9	94.1	89.2
	2010	93.6	111.8	98.0	95.5	114.1	83.7
	2015	100.0	100.0	100.0	100.0	100.0	100.0
	2016	104.1	103.8	103.2	100.9	100.6	100.3
	2017	110.7	112.8	108.1	102.4	104.3	98.2
	2018	118.0	125.7	112.9	104.6	111.4	93.9
	2019	124.6	125.7	116.5	106.9	107.9	99.1
Spain	1970	1.6	3.4	32.3	4.9	10.6	46.7
(Euro)	1975	3.7	9.6	41.9	8.8	22.9	38.3
	1980	9.3	19.5	46.2	20.2	42.2	47.8
	1985	17.1	15.1	49.5	34.6	30.6	113.3
	1990	30.5	44.9	61.7	49.5	72.8	67.9
	1995	42.7	51.4	66.5	64.3	77.4	83.1
	2000	60.1	49.9	81.2	74.0	61.5	120.4
	2005	86.1	96.5	95.5	90.1	101.1	89.2
	2010	99.5	118.9	100.1	99.4	118.7	83.7
	2015	100.0	100.0	100.0	100.0	100.0	100.0
	2016	103.4	103.1	103.0	100.3	100.1	100.3
	2017	107.8	109.8	106.1	101.6	103.5	98.2
	2018	111.8	119.0	108.7	102.8	109.5	93.9
	2019	115.5	116.6	110.8	104.3	105.2	99.1
Sweden	1970	4.6	7.5	38.8	11.9	19.4	61.3
(Swedish Krona)	1975	8.1	16.4	44.1	18.3	37.2	49.2
	1980	14.1	28.1	47.1	29.9	59.7	50.1
	1985	23.0	22.6	52.0	44.3	43.4	102.0
	1990	36.4	51.8	58.6	62.1	88.5	70.2
	1995	44.8	52.9	60.5	73.9	87.4	84.6
	2000	56.5	52.0	72.2	78.3	72.0	108.6
	2005	68.8	77.7	82.2	83.7	94.4	88.6
	2010	83.9	98.2	89.8	93.4	109.3	85.4
	2015	100.0	100.0	100.0	100.0	100.0	100.0
	2016	103.6	102.1	102.1	101.5	100.0	101.5

Table 7. Implicit price deflators of Gross Domestic Product in US Dollars and National Currency (2015 = 100)

Major area, region and country	Year	GDP in Current Prices: National Currency (1)	GDP in Current Prices: US Dollars (2)	Gross Domestic Product at Constant Prices (3)	GDP Implicit Price Deflators (2015 = 100): National Currency (4)	GDP Implicit Price Deflators (2015 = 100): US Dollars (5)	Exchange Rates (6)
	2017	108.6	107.1	104.7	103.7	102.3	101.4
	2018	113.3	110.0	106.7	106.2	103.0	103.1
	2019	117.9	105.1	108.1	109.0	97.2	112.1
Switzerland (Swiss Franc)	1970	15.7	3.5	47.6	33.0	7.3	454.4
	1975	24.3	9.1	49.6	49.0	18.3	268.2
	1980	29.5	16.9	53.9	54.8	31.4	174.1
	1985	39.2	15.3	58.1	67.5	26.4	255.3
	1990	53.1	36.8	67.1	79.0	54.7	144.3
	1995	61.8	50.3	67.6	91.4	74.4	122.9
	2000	69.9	39.9	75.7	92.4	52.6	175.5
	2005	77.5	59.9	81.3	95.3	73.6	129.4
	2010	93.1	85.9	91.4	101.9	94.0	108.4
	2015	100.0	100.0	100.0	100.0	100.0	100.0
	2016	101.4	99.1	102.0	99.4	97.1	102.4
	2017	102.7	100.3	103.7	99.0	96.8	102.3
	2018	106.5	104.8	106.8	99.7	98.1	101.6
	2019	107.6	104.2	107.9	99.7	96.5	103.3
Ukraine (Hryvnia)	1990	0.0	102.7	176.7	0.0	58.1	0.0
	1995	2.8	55.3	84.4	3.4	65.6	5.1
	2000	8.9	35.6	76.3	11.6	46.6	24.9
	2005	23.0	98.0	110.8	20.8	88.5	23.5
	2010	54.3	149.4	112.2	48.4	133.1	36.3
	2015	100.0	100.0	100.0	100.0	100.0	100.0
	2016	120.0	102.6	102.4	117.1	100.1	117.0
	2017	150.1	123.2	105.0	143.0	117.4	121.8
	2018	179.1	143.8	108.5	165.0	132.5	124.5
	2019	199.9	168.9	112.1	178.4	150.8	118.3
United Kingdom (Pound Sterling)	1970	2.8	4.5	36.3	7.8	12.3	63.7
	1975	5.7	8.2	40.1	14.2	20.6	69.1
	1980	12.7	19.3	44.8	28.3	43.0	65.7
	1985	19.9	16.7	50.3	39.5	33.2	119.1
	1990	32.1	37.3	59.7	53.7	62.4	86.0
	1995	44.3	45.7	64.7	68.4	70.7	96.8
	2000	57.1	56.5	77.2	73.9	73.2	101.0
	2005	72.6	86.4	88.2	82.3	97.9	84.0
	2010	83.7	84.6	90.5	92.5	93.5	98.9
	2015	100.0	100.0	100.0	100.0	100.0	100.0
	2016	103.9	91.8	101.7	102.2	90.3	113.2
	2017	107.8	90.8	103.5	104.1	87.7	118.7
	2018	111.6	97.4	104.8	106.5	93.0	114.5
	2019	115.4	96.4	106.1	108.7	90.8	119.7
Oceania							
Australia (Australian Dollar)	1970	2.4	3.6	25.2	9.6	14.4	67.1
	1975	5.0	8.7	29.1	17.2	30.0	57.4
	1980	9.2	13.9	33.7	27.2	41.2	66.0
	1985	15.7	14.6	39.0	40.2	37.4	107.6
	1990	25.0	25.9	45.3	55.1	57.3	96.2
	1995	31.8	31.3	53.0	59.9	59.1	101.3

Table 7. Implicit price deflators of Gross Domestic Product in US Dollars and National Currency (2015 = 100)

Major area, region and country	Year	GDP in Current Prices: National Currency (1)	GDP in Current Prices: US Dollars (2)	Gross Domestic Product at Constant Prices (3)	GDP Implicit Price Deflators (2015 = 100): National Currency (4)	GDP Implicit Price Deflators (2015 = 100): US Dollars (5)	Exchange Rates (6)
	2000	42.5	32.8	64.2	66.1	51.0	129.6
	2005	60.0	61.0	75.9	79.0	80.3	98.4
	2010	85.3	104.2	87.1	97.9	119.6	81.9
	2015	100.0	100.0	100.0	100.0	100.0	100.0
	2016	106.1	105.0	102.3	103.7	102.6	101.1
	2017	111.3	113.6	105.3	105.7	107.8	98.0
	2018	117.6	116.9	107.6	109.3	108.7	100.6
	2019	119.6	110.6	107.3	111.4	103.1	108.1
Cook Islands (New Zealand Dollar)	1970	2.3	3.7	36.9	6.2	10.0	62.3
	1975	3.3	5.7	30.3	11.0	19.0	58.0
	1980	6.6	9.2	38.6	17.1	23.9	71.6
	1985	14.4	10.2	47.9	30.0	21.3	141.1
	1990	28.1	24.0	58.6	47.9	41.0	116.9
	1995	40.6	38.2	68.6	59.2	55.7	106.3
	2000	50.8	33.1	77.6	65.5	42.7	153.5
	2005	65.3	65.9	87.8	74.3	75.1	99.0
	2010	77.1	79.7	88.0	87.7	90.6	96.8
	2015	100.0	100.0	100.0	100.0	100.0	100.0
	2016	102.7	102.5	104.9	97.9	97.7	100.2
	2017	112.3	114.4	114.9	97.7	99.5	98.1
	2018	121.0	120.0	121.4	99.7	98.9	100.8
	2019	132.8	125.5	127.2	104.4	98.6	105.9
Fiji (Fiji Dollar)	1970	2.0	4.7	22.6	8.7	20.9	41.5
	1975	5.7	14.6	30.3	18.9	48.3	39.2
	1980	10.0	25.7	36.5	27.5	70.6	39.0
	1985	13.4	24.4	38.3	35.0	63.7	55.0
	1990	20.2	28.6	47.8	42.2	59.8	70.6
	1995	28.5	42.6	53.0	53.9	80.3	67.0
	2000	37.0	36.5	58.9	62.9	62.0	101.5
	2005	51.3	63.7	66.3	77.3	95.9	80.6
	2010	61.3	67.1	68.7	89.3	97.6	91.5
	2015	100.0	100.0	100.0	100.0	100.0	100.0
	2016	105.1	105.3	102.5	102.6	102.7	99.9
	2017	112.7	114.3	108.1	104.2	105.8	98.5
	2018	117.7	118.2	111.9	105.2	105.7	99.5
	2019	121.1	117.6	112.4	107.7	104.5	103.0
French Polynesia (CFP Franc)	1970	4.6	4.9	27.3	17.0	18.1	93.9
	1975	9.7	13.4	35.2	27.6	38.1	72.4
	1980	20.9	29.3	44.7	46.8	65.5	71.4
	1985	48.9	32.2	62.4	78.4	51.7	151.8
	1990	61.7	67.0	76.4	80.7	87.7	92.0
	1995	70.0	83.0	82.1	85.3	101.2	84.3
	2000	85.0	70.6	95.1	89.4	74.2	120.4
	2005	95.5	107.1	105.5	90.5	101.5	89.2
	2010	95.6	114.2	101.2	94.5	112.9	83.7
	2015	100.0	100.0	100.0	100.0	100.0	100.0
	2016	103.5	103.2	102.3	101.1	100.9	100.3
	2017	106.2	108.1	104.8	101.3	103.2	98.2
	2018	108.9	116.0	107.4	101.4	108.0	93.9
	2019	112.1	113.1	110.0	101.9	102.9	99.1

Table 7. Implicit price deflators of Gross Domestic Product in US Dollars and National Currency (2015 = 100)

Major area, region and country	Year	GDP in Current Prices: National Currency (1)	GDP in Current Prices: US Dollars (2)	Gross Domestic Product at Constant Prices (3)	GDP Implicit Price Deflators (2015 = 100): National Currency (4)	GDP Implicit Price Deflators (2015 = 100): US Dollars (5)	Exchange Rates (6)
Kiribati (Australian Dollar)	1970	8.0	11.9	80.3	10.0	14.9	67.1
	1975	26.3	45.8	162.8	16.2	28.2	57.4
	1980	13.1	19.8	56.5	23.1	35.1	66.0
	1985	19.1	17.7	55.6	34.3	31.9	107.6
	1990	22.8	23.6	60.5	37.6	39.1	96.2
	1995	33.5	33.1	65.2	51.4	50.8	101.3
	2000	57.2	44.2	80.4	71.2	55.0	129.6
	2005	65.2	66.3	82.5	79.1	80.4	98.4
	2010	75.6	92.3	82.3	91.9	112.2	81.9
	2015	100.0	100.0	100.0	100.0	100.0	100.0
	2016	108.5	107.3	101.1	107.3	106.1	101.1
	2017	108.5	110.7	106.1	102.3	104.4	98.0
	2018	117.0	116.3	108.5	107.8	107.2	100.6
	2019	124.5	115.2	111.0	112.1	103.8	108.1
Marshall Islands (US Dollar)	1970	4.7	4.7	22.6	20.7	20.7	100.0
	1975	9.3	9.3	36.1	25.7	25.7	100.0
	1980	14.9	14.9	37.2	40.0	40.0	100.0
	1985	24.4	24.4	46.6	52.4	52.4	100.0
	1990	43.7	43.7	69.1	63.2	63.2	100.0
	1995	66.9	66.9	90.0	74.3	74.3	100.0
	2000	61.2	61.2	76.7	79.7	79.7	100.0
	2005	77.3	77.3	87.1	88.8	88.8	100.0
	2010	92.8	92.8	94.5	98.1	98.1	100.0
	2015	100.0	100.0	100.0	100.0	100.0	100.0
	2016	109.0	109.0	101.8	107.1	107.1	100.0
	2017	114.5	114.5	106.4	107.6	107.6	100.0
	2018	121.9	121.9	127.7	95.5	95.5	100.0
	2019	130.8	130.8	134.5	97.3	97.3	100.0
Micronesia (FS of) (US Dollar)	1970	6.7	6.7	32.4	20.6	20.6	100.0
	1975	15.5	15.5	51.8	29.8	29.8	100.0
	1980	21.5	21.5	53.3	40.3	40.3	100.0
	1985	34.2	34.2	65.0	52.5	52.5	100.0
	1990	49.9	49.9	79.5	62.7	62.7	100.0
	1995	70.1	70.1	98.8	70.9	70.9	100.0
	2000	73.7	73.7	98.2	75.0	75.0	100.0
	2005	79.2	79.2	101.5	78.0	78.0	100.0
	2010	93.8	93.8	100.3	93.5	93.5	100.0
	2015	100.0	100.0	100.0	100.0	100.0	100.0
	2016	105.0	105.0	100.9	104.1	104.1	100.0
	2017	115.9	115.9	103.6	111.8	111.8	100.0
	2018	127.0	127.0	103.8	122.3	122.3	100.0
	2019	130.9	130.9	105.1	124.6	124.6	100.0
Nauru (Australian Dollar)	1970	9.9	14.7	178.6	5.5	8.2	67.1
	1975	18.5	32.2	206.1	9.0	15.6	57.4
	1980	26.5	40.2	178.6	14.8	22.5	66.0
	1985	34.1	31.7	154.9	22.0	20.4	107.6
	1990	45.4	47.2	134.2	33.8	35.2	96.2
	1995	33.9	33.4	67.6	50.1	49.4	101.3
	2000	27.0	20.8	41.7	64.7	50.0	129.6

Table 7. Implicit price deflators of Gross Domestic Product in US Dollars and National Currency (2015 = 100)

Major area, region and country	Year	GDP in Current Prices		Gross Domestic Product at Constant Prices (3)	GDP Implicit Price Deflators (2015 = 100)		Exchange Rates (6)
		National Currency (1)	US Dollars (2)		National Currency (4)	US Dollars (5)	
	2005	24.8	25.2	29.5	84.0	85.4	98.4
	2010	46.5	56.8	43.2	107.8	131.6	81.9
	2015	100.0	100.0	100.0	100.0	100.0	100.0
	2016	114.4	113.2	103.6	110.5	109.3	101.1
	2017	120.9	123.4	97.9	123.5	126.0	98.0
	2018	133.2	132.4	103.5	128.7	128.0	100.6
	2019	137.6	127.3	104.5	131.6	121.8	108.1
New Caledonia (CFP Franc)	1970	4.0	4.3	27.6	14.6	15.6	93.9
	1975	6.7	9.3	32.5	20.7	28.6	72.4
	1980	9.6	13.5	32.0	30.0	42.0	71.4
	1985	14.8	9.7	31.8	46.4	30.6	151.8
	1990	26.5	28.8	51.5	51.4	55.8	92.0
	1995	34.8	41.3	59.4	58.7	69.5	84.3
	2000	46.7	38.8	63.0	74.2	61.6	120.4
	2005	63.3	70.9	74.3	85.1	95.5	89.2
	2010	89.1	106.4	90.1	98.9	118.1	83.7
	2015	100.0	100.0	100.0	100.0	100.0	100.0
	2016	102.7	102.4	102.1	100.6	100.3	100.3
	2017	105.6	107.6	103.8	101.8	103.7	98.2
	2018	108.7	115.7	105.5	103.1	109.8	93.9
	2019	111.3	112.4	107.1	104.0	105.0	99.1
New Zealand (New Zealand Dollar)	1970	2.3	3.7	33.4	6.8	11.0	62.3
	1975	4.5	7.8	40.9	11.1	19.1	58.0
	1980	9.4	13.2	41.2	22.9	32.0	71.6
	1985	19.2	13.6	47.9	40.0	28.4	141.1
	1990	29.9	25.6	48.6	61.6	52.7	116.9
	1995	37.8	35.6	56.7	66.6	62.7	106.3
	2000	47.1	30.7	65.7	71.7	46.7	153.5
	2005	64.0	64.6	79.9	80.1	80.9	99.0
	2010	79.9	82.6	86.2	92.8	95.9	96.8
	2015	100.0	100.0	100.0	100.0	100.0	100.0
	2016	106.2	106.1	103.8	102.4	102.2	100.2
	2017	113.6	115.7	107.9	105.3	107.2	98.1
	2018	118.1	117.2	111.0	106.4	105.6	100.8
	2019	123.4	116.6	113.4	108.8	102.8	105.9
Palau (US Dollar)	1970	3.3	3.3	47.4	7.1	7.1	100.0
	1975	5.4	5.4	47.8	11.2	11.2	100.0
	1980	8.6	8.6	47.8	18.0	18.0	100.0
	1985	14.8	14.8	53.4	27.7	27.7	100.0
	1990	28.3	28.3	69.6	40.6	40.6	100.0
	1995	39.6	39.6	82.0	48.3	48.3	100.0
	2000	53.0	53.0	86.7	61.2	61.2	100.0
	2005	66.2	66.2	93.8	70.5	70.5	100.0
	2010	65.8	65.8	83.1	79.2	79.2	100.0
	2015	100.0	100.0	100.0	100.0	100.0	100.0
	2016	106.4	106.4	99.6	106.9	106.9	100.0
	2017	103.1	103.1	97.1	106.2	106.2	100.0
	2018	102.3	102.3	102.1	100.2	100.2	100.0
	2019	100.6	100.6	102.4	98.2	98.2	100.0

Table 7. Implicit price deflators of Gross Domestic Product in US Dollars and National Currency (2015 = 100)

Major area, region and country	Year	GDP in Current Prices: National Currency (1)	GDP in Current Prices: US Dollars (2)	Gross Domestic Product at Constant Prices (3)	GDP Implicit Price Deflators (2015 = 100): National Currency (4)	GDP Implicit Price Deflators (2015 = 100): US Dollars (5)	Exchange Rates (6)
Papua New Guinea (Kina)	1970	1.6	5.1	25.6	6.4	19.7	32.3
	1975	2.9	10.7	29.3	10.1	36.5	27.6
	1980	4.8	19.6	29.3	16.3	67.1	24.2
	1985	6.2	17.0	31.2	19.7	54.6	36.1
	1990	7.9	22.9	33.3	23.6	68.6	34.5
	1995	15.6	33.7	50.3	30.9	66.9	46.2
	2000	24.5	24.3	52.3	46.8	46.6	100.5
	2005	37.9	33.9	58.2	65.2	58.2	112.0
	2010	64.4	65.6	75.2	85.7	87.2	98.2
	2015	100.0	100.0	100.0	100.0	100.0	100.0
	2016	108.1	95.6	105.5	102.5	90.6	113.2
	2017	120.6	104.7	109.2	110.4	95.9	115.2
	2018	132.0	111.5	108.9	121.2	102.4	118.4
	2019	140.6	114.9	116.0	121.2	99.1	122.4
Samoa (Tala)	1970	1.5	5.3	41.7	3.5	12.6	28.2
	1975	2.7	10.9	44.3	6.1	24.5	24.7
	1980	5.3	14.6	54.3	9.7	27.0	35.9
	1985	9.8	11.1	51.7	18.9	21.5	87.7
	1990	13.2	14.6	53.5	24.7	27.4	90.2
	1995	24.7	25.6	56.2	44.0	45.6	96.6
	2000	38.8	30.2	69.1	56.1	43.7	128.3
	2005	60.1	56.8	89.3	67.3	63.6	105.8
	2010	85.3	88.0	94.2	90.6	93.4	97.0
	2015	100.0	100.0	100.0	100.0	100.0	100.0
	2016	104.6	104.4	103.7	100.9	100.7	100.2
	2017	104.5	104.8	103.0	101.4	101.7	99.7
	2018	107.0	105.9	103.7	103.2	102.1	101.0
	2019	111.0	107.3	106.0	104.7	101.2	103.4
Solomon Islands (Solomon Islands Dollar)	1970	0.3	3.0	16.1	2.1	18.5	11.3
	1975	0.6	6.1	20.8	2.8	29.1	9.7
	1980	1.4	13.4	33.1	4.3	40.5	10.5
	1985	2.8	14.9	35.7	7.8	41.9	18.7
	1990	6.2	19.4	43.6	14.3	44.6	32.0
	1995	14.7	34.1	60.1	24.4	56.6	43.0
	2000	20.3	31.6	52.3	38.8	60.3	64.3
	2005	38.2	40.1	60.8	62.7	65.9	95.1
	2010	68.5	67.2	84.8	80.7	79.2	101.9
	2015	100.0	100.0	100.0	100.0	100.0	100.0
	2016	105.9	105.5	105.9	100.0	99.6	100.4
	2017	113.1	113.5	111.5	101.4	101.8	99.7
	2018	122.5	122.0	115.9	105.7	105.2	100.5
	2019	125.6	121.6	117.3	107.1	103.7	103.3
Tonga (Pa'anga)	1970	1.8	4.2	32.3	5.6	13.1	42.4
	1975	3.8	10.5	36.3	10.5	29.0	36.3
	1980	8.2	19.6	46.1	17.7	42.4	41.7
	1985	12.3	18.1	69.2	17.8	26.2	68.0
	1990	24.4	40.2	70.2	34.8	57.2	60.8
	1995	31.3	51.8	83.9	37.2	61.7	60.4
	2000	39.5	47.4	90.6	43.6	52.2	83.5

Table 7. Implicit price deflators of Gross Domestic Product in US Dollars and National Currency (2015 = 100)

Major area, region and country	Year	GDP in Current Prices		Gross Domestic Product at Constant Prices (3)	GDP Implicit Price Deflators (2015 = 100)		Exchange Rates (6)
		National Currency (1)	US Dollars (2)		National Currency (4)	US Dollars (5)	
	2005	59.8	64.8	93.9	63.6	68.9	92.3
	2010	83.3	92.1	89.7	92.9	102.7	90.5
	2015	100.0	100.0	100.0	100.0	100.0	100.0
	2016	109.8	104.4	106.6	103.1	97.9	105.2
	2017	119.8	114.4	110.1	108.8	103.9	104.8
	2018	126.4	119.0	110.4	114.4	107.7	106.2
	2019	137.1	126.1	111.3	123.2	113.3	108.7
Tuvalu (Australian Dollar)	1970	4.9	7.4	31.6	15.6	23.3	67.1
	1975	6.3	11.0	29.0	21.7	37.9	57.4
	1980	8.1	12.3	26.9	30.1	45.6	66.0
	1985	10.8	10.0	26.6	40.5	37.7	107.6
	1990	26.2	27.2	49.4	53.0	55.1	96.2
	1995	34.0	33.6	57.4	59.2	58.4	101.3
	2000	51.2	39.5	77.0	66.4	51.3	129.6
	2005	60.9	61.9	76.9	79.2	80.5	98.4
	2010	73.4	89.6	83.5	87.9	107.3	81.9
	2015	100.0	100.0	100.0	100.0	100.0	100.0
	2016	114.1	112.9	105.9	107.7	106.6	101.1
	2017	122.8	125.3	112.2	109.5	111.7	98.0
	2018	132.1	131.4	120.0	110.1	109.5	100.6
	2019	145.0	134.1	127.6	113.7	105.2	108.1
Vanuatu (Vatu)	1970	4.6	5.0	15.6	29.8	32.1	92.7
	1975	6.7	10.6	24.7	27.2	42.9	63.6
	1980	10.2	16.3	26.9	38.0	60.7	62.7
	1985	17.0	17.5	44.2	38.4	39.5	97.3
	1990	24.2	22.6	47.4	51.1	47.6	107.4
	1995	36.9	35.9	59.2	62.3	60.6	102.9
	2000	44.0	34.9	67.3	65.4	51.8	126.3
	2005	52.1	52.0	72.9	71.5	71.3	100.2
	2010	82.0	92.2	92.9	88.3	99.3	88.9
	2015	100.0	100.0	100.0	100.0	100.0	100.0
	2016	105.4	105.9	103.5	101.8	102.3	99.5
	2017	114.6	115.8	108.0	106.1	107.2	98.9
	2018	121.7	120.4	111.2	109.5	108.3	101.1
	2019	125.1	119.3	114.3	109.5	104.4	104.8